# Professional K2 blackpearl®

*(continued)*

## Part IV: Administration of K2 blackpearl

## Part V: Advanced K2 blackpearl Concepts and Platform Extensions

Professional

# K2 blackpearl®

# Professional
# K2 blackpearl®

Holly Anderson
Jason Apergis
Sergio Del Piccolo
Chris Geier
Codi Kaji
Shaun Leisegang
Igor Macori
Gabriel Malherbe
Jason Montgomery
Colin Murphy
Chris O'Connor
Anthony Petro
Eric Shaffer
Mike Talley

WILEY

**Wiley Publishing, Inc.**

# Professional K2 blackpearl®

Published by
Wiley Publishing, Inc.
10475 Crosspoint Boulevard
Indianapolis, IN 46256
www.wiley.com

Published simultaneously in Canada

ISBN: 978-0-470-29305-8

Manufactured in the United States of America

10 9 8 7 6 5 4 3 2 1

Library of Congress Cataloging-in-Publication Data.

Professional K2 Blackpearl / Holly Anderson ... [et al.].
   p.   cm.
   Includes bibliographical references and index.
   ISBN 978-0-470-29305-8 (alk. paper)
    1. K2 Blackpearl.   2. Application software—Development—Computer programs.   3. Business—Computer programs.   I. Anderson, Holly, 1975-
QA76.76.D47P7647 2009
005.365—dc22                                                        2008048458

# About the Authors

**Holly Anderson** is the product marketing manager for K2. Holly began working with K2 software in 2004 as a technical consultant building complex workflow applications for clients and joined K2 as a technical specialist in 2006. With her technical and marketing background, Holly is able to provide a unique perspective on K2 products for both business and technical audiences. You can reach her at holly@k2.com.

**Jason Apergis** is a software consultant who has lived in the Washington, DC, area his entire life. Jason currently works for a Microsoft Gold Partner named RDA Corporation as a technical project manager and has worked for various other consulting firms like BearingPoint and AMS. One of Jason's solutions, which integrated K2, BizTalk, SharePoint, and InfoPath, was nominated as a finalist for a Microsoft solution of the year award in 2006. Jason completed both his undergraduate and graduate degrees in Information Technology from Virginia Tech. Jason plays ice hockey on a weekly basis and is both an avid fan of the Washington Capitals and a Virginia Tech Football fan. Jason dedicates this book to his wife, Catherine, and both his children, Ethan and Caroline.

**Sergio Del Piccolo** is an experienced business process consultant and a partner at Avantage Partners in Vancouver, Canada. He has led business process integration engagements of all sizes and brings over 10 years of hands-on experience as a technical and business solutions architect. Sergio has acted as a trusted advisor for multiple clients, providing guidance and leadership on successful process-driven and integration solutions. As a well respected consultant within the community, Sergio has achieved a number of accreditations that have further established his expertise, including being a K2 Insider and a Microsoft Virtual Technical Specialist for BizTalk Server. He is an expert on the Microsoft Connected System and K2 platforms. Sergio leads the Partner Integrated Workflow program, focusing on getting organizations to streamline their business processes and helping them gain a competitive edge in today's global market. You can reach him at sergio.delpiccolo@avantagepartners.com, and you can take a look at his blogs at http://delpiccolo.com and http://avantagepartners.com/team-profiles/sergio-del-piccolo.

**Chris Geier** evangelizes K2, helps build and nourish the broader K2 community, and coordinates global readiness efforts internally. He's worked in the technology industry for 14 years — for several companies, including Microsoft — and has focused primarily on infrastructure and security. Chris lives in the suburbs of Chicago with his ever-so-patient wife, Sara, and their three children: Leah-Rose, Carter, and Ella Claire. Chris is a history buff, ashamed to admit he loves reality television, and loves the soon to be world champion Chicago Cubs.

**Codi Kaji** is a technical writer for K2, where her main responsibility is translating the features and functionality of the K2 platform into things business people can understand, in other words, translating geek to human. With a background of consulting and training on various Microsoft based technologies, she enjoys the challenge of installing and testing the latest products and writing information that helps people get the most out of their K2 experience. Codi and her husband have three cats and enjoy fishing. When she's not testing the latest build, writing words, or landing a trout, Codi enjoys the soothing craft of knitting. Watch out for the pointy sticks.

**Shaun Leisegang** is the presales manager for K2 and is responsible for technical presales across Europe. Shaun is responsible for product evangelism, solution design, and specifications as well as for solution consulting. Shaun has vast experience within the Microsoft ecosystem; designing and building .NET-based enterprise and system architectures that include workflow or business process automation as well as consulting and working with the full Microsoft stack of technologies. Shaun is a true stage performer of the IT world: immensely capable, adaptable, confident, an excellent communicator, who is equally comfortable in front of large crowds and intimate groups. Shaun has a passion for both people and technology, which allows him to convey dynamic new products in an infectious way, while at the same time knowing the IT business as a whole in order to speak authoritatively across multiple products and platforms. He began his career as a software developer, moved on to lead a team of application developers, and now runs a presales team where he has found a perfect mix between two of his passions: people and technology.

**Igor Macori** lives in Bologna, Italy, with his three girls (his partner and his two cats). He is cofounder and Training and Consulting Manager for GreenTeam (`www.greenteam.it`), an Italian Microsoft Gold Certified Partner founded in 1991. He has managed various IW Solutions projects (SharePoint, LCS/OCS, Project Server, WWF, and others) and completed various solutions implemented for enterprise companies and public sector organizations. He is a regular trainer and speaker for Italian Microsoft courses and events dedicated to partners and customers and has achieved various technical certifications since 1996 (MCP, MCSA, MCSE, MCTS SharePoint, MCAS, MCT, and MOS Master Instructor). In 2008, he received the Microsoft MVP (Most Valuable Professional) Award for Microsoft SharePoint Server — Architecture. He is the owner of one of most visited Italian SharePoint and Collaboration Internet Blogs (`www.macori.it`). He is co-organizer of the Italian SharePoint Technical Conference (`www.sharepointconference.it`). He has written 14 books about the Microsoft Office System and Microsoft Windows Vista, and since 2007 has been a K2 Insider.

**Gabriel Malherbe** is a .NET solutions architect in the Thames Valley, UK. He currently works with the amazing team of K2 professionals at Dynamyx, where they service some multinational clients across Europe in the manufacturing and financial sector. He built his process management experience by codesigning system integration components that are used by airports worldwide. Broadening his horizons, he and his wife, Sharm, moved to the UK where Gabriel has delivered K2 training and seminars since 2004. He is one of the founding members of the K2 Insiders program. He can be contacted at `gabriel.malherbe@dynamyx.com`, and you can follow his K2 dedicated blog at `http://nakedprogrammer.blogspot.com`.

**Jason Montgomery** is a principal of Active Technologies Group, Inc. (ATGi — `www.atgi.com`), an international technology consulting firm based in Columbus, Ohio, working with clients ranging from Fortune 500 companies to government agencies, including the U.S. Department of Defense. His skills cover a broad range of technologies with specializations in information security, Microsoft technologies, Microsoft .NET, and K2 Workflow solutions, as well as Linux and FreeBSD system administration. Currently, Jason serves on the Global Information Assurance Certification (GIAC) Advisory Board as well as on the Global Information Assurance Professional (GSSP) Steering Committee for the .NET Security Certifications for SANS Institute. He additionally holds the CISSP Certification and the GIAC .NET Security (GNET) and GIAC Security Essentials (GSEC) Certifications.

**Colin Murphy** is a principal architect with RDA Corporation, is a Microsoft Gold Certified Partner, and has been working in the industry for about 12 years. Colin's areas of specialization are Microsoft Office SharePoint 2007, Smart Clients, and Workflow. Colin has been working with K2.net 2003 since early 2006 on projects for a variety of clients.

**Chris O'Connor** began programming on a Commodore 64 as an avid 12 year old, entering listings from computer magazines. He has spent the last 15 years or so developing Web sites, Windows applications, and other solutions using Visual Basic, C#, SQL Server, and other products within the Microsoft arena. He is currently employed as a SharePoint solution architect and has implemented many SharePoint Content Management and Document Management Solutions, as well as K2.net 2003 and K2 blackpearl.

He is also a Microsoft Certified Professional and Microsoft Certified Application Developer, and K2 Insider. With so many new products and technologies from Microsoft, it's hard to keep up; Chris follows with great interest to the happenings of Microsoft and the Web 2.0 community, especially with regard to SharePoint, Silverlight, and "Software+Services." He updates a blog of SharePoint related articles, other technical bits and pieces, and fun and family at www.grumpywookie.com. To keep up with the K2 community, Chris hosts a K2-related blog, located at www.devk2.net. He is a keen photographer, with his favorite subjects being his wife and two young sons. Spending weekends with family is his favorite pastime, with house renovations, gardening, kids' activities, and such. He can be contacted at chris@grumpywookie.com.

**Anthony Petro** resides in Silverthorne, Colorado, and is the Technical Product Manager for K2. He started his professional career in the consulting world 14 years ago and has always remained focused on Microsoft technologies and solutions. He joined Microsoft in 2001 and spent the next 5 years heavily immersed in SharePoint Joint Development Programs bridging the gap between the product development teams in Redmond and the enterprise customers around the world. He was a strong contributor to the SharePoint community in its infancy and focused on teaching the masses about the complexities of search and enterprise scale issues and about using products such as K2 to fill the enterprise workflow gaps of SharePoint. He joined K2 in 2006 to help bring K2 blackpearl to market through early adopter programs that spanned the alpha and beta cycles through to RTM. Anthony remains actively involved in early adopter programs for K2 blackpoint and K2 connect, and in planning the future releases of all product lines.

**Eric Schaffer** has been working with K2 since early 2005 when he helped formalize the K2 North America technical support team. He now spends his time working on new ways to showcase the power of the K2 platform as a presales technical specialist with K2. Eric holds a bachelor's degree in Computer Science from Washington State University. Prior to joining the K2 family Eric contracted with Microsoft in both the Xbox certification testing department and developer technical support department. Eric lives in Seattle with his wife, Dara, and daughter, Kayla.

**Mike Talley** joined K2 as a technical writer in February 2007, working on whitepapers, training content, wizard text, and a variety of other things in his time with K2. Prior to K2 he spent 8 years at Microsoft, where at various points he was a programming writer, beta lead, and support professional. While at Microsoft he worked with product teams on supportability issues and wrote about InfoPath, InfoPath Forms Services, SharePoint, and Excel. He currently resides in Highlands Ranch, Colorado, with his wife and two sons. You can reach him at miket@k2.com.

# Credits

**Acquisitions Editor**
Katie Mohr

**Senior Development Editor**
Kevin Kent

**Development Editor**
Jeff Riley

**Production Editor**
Kathleen Wisor

**Copy Editor**
Jeri Freedman, Foxxe Editorial Services

**Editorial Manager**
Mary Beth Wakefield

**Production Manager**
Tim Tate

**Vice President and Executive Group Publisher**
Richard Swadley

**Vice President and Executive Publisher**
Barry Pruett

**Associate Publisher**
Jim Minatel

**Project Coordinator, Cover**
Lynsey Stanford

**Proofreader**
Nancy Carrasco

**Indexer**
Jack Lewis

# Acknowledgments

K2 and the book's authors wish to thank everyone who made this publication possible. K2 would like to extend a special thanks to each author who worked so hard on this, and also thanks to the authors' families for giving them the time to work on this. We also need to send out a special thanks to the following people, without whom this book would not be possible:

Adriaan Van Wyk

Hennie Laubscher

Dennis Parker

Josh Swihart

Katie Mohr

Kevin Kent

Hubert Cheng

Pieter Janson

Johan Van Heerden

Lardus Brooks

Ben Fourie

Koos Du Preez

Wynand du Toit

Jaco Lubbe

Jan Joubert

Michael Erasmus

Leon Geldenhuys

Schalk de Jager

Bob Maggio

Joseph Dunagan

David Loomis

Murray Foxcroft

# Contents

# Contents

# Contents

# Contents

# Contents

# Part IV: Administration of K2 blackpearl

# Contents

Contents

# Contents

# Introduction

K2 blackpearl and the K2 platform is a large, powerful, "game-changing" application platform built on Microsoft technologies. Understanding it from top to bottom would be a great task for a single person, which is why we have gathered more than a dozen authors to supply you with the information to successfully transform your company into a process-oriented, efficient business that can grow with the K2 platform.

## Who This Book Is For

Since this is the first book on K2 blackpearl, you will find a broad range of topics in this book, from the market in which K2 blackpearl is aimed to the architecture of the platform, from how to approach process design to developing your own custom user manager.

The first part of the book is meant for everyone and provides an understanding of K2 blackpearl and where it fits in the marketplace. It is included to provide a framework for thinking about various aspects of process-driven applications, including how they differ from business process management techniques; identifying processes in your company to automate, the different pieces that make up a process; measuring the success of your efforts; and finally shifting your company's culture in the direction of process efficiency. This section may be the only section you need to read if you are sponsoring a process improvement effort in your company. If you are responsible for leading the effort, make sure to read Chapters 3 and 4.

The other parts are meant to provide details on how to effectively deploy and use K2 blackpearl and include a broad range of topics. Read what you are most interested in, but also make sure to read Chapter 8, which will give you a great foundation to start designing processes with K2 blackpearl. Chapter 14 is also recommended for everyone because it provides an overview of the available K2 Designers and how you can share projects among them.

If you are a developer, you may be tempted to flip through the book looking for code, and you will find some, but we also recommend reading much of the rest of the book to learn how the API and the K2 platform extensions fit within the overall process-driven application environment. Pay particular attention to Chapter 22 and the Appendix, which may save you hours of coding or give you a no-code solution to something that you may have thought would take hundreds of lines of code to accomplish.

If you are an administrators, focus on Parts II and IV, but also take a look at the other chapters to gain an understanding of how your users will be using K2.

## What This Book Covers

K2 blackpearl is the main subject of this book, although we devote an entire chapter, Chapter 23, to the add-on product K2 connect to give you an understanding of how to bring SAP data into your processes. We also talk a bit about K2 blackpoint, particularly in the SharePoint chapters. Since K2 blackpoint is built on the K2 blackpearl foundation, many of the same concepts apply to that product as well, but we do not point out the differences between K2 blackpearl and K2 blackpoint. For that information browse to www.k2.com.

# How This Book Is Structured

We recommend that you approach this book in parts and perhaps read or reference each part differently. If you are working on a team, each member of the team may find one part more interesting to them than the other sections; that is expected and is how we designed the book.

❏ **Part I, "Introduction to K2 blackpearl and Process-Driven Applications":** The first four chapters discuss what K2 blackpearl is, how the applications you can design may or may not fit the business process management (BPM) model, how to go about identifying and designing processes, and last how to measure results and shift the culture of your company to a more process-oriented business.

❏ **Part II, "Architecture and Installation Options for K2 blackpearl":** Chapters 5 and 6 will get you started. Installing the K2 blackpearl components is a necessary step before you can start designing processes, so in these two chapters you will gain an understanding of all of the pieces of the platform, the architecture, and the supporting technology, as well as ideas on how to plan out your development, QA/staging, and production environments.

❏ **Part III, "K2 blackpearl Process Planning and Design Essentials":** Chapters 7 through 14 give you a ton of information about how to design, build, extend, and generally work with the main pieces of the platform. From a step-by-step tutorial on building your first process to how to share processes across the different K2 Designers, you'll learn all of what you need to really get ramped up. Pay particular attention to Chapters 8 and 11, which cover the basic things you need to know about process planning and the various concepts of process design with K2 blackpearl and then provide an in-depth view of the available forms technologies that you can use for user interaction with your processes. If you are particularly interested in SharePoint, make sure to read Chapters 12 and 13.

❏ **Part IV, "Administration of K2 blackpearl":** Chapters 15 through 20 offer an administrator's view into the platform. Things like disaster recovery, logging, security, and using the K2 Workspace for notifications, reports, assigning process permissions, and recovering from errors are all key aspects of the platform that you or someone in your company will have to understand. This section gives you everything you need to know and probably more, including how to build your own user manager to plug into the K2 platform.

❏ **Part V, "Advanced K2 blackpearl Concepts and Platform Extensions":** The last part includes Chapters 21 through 23, and these chapters are there to round out the discussion of the platform. You'll find information about using the Event Bus to surface outside events to the K2 server and a discussion of tailoring the platform and your processes to your particular needs by going beyond the default settings of the components that you learned about in Chapter 8. Finally you'll learn about the K2 connect platform extension, which allows data from SAP (and eventually any system for which a WCF LOB adapter is released) to be used within your processes.

Last but not least, we've combed through the various K2 blog entries available at the time of this writing to give you what we think are some of the greatest tips and tricks out there for working with K2 blackpearl in the appendix. Of course you could go out and find these yourself (and we give you the links to do so), but we thought that including the best of the best right here in the book would give a complete picture of K2 blackpearl. Also take a look at the "Other Resources" section later in this introduction.

# What You Need to Use This Book

There are some pieces of this book that you can sit down and read without needing a computer or access to K2 blackpearl at all, but much of this book requires you to have access to K2 blackpearl and the supporting applications as well. Whenever we talk about designing processes, we do so in the context of the K2 Designer for Visual Studio. To install this component you will need Visual Studio 2005. Support for Visual Studio 2008 may be available by the time this book is published, so look for that on www.k2.com.

For the server pieces of the platform, you will need a Windows Server 2003 environment (virtual or otherwise) and the additional components required by the K2 server. For detailed information about the K2 blackpearl requirements see the K2 blackpearl *Getting Started* guide available on the customer portal. For access to the portal you need a customer account, which may be obtained by contacting your nearest K2 representative. If you don't know who that is, browse to www.k2.com and click Contact. Evaluation licenses are available for K2 blackpearl.

# Other Resources

There are a great number of resources available to learn more about K2 blackpearl. Here we'll give you some pointers.

**K2 blackpearl Help:** The collection of Help files included in K2 blackpearl is broken down into the following:

❑ **The Getting Started Guide:** Includes everything you need to install K2 blackpearl, from a single server installation all the way up to a fully distributed, load-balanced server farm. It even includes tips for troubleshooting Kerberos issues.

❑ **The User Guide:** Includes information on every page of every wizard as well as overviews of each wizard to help you know how to use each wizard. The User Guide also includes information about using every other piece of the platform, from client to server, so this should be your first stop for getting "how to" information about each piece of the platform.

❑ **The Developer Reference:** Includes information about common developer tasks, from working with design time and run-time APIs to extending the platform with custom wizards, service objects, and third-party event recorders. It's a work in progress because there are over 30,000 properties, methods, and events across the entire platform, but it's a great place to start learning about developing on the K2 platform.

**K2.com** (www.k2.com)**:** The public Web site where you can find company information, product information and videos, and customer case studies, among other things, completely built on K2 SmartObjects.

**The K2 Customer Portal** (portal.k2workflow.com)**:** This is where you can download the available beta products and submit support tickets. It requires a login, so if you are a customer and don't know your login, contact your nearest K2 office. The customer portal is also a place for reading the K2 Knowledge Base articles.

**The K2 Underground** (www.k2underground.com)**:** The place where the K2 community meets to exchange ideas, questions, tips, videos, and code. You will find interest groups, ranging from

K2 user groups to public betas, and forums, blogs, whitepapers, and most importantly the K2 blackmarket, which is where really smart developers come to browse and share their code projects. There is some great stuff up there, and it's constantly growing. So, don't miss this site.

**The Blogosphere:** There are many blogs out there either dedicated to K2 or with recurring posts about K2. Here is a listing of a few of them from K2 and non-K2 employees alike. Perhaps you will recognize some names:

### Blogs by K2 Insiders

- **Bob Mixon** (http://masteringsharepoint.com/blogs/bobmixon/default.aspx)
- **Daniel Gocsman** (http://danielgocsman.com/)
- **Grumpy Wookie** (http://www.devk2.net/) Chris O'Conner
- **Igor Macori** (http://blogs.devleap.com/igor/default.aspx)
- **No Intelligent Life** (http://charlesemes.blogspot.com/) Charles Emes
- **Naked Programmer** (http://nakedprogrammer.blogspot.com/) Gabriel Malherbe
- **—=[security through absurdity]=—** (http://choosing-a-blog-url-sucks.blogspot.com/) Jason Montgomery
- **Sergio Del Piccolo** (http://delpiccolo.com/)
- **Stumbling Through** (http://blogs.claritycon.com/blogs/tim_byrne/default.aspx) Tim Byrne
- **SOA What!** (http://allsoa.wordpress.com/) Craig Butler

### Blogs by K2 Employees

- **From the Bench** (http://k2underground.com/blogs/fromthebench/default.aspx) K2 Consultants in North America
- **Pitchblack** (http://k2underground.com/blogs/pitchblack/default.aspx) K2 Technical Specialists in the UK and Europe
- **Ramble On** (http://k2underground.com/blogs/rambleon/default.aspx) K2 Consultants in the UK and Europe
- **Chris Geier** (http://k2underground.com/blogs/chrisg/default.aspx) K2 Program Manager
- **How To K2** (http://k2underground.com/blogs/howtok2/default.aspx) Chris Geier
- **Why K2?** (http://k2underground.com/blogs/why_k2/default.aspx) Holly Anderson, K2 Product Marketing Manager
- **Johnny's K2 Blog** (http://k2underground.com/blogs/johnny/default.aspx) Johnny Fang, K2 Solutions Manager, Singapore
- **blacktop: Writings from the Road** (http://www.k2underground.com/blogs/blacktop/default.aspx) David Loomis, Consultant, North America
- **jEy on K2** (http://jeylabs.com/) Jey Srikantha, K2 Technical Specialist, Australia

If you search around you're bound to find more blogs with topics on K2 or even dedicated to K2 technologies. Try Google or Technorati for those.

# Conventions

To help you get the most from the text and keep track of what's happening, we've used a number of conventions throughout the book.

> **Boxes like this one hold important, not-to-be forgotten information that is directly relevant to the surrounding text.**

*Notes, tips, hints, tricks, and asides to the current discussion are offset and placed in italics like this.*

As for styles in the text:

❑ We *highlight* new terms and important words when we introduce them.

❑ We show keyboard strokes like this: Ctrl+A.

❑ We show file names, URLs, and code within the text like this: `persistence.properties`.

❑ We present code in two different ways:

```
We use a monofont type with no highlighting for most code examples.
We use gray highlighting to emphasize code that's particularly important in the
present context.
```

# Source Code

As you work through the examples in this book, you may choose either to type in all the code manually or to use the source code files that accompany the book. All of the source code used in this book is available for downloading at `www.wrox.com`. Once at the site, simply locate the book's title (either by using the Search box or by using one of the title lists) and click the Download Code link on the book's detail page to obtain all the source code for the book.

*Because many books have similar titles, you may find it easiest to search by ISBN; this book's ISBN is 978-0-470-29305-8.*

Once you download the code, just decompress it with your favorite compression tool. Alternately, you can go to the main Wrox code download page at `www.wrox.com/dynamic/books/download.aspx` to see the code available for this book and all other Wrox books.

# Errata

We make every effort to ensure that there are no errors in the text or in the code. However, no one is perfect, and mistakes do occur. If you find an error in one of our books, such as a spelling mistake or faulty piece of code, we would be very grateful for your feedback. By sending in errata you may save another reader hours of frustration and at the same time you will be helping us provide even higher-quality information.

To find the errata page for this book, go to www.wrox.com and locate the title using the Search box or one of the title lists. Then, on the book details page, click the Book Errata link. On this page you can view all errata that has been submitted for this book and posted by Wrox editors. A complete book list including links to each book's errata is also available at www.wrox.com/misc-pages/booklist.shtml.

If you don't spot "your" error on the Book Errata page, go to www.wrox.com/contact/techsupport .shtml and complete the form there to send us the error you have found. We'll check the information and, if appropriate, post a message to the book's errata page and fix the problem in subsequent editions of the book.

# p2p.wrox.com

For author and peer discussion, join the P2P forums at p2p.wrox.com. The forums are a Web-based system for you to post messages relating to Wrox books and related technologies and interact with other readers and technology users. The forums offer a subscription feature to e-mail you topics of interest of your choosing when new posts are made to the forums. Wrox authors, editors, other industry experts, and your fellow readers are present on these forums.

At http://p2p.wrox.com you will find a number of different forums that will help you not only as you read this book but also as you develop your own applications. To join the forums, just follow these steps:

1.  Go to p2p.wrox.com and click the Register link.

2.  Read the terms of use and click Agree.

3.  Complete the required information to join as well as any optional information you wish to provide, and click Submit.

4.  You will receive an e-mail with information describing how to verify your account and complete the joining process.

> *You can read messages in the forums without joining P2P but in order to post your own messages, you must join.*

Once you join, you can post new messages and respond to messages other users post. You can read messages at any time on the Web. If you would like to have new messages from a particular forum e-mailed to you, click the Subscribe to this Forum icon by the forum name in the forum listing.

For more information about how to use the Wrox P2P, be sure to read the P2P FAQs for answers to questions about how the forum software works as well as many common questions specific to P2P and Wrox books. To read the FAQs, click the FAQ link on any P2P page.

# Part I

# Introduction to K2 blackpearl and Process-Driven Applications

# 1

# Introduction to BPM and the K2 Platform

Mike Talley

Businesses run on processes. Processes develop out of necessity and become part of a company's culture, or a way of doing things, and define its day-to-day operations. How those processes work determines a company's success. Efficient processes enable the business to thrive. Inefficient processes drag the business down and can ultimately ruin it if the competition is more efficient.

Everything from making phone calls, to sending e-mails and instant messages, to filling out electronic and even paper forms, most actions that employees take are a part of a larger process. Whether that process is bringing a new employee onboard or paying a supplier, from start to finish the process can be described and documented. Often the details of a particular process are known by a handful of people, and sometimes by just a single person. In large processes involving many people, the full details of the entire process may not be known by any one person, which makes it more difficult to document. In fact, determining the exact nature of a process in large organizations is not easy. But writing the process down pays big dividends, because once the process is documented it can be optimized and improved, which helps the business become more efficient. Parts of the process may remain a manual task for an employee, but many parts can be automated, which can take the efficiency of the business to another level.

What if your business has other needs? Maybe efficiency is not the most important issue facing your company today. Maybe you need to streamline operations, improve responsiveness, make better decisions, increase the visibility of process operations, reduce IT costs, minimize risk, or enforce governance. These are all critical aspects of your business that, if resolved, would make your business run more efficiently. You would be meeting your business requirements — the requirements to run your business — more effectively and more efficiently.

The K2 platform enables businesses to be more efficient. This may sound like a bold statement, but think about how your own company operates. You know that there are big efficiencies to be gained if you could identify all the processes in your business and start automating the most critical pieces of those processes. For example, to be able to optimize a process to avoid bottlenecks or to identify how an employee's absence affects the functioning of the business is something that many companies believe is beyond their reach. But through process discovery, automation and the right tools, getting the business to operate more efficiently is no longer beyond the reach of most, if not all, companies.

To begin your look at process management and K2, this chapter covers the following topics:

- ❑ Defining workflow
- ❑ Exploring the history of K2
- ❑ Examining the K2 platform, including the anatomy of K2 blackpearl and its key features
- ❑ In terms of workflow, making the build versus buy decision
- ❑ Evolving workflow

# Defining Business Applications and Workflow

There are many terms that describe the methodology and technology around processes and process management. Some equate the term *workflow* with Business Process Management (BPM). Since Microsoft introduced the Workflow Foundation (WF) in .NET 3.0, more companies are trying to figure out how workflow can enhance their business. There is also a buzz in the marketplace around business process automation, process-driven applications, and workflow-enabled applications — all of which, at the end of the day, mean the same thing. Analysts predict strong growth for technology solutions and add-on applications that integrate with traditional applications to provide process automation, but how can you make sense of what is real and what is just buzz? It helps to understand the history of business applications.

## A Very Brief History of Business Application Development

In the recent past, line-of-business (LOB) application development and implementation happened in the IT shop, where applications were developed from the ground up or custom development occurred on an application from a vendor. The initial request would come from the business or be pushed down from upper management. After application requirements were gathered, IT developers would architect the solution and, through a handful of builds and revisions of the application, deliver it back to the business. This process could take anywhere from 6 months to many years. Maintenance of the application became a much lower priority for IT as other business requests became a priority, and changes to the initial application became very difficult, if not impossible, to make. Over time, these changes would occur, and eventually the price to pay, either in a direct charge to the business or from a resource- and time-investment perspective, became too high for the business. The application became a "legacy" application that IT no longer had to modify, although they still had to spend resources to keep it running.

As custom and off-the-shelf LOB systems became more feature-rich and information technology grew more sophisticated, a new form of business need emerged, namely workflow. Arguably the need was always there. People were responsible for understanding and maintaining complex relationships and processes in the business. Often those processes were documented so that the organization wouldn't forget. Often that documentation wasn't read. The advent of systems helped codify some things, but usually this happened in silos. Software was needed to help bridge the silos of people and information and to help organizations move processes from paper and tribal knowledge to something codified, enforceable, and trackable.

If it wasn't workflow by name, it involved the integration of multiple applications with processes and contracts for how they worked together. It was around this time that Enterprise Application Integration (EAI) and Service-Oriented Architecture (SOA) became popular concepts. By this time, many businesses had moved away from paper-based documents. Electronic versions of documents and business forms came to be used to capture information because this was cheaper and the technology was readily available. This exposed the need to capture the remaining human interactions with these electronic business entities. Whether a document and data were stored haphazardly on a file share or checked in to a line-of-business document management system, the need to manage the chain of human interaction with the data was the next challenge.

Even a decade ago, automation of a human-to-human or human-to-system workflow was virtually impossible for most companies, except for those with a lot of time and money to spend. But in the recent past, many workflow solutions have entered the marketplace that allow small to medium-sized companies, as well as large organizations, to benefit from process applications. The latest versions of SharePoint and Microsoft Dynamics CRM (Customer Relationship Management) include the ability to create workflows out of the box. Creating and running workflows has become commonplace, at least for those companies who adopt some of the latest technology.

The question that hasn't been answered by these solutions, however, is how do you create and automate processes to transform a business? Sure, you may be able to automate the gathering of feedback or the sending of an e-mail based on some action a user takes, but is that really creating efficiencies in the business? The need to discover, optimize, automate, monitor, and improve business processes, or workflows, is known as Business Process Management (BPM), and this can mean many things to many people. At its core, it has nothing to do with technology, as business processes can be optimized and remain completely paper- and human-based. For most businesses, however, technology plays a central role in the way that processes are identified, created, and delivered to those involved in the processes, that is, "the business," and a solution is needed for that. *Business Process Management System (BPMS)* is the term for technology platforms used to implement BPM.

## *Clarifying the Definition of Workflow*

The term *workflow* can mean different things to different people. You may see the term *workflow* in graphics- and video-editing applications, in SharePoint, or in a description of an assembly line. Workflow, as it relates to K2, BPM, and process-driven applications means one thing: *the automation of all or part of a business process involving human actions and/or system functions.*

Some would argue that workflows involving humans can't be automated, but capturing that interaction of the user within the business process is a critical piece of a workflow. A workflow is not a task that begins and ends with a single user and contains information that nobody else will ever use. This type of workflow is a matter of personal productivity, not business productivity. However, a workflow that integrates disparate applications to improve the business process and increases the transparency of that process is a workflow that is interesting to the business, even when there is no human interaction with that process. An example of this is an event that creates a file in a location on the network, which in turn creates an instance of a workflow to extract data from the file and update two different LOB systems. No human interaction was necessary for that process to happen. System (or system-only) workflows do increase business efficiency, and the data captured can be used by someone to make better decisions about the business. More common than system workflows is the need to capture human-system interactions, where an action taken by a user creates an instance of a workflow, which in turn creates tasks for other users and records data for reports and other business systems.

# K2 and the K2 Platform

K2 blackpearl, the core of the K2 platform, enables businesses to build process-driven applications that improve business efficiency. Started in 2001 in South Africa, the first version of K2 was a visionary product that enabled businesses to leverage information and resources for increasing business efficiencies and making better decisions about the business. K2.net 2003 followed and offered strong integration with Microsoft business applications such as BizTalk, SharePoint, Exchange, and the Office 2003 product line, as well as SQL Server and Active Directory. Along with an extensive API to extend the platform, K2.net 2003 became a market leader in building business applications.

K2.net 2003 included a business process design canvas, K2 Studio, where designers could build processes and modify the code behind each process element, otherwise known as an activity. Those familiar with K2.net 2003 know that this ability to modify and extend the code was necessary in many cases to tailor the process to the business requirements. While powerful, this model also led to longer development times and greater maintenance of the application once deployed to production. K2.net 2003 did not feature out-of-the-box reporting capabilities and encouraged a data model that was tightly coupled to the process itself. K2 blackpearl, released in 2007, addressed many of these concerns and extended the vision of enabling business to be more efficient and make better decisions.

As Adriaan Van Wyk, CEO of SourceCode Technology Holdings, said in response to K2 blackpearl being named a finalist for the 2008 American Business Award (otherwise known as the Stevie Awards), "When we set out to build K2 blackpearl, we set out to create something simple, so that nontechnical people can contribute to and participate in the application-building process; and flexible, because business needs constantly shift; and fast, because time is money. We feel like we accomplished all of that and that it is a unique product in the industry."

## K2 blackpearl: Three Key Features

K2 blackpearl comprises three key features:

❑ **By building on .NET 3.0 technologies, the most important of which is the Workflow Foundation (WF), K2 blackpearl uses a declarative model for building processes.** The declarative model, based on WF constructs, allows more flexibility and power when designing the process, while at the same time reducing the amount of custom code required. While modifying the workflow activities and code behind the WF constructs is supported and is similar to what you find in K2.net 2003, the need to use code is minimized to the extent that you can build and deploy even complex processes without a single line of code.

❑ **K2 blackpearl includes many reports for common process-related reporting scenarios, including a View Flow report that allows real-time visualization of the state of a process instance.** Based on Microsoft SQL Server Reporting Services, all reports are built using the Report Definition Language (RDL) file format and, thus, can be modified and extended using common report design tools. Custom reports can also be imported into the K2 reporting environment following deployment to the SQL Server Reporting Services server. More details of the reporting features are covered in Chapter 20.

❏ **Data, a key aspect of all business applications, is managed by K2 blackpearl in an innovative way.** Data is stored in the process and can be managed in a similar manner to the way that it was managed in K2.net 2003. However, K2 blackpearl includes new data-handling features that allow the important data to be abstracted from the process and, if it is data from a LOB system, to remain in the LOB system. This is useful in many scenarios, including reporting, process management, process design, and providing access to process data to other applications or LOB systems. The key features that enable these scenarios are SmartObjects and SmartObject Services, details of which are covered in Chapter 7.

## *Anatomy of the K2 Platform*

While those three key features give you a high-level overview of what K2 blackpearl offers, there are other important concepts to understand about the K2 platform. We're going to refer to it as the anatomy of the K2 platform because it's not an architecture per se but rather a view of the entire technology stack that K2 is built on and extends.

On the server, the K2 foundational technologies leverage standard Microsoft server technology, such as Internet Information Services (IIS) and Microsoft Message Queuing (MSMQ), and .NET 3.0. At the heart of K2 is the server, sometimes referred to as the Host Server, which hosts not only the .NET 3.0 WF run time but many K2 services and servers.

> *More detail of these servers and services is covered in Chapter 5.*

Chief among these servers and services are the Workflow server, the SmartObject server, the core servers such as the Dependency server and the User Role server, and the Communication and Discovery services. The Host Server allows all hosted servers and services to communicate using a common framework for sharing data, user credentials, and Single Sign-On (SSO) security tokens. This common framework also provides a mechanism for discovering other Host Servers on the network.

You can also develop custom servers and services to extend the platform.[1] You can substitute custom security providers, logging mechanisms, SmartObject Services, and thread management for the out-of-the-box services that the K2 platform provides. This modular, extensible, pluggable, and scalable design of the K2 platform enables partners and customers to customize and tailor the K2 installation to meet almost any network architecture or security requirements. Moreover, since the core features of the server are built on the common Microsoft framework of Windows server technologies and .NET 3.0, the K2 platform benefits from the scalable and secure framework that those components provide.

The key features of the K2 platform include:

❏ **A highly-scalable and robust process engine:** The engine provides the core business application processing and logic and is built to handle large volumes of processes on a single server. With a distributed topology, the platform is capable of handling an enterprise-class level of processes on a daily basis.

❏ **A common communication and messaging platform:** Built on common protocols, such as HTTP, DTC, and RPC, the K2 platform can be installed in the most demanding environments by using common protocols for server communications.

❏ **Deep integration with Microsoft products and technologies:** This includes SQL Server, Reporting Services, Exchange, Windows SharePoint Services 3.0, and Microsoft Office SharePoint Server (MOSS) 2007, the Microsoft Office 2007 System, Visio 2007, BizTalk 2006, and Visual Studio 2005 and 2008. This also extends to core Microsoft technologies such as Microsoft Message Queuing (MSMQ), Internet Information Services (IIS), SMTP, Network Load Balancing and Clustering, Kerberos, Active Directory, and SQL user manager and the .NET 3.0 and 3.5 technologies such as AJAX, WF, Windows Communication Foundation (WCF), Windows Presentation Foundation (WPF), and Silverlight.

❏ **Integration with line-of-business systems:** This includes both the out-of-the-box capabilities and the additional products like K2 connect for specific systems, such as SAP, Siebel, and Oracle.

❏ **Real-time data flow:** By default, data in the K2 platform isn't cached, which provides the most up-to-date view of business information regardless of the source of that information. The robustness of this aspect of the K2 platform not only allows LOB information to be used in processes but also enables that LOB information to be updated according to business rules and back-end data constraints, which are controlled by the data engine. The same engine also allows snapshots of the data to be captured for compliance or reporting purposes.

❏ **A highly secure platform:** The platform, built on Microsoft technologies, provides out-of-the-box support for fine-grained permissions and role-based task assignment, and a method for handling primary and secondary identifications for each user, all of which are configurable by the administrator.

❏ **Forms and UI:** A dynamic forms capability based on a number of technologies allows custom forms to be rapidly developed for capturing and validating data entered by users.

❏ **Business Involvement:** Involving business users who know more about their job than anyone in the IT department is a key aspect of the K2 platform. Enabling business owners to model, design, and improve their own processes may require some support from the administrators of the technology itself, but it is a vast improvement upon the sometimes antagonistic relationship that business owners have with the owners of the technology development and management staff.

❏ **A continuous Return on Investment:** Through continued quality improvements, additional functionality and entirely new components are incorporated into the K2 platform for the benefit of new and existing customers. Two examples of this include the Out of Office functionality and the updated K2 Designer for SharePoint.

The K2 platform is built on proven technologies and is a reliable, secure platform to build on and extend. Even the most demanding environments can employ K2 to automate and optimize their business processes, and tailor the platform to meet the current and future needs of the business.

---

**Workflow: Build or Buy?**

For many companies, the decision to write workflow applications using the .NET 3.0 Workflow Foundation seems like a good choice, especially if their developers have the skills. After all, the K2 blackpearl server is just a host for the .NET 3.0 Workflow Foundation, right?

There are some scenarios where building custom WF applications is the right choice. Even SharePoint Designer 2007 has the ability to create custom workflows in SharePoint that offer some advanced functionality. Paul Andrew, a technical product manager for the SharePoint Developer Platform at Microsoft, sums the "build versus buy" decision up nicely in his January 16th, 2007, post:[2]

"Ask yourself whether you want to build a software development project or whether you would prefer to buy software from a vendor. WF is a technology that you could use to build the software yourself and by releasing it as part of the .NET Framework Microsoft has essentially made the build argument stronger. But we also made WF available for independent software vendors (ISVs) who are building the products you might otherwise consider. And that means they can build on top of it to provide all the higher level features and business value that isn't in WF."

The higher-level features of K2 blackpearl will be covered extensively in this book, from reporting to process versioning, from LOB integration to processes that communicate with each other, as well as parallel and serial task allocation and dynamic roles. The K2 blackpearl platform provides many simple and advanced features that you can start using right away.

---

# Process-Driven Applications, Today and Tomorrow

By now, you should have a good idea of how workflow and BPM fit together, the basic technical underpinnings of the K2 platform, and a general idea of how businesses can benefit from process automation. In subsequent chapters, you will learn how to identify and build processes that transform your business. For the purposes of this discussion, it is necessary to identify where BPM is today and look forward to where it is going.

By whatever name you give it, applications that are "process-aware" don't look or function like other applications. To the end user involved at a particular step in a process, it may look very much like a traditional application, such as a Web page, a form in InfoPath, or even an instant message that reminds them they have work to do. As such, a process-driven application can act and look like one or more standard applications.

What sets a process-driven application apart from other applications is that it is aware of business rules and the next step in the process. For example, a user may create a Word document in a SharePoint library and fill in some data about that document but have no idea that the information contained within that document, coupled with the data they filled in about that document, allows the process engine to determine what happens next in the process. Process-driven applications can be very dynamic in this way, but of course, that depends on how they were originally designed.

K2 blackpearl provides all of the components to build simple to very complex and dynamic process-driven applications. It also provides the tools for business owners to see where an instance of a process is at any given time and to generate a report of all instances of a single process; all instances of multiple processes for a given department, user, or time of day; or all instances of every process in the organization. Based on that report, instances can be redirected to another user or delegated to a group of users depending on the business need. If the design of a process needs to be updated based on changes in the business, those changes can be made to the process. New instances of the process will reflect the changes in the process, and business owners may also choose to alter existing instances of the process with the new changes (often referred to as "in-flight" changes).

Realizing this vision of operational efficiency and agility is the future of business. BPM and process-driven applications is the road to that future. We contend that it is a future that requires the use of technology, simply because managing business processes and getting the level of transparency that is necessary to make sound business decisions can only be enabled by technology, even in small companies.

The following is a broad sketch of the landscape of the future of process-driven applications. Some of these capabilities are available today in applications that are not process-based, while others define a crucial aspect of process-driven applications that you will learn more about in the next chapter.

- ❏ Applications that leverage existing technologies and employee skill sets to enhance business efficiency
- ❏ Declarative process models that allow in-flight changes and business agility, decoupled from strict code-based models
- ❏ Processes that expose business information in context with a user's task and enable corporate data to be retrieved and updated without the need to switch applications
- ❏ Better insight and visualization of day-to-day business operations for decision makers
- ❏ A robust, scalable, reliable, and secure platform that is easier for IT to manage because it is built using standard technologies
- ❏ Loosely coupled integration with third-party servers and services to enable events, rules, and policy changes to affect processes without needing to alter the process itself
- ❏ Rapid application design and testing with robust simulation capabilities that allows a business to model processes and estimate a Return on Investment before deploying the solution

# Summary

Unlike many books in the Wrox *Professional* series, not all of the chapters in this book dive into code. This book is not meant for a developer-only audience, although developers will find a lot of useful information in this book, including code samples and discussions of the K2 platform API. However, because of the nature of the K2 platform and the fact that for many people the Business Process Discovery phase of implementing a BPM solution may be new, this book attempts to orient and educate both business users and developers about what it means to employ a BPM solution, in particular K2 blackpearl, successfully. Transforming a business to operate more efficiently and enabling better decision making are the key goals of this book. It is our hope that gaining confidence and knowledge of the K2 platform will allow a business process methodology to transform your business, and this book intends to address the full spectrum of ideas, methods, and information to make achieving those key goals a reality.

# Notes

1. At the time of this writing, the Host Server can load only servers and services signed by SourceCode Technology Holdings.

2. "How does Windows Workflow Foundation (WF) compare to product X?" by Paul Andrew, Microsoft Corporation, 2007. `http://blogs.msdn.com/pandrew/archive/2007/01/16/how-does-windows-workflow-foundation-wf-compare-to-product-x.aspx`

# 2

# Evolving Workflow and BPM into Process-Driven Applications

Mike Talley

The evolution from traditional application development to workflow and Business Process Management (BPM) resulted in a much more human-aware application design. Toward the end of this chapter we take a look at the next step in the evolution, setting the stage to get a clear vision of what that application is and how we can refer to it.

In this chapter, we cover the following topics:

- ❏ Defining BPM
- ❏ Common failures of traditional applications
- ❏ Defining a new type of application
- ❏ Approaching process design
- ❏ Process-driven application examples

## What Is BPM?

You might have a good idea of how workflow and BPM are related, but we haven't defined yet what BPM means. According to the article "ABC: An Introduction to Business Process Management (BPM)"[1] published on CIO.com:

BPM is a systematic approach to improving a company's business processes. For example, a BPM application could monitor receiving systems for missing items, or walk an employee through steps to troubleshoot why an order did not arrive. It is the first technology that fosters ongoing collaboration between IT and business users to jointly build applications that effectively integrate people, process and information.

BPM gives an organization the ability to define, execute, manage, and refine processes that:

❑   Involve human interaction, such as placing orders

❑   Work with multiple applications

❑   Handle dynamic process rules and changes, not just simple, static flows (think tasks with multiple choices and contingencies)

Important components include process modeling (a graphical depiction of a process that becomes part of the application and governs how the business process performs when you run the application) and Web and systems integration technologies, which include displaying and retrieving data via a Web browser and which enable you to orchestrate the necessary people and legacy applications into your processes. Another important component is what's been termed business activity monitoring, which gives reports on exactly how (and how well) the business processes and flow are working.

Optimizing processes that involve people and dynamic change has been difficult historically. One barrier to optimization has been the lack of visibility and ownership for processes that span functional departments or business units. In addition, the business often changes faster than IT can update applications that the business relies on to do its work, thus stifling innovation, growth, performance, and so on.

Alluded to in the brief history of enterprise application development in the first chapter, the struggle between the business and IT causes friction that, in the modern business environment, is counterproductive, potentially harmful, and unnecessary.

By adhering to an outdated method of application development, companies will find themselves involved in the same struggle that leads to common problems with traditional applications as outlined in the following table:

| Problem | Description |
| --- | --- |
| Inflexibility | When the business changes, the representation of the business must be changed in the application. Rules, processes, roles, and logic that are hardcoded into the application require a lot of effort to alter and redeploy. This long turnaround time makes the business less agile in responding to changes. |
| Lack of visibility | Reporting, tracking, and auditing are often afterthoughts for traditional applications. These things are seen as a "nice to have" feature for the next version. In a process-based application these items are critical for seeing how the business is doing and making good decisions. |

| Problem | Description |
|---------|-------------|
| Strict functional boundaries/no collaboration | Traditional applications are often departmental in nature, limiting the scope of the application to a subset of the company's users. Furthermore, active collaboration among departments, from design to deployment to the production use of the application, is not possible because the toolsets for each department are different. |
| External partners not involved | The application and sometimes the infrastructure are unable to handle variability when it comes to involving those outside of the firewall. |
| Business forced to adapt to the application | Many applications, either built or purchased, require the business to adapt to the application, not the other way around. For some industries this is acceptable, but for most industries an application that can incorporate industry-specific data, methods, and context is more likely to be successfully deployed and to increase the efficiency of the business. |

BPM is a methodology for improving application development that allows for rapid business change and crosses functional boundaries. But not all BPM strategies and software suites are the same, and they cannot be compared across feature sets or product capabilities. In contrast to traditional application development, following a strict "workflow" or "BPM" strategy may be difficult for companies that don't have a process management team. Some common mistakes that companies find when trying to introduce BPM to the organization are:

- ❑ **Trying to do all departments and all processes at once:** It is better to start small and identify those areas of the business that are most critical to the functioning of the business. Then, start with one complex process or a handful of smaller processes.

- ❑ **Getting lost in the implementation phase:** There is sometimes a complex mix of systems, departments, internal and external customers, and data requirements for processes. Following a strict BPM method may prove too time-consuming and ultimately end with a failed project.

- ❑ **User revolt:** Many times, if the interface of the business application is too difficult to use, if it doesn't save people time, or if it interferes with a user's actual job, the system will not be used. Users will find ways to short-circuit the application or process, using backchannels to get their work done. Since Return on Investment (ROI) is in many respects based on an application's adoption rate, this can have a drastic effect on the business value an application brings.

K2 blackpearl, while not a panacea for all BPM implementation problems, allows for rapid application development by both business users who understand their work and more technical users who can solve some of the data and process problems that may exist when integrating data from other systems into a single user interface. Calling K2 blackpearl a BPM platform, while accurate in many ways, does not illustrate the full power of the platform for delivering business applications. K2 blackpearl is a different type of platform for quickly assembling business applications that people will use. Furthermore, the business applications that you can design with K2 blackpearl may not have any processes associated with them, or may have processes that are only instantiated when certain conditions are met. These types of business applications would use the K2 platform to aggregate information from line-of-business (LOB) systems and present a user interface that allows for easy data aggregation, retrieval, and updating. If processes such as escalations or management approval were required, the user could launch a process to handle that aspect of the application. These types of applications are sometimes referred to as *composite applications* and bear resemblance to Web 2.0 and mash-up applications.

Whatever the type of business application, developing them with K2 blackpearl is advantageous for a number of reasons, including:

- ❑ **The business is involved:** When the business is involved in the design and testing of the application, the user interface (that is, forms and reports) can be designed in a way that the users of the application will be comfortable with and actually use. This, combined with the next point, solves two of the problems of traditional applications discussed earlier.

- ❑ **IT is involved:** IT can use the features of the platform to bring together disparate systems through Web services and the built-in SmartObject Services data layer; the entire process builds upon the existing investments but is modeled at the business level rather than being limited at the technology level. For more information about SmartObjects, see Chapter 7. Active collaboration between the business and IT results in a better application that is tailored to the business. The business can draw their process in Visio or K2 Studio and hand that project over to IT, who can then extend it in Visual Studio. For more information about how this collaboration works, see Chapter 14.

- ❑ **Processes can be rapidly built and deployed:** Processes that don't require a lot of design and collaboration between business and technical users can be quickly put into production use. Even those that require a lot of collaboration are much faster to develop than traditional applications. The platform and the infrastructure on which it operates enable an incremental approach for process-driven applications to enter production.

- ❑ **Maintaining the process is simplified:** When business rules change, the process needs to account for those changes. Processes designed with K2 blackpearl can be very dynamic, but sometimes the process design must be updated and redeployed. Often this type of change can be handled by the business without the need to involve IT.

Subsequent chapters will discuss process design best practices, including how K2 blackpearl enables collaborative design (see Chapter 14), how processes can integrate with enterprise systems through SmartObjects (see Chapter 7), and how to design very flexible processes that are easy to maintain and actually get used in the day-to-day operations of the business. You will also learn much more about the K2 blackpearl platform and how to take advantage of it to make your business more successful. But the key points to be made here are that your K2 blackpearl application design should:

- ❑ **Not be stifled by traditional application development approaches or by adhering to a strict BPM-based approach.** While using BPM methodologies is very important, if an aspect of BPM does not fit with your business application, ask yourself "Can I safely ignore this point?" If the answer is "Yes," continue on with more important aspects of the project.

- ❑ **Have business ownership.** A successful project almost always has executive level sponsorship if not outright ownership.

- ❑ **Not underestimate the time it will take to gather business requirements.** Often identifying key players, data, and metrics is more time-consuming than actually building and deploying the process.

❑ **Be made up of a cross-functional team and builds high-value applications quickly.** These applications should be designed to provide immediate value and possibly tie in to corporate goals and current strategies. Once people from all levels in your company see the value this new type of business application provides, they will want more and more process-driven applications identified, built, and deployed.

So what is this type of application?

# A New Type of Application

This new type of application has many names and is supported by evolutions in the underlying information systems. Referred to by some as a dynamic business application, by others as a process or process-driven application, and by still others as a business process solution, this type of business application combines aspects of a traditional BPM solution with a collaborative, multidisciplinary implementation team that can work toward a common goal. Many technologies and methodologies have given rise to this type of application. All of these methodologies identify the need to discover, optimize, and improve complex business processes. These include Business Process Reengineering (BPR), Business Process Discovery (BPD), Process Driven Development (PDD), and Workflow Management (WFM). Though these methodologies are beyond the scope of this book, there are many resources available online for learning about them.

Technologies that support these methods include generic and well-understood architectures such as Web services, Extensible Markup Language (XML), Service-Oriented Architecture (SOA) and Enterprise Application Integration (EAI), as well as the more specific terms such as Process Aware Information Systems (PAIS). PAIS is defined as a "software system that manages and executes the operational processes involving people, application, and/or information sources on the basis of process models."[2] Microsoft defines the evolution and state of a business's infrastructure in their Business Productivity Infrastructure Optimization (BPIO) campaign.[3] The following table illustrates the evolution of a Microsoft-based infrastructure and how K2 blackpearl fits in:

| BPIO Model | Basic | Standardized | Rationalized | Dynamic |
|---|---|---|---|---|
| Business application capability | Document Routing | Workflow | BPM | Process-Driven Applications |
| Microsoft products | Windows SharePoint Services (WSS) v3 | WSS/Microsoft Office SharePoint Server (MOSS) 2007 Visio | WSS/MOSS Visio InfoPath | WSS/MOSS Visio InfoPath OCS BizTalk SQL BI PerformancePoint |
| K2 products | K2 blackpoint | K2 blackpoint K2 blackpearl | K2 blackpearl | K2 blackpearl K2 connect |

The Dynamic column represents a process-oriented, flexible infrastructure that can adapt to a changing business environment. Yet, according to Microsoft, most companies are at the Basic or Standardized level.

According to Forrester,[4] a dynamic business application is:

❏ A software system that embodies a business process

❏ Built for change

❏ Adaptable to business context

❏ Information-rich

These applications are built for rapid modification and extension, to change as the business rules change. The processes adapt their behavior to respond to variable conditions, and contextualize information and processes for people. These processes may be short-lived, ad hoc tools as the situation demands.

There are two key requirements of dynamic business applications:

❏ **Design for people:** The application should be dynamic and developed by business people and IT together, with appropriate contextualization of information and tasks. The application interface is designed for the work, not dictated by application boundaries or a strict adherence to an interface standard.

❏ **Build for change:** The application must be able to evolve at a pace designed to match the business change, with flexible points built into the structure of the design.

Building a dynamic business application requires that the business users and the IT department work together to design the application. Because this collaboration crosses organizational boundaries, the team dynamics can be challenging. However, the K2 platform provides different design experiences for different types of people with varying technical skills. The platform is designed with collaboration as a key value point, and every K2 Designer generates the same underlying project structure to facilitate collaboration and reuse of design work.

Some organizations have fairly rigid standards for building and deploying business applications. It does not matter whether you mandate that IT must be responsible for all software builds and changes or you allow other people in the business to actively participate. K2 blackpearl is designed to handle these scenarios and all variations in between. The next sections take a closer look at the scenarios.

## Designed and Delivered by IT

IT teams can design, build, and deploy dynamic business applications within the context of a team. K2 includes libraries for sharing environmental information and items within the K2 design environments. Developers can also version code and deploy the solution through multiple development and production environments.

## Business Collaboration with IT

IT deploys the K2 server environment and set of core items that can be shared and used by the business to create solutions. The solutions created may include some business-user-defined logic (built with wizards and browser-based tools) but also require some customization available only with developer tools (K2 Designer for Visual Studio). IT may also require that its own staff manages quality assurance (QA) and deployment for the organization. Reports can be designed and deployed by either the business users or IT.

## Business Designed, IT Delivered

IT provides the business users with a set of tools that they can use to model what they need. For example, business users can leverage Visio to model a business process or write policies in common language. IT has the ability to leverage these designs and quickly bring them to life by consuming them within K2 Designer for Visual Studio, extending the applications and then managing the QA and deployment process. IT can deliver a standard set of reports that allows for some personalization.

## Business Empowered by IT

IT deploys the K2 server environment and a set of core items that can be shared and used by the business to create solutions. For example, the IT team may create reusable wizards, business entities, and policies for use by all business users. A business user could then design, deploy, modify, and report on a process-driven application that leverages these items through Visio or a browser-based designer without any IT involvement.

---

### The Spreadsheet Analogy

The last scenario, "Business Empowered by IT," represents a key step forward for business applications in general, both for IT and for the business. For this analogy, picture in your head the spreadsheet jockey who does everything in Excel. Everyone knows somebody like this. He's the guy you pay a visit to when you want to do a quick analysis of your data or add another column to your spreadsheet to do a slightly different calculation. He's the guy who wants to solve all problems in Excel because (a) he's really good at Excel, and (b) he can usually solve the problem with this Swiss Army Knife of office applications. That represents a business user solving the business problem, adapting the application to fit the need, without the need for a big system change or IT involvement. It's also the vision of business user empowerment. It's not the out of control "who has the latest version?" spreadsheet problem but the business user making a change to the application when the change needs to happen. Changes to applications are often minor — a new field here, a different option there — that can easily be accomplished by those who know their business. Empowering them to modify the application makes them more effective.

Where the spreadsheet analogy fails, thankfully, is that the change to the process-driven applications happens in an auditable, secure, and revertible manner, and in a way that can immediately benefit other users of the process, as well as IT, management, and the entire business

---

# Approaching Process-Driven Application Design

Regardless of the physical makeup of the team building it, who ultimately maintains it, or which department drives the adoption of process-based applications within the company, a successful process-based application is different from a traditional application. Other chapters (including Chapters 3 and 8) include more specific details about how to successfully design process-based applications, but at a high level they include the following aspects:

❑ **Pursue an incremental adoption.** Each initiative is focused on a specific goal that provides value to the business. Don't try to automate everything right away. Start with one department and a few processes that can show immediate value. Not being able to show some tangible value from the first few process-driven applications that you create, while unlikely, does not help users of the application or decision makers have faith in the platform.

❑ **Give people tools and applications they already know.** Making people who are designing and using process-driven applications use a different toolset than they normally use will make them uncomfortable. This will dramatically slow adoption of process-driven applications. A slow adoption means that the first point will be more difficult to achieve.

❑ **Leverage the platform you already have.** Many companies already have an infrastructure that enables process-based applications to thrive. Some companies may have to increase some of the infrastructure's capabilities with some custom development or product purchases. However, if your company uses a Microsoft-based platform and has enterprise licenses, most of the capability should already be in place to deploy K2 blackpearl.

❑ **Make the application easy to use and relevant to the people using it.** Design the application from the user's perspective. Contextualize information and business data as it relates to each task in the process. This aspect of a successful process-driven application is enhanced by the two previous points, that is, integrating task-based information in the environment and applications people already know that leverage your existing systems. Users will require less training and recognize how the application makes it easier for them to get their job done.

These aspects of a successful process-driven application make sense from business investment (ROI) and user adoption perspectives. They are interrelated and build on each other, and once you internalize a successful approach to process-driven application design, you may start accepting these as common sense. From a historical perspective this approach to application design might seem unattainable or even a bit nonsensical. But given the Web 2.0, the growing technical skills of the average employee, and the state of the typical infrastructure in a company today, this dynamic approach to application design is achievable.

# Evolving Workflow: Two Scenarios

Two examples of real-world scenarios can illustrate the power of this dynamic approach to application design. Both of these scenarios have a few things in common, namely:

- ❑ They were relatively quick to implement.

- ❑ The efficiency of the process increased dramatically.

- ❑ New scenarios for reporting and decision making were enabled.

- ❑ The application included LOB system integration.

- ❑ Previous attempts to automate the process failed.

## Scenario 1: SOX Compliance

A Fortune 500 company found itself navigating the Sarbanes-Oxley compliance waters around IT User Access and Provisioning. This included creating new accounts for contractors and employees and granting access to the various applications and systems that were used within the company.

The first attempt was a quick-and-dirty, one-page Word document where end users were required to fill out cryptic fields, get the document signed by their manager and whoever was responsible for the application, then put it in an inbox next to the IT secretary's desk. Someone on the IT Help Desk staff would check the box when they remembered and then grant the access, if they could read the form. Requests for new accounts generally took 3–5 business days. The onus was put back on the business to request access well ahead of the time when they would actually need the access, which with new employees was generally set by a start date. But for contractors, this was always difficult and usually ended up with the contractor being on-site, billing the company for hours wasted while waiting for IT access to be granted.

The second attempt was the first attempt at automation and just involved adding a fax number to the equation. Now, users could fax the filled-out request to the number, which would send the electronic copy to the inboxes of the IT Help Desk staff. This was marginally better, as there wasn't a reliance on checking a physical inbox for forms.

However, both of these attempts failed miserably when it came to the IT audit. Once a quarter, Internal Audit would come through and demand to see the stacks of forms and would ask IT to cross-reference them against a list of new employees. Digging through stacks of forms and file cabinets and people's desks took up to 2 weeks of the Help Desk's time, adding further delay to the backlog of IT access requests.

The company decided to automate the process using K2. Over the period of 6 months, a team came together to define the process and the actors. A list of all the applications, roles, and the information owners was collected for the corporate office. This was the first time that all of the data was collected into a single source of "the truth." The act of defining the approvers and roles for each application was a huge boost to the IT staff, as before they had to track down someone to sign an application, and they were never sure who to ask in the first place. Once that list of applications, roles, and approvers was in a single place, the process was automated rather quickly. Using SharePoint lists to store the data, IT used InfoPath forms to surface the list of applications and roles for the end user to select from. A Web service allowed tight integration with Active Directory and allowed new accounts to be created, complete with Exchange mailboxes and access to certain default distribution lists and groups. For application access, if membership in an Active Directory group was all that was required, upon approval the access was granted immediately, with no human interaction required. If the system had other authorization mechanisms built into the software, the fully approved request was sent to the system administrator to be fulfilled. After the request was fulfilled, it was archived in a document library in SharePoint.

Towards the end of the project, lunch and learns were held with the staff members to describe the new process and forms. Each session ended with a standing ovation. After the forms and workflow were rolled out, department secretaries could go back to doing their regular job and didn't have to fight with IT access forms. New accounts were created in 20 minutes after approval. Access to many systems was almost immediate. Because all requests were stored electronically, when Internal Audit came through it was a matter of minutes to pull a report and print out the evidence they requested. No forms were misplaced, and no form was approved by the wrong person. Bottlenecks were identified for those requests that took a long time to get approval, and adjustments were made to ease the burden on the business owners.

## Scenario 2: Design Review Process and LOB Integration

A global manufacturing organization had three main needs:

❏ **Document Management:** They needed a single place to store and manage documents. They were trying to move away from network file shares.

❏ **Workflow:** They needed a workflow system that would tightly integrate with the document management system to allow for true document-centric workflow. The ability to control access to documents at various steps in the approval process was also a requirement. They needed a system that was flexible enough to integrate with existing LOB systems, including custom and off-the-shelf systems like SAP.

❏ **Dashboards:** IT needed a way to build meaningful reports against information in various systems to surface to management. The current system was comprised of paper-based wall charts that engineers manually updated using a pen.

They needed to start a design review process from an existing in-house application. The data collected during the review process had to be uploaded to SAP upon completion of the review. They also needed to surface reports that combined LOB data from SAP with data about the workflow, including metrics collected on the workflow itself. The current review process was manual, so the opportunity for gaining efficiency was great.

They spent a significant amount of time and money attempting to develop this solution with a different product. However they were not able to seamlessly integrate the various workflow, user interface (UI), reporting, and SAP pieces in a timely manner.

The development of the process-driven application lasted a total of 2 weeks. In this timeframe, K2 blackpearl and K2 connect were installed. K2 connect SmartObjects were developed against the appropriate SAP function modules. The workflow and an InfoPath form were created to interact with the process and the LOB data. Finally reports were created to display the SAP and K2 workflow data within a SharePoint dashboard.

# Summary

Forrester summarizes in the report cited earlier that dynamic business applications "can provide much more productive experiences for businesspeople, make breakthroughs in the automation of decisions and business processes, and provide the points of flex that businesses need. Our applications don't do this today. Our businesses need them to."

The evolution of the business application, by whatever name, is the next step for companies. There are many advantages to this approach. The next chapter provides a high-level overview of identifying processes in your company, a framework for thinking about the various pieces of the process, and some best practice guidance on how to put a project team together.

# Notes

1. "ABC: An Introduction to Business Process Management (BPM)" by Mark Cooper and Paul Patterson. CIO.com, 2007. www.cio.com/article/106609/ ABC_An_Introduction_to_Business_Process_wManagement_BPM_/1

2. *Process Aware Information Systems: Bridging People and Software through Process Technology* by Marlon Dumas, Wil M. P. van der Aalst, and Arthur H. M. ter Hofstede (Wiley, 2005).

3. Microsoft Corporation, Business Productivity Infrastructure Optimization: Overview. Accessed at www .microsoft.com/business/peopleready/bizinfra/campaign_overview.mspx

4. "The Dynamic Business Applications Imperative" by John R. Rymer and Connie Moore (Forrester Research, 2007).

# 3

# Designing Process-Driven Applications

Mike Talley

Identifying and designing process-driven applications is both an art and a science. Many times you will know which departments could benefit most when pursuing an incremental adoption of K2 blackpearl. Other times you will need to take a look at your company's organizational entities, how they interact with each other, and which ones are the most process-based already.

Take a minute to think about a process in your company. Keep that process in mind as you read this chapter. When you are finished reading, write down the major pieces of the process and ask yourself some of the questions included at the end of this chapter. Does your process fit some or most of the criteria of a good process for automation?

Also keep in mind that the methodologies and project roles identified in this chapter are meant for an organization that has a relatively mature Business Process Management (BPM) initiative in place. While you can strive toward this "ideal" environment, don't let a few missing pieces discourage you from designing your first process-driven application. Many times the first few applications that you build will be a great learning experience and can help you identify what you realistically need to build your next process-driven application.

This chapter covers the following topics:

- ❑ Evaluating potential processes for automation
- ❑ Running a process-driven application project, including methodologies, time estimation, and project roles
- ❑ Identifying the business requirements of a process
- ❑ Evaluating potential benefits of process automation

# The Typical Enterprise

While there is no "typical" enterprise, many enterprises share a common organizational structure. An enterprise is nothing without employees or customers. You are in business for a reason, whether that is to sell a physical product or a Service. You probably have partners, suppliers, one or more banks that you deal with, and possibly a manufacturing plant and a warehouse. All of these departments, or business entities, form a critical part of your organization. They all interact with one or more of the other entities in your organization. The bank issues payroll checks to your staff, your sales staff contacts your customers to identify new business, and your customers contact your staff for support; every day there are many points of contact that each business entity makes with the other business entities. Figure 3-1 shows a high-level view of a company.

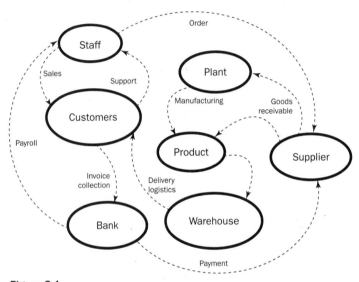

**Figure 3-1**

Drilling in to a particular business entity (see Figure 3-2), you'll find more points of contact with other business entities, which will lead you to even more business entities. In addition to your sales and support staff interacting with your customers, when you look closer you'll see that Finance also has a key role to play when making payments and collecting invoices. At the macro-level, Finance and HR didn't appear at all. This is the nature of every business — the more you look, the more points of contact you will find among your employees, customers, and partners. Each of these points of contact is a process. You may be surprised at the number of processes that you will be able to identify in just a few hours.

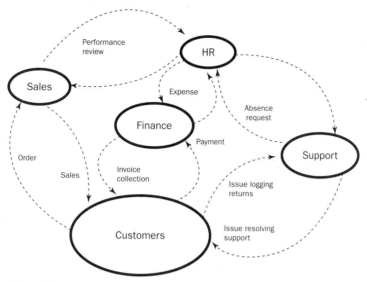

Figure 3-2

# Getting into a Process

Earlier in the chapter, we asked you to identify a process that you want to investigate further. Now it's time to take that process and break it down into some pieces (see Figure 3-3). What are the building blocks? Common to almost all processes are the following items:

- ❏ **Forms:** The way information is gathered and displayed.

- ❏ **Information:** The data that is gathered, displayed, or collected while the application is running.

- ❏ **People:** People are involved in all business processes, either directly through taking some action or indirectly by monitoring performance and viewing a report.

- ❏ **Policies:** The rules that govern a process and the business.

- ❏ **Actions:** Steps users take to move the process along.

- ❏ **Reports:** A view of related information useful to decision makers and process optimizers.

- ❏ **Event Monitoring:** The ability for a process to respond to external events.

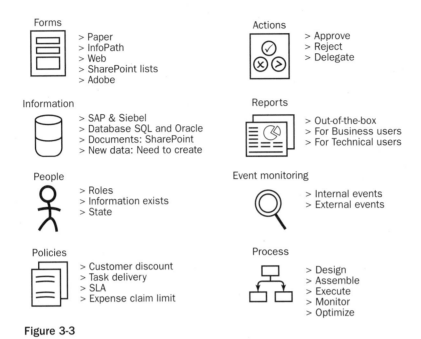

Forms
> Paper
> InfoPath
> Web
> SharePoint lists
> Adobe

Actions
> Approve
> Reject
> Delegate

Information
> SAP & Siebel
> Database SQL and Oracle
> Documents: SharePoint
> New data: Need to create

Reports
> Out-of-the-box
> For Business users
> For Technical users

People
> Roles
> Information exists
> State

Event monitoring
> Internal events
> External events

Policies
> Customer discount
> Task delivery
> SLA
> Expense claim limit

Process
> Design
> Assemble
> Execute
> Monitor
> Optimize

**Figure 3-3**

These building blocks, in turn, bring up some good questions about the process, such as:

❑ What type of forms does your organization currently use?

❑ What type of information is gathered and used in those forms?

❑ Where is the information stored?

❑ Who is using those forms?

❑ What are they doing with that information or those forms?

❑ Who gets alerted when there is a problem with the form or data?

❑ Who needs to see the aggregated view of the data?

❑ What type of aggregation of the data is needed?

When you start learning about the process there will be more questions than answers. There are individuals within your organization who know the answers to one or more of these questions, and you will have to find them and ask them more about the process. Be thorough and cautious in this process discovery phase. A thorough approach allows you to put together a complete picture of the process, or as complete as you can get. This allows you to identify noncritical or potentially wrong information that you receive from people. It also allows you and the business owners, if that isn't you, to take a critical, objective view of the process. You don't want to automate a bad process; it will just go bad quicker than it used to.

While being thorough and cautious is good, it's not something that has to introduce anxiety or overwhelm you. Keep pushing through the process until you have enough information to work with. As you begin to understand the process, you and those you are working with will already begin to identify pieces of the process that can probably be improved. That's good. Write those down. These are precisely the items that process discovery helps illustrate.

Many times you will find people who know the "what" or "how" of the process, but the "why" of the process is "because that's the way we've always done it." This is not necessarily bad. If the culture of your company typically takes a critical eye to how it does business, the accepted way of doing things is probably okay (but maybe it could be improved). If your company does not typically pursue best practices, then your job of separating out the real process from noncritical aspects of the process will be more difficult.

Speaking of culture, many businesses are open and accepting of change. In this type of environment, making a complete assessment of a process will be less difficult than in a business environment that is not open and accepting of change. The best option in these latter environments is to pick a department that seems more likely to accept change (the "least bad" option), get executive-level support, or better yet, ownership of the process, and identify a process that will add immediate value.

A lot of this sounds more like project management than identifying and building a process-driven application. That's because it is. Therefore, it's useful to spend some time looking at project management and get back to the process itself toward the end of the chapter.

# Project Management Fundamentals

Like any successful project, having a strong methodology for process-driven application design will help ensure a successful deployment. We all know that we should follow a strict methodology and not skip any steps. Theoretically that makes sense, but it is hard to be disciplined with the documentation when deadlines are looming. There are many excuses why people shortcut the project methodology, but without proper planning and a structured design and development methodology, project success is at risk.

There are several reasons why development projects fail:

- ❑ Corporate goals are not understood at the lower organizational levels.
- ❑ Plans encompass too much in too little time.
- ❑ Plans are based on inefficient data.
- ❑ No attempt is made to systematize the planning process.
- ❑ No one knows the major milestone dates and the ultimate goal of the project.
- ❑ Project estimates are best guesses, not based upon standards or history.
- ❑ Not enough time is given for proper estimation.
- ❑ Resources are not available with the necessary skills.
- ❑ People are not working toward the same specifications.
- ❑ There is high turnover in the project team, without regard to schedule.
- ❑ There is poor risk foresight.

These are some of the major pitfalls that many projects encounter. The basis for all of these is poor planning or no proper insight into a project methodology. A well structured methodology can ensure the successful delivery of any project and can steer the project clear of the pitfalls just mentioned.

## *Methodology and Approaches*

In the last section of Chapter 2, we talked about a very agile method of developing and deploying process-driven applications. But agile development methodologies are not always suited to business process development projects, especially when the project team and the processes are large. In the end, the processes need to be well understood and analyzed before any development can begin. The following approaches can be successfully employed:

❑ **Big bang approach:** Develop all forms, processes, and subprocesses and integration components.

  ❑ **Pros:** If processes and technology are very well understood, this approach will bring about major changes at once.

  ❑ **Cons:** Business processes can change between analysis and deployment phases, which may be a longer elapsed time than in iterative approaches.

❑ **Iterative approach:** Develop a small number of workflow steps, with only the corresponding forms, and then keep reworking this based on stakeholder feedback.

  ❑ **Pros:** Technology is understood rapidly by stakeholders, and small changes in business process appear almost immediately.

  ❑ **Cons:** Feedback loop can be long, and requirements can change more rapidly than the project team can keep up with.

❑ **Quick wins approach:** Develop the simplest processes first.

  ❑ **Pros:** Technology can be proven, and the platform can be adopted faster.

  ❑ **Cons:** More complex processes will lead to refactoring steps that might push the need to revisit the simple processes.

❑ **Slice approach**: Develop a single process from the front end through the workflow all the way to the system integration.

  ❑ **Pros:** Entire architecture proven and risks and problems identified up front, making subsequent processes faster to deploy.

  ❑ **Cons:** In some organizations, this approach can be challenging when all stakeholders have to be involved in a short period of time.

The best approach can be different for each organization, and the methodology will evolve as the process team becomes more mature. Many organizations choose to combine aspects of these approaches. For example, an iterative/simple/slice approach will automate a simple process from the front-end to the back-end integration in an iterative fashion.

# Linear vs. Nonlinear Processes

Another important aspect of your approach to process design is whether your process is linear or nonlinear. Linear processes typically follow the same set of steps that remain constant over time, such as procurement within a government agency. Other processes (nonlinear ones) change frequently, adjusting to outside business factors. Some are long running, and some are temporary. Others are ad hoc, requiring reallocation of work and flexibility in the number of users involved. When designing process-driven applications, it is important to consider dynamic activities, reassignments, unanticipated events that change actions or information, integration with other systems, nonlinear communication, and other unanticipated activities.

Just as with business processes, the BPM implementation process can sometimes be linear, following the standard flow of design: assemble, execute, monitor, and optimize (see Figure 3-4).

Figure 3-4

However, many times the implementation process looks more like a spiral. There may be multiple, coexisting spirals that have dependencies on one another. Or, the first process may be a subprocess of another with dependencies on others. Figure 3-5 illustrates a nonlinear model of process-driven application development.

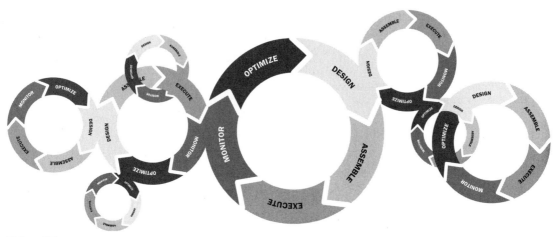

Figure 3-5

# Project Roles

For a successful project, there are several key roles that must be filled on your project team. A single person may fill more than one of these roles, or many people may play a single role. If you are just starting down the BPM path, your entire team could be two or three people, which is fine for now.

- ❑ **Project Manager (PM):** The Project Manager is responsible for the project timeline and plan, organizing meetings, ensuring the project stays on time and on budget, filling roles with available project resources, identifying risks, and removing obstacles to the success of the project.

- ❑ **Business Owner:** The Business Owner is responsible for the business process, which may span multiple departments or areas of responsibility. The Business Owner works closely with the PM to ensure that resources from the business are available and are responding promptly to the needs of the project. The Business Owner is also responsible for all approvals, or sign-offs, of the project. If the Business Owner is not an executive-level employee, they are responsible for getting executive-level sponsorship of the project, when necessary.

- ❑ **Subject Matter Experts (SMEs):** SMEs have intrinsic knowledge of the business process or technical system and play a critical role in the design of the application. They can also play a key role in making decisions during the building and testing of the application.

- ❑ **Information Owner:** The Information Owner is responsible for the underlying technology and knows the system and data better than anyone.

- ❑ **Business Analyst:** The Business Analyst is responsible for the documentation of the process, including the business requirements, use cases, form design, and data requirements. The Business Analyst is a key conduit of information from the SMEs and Business Owners to the Process Designers.

- ❑ **Process Designer:** The Process Designer is responsible for the design of the application. Many times, a Process Designer can also be the Business Analyst and can use tools like the K2 Designer for Visio to develop the business processes. It is the role of the Process Designer to translate the business requirements to the K2 features that will fulfill the needs of the application.

❑ **Developer:** The Developer is responsible for developing any custom code that is needed as well as the integration points into line-of-business systems. The Developer will use tools such as the K2 Designer for Visual Studio to leverage the K2 API to build custom forms, custom reports, or custom applications to support the application.

❑ **Tester:** The Tester is responsible for documenting the test cases based on the use cases provided by the Business Analyst. Once the system has been developed, the Tester will test the application and provide feedback to the project team. The Tester is responsible for sign-off that the application has passed all critical test cases and is ready for release.

❑ **Change Management:** Change Management is responsible for the communication and training plan for the application. While usually an afterthought, the change management portion of a project is critical for the successful implementation.

❑ **Releaser:** The Releaser, sometimes referred to as the Product Manager, is responsible for the release of the application. They are usually not a dedicated member of the project team, but it is critical that the Product Manager clearly communicates to the Project Manager what the release guidelines and regulations are to avoid any surprises near the release date.

The preceding roles are those most commonly found in business process projects. For a large project, each role listed could be a team in and of itself, with a team lead and team members. For a small project, a single person may play more than one role listed. The important part is not how many people make up the team, but that each role is filled and that resources are not over allocated.

## Time Management and Estimation

Time management is important for all members of the project team. A culture of effective time management must be created in order to ensure the success and promptness of milestones within a project' lifecycle. There are several rules for time management that should be practiced during the project:

❑ Conduct time analysis.

❑ Plan solid blocks for important things.

❑ Classify activities.

❑ Establish priorities.

❑ Establish opportunity cost on activities.

❑ Practice delegation.

❑ Practice calculated neglect.

❑ Practice management by exception.

❑ Focus on opportunities, not on problems.

Alongside the rules, there are several questions that team members can ask when trying to manage their time effectively:

❑ What am I doing that I don't have to be doing at all?

❑ What am I doing that can be done better by someone else?

❑ What am I doing that could be done sufficiently well by someone else?

❑ Am I establishing the right priorities for my activities?

While time management is crucial for ensuring the project is delivered on time, proper estimation of the project tasks is also essential. In order for the Project Manager to effectively plan and control a project, it must be estimated correctly from the beginning. The Estimator's task is to predict the project's parameters by building a model of the project on paper. The quality and accuracy of the estimate should be seen as the best approximation based on:

❑ Time available

❑ Information available

❑ Techniques employed

❑ Expertise and experience of available resources

Because of the nature of any business, it is expected that the project is committed to a budget and a deadline early in the project's life. Limited information regarding a project is available during the beginning phase of a project. This makes it very important that all resources participating in the estimation process be skilled in time estimates to provide accurate estimates based on incomplete information.

Due to organizational nuances, it is important to estimate projects based on the known constraints of an organization. For example, if the Releaser for your project works only on Fridays, it is important to take that restraint into account when setting up your timeline.

## Set Expectations

One of the key success criteria for a project is that expectations are met with the final project. The Project Manager should start setting expectations early when you are defining your project methodology and team members. This should include:

❑ **Meeting schedule:** Be sure to let people know when and where the project meetings will occur, as well as an agenda ahead of time.

❑ **Communication schedule:** Publish the communication schedule, for both internal project communications and external communications. Be sure to include review and approval time for external communications.

❑ **Deliverable checkpoints:** Publish the checkpoints and deliverable dates and hold meetings for feedback. Be sure to allow enough time for the Business Owners and SMEs to review. Remember, this project may not be their full focus and be respectful of their other obligations.

❑ **Collaboration mechanism:** Decide where documents, decisions, issues, and all project-related information will be stored.

Once you've set the expectations, be sure to hold to what you promise. Having a good track record with your Business Owner and SMEs will ensure that future projects will be more predictable.

# Defining the Business Requirements

Now that you understand the project methodologies and roles, you can get back to the business process itself. Note that the methodology and roles are completely independent of the business process you will tackle in this project; they are common across all projects.

If the process is large and complex, this phase will take significantly longer to complete than you might first estimate. Plan for and expect a long discovery phase. The amount of time and effort that you put into this phase will make the rest of the process implementation phase much faster and less prone to errors and rework.

The best way to find out the answers to your questions is to ask. There are three basic categories of questions that you want to ask and the next three sections give some examples. Though not an exhaustive list of the types of questions you need to ask, these can give you a good start toward identifying your process requirements and building the basis for evaluating the benefits of automating the process.

## Process Questions

It is always good to know as much as you can about the process. This can give you insight into where the process is currently working and perhaps where it is not. It also helps you start to identify the requirements of the process and eventually, its main goals. Process questions include the following:

❏   What is the process today?

❏   Where does stuff live (that is, Where is the data? Where are the forms?)

❏   How do people interact with the application and/or process?

❏   What are the external requirements (for example, Audit, Legal)?

❏   What are some of the issues or bottlenecks with the process today?

## People Questions

Without people a process is just a programming exercise. People are key to understanding the business process and often have knowledge about the process that no one else does. People questions include the following:

❏   Who owns which aspects of the process?

❏   Who participates in the process?

❏   Who knows how this process works today? Should work tomorrow?

## Entities Questions

Your entities could simply be the departments within your company, or they could represent functional roles that span multiple job titles and departments. They could also encapsulate internal business policies, or external governmental laws, or business association standards. Understanding your entities helps you round out the process requirements. Entities questions include the following:

- ❏ What are the primary organizational entities in this process?
- ❏ What are the business entities or objects associated with this process?
- ❏ What are the business rules that govern this process?

## Evaluating Potential Processes

When an organization is looking at process automation, the reality is that any process can be automated. It is a matter of deciding whether or not it makes sense to the business to automate the process.

The following questions can be used as guidelines and criteria for determining if your processes should be automated:

- ❏ **If this process did not exist, what would the impact be to your business?** With the response to this question, the perceived value of the process can be determined. Based on this perceived value, you can perform a cost/benefit analysis either to justify the project or to discard the process from the selection. In the next chapter we discuss ROI calculations. Make these numbers part of your project plan.

- ❏ **Has this process been mapped or optimized before?** If yes, then there is probably a good definition of the process that can be used as a starting point for the project. Even a Visio diagram of the process can help identify where additional questions should be asked to see if the process is a good fit. If no, then the process probably needs to be defined in more detail to understand if it is a good fit.

- ❏ **Do you have disparate business systems that need to participate within a single business process? Do you need to obtain data from other information systems?** If yes, then it is a good candidate for a process-driven application as integration with LOB systems is a key component of the K2 platform. Additional questions around this topic will help clarify the data requirements and determine if custom development work is required to retrieve and update data in the line-of-business (LOB) systems.

- ❏ **Is there data or a form that needs multiple people to review and/or approve?** If yes, then it is a good candidate for a business process. Additional questions around this topic will help identify the data and form requirements, tracking and auditability, as well as the process roles.

- ❏ **Does this process require more than one type of review or decision at the same time?** If yes, then it is a good candidate for a process application as handling the routing and tracking of decisions is a key component to the platform. Additional questions around this topic will help identify parallel or serial processing for activities.

- ❏ **Is this process time sensitive? For example, are there Service Level Agreements (SLAs)?** If yes, then it is a good candidate for a process application, as escalations are a key component of the platform. Additional questions around this topic will help identify escalations and notifications to enforce SLAs in the process definition.

❑ **Is it important to notify the process users of the status? Is overall process visibility important?** If yes, then it is a good candidate for a process application, as notifications and process visibility are key components to the platform. Additional questions around this topic will help identify interfaces such as e-mail notifications, dashboards, and reports based on the audience.

❑ **Does this process require reporting across systems or auditing for compliance?** If yes, then it is a good candidate for a process application. Additional questions around this topic will help identify the integration pieces for the process as well as the reporting and auditing requirements.

❑ **Do you believe that automating this process is going to be more cost-effective in the future?** If yes, then it is a good candidate for a process application. If you do not believe that automating the process will be beneficial, then do not try to force it as a solution. However, if you do see some benefits to automation, those can be key selling points to get business owner and process user buy-in, especially when the benefits of automation tie in with departmental or even corporate goals.

## User Benefits and Process Considerations

Aside from questions that you ask yourself about the process, think about other benefits to the users of the process as well as to the business.

### Benefits to Users

A process may be a good candidate for a process-driven application if such an implementation can produce some of the following benefits for users who will be involved in the process:

❑ **Hide business processes:** To some users, particularly those involved in a single step, the process may not look like a process at all; they will not know what the next step is or where the data came from. They are just filling out an InfoPath, SharePoint, or ASP.NET form that they received a link to in an e-mail.

❑ **Consistency:** The ability to design and consolidate user interfaces and views of data, while maintaining the core of the process can make it easier to standardize a series of forms and reports.

❑ **Transparent applications:** Information about process-driven applications with the K2 blackpearl platform can be easily surfaced in a report or in a graphical way using the View Flow component. Anyone who has the right security can find out where the process is and get data about the process, whether that is tracking information or business information.

❑ **Reduced inefficiencies:** When designing the process, you may be able to streamline and optimize some of the steps.

### *Other Considerations*

If the following aspects of the process are true, it increases the chances that the process you have identified is a good candidate for automation:

- ❑ Large number of participants

- ❑ Process crosses organizational boundaries

- ❑ Large number of instances that must be tracked

- ❑ Geographically dispersed participants

- ❑ Processes that last over long periods of time ("long-running" processes)

- ❑ Processes that currently involve costly mistakes, such as legal ramifications, fines, damage to the business's reputation, and sensitive intellectual property leaks.

Each one of these aspects of a current process can benefit from automation, if only to improve tracking and increase security in relation to which users have the necessary rights to view data about the process.

# Summary

Identifying the process and forming a project team are the first steps towards delivering a process-driven application. From a project management perspective, it's not all that different from other projects. The same diligence and thoroughness are required for a successful process-driven application project as they are for other technical and nontechnical projects alike. If you are just starting down the road of process-driven applications, do not let the methodologies and roles overwhelm you. Gain some experience with delivering a few simple process-driven applications before you tackle the larger, more complex ones. In this way, you will learn what works for your company. While the best practices are outlined here, the only thing that really matters at the end of a project is whether or not it is successful.

In the next chapter, we'll look at how to measure the success and Return on Investment (ROI) of a process-driven application project.

# 4

# Process-Driven Applications and K2 blackpearl

Mike Talley

We outlined some of the key benefits of the K2 platform at a high level in Chapter 1. Chapters 2 and 3 discussed how workflow and Business Process Management (BPM) evolve into process-driven applications and designing process-driven applications. Now it's time to bring these elements together and take a closer look. In this chapter:

- ❏ We're going to take a lower-level look at the key benefits of K2 blackpearl to give you the tools you need to take advantage of and extend many features of the platform.

- ❏ Then we'll look at what it means to implement a successful process-driven application and how to measure your Return on Investment (ROI).

- ❏ Last, we'll give you some ideas of how to expand awareness of process-driven applications throughout your company.

## A Closer Look at Key Benefits of the K2 Platform

There are key features of the K2 platform that you should think about when evaluating and implementing a process-driven application. Most of these features also represent extension points that enable a number of tailored scenarios in both the design-time and run-time aspects of the platform, allowing you to leverage the platform even further. Architectural details of the platform are covered in later chapters (chapters covering specific details of the platform are referenced in the sections that follow). This section is meant to provide the business value of the platform, broken down by feature areas.

## Wizards and Templates

For process designers, K2 blackpearl includes a number of wizards that provide step-by-step configuration of process integration, activities, and events. All design-time aspects of a particular step in the process can be configured using static or dynamic values, and common fields, including information about users, the process, the server environment, and SmartObjects, are surfaced through the K2 Object Browser. Every wizard that is available in the K2 Designer for Visual Studio is also available in the K2 Designer for Visio 2007 and in K2 Studio. Custom wizards can be created by developers and deployed for all process designers to use. Backward-compatible templates from K2.net 2003 can also be added to the K2 Designer for Visual Studio by installing K2.net 2003 Studio.

*For more information about wizards and templates, see Chapter 9.*

**Business Value:** All designers can be extended with custom wizards tailored to your environment. Except for the K2 Designer for SharePoint, the designers use the same wizard extension mechanism, allowing you to invest once and reuse the same interface for multiple audiences.

## SmartObject and SmartObject Services

SmartObjects provide two key value propositions: They are a mechanism to:

1. Abstract data from the process
2. Surface data from multiple systems through a single interface

This second point allows data objects to be created for quick analysis and reuse in other systems as well as K2 processes. SmartObjects can be accessed directly in processes using the SmartObject Event Wizard. They can also be accessed using the .NET Framework Data Provider for K2 SmartObjects, which is an ADO.NET provider used to query and update data surfaced through SmartObjects. SmartObject Services provides the ability to query and update information from other systems, such as SalesForce.com, SQL, SharePoint, and others. K2 connect provides access to SAP data and will provide access to any BizTalk adapter with version 2. Windows Communication Foundation (WCF) endpoints can also be created for SmartObjects by using the K2 EndPoint Designer.[1]

*For more information about SmartObjects and SmartObject Services, see Chapter 7.*

**Business Value:** Provides a single point of access for data from multiple systems, allows data to be abstracted from the process, and the mechanism can be extended to connect to custom line-of-business (LOB) systems.

## Collaborative Designers

Collaboration between the business and IT is critical for process-driven applications. All K2 Designers generate the same project structure so that process and SmartObject designs can be shared among designers.

*For more information about this platform feature, see Chapter 14.*

**Business Value:** All designers generate the same project file, allowing workflow and SmartObject designs to be shared among project team members. One of the key benefits of K2 blackpearl is bridging the IT–business user gap and allowing business users to perform a majority of the work, lessening the involvement of IT and, in turn, reducing costs.

## SharePoint and Office Integration

Deep integration with the Microsoft Office system allows you to leverage your existing client and server applications to derive more business value from them. This integration also allows you to tailor your application to familiar applications to increase user acceptance.

*For more information about the Microsoft Office System integration, see Chapters 9, 12, and 13.*

**Business Value:** The tools that your employees are familiar with are used extensively in process-driven applications. Extensive SharePoint, Word, and Outlook integration means that tasks can be actioned by users in their preferred environment. Office Communications Server integration provides presence-based routing of tasks.

## The Event Bus

The Event Bus represents a mechanism for surfacing events from third-party servers or systems that can alter a business rule, a process instance, or create an entirely new instance of a process. A second feature of the Event Bus is that it can be used to schedule custom events, whether they are single events or repeating events such as the first Monday of every month. Last, the Event Bus is used to send custom notifications to users when certain events occur. The Event Bus provides a powerful mechanism for system integration, scheduling, and management alerts.

*For more information on the Event Bus, see Chapter 21.*

**Business Value:** Allows the business user and managers to choose when, why, and how to be notified of process events. Also allows third-party servers to participate in process events and provides a scheduling mechanism for notifications and custom methods.

## Reporting

Based on the Microsoft Report Description Language (RDL) specification, all out of the box reports in K2 blackpearl use SQL Servicer Reporting Services to render reports. Moreover, the out-of-the-box reports can be customized based on your business requirements, or new reports can be designed in K2 Workspace and in Visual Studio. In Visual Studio, custom reports can be written to aggregate process data and data from other systems into a single report. Once deployed to the report server, this report can then be imported into the K2 Workspace.

*For more information, see Chapter 20.*

**Business Value:** Flexible and customizable reports based on process data and SmartObjects allow very rich reporting capabilities. Built on standard reporting technology from Microsoft, reports can be tailored to business needs and exported to multiple formats, including Excel and PDF.

## Extending the Platform and the API

The K2 platform would not be a platform if it could not be extended. There are many extension points that allow the platform to be tailored to a particular environment. Custom SmartObject Services, user providers, wizards, and integration with LOB systems can be written by partners or a business's internal development team for use with the platform. A list of current projects and their source can be found on the community site, k2underground.com. Sign in or create an account, and then click **K2 blackmarket** to see all projects.

The extension points mimic most of the key business value propositions of the platform as outlined earlier in this chapter. Reference the chapters in this book for more information on a particular topic. Also see k2underground.com, the K2 Knowledge Base, and the Help files available in the product and on the K2 customer portal for more information.

## The API

The K2 platform application programming interface (API) is used throughout the K2 platform and is the key mechanism for extending it. The main run-time assemblies are the `SourceCode.Workflow.Client` and `SourceCode.SmartObjects.Client`. The design-time assemblies allow programmatic process and SmartObject authoring, even visually. They also work with the management assemblies for the deployment of a process or SmartObject. The Event Bus includes its own assemblies to schedule custom events, and the wizard and SmartObject Services assemblies round out the K2 platform API. For more information about the API, see the K2 blackpearl Developer Reference.

# Measuring Success and Achieving a High ROI

"If you don't measure it, it will not improve; if you don't monitor it, it will get worse."

At all levels, from the factory floor to the corporate boardroom, companies want to know how their business is doing. They also want to make good investments. There are probably initiatives within your company to improve customer service, to decrease the time it takes to process an order, to streamline the data gathering and upper-level management reporting, and to reduce staffing requirements.

The good news is that companies which have not implemented a BPM solution should expect to see a higher rate of return than those who have pursued process improvement initiatives in the past. Companies new to BPM will probably find it more difficult to identify the right processes to automate and implement those processes, simply because they have never done it before. The returns on the investment in a BPM strategy, combined with the right approach, can be significant for all companies that choose to pursue it. This section takes a look at how to measure success and get a high rate of return using K2 blackpearl.

## Identifying Key Performance Indicators (KPIs)

Key Performance Indicators (KPIs) are measurements of critical business operations. The types of measurements that you decide to use for your business will be very different from the types of measurements that another company will choose. The data that you want to track should be relatively easy to measure. You don't want to waste a lot of resources trying to gather data when it can be inferred from other, more readily available, measurements. You may have to interpret some of the data and communicate that interpretation in a report.

For example, if the goal of a process-driven application is to improve customer satisfaction, how would you measure customer satisfaction? It may be too expensive to conduct surveys to measure customer satisfaction on an ongoing basis for every transaction, but you could infer that customers are more satisfied by measuring other aspects of the transaction. These might be the time it takes to complete a transaction, if and when customers return to purchase another product, if they contact you for support of the product, and whether they refer your product to their friends.

Prioritize and limit the number of KPIs that you measure. KPIs should be just that — Key Performance Indicators. It's not every performance indicator, just those that matter to your business goals and strategies. They are meant to give you an indication of where your business is today and how it is moving towards your goals and strategies.

Process-driven applications can supply some of the information that goes into your KPIs. This data is usually aggregated across all instances of a particular process, especially if that process is one of the critical processes for your business. Getting to that data is relatively easy, since workflow-reporting SmartObjects are created by default for every process. Out-of-the-box or custom reports can also surface this type of data. If you need to aggregate additional data, a custom SmartObject can be used.

> *For more information about SmartObjects, see Chapter 7.*

Measuring the success of the automation of a process involves identifying KPIs at the process level and then comparing that with the historical data that you may have for the process. Because the process may not have been completely understood before it was automated, the comparison between pre-automation and post-automation cannot be objectively measured. To measure success in this case, you will have to look at other aspects of the business that are affected by the process. For example, if you automate a customer service operation, are your customer service representatives able to service more customers? Do they have more time to do other work? Do you see an increase or decrease in the volume of customer service requests? You want to monitor the right data points as your new process continues to run.

Another option to measure success is to interview the process users. The value of this may not be directly measurable but will provide some anecdotal information about the success of the application. It may provide data that can be used in improving the current process and in approaching new processes, within the same department or throughout the company. This type of data gathering can also provide a quasi-quantifiable measurement of user acceptance, especially if users are surveyed and their responses are statistically valid.

## *Calculating Your Return on Investment (ROI)*

Steven Minsky, CEO and founder of LogicManager Inc., makes the following point in his 2005 article "The Challenge of BPM Adoption": "Companies in a broad range of industries are reporting measurable payback from this [BPM] technology. Ninety-eight percent of those who have implement workflow improvement tools say the solution meets or exceeds their expectations, according to Gartner Group reports. In industry assessments and other printed reports, improvements cited include:

- ❑   30–45% reduction in process operating costs
- ❑   50–75% reduction in end-to-end process completion time

❏   60–90% reduction in time to change business requirements

❏   75–90% reduction in manual operations errors"[2]

Calculating your ROI of the K2 platform starts with measuring how much you invested in the platform. There are a number of expenses, including:

❏   The cost and terms of the software license

❏   The cost of installing the software

❏   The cost of the hardware and other related setup costs

❏   The cost of implementing each process

❏   The cost of training and supporting users

❏   The cost of maintaining the system, including administration

On the other side of the equation, you have to measure the tangible benefits of the overall solution. Typically, this is measured on a process-by-process basis. A simple calculation would take into account the following measurements:

❏   The time saved per employee

❏   The average salary of your employees

❏   The number of participants in the process

❏   The number of process instances per year

❏   The amount of paper saved (if your current process uses paper)

This example is typically referred to as soft ROI, where you may save an employee some time but not be able to measure what that employee will do with their saved time. Other "hard ROI" benefits should also be measured, such as bringing your product to market more quickly and improving revenue earlier in the fiscal year, or saving costs associated with vendor contracts for work that can now be done in-house. Other hard benefits include reduced staffing needs and the ability of the same number of employees to service a greater number of requests. These two factors represent different sides of the same coin. If you are trying to measure the increase in volume that a department can handle, calculate how many employees would be needed to service that number of requests before the automation of the process.

The equation shown in Figure 4-1 takes into account how long you expect the benefits to accrue. Future benefit amounts should be reduced by the present value of the anticipated cost savings, here estimated to be 10% per year. The following 3-year ROI calculation can be expanded or scaled back, depending on how you need to calculate your return.

$$\frac{\frac{\text{Year 1 Cost Savings}}{1} + \frac{\text{Year 2 Cost Savings}}{1.10} + \frac{\text{Year 3 Cost Savings}}{1.20}}{\textit{Total K2 Platform Cost}}$$

**Figure 4-1**

This simple ROI calculation takes into account the following benefits:

❑ The automation of the process (the person-day calculation)

❑ Scalability, or increasing the number of work items a person can process

If you are moving from a paper-based system to an electronic forms system, summarize the data in a way that makes sense for businesses. For example, you have a paper-based process that every employee uses; start by writing down the facts:

❑ 30,000 employees.

❑ Each employee submits two forms a week.

❑ There are 45 working weeks in a year.

❑ Approximately 90 working forms per employee per year.

❑ 2.7M paper forms per year.

Ask yourself this about 2.7M paper forms:

❑ How much does it weigh?

❑ How much does it cost?

❑ How many trees does it kill?

❑ How much space does it take up?

❑ How do you aggregate information from 2.7M paper forms? per year?

Measuring this type of automation benefit is easy and shows the immediate value of the process-driven application.

## The Intangible Benefits

Measuring all of the tangible benefits is necessary and should be part of your overall project plan. But there are other benefits that can be found in implementing K2 blackpearl with a BPM methodology. Some of these benefits can be associated with costs and risks that should be incorporated into your ROI calculation, while other benefits are intangible and should be expressed as part of your company's strategy versus its bottom line:

❑ **Better business intelligence:** Improved data consolidation and reporting, especially compared to paper or simple Web forms, process improvement, and automation provide much better insight into your business.

❑ **Risk reduction:** Knowing what happened — the when, where, and how — and having the data to report, reduce chances of fraud, missed steps, forgotten items, and other mistakes.

❑ **Improved auditing compliance:** Allows you to track who did what, when, and how for detailed record keeping and regulatory compliance.

❑ **Higher-quality execution:** Ensures that the correct process is adhered to and measures the execution and lag times for each step as well as the overall process.

❑ **Assistance with streamlining and reengineering:** Helps reduce bottlenecks and makes your processes run faster and more efficiently.

❑ **Leveraging of existing investments:** The platform you already own may be underused, and the K2 platform will help you leverage that platform.

❑ **Competitive differentiation:** Companies are always trying to be better than their competition, and increasing your efficiency could be a way to make your company stand out from your competitors.

❑ **Improved product quality:** Efficient businesses can address problems when they occur, and sometimes even before they occur, resulting in less product reworking at the end of the manufacturing process and a higher-quality product.

❑ **Better customer service:** Customers will rate your customer service (and the type of services you offer your customers, such as real-time and self-help services) relative to the service they receive from other companies. More efficient applications result in quicker turnaround times for servicing customers.

❑ **Decreased time-to-market:** Business applications that improve collaboration and decrease the time it takes for the various departments in your company to create a new product or Service, including the business plan to go along with it, allow you to get the product to market faster. It may also allow you to enter new markets.

There is one last area of intangible benefits that should be considered — the hidden inefficiencies. There are a number of processes that employees do every day that are very manual in nature. Employees may not feel like they are being inefficient, or they may feel like these manual things are just part of their job. Just the exercise of identifying and improving a process that has been part of a manual system for years brings benefits that you won't realize until you are finished with the exercise and the new process has been in place a few weeks to a few months. Achieving success with future processes becomes easier when employees and management can see how reducing manual steps and running the business more efficiently actually frees up time to work on more valuable tasks, or to achieve a better work-life balance for overworked employees.

# Orienting the Business to Process Improvement

Capturing and documenting business processes is a difficult process, especially for medium to large businesses. Changing the culture of a business is even more difficult. But everything doesn't have to be done all at once.

K2 blackpearl can close the gap between the business and IT. However, typically when K2 software is first brought into a business, it is for the automation of a single business process that is built and managed by IT. During the construction of that first process, IT starts seeing the K2 platform as a solution to many of their process automation needs rather than as a vertical solution for a single type of process. At that point, they realize other values of the platform, including the collaborative process design that can take place between business and IT. Although it may take a progressive IT department to let business users design and deploy their own applications, many IT departments realize that collaborating with business users can be a lot more efficient than gathering requirements and pursuing a traditional application design and release approach. Refer to Chapter 2 for more information about the various ways in which IT can work with and enable the goals of the business. In the end, narrowing the gap between the business and IT is critical to the overall success of a process-driven business.

Automating some very visible processes can provide some "quick wins" that allow process improvement to seep into the culture of the business in ways that may be difficult to imagine. Much of this will happen by allowing business users to model and design their own processes, turning the traditional application engineering modality on its head. It brings the application design effort to a grass-roots level, where the benefits and adoption mechanism can spread with word of mouth rather than an executive memo.

This does not mean that executive-level awareness and even sponsorship of a project is not necessary. In many cases, it will be one of the main factors in determining the overall success of the project. Awareness at this level will also help BPM awareness and methodologies become more widespread in the company. This is particularly important for those business processes that cross functional or departmental boundaries. As identified in Chapter 3, these types of processes lend themselves well to automation.

Some companies already have a Process Improvement department, or maybe it's a "virtual" team that meets once a month to identify processes and ways to improve them. If you participate in one of these teams and want to start down the road of process automation, take some of the ideas, examples, and calculations in this book and present them to your team. A Process Improvement team is completely viable without any process automation, but if you have already identified your businesses core processes, as well as the costs and risk associated with those processes, technology can take your improvement metrics to a new level. Especially if your company runs on the Microsoft platform, K2 blackpearl can make a lot of sense as an investment that will pay high returns.

If your company does not have a Process Improvement department or team, you can identify some forward-thinking individuals in your organization, from different roles and different backgrounds, and form a team to explore the benefits that K2 blackpearl can bring to your business, whether you start with a single department or a handful of departments that work closely together. Once you get business users collaborating with IT, and people see the advantage of process-driven applications over traditional ones, you will be improving your operational efficiency and changing the way people think about their work.

The rest of the book will fill in the details of the platform so that developers, designers, and managers can use the chapters as a reference for what is possible with the platform. Business users should also use this book to gain a deeper understanding of the platform in order to use it more effectively. K2 blackpearl ships with a number of tutorials, which are step-by-step guides for doing particular tasks with the platform. k2underground.com provides forums for the community, blogs, and the code-sharing of K2 blackmarket and represents the strong community that is building up around the software. There are people in your company that may want to participate in the community, learning from other people's experience and becoming more adept at using K2 blackpearl. These are the people who will become advocates of process-driven applications in your company.

# Summary

Hopefully, you now have a better understanding of the tools you need to take advantage of the K2 platform. Keep focused on the right processes and the right process measurements, and make it easy for managers to get reports and business information when they need it. Start reaping the benefits of your investment in the platform and, over time, you will change the culture of how work gets done in your business.

# Notes

1. K2 connect v2 and the K2 EndPoint Designer are scheduled to be released in Q2 2008.

2. "The Challenge of BPM Adoption" by Steven Minsky, LogicManager Inc., 2005. Accessed at www.ebizq.net/topics/bpm/features/5757.html

# Part II

# Architecture and Installation Options for K2 blackpearl

# 5

# Planning an Effective Deployment

## Chris Geier

Like many people, you probably have questions about planning a solid K2 deployment. You don't want to underplan for a deployment by not taking into account the different moving parts that make up K2. And it's easy to become overwhelmed by looking at the architecture diagrams and listing out all the different services, databases, and integration points. You may wonder how scalable K2 is, can it run on one box, can it scale, and even how does it scale? The answer is always the same: It depends.

While K2 has much in common with many other three-tier applications, it is also different. It is different in that the workload profile can change dramatically from customer to customer and even from process to process. Some customers may use SharePoint; some may not; some may use ASP.NET forms, and some may use InfoPath. Some may use K2 to integrate with many back-end systems; some may not integrate it at all. There are too many variables to accurately predict, with any degree of certainty, a formula for how to scale.

While the architecture of K2 does correlate to a normal three-tier server application, it also differs in that the tiers can vary.

The front tier can be Web forms, InfoPath forms services, SharePoint, or virtually anything you can imagine. The application tier is the K2 server along with its ancillary services, such as SmartObjects interfaces and the Web services for SharePoint. The data layer is the set of K2 SQL Server databases. However K2 can also use various back-end systems as a data layer where the K2 server acts a broker to the other backed systems and their data.

This chapter will not give you a magic formula for how to calculate the exact deployment model and configuration that will work best in your particular situation. Rather it will attempt to give you guidance on particular aspects of your environment to consider, and particular things to plan and watch for. It will also explain the architecture and attempt to point out the most important aspects according to how you plan to use the platform.

There is a significant advantage to understanding the K2 architecture before you start to examine different deployment models. You need to understand the various K2 blackpearl components that are involved in a deployment of K2 before deploying it or updating an existing deployment.

This chapter covers the following topics:

❑   An overview of the K2 architecture

❑   Considerations for building a K2 plan

❑   Guidance on choosing a K2 deployment architecture

❑   Infrastructure considerations in a K2 environment such as Kerberos, AD, and DNS

# K2 Architecture

The overall K2 architecture is built on and includes different Microsoft components so it is important that we include them in any discussion on the architecture of K2. Depending on the different components being utilized, all or some of these components will be installed. When you are designing your environment, you should be aware of each of these pieces and what functions they perform, so that you have an environment that performs well today and is ready for tomorrow.

At a high level, the K2 blackpearl server uses common Microsoft components, such as the .NET 3.0 Framework, which includes Windows Workflow Foundations (WF) and Windows Communication Foundation (WCF). The K2 blackpearl components are discussed in further detail in following sections.

You can think of the K2 blackpearl components as being divided into two categories:

❑   Client components refer to the designer tools installed on a client machine, such as the K2 Designer for Visual Studio and K2 Designer for Visio.

❑   Server components are installed on a server either sharing the resources or functioning independently.

We next take a look at these different components in some detail.

## Client Components

The client components include K2 Designer for Visual Studio and K2 Designer for Visio and K2 Studio.

### K2 Designer for Visual Studio

The K2 Designer for Visual Studio is a design environment for creating process-driven applications that may be extended with custom code. The K2 Designer is built on top of Visual Studio 2005 and is geared primarily towards the developer audience. Be sure to check out the system requirements in either the *Getting Started Guide* or other installation documentation, as there are several different requirements you must address before installation.

*Support for Visual Studio 2008 should be available in beta by the time this book is published.*

## K2 Designer for Visio and K2 Studio

The K2 Designer for Visio allows Visio diagrams to be extended with workflow design capabilities. The K2 Designer for Visio and K2 Studio are the design tools for the business analysts. Processes designed in K2 Studio and Visio can be opened later in the K2 Designer for Visual Studio for more advanced functionality and allow the developer and the business analyst to collaborate on a design. For more information on collaborative development see Chapter 14. From the installation perspective, the K2 Designer for Visio can be installed by itself on a client machine without other K2 components. Obviously, Visio 2007 (Standard or Professional) is a prerequisite.

# Server Components

Server components are the principle components responsible for running the processes that are deployed from the designers. The primary component is the K2 server itself. The K2 server requires access to the K2 databases to run successfully.

In addition to the K2 server, the server components include:

- ❏   Workspace and Web Components
- ❏   K2 for SharePoint
- ❏   K2 integration with SQL Reporting Services

## K2 Workspace and Web Components

K2 Workspace and Web Components allow you to design reports, manage servers, and manage security and notifications. All of these can be accomplished in the K2 Workspace. Figure 5-1 shows K2's Workspace architecture.

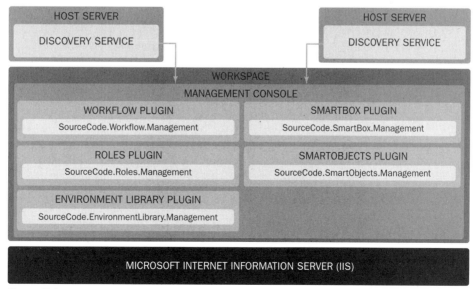

Figure 5-1

Some features included in the K2 Workspace are:

- ❏ Worklist
- ❏ Management Console (SmartObject Services, Environment Library, Workflow server, SmartBox, Roles)
- ❏ Report Designer
- ❏ Notification Event Designer

Carefully think through how you plan to leverage the Workspace. You can use it to surface user worklists or you can do this in other ways, for example in the SharePoint Web part or a custom application. Also consider your use of the Workspace for its reporting function and how much it will be used for this purpose. The Workspace is built in a modular fashion to allow different functionality for the K2 platform. Access to each module can be controlled by a server administrator using the Security module.

The Management Console is a mechanism through which one or more K2 blackpearl servers can be managed. This includes setting security rights on the server and on processes, accessing the global worklist, creating Service Object instances, managing Environment Library templates and fields, creating user roles, creating process instances, configuring working hours, and troubleshooting process errors.

*For more information about administrative tasks, see Chapter 15.*

## K2 for SharePoint

The K2 for SharePoint component is split into two separate versions. The installer will install only the component that corresponds to the version of SharePoint you have installed. There are two versions, for Microsoft Office SharePoint Server 2007 or Windows SharePoint Services v3.0. They are installed on the SharePoint servers and enable interaction and communication between K2 server and functions found in SharePoint, including Microsoft InfoPath processes.

The following integration features require Microsoft Office SharePoint Server 2007:

- ❏ Business Data Catalog
- ❏ InfoPath Forms Services
- ❏ Publishing sites and pages
- ❏ Records management

The remaining integration features that K2 for SharePoint provides are available on any edition of Windows SharePoint Server v3.0:

- ❏ K2 Web Designer for SharePoint
- ❏ Workflow integration
- ❏ Site management
- ❏ User management
- ❏ List and library management

- ❏ Events
- ❏ Document manipulation
- ❏ Search results

### K2 Integration with SQL Reporting Services

This component allows K2 blackpearl to interact with Reporting Services of Microsoft SQL Server 2005 SP2 or greater. The .NET Data Provider for K2 SmartObjects allows custom applications to query SmartObject and workflow data from the K2 server. Reports can be hosted in Reporting Services to provide scalable reporting capabilities.

## Architecture of the K2 Platform

The entire K2 platform architecture is depicted in Figure 5-2. We will now break it down to give you a better idea of what you will be using. To begin let's talk about the hosted servers.

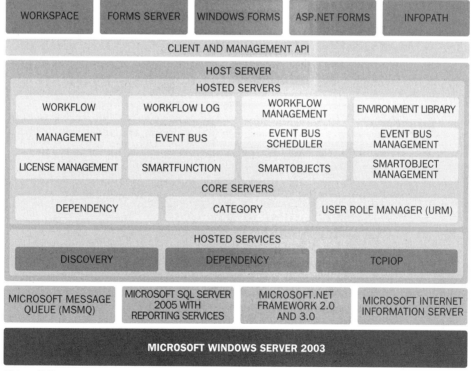

Figure 5-2

## *The Hosted Servers and Services*

While the hosted servers can be disabled on each K2 blackpearl installation, the core servers and hosted services are required on every installation of K2 blackpearl. In this section, we'll describe each "server" and give you a high-level overview of each component.

### Workflow

This server is responsible for all workflow-related tasks as its name suggests. These can be actions, such as the starting of a process or kicking off a specific activity or user task assignment. This server would also be responsible for evaluating each Line Rule in a process or assigning the tasks of an event to participants.

### Workflow Log

The logging component is responsible for reading from the K2server database and writing all necessary audit and logging information to the K2serverLog database. See the database breakdown chart for more information on this later in the chapter to understand this relationship better.

### Workflow Management

The Workflow Management server component is responsible for overall management of the workflows. These tasks can include such things as managing rights and permission to the process, and managing permissions to the global worklist that is surfaced in the K2 Workspace.

### Environment Library

The Environment Library is a very critical component in K2 blackpearl and will be discussed in more detail in Chapter 10. Essentially, the Environment Library provides the K2 platform with the ability to deploy to different environments based on the stage of the development process.

### Management

Currently not used but is reserved for future functionality.

### Event Bus

The Event Bus allows a person to set notifications or actions based on events, thus increasing visibility into the business. These notifications can be set to occur when there is a change to specific data, when a process starts, finishes, or changes. These events can be raised by third-party servers, from a process, or from a single or recurring schedule. There are three hosted servers that compose the broader Event Bus component. The first is the run-time component, which in the diagram is simply referred to as Event Bus. The other two are Event Bus Scheduler and Event Bus Management.

### Event Bus Scheduler

This uses the `SourceCode.EventBus.ClientRecorder` to schedule events on specific schedules. For example, you can have events fire on the first of every month.

### Event Bus Management

This is the management component of the Event Bus and is used in conjunction with the Event Bus Scheduler for scheduling new events.

## SmartFunction

This is the policy component for logical evaluations of Event Bus notifications.

## SmartObjects

You will learn more about SmartObjects throughout the rest of the book. (Pay special attention to Chapter 7.) SmartObjects are building blocks of data that can encapsulate information from multiple sources and can be used and reused to build process-driven applications. For the purposes of talking about the hosted servers and SmartObjects, there are two main elements:

❑    The run-time component for working with deployed SmartObjects, shown in Figure 5-2 as SmartObjects.

❑    The management aspect of SmartObject services, shown in Figure 5-2 as SmartObject Management. This loads each Service and Service Object instance, while the run-time aspect executes and performs data brokering between the K2 server and the line-of-business (LOB) system.

# Core Servers

The core servers are fundamental pieces of the infrastructure that the "hosted services" can all leverage. For example, the User Role Manager (URM) provides the ability to authenticate and authorize users. Thus, all the hosted servers can leverage it any time they need that functionality.

## Dependency

This is the service that all objects use to register their dependencies. For example, when you are deleting an object or incrementing its version, this service will manage the interdependencies of that object with other objects.

## Category

This hosted server provides the hierarchical system for deploying processes and SmartObjects as well as for categorizing reports and notifications.

## User Role Manager (URM)

This is the hosted service that provides role creation and resolution capabilities.

# Hosted Services

Notice in Figure 5-2 that three services are categorized as hosted services. These serve as communication bridges between servers.

## Discovery

The Discovery service is K2's way of finding other blackpearl services that have been distributed. The Discovery service actively listens on port 49599 (this is the default but can be changed in the `DiscoveryService.config` file). The Discovery service does not send out a broadcast. There is an API in place that allows for the discovery of hosts. When a component wishes to locate other servers on the network, they send out a broadcast, via the API, to the configured port (49599). Each HostServer that is running the Discovery service on that port will then respond back to the individual IP address that made the search request. The response to the search request includes the HostServer machine name and the port, which the HostServer is listening for connections on.

### Dependency

The Dependency Service is the hosted service for objects, such as processes and SmartObjects, to register their dependencies. It is also used to determine interdependencies of K2 objects, such as processes and SmartObjects.

### TCPIOP

The TCPIOP layer handles all communication from the standard client APIs typically used by developers, such as `SourceCode.Workflow.Client` and `SourceCode.SmartObjects.Client`. Those API calls are then handed off to the run-time component of the particular hosted server using the internal marshaling provided by the Host Server. The K2 server pictured above it in Figure 5-2 shows the run-time architecture of the server, including the management portions. Design-time components are provided by the various APIs. Currently all client and management API communications occur over TCP port 5555, except for the workflow communications, which occur over TCP port 5252. This is for backward-compatibility reasons with K2.net 2003. Essentially there are two integrated communication services (one for each port), but only the Workflow hosted server is able to use the backward-compatible 5252 port. All other hosted servers, including the Workflow Log and Workflow Management servers, use port 5555.

## Databases: The Heart of K2

Sitting behind it all and at the heart of any K2 deployment are the databases. Keep in mind that in any deployment, each database (see the following table) can be separated to run on different servers, which may be desirable depending on how much each database will be accessed.

| Database | Description and Notes |
|---|---|
| Categories | Stores information for the Category hosted server, which allows K2 objects to be managed and categorized. |
| Dependencies | Stores information for the Dependency hosted service, which allows a K2 object to register its dependencies on other objects. Also allows the server to discover an object's dependencies, such as a process that has a dependency on another process or SmartObject. |
| Environment Settings | Stores information about the Environment Library, such as templates and configured environments. |
| | Environment names and their various fields, field types, and values. Typically a read profile, because these values rarely change once the environments have been configured. |
| EventBus | Stores information about the Event Bus and configured notifications. |
| | Information about the configuration or the Event Bus and various Events that are created in it. A read-write profile would be based on an organization's adoption of this feature. |
| EventBus Scheduler | Stores information about Event Bus Scheduler, which provides a mechanism to raise events to the Event Bus using a recurrent pattern. |
| | Schedule and the status of Event Bus entries. |

| Database | Description and Notes |
|---|---|
| HostServer | Stores information about the Host Server, which provides services and a common framework for each hosted server and service. |
| | The Host Server database contains important functions such as storage of information on Roles and various Security Provider's Registration. Depending on the frequency of changes to this type of information, this database could have a high rate of reads. |
| K2server | Stores information about processes including rights, instances, destinations, actions, and other data. |
| | Stores everything to do with running processes on a K2 blackpearl server. This is one of the most critical and used databases in the entire platform. |
| | This database has a heavy read IO profile during process execution and a write IO profile during process deployment. |
| K2serverLog | Stores logging information from the K2server database. |
| | Processes will be written here as they are completed. This database will be heavily written to. However, environments that make heavy use of reporting will also see this database used heavily, as it is queried to return data for those reports. |
| K2SQLUM | Stores information for the SQL user provider. |
| | Only used if configured; if used, it would be heavily read, since K2 would be using this to query for people's user information. |
| SmartBox | Stores information and data for SmartBox-based SmartObjects, which are SmartObjects that have some or all of their data stored directly in K2 versus other LOB data sources. |
| | This could vary dramatically, depending on how one uses it in their environment. Think of each SmartBox SmartObject as a table in a database. Then based on how you collectively use those tables, estimate how this profile would appear. |
| SmartBroker | Stores information about SmartObjects that use Service Objects to retrieve and update data from LOB systems. |
| | This database would most likely have a high read profile, as it stores information about the systems to which you have established a service object link. It is used by the broker layer of SmartObjects. |
| SmartFunctions | Stores information for policies used in conjunction with the Event Bus. |
| | At the time of writing, primarily used in the Event Bus and depending on how your environment takes advantage of that feature this database could see very light use. If this feature is used heavily, expect this database to get a balance of read-write activity. |
| WebWorkflow | The WebWorkflow database stores only data related to the designer (design-time data), for example, the XML representing the process designer in WebWorkflow, and favorites you added in the designer. No run-time data is stored within this database. |
| Workspace | This database stores information about the Workspace Web site, including user preferences, for example any worklist filters that a user has setup. |
| | This database could get some heavy use if your organization uses the Workspace Web site widely and your users set up preferences. |

The two databases that should be considered the most important are K2server and the K2serverLog (these are default names and can be changed). K2 needs these databases to store its state data. The data must be held both in current instance form and historical (audit) form in order to log all transactional data. These databases contain the transaction and log data, respectively.

*These databases can physically reside on the same or different servers.*

The purposes of the two databases are very different. The transaction database (K2server) directs internal transactional processing and should not be modified or accessed directly.

The K2serverLog database can be divided into two halves:

❑ **The design-time data:** The *design-time data* contains all the process definitions. The reason that this data is duplicated here is that reporting components (such as K2 View Flow) make use of this definition data in order to render a view of the process definition, and then overlay the run-time data on it. Without the design-time data, there would be no definition data (such as the coordinates of process elements), which allows the design view to be rendered.

❑ **The run-time (instance) data:** The *run-time data* (also called the *instance data*) contains all the data for the running instances of processes and their components. This includes details all the way down to audit information for when process and activity data are changed. The level of data logging is set in the K2 Workspace, and can be set per process. By default, all details for each process are logged.

# Building Your Deployment Plan

Now that you have a good understanding of the pieces that make up K2, you will be better prepared to start the exploration of what a good deployment model is for your environment.

When determining architecture for your K2 infrastructure, there are many considerations, according to how you plan to use the different components. You need to develop a profile of the processes planned and how they will be leveraging the K2 infrastructure. You need to understand not only the processes themselves but also their users. If this is not possible, you should ensure that you keep the design as flexible as possible, thus allowing for changes as the user population grows or changes. These questions will form the basis on which you make decisions about your architecture. Keep in mind, when creating a plan and picking an architecture, that the most critical component of any K2 deployment is the database, as is the case with many data-intensive applications. K2 relies heavily on the database for everything that it does, and requires information to be read from and written to the various databases constantly. If you have to pick one layer of the architecture to focus on from a resources and hardware perspective, this is the layer to choose.

❑ **How many users will there be?**

Consider how many total users there will be and how many may be using the system concurrently at any given time.

Take a look at the mix of user interactions with the processes you plan. Effects can be starting processes, reporting on processes, and including out-of-the-box and custom reports.

Having users performing different tasks at the same time will have a different effect on overall system load as opposed to users acting on and interacting with the system in different ways at different times. For example, consider the difference between a user running a report through the Workspace, thus accessing and putting overhead on the system via a Web site, and a user actioning interacting with a process via an InfoPath form through the InfoPath K2 Web service. Each of these components can be on different servers and can be accessing different databases.

❏ **Where is the data for the processes coming from?**

Having data stored within the process in SmartObjects vs. having to go to back-end systems to retrieve necessary data will affect response time. Having a significant number of these processes may require you to add additional hardware resources.

❏ **Where is it being stored?**

Data storage requires long-term capacity planning on the database side. Take this into account if you are increasing the storage within the process or within SmartObjects.

❏ **If you are doing any type of document workflows, what are you doing with attachments?**

Storing these with the process data is not recommended because it will greatly increase the amount of data being moved by the server.

❏ **What number of processes do you have today, planned for this quarter, next quarter, and this year, and how many total people will be involved in those in all aspects of system usage?**

You need to make sure that you appropriately gauge the level of adoption of K2 in your organization and work to make sure that you size appropriately for growth.

❏ **What about in 18 months?**

You have to decide, as an organization, how far out you wish to plan before you would feel comfortable taking a look at rearchitecting the system (which may happen when there is a significant change in needs).

❏ **Will you need to add layers or resources to the environment to adapt to this?**

To help alleviate load, many organizations scale out, add additional Workspace servers, or add servers to their SharePoint farm

❏ **What components or architecture layers will be the most important in your environment?**

Layers that will get heavy use or are to be considered especially important to the value that the business receives from the K2 solution and should be given heavier priority when allocating hardware resources. For example, if the Workspace will be a heavily used component, you should dedicate a server or multiple servers to that role.

Keep this in mind for the architectural section, as you may want to add redundancy or additional hardware resources to that component.

❏ **What will be the most common components used?**

This may also affect your architecture, as they may need to have additional hardware resources.

❏ **Based on the processes and the users involved, what is the level of business criticality that will be assigned to these systems?**

This is a critical decision to be made, and one that requires much thought. This is also a decision that should be made by the business, not IT.

Make sure that you fully understand the people and the systems that will be involved in the processes managed by K2. One of the most important aspects of your deployment will be the level of availability and the criticality with which it is treated. You may be surprised by the level of business criticality that these systems end up having after several processes are running. You may start out by thinking that the criticality level is low; however, down the road, and often very quickly, the processes become critical and need an ever-increasing level of both performance and availability. It is important that you begin with this in mind so that you are not rearchitecting your K2 installation six months after completing it.

Plan above the level of performance and availability that you initially estimate (to allow your system the easiest path to evolve). If you think that the processes and systems could become critical, it is important that you start off with a system that supports it, such as a Network Load Balanced (NLB) farm. This does not mean that you must start out with a full NLB farm. You can configure K2 to be in a single node farm (as shown in Figures 5-3 and 5-4). Simply select the install K2 server farm option and input the farm name. Even if you have one server for now, you can still add servers later that will make the system a true NLB farm. Configuring it in this way makes it much easier to add nodes later without having to reconfigure the K2 installation.

**Figure 5-3**

Figure 5-4

The previous questions all dealt with areas specific to the K2 components. Now it's time to expand on a couple of key integrations that you may have. Each integration will be addressed in the next section.

❑ **Will SharePoint be used?**

If SharePoint is used, one common decision is whether the same SQL database will be shared between K2 and SharePoint. If you will be using the same SQL database, it is very important that you ensure that this database is very scalable. Adding significant load to SharePoint with K2 and possibly other applications may significantly affect the overall performance of both K2 and SharePoint.

❑ **Will K2 share a server with the SharePoint servers themselves?**

This can be at the application server level or with the Web front end. Either is technically feasible, but once again, if both K2 and SharePoint are heavily used you will run into bottlenecks. It is best to start off with K2 on a dedicated server for most situations, which allows easier scaling of K2 if and when needs arise. If you don't put K2 on a dedicated server, you may have to perform additional activities, such as establishing Web site Host Headers, dedicated IP addresses, or ports. In some environments this is not desirable, and you may choose to dedicate a server to K2 for this reason alone. Again, this depends on your particular environment, but it is always preferable to dedicate a server to K2 to give you the ability to easily expand its capabilities in the future, rather than having to build a new dedicated server for K2 down the road.

❑ **How heavily will you take advantage of SmartObjects?**

This question primarily needs to be answered for SmartBox SmartObjects, as they will be stored on the same SQL box as the other K2 databases (refer back to the database table earlier in the chapter).

# Choosing a K2 Architectural Template

In this section, we will describe three main architectural approaches. Each approach can be "tuned up," so to speak, to bring more performance and scale to the overall system. Use these templates as a starting point for planning the architecture of your K2 installation. No single template will describe the exact system that you will ultimately build, but they will help you think about the types and configuration of servers that you need for your environment.

The primary focus of planning K2 should be the databases. No component of the entire environment is as critical to the overall success, performance, and scalability as the database. Every decision you make in your processes is directly affected by or has a direct effect on the K2 databases.

Deployment architectures typically fall into one of three general architectural categories:

- ❑ Small scale
- ❑ Medium scale
- ❑ Large scale

Your specific particular configuration may differ slightly, but these should cover the majority of deployments.

These small-, medium-, and large-scale architectures are important when planning a K2 installation in your production environment, but what about your development, test, and staging environments? Most companies already have one for SharePoint or other Web applications. Often these environments can be reused. See Chapter 6 for more information on planning these environments.

## Small-Scale Architecture

The most basic of the small-scale architectures is the standalone install, so that's where we'll start.

### Standalone Architecture

A standalone K2 install (see Figure 5-5) is where all the K2 components are on the same server. This would include all K2 components and SharePoint components, if used. This architecture should only be used in nonproduction scenarios because this configuration offers no redundancy of any kind. Furthermore, since all pieces of the architecture are on one server, there is little to no optimization for performance.

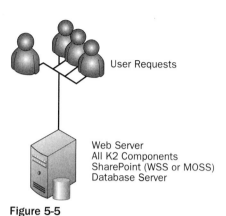

**Standalone Install**

In this configuration all components are on one box. This should be used for quick development and proof of concept environments, but is not recommended for production use.

User Requests

Web Server
All K2 Components
SharePoint (WSS or MOSS)
Database Server

**Figure 5-5**

This type of architecture could not support a high number of users, even when used in a SharePoint-only capacity. In addition, because there is no redundancy or distribution of services, rerouting traffic from this server to perform maintenance is difficult. If you were to use a standalone server in a production environment, do not deploy processes to this sever that are critical to your business.

## Basic Small-Scale Architecture

In the basic small-scale architecture (see Figure 5-6), we break out the SQL server, often using a database that already exists to support other applications. This helps with the overall workload, given the database-intensive nature of K2. However, for an environment where any of the processes could be deemed critical to the business in any way, this architecture should not be considered. Performance will increase given that the database is separated. However, with SharePoint and K2 on the same server, scale is limited as well as the ease in which maintenance and other operational tasks can be performed. If you need some additional performance, you can move the K2 server to a separate server as depicted in the next version of small-scale architecture.

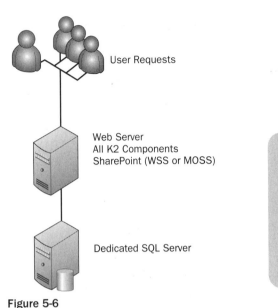

User Requests

Web Server
All K2 Components
SharePoint (WSS or MOSS)

**Small-Scale Install**

Components scaled to at least two servers on two tiers.

Most commonly, K2 is installed on an existing SharePoint installation, using an existing SQL Server instance.

Dedicated SQL Server

Figure 5-6

## Small-Scale Architecture with Performance Enhancement

In this architecture (see Figure 5-7) the major components — Web, K2, and Data — are separated onto their own servers. This should be considered an entry-level departmental small business deployment architecture, as it does offer some degree of separation and a minimal level of operational activity, such as performing maintenance of some layers while allowing other layers to stay running. While this separation may be the most minimal for a production environment, problems in one area may not as readily affect others.

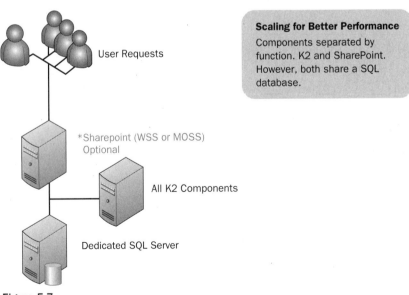

User Requests

**Scaling for Better Performance**

Components separated by function. K2 and SharePoint. However, both share a SQL database.

*Sharepoint (WSS or MOSS)
Optional

All K2 Components

Dedicated SQL Server

Figure 5-7

# Medium-Scale Architectures

In the medium-scale architecture, we begin to focus on some of the functionality needed for today's important applications. The first entry into the medium-scale architecture focuses on data availability.

## Basic Medium-Scale Architecture

This architecture (see Figure 5-8) is very similar to the initial small-scale deployment with the exception that the database layer is redundant. This can often occur because the databases are sharing a cluster with other application databases, including the SharePoint database if present. Having the databases clustered can help in scaling, given the data-intensive nature of both SharePoint and K2. However, with only the data layer being redundant and everything else being on the same server, this architecture has minimal flexibility for operational tasks. If data availability is not a key factor in your architecture, you can focus more on the front-end page-rendering performance.

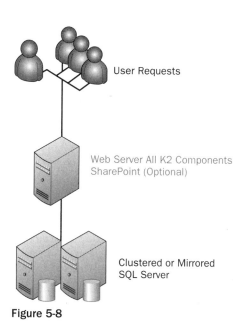

User Requests

Web Server All K2 Components
SharePoint (Optional)

Clustered or Mirrored
SQL Server

**Scaling for Data Availability**
This topology focuses on data availability through the use of clustering. Use this topology when availability of your data is critical, and you are satisfied with the small-scale performance.

Figure 5-8

## Medium-Scale with Focus on Page Rendering

This architecture (see Figure 5-9) has a load-balanced Web layer, which can be ASP.NET, SharePoint, or Workspace, or a combination of these components. This is great for operational tasks as you can take individual servers out of the NLB cluster for routine maintenance tasks. This makes the Web layer performant and scalable. This layer can be easily expanded by adding additional new nodes. This architectural tradeoff is appropriate if your Web forms, SharePoint sites, and Workspace will be the most heavily utilized components.

We can then take it one step further and combine the two medium-scale options.

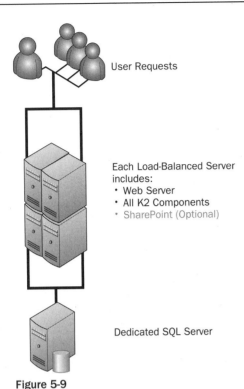

User Requests

Each Load-Balanced Server includes:
• Web Server
• All K2 Components
• SharePoint (Optional)

**Scaling for Page Rendering**
This topology adds additional servers to increase the overall performance. Use this topology when performance is more important than data redundancy.

Dedicated SQL Server

Figure 5-9

## Medium-Scale, Full Architecture

This should be considered the entry-level enterprise architecture, as it provides redundancy at both the Web tier and the data tier, thus increasing two very important aspects of the three tiers. This architecture (see Figure 5-10) offers good operational ability and ease of scale. This would be a good choice for an enterprise with a short-term goal of heavy front-end usage involving a heavy dose of SharePoint, and offers good scaling for front-end page rendering and reporting.

This architecture can easily handle a large number of users who interact both with forms, workslists, and reports.

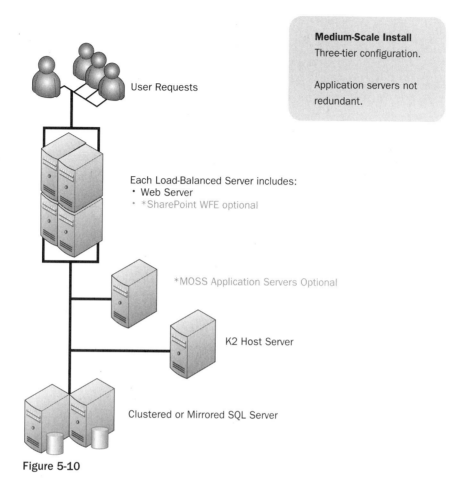

Medium-Scale Install
Three-tier configuration.

Application servers not
redundant.

User Requests

Each Load-Balanced Server includes:
• Web Server
• *SharePoint WFE optional

*MOSS Application Servers Optional

K2 Host Server

Clustered or Mirrored SQL Server

Figure 5-10

# Large-Scale Architectures

When you surpass the abilities of an entry-level K2 architecture for an enterprise, you must move to a
large-scale system. These systems offer additional levels of performance by increasing the components
that are set up with NLB in addition to having SQL in a single cluster at a minimum.

## Basic Large-Scale Architecture

This architecture (see Figure 5-11) is similar to the medium scale, full architecture except that K2 is not
separated from the other front-end servers. You have a load-balanced front end that also is running K2
on each server. This provides good availability; however, you may still run into issues where problems in
one part of the Web application layer take down the others, since there is no separation between them.
Maintenance tasks may still be problematic.

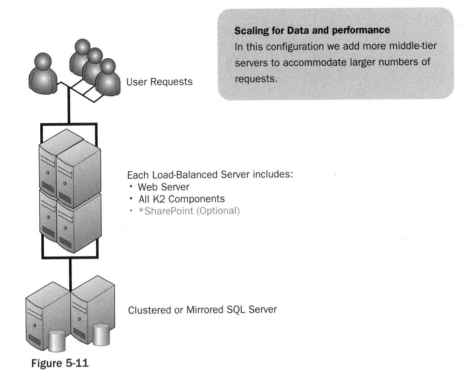

User Requests

**Scaling for Data and performance**
In this configuration we add more middle-tier servers to accommodate larger numbers of requests.

Each Load-Balanced Server includes:
• Web Server
• All K2 Components
• *SharePoint (Optional)

Clustered or Mirrored SQL Server

Figure 5-11

## Large-Scale with Maximum Redundancy Using the Fewest Servers

This can be thought of as the ideal implementation for the enterprise or for any organization that will deploy business-critical process-driven applications. This architecture (see Figure 5-12) offers:

❑ Load balancing for performance and redundancy

❑ Layer separation and isolation

❑ Clustered database for availability and performance

Obviously, one of the main drawbacks to this architecture would be cost. Not every company has the requirements or budget to accommodate such a deployment. However, you may find that as your company grows its use of process-driven applications, this architecture will become necessary. Keeping this in mind will help you choose the right initial architecture.

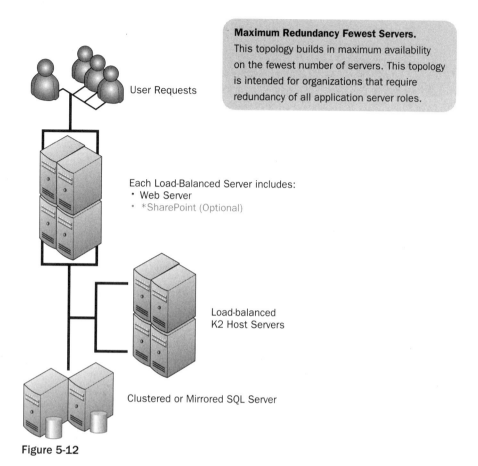

User Requests

**Maximum Redundancy Fewest Servers.**
This topology builds in maximum availability
on the fewest number of servers. This topology
is intended for organizations that require
redundancy of all application server roles.

Each Load-Balanced Server includes:
• Web Server
• *SharePoint (Optional)

Load-balanced
K2 Host Servers

Clustered or Mirrored SQL Server

**Figure 5-12**

If you need to increase performance in this architecture, simply add nodes to the existing NLB clusters.
You may also further separate the databases across different clusters.

### What's the Difference between Load Balancing and Clustering?

There are lots of misconceptions about load balancing (NLB) and what the differences are between it and true clustering. It is important for you to understand the difference between the NLB Service and the Cluster Service. Setting up NLB in your environment means establishing the ability to distribute TCP/IP traffic among multiple servers in an NLB cluster. Any servers that are participating in the NLB cluster do not share resources, but instead run their own instances of the applications to be load balanced. For example, each server would independently run K2Server or Workspace, or SharePoint. Each instance would essentially be a separate copy. NLB simply manages the incoming traffic in order to balance it out and distribute the traffic/performance load. NLB by itself provides no failover capability, rather it distributes load, and if one of the nodes is removed, the overall farm does not go down, but its load capacity does.

True clustering provides redundancy and failover capability. Servers in this type of cluster generally share common storage and function as a single, logical unit. A server cluster is a collection of servers that together provide a single, highly available platform for hosting applications. Applications can be failed over to ensure high availability in the event of planned downtime because of maintenance, or unplanned downtime because of hardware, operating system or application failures. Server clusters provide a highly available platform for applications such as SQL Servers. Server clusters are used for stateful applications that rely on some state context from one request to the next.

Important: The K2 server is not supported in the Windows server cluster environment. The K2 server is only supported on NLB clusters.

NLB and server clusters complement each other in complex architectures: NLB is used for load balancing requests between front-end Web servers, while server clusters provide high availability for back-end database access.

Now that you understand the architecture and you have chosen a deployment model, you should take steps to understand how your system operates and ensure that you have appropriate capacity as the use of the system expands. For more information about monitoring your servers, see Chapter 19.

# Integrating K2 into Your Existing Environment

Once you have settled on a deployment architecture, there are many additional considerations that you need to take into account when planning administrative tasks and analyzing your existing infrastructure.

Take a look at the following aspects of your existing infrastructure while making decisions about how you will install K2:

- **Physical network configuration:** Where are your servers and users physically located, and what is the link between them?

- **Kerberos:** How many servers do you have and how can they readily impersonate users across all of them? Kerberos is a necessity that requires planning and, most likely, a good dose of troubleshooting.

- **IIS locations, ports, IP addresses, Host Headers, DNS:** How is network traffic routed?

- **Domain configuration:** How many domains do you have? Do you have more than a single forest? There are important decisions to make about K2 when you have a nonstandard domain configuration.

- **Database configurations:** As stated before, K2 is a data-intensive platform; the data layer needs special attention to ensure that the K2 databases are appropriately designed.

- **Service accounts:** Will you use a different account for each service? Do you have the accounts configured already?

Methodically working through an infrastructure appraisal phase with the above considerations in mind will ensure that nothing important is overlooked and there are no surprises when you get to actually installing and configuring K2. Ensure that you look through the hardware and software prerequisites that are included in the K2 *Getting Started Guide*. This is a great resource that includes specific steps to configure and troubleshoot pre- and post-K2-installation.

Often something that is overlooked is the physical network, so it will help to point out a few issues that can become a problem later on.

- **WAN bandwidth and component location:** You need to understand where your users are located relative to the server components. You also need to understand usage patterns across the entire network (time of day, peaks and valleys). You do not want peak usage times for critical processes to coincide with network backups or other types of activities that may take away vital resources needed by your processes.

- **Network latency:** This can affect component location and has the potential to cause a poor user experience if not addressed.

- **User locations:** As stated previously, you need to think about how users will view and interact with items such as worklists and forms that are involved in a process-driven application and optimize the system for the best possible experience.

From a network perspective, you need to understand the network constraints to appropriately place various components for K2. For example, K2 blackpearl and SharePoint network traffic may consist of large documents moving between servers. Furthermore, traffic to and from a SharePoint site or the K2 Workspace involves a considerable amount of communication from the Web servers to the back-end servers running SQL Server. Good connectivity between them is required. Take into account your processes, what forms they use, and how the forms are used. For example how will forms with large attachments being passed form remote office locations over the wide area network (WAN) to the K2 server affect overall WAN performance? Possible solutions to this are regional SharePoint sites, but this is not always the best answer.

Ensure that you plan for appropriate response time for each of these components. You can certainly have each component of K2 across a WAN link to move the layer closer to the user population. However, be sure that the link can support the amount of traffic, particularly when it also involves SharePoint. This choice can often be a double-edged sword because you may move the Web front end closer to your primary user population, thus increasing response time, but the link between the front end and the back end can become saturated and unable to handle the traffic. This will often result in timeouts and user complaints to the Help Desk.

# Active Directory Integration

K2 makes extensive use of Active Directory for authentication and authorization, which is why it's an important area to focus some of your attention when planning a K2 installation. For a large percentage of K2 customers, Active Directory plays a crucial role in task assignment. K2 can use Active Directory in task assignment through Active Directory groups or K2 roles and even down to individual static user accounts. It is important that you take this into account before deploying K2 to a production environment. You should make sure that you involve your Active Directory team when architecting the environment so that they know what is going on and can advise you. Here are some aspects that you will need to pay special attention to:

❑ Querying Active Directory for groups and roles used for destination users and for permissions

❑ Multi-domain effects for resolving groups, adding roles, authenticating users

❑ Multi-forest elements for K2 server management of documents in one forest and users in another, for example

❑ DNS to ensure consistency, accuracy, and completeness

❑ Site configuration to ensure that K2 has quick and easy access to Active Directory

Ideally, you should have a domain controller assigned to the same site as your K2 server or servers. This will dramatically increase response and query times between K2 and Active Directory. Queries to domain controllers and the DNS server will be very common in most K2 processes as well as with users and roles. This becomes more complicated when dealing with large Active Directory infrastructures, such as those with many domains or even multiple forests. You should understand how a generic query is handled in Active Directory, especially those that span domains within a forest and have users from multiple forests. Problems in this area can affect how your processes function.

## A Complex Active Directory Scenario

In an extreme case — let's say your process has only three steps, but each step has a destination where users are assigned from different forests. These different users are contained in a role that is assigned as the destination. K2 must regularly query and resolve these users or groups to ensure that the role stays up-to-date. If the name resolution process fails, your process may not be able to function properly.

Also consider where users access K2 processes and where they are in relation to a domain controller (DC) and a Global Catalog (GC). This may make a difference in planning. If you have a DC in the same office as the K2 servers and the WAN link goes down, all the users in that office will still be able to use K2, since they will be able to renew Kerberos tickets at the DC. If there is no DC in that location, they will cease to be able to access K2.

> ### Active Directory Domain Controllers and the Global Catalog
>
> Global Catalog (GC) servers are an important part of not only your Active Directory infrastructure, but as it turns out, they are also important to K2. The Microsoft Windows authentication system depends on the GC in order to retrieve Universal group membership. In a multi-domain architecture, K2 depends on the GC for information about users throughout the forest. Having a GC in the same site as the K2 server will help in query and resolution performance, since LDAP queries will take greater amounts of time if K2 is required to walk the domain tree, as opposed to going directly to the GC. Perhaps you need to understand this a tad better to get the impact.
>
> The GC can be described as a database of Active Directory objects in the forest. This database can be large or small, depending on the organization. Each domain controller (DC) in a domain holds a subset of the information that is contained in the GC. This subset is restricted to all objects in its specific domain. The GC, however, has a full copy of all the objects across all domains in the forest. If your environment has multiple domains and these multiple domains contain users that will participate in your processes, this may affect your K2 installation. A typical rule of thumb is to have a GC server in every site.
>
> How would this be bad, you ask?
>
> Well, let's say your K2 server needs to issue a search for a user or a user's manager. K2 queries its assigned DC through a locator process. If the target of the search is in one of the other domains, the DC queries the DC holding the GC of the other domain and returns the results to the user. This process of going outside that domain, and possibly outside the local site and across WAN links, can take time and reduce the overall performance of your process.
>
> Work with your internal Active Directory team to figure out what is right for your organization.

## DNS

DNS plays a vital role in any network infrastructure and with many distributed applications. In order for K2 to communicate with various servers on which its own or other components are installed, it must be able to resolve their addresses. Additionally, given the reliance on Kerberos in a distributed architecture, your DNS infrastructure must be solid if K2 is going to perform well and without error. This is usually not a problem as many Microsoft servers are set to self-register with their DNS server. However, in cases where you are using Host Headers or aliases, you will need to make sure you work closely with your DNS administrator in planning your K2 installation to ensure that these entries are added as needed. Having a solid DNS infrastructure will also help with performance, reducing the amount of time that servers have to wait until addresses are returned. If K2 has to go through many hops in order to retrieve DNS information, overall performance will suffer.

## Authorization and Authentication

Authorization and authentication are important aspects to your Active Directory but also important to K2. Two common aspects that need clarification in this arena are:

❑   Kerberos

❑   SSO

*SSO will be covered more in Chapter 17. For more information see that chapter.*

A significant aspect of planning a distributed install is Kerberos. You must understand how it affects your environment, and you must prepare for it. Once again, it will be wise to involve your Active Directory and/or Security group in this conversation. There are many good Microsoft resources available to help you, including the following:

```
http://www.microsoft.com/technet/prodtechnol/windowsserver2003/technologies/
security/tkerberr.mspx
```

```
http://www.microsoft.com/windowsserver2003/technologies/security/kerberos/
default.mspx
```

```
http://technet2.microsoft.com/windowsserver/en/library/
b748fb3f-dbf0-4b01-9b22-be14a8b4ae101033.mspx?mfr=true
```

## What Is Kerberos?

There has been a lot of bad press about Kerberos, and most of it is due to a lack of understanding. When it comes to Windows, Kerberos is not something that you install and or enable. Kerberos (see Figure 5-13) is there by default and is typically used when you log in to the domain from a Windows PC. The interesting part comes into play when you need Kerberos to help with some of the advanced authentication scenarios that are becoming more common in the enterprise, such as impersonation and delegation of authentication. Kerberos is Microsoft's way of solving the "double-hop" authentication problem.

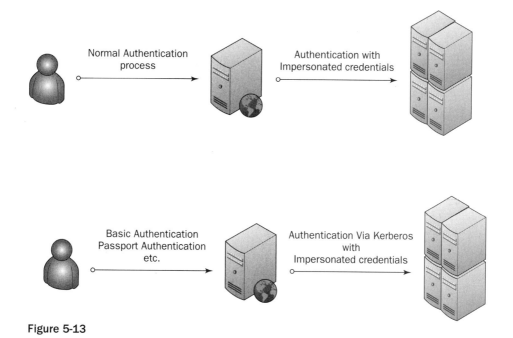

**Figure 5-13**

As a client, you can browse to a Web page or any other front-tier application and use Kerberos for authentication. This part is easy and will rarely give you problems. However, what if you need to go beyond this front tier? What if you need to, as part of that application, go to the application server as well? How do authentication and authorization work? You don't browse to the application server. Will the front tier of the application prompt you for credentials again? You do not have many options if you want this to work seamlessly. The best, most accepted, and easiest approach is to use impersonation. But because of the double-hop problem, impersonation is not possible. That's where Kerberos comes in.

With Kerberos impersonation becomes easy again, and it can work with Windows authentication and even Basic or Passport authentication, for example.

We highly recommend reading up on Kerberos and some of the technology behind it. Before we get into how K2 uses Kerberos, let's talk about some of the benefits of Kerberos:

❑ **Impersonation (delegated authentication):** As mentioned, you can use impersonation with Kerberos much more easily now. In Kerberos, different services can impersonate a user when accessing resources on the user's behalf. Previously, this was not possible with Windows, as there is no similar ability with NTLM. Impersonation is leveraged by K2 in all "double-hop" scenarios, such as when a user opens their worklist in a SharePoint site.

❑ **Authentication interoperability:** The Microsoft implementation of the Kerberos protocol is compliant with the Internet Engineering Task Force (IETF) Standards-track specifications. This compliance allows interoperability with other networks that use Kerberos.

❑ **Increased authentication efficiencies:** In systems that use NTLM for authentication, the application server must connect to a domain controller in order to authenticate each client. With Kerberos authentication, the application server does not have to contact a domain controller each time. With Kerberos, the application server can authenticate the client by the credentials presented to the server by the client. The clients get credentials for a particular server only once in a given time period, then they are able to reuse those credentials.

❑ **Mutual authentication:** By using Kerberos, the server can be sure that the client has the appropriate access to the data, services, and applications that the server provides. In addition the client can be sure that the server it is trying to connect to is actually the server it expects it to be.

Taking Kerberos one step further and making it even more valuable, Microsoft added two new Kerberos features in Windows 2003:

❑ **Protocol transition:** Enables applications to support several different authentication mechanisms at the user authentication tier, Windows will then switch to the Kerberos protocol to move on further into the other subsequent application tiers.

❑ **Constrained delegation:** Gives administrators the ability to specify authentication limits by specifying where application services can impersonate and act on a user's behalf. This is a huge benefit in high-security environments because it allows administrators to limit an application's impersonation boundaries to only other services that the application uses.

Some notes to keep in mind about constrained delegation:

❑ Constrained delegation is possible only if the domain is at the Windows Server 2003 functional level.

❑ Constrained delegation cannot be used between services whose accounts are in different domains. All domain controllers in the domain must be running Windows Server 2003, and the domain must be operating at the Windows Server 2003 functional level. The accounts of users accessing the services do not have to be in the same domain as the services.

The authentication model implementation is dependent on whether user credentials must be passed from one system to another. When they are passed, the system that is attempting to pass the credentials must be trusted for delegation. For this step to take place successfully, Kerberos delegation must be configured. There are some requirements for Kerberos delegation to occur:

❑ A domain user for the application must not have the Account is sensitive and cannot be delegated option checked.

❑ SPNs (Service Principal Names) must be registered for the services on the middle-tier servers. The service's SPN must be registered by a domain administrator if the service account is a domain user account. If the service account uses the computer's account, then the process can register by itself or the local administrator can register it by using the Setspn.exe utility. SPN's can also not be duplicated anywhere within a forest. Duplicate SPNs will cause Kerberos authentication to fail.

❑ Middle-tier service accounts must be trusted for delegation.

❑ An SPN must be registered for the service on the back-end server.

❑ If using constrained delegation, then middle-tier services and back-end services must be in the same domain.

## The Requirements for Kerberos

Now that you know why Kerberos is so good, we can go through some of the prerequisites for a good Kerberos experience:

❑ **Operating system:** Kerberos authentication relies on client functionality that is built into the Windows Server 2003 operating system, the Microsoft Windows XP or Vista operating system, and the Windows 2000 operating system. Earlier versions of the operating system will not work with Kerberos. K2 blackpearl is recommended to run on Windows 2003.

❑ **TCP/IP network connectivity:** For Kerberos authentication to occur, fully functional network connectivity (over TCP/IP) must exist between the client, the domain controller, and the target server, and they must communicate in a timely manner. TCP/IP is also a requirement for K2 blackpearl.

❑ **Domain Name System (DNS):** Kerberos clients will use fully qualified domain names (FQDN) to access resources such as the domain controller. In order for Kerberos to work properly DNS must be functioning properly.

❑ **Active Directory domain/forest:** All accounts that are to be used in a Kerberos authentication session must reside in a valid Active Directory domain. The current version of Microsoft Kerberos does not support the use of local Windows accounts.

❑ **Time service:** Kerberos is very sensitive to time differences between machines. In order for Kerberos authentication to function correctly, all domains and forests in a network should need to keep time synchronized. Time differences can cause Kerberos authentication to fail. By default, the time differences accepted is < 5 minutes.

❑ **Service Principal Names (SPNs):** An SPN is a unique identifier for a Windows service. Any service that is going to participate in Kerberos authentication will need to have an SPN. This is so clients can properly identify the service on the network. If you have a service that needs to participate in Kerberos authentication, and it does not have an SPN set for it or it is not set properly, clients who need to connect to it will not have a way of locating that service. Without correctly set SPNs, Kerberos authentication is not possible.

SPNs can be set both with the Microsoft SPN utility and through the `ADSIEDIT.MSC`, the latter of which is shown in Figures 5-14 and 5-15.

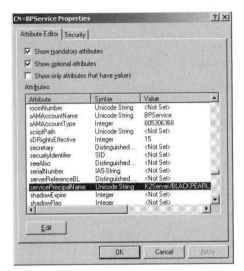

Figure 5-14

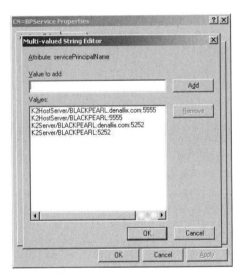

Figure 5-15

> **More on SPNs**
>
> An SPN is registered in Active Directory under a user account as an attribute called `Service-Principal-Name`. The SPN is assigned to the account under which the service the SPN identifies is running. Any service can look up the SPN for another service. When a service wants to authenticate to another service, it uses that service's SPN to differentiate it from all of the other services running on that computer.
>
> SPNs are also involved in constrained delegation. When you set up a domain computer or user account for delegation, one step of the process is to list the SPNs of services on other computers that the computer is allowed to delegate to. This list forms a type of ACL. The services running on the other computers are identified by the SPNs that are issued to those services.

## Planning Kerberos and K2

When talking about Kerberos, it is important to understand how K2 uses Kerberos and when. Let's take a look some of the different components of K2 and how they use Kerberos.

### The Web Services (Run-Time Services)

K2 makes extensive use of Web services for integration into both InfoPath and SharePoint:

- ❑ **SharePoint Web service (`SharePointService.asmx`):** The SharePoint Web service is used to initiate process instances from SharePoint Events. This service will require Kerberos authentication in any distributed environment to pass credentials from SharePoint sites to the K2 SharePoint Web service and then to the K2 blackpearl server. This is also used in the SharePoint Integrated workflow to pass credentials from the Web service to the K2 blackpearl server. During the design process, the K2 SharePoint wizards also use this Web service to interact with Microsoft Office SharePoint Server/Windows SharePoint Services (MOSS/WSS).

- ❑ **InfoPath Web service (`InfoPathService.asmx`):** The InfoPath Web service passes credentials to the blackpearl server using Kerberos to interact with processes, including starting new processes.

*When using browser-enabled forms the InfoPath Service Web service must be installed on the MOSS/WSS server because of an InfoPath Forms Services limitation.*

### Reporting

K2's use of Kerberos, as it pertains to reporting, varies according to how the reports are surfaced.

- ❑ **For Non-SRSS reports:** Authentication occurs as the end user via Kerberos. K2 Workspace delegates the user's credentials to the blackpearl server to execute the desired action.

- ❑ **K2 reports (published to SSRS):** SSRS delegates the users credentials to blackpearl to obtain and return the report data based on the user's View and Participate permissions. When publishing a report from Workspace Report Designer, both the blackpearl server and the SSRS server are accessed as the Workspace Application Pool account.

❏ **SSRS Reports that are imported into Workspace:** A user accesses the reports on the Workspace home page. Authentication occurs via Kerberos as the end user opens the report on the Workspace. The Workspace service then delegates the user's credentials to the SQL Reporting Services Web site to run the report. The user must have appropriate permissions (at minimum Browser) in SSRS to run the report. SSRS then delegates the user's credentials to the blackpearl server to run the report and return the data, as long as the user has correct permission to view it.

## Other K2 Components

There are also other components that need to be taken into consideration for the same planning process.

**The K2 Web Designer:** Deploying a process will use the MOSS or WSS Application Pool account, which must have Export server rights on the K2 blackpearl server. The blackpearl WebWorkflow database is also accessed directly using the identity of the MOSS Application Pool account. This account must have at least the db_datareader and db_datawriter roles in the WebWorkflow database.

**SQL Server (for blackpearl):** The blackpearl server accesses the blackpearl databases using the blackpearl service account or via SQL Authentication as specified during the install. SPNs for MSSQLSERVER may or may not be required, depending on the environment. In many cases, SQL creates SPNs and in other cases, such as when using a named instance, SPNs must be manually created.

**Workspace:** A user accesses the Workspace Web site from a remote client and must be authenticated using Kerberos. If the Workspace is on a separate server, it will delegate the user's credentials to the blackpearl server and authenticate them using Kerberos.

---

### Farm Options for the K2 Workspace

Similar to a K2 server farm, a K2 Workspace farm is Internet Information Server (IIS) configured in a Web cluster with multiple Web servers. All of the associated Web servers must have K2 blackpearl Workspace installed and be configured to use the same application pool identity account. HTTP SPNs must be created for the K2 Workspace farm name under this application pool identity account.

---

**SharePoint SmartObject Service Instance:** If a security provider, username, and password are not configured for the Service Instance, and Impersonate is not checked, the Service Instance will run under the context of the blackpearl service account and authenticate in MOSS as such. If the Impersonate checkbox is checked, it will try and connect using the user that is logged in to the Host Server, that is, the one executing the SmartObject.

*The Impersonate checkbox should not be used when configuring the service instance as there typically will not be a user to impersonate.*

**K2 blackpearl Worklist Web part:** A user accesses a page in SharePoint that is configured with the K2 Worklist Web part; if the Web part is running on a different server from K2, it must be authenticated using Kerberos. The Web part will delegate the user's credentials to the blackpearl server and authenticate them using Kerberos to retrieve the worklist, and open the worklist items and action worklist items.

**Forms Generation Client Event:** When a user opens a Forms Generation Client Event .ASPX Web page, they are authenticated using Integrated Windows Authentication. The RuntimeServices Application Pool account authenticates against the blackpearl server and impersonates the user to retrieve the worklist item. The same thing occurs when the user actions the workflow using the form; actioning the item also calls the ClientEventServer.asmx Web service. This Web service is not used if the process is actioned from the context menu in the Workspace worklist. The identity used for the RuntimeServices Application Pool must have "Impersonate" server rights in the Workflow server. Since the ClientEventService .asmx Web service uses impersonation when communicating with the blackpearl server, it will not work with Kerberos alone in a distributed environment as they work in conjunction for authentication and authorization.

---

### Need Help Figuring Out When Kerberos Is Needed?

The rule of thumb for when Kerberos configuration is required falls to one question: Does a system need to impersonate a user? If the answer to that question is yes, then Kerberos is required. An alternative approach to the need to configure Kerberos would be to assess whether more than one hop between servers is required. In such a case, Kerberos is required.

---

## Setting SPNs for Kerberos

Now that you have a good idea of where K2 uses Kerberos, we can dig into setting SPNs for Kerberos. In order to help you with this, use the following SPN table as a reference.

*Kerberos configuration can occur either before or after the installation of K2 blackpearl. The configuration of K2 blackpearl, which occurs directly after installation, allows for the automatic setting of the K2 blackpearl Server SPNs.*

| SPNs Needed for | From a Command Prompt |
|---|---|
| Host Server | `K2HostServer/[MachineName]:5555`<br>`[DomainName]\[ServiceAccount]` |
| | `K2HostServer/[MachineName.FQDN]:5555`<br>`[DomainName]\[ServiceAccount]` |
| Workflow Server | `K2Server/[MachineName]:5252`<br>`[DomainName]\[ServiceAccount]` |
| | `K2Server/[MachineName.FQDN]:5252`<br>`[DomainName]\[ServiceAccount]` |
| Workspace Application Pool Identity Account | `HTTP/[MachineName]`<br>`[DomainName]\[AppPoolAccount]` |
| | `HTTP/[MachineName.FQDN]`<br>`[DomainName]\[AppPoolAccount]` |
| | **If the Web site uses Host Header, create SPNs as follows:** |
| | `HTTP/[HostHeaderName]`<br>`[DomainName]\[AppPoolAccount]` |
| | `HTTP/[HostHeaderName.FQDN]`<br>`[DomainName]\[AppPoolAccount]` |
| SQL Server 2005 Service Account | `MSSQLSvc/[MachineName]:[Port]`<br>`[DomainName]\[ServiceAccount]` |
| | `MSSQLSvc/[MachineName.FQDN]:[Port]`<br>`[DomainName]\[ServiceAccount]` |
| SQL Reporting Service Application Pool Identity Account | `HTTP/[MachineName]`<br>`[DomainName]\[ServiceAccount]` |
| | `HTTP/[MachineName.FQDN]`<br>`[DomainName]\[ServiceAccount]` |

When setting up K2 in a farm environment some of the SPNs need to be set up differently. In a farm environment, use the following table as a reference:

| SPNs Needed for | From a Command Prompt |
|---|---|
| Server Farm Option for K2 Host Server (SP1 or higher) | In addition to blackpearlserver/K2server SPNs for each farm node, create SPNs for the farm name like this:<br><br>`K2HostServer/ FarmName]:5555`<br>`[DomainName]\[ServiceAccount]`<br><br>`K2HostServer/ FarmName.FQDN]:5555`<br>`[DomainName]\[ServiceAccount]` |
| Workflow Server | `K2Server/[FarmName]:5252`<br>`[DomainName]\[ServiceAccount]`<br><br>`K2Server/[FarmName.FQDN]:5252`<br>`[DomainName]\[ServiceAccount]` |
| Server Farm Option for Workspace | `HTTP/[WorkspaceFarmName]`<br>`[DomainName]\[ServiceAccount]`<br><br>`HTTP/[WorkspaceFarmName.FQDN]`<br>`[DomainName]\[ServiceAccount]` |
| SharePoint Server Service Account | `HTTP/[MachineName]`<br>`[DomainName]\[ServiceAccount]`<br><br>`HTTP/[MachineName.FQDN]`<br>`[DomainName]\[ServiceAccount]`<br><br>If the Web site uses Host Header, create SPNs as the following:<br><br>`HTTP/[HostHeaderName]`<br>`[DomainName]\[ServiceAccount]`<br><br>`HTTP/[HostHeaderName.FQDN]`<br>`[DomainName]\[ServiceAccount]` |

*Running K2 Host Server in console mode can be an effective way to verify if the K2 Host Server has started up successfully, or failed to do so. Console mode also reports the reason for the startup failure, thus making troubleshooting simpler.*

## Kerberos Checklists

To help you through a Kerberos delegation setup, use this checklist to ensure that you complete each step.

## *Kerberos Delegation Checklist*

Recommended domain configuration:

- ❑ Middle and back-end tiers are in the same domain.
- ❑ Domain must be Windows 2003 functional mode.
- ❑ Middle tier and DCs must be Windows Server 2003.

### Back-End Systems (K2 Server)

Set Service Principal Names using SETSPN for each account. When setting these SPNs, ensure you use NetBIOS and FQDN names (Host Header, Port Info). This process will not be necessary if these services are running as built-in accounts such as local system; however, this is not a recommended best practice.

### Middle-Tier Systems

This is typically the Web or SharePoint layer. If you are using named user accounts as the AppPool identities at this layer, set Service Principal Names using SETSPN for each account. When setting these SPN's ensure you use NetBIOS and FQDN names.

- ❑ Ensure that the Kerberos Authentication method is used by IIS virtual server or SharePoint by querying the metabase settings as shown in Microsoft KB articles Q248350 and Q832769.
- ❑ Ensure that any service account involved with delegation (for example, AppPool identities) is not marked as sensitive (Kerberos delegation will not work if accounts are marked as sensitive).
- ❑ Using Active Directory Users and Computers, ensure that all service accounts involved with delegation are set to Trust this user for delegation.
- ❑ If you will be using constrained delegation (in 2003), you must also ensure that the "specified services only" additional checkbox is checked in addition to the back-end system's SPN being listed as the specified service.
- ❑ The service accounts involved with authentication must be given the Act as Part of the OS or Impersonate a Client after Authentication user rights.
- ❑ All service accounts at this layer must be added to the local IIS_WPG group.
- ❑ IIS must be set to use only Integrated Windows Authentication; also make sure that all other authentication methods are cleared, unless you will be using protocol transition.
- ❑ Load balancing can be done in Win2k3 in some scenarios. See the Microsoft article "Kerberos authentication for load balanced Web sites" at http://technet.microsoft.com.
- ❑ Set up SPN for Virtual Host Name (cluster name) mapped to service acct.
- ❑ For ASP.NET applications, Authentication settings must be entered into the appropriate Web.config file (see Microsoft KB article Q810572).

### Client Tier

- ❏ Middle-tier Web sites must be in Local Intranet zone. By default, machines will not use Kerberos in the Internet zone.

- ❏ If proxy servers are in use, you must make sure that you configure IE to bypass proxy server for local addresses.

- ❏ All clients must be running Internet Explorer version 5.5 or greater.

- ❏ In Internet Explorer, ensure Integrated Windows Authentication is enabled. This will require a restart of Internet Explorer.

- ❏ Client must use Kerberos.

- ❏ To ensure that it's operational, use the resource kit utility `kerbtray`.

---

#### A Note about Configuring Internet Explorer for Client Machines

For an Internet Explorer client to browse to either K2 Workspace or a SharePoint page containing K2 blackpearl components (such as MOSS components or WSS components), IE client settings must be configured as follows:

1. Enable Integrated Authentication.

2. Add the Workspace site URL to the list of trusted sites.

---

## Troubleshooting Checklist

If you are having trouble with authentication, complete the following Kerberos checklist to ensure that all points are set up correctly.

- ❏ Ensure that you set up all SPNs correctly and there are no duplicates. Use `LDIFDE` to search for and find these. These types of errors can cause the user to be continuously prompted for credentials and fail authentication. (Also check out Microsoft KB article Q871179: `http://support.microsoft.com/kb/871179`).

- ❏ Confirm the Identity User account and Password.

- ❏ Review AppPool consistency (compare/contrast AppPools used across all blackpearl resources, MOSS resources, and Web applications).

- ❏ Check permissions of the AppPool identity account.

- ❏ Confirm that Web application configurations are set properly

- ❏ Check the FQDN being used or defined (DNS).

- ❏ Check the Host Header being used or defined.

- ❏ Check browser settings (Trusted Sites, Login settings, Security settings, and so on).

- ❏ Confirm the K2 server Service account permissions and membership.

- ❑ Check the IIS AppPool permissions and membership.

- ❑ Check the User permissions for K2 processes, MOSS sites, and MOSS permissions.

- ❑ Check that HTTP and Machine SPNs are set for proper accounts.

- ❑ Check for duplicate SPNs.

- ❑ Confirm that there is a pair of SPNs for each account (HTTP and Machine).

# Summary

Hopefully, the preceding sections have helped you to identify the various K2 components and to familiarize yourself with installation and architectural requirements of K2 blackpearl products. Along with understanding the various K2 components, you also need to know the organization's existing network and architecture.

The successful development and use of processes with K2 blackpearl not only depends on your ability to know the process and develop it but also on ensuring the infrastructure that it runs in and depends on. This chapter has given you insight into the underlying architecture that is K2 blackpearl, and hopefully has led you down the right path to choosing a K2 blackpearl deployment model. In the next chapter, you will learn what it takes to also be successful in choosing a testing environment to begin testing the processes you build in.

# Planning an Effective Development, Testing, and Staging Environment and Strategy

**Gabriel Malherbe**

Planning an effective approach to a K2 blackpearl solution from an environment perspective is the key to successful delivery. The nature of the solution, size of the audience, and your development approach play a role when selecting the required environments. Capturing non-functional requirements often dictate the project approach. This approach will in return help formulate a strategy that can be applied when setting up an effective environment.

Planning and deploying a successful K2 blackpearl project is not only about having a running server. Methodology, solution footprint, and technology dependency will dictate environment requirements.

When picking a strategy, consider some of the following factors:

❑   **The project and development methodology:** Are you involved in a large waterfall style development where specification and construction cycles are long and delivery positioned at the end of the project, or are you required to deliver short, continually integrated development cycles?

❑   **The infrastructure footprint of the solution:** Is your solution a standalone development with minimal dependencies on external infrastructure, or is the list of systems, data sources, and technologies your solution depends on as long as the list of requirements?

❑ **Continual development and maintenance:** After you have delivered the solution are there subsequent phases to the project or will continual support and incremental development be required?

❑ **Corporate policy:** Are your developers allowed to wander around productions systems at will, or does a corporate policy or compliance issues require that environments are isolated and governed by strict staging and deployment procedures?

For completeness, this chapter will cover some common environments required for turnkey solution development. We will introduce four environments and cover the use of them in a test-driven development methodology. We will indicate what variations are available for each environment if the methodology is not test driven.

Specifically, this chapter covers the following topics:

❑ Project methodology and the impact it has on the required methodology and development approach

❑ Planning and implementing K2 blackpearl environments

❑ Development best practices including source control, versioning, and release management

❑ Debugging and monitoring suggestions

# Methodologies and the Impact on Environments

K2 blackpearl development projects can differ in size. Development can be done by a single person or a team of developers and infrastructure specialists.

As an example, it is possible to use K2 blackpoint to develop, test, and deploy a solution into SharePoint using only a production server. Using the end-user design surfaces of K2 blackpoint, there might be no requirement for a development environment to be introduced. Developing a solution where there are multiple disciplines involved is likely to include a development methodology that will require a host of environments to be configured. These will include an area for a developer to build the solution and an area to execute development testing. Before deploying the solution, it will be necessary to gain acceptance and mitigate production risks, typically at some staging environment before deploying the final solution into the production environment.

The selection of your environment should be appropriate to the requirements. Creating and maintaining environments takes time and money. Avoid an overly complex configuration. Likewise, not covering all the environments for your requirements could be problematic and might result in a low-quality or untested solution reaching the production system.

This chapter will focus on creating an effective development, testing, and staging environment and will assist in picking the strategy most applicable to your requirements.

# Formulating a Strategy

When we do whiteboard planning sessions with project stakeholders, the focus naturally remains on capturing and understanding functional requirements. We remain focused on statements like "if the amount is more than $1,000.00 then the system should route approval to a director," or "when the purchase order is approved, the system should update the financial record in our accounts system."

Non-functional requirements can be as important in a project as the functional requirements: statements like "the system should run on this version of Windows" or "our aim is to improve the rate of purchase order approvals threefold by introducing this system" or even "we will require that phase 1 is released to production while phase 2 is continuing to be developed and tested." These requirements have an impact directly on what environments will be required.

A checklist of non-functional requirements should include the following:

- ❑ Project methodology including details of planning, building, testing, and deployment strategy
- ❑ Construction team considerations, including team size, location, structure and standards for source control, release management, and continual integration testing
- ❑ Expected system performance, testing, and measurements
- ❑ Data growth, capacity planning, data retention, and reporting requirements on historical data
- ❑ Technology required, including the versions of platforms, systems, operating systems and dependent systems, or data sources
- ❑ Security, access restrictions, encryption, authentication, and authorization models
- ❑ Client platform including browser versions, mobile device access, and bandwidth restrictions
- ❑ Postdeployment development, support, and maintenance requirements

Having a view of these requirements will enable the team to design and implement an effective development and testing strategy and commission the required environments. We will focus on some common environment configurations and how you can best use them with K2 blackpearl.

# Common Environment Configurations

In this section we want to cover four common environment configurations. Not all scenarios will require four environments and some might require more, including an environment for performance, load, or security testing.

This chapter covers each of the four most common environments and explains how your project approach and development methodology dictate what environments you should consider and how they should be configured.

We will categorize our environments into two main areas; development and production. The development area includes a development and testing environment. Production includes a staging and production environment. Figure 6-1 indicates the location of a four-environment setup. They include:

❑ A development environment, including an infrastructure dependency host. This environment should be a standalone, sandboxed environment that allows a developer to build the solution with access to test or offline instances of dependent infrastructure and integration points.

❑ Testing environment, including automated building, deployment, and testing strategies.

❑ Staging environment used to mitigate production risks.

❑ Production environment and best practices for production.

**Figure 6-1**

Within the development environment, business analysts and developers should have the freedom to construct the solution having all the required tools available. The development and testing environment needs to reflect the infrastructure that will be available in production. By sandboxing the development and testing environment, changes and experiments in these environments can be isolated from other development environments and importantly, the production environment.

> *A sandbox is a testing (or virtual) environment that isolates untested code changes and outright experimentation from the production environment or repository, in the context of software development, including Web development and revision control, and by extension in Web-based editing environments including wikis.*

In BPM solutions a company's dependency on a stable and running production environment should not be underestimated. A workflow solution can span a wide audience, and instability in a production environment can have a far reaching impact on your business. As important as it is for a company to have online systems, it is just as important for these systems to adjust to changing business needs. All business solutions will need maintenance in the form of upgrades or issue fixing. These are contradicting requirements, and a staging server that operates within the production environment will allow project and business system sponsors to mitigate the risk of making changes to a production system without impacting the production system.

It is important to realize that a staging environment is not a development platform. A complete strategy should allow development to test freely and production risks to be mitigated by staging.

Figure 6-2 shows the deconstruction of the development area where multiple development environments share a common infrastructure. The testing environment that is used for incremental build releases and development testing also shares this environment.

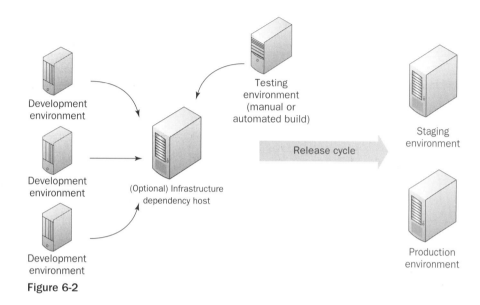

**Figure 6-2**

The release cycle is executed when a stable and tested build is released from the testing environment onto the staging environment.

## Development Environment

This is one of the most important parts of an infrastructure. Development should not be hampered by infrastructure and access issues. Developers should have an environment that replicates access to everything they will need to have a productive construction experience. The setup should reflect the environment that the solution will run in. Dependent infrastructure that is replicated in the development environment will allow you to mitigate any integration risks early in the development cycle.

By sandboxing the development environment, developers can build the solution without impacting each other or the production environment. An ideal solution is to create a virtualized development environment prior to project kick-off. By building a virtual development environment template, it allows you to make multiple copies of the environment for different team members without having to reinstall and configure all the developer tools required. This could speed up the process of getting new developers joining the team ready to work and ensuring that everybody uses the same environment.

Using a virtualization technology the development team can build and use a virtual environment that can be reused for projects that require the same setup and infrastructure. It is a useful practice to store copies of each virtual environment for use in future development projects.

## *Isolated Development or Shared Infrastructure*

A typical development environment should include technology components as determined from the non-functional requirements. Version mismatch during development will create problems during staging and testing, if the development environment's version does not match the version used in production.

A recommended developer environment should include the components listed in the following table:

| Operating System | Windows Server 2003 |
|---|---|
| K2 blackpearl, including development tools | Latest (or applicable for solution maintenance) of K2 blackpearl server |
| | Visual Studio 2005 or 2008[1] |
| | K2 blackpearl Visual Studio components |
| | SQL Server 2005 and SQL Reporting Services |
| | SharePoint and InfoPath components as required |
| Infrastructure components | Active Directory |
| | .NET 2 and 3.0 or .NET 3.5[2] |
| | Microsoft Office SharePoint Server 2007 (or Windows SharePoint Services 3.0) if required |
| | InfoPath or InfoPath Forms server if required |
| Source control and build tools | Source control client |
| | Automated build tools |
| | Testing tools for unit testing and scenario testing |
| Debug tools | Visual Studio 2005 debug tools |
| Dependency infrastructure | Any dependent infrastructure and systems identified during your non-functional requirements gathering |

[1] Support for Visual Studio 2008 is expected in the fourth quarter of 2008.

[2] Support for .NET 3.5 will be available with Visual Studio 2008 support.

For a small development team, this is an effective way of building a solution that might contain multiple dependent components. However, for larger teams it might become ineffective to create a full development environment for each team member. Restrictions could include software licensing requirements or practical limitations of a virtualized environment. A development server that will host dependent infrastructure components will allow a team to work with local components where possible and shared components that cannot be virtualized or require a group effort around configuration. As an example using a single Active Directory instance in development will ensure that changes made to Active Directory are available to all developers.

Figure 6-3 shows multiple development environments that share a common set of infrastructure components on an infrastructure Host Server.

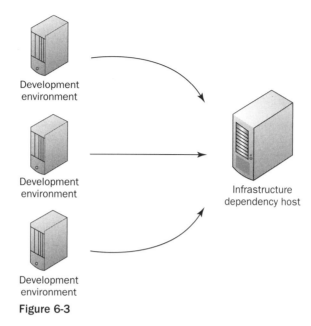

**Figure 6-3**

Some other infrastructure components that could be shared include database servers, directory services, document management systems, and service bus endpoints.

In the automated build section of this chapter, we will look at how to create tools that will ease configuration in a development environment where infrastructure components need to be kept in sync on the development environments.

## Source Control and Version Management

A member of our team once said that the first question when interviewing a technical candidate for a development job should be about source control.

Managing a successful development methodology cannot be done without proper source control and version management. The overriding motivation for source control adoption is code management (versioning, backup, change tracking, etc.) and not necessarily the requirement for team working. Even a single developer should adopt a source control discipline for these reasons.

BPM solutions are complex and often include components other than code. In order to manage your development cycles; introduce effective source control tools and policies in your development environment. K2 blackpearl solutions are no exception and with the integration of K2 blackpearl Designer for Visual Studio being available inside the integrated development environment (IDE), source control is made easy. A few strategies exist and some best practices recommend that you create a separate Visual Studio solution for your workflow components. Refer to Chapter 9 to learn about creating a solution in Visual Studio.

Once a solution is under source control, managing changes to a solution is easy. Other features include version and build label management, check-outs, source code history, and blame (depending on your source control provider).

*Blame is the ability of a source control provider to store the responsible team member for each line of committed source code in the source control repository.*

Figure 6-4 shows a solution under source control and lists the available options offered by the source control client.

**Figure 6-4**

Because process definition (`.kprx`) files and SmartObject definition (`.sodx`) files are large XML structures that include logic, layout, and documentation about the entity, it is recommended that you enable exclusive check-out when editing these files. Automatic merging is often unsuccessful when multiple developers worked on the same entity.

The K2 blackpearl project file (`.k2proj`) file contains deployment information including the deployment label and version description. For this reason it is required that this file is also exclusively checked out when deploying the solution to the K2 blackpearl server. To avoid developers competing for a single project file when under source control, break your K2 blackpearl solution into smaller projects under a single solution file if required.

## K2 blackpearl Deployment Versioning

When deploying a solution to the K2 blackpearl server, the server will automatically store a copy of your source code and a description of your version. For more information on workflow and SmartObject deployment, refer to Chapter 10.

The version description should be used together with your source control service to link a specific version of a process back to code base and other solution components. Figure 6-5 shows how a developer is exporting a process version to the K2 blackpearl server and indicating the description of the version to be related to a specific functional requirement.

To view the Server and Project Settings step in the deployment wizard (see Figure 6-5), run the Deploy Project Wizard in Advanced Mode.

Figure 6-5

This version comment will apply only to the K2 blackpearl process and SmartObjects exported. To link the changes back to the rest of the code base, use the code labeling or check-in comments feature of your source control client. This will create a link between a specific version of your process and the rest of the solution under source control.

## Testing Environment

How this environment is used will differ, depending on the size of your team and the development methodology. Later in this chapter we explore different methodologies and how the testing environment can used to benefit them.

The use of a testing environment in development is equivalent to using a staging environment in production, as shown in Figure 6-6 (which repeats the four-environment setup shown in Figure 6-1). It is a risk-mitigating environment.

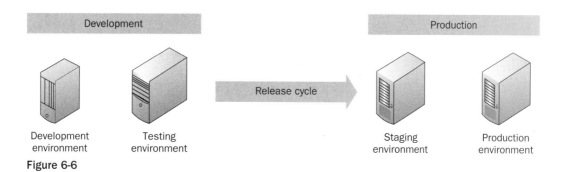

Figure 6-6

In a test-driven methodology, the testing environment is normally an instance of your development environment. It allows testers and developers to do integration testing on a clean instance of your infrastructure. Depending on the testing methodology, automating the setup and execution of test scenarios on your testing environment will reduce manual effort required to test a solution.

The reason that the testing environment should be separated from development is to create a blank environment prior to deployment and testing. Development environments might include configurations that are not available on the testing environment. This will immediately become clear once the solution is deployed. By creating a separate environment for testing, you ensure that infrastructure skew that might happen on a development environment (as developers fiddle with the database or other services on the development environment) does not create a false sense of security that your solution is actually working the way it will when it is configured on a blank server. The effort required for moving a solution from a development environment should not be underestimated. The introduction of a testing environment and using a complete deployment package to deploy to the testing environment will mitigate this risk early in your project.

In the absence of a testing environment, it is possible to execute unit testing only on your development environment and not have a dedicated testing environment. In this scenario, you would use the staging environment to execute integration and acceptance testing, as outlined in Figure 6-7.

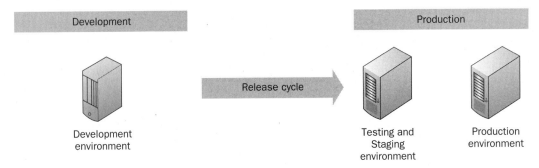

Figure 6-7

## Automated Testing

Test-driven development and the automated execution of those tests can greatly improve the quality of your solution and minimize the effort spent on testing. Current industry standards dictate that 40 to 50% of the man-hours spent on development be spent on testing. We have found that more is required for BPM solutions. The reasons for this are that business process automation is human driven and greatly dependent on the external infrastructure components over which the business process is executed. Because these external infrastructure components are normally only available in the production area, the testing effort required during staging can be disproportionally large. We often see testing efforts equivalent to or greater than the development effort.

A workflow with human steps in it is time-consuming to test. A user will need to start the workflow and then confirm that each subsequent human step is routed to the correct person, and that each of those steps is presented as required. This includes confirming that e-mail notifications were sent, tasks were allocated correctly, the user interface renders the data correctly, and that the required actions available can be taken.

Just imagine a user requirement in your workflow that states a person should get a task only 2 hours after the workflow started. Your testers will become master foosball players! By automating testing, you can save a lot of time.

The K2 blackpearl client API is a .NET assembly that gives the developer access to the run-time features of the K2 blackpearl Workflow server. By using the K2 blackpearl client, API developers are able to create automated test scenarios that can be executed unattended. This approach allows you to treat the testing of your workflow process like testing a code module using a unit testing approach.

The K2 blackpearl client API exposes the following core functionality:

❑ Simulate different named connections to the K2 Workflow server.

❑ Instantiate and start a new process instance.

❑ Find a process instance based on the instance ID of the instance.

❑ Interact with the data stored inside a process instance.

The client API is normally used to build custom functionality, such as a custom worklist or a user interface that interacts with K2 blackpearl. However, the functionality exposed by the client API allows you to build tests that simulate the activity that users or a system would perform against a workflow solution. We refer to this as *scenario testing*.

The following section provides an example of how to automatically execute steps in a workflow and simulate user interaction using the K2 blackpearl client API.

## Creating Your Own Automated Test Scenario — the Problem

Consider the following scenario: Payment is requested for a supplier, and all requests must be approved by a manager. If the request is for more than $1,000.00, a director's approval is also required.

The resulting workflow in Figure 6-8 represents the solution to this use case. Once the solution is built and deployed, the only way to test this would be to manually execute the workflow and run four different scenarios to cover all the possible outcomes of the workflow:

❑ The amount is less than $1,000.00, and the Manager approves the request.

❑ The amount is less than $1,000.00, and the Manager declines the request.

❑ The Manager approves an amount more than $1,000.00, and the Director also approves the request.

❑ The Manager approves an amount more than $1,000.00, and the Director declines the request.

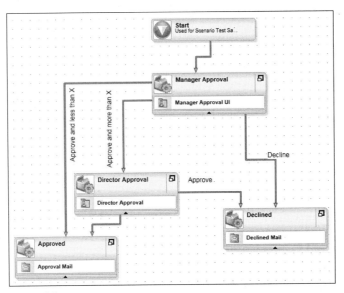

**Figure 6-8**

This is a simple solution but with four different scenarios to test. By adding another requirement that allows the Director to route the approval back to the Manager, you have at least eight scenarios to test, effectively doubling the testing effort required. This effort contributes to the cost of the project because it's labor intensive. By automating these scenarios, developers can execute a scenario unattended to assess if the solution meets the requirements. It also helps to validate that a change to the solution did not introduce other bugs, by acting as a regression test.

## Creating Your Own Automated Test Scenario — the Solution

We can now look at using the K2 client API to write an automated test. The scenario to be tested is to ensure that the Director's Approval activity is active and that the Director has a work item if the purchase request is more than $1,000.00.

First, we start the workflow by using the K2 blackpearl client API, and then we simulate actions on the workflow, using the client API, in the same way that the the workflow would execute under human interaction.

```
01 internal void MyTestScenario()
02 {
03    // start a process instance
04    int myProcessID = StartMyProcess(1500);
05
06    // do the manager approval
07    ManagerApproveMyProcess(myProcessID);
08
09    // check if the process is at directors approval
10    Assert.IsTrue(ProcessAtDirectorsApproval(myProcessID));
11 }
```

In this scenario, line 4 creates a new instance of the workflow and sets the purchase request amount to $1,500.00 and returns the ID of the workflow. This ID is used in the subsequent steps to distinguish this instance of My Process on the K2 blackpearl server.

Using the K2 blackpearl client API, we can break the code executed by line 4 down into the following call on the client API:

```
// create a connection that supports IDisposable
using (Connection myConnection = new Connection())
{
  try
  {
    // open a connection to the local server
    myConnection.Open("127.0.0.1");

    // create a process instance using the full name of the process
    ProcessInstance myProcess =
        myConnection.CreateProcessInstance(@"My Workflow Project\My Process");

    // set some data in the process instance
    myProcess.DataFields["Amount"].Value = amount;

    // start the process instance and return the instance ID
    // to ensure the process is in a stable state, set the sync
    // parameter to true. for async systems, this should
    // be left at the default value.
    myConnection.StartProcessInstance(myProcess, true);
    return myProcess.ID;
  }
  finally
  {
    // release the connection to the K2 workflow server
    myConnection.Close();
  }
}
```

Note that we start the process instance using the connection instance. We also pass a Sync parameter of true into the StartProcessInstance method. This ensures that the StartProcessInstance method returns only once the process instance has reached a stable state (client event, end of process, or process is in error state). This pattern should be used only if you require this specific functionality. Under normal circumstances, the process instance on the K2 server should be allowed to execute asynchronously. For this reason, the default value for the Sync parameter is false.

Line 7 does the manager approval step and routes your instance to the Directors Approval activity. Line 10 checks if the instance is indeed at the Directors Approval activity, and the test scenario creates a unit test failure if this is not the case.

Also note that this automated test code does not test any back-end integration. It executes the workflow instance and checks that the desired path is followed within the workflow by simulating a specific scenario. Although an effective test, this should not replace unit testing that needs to be executed on back-end integration points even if the path in the workflow does interact with a back-end system.

Unit testing frameworks such as Microsoft Unit Testing Framework or nUnit are great tools for creating test scenarios that can be automatically executed during the automated build cycle. This section illustrates a sample scenario test using custom .NET code.

This code can be downloaded from the book's Web site at www.wrox.com.

## Automated Building

To reduce the effort involved in keeping the testing environment up to date, consider creating an automated build and deployment package for your solution. Automated building and deployment tools can help with this strategy. Examples include Visual Studio Team System and CruiseControl.NET. An effective automated building and deployment tool should be able to extract the latest source files from your source control service, build the solution, and deploy the different pieces of the solution in your testing environment. It should also be able to automatically execute your test scenarios and report on the outcome of each test scenario.

When deploying a solution to a clean testing environment, other items also need to be configured. Automating these tasks will assist in creating a fully automated testing environment. Use the following checklist to consider that items should be configured during deployment:

❑ Active directory users and groups

❑ Application database and application data

❑ Integration points, including XML Web services and Windows Commutation Foundation endpoints

❑ SharePoint sites, lists, libraries, content types, users, and groups

❑ Other infrastructure endpoints that your solution will depend on or integrate with

The K2 blackpearl Designer for Visual Studio allows you to create a deployment package. This deployment package can be executed unattended on your target environment. To create a deployment package, select Create Deploy Package from the context menu of the K2 project in Solution Explorer. This will allow your operations team to deploy the workflow and workflow dependencies without the Visual Studio .NET dependency.

Some items are not included in the deployment package and need to be manually configured on the server. Take note of the following:

❑ Although String Table entries are deployed for a specific environment, the environment configuration is excluded from the package.

❑ Roles used by your process are not included in the package. These need to be configured on the environment before running the package.

❑ Time zones specific to your environment are not included in the package.

You can use MSBuild to deploy your package. To comply with deployment policies or corporate governance, some organizations create a clear boundary between the development and production environments. To comply with these policies, it's important that your whole solution can be packaged and deployed unattended. Because K2 blackpearl's compilation and deployment processes are executed by MSBuild, you can create a full MSBuild package that can build and deploy your solution unattended.

# Staging and Production Environments

A production environment should be stable and scalable according to the non-functional requirements of the solution. This section will cover recommendations on how a production environment should be configured to allow for redundancy and scalability. To mitigate risks before deploying to production, a staging environment is required.

A production environment will place certain requirements and restrictions on a solution that might not exist within the development and testing environment. To indentify and test these restrictions, a staging environment is used. The staging environment should be an exact duplicate of the production environment. This includes any requirements for security, load balancing, redundancy, and infrastructure configuration.

If, for example, a hardware load balancer will be used for production, attempt to have the same hardware and configuration on the staging environment (as shown in Figure 6-9). Certain items of a solution can only be tested with the real thing, and there are obvious differences between hardware and software load balancing. The risk of introducing problems in production is greatly mitigated by having an environment where final acceptance of a solution can be made.

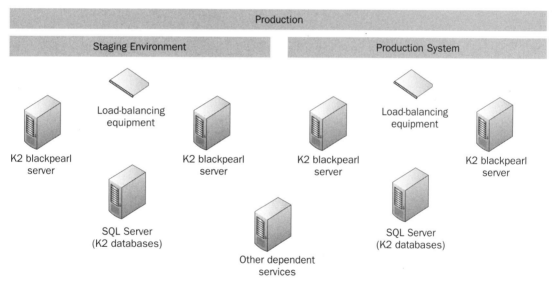

Figure 6-9

Some restrictions and requirements exist in a production environment. These restrictions should be noted and planned for prior to deploying a solution in production. Ensure that the following items are considered:

❏ **Security:** Is the production environment a distributed installation of your solution? Will the application code, forms generator, K2 blackpearl server and databases all be available on a single machine or will they be installed on different servers with specific security restrictions between the servers?

❑ **Configuration:** The solution configuration settings for development are normally different from those for production. Ensure that all configuration values used during development can be extracted and that the production values can be applied when transferring the solution to production. Using the K2 blackpearl Environment tables and templates, common configurable settings can be extracted from the solution. Chapter 10 provides a detailed overview of how to set up different environment templates to represent the various environments you have configured.

❑ **Encryption and data security:** Your solution might have to encrypt configuration files or data sent between interfaces. This requirement should be reflected in development and testing on the staging environment.

❑ **Rights:** During development assume limited rights to K2 blackpearl server components and process access. By starting with maximum rights available, effort might be required to limit these rights during production. By taking a "grant as required" approach during development, you will end up with the smallest footprint of rights required for production.

❑ **Redundancy and scalability:** Your development environment will not represent the real strain that your solution will be placed under. Equipment and infrastructure that address redundancy and scalability should be tested in the staging environment. A good rule is to always design any solution with redundancy and scalability in mind. Develop your solution assuming that horizontal and vertical scaling will be required even if it is not stated as a non-functional requirement at design time.

Review Chapter 5 and implement a stable and scalable production environment along the guidelines set out during the requirements-gathering phase of your solution. Bad solution design can lead to performance problems that can be hard and expensive to fix postproduction. Throwing hardware at a problem is not always possible, and even then the problem might not go away. Capturing performance metrics during requirements gathering and implementing proper design approaches during development for good performance can mitigate these risks in production.

# Debugging and Monitoring Strategies

An effective development strategy should include mechanisms to monitor and debug code during development. It must be possible to debug parts of your BPM solution. Every part of a BPM solution should be able to report on its health by outputting and reporting on exceptions that occur within the solution. This section will cover mechanisms for debugging, error reporting, and logging.

*Chapters 19 and 20 provide coverage of the features available on K2 blackpearl for error logging and error reporting.*

## Error Reporting from the Workspace

The Workspace provides a details overview of your process status, allowing you to monitor the health of a process. The Process Overview report reports on all active and completed processes and indicates if a process is in an error state (as shown in Figure 6-10).

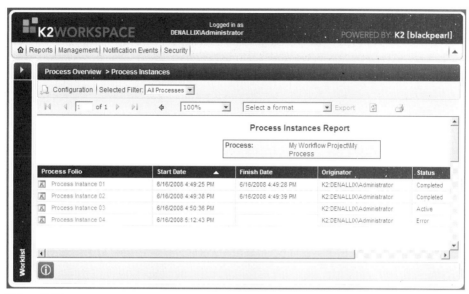

Figure 6-10

Two instances are currently running, one instance is complete and one is in an error state. Processes going into an error state provide some information to the developer other than the description of the exception that was generated.

When a process instance does go into an error state, the Error Profile in the Workspace will report the error message (as shown in Figure 6-11). By adding an exception-handler to the process all relevant business data and state can be logged for further debugging. This will assist in finding the source of the error as discussed in the next section.

Figure 6-11

## *Error Reporting from Inside the Process*

Process instances that generate an exception in any part of the process will result in the instance being suspended by the K2 server. The server reports the state of the current instance, the location of the error, and the details of the error in the K2 Workspace.

By adding an exception rule to a process and capturing and reporting as much information as possible, you can review the details to find the source of the problem. The details can be reported to the server log file (see the next section of this chapter "Running the Server in Console Mode") or to a custom log repository.

> *Hint: A common exception-handler I normally add to my own processes sends me a support e-mail, including everything I might need to know to find the source of the problem. In this way, I'm notified of the error and error details before the client has even realized something's gone wrong.*

To add an exception-handler to your process, use the Exception Rule property of the process (as shown in Figure 6-12). The purpose of the exception rule is to recover from the error but it is also a great location to report on the error. If the error cannot be recovered, the exception should be logged and thrown.

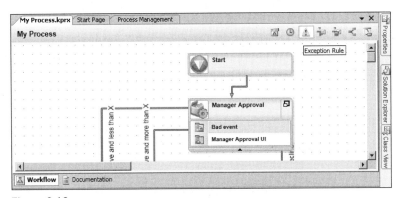

Figure 6-12

To output information from the inside of a process, you can add the following code to any process component:

```
K2.ProcessInstance.Logger.LogDebugMessage("Event Name", "Log Message");
```

Process health reporting and auditing is a powerful way of tracking problems when something goes wrong. Having your process report on its internal state is a good way to accomplish this.

A good practice is to design your process to be modular. In other words, if a specific step or rule in your workflow needs external data or needs to configure data prior to executing, it should do that at the location that the data is needed. If the specific module then fails, reexecuting the module from the K2 Management Console will ensure that all steps required are retried. This approach also makes moving the current execution point in the process instance easier.

## *Running the Server in Console Mode*

The K2 blackpearl server is capable of outputting detailed information about the execution of running processes. By default, this log is written to the install folder of the server.

Developers and testers can have a real-time view of the server output by starting the K2 blackpearl server in console mode. To run the server in console mode, ensure that the K2 blackpearl Service is stopped and then run the server application by starting the K2Server.exe process directly from Windows Explorer (as shown in Figure 6-13). The server will start in a console, and all information normally written to the server log files will be visible in the console.

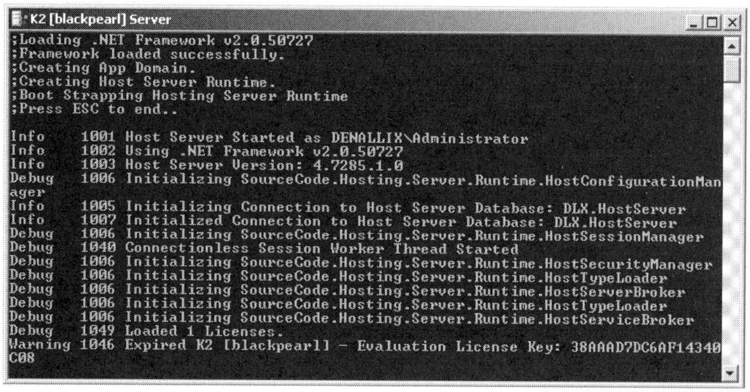

Figure 6-13

Real-time monitoring of activity on the K2 blackpearl Host Server is a powerful way of debugging run-time issues during the development phase of a project.

> *Refer to Chapter 19 for details about the logging framework configuration file. This file controls the level of detail that is logged to the Host Server console.*

## *Debugging K2 blackpearl Components*

Various debugging mechanisms exist for K2 blackpearl. This section will cover some of the basic techniques for enabling developers to debug K2 blackpearl components.

A K2 blackpearl solution consists of various code components. They include items such as:

❑   Process components, including server events, destination and Line Rules, and exception rules

❑   Custom server events

❑   Custom service brokers

Because the execution of these components is hosted by the K2HostServer.exe process, the process needs to be attached to Visual Studio. This allows the developer to set breakpoints and stepover code.

To be able to set breakpoint or stepover code, the K2 blackpearl server process needs to be attached to Visual Studio. Figure 6-14 shows how to attach the K2 blackpearl server process to Visual Studio by selecting the Debug ⇨ Attach to Process . . . option in Visual Studio. By attaching the K2 blackpearl server process to Visual Studio, developers can debug code components, including process rules, SmartObject Services, and custom code.

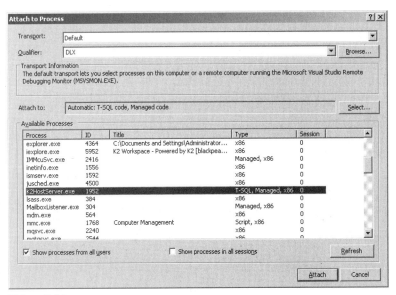

Figure 6-14

Using performance monitors allows developers and infrastructure owners to report on the health of the K2 blackpearl server (review Chapter 19 for a detailed list of performance counters available).

# Summary

In theory, an effective project strategy and environment configuration sounds great. In practice, it requires planning time and effort. Projects differ greatly; some require a single business analyst to put together a business-facing workflow, while others use a solution development consisting of many team members covering various disciples. Hopefully, this chapter has given you a good start toward planning your own approach to a K2 blackpearl solution.

# Part III

# K2 blackpearl Process Planning and Design Essentials

# 7

# Building and Using SmartObjects

**Jason Apergis**

One of the newest and most significant features of the K2 platform is SmartObjects. SmartObjects provide process designers the ability to provision data from line-of-business (LOB) data sources in a drag-and-drop fashion. Now that data is more accessible, business users can make more informed and better decisions in their workflows. Also, business processes can be built using SmartObjects, which focus on management of data itself. The SmartObject framework is not scoped to K2 blackpearl; SmartObjects can be used with all applications that participate in a process, even disparate ones on different platforms. When using SmartObjects, designers now have the ability to gain access to data that resides in Active Directory, SharePoint, SQL Server, Oracle, SAP, and so on and to build business objects using data harvested from these locations. The SmartObject framework is also extremely flexible, as it provides the ability to create composite views from any LOB application. For instance, a designer may create a composite employee SmartObject that uses data from both Active Directory and a human resources database.

In addition to providing a framework in which data services can be written, K2 blackpearl provides a designer tool that allows for rapid construction of SmartObjects. There are visual design tools for building, deploying, and maintaining SmartObjects. These tools literally enable a designer to author fully functional SmartObjects in minutes. When authoring K2 blackpearl processes, designers have the ability to drag-and-drop data and use it within the process. SmartObjects are designed to be completely decoupled and deployed independently from the K2 process. Since SmartObjects are separate from the process definition, with time, a catalog of SmartObjects for the enterprise is created. This catalog of SmartObjects can be reused in future K2 processes or referenced in other LOB applications. This will create continuity between enterprise applications because now business objects are defined outside of the applications that use them.

This chapter:

❑ Discusses the history of K2 prior to SmartObjects and provides insight as to why SmartObjects have become an indispensible component when writing new workflows.

❏ Discusses the architecture of SmartObjects along with how they may be created, customized, and leveraged within a K2 process.

❏ Explores the SmartObject API to show you how it can be used in custom code such as an ASP .NET Web page.

❏ Gives an introduction in writing custom SmartObject Services that can be used to access data in any LOB database.

# SmartObjects Background

SmartObjects were introduced into the K2 platform to solve the challenge of provisioning data to make business decisions. K2.net 2003 was the version prior to the release of K2 blackpearl. To access data in K2.net 2003, you had to build custom data services from scratch, and it was common that designers would not create reusable data access frameworks. There were event templates for SQL Server and Web services in K2.net 2003; however, designers quickly started to build custom frameworks and code libraries to gain access to this and other data. These services would be used for many things, such as making Line Rule decisions, setting destination users, and creating business logic for escalation rules to name just a few. Custom data access layers are typically vertically aligned to the process and not reusable in other processes. This required significant time in every project plan to gain access to data, increasing the level of effort for the project. K2 recognized this as a missing piece of the puzzle. K2 was providing a powerful business process automation modeling tool, but there was no support for retrieving business data just as easily. Potentially every piece of data in the entire enterprise is a candidate for usage inside of K2 workflow. With the introduction of the SmartObjects framework, this hurdle has been overcome.

Along with challenges in reading data from LOB databases, K2.net 2003 also had challenges with publishing data it had captured for enterprise reporting. Commonly rich business data about the business process would be captured within the K2 server, but it was challenging for nontechnical designers to get the data back out. Much of the process data would be embedded directly within the process and stored in the K2 database as process or activity fields. Developers were faced with the challenge of getting that data back out of the K2 database. The K2 process database does use SQL Server; however, its database schema is geared towards supporting a workflow server rather than a reporting database. Designers would believe that data stored in the K2 process database was redundant and inefficient when, in fact, it was doing things like protecting transition boundaries between concurrent threads of process and activity instances. Designers for K2.net 2003 solutions realized this and started externalizing all business data to a custom database, thus allowing the K2 database to do what it does best, manage a workflow server. This was recognized as a best practice for K2.net 2003 and still is a good practice for K2 blackpearl. As already mentioned, process designers had to build up custom frameworks again to persist data to these external custom databases, increasing the level of effort for projects. With SmartObjects, designers no longer have to spend nearly as much time building these data access layers as the SmartObject infrastructure provides all the plumbing to hook into external data sources in a consistent and reusable fashion.

# SmartObject Architecture

Before diving into how to create and use SmartObjects in a process, it's valuable to understand where they fit within the enterprise architecture. Simply put, there are three traditional layers for application architecture: the user interface, business, and data layers, as shown in Figure 7-1. The K2 blackpearl platform resides in the business layer. The K2 blackpearl platform allows you to visually organize business events that will be raised in a specific order based upon business rules. Traditionally, K2 provided many accelerators (wizard templates) that allowed designers to hook into user interface layers using events like InfoPath, SharePoint, ASP.NET, and so on. Designers would simply use these wizards, provide the necessary configurations, and deploy the process. However, that was only half of what was needed. What was missing was designers did not have a framework to rapidly integrate K2 processes and LOB data to make business decisions.

Figure 7-1 is a contextual diagram that shows where K2 blackpearl and the SmartObjects reside in a layered view of an enterprise's architecture. The diagram is generic and is not meant to cover every permutation of how data can be provisioned using the K2 SmartObject framework. Also, it does not account for the various layers that may reside within an enterprise application or Web service. This diagram does demonstrate how K2 SmartObjects can be used as an enterprise facade to access all data across the enterprise.

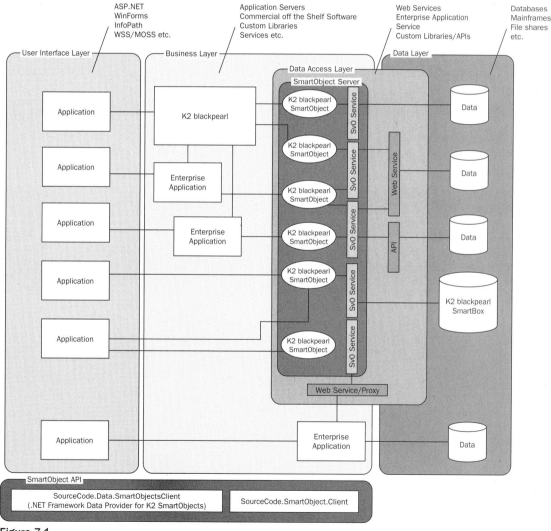

Figure 7-1

*Chapter 17 discusses Single Sign-On that is provided by the SmartObject framework.*

The K2 blackpearl Server in Figure 7-1 is part of the business layer. This is because it executes all of the business rules and process definitions that are used to build enterprise applications and services. Based on these process definitions, the K2 blackpearl server collects rich data associated to the execution of these business process such as who were the assigned participants, who took action (which can be a person or system), what actions were taken and in what order, and how long it took to complete the process. This data can then be used to improve the business processes, introduce efficiencies, and resolve bottlenecks.

In the standard three-tier architectural model, a thin layer, often referred to as the data access layer, resides between both the business and data layers. The data access layer, shown in Figure 7-1, commonly contains all infrastructure logic to enable the exchange of data to LOB data. The data access layer focuses on managing transactions of data and does not contain business contextual logic (that is, business rules are not applied there). The SmartObject framework provides this data access layer, which is sometimes written from scratch. There are two important concepts within the SmartObject framework shown in the data access layer. They are SmartObject Services and SmartObjects themselves.

❑   SmartObject Services are the data providers that implement actual connections to data sources and perform operations against them.

❑   SmartObjects define business entities that use the service methods.

Having the SmartObject framework significantly reduces the amount of time required to implement a solution, allowing more time to be spent on business process modeling. This is because a standardized framework, an interface, and tools are provided to both designers and developers.

## *The Advantages of SmartObject Architecture*

One of the advantages of using the SmartObject framework is that it forces designers to create highly decoupled data access layers. It is not uncommon for developers to violate the tenants of a custom data access layer by slipping in business contextual logic into the wrong place. SmartObject Services can be developed without knowledge of the SmartObject that will use it. SmartObjects are not dependent on the SmartObject Service because SmartObject Services must be published using standard interface guidelines. SmartObjects can easily map from one service to another without concern for where the data originated from or where it is going to. SmartObject Services serve primarily as a facade to LOB data, and SmartObjects are both scalable and maintainable over their lifetimes. For instance, an organization can create a SmartObject that uses a SmartObject Active Directory Service to expose data. If the organization were to change its direction and store data in a Human Resources database, the SmartObject would simply have to change its mapping to a different SmartObject Service that has access to the Human Resources database. None of the calling applications in the business or user interface layers would have to change their implementation unless the new Human Resources application had different business rules (that is, new required data, different data types, or so on).

SmartObjects also create more agile business processes. Without SmartObjects, it becomes challenging to create business rules that are dynamic. For instance approval tasks can be assigned dynamically based on external data such as a purchasing database. The purchasing database may have data that knows which purchasing officer must approve purchase orders, according to the types of parts being ordered. If you use SmartObjects, the process logic to assign approval tasks is not hardcoded.

Another important concept within the SmartObject framework is composite SmartObjects, which are shown in Figure 7-1. It is very common when building a process that data to be used originates from many different places. For a SmartObject, some data could originate from an enterprise resource planning (ERP) system, while other data originated from a SharePoint list. The decoupled nature of the SmartObject framework provides the ability to build SmartObjects that use all of these data sources. A very common scenario would be retrieving employee data from both Active Directory and a Human Resources database. Another common scenario would be a SmartObject that can save data across a purchasing and inventory databases in a single transaction. SmartObjects allow for the ability to create methods that use multiple services and hide from you the fact that many data repositories are being used.

However, the SmartObject framework is not intended to be a data brokerage server like Microsoft BizTalk. If there are really complex transactions, you can create a SmartObject Service that calls a BizTalk Orchestration that has been published as a Web service. Then the complexity of a BizTalk can be hidden by the SmartObject Service. Also, if there are complex data reads from multiple ERP systems, it would be highly recommended that you create a data warehouse and then create a SmartObject to read from the data warehouse.

SmartObjects are not scoped either to the K2 or .NET platforms either. All SmartObjects can be executed as a Windows Communication Foundation (WCF) endpoint or even executed using K2's SmartObject Method execution Web service that InfoPath uses. This now enables K2 processes to be initiated from other platforms and allows K2 processes to coordinate operations across platforms.

Figure 7-2 shows all of the components of the K2 SmartObject architecture. K2 Visual Studio and the K2 Workspace use the same APIs to work with SmartObjects. The SmartObject APIs access the SmartObject server, which is one of the many servers hosted with K2 platform. There are two SmartObject servers:

- ❏  The **Management Server**, which is responsible for loading SmartObject Service and SmartObject instances

- ❏  The **Run-time Server**, which is responsible for the execution of the SmartObjects with LOB applications

Figure 7-2 shows a few SmartObjects services like SmartBox, Salesforce, Workflow, and Active Directory; however, additional SmartObject Services can be added to the server over time. The Service SDK is the framework SmartObject Services must implement so that they can be hosted with the SmartObject server. Finally, the SmartObject Host Server uses a SQL Server database to manage all of the SmartObject Service instances and their definitions.

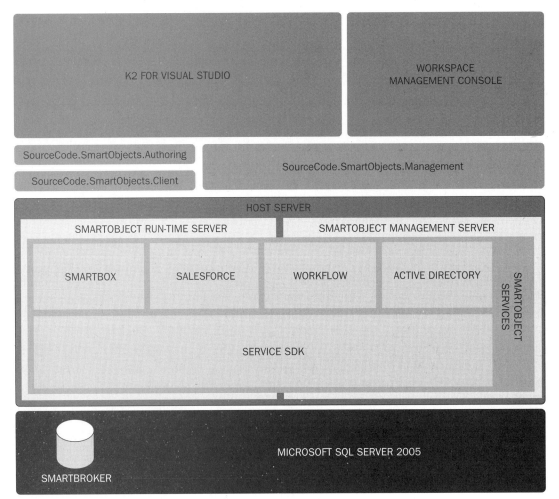

Figure 7-2

## SmartObject Services

The following are the current out of the box SmartObject Services provided by K2 blackpearl! This list will expand with future planned releases of K2 blackpearl:

❏ **SmartBox:** When you are using the SmartBox, all SmartObjects will have a dedicated database table generated in SQL Server with columns for each property defined for the SmartObject. This service provides the ability to rapidly store data using SmartObjects.

❏ **SharePoint:** This service supplies methods to support operations on lists and libraries that are located within a SharePoint site. This service is extremely useful because now SharePoint data is being exposed without having to go to SharePoint Web services or API. Since SmartObjects can be used with the .NET Framework Data Provider for K2 SmartObjects, data within SharePoint is now easily accessible.

❑ **Active Directory:** This service provides several methods to read information from an Active Directory schema. Methods such as looking up user detail information, finding a user's manager, or getting all users in a group are provided.

❑ **K2 blackpearl:** This service provides access to representations of K2 workflow data as business objects.

❑ **Salesforce.com:** This service provides access to data and methods available in Salesforce.com.

The K2 community also supports several SmartObject Services through the K2 Underground Web site (www.k2underground.com). This list will grow, but here are some of the more popular services:

❑ **Dynamic SmartObject Services:** This service dynamically reads the schema of a custom SQL Server database and provides methods for each table in the database.

❑ **Dynamic SQL Stored Procedure Service:** This service dynamically reads the definition of each stored procedure on a SQL Server database and provides methods to execute the stored procedures.

❑ **Dynamic Web Service:** This service dynamically reads the definition of a Web service and creates a method for each Web method on the Web service.

❑ **SharePoint Users in Groups ServiceObject:** This service exposes SharePoint User Groups for SmartObjects.

❑ **Office Communication Server Service:** This service allows for the creation of a SmartObject to send notifications via Microsoft Office Communications Server 2007.

❑ **SmartObject Service Provider for Oracle:** This service dynamically reads the schema of a custom Oracle database and provides methods for each table in the database.

❑ **Dynamic SmartObject Service:** This service dynamically builds a service using existing SmartObjects as the data source. This can be used to create inheritance between SmartObjects.

# Designing a SmartObject

The approach taken to design a SmartObject is similar to designing a database. Even though SmartObject has the word *Object*, which is associated with object-oriented principles, concepts such as inheritance, overloading, overriding, and polymorphism do not apply. Think of SmartObjects simply as a business objects or entities. Remember the SmartObject will use SmartObject Services to populate it with data, and the SmartObject is not concerned with data origination.

We're going to use as an example a business opportunity assessment process that requires automation, and K2 blackpearl is selected to manage the process. In this process, an Account Executive identifies an opportunity and must gather information prior to a meeting with the Business Development Director, the Program Director, and the Project Manager. The goal is to obtain sign-off before the Account Executive is allowed to author a proposal for services. To support this process, a few simple SmartObjects need to be created.

❑    First, a SmartObject needs to be created for the company for whom the proposal will be written.

❑    Second, an Opportunity SmartObject needs to be created to capture specific information associated with the opportunity.

❑    Third, an OpportunityEmployee SmartObject is needed to retrieve information for the participants in the workflow.

Figure 7-3 shows a model of this example. In this model, a Company SmartObject will have associations to many Opportunities, while an Opportunity will be associated to a single Company. The Opportunity SmartObject will have associations for each of the OpportunityEmployee SmartObjects that participate in the workflow.

Figure 7-3

# Creating SmartObjects

Creating SmartObjects is simple when you use the K2 Designer for Visual Studio or K2 Studio. For the purpose of this example, Visual Studio will be used and it assumed that readers have a developer's understanding of how to use Visual Studio. Figure 7-4 shows New Project window from Visual Studio. To start making SmartObjects, you need to create a new Visual Studio project using K2's SmartObject Project Template. In the New Project window, select K2 in the Project Types tree and then select K2 SmartObject Project template.

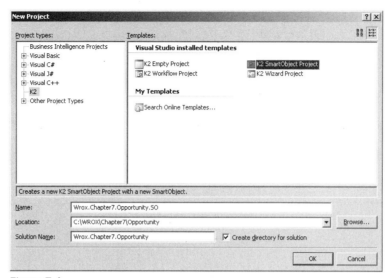

Figure 7-4

*Naming conventions are very important and should not be an afterthought. Typically, when writing C# code libraries, developers adopt the namespace into the name of the project, which subsequently names the .dll the same. The same approach should be taken for a SmartObject project. A good project naming convention would be* CompanyName.Division.ProcessName.SmartObjectProjectName. *However, this may not always apply because the SmartObjects being defined may have a global context. The point is to recognize that the same naming standard approach should be taken because these SmartObjects will be deployed centrally to a K2 server. The name of the SmartObject must be unique, and it is highly likely that SmartObject names will conflict as more and more are created.*

Once the SmartObject project is created, a new default SmartObject file called SmartObject1.sodx will be in the project, as shown in Figure 7-5. Notice that in the visual design interface, you can add properties and methods to the SmartObject. First, rename the default SmartObject by going to the Name textbox and changing **SmartObject1** to **Company**. Note that after changing the name of the SmartObject, the filename of SmartObject1.sodx changes to Company.sodx.

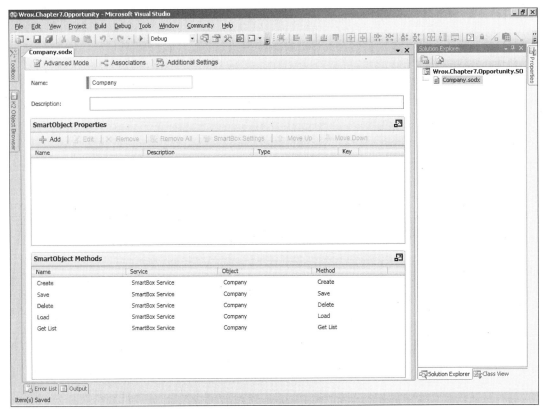

Figure 7-5

You now need to add properties to the Company SmartObject using the Add SmartObject Properties window shown in Figure 7-6. Think of properties as fields in a database table, because in many instances that is exactly what they will be. Properties are things like first name, last name, and e-mail. Keeping this simple, you'll add an ID and a Name property to the Company SmartObject. To add the property, click the Add button, and the Add SmartObject Properties window appears. Then enter **ID** into the Name column, enter an optional description, and then select the Autonumber type from the drop-down. This automatically checks the Key column. Making the ID column autonumbered ensures that the ID property is populated with a unique number generated from the database. Add the Name property in the same manner; however, make the type Text.

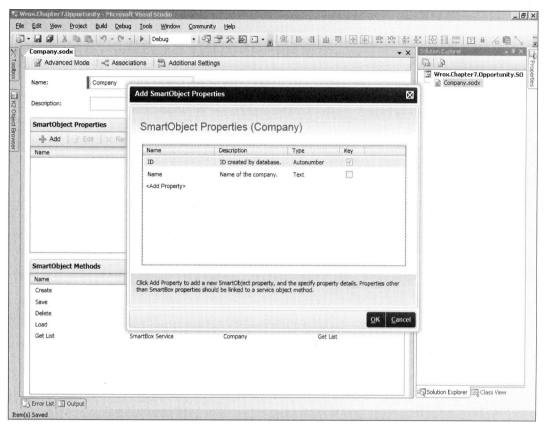

Figure 7-6

There are many data types that can be selected. The supported data types for a SmartObjects are as follows:

| Data Types | SmartBox Data Type (SQL Server 2005) |
| --- | --- |
| Autonumber | bigint (with Identity Increment) |
| AutoGUID | uniqueidentifier |
| DateTime | datetime |
| Decimal | decimal(18, 2) |
| File | nvarchar(MAX) |
| GUID | uniqueidentifier |
| Hyperlink | nvarchar(400) |

(continued)

(*continued*)

| Data Types | SmartBox Data Type (SQL Server 2005) |
|---|---|
| Image | nvarchar(MAX) |
| Memo | nvarchar(MAX) |
| Multivalue | nvarchar(MAX) |
| Number | bigint |
| Text | nvarchar(100) |
| Yes/No | bit |

To create an Opportunity SmartObject, right-click the project, select Add New Item, select SmartObject type, and give the SmartObject the name of **Opportunity.sodx**. Once the new SmartObject has been created, add the following properties to the Opportunity SmartObject:

❑ ID (Autonumber)

❑ CompanyID (Number)

❑ Name (Text)

❑ Point of Contact (Text)

❑ Account Executive (Text)

❑ Business Development Director (Text)

❑ Program Director (Text)

❑ Project Manager (Text)

❑ Estimated Project Value (Decimal)

❑ Estimated Project Start Date (Date Time)

❑ Comments (Memo)

Figure 7-7 shows the completed Opportunity SmartObject. Take note of how quick it was to design both the Company and Opportunity SmartObjects. Code was not needed, and both are ready to be used anywhere once they have been deployed. Since these SmartObjects are using the SmartBox Service by default, when they are deployed, tables are generated in the SmartBox database, and data can be retrieved from and written to these tables.

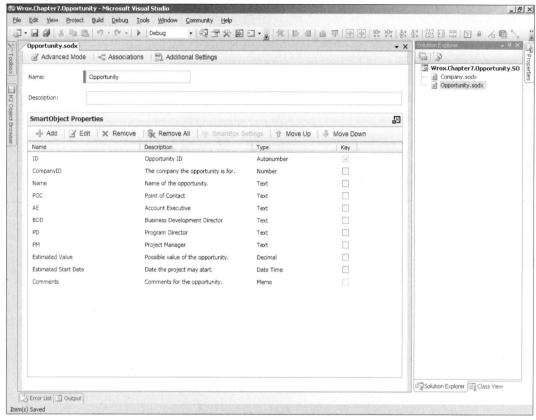

Figure 7-7

# Creating Associations

If you review the requirements for this opportunity process, you will see it was stated that there is a relationship between Company and Opportunity. An association can be created between both the Company and Opportunity SmartObjects. An association can be created immediately if both SmartObjects are in the same project. It is possible to create associations between SmartObjects in different projects; however, they both must be deployed first. When creating an association between Company and Opportunity, it does not matter which SmartObject is selected in the designer as both will have their definitions updated. If the SmartObjects were in a different project, understand that the definition of the second SmartObject will be updated on the server and that you will need to synchronize that SmartObject definition with the other project. To create an association, click the Associations button, and the Add SmartObject Associations window appears. Figure 7-8 shows the Add SmartObject Association window.

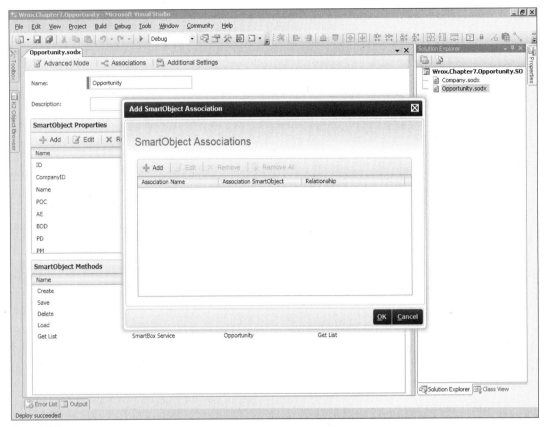

Figure 7-8

Click the Add button and the Association Wizard appears (see Figure 7-9). Click the Next button, and find the SmartObject to associate to by clicking on the ellipse. The Context Browser appears. This is where the designer can drill down and find the Company SmartObject. Initially, the Context Browser shows only SmartObjects that have been deployed to the server. A node called Local appears for SmartObjects that are in the project that have not yet been deployed.

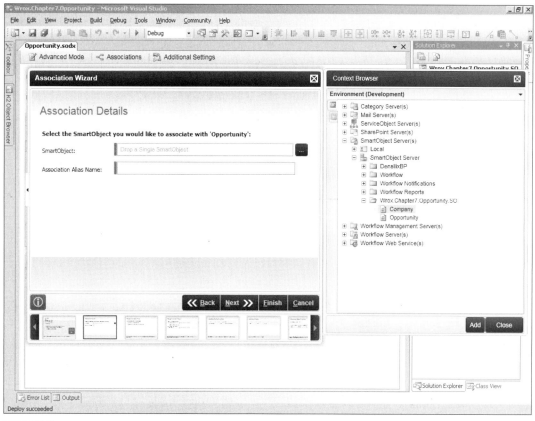

Figure 7-9

Once you select the Company SmartObject, the association cardinality between it and the Opportunity can be defined (see Figure 7-10). In this case, the "Each Opportunity has a single Company" and "Company can have many Opportunity SmartObjects" should be selected, in essence creating a one-to-many relationship between Company and Opportunity SmartObjects similarly to what would be done in a database constraint with a primary and foreign key.

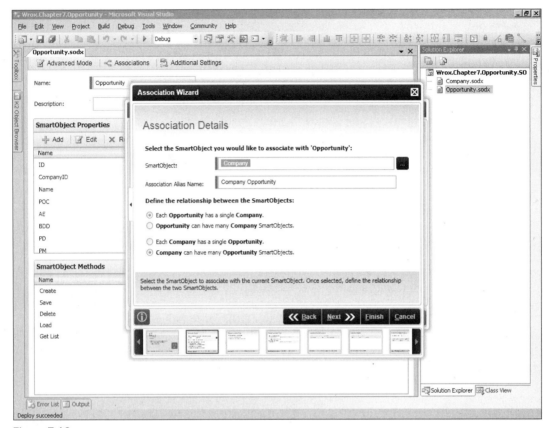

Figure 7-10

The next step in the wizard is where the Association Type between the Company and Opportunity can be selected. Figure 7-11 shows there are two options: Automatically associate SmartObjects or Manually associate SmartObjects on existing properties. If the first option is selected, the wizard creates new properties on the SmartObject to create a foreign-key relationship between the Company and Opportunity SmartObjects. However, automatic association is not needed because the CompanyID property has already been created on the Opportunity SmartObject. In this case, the manual option should be selected.

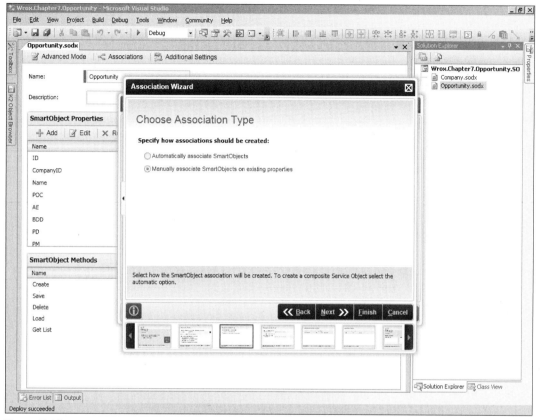

Figure 7-11

Figure 7-12 is the Association Mappings step of the wizard, where the CompanyID property of the Opportunity SmartObject needs to be mapped to the ID property of the Company SmartObject. Click the Assign button and a prompt appears with all of the properties from the Company SmartObject. Select the ID property. Through this action, an association between the Company and Opportunity SmartObjects is created.

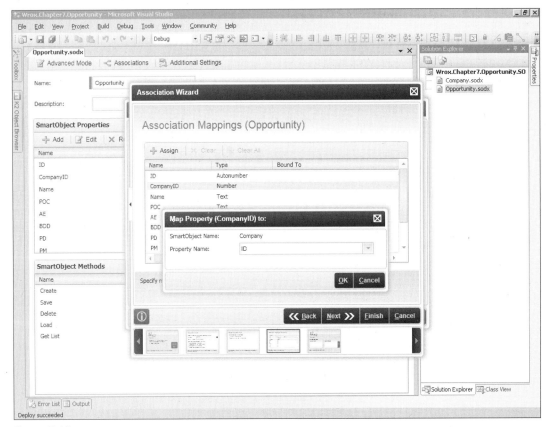

Figure 7-12

Now you have seen how simple it is to create an association between a `Company` and an `Opportunity` SmartObject. If you noticed, creating associations is similar to creating a foreign-key relationship between two tables in a database. Creating associations between SmartObjects is a good practice because these associations can later be leveraged in such things as the Report Designer in the K2 Workspace.

## Using SmartBox

By default, all SmartObjects are configured to use K2's SmartBox Service, which is based on SQL Server. The SmartBox database is a single database instance that is created when K2 blackpearl is first installed and configured. When SmartObjects are deployed, the SmartBox database has a table dynamically generated for each SmartObject. By default, SmartBox SmartObjects are configured to use five methods:

❏ **Create:** Runs a create SQL statement.

❏ **Save:** Runs a select SQL statement and returns a single column of data.

❏ **Delete:** Runs a delete SQL statement.

❏ **Load:** Returns a select SQL statement returning a single record.

❏ **Get List:** Returns a select SQL statement and returns many records.

Figure 7-13 shows all of the methods for a SmartObject that is initially using the SmartBox Service. Note the Service column states which SmartObject Service type it is using, and the methods are shown, too.

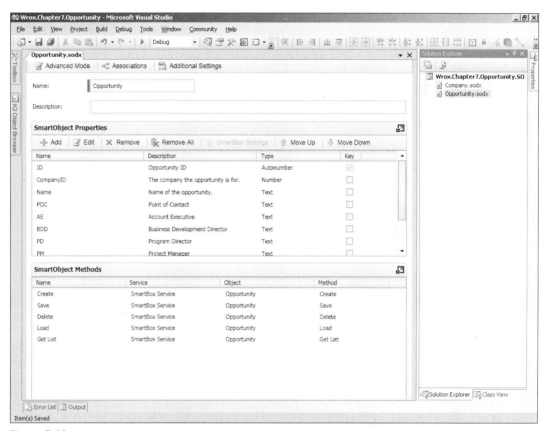

Figure 7-13

It is important to understand the inner workings of the SmartBox database with SmartObjects. The dynamically generated database table for the SmartObject is updated every time the SmartObject is redeployed. When new properties are added to the SmartObject, a new column is created on the existing table. If the data type or name of a SmartObject property were to change, this would result in a new column being created in the database. If a property is ever removed, the existing column in the database table is not deleted. This is to support version control of the SmartObject that uses the SmartBox. The SmartBox makes no assumptions on what processes or applications are using it, and it ensures that all callers of the SmartObject can continue to use it even though its data model may have changed.

## SmartBox Considerations

The SmartBox is a fantastic tool that allows you to create SmartObjects without having to consider how to build a database and a data persistence tier to store the data. Even if you are nontechnical, you are empowered with the ability to create data objects and start hooking them into your workflows.

SmartObjects that use the SmartBox are scalable from a performance perspective. Using SmartBox SmartObjects saves significant time in a project plan, literally taking the time down to minutes to create a SmartObject and having it use data from SQL Server. Also, SmartObjects using the SmartBox are backward compatible with all versions of callers that may use them.

However, there are some tradeoffs that must be considered when using the SmartBox versus a traditional database design approach.

❑   First, the table names and columns cannot be controlled and cannot be changed to adhere to naming conventions that may be instituted within an organization.

❑   Second, data tables cannot be organized logically based on their context. Usually, when you are building an application, a new database is created for the application. Typically, an accounting system only has accounting data in the database. When you are using the SmartBox, all data is stored in the same database, regardless of its business context.

❑   Third, database administrators may have specific security mandates they put on a database such as "all data must be accessed through a stored procedure and not from a table directly." This is not the case with the SmartBox.

❑   Fourth, custom databases cannot be used with the SmartBox, and only one instance of the SmartBox database can be created. There are plans to greatly improve this in future releases.

These tradeoffs are not limitations to the SmartObject framework, just to the SmartBox implementation itself. The primary goal of the SmartBox is to empower you to quickly hook into an external database and use it within your K2 processes. A secondary goal of the SmartBox is to support composite SmartObjects. For instance Active Directory (AD) may not contain all the data needed to make a business decision, and changing the schema of AD may not be possible. A similar example would be an application server that has a database, but the database schema is "owned" by the software vendor and cannot be changed (that is, they will not support the software if any changes are made to their database schema). The SmartBox is designed so that you can get around this issue by creating composite SmartObjects that use both AD and product data with SmartBox data.

There are several other SmartObject Services that are provided by K2 and the K2 community that provide the ability to work with enterprise data. For instance, a SharePoint SmartObject Service provides access to much of the data within SharePoint, and you can build SmartObjects for them in the same manner as building a SmartObject that is using the SmartBox Service. In the case of a SmartObject using the SharePoint SmartObject Service, a SmartObject treats a SharePoint list like a table of data. As mentioned before, SmartObject Services can be custom written to access products like SAP, Oracle, SQL Server, Business Objects, COGNOS, and so on. There are literally no limitations on where the data can originate from or go to because the SmartObject Service platform is built on a facade pattern.

> ### SmartObject Versioning
>
> SmartObjects that are deployed to the K2 blackpearl server are versioned. However, it is the responsibility of the SmartObject Service method that is being used by the SmartObject to support versioning. As previously discussed, the SmartBox Service supports versioning, but that does not mean that all custom SmartObject Services or ones used from the K2 Underground Community support versioning. Supporting versioning is more of a Service-Oriented Architecture (SOA) discussion, which is outside the scope of this book. Some ways that versioning can be accomplished are by requiring a version number to be a parameter in the SmartObject Service method or creating a new SmartObject Service method for modification.

## *Creating Active Directory SmartObjects*

For this example, to support the requirements for the Opportunity process, you need to create an OpportunityEmployee SmartObject. This SmartObject could use the SmartBox; however, much of the data needed, such as the e-mail address, Active Directory account, first name, and last name are already stored within an Active Directory. K2 provides an Active Directory SmartObject Service with methods that can be used to retrieve data from the Active Directory.

To create a new employee SmartObject that will use Active Directory, add a new SmartObject to the project and name it OpportunityEmployee. By default, all new SmartObjects use the SmartBox. Therefore, the first step is to configure the SmartObject so that it does not use the SmartBox. As shown in Figure 7-14, clicking on the Advanced Mode button in the SmartObject Designer allows you to reconfigure the SmartObject so that it does not refer to the SmartBox. After clicking the Advanced Mode button, two things change:

❑ First, a column is added to the SmartObject Properties called SmartBox. This provides the designer the ability to mark which properties of the SmartObject will use the SmartBox and which properties will not. It is possible that a SmartObject may have some data originate from the SmartBox, while other data originates from other locations.

❑ The second change is that a toolbar is added to the SmartObject Methods section that allows you to add other SmartObject Service methods. Notice that, by default, all of the methods for the SmartObject are configured to use the SmartBox.

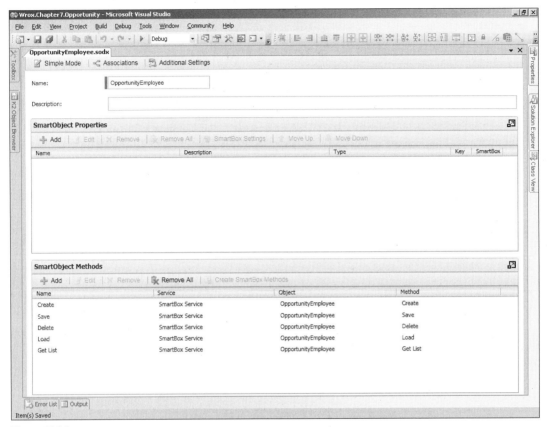

**Figure 7-14**

The first thing you need to do for the `OpportunityEmployee` SmartObject is to add properties. Add the properties shown in Figure 7-15 to the SmartObject, and make sure that the SmartBox checkbox is not checked. This ensures that the SmartBox is not used because these data fields should be mapped from Active Directory.

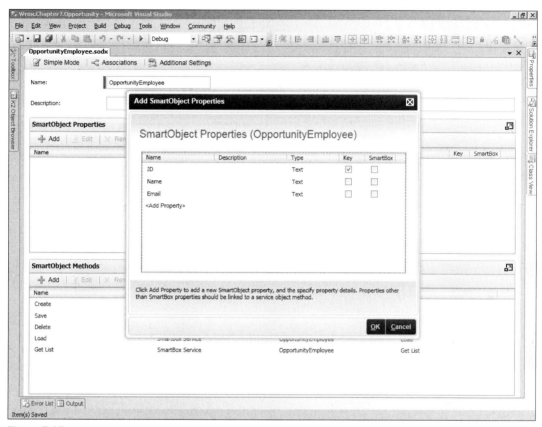

Figure 7-15

The OpportunityEmployee SmartObject needs three methods, one to get employee details, one to get an employee's manager, and another to get all users in an Active Directory Group. Since this SmartObject is not using the SmartBox, the default methods should be removed by clicking the Remove All button in the toolbar of the SmartObject Methods section.

### Creating the GetDetails Method

To populate the OpportunityEmployee SmartObject with data, you must configure it to work with the Active Directory SmartObject Service method. The first method loads all the data based on the primary key of the SmartObject. The primary key of the OpportunityEmployee SmartObject is a text field that will contain the Active Directory account name of the employee. The Active Directory SmartObject Service method uses the account name to retrieve detail information such as full name and e-mail address. A new method is added by clicking the Add button, which starts the SmartObject Method Wizard (see Figure 7-16). When the wizard begins, select the checkbox to run the wizard in Advanced Mode. This wizard then runs in Advanced Mode to show all configuration screens that are part of the wizard. When you are creating SmartObjects that require custom parameters or composite SmartObjects, you need to run the SmartObject Method Wizard in Advanced Mode.

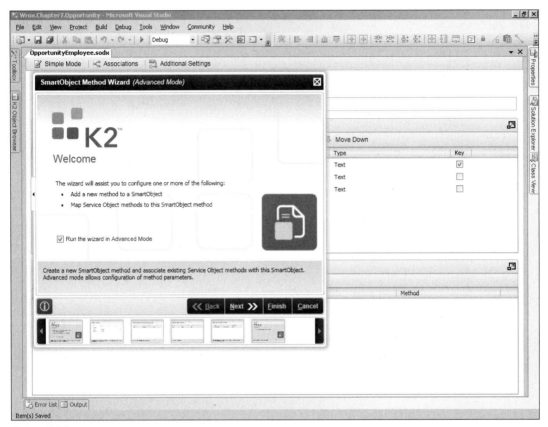

Figure 7-16

Figure 7-17 is the Methods Details step of the wizard. Here is where you set the Name of the method to **GetDetails** and the Type to Read. There are several other method types you can select, for example, Create, Update, List, Execute, and Delete. This type must correspond to the type of service method that is selected. It is not possible to select a Read type if the service method is an Update type. The default value for the Transaction field should be set to Continue, since this is a Read method. If an exception occurs during execution of the transaction, the Transaction field controls the behavior of the method. If this method is an Update or Delete method, where complex commits must succeed across multiple service methods, the Transaction type can be set to Rollback. However, the SmartObject Service must implement rollback procedures in order to support this.

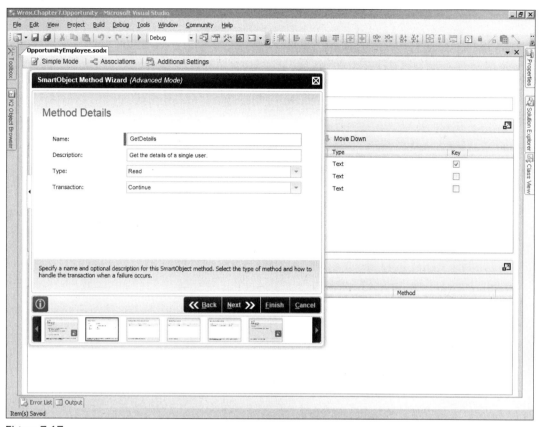

Figure 7-17

The Configure Method Parameters step of the wizard is used to add parameters, which are used to provide values from the SmartObject in a SmartObject Service method (see Figure 7-18). This step will be shown only if the wizard is running in Advanced Mode, and it is optional. You should use this step when you have a value that is not a property of the SmartObject and must be provided to a SmartObject Service method. In the case of the GetDetails method, the ID property of the OpportunityEmployee SmartObject will have the account name, so this step does not need to be used. Press the Next button to go to the next step in the wizard.

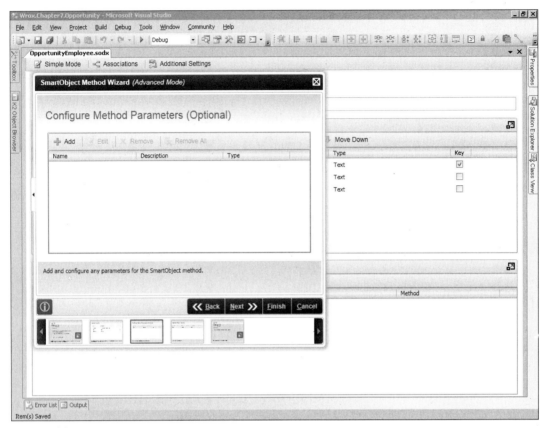

Figure 7-18

The Service Object Methods step of the wizard is where the configuration to the Active Directory Service occurs. Currently, there are no methods that have been assigned to the SmartObject. Figure 7-19 is the screen where methods can be added by clicking the Add button.

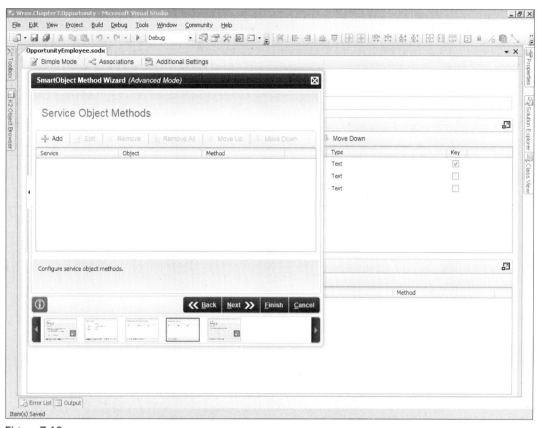

Figure 7-19

The Add Service Object Method window appears as shown in Figure 7-20, and this is where you can select a SmartObject Service method to be used by the SmartObject. Clicking the ellipse next to the Service Object Method field opens the Context Browser. In the Context Browser there is a node called the ServiceObject Server(s) that shows all of the SmartObject Service instances running on the server. Among others in Figure 7-20, there is an Active Directory Service, a SharePoint Service instance called Denallix Collaboration Portal, and a SmartBox Service Instance. Within each Service instance are Service Objects. In the case of the Active Directory Service instance there is the Active Directory Base, Group, and User Service Objects. Service Objects are no more than a logical grouping of Service Object methods. In the case of the Active Directory User Service Object, there are methods associated to getting user information from Active Directory. To get data about the user, in the Context Browser, open the ServiceObject Server(s) node, drill down to the Active Directory Service, open the Active Directory User node, and add the User Details method. This method then returns the core data associated with a user who is stored in Active Directory.

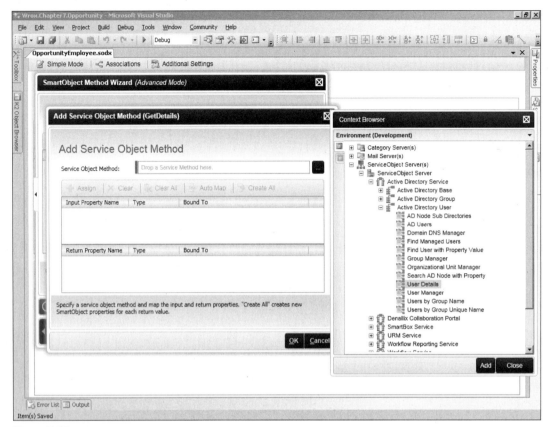

Figure 7-20

Clicking the Add button closes the Context Browser, and the Input and Output Properties of the method are filled in. Figure 7-21 shows all of the input and output parameters of the User Details Service Object method. The parameters of the Service Object method need to be mapped to the `OpportunityEmployee` SmartObject properties. The Auto button maps all of the method properties to SmartObject properties if they have the same name. In this case, clicking the Auto Map button maps only the e-mail property, and the other ones have to be manually mapped. The Account Name input property has a star next to the name to signify that it is required and must be mapped or populated with data.

There is also a Create All button. If this button were clicked, a property would be generated on the SmartObject for each and every Input and Return parameter of the Service Object method. This is useful if the properties of the SmartObject were not defined prior to adding the Service Object method or if there are lots of parameters that need to be read into the SmartObject. The one disadvantage of this is that the properties of the SmartObject will have the same name as those of the Service Object method parameters, which may not always be desirable.

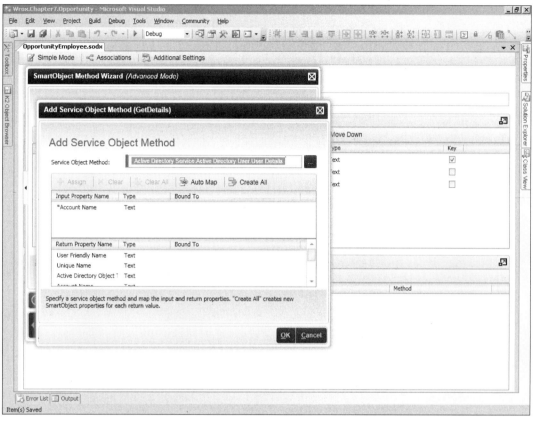

Figure 7-21

To map the ID and the display name, select the property and then click the Assign button in the toolbar, which opens the Map Service Property window (see Figure 7-22). The Map To field is used to map where the data will be pulled from. Data can come from a SmartObject method parameter, a SmartObject property, a system value, or a specific value that can be hardcoded. In this case, select SmartObject Property in the Map To field, and in the second drop-down, select the property on the SmartObject. The Account Name parameter needs to be mapped to the ID, while the User Friendly Name parameter must be mapped to the Name. Once this is done, the Add Service Object window should be closed. After these mappings have been completed, the wizard is finished, and the SmartObject can query and update data from Active Directory.

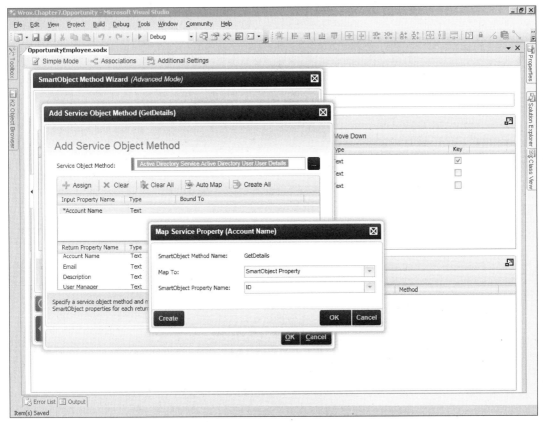

Figure 7-22

*At the K2 Underground Web site there is a tool called the Amazing K2 SmartObject. What this does is generate SmartObjects-based SmartObject Service method definitions. This can save you several manual steps if there are lots of fields that needed to be mapped to the SmartObject.*

## Creating the GetManagerDetails Method

The second method that you need to add is a method that gets a user's manager from Active Directory. This may not make sense for every organization because Active Directory may not be the place where this type of data is stored. Also, depending on the business process that will use the SmartObject, an employee may have different managers. To add this method, click Add Method on the SmartObjects Methods toolbar and name the method **GetManagerDetails.** Complete the same steps as laid out in the `GetDetails` method; however, when you are selecting the Service Object method, select the User Manager method from the Active Directory service (see Figure 7-23). Complete the same prior mapping and complete the wizard.

*It is important to point out that in the `GetDetails` method, the User Details service method does return a User Manager property. This cannot be used because it returns the display name of a manager from Active Directory, not the account name. The account name is needed to make that person a destination user in a process activity.*

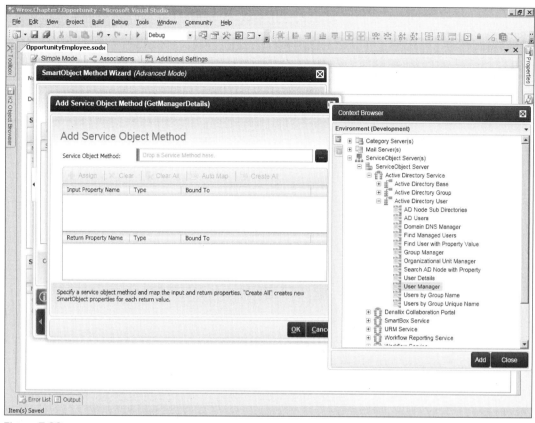

Figure 7-23

## Creating the GetUserInGroup Method

The third method you are going to create retrieves all users in an Active Directory group. This method is very similar to the GetDetails method. Again, click the Add button to start the SmartObject Method Wizard and run the wizard in Advanced Mode. Name this method **GetUserInGroup** and in the Type drop-down, select List. List must be chosen because this method is going to return more than one record. In contrast to the earlier methods, this time the Configure Method Parameters step of the wizard must be used. In this case (see Figure 7-24), you need to add a parameter for the name of the Active Directory group. The name of the Active Directory group is not a property of the OpportunityEmployee SmartObject, and because of this fact, the parameter must be added. As shown in Figure 7-24, a parameter named GroupName is created.

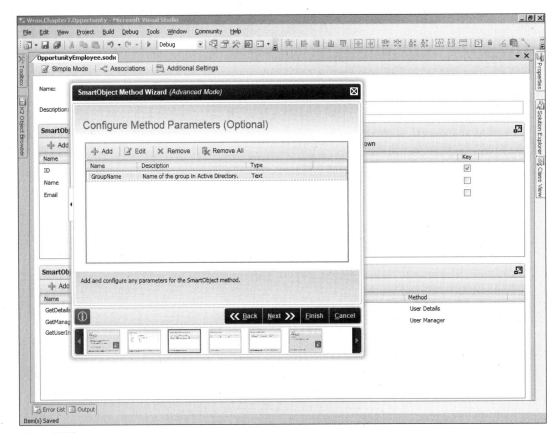

Figure 7-24

When you are configuring the Service Object method, this time select Get Users by Group Name service method and map all of the properties in the same fashion as the prior two methods. The one exception is that the Group Name input parameter needs to be mapped to the SmartObject method parameter called GroupName that was created in the previous step. Figure 7-25 shows the parameter window that is used to set the group name into the SmartObject Service method.

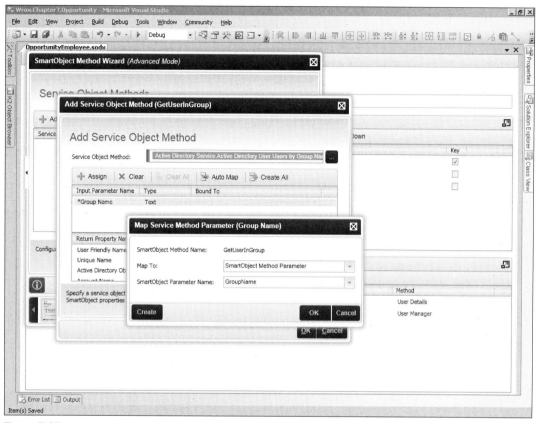

**Figure 7-25**

Once you have completed all of the steps, the SmartObject should be similar to the following Figure 7-26. In the SmartObject Methods section, only the three methods that were created are configured. From here, you can see the name of the OpportunityEmployee method and what SmartObject Service method it is mapped to.

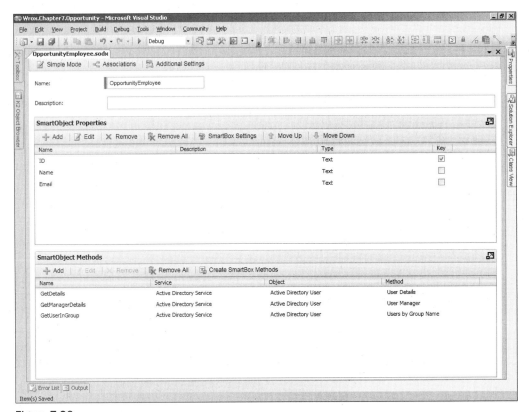

Figure 7-26

The purpose of this section was not to just show you how to connect a SmartObject to an Active Directory SmartObject Service; it was to show you various ways in which a SmartObject can call a SmartObject Service method. This section covered only SmartObject Services that were performing Read transactions; however, all other method types would be done in the same manner. What this SmartObject Wizard method facilitates is the configuration of how values are moved back and forth between a SmartObject and a SmartObject Service data provider.

## Composite SmartObjects and Associations

One of the value-adds of using SmartObjects is that creating SmartObjects that connect to multiple data sources is a trivial task. SmartObjects are completely decoupled from the implementation, and K2 blackpearl provides an extremely flexible design environment that allows you to easily model business entities. You are required to use the SmartObject service facade to retrieve data.

Historically, developers had to create solution-based data access tiers, and they would rarely be consistent in their implementation. In these solutions, developers would commonly create complex mapping tools that would map properties of an object to columns in a database table. One common way of doing this is using an XML file and using reflection to get all of the data out of the objects so that they could be committed to a database. Even worse, most of the time, there would be no mapping code, and the logic to write to one table or another would need to be hardcoded. These are typically called Object Relational

Mapping (ORM) tools. Sometimes a third-party tool would be purchased, open-source frameworks like Hibernate would be used, and now Microsoft provides LINQ and Entity as part of .NET 3.5.

The SmartObject framework is inherently not an ORM; it is a framework to build data service facades that provision data. The SmartBox Service implementation does provide a lot of the features present in ORM. The value proposition of SmartObjects is their ability to integrate with K2 processes in the visual designer. There is no reason why a SmartObject Service cannot be written using LINQ or some other third-party ORM. It does introduce a new layer into the architecture; however, not all data sources will be accessible by LINQ. Using SmartObjects creates a consistent interface for retrieving data and using that data in K2 processes. Notice that while these SmartObjects were being created, there was no mention of the K2 process, the user interface, or any other tier of the architecture. This demonstrates that this is truly interface-driven development.

A mentioned earlier, a very common example for creating a composite SmartObject is when an OpportunityEmployee SmartObject may need to retrieve data from both Active Directory and a Human Resources database. Figure 7-27 shows a SmartObject that has a method called GetDetails that is reading from two different SmartObject Service methods. To create composite SmartObjects, you simply select the GetDetails method of the OpportunityEmployee SmartObject in the designer, and in the wizard add another service method that connects to the Human Resources database. When GetDetails is called, both the Active Directory and the HR database are used to fill the SmartObject, effectively creating a view from disparate locations. The only thing that is required is a common field across both the Active Directory and the Human Resources database. There is nothing done specifically to make the SmartObject a composite one; it is just termed composite because it has a method that uses multiple service methods.

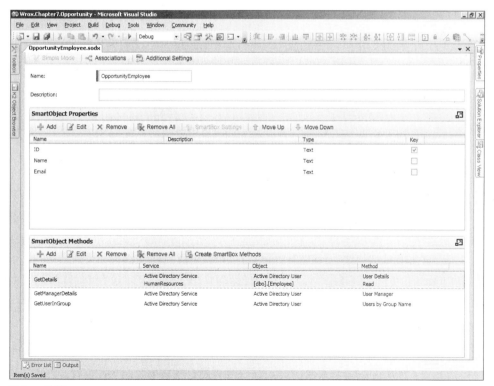

Figure 7-27

By contrast, associations, which were introduced earlier in the chapter, are not the same as creating a composite SmartObject. Associations are simply a reference created between two SmartObjects, similar to a foreign-key relationship between two database tables. With SmartObjects associations, you can build relationships between SmartObjects; however, they are not enforced at the database layer because the SmartObject may not be using a database to load data. The SmartObject's associations are enforced by the SmartObject server. The nice thing about this is that SmartObject associations can be created across data sources that may reside on different platforms.

Performance must be taken into consideration when modeling both composite SmartObjects and associations. If you understand that the SmartObject data access layer is executing the filtering and joining of data, it may not be wise to retrieve hundreds of thousands of records from various data sources and join them together in SmartObjects. SmartObjects should not be positioned as a way to get around making an investment in a data warehouse. Keep in mind that the purpose of SmartObjects is to provision data and provide developers a quick way to access data and perform operations on that data.

## Taking Advantage of SmartObject Agility

Another powerful attribute of SmartObjects is their ability to support a dynamic and agile environment. Because SmartObjects provide a plug-and-play environment, if the data source of the SmartObjects needs to change, applications using the SmartObject will not be affected. For instance, if it is decided that both the Company and Opportunity SmartObjects should be connected to a Customer Relationship Management (CRM) database, the SmartObjects can simply be modified to use a SmartObject service that accesses the CRM database.

## Modifying and Deleting SmartObjects

After a SmartObject has been deployed, you can download the SmartObject's definition directly from the SmartObject server, modify it, and then upload it back to the server. This can be accomplished by going to the SmartObject in the K2 Object Browser, right-clicking the SmartObject, and clicking the Save as Local menu item. The .sodx file that was deployed to the server can then be saved locally and modified. It is important to still be using a source code control application to manage the .sodx files.

SmartObjects can be deleted from the server using the K2 Object Browser. Again, right-click on the SmartObject, select delete, and it is removed. It is again important to plan on how the delete of the SmartObject may affect applications that are referencing it.

# Using a SmartObject in a Process

SmartObjects can be used anywhere inside of a K2 process when data is needed. They can be called upon to accomplish a ton of activities; from calling the methods to performing a standard operation like saving data or making a Line Rule decision. This section covers a few common ways in which SmartObjects can be used within a K2 process.

Figure 7-28 shows a simple K2 process that needs to be wired up to use SmartObjects. There are some very simple business rules that need to be implemented.

❑ First, an Opportunity record needs to be created in a database using a SmartObject.

❑ Second, if the expected amount of the Opportunity will be greater than $500,000, the manager of the account executive needs to be notified and make a decision whether to approve or deny the Opportunity. To implement this:

    ❑ A SmartObject Event will be used to create a record in the database.

    ❑ The Line Rule from the Create Record activity to the Review Opportunity activity will be modified to retrieve the Opportunity dollar amount and check to see if it is greater than $500,000.

    ❑ The Send Email Event in the Review Opportunity activity will be used to retrieve the e-mail address of the Account Executive's Manager.

    ❑ Finally, the Destination Rule for the Review Opportunity activity will be updated to retrieve the Account Executive's Manager in order to assign the Approve Opportunity worklist item to that user.

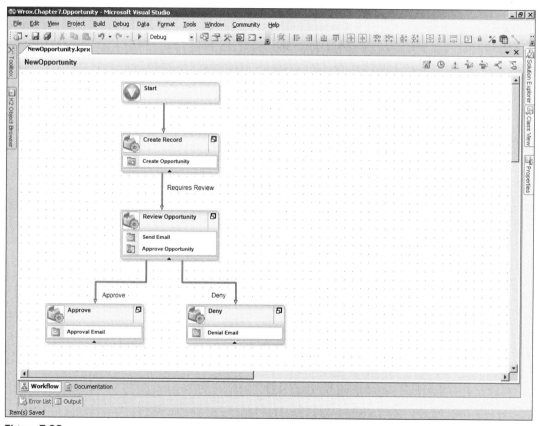

Figure 7-28

## Using a SmartObject Event

To use a SmartObject Event in a K2 process, drag-and-drop a SmartObject Event onto the design canvas from the toolbox, as shown in Figure 7-29. This starts a SmartObject Event Wizard, as you can see in the figure. A SmartObject Event allows the designer to run any method of a SmartObject. A SmartObject Event can be used to get data, create a new record in a database, and update or delete data. Remember, though, SmartObject methods are not scoped to doing just database operations. SmartObject methods can be a proxy to other enterprise services. The SmartObject Event supports the execution of any SmartObject method.

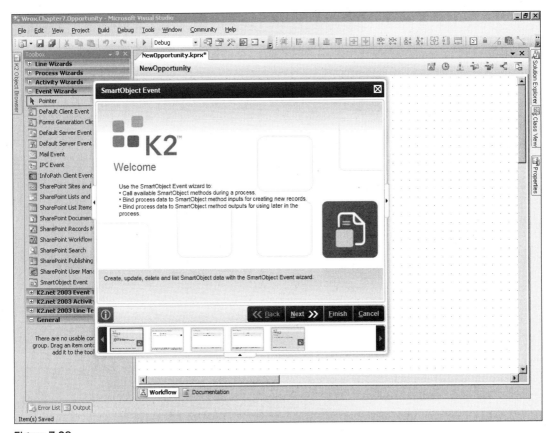

Figure 7-29

To start, change the name of the event to **Create Opportunity** and then click on the ellipse next to the SmartObject method, which opens the Context Browser. This is where the designer searches for the SmartObject method. In the Context Browser, open the SmartObject server(s) node and drill down to the `Opportunity` SmartObject, select the Create method, and press the Add button. Figure 7-30 shows that the `Opportunity.Create` method has been selected.

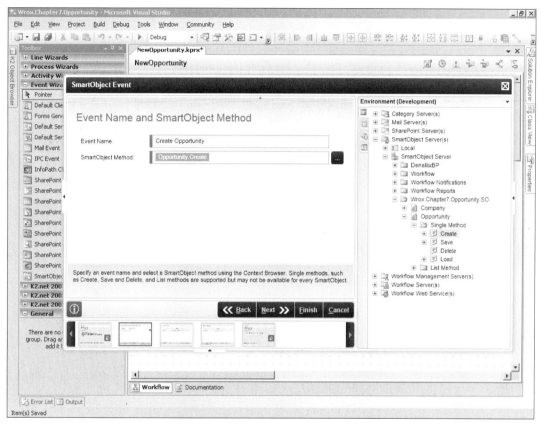

Figure 7-30

When you move to the next step in the wizard, all of the parameters of the SmartObject method will be visible, and this is where you can set values. You can select a parameter of the SmartObject method and then press the Assign button. Figure 7-31 shows the Assign Mapping window where a value can be set. You can then click the ellipse to open the Context Browser and select any data field that is available in the K2 process. For example, XML from an InfoPath form, Process or Activity fields, another SmartObject, or a static value can be set.

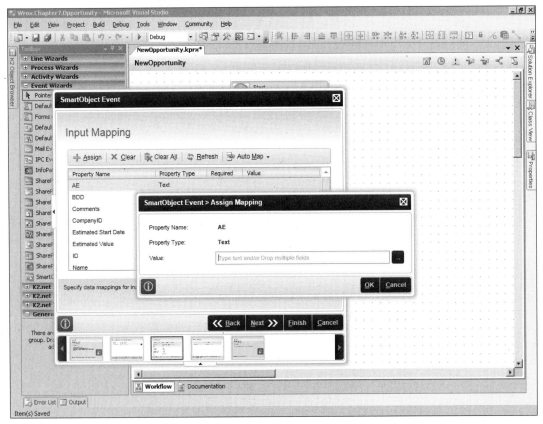

Figure 7-31

Once all of the input parameters have been set, the next step in the SmartObject Event configuration is the Return Mapping screen. This allows you to take any values returned and store them locally in the process. Since this event is using the Opportunity Create method, the auto-generated ID of the new SmartObject is returned. This value should be stored in the K2 process so that it can be used later for update or read operations. In this case, assigning the Opportunity ID to a process field can allow for this SmartObject to be loaded later using that ID. Figure 7-32 shows that the OpportunityID field of the process has been mapped to the ID return value.

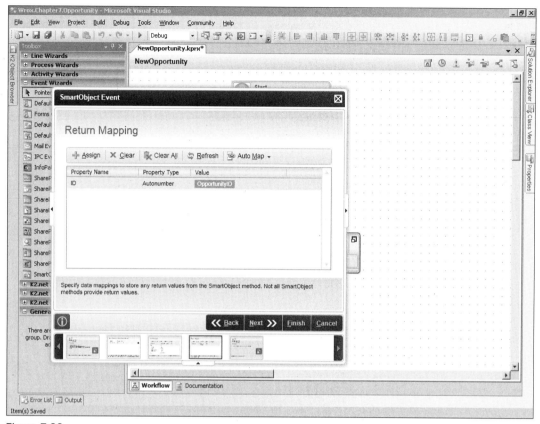

Figure 7-32

## Implementing a SmartObject Line Rule

In the example you are using, if the amount of the Opportunity is greater than $500,000, the Review Opportunity activity must be executed. To do this, the Line Rule is modified to get the Opportunity SmartObject, using the ID that was earlier stored in the K2 process field. To implement this, right-click on a line, select Properties, go to the Line Rule tab, and click the Add button to open the Add/Edit Rule window. Figure 7-33 shows the Line Rule window that has no rules specified yet.

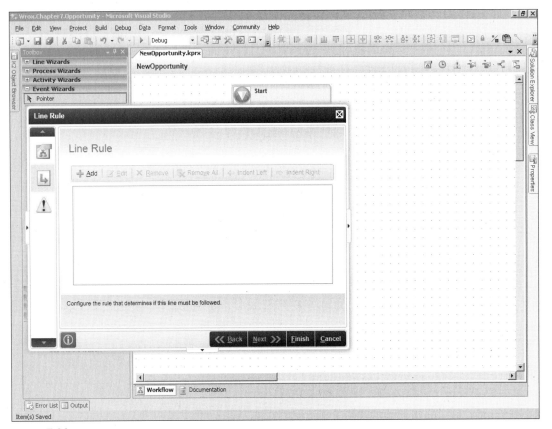

Figure 7-33

Figure 7-34 shows the Add/Edit Rule window where designers and design conditional logic statements are visually displayed. In this case, the Opportunity SmartObject amount needs to be retrieved and then checked to see if it is over $500,000. To do this, click the ellipse next to the First Variable to open the Context Browser. Use the Context Browser to locate the Opportunity SmartObject, select the Estimated Value property underneath the Load method, and click the Add button.

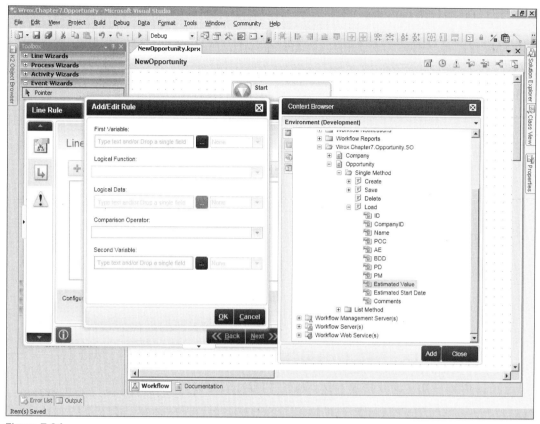

Figure 7-34

This opens the Smart Properties window, allowing you to set the Key identifier fields of the SmartObject shown in Figure 7-35. In this case, you need to set the ID of the Opportunity. In the Inputs section of the window, press the ellipse next to the ID to open the Context Browser. Instead of finding a SmartObject, select the Process/Activity Data tab and get the ID of the `Opportunity` SmartObject that was saved earlier. Click the Add button and then click the OK button on the Smart Properties window. Now the Opportunity ID that was saved earlier is being used to look up the Estimated Project Value.

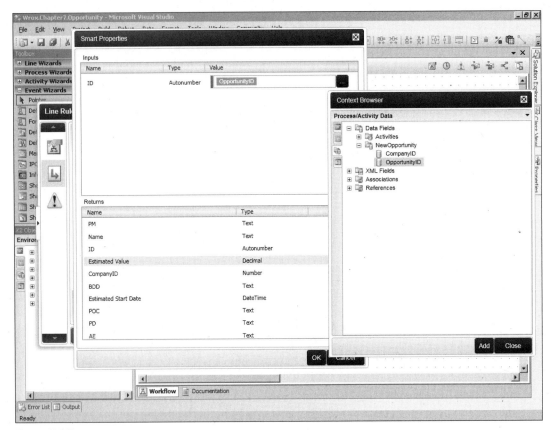

Figure 7-35

To complete the rule in the Add/Edit Rule window, simply finish the form to check if the value of the Opportunity is greater than $500,000 (see Figure 7-36). If you wanted to make sure that the $500,000 value was not hardcoded, you could load that value from another SmartObject or from an Environment field.

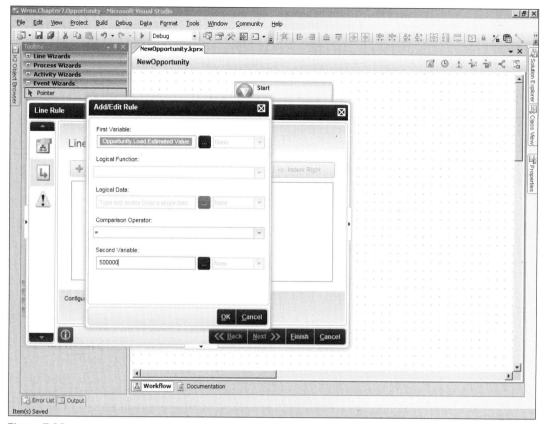

Figure 7-36

*It is a best practice to avoid hard-coding values wherever possible in a business because the business process can always change. If a change was to occur and a value like this was hardcoded, the entire business process would have to change, and then be redeployed. And that still does not account for running process instances that may have to be restarted so that they will adhere to the new rule. However, if the value were dynamic, all that would need to be changed is the amount.*

Once this form is complete, click the OK button and the Line Rule has now been configured to retrieve data using a SmartObject.

Figure 7-37 shows a completed Line Rule that has been configured to use a SmartObject method. Notice that the `Opportunity.Load.EstimatedValue` is displayed. This communicates which field of the SmartObject method is used to compare to the dollar amount of $500,000.

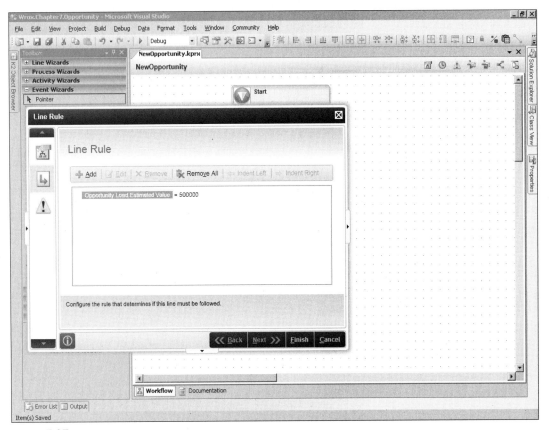

Figure 7-37

## Configuring E-Mail and Destination Rule

This section shows how you can use a SmartObject to have an e-mail sent to the Account Executive's Manager who is responsible for the Opportunity. Figure 7-38 shows the E-mail Settings window of a Mail Event. Click the ellipse next to the To field to open the Context Browser, and drill down to the OpportunityEmployee SmartObject. Click the GetDetails method, select the Email property, and then click the Add button. This will retrieve the e-mail address for a user; however, this is not complete.

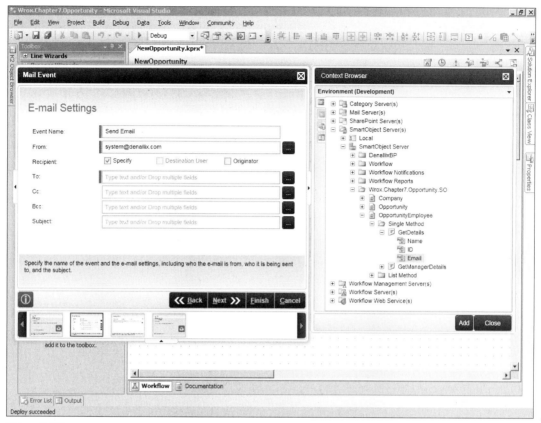

Figure 7-38

After you select the e-mail address property, the Smart Properties window opens (see Figure 7-39). This is where you must set the Account Executive Manager's ID. To get that value, you must find the Account Executive for the Opportunity. Click the ellipse next to the ID field in the Inputs section to open the Context Browser. This time, go to the OpportunityEmployee SmartObject again and select the ID field for the GetManagerDetails method.

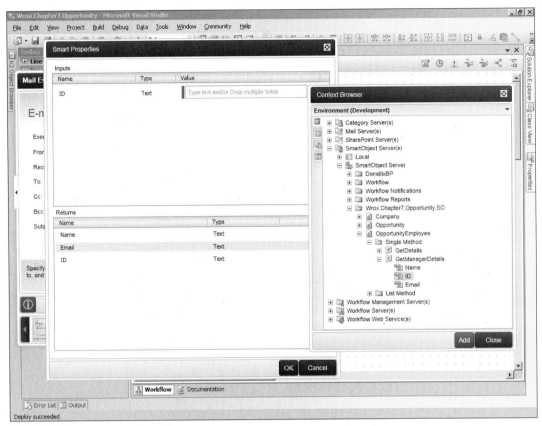

**Figure 7-39**

When you select the ID of the Manager, another Smart Properties window opens (see Figure 7-40). In this window, again go to the ID field and click the ellipse, but this time, go to the `Opportunity` SmartObject to find the Account Executive for the Opportunity. Locate the `Load` method, click the AE field, and then click the Add button. At this point you have the e-mail address for the Account Executive's Manager, but you have not set the Opportunity.

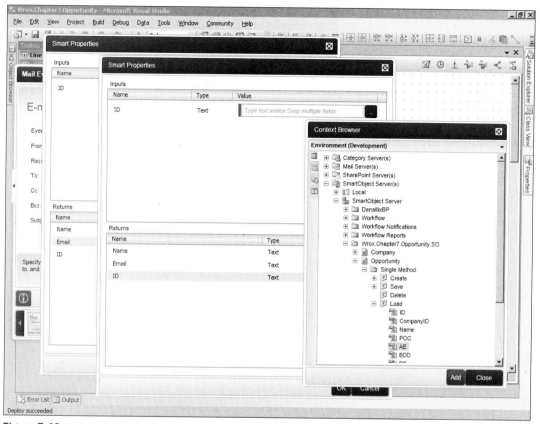

Figure 7-40

A third Smart Properties window appears (see Figure 7-41), and in this window, you need to set the Opportunity ID from the K2 process. This time for the ID field, click the ellipse to open the Context Browser and find the OpportunityID in the Process/Activity Data tab. Click the Add button.

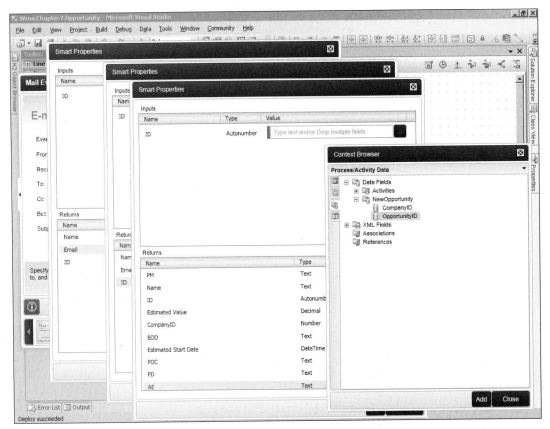

Figure 7-41

Click the OK button on all the Smart Properties windows to complete the lookup of the Account Executive's Manager based on the OpportunityID of the process. Assigning the destination user for the Review Opportunity activity requires the same steps to get the Account Executive's Manager e-mail address; however, instead of selecting the e-mail address, the ID should be selected.

These configuration steps are similar to writing a SQL join clause where the `OpportunityEmployee` and `Opportunity` SmartObjects are joined together to find a specific value. This demonstrates the real power of using SmartObjects inside of a K2 process. You have a visual experience where you can configure the K2 process to obtain data to make business decisions. In the E-Mail Event configuration example, you can use SmartObjects to obtain data across multiple data sources and have the data access layer completely hidden from you. In this example, Active Directory and SQL Server databases were used together to retrieve an e-mail address.

# Process-Generated SmartObjects

SmartObjects are not just used by the designers as a way to access data in a K2 process; SmartObjects are used throughout the K2 platform. For instance all of the reports in the K2 blackpearl Workspace use SmartObjects. Also, when a K2 process is deployed, SmartObjects are dynamically generated using the process definition. These SmartObjects are able to perform operations on the process like starting a new process instance. There will be other SmartObjects that are created geared specifically towards supporting reporting on the K2 process. This section discusses SmartObjects as they relate to the process.

When a process is deployed to the K2 server, K2 provides an option to dynamically generate SmartObjects based on the definition of the process. To control whether these SmartObjects are created, click on the SmartObject Association icon above the process canvas and the SmartObject Association window appears, as shown in Figure 7-42. There are two checkboxes, the first is Create Workflow SmartObjects and the second is Create Workflow Reporting SmartObjects, which is checked by default. The Reporting SmartObjects option is checked by default to support reporting in the K2 Workspace. If this is not checked, reports for the process are not supported. The Workflow SmartObjects checkbox is not checked because they are not required unless you have external applications that are going to be created to call the K2 process.

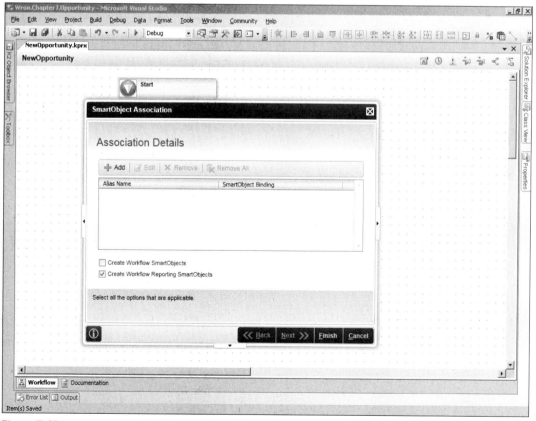

Figure 7-42

## Workflow SmartObjects

Checking the Create Workflow SmartObjects and then deploying the process results in SmartObjects being dynamically generated based on the process definition. Figure 7-43 shows the K2 Object Browser where SmartObjects can be found. The Workflow SmartObjects are located underneath the Workflow node in the SmartObjects Server(s) node of the K2 Object Browser. There are a few types of SmartObjects that are created. First, a Process Instance SmartObject is created, which has a Start Process method. All of the process data fields are exposed along with the Folio and the Process Instance ID.

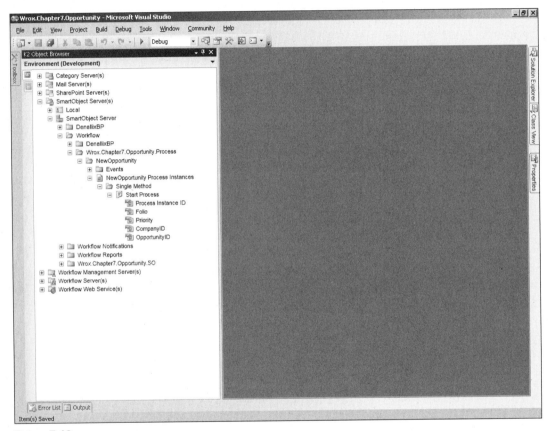

**Figure 7-43**

Figure 7-44 shows the Events folder, which is underneath the Process SmartObject folder. Only client-based events are created; none of the server-side events are exposed through a SmartObject. For every Event Instance SmartObject, there is a List Worklist Items method and a Load Worklist Item method as well as methods for each Action that is configured for the client event. In Figure 7-44 the Approve Opportunity Event Instances SmartObject has been created. There are the two Worklist methods and a method for each action that can be taken on the client event. The methods for the actions are dynamically generated each time the process is deployed.

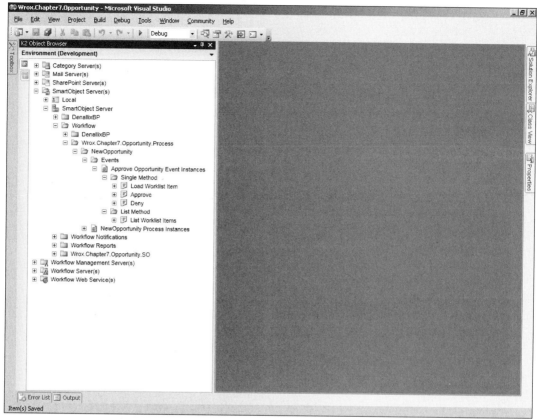

**Figure 7-44**

These Process and Event Instance SmartObjects provide the ability to perform standard operations that external applications may need to refer to. For instance, a custom ASP.NET dashboard page or a SharePoint Web part can start a K2 process and show all Worklist items based on these methods. In addition, these custom Web pages can use these SmartObject methods to allow users to complete actions. This can be done through the K2 API. However, an interesting point to highlight is that SmartObjects can be exposed as Windows Communication Foundation (WCF) endpoints, which are discoverable through Universal Description Discovery and Integration (UDDI). This would then allow these methods to be called from non-Microsoft platforms.

## Reporting SmartObjects

If the Create Workflow Reporting SmartObjects checkbox is checked, SmartObjects used for reporting are generated when the process is deployed. To view the Process Reporting SmartObjects, go to the K2 Object Browser and find the Workflow Reports folder underneath the SmartObject server(s) node, as shown in Figure 7-45. Within that folder, open the Workflow Solutions folder. Underneath that is a folder for each and every K2 solution deployed. Underneath the solution folder is a process folder that has activity and event folders that correspond to all the activities and events defined on the process (whether they are server-side or not).

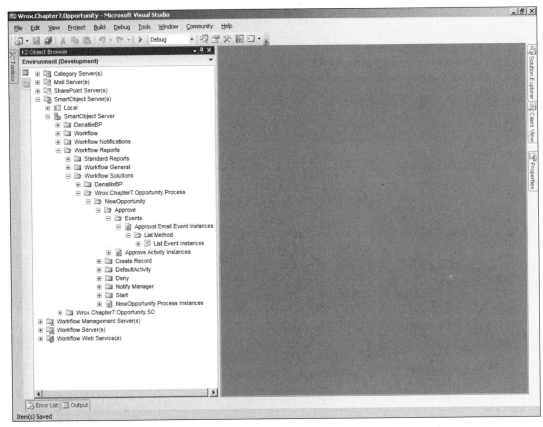

**Figure 7-45**

*Note that if the process has lots of activities and events and the reporting SmartObjects are being created, the deployment of the process will slow down. Removing the creation of these SmartObjects allows the deployment to go quicker, but reports will not work for the process if they are removed.*

Figure 7-46 shows the generic reporting SmartObjects in the K2 Object Browser. These SmartObjects expose all of the data from the K2 process database.

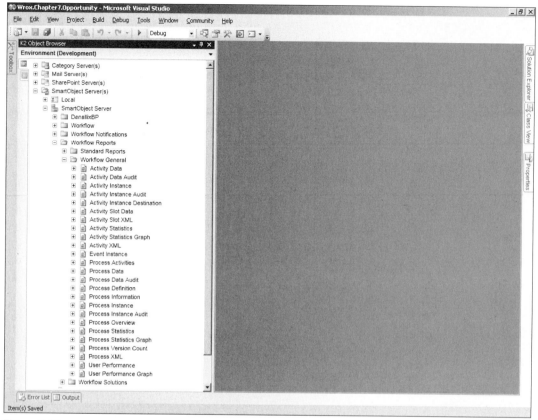

Figure 7-46

## Process SmartObject Associations

Process SmartObjects can be associated with other SmartObjects that have been deployed. For instance, the Opportunity Process SmartObject could have an association to the Opportunity SmartObject using the OpportunityID process field. To add an association to the Opportunity SmartObject, go to the SmartObject Association window by clicking on the SmartObject Association icon at the top of the process design canvas. Figure 7-47 shows the SmartObject Association window where new associations can be created to existing SmartObjects.

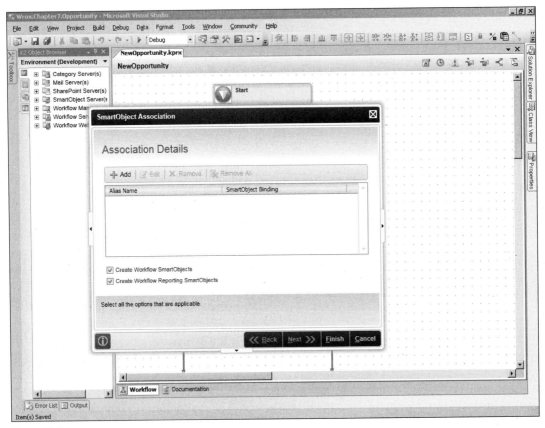

Figure 7-47

When the SmartObject Association window opens, click the Add button to find the Opportunity SmartObject using the SmartObject Association Wizard. On the Association Details step, click the ellipse next to the SmartObject field and use the Context Browser to find the Opportunity SmartObject (see Figure 7-48). Once the Opportunity SmartObject has been selected, a relationship is defined between the process and the Opportunity SmartObject. For this relationship, the process should be related to a single Opportunity SmartObject (that is, a one-to-one relationship).

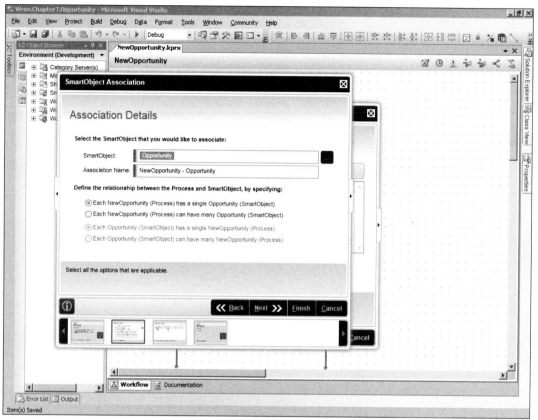

Figure 7-48

On the next Association Details step of the wizard, it lists all of the process fields that have been defined for the process. The OpportunityID field is used to bind the relationship to the OpportunityEmployee SmartObject. This effectively creates a join between the Opportunity and Process Opportunity SmartObjects. Figure 7-49 shows the OpportunityID being used to do a join to the Opportunity.ID.

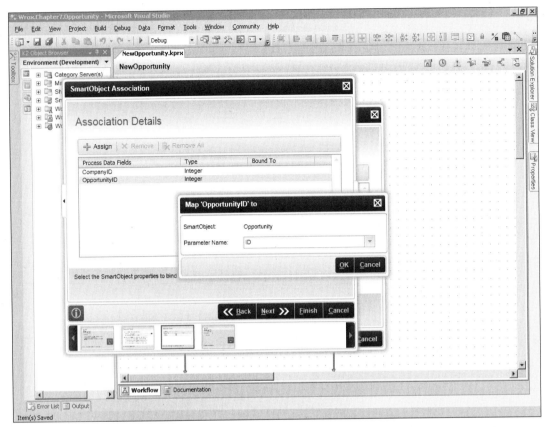

**Figure 7-49**

An association has now been created between the Opportunity Process and the Opportunity SmartObjects in the same way the Company SmartObject was associated to the Opportunity SmartObject. This is advantageous when executing reporting within the K2 Workspace. For instance in Figure 7-50, when you are selecting a Process Instance SmartObject in the report-building tool in the K2 Workspace, the Opportunity SmartObject is available, allowing for easy report building.

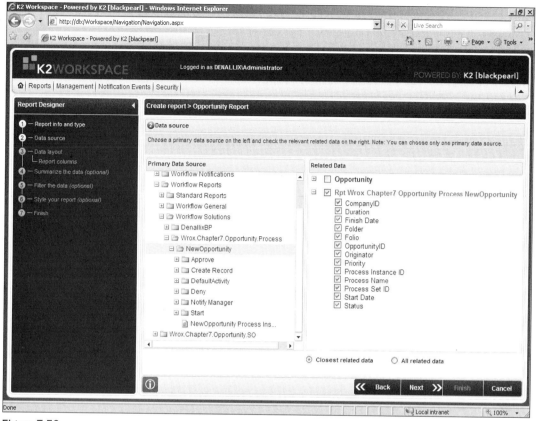

Figure 7-50

# SmartObject Process References

SmartObject process references can be added to a K2 process. This allows you to pick a SmartObject method that will be used many times throughout the process. There are several advantages for referencing SmartObject methods in this manner. One advantage is the SmartObject method can be quickly selected without having to use the Context Browser. Another advantage is that it creates performance efficiencies if the SmartObject method is used multiple times within a single event. If a SmartObject reference is not used, each time the SmartObject method is referenced in an event, a distinct call is made. This is important because if a SmartObject method is called in an event 20 times, there will be 20 concurrent calls made to the K2 server. That may not seem burdensome, but if there are many process instances running concurrently, and the SmartObject Service is using a data connection that cannot handle high volumes, the server can become flooded. This will not occur when a SmartObject reference is used because it will make a single call per event.

To make the reference to a SmartObject method, go the K2 Object Browser and select the Process/ Activity Data tab. Right-click the References node, click Add, and the SmartObject Method Reference Wizard opens, as in Figure 7-51. On the SmartObject Details tab, find the Opportunity SmartObject method and click the Load method.

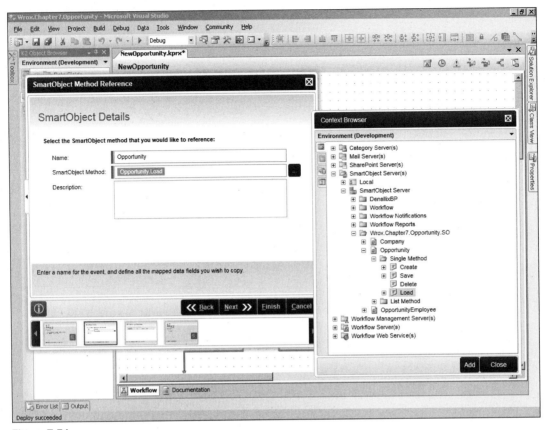

Figure 7-51

In the Bind Method Input Parameters step of the wizard (see Figure 7-52), find the ID parameter of the Opportunity SmartObject's Load method and bind it to the process's OpportunityID data field. The SmartObject Reference to the Opportunity Load method is completed, and it can be used throughout the K2 process.

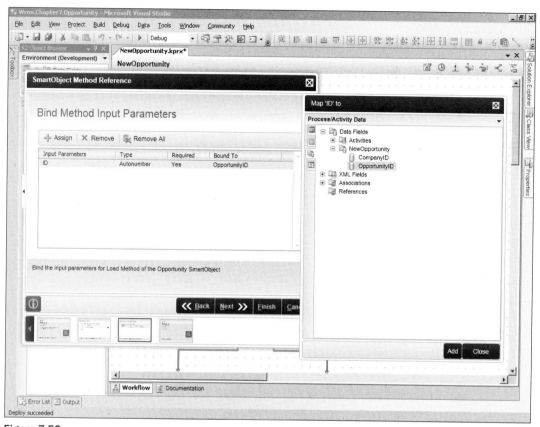

Figure 7-52

Using the SmartObject Reference to the Opportunity Load method is simple. For example in Figure 7-53, in an E-Mail Event body, open the Context Browser and go to the Process/Activity Data tab. Open the Reference node and drag-and-drop the return parameters from the Load method into the body of the e-mail. Before using the SmartObject Reference, make sure the OpportunityID has been populated. Otherwise, a run-time error will occur because the Opportunity SmartObject has not yet been created.

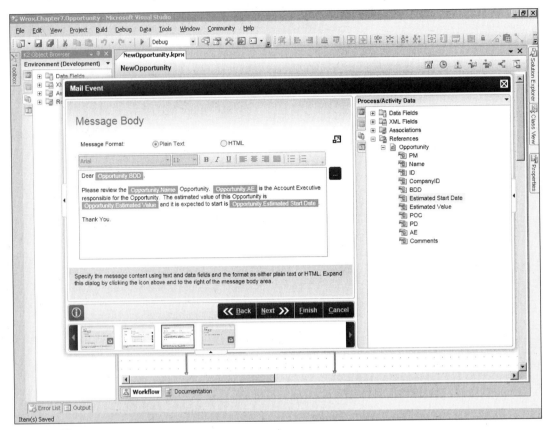

Figure 7-53

# Advanced SmartObjects

Up to this point, SmartObjects have been used to perform operations within a K2 process; however, SmartObjects can be easily referenced outside of K2. When you are automating a business process using K2, it is very common to have several external applications integrated with K2, such as a custom ASP .NET Web site, a Web service, or even a Windows application. Since K2 provides a data access layer that is used in the K2 process, there is no reason why it could not be reused within other applications. Using the same data services adds consistency and logic reuse throughout the entire solution. Using the SmartObject API is not difficult to learn for .NET developers because it uses many design patterns found in data access layers such as ADO.NET.

## *SmartObjects Are Not Cached*

Before discussing how SmartObjects are used in code, you need to know that they are not cached. The SmartObject framework loosely follows a Proxy pattern where SmartObject methods point to SmartObject Services. Most of the time the SmartObject Services are a simple pass-through to retrieve or commit data. SmartObjects provide the ability to define entities that use the SmartObject Services.

When loading a SmartObject, understand that the SmartObject is loaded when the method is executed. If data for SmartObjects needs to be cached, the SmartObject Service can be implemented to support a caching pattern or the data source itself can implement some form of caching.

However, it would be incorrect to compare SmartObjects to the Business Data Catalog (BDC), which is provided in the Microsoft Office SharePoint Server (MOSS). There are some limitations of the BDC, limitations that are not shared by SmartObjects. First, the BDC is a component of MOSS that can be used to consume read-only external data. When data exposed through the BDC is indexed by MOSS's Enterprise Search, a user performing a search will not retrieve real-time results. Users get only the data results from the last time the BDC content source was last indexed by the MOSS Search Server. Second the BDC cannot easily support insert, update, and delete operations, which is not the case for SmartObjects.

*SmartObjects can be indexed as part of the Enterprise Search of MOSS. Within the Central Administration of MOSS is a K2 tab where SmartObjects can be selected and an Application Definition File (ADF) is generated. This ADF file contains Entity definitions that are used by BDC.*

## Creating a SmartObject Instance

Creating a SmartObject instance is a relatively simple task that is started by adding references to both the `SourceCode.SmartObjects.Client` and `SourceCode.HostClientAPI` libraries found in the Global Assembly Cache. The following code creates an instance of a `Company` and `Opportunity` SmartObject. The logic flow is that a `Company` SmartObject is created first and then the auto-generated identifier is used from the `Company` in the `Opportunity` SmartObject.

```
SmartObjectClientServer server = new SmartObjectClientServer();

try
{
    //Make the server connection
    SCConnectionStringBuilder cb = new SCConnectionStringBuilder();
    cb.Host = "DLX";
    cb.Port = 5555;
    cb.Integrated = true;
    cb.IsPrimaryLogin = true;

    //Create the connection
    server.CreateConnection();
    server.Connection.Open(cb.ToString());

    //Get the Company SmartObject definition
    SmartObject company = server.GetSmartObject("Company");

    //Set properties
    company.Properties["Name"].Value = "Denallix";

    //Create the SmartObject
    company.MethodToExecute = "Create";
    server.ExecuteScalar(company);

    int companyID = Convert.ToInt32(company.Properties["ID"].Value);
```

```
    //Get the Opportunity SmartObject definition
    SmartObject opportunity = server.GetSmartObject("Opportunity");

    //Set properties
    opportunity.Properties["CompanyID"].Value = companyID.ToString();
    opportunity.Properties["POC"].Value = "Catherine";
    opportunity.Properties["Name"].Value = "K2 Opportunity";
    opportunity.Properties["AE"].Value = "Ethan";
    opportunity.Properties["BDD"].Value = "Caroline";
    opportunity.Properties["PD"].Value = "Winston";
    opportunity.Properties["PM"].Value = "Becky";
    opportunity.Properties["Estimated_Value"].Value = "500000";
    opportunity.Properties["Estimated_Start_Date"].Value =
            DateTime.Today.AddYears(1).ToString();
    opportunity.Properties["Comments"].Value =
            "This is a big opportunity with a new client.";

    //Create the SmartObject
    opportunity.MethodToExecute = "Create";
    server.ExecuteScalar(opportunity);
}
catch (Exception ex)
{
    throw new Exception(ex.Message);
}
finally
{
    server.Connection.Close();
}
```

In the code, a connection string to the SmartObject server must be created using the SCConnectionStringBuilder helper class. This class provides all the properties needed to build a connection string. Once the connection string has been created, a connection object is created using the CreateConnection() method of the SmartObjectClientServer object. The connection string from the SCConnectionStringBuilder object is passed into the Open() method.

Now that the connection has been made, the definition of the SmartObject needs to be loaded. This definition is retrieved from the SmartObject server. Once the definition has been retrieved, a method can be selected and executed. The SmartObject is then populated with instance data from the SmartObject server. There is a GetSmartObject() method on SmartObjectClientServer class that is used to retrieve the SmartObject definition. The GetSmartObject() method takes the name of the SmartObject. Once the SmartObject definition has been returned, properties can be set on the SmartObject. Properties are accessed through the Properties collection on the SmartObject.

*Take note that when you are using a SmartObject that is using the SmartBox Service, the properties that have spaces in their names are replaced with an underscore.*

Once all of the properties have been set, it is time to create data. The MethodToExecute property of the SmartObject is used to designate which method should be called. In this example, the Create method for both the Company and Opportunity is called. Finally, the method is executed by calling the ExecuteScalar method on the SmartObjectClientServer object. The SmartObject must be passed into `ExecuteScalar`, which sends the data and method to the SmartObject server to be executed. Once the method is complete, a new record should be created in the SmartBox database. In this code sample, notice that after the `ExecuteScalar` method is called for the Company SmartObject, the `ID` property is referenced. This is because the database has generated the ID, and it was returned from the `Create` method.

Other methods of the SmartObject can be executed in the same fashion. This would include operations such as update, delete, or read. As mentioned before, when you are performing these operations, you find no indication that the K2 SmartBox database is used. Regardless of whether SQL Server, Oracle, Active Directory, or some other data source is used, it is hidden by the SmartObject. You may also encounter instances during the lifecycle of the application that the data source may move. Such an occurrence will not affect the preceding code because the SmartObject method can simply be modified to use a different service. For instance data may originally be pulled from Active Directory but later a Human Resources database might be created to house all Active Directory data and more. To reference the Human Resources database the SmartObject method is modified to call the correct SmartObject Service, but this code here doesn't have to change.

## Inserting with the .NET Data Provider for K2 SmartObjects

In the previous section, you saw how data was created using the SmartObject API; however, the same operation can be done using the .NET Framework Data Providers for K2 SmartObjects. This is done by adding a reference to the `SourceCode.Data.SmartObjectsClient` library located in the Global Assembly Cache where K2 Studio tools have been installed. This is the same library that is used for reporting in the K2 Workspace. There are actually two ways the SmartObject can be created. One way is by executing a SQL statement; the second is by making a stored procedure call. Pay careful attention to the fact that this is not an actual SQL statement or a stored procedure. SmartObjects may or may not be using a relational database, for example, like Active Directory or a mainframe.

The two important classes used to perform these operations are `SOConnection` and `SOCommand`. The `SOConnection` is responsible for creating a connection to the SmartObject server, while the `SOCommand` is responsible for executing a command. The following code creates an Opportunity SmartObject instance, using the SQL statement approach.

```
SOConnection conn = null;
SOCommand cmd = null;

try
{
    //Make the server connection
    SOConnectionStringBuilder cb = new SOConnectionStringBuilder();
    cb.Server = "DLX";
    cb.Port = 5555;

    //Create connection and command
    conn = new SOConnection(cb.ToString());
    cmd = new SOCommand();
    cmd.Connection = conn;
```

```
//Insert Opportunity
cmd.CommandText = "INSERT INTO [Opportunity] (CompanyID, POC, AE, BDD, PD, PM, " +
    "Estimated_Value, Estimated_Start_Date, Comments)" +
    "VALUES (@CompanyID, @POC, @AE, @BDD, @PD, @PM, " +
    "@Estimated_Value, @Estimated_Start_Date, @Comments)";

//Set properties
cmd.Parameters.Add(new SOParameter("CompanyID", companyID));
cmd.Parameters.Add(new SOParameter("Name", "K2 Opportunity"));
cmd.Parameters.Add(new SOParameter("POC", "Steve"));
cmd.Parameters.Add(new SOParameter("AE", "Justin"));
cmd.Parameters.Add(new SOParameter("BDD", "Nick"));
cmd.Parameters.Add(new SOParameter("PD", "John"));
cmd.Parameters.Add(new SOParameter("PM", "Helen"));
cmd.Parameters.Add(new SOParameter("Estimated_Value", 500000));
cmd.Parameters.Add(new SOParameter("Estimated_Start_Date",
                    DateTime.Today.AddYears(1)));
cmd.Parameters.Add(new SOParameter("Comments",
                    "This is a big opportunity with a new client."));

//Create SmartObject
cmd.ExecuteNonQuery();
}
catch (Exception ex)
{
    throw new Exception(ex.Message);
}
finally
{
    conn.Close();
}
```

The SOConnection object is created using a connection string from the SOConnectionStringBuilder helper class, and then the SOCommand object is created using the SOConnection object. The Insert statement is very similar to SQL and is set into the CommandText property of the SOCommand object. Notice that in place of a table name is the name of the SmartObject, and instead of referring to column names, the properties of the SmartObject are used. Actual values are then set using the Parameters collection of the SOCommand object.

Finally, the ExecuteNonQuery method of SOCommand object is called, executing the insert statement. Update, delete, and select operations can all be executed in a similar fashion.

As previously indicated, the other technique of using the .NET Data Provider is to insert the Opportunity SmartObject using a stored procedure call. The following code gives an example of that technique.

```
SOConnection conn = null;
SOCommand cmd = null;

try
{
    //Make the server connection
    SOConnectionStringBuilder cb = new SOConnectionStringBuilder();
    cb.Server = "DLX";
    cb.Port = 5555;

    //Create connection and command
    conn = new SOConnection(cb.ToString());
    cmd = new SOCommand();
    cmd.Connection = conn;

    //Insert Opportunity Method
    cmd.CommandText = "Opportunity.Create";
    cmd.CommandType = System.Data.CommandType.StoredProcedure;

    //Set properties
    cmd.Parameters.Add(new SOParameter("CompanyID", companyID));
    cmd.Parameters.Add(new SOParameter("Name", "K2 Opportunity"));
    cmd.Parameters.Add(new SOParameter("POC", "Terri"));
    cmd.Parameters.Add(new SOParameter("AE", "Raymond"));
    cmd.Parameters.Add(new SOParameter("BDD", "Gene"));
    cmd.Parameters.Add(new SOParameter("PD", "Ethan"));
    cmd.Parameters.Add(new SOParameter("PM", "Caroline"));
    cmd.Parameters.Add(new SOParameter("Estimated_Value", 500000));
    cmd.Parameters.Add(new SOParameter("Estimated_Start_Date",
                    DateTime.Today.AddYears(1)));
    cmd.Parameters.Add(new SOParameter("Comments",
                    "This is a big opportunity with a new client."));

    //Create SmartObject
    cmd.ExecuteNonQuery();
}
catch (Exception ex)
{
    throw new Exception(ex.Message);
}
finally
{
    conn.Close();
}
```

In this code, the only differences are with the SOCommand object. The CommandText property is set to Opportunity.Create, which calls the Create method of the Opportunity SmartObject (format [SmartObject Name].[SmartObject Method]). Also, the CommandType property is set to CommandType.StoredProcedure. Again, any method (regardless of type) on a SmartObject can be executed in this fashion, regardless of whether the SmartObject is using a database or not.

# Getting a SmartObject Instance(s)

The code for reading a single Company SmartObject is similar to the code presented earlier to insert a Company SmartObject. The following code will get a single Company SmartObject and then retrieve all of the Opportunities for the Company.

```
SmartObjectClientServer server = new SmartObjectClientServer();

try
{
    //Make the server connection
    SCConnectionStringBuilder cb = new SCConnectionStringBuilder();
    cb.Host = "DLX";
    cb.Port = 5555;
    cb.Integrated = true;
    cb.IsPrimaryLogin = true;
    server.CreateConnection();
    server.Connection.Open(cb.ToString());

    //Get the Company SmartObject definition
    SmartObject company = server.GetSmartObject("Company");

    //Set properties
    company.Properties["ID"].Value = companyID.ToString();

    //Get the SmartObject
    company.MethodToExecute = "Load";
    server.ExecuteScalar(company);

    //Write out Company Values
    foreach (SmartProperty property in company.Properties)
    {
        System.Diagnostics.Debug.Write(property.Name + "=" + property.Value);
    }

    //Get a list of Opportunities for a company
    SmartObject opportunity = server.GetSmartObject("Opportunity");

    //Set properties
    opportunity.Properties["CompanyID"].Value = companyID.ToString();

    //Get the SmartObjects
    opportunity.MethodToExecute = "GetList";
    SmartObjectList opportunities = server.ExecuteList(opportunity);

    //Write out Opportunities for the Company
    foreach (SmartObject companyOpportunity in opportunities.SmartObjectsList)
    {
        foreach (SmartProperty property in companyOpportunity.Properties)
        {
            System.Diagnostics.Debug.Write(property.Name + "=" + property.Value);
        }
    }
}
```

```
    }
catch (Exception ex)
{
    throw new Exception(ex.Message);
}
finally
{
    server.Connection.Close();
}
```

Again, a `SmartObjectClientServer` object is created, the `Company` SmartObject definition is retrieved, and the `ID` property of the `Company` SmartObject is set. The `MethodToExecute` property is set to `Load`, and the `ExecuteScalar` method is called, populating the `Company` SmartObject with data. The `Company` SmartObject uses the SmartBox service to dynamically build a query using the fields that have been set prior to the call of `ExecuteScalar`. In this case, a query would be built using the ID and the value that was set. Retrieving a collection of `Opportunity` SmartObjects for a `Company` SmartObject is a similar approach; however, instead of calling the `ExecuteScalar` method, you call the `ExecuteList` method to return a collection called `SmartObjectList`.

## Getting a SmartObject Instance(s) with a Filter

In the previous example the SmartObject properties were used as a filter for the selection of SmartObjects. A more effective way of doing this is by using the `SourceCode.SmartObjects.Client.Filters` namespace. In the following code, a query has been set up to retrieve all `Opportunity` SmartObjects for a company greater than a specified amount.

```
SmartObjectClientServer server = new SmartObjectClientServer();

try
{
    //Make the server connection
    SCConnectionStringBuilder cb = new SCConnectionStringBuilder();
    cb.Host = "DLX";
    cb.Port = 5555;
    cb.Integrated = true;
    cb.IsPrimaryLogin = true;
    server.CreateConnection();
    server.Connection.Open(cb.ToString());

    //Get Opportunity Definition
    SmartObject opportunity = server.GetSmartObject("Opportunity");

    //Get the List Method
    SmartListMethod getList = opportunity.ListMethods["GetList"];
    opportunity.MethodToExecute = getList.Name;

    //Find all Opportunities for a specified company
    Equals companyEqual = new Equals();
    companyEqual.Left = new PropertyExpression("CompanyID", PropertyType.Number);
    companyEqual.Right = new ValueExpression(companyID, PropertyType.Number);
```

```
//Find all Opportunities greater than a specified amount
GreaterThan amountGreater = new GreaterThan();
amountGreater.Left = new PropertyExpression("Estimated_Value",
                                            PropertyType.Decimal);
amountGreater.Right = new ValueExpression(amount, PropertyType.Decimal);

//Get the Opportunities for a Company Greater than a specified amount
And and = new And();
and.Left = companyEqual;
and.Right = amountGreater;

//Apply the filter
getList.Filter = and;
```

```
//Get the data
SmartObjectList opportunities = server.ExecuteList(opportunity);

//Write out values
foreach (SmartObject companyOpportunity in opportunities.SmartObjectsList)
{
    foreach (SmartProperty property in companyOpportunity.Properties)
    {
        System.Diagnostics.Debug.Write(property.Name + "=" + property.Value);
    }
}
}
catch (Exception ex)
{
    throw new Exception(ex.Message);
}
finally
{
    server.Connection.Close();
}
```

First the `Opportunity` SmartObject definition is retrieved and then the `GetList` method of the SmartObject is referenced using a `SmartListMethod` object. Then an `Equals` filter object is created, which has both a `PropertyExpression` and `ValueExpression` objects set to it. The `PropertyExpression` object is used to reference the `ComapnyID` property of the `Opportunity` SmartObject, while the `ValueExpression` contains the value that will be searched on. The next filter used is a `GreaterThan` filter, which checks to see if the `Estimated_Value` is greater than a certain amount. Once both of the filters have been created, they are put together in an `And` filter, which is set into the `Filter` property of the `SmartListMethod` object. Then the SmartObjects can be retrieved just as before by calling the `ExecuteList` method.

There are several more types of logical filters that can be created. The available logical filters are `And`, `Contains`, `EndsWith`, `Equals`, `GreaterThan`, `IsNull`, `LessThan`, `Not`, `Or`, and `StartsWith`. One advantage of writing code in this manner is that the code is more intuitive than the code presented in the previous section. This type of filtering can be done only on list methods, so a `Load` type method does not supporting filtering.

In essence what the code example is doing is building up a traditional SQL statement similar to:

```
Select * From Opportunity Where CompanyID = X And Estimated_Value > Y
```

But this SQL statement is logical because this SQL statement will not actually get built and executed. However, both the SmartObject Services and the SmartObject server use the defined filter to whittle down the results returned. First, if the SmartObject Service implements filtering, this means that it applies the filter set to the SmartObject method as previously shown. For example, to apply the filter the SmartObject service would dynamically generate SQL based upon the filter provided. The SmartBox Service does this by adding the filter to the SQL statement before it calls the database. The second place where filtering is applied is on the SmartObject server when the data is returned from the SmartObject Service. SmartObject Services return data in the form of an ADO.NET `DataTable`, which the SmartObject server can apply the filter to.

*As alluded to earlier in this chapter, if there are significant amounts of records that could be returned, it would be better to do the filtering lower down the call stack directly on the database and not rely on the SmartObject server to do this filtering.*

## Getting SmartObjects with the .NET Data Provider

The following code again shows how to get the `Company` and `Opportunity` SmartObject, this time using the .NET Data Provider.

```
SOConnection conn = null;
SOCommand cmd = null;

try
{
    //Make the server connection
    SOConnectionStringBuilder cb = new SOConnectionStringBuilder();
    cb.Server = "DLX";
    cb.Port = 5555;

    //Create connection and command
    conn = new SOConnection(cb.ToString());
    cmd = new SOCommand();
    cmd.Connection = conn;

    //Opportunities for a Company
    cmd.CommandText = "SELECT [Company].Name AS CName, [Opportunity]
.Name AS OppName, " +
        "[Opportunity].Estimated_Value " +
        "FROM [Company], [Opportunity] " +
        "WHERE [Company].ID = [Opportunity].CompanyID " +
        "AND [Company].ID = @ID";
    cmd.Parameters.Add(new SOParameter("ID", companyID));

    //Get data
    SODataReader reader = cmd.ExecuteReader();
```

```
    while (reader.Read())
    {
        //Write out Opportunities for Company
        System.Diagnostics.Debug.Write(
            "Company Name=" + reader["CName"].ToString() + " " +
            "Opportunity Name=" + reader["OppName"].ToString() + " " +
            "Value=" + reader["Estimated_Value"].ToString());
    }
}
catch (Exception ex)
{
    throw new Exception(ex.Message);
}
finally
{
    conn.Close();
}
```

In the preceding code, the `CommandText` property is set with a `Select` statement where the SmartObjects and its properties are treated as database tables and columns. Notice in this example, a join between the two SmartObjects is made, and the column names use an alias. This time, the `ExecuteReader` method is used, returning a `SODataReader` that can be iterated over. To use the `Select` command, the SmartObject must have a method of `List` type because it is expected that a `Select` command will return a collection of data. However, there are limitations (see the note following this paragraph) surrounding the use of the .NET Data Provider as this is not a SQL-based language. If there is a complex query that needs to be written to retrieve data, it would be better to write a custom service that could execute those queries through a real stored procedure call.

> Notice in the SQL query for the SmartObjects the join is done in the where clause. Currently SQL syntax like Left Join is not supported. Also, these queries cannot be indexed either, so it is recommend that you use the SmartObject Service to run queries that may have a high performance cost.

## Using SmartObjects with Required Method Parameters

When working with SmartObject methods with custom parameters, you must do a few steps differently. Earlier in this chapter, a SmartObject called `EmployeeOpportunity` was created using the Active Directory SmartObject Service. There was a method called `GetUsersInGroup`, which has a parameter called `GroupName`. The following code calls that method:

```
SmartObjectClientServer server = new SmartObjectClientServer();

try
{
    //Make the server connection
    SCConnectionStringBuilder cb = new SCConnectionStringBuilder();
    cb.Host = "DLX";
    cb.Port = 5555;
    cb.Integrated = true;
    cb.IsPrimaryLogin = true;
    server.CreateConnection();
    server.Connection.Open(cb.ToString());
```

```
        //Get SmartObject Definition
        SmartObject opportunityEmployee = server.GetSmartObject("OpportunityEmployee");

        //Set properties
        opportunityEmployee.ListMethods["GetUserInGroup"].InputProperties["GroupName"]
.Value = groupName;

        //Get the SmartObjects
        opportunityEmployee.MethodToExecute = "GetUsersInGroup";

        //Write out users in the group
        SmartObjectList opportunityEmployees = server.ExecuteList(opportunityEmployee);
        foreach (SmartObject so in opportunityEmployees.SmartObjectsList)
        {
            foreach (SmartProperty property in so.Properties)
            {
                System.Diagnostics.Debug.Write(property.Name + "=" + property.Value);
            }
        }
    }
    catch (Exception ex)
    {
        throw new Exception(ex.Message);
    }
    finally
    {
        server.Connection.Close();
    }
```

This code is very similar to methods presented earlier except for the setting of the parameter value. In those examples the parameters were set directly onto the Properties of the SmartObject instance. In this case, the InputProperties property is used to set the GroupName parameter. The InputProperties property is accessed through the ListMethods property because the method returns a collection of SmartObjects. The ExecuteList method is called by using the SmartObject, but this method returns a SmartObjectList collection.

## Using SmartObject Required Method Parameters with .NET Data Provider

In the previous sections, you saw that both the SQL and stored procedures can be used to execute SmartObject methods; however, this is not the case with SmartObjects that have custom parameters. If there is a required parameter for a SmartObject method using SQL with the K2 .NET Data Provider, an exception is thrown. In the following code the GetUsersInGroup method of the OpportunityEmployee SmartObject throws an exception stating that the GroupName parameter has not been set.

```
SOConnection conn = null;
SOCommand cmd = null;

try
{
    //Make the server connection
    SOConnectionStringBuilder cb = new SOConnectionStringBuilder();
    cb.Server = "DLX";
    cb.Port = 5555;

    //Create connection and command
    conn = new SOConnection(cb.ToString());
    cmd = new SOCommand();
    cmd.Connection = conn;

    //Get Users in Group
    cmd.CommandText = "SELECT * FROM OpportunityEmployee " +
        "WHERE GroupName = @GroupName";
    cmd.Parameters.Add(new SOParameter("GroupName", groupName));

    SODataReader reader = cmd.ExecuteReader();

    //Write out values
    while (reader.Read())
    {
        System.Diagnostics.Debug.Write(
            "ID=" + reader["ID"].ToString() + " " +
            "Email=" + reader["Email"].ToString());
    }
}
catch (Exception ex)
{
    throw new Exception(ex.Message);
}
finally
{
    conn.Close();
}
```

Putting the GroupName parameter into the where clause will not work because the GroupName parameter is not a property of the OpportunityEmployee SmartObject. Only SmartObject properties can be used in SQL. However, the .NET Framework Data Provider for K2 SmartObjects can use a stored procedure to execute a SmartObject method with a custom parameter. The following code sets the groupName value into the Parameters collection of the SOCommand object. This then sets the group name into the SmartObject OpportunityEmployee.GetUserInGroup custom parameter correctly.

```
SOConnection conn = null;
SOCommand cmd = null;

try
{
    //Make the server connection
    SOConnectionStringBuilder cb = new SOConnectionStringBuilder();
    cb.Server = "DLX";
    cb.Port = 5555;

    //Create connection and command
    conn = new SOConnection(cb.ToString());
    cmd = new SOCommand();
    cmd.Connection = conn;

    //Get Users in Group
    cmd.CommandText = "OpportunityEmployee.GetUserInGroup";
    cmd.CommandType = System.Data.CommandType.StoredProcedure;
    cmd.Parameters.Add(new SOParameter("GroupName", groupName));

    SODataReader reader = cmd.ExecuteReader();

    //Write out values
    while (reader.Read())
    {
        System.Diagnostics.Debug.Write(
            "ID=" + reader["ID"].ToString() + " " +
            "Email=" + reader["Email"].ToString());
    }
}
catch (Exception ex)
{
    throw new Exception(ex.Message);
}
finally
{
    conn.Close();
}
```

## Writing a SmartObject Service

SmartObject Services are the conduit for provisioning data from data sources into SmartObjects. A SmartObject Service is simply a class that must override several methods that are K2 blackpearl SmartObject server requirements. The implementation of these methods can be simple or complex as needed. This section delves in detail on how to create a stub for a SmartObject Service but does not go into the details of an actual implementation for getting data from a data source.

*Chapter 10 covers the deployment of SmartObject Services.*

*An alternative to developing a custom service as described in this chapter is to use code attribution in a class library that is used to communicate with the LOB system. For more information about how to do this, see the articles "Developing a Custom Service"* (www.k2underground.com/files/folders/ technical_product_documents/entry21898.aspx) *and "Creating Custom SmartObjects Services Part 2"* (http://k2distillery.blogspot.com/2008/09/ creating-custom-smartobjects-part-2.html).

To create a SmartObject Service, first create a code library project in Visual Studio and then add a reference to `SourceCode.SmartObjects.Services.ServiceSDK`, which is located in `\\Program Files\ K2 blackpearl\Host Server\Bin\`. Once this library is referenced, right-click the reference in Visual Studio Solution Explorer, go to properties of the reference, and change Copy Local property from True to False, then add a reference to the `System.Transactions` library. Once both of the libraries have been added, create a class that inherits from `ServiceAssemblyBase`. There can only be one class of `ServiceAssemblyBase` per code project. All classes that inherit from `ServiceAssemblyBase` must override the following methods: `GetConfigSection()`, `DescribeSchema()`, `Execute()`, and `Extend()`.

```
public class MyCustomService : ServiceAssemblyBase
{
    public MyCustomService()
    {
    }

    public override string GetConfigSection()
    {
    }

    public override string DescribeSchema()
    {
    }

    public override void Execute()
    {
    }

    public override void Extend()
    {
    }
}
```

## GetConfigSection Method

The `GetConfigSection()` is a method used to define configuration values for the service instance after it has been deployed. It is similar to a configuration file that is used by an instance of a SmartObject Service. Defining configuration keys is very important because the location of a data connection may change over time. If the service needs to make a connection to a database or Web service, that connection information could be defined in this method.

```
public override string GetConfigSection()
{
    this.Service.ServiceConfiguration.Add("Server", true, "Default Value");

    return base.GetConfigSection();
}
```

In this implementation, the `ServiceConfiguration` property is accessed from the base, and a key and default value are added. Also, configurations can be marked as required. When the service instance is created, it can require that the field be populated.

There are reasons why a config file should not be used with SmartObject Services. A SmartObject Service may be implemented in a generic fashion so that many instances of the service can be created. But because each SmartObject Service instance is different from every other, these configuration values are stored on a per service instance basis (that is, the values are not shared between service instances). An example would be the Active Directory SmartObject Service. By default, an instance of that service is created when K2 is installed, and it sets the LDAP path configuration to the current domain. However, some companies have multiple Active Directory Domains. So, this service has a configuration to specify the LDAP path, making it possible to have different service instances for each Active Directory Domain.

## DescribeSchema() Method

The `DescribeSchema()` method defines the public interface for the SmartObject Service. The first thing that should be added to the `DescribeSchema()` is the description of the service. This information is then presented to developers when they are searching for a service to use with a SmartObject method. In the following code, the name and description are assigned to the service.

```
public override string DescribeSchema()
{
    //set base info
    this.Service.Name = "WroxCustomService";
    this.Service.MetaData.DisplayName = "Wrox Custom Service";
    this.Service.MetaData.Description = "Custom service for Wrox.";
```

After this has been set, one-to-many `ServiceObjects` need to be created. `ServiceObjects` are no more than a logical grouping of methods. Think of them as a class definition. For the `ServiceObject`, the display properties are values that are shown to the developer when they are creating a SmartObject. The `Active` property of the `ServiceObject` must be set to true for it to be used. In the following code, the service is called the `"Wrox Stub Service"`.

```
    //Create the service object
    ServiceObject so = new ServiceObject();
    so.Name = "WroxCustomServiceObject";
    so.MetaData.DisplayName = "Wrox Stub Service";
    so.MetaData.DisplayName = "Use for Wrox stub service.";
    so.Active = true;
    this.Service.ServiceObjects.Add(so);
```

Next, property definitions are created, using the `Property` object. `Property` objects are used to define the input and output parameters for service methods. Two properties are defined in the following code block, the first is an integer and the second a string. The properties must be added to the SmartObject list of properties.

```
//Create field definition
Property property1 = new Property();
property1.Name = "MyField1";
property1.MetaData.DisplayName = "My Field 1";
property1.MetaData.Description = "My Field 1";
property1.Type = "Integer";
property1.SoType = SoType.Number;
so.Properties.Add(property1);

//Create field definition
Property property2 = new Property();
property2.Name = "MyField2";
property2.MetaData.DisplayName = "My Field 2";
property2.MetaData.Description = "My Field 2";
property2.Type = "System.String";
property2.SoType = SoType.Text;
so.Properties.Add(property2);
```

Finally, once the properties have been created, you can define methods. `Property` objects have to be created first because all of methods reuse `Property` objects. The `Method` class defines things such as the name, metadata, type, required properties, and input/output properties. The method type enumeration has the following method types: Create, Read, Update, Delete, List, and Execute. In the following code, `Load` and `List` methods are created, and both require the integer as an input parameter. In addition, both methods return the integer along with a string value. Once the method object has been created, you must add it to the `ServiceObject` object methods collection.

```
//Create Load method
Method method1 = new Method();
method1.Name = "Load";
method1.MetaData.DisplayName = "Load";
method1.MetaData.Description = "Load a single record of data";
method1.Type = MethodType.Read;
method1.Validation.RequiredProperties.Add(property1);
method1.InputProperties.Add(property1);
method1.ReturnProperties.Add(property1);
method1.ReturnProperties.Add(property2);
so.Methods.Add(method1);

//Create List method
Method method2 = new Method();
method2.Name = "List";
method2.MetaData.DisplayName = "List";
method2.MetaData.Description = "Load collection of data";
method2.Type = MethodType.List;
method2.Validation.RequiredProperties.Add(property1);
method2.InputProperties.Add(property1);
method2.ReturnProperties.Add(property1);
method2.ReturnProperties.Add(property2);
so.Methods.Add(method2);

return base.DescribeSchema();
}
```

This implementation is building up a static list of methods; however, the list of ServiceObjects, Methods, and Properties can be created dynamically. For instance, this method could read a database or Web service schema and dynamically generate the entire interface. This is a common practice with many of the SmartObject Services that are provided by K2 or the K2 community.

## Execute() Method

The Execute() method of the ServiceObject Service has the implementation code to perform an operation. The following code shows a basic implementation of the Execute() method. When a method is called from a SmartObject, the Service.ServiceObjects collection is filled with the ServiceObjects that were called. The same is true for the Methods collection of the ServiceObject. Currently, these two collections are only ever filled with a single ServiceObject and a method. It is good practice still to iterate over the collection because future enhancements may support more.

The implementation of this Execute() method loops over these two collections and determines what code should be executed. In the catch block of this code, the ServicePackage object of the base class is used to return an error message to the caller and flags the transaction as being unsuccessful.

```
public override void Execute()
{
    try
    {
        //Loop over called ServiceObject(s)
        foreach (ServiceObject so in Service.ServiceObjects)
        {
            switch (so.Name)
            {
                case "WroxCustomServiceObject":
                    //Loop over the method(s) that were called.
                    foreach (Method method in so.Methods)
                    {
                        switch (method.Name)
                        {
                            case "Load":
                                LoadMethod(so, method);
                                break;
                            case "List":
                                ListMethod(so, method);
                                break;
                            default:
                                throw new Exception(
                                  "Service method undefined");
                        }
                    }
                    break;
                default:
                    throw new Exception("Service Object Not Found");
            }
        }
    }
```

```
        catch (Exception ex)
        {
            string errorMsg = Service.MetaData.DisplayName +
                " Error >>  " + ex.Message;
            this.ServicePackage.ServiceMessages.Add(
                errorMsg, MessageSeverity.Error);
            this.ServicePackage.IsSuccessful = false;
        }
    }
```

The `ServicePackage` object has another property called the `ResultTable`. This should be populated with all the data that needs to be returned to the SmartObject. A `ResultTable` table is a `System.Data.DataTable` that simply needs to be filled with data. In the `ListMethod()`, the `ResultTable` is initialized by calling `InitResultTable()`, and then the `ResultTable` can be filled with data (this topic is outside the scope of this chapter).

In the `LoadMethod()` method, the `ResultTable` is initialized by calling `InitResultTable()`; however, in this example, all of the values are set to the properties of the `ServiceObject`. Once all of the values have been set into the `ServiceObject`, the values need to be moved to the `ResultTable`. This can be accomplished by calling `BindPropertiesToResultTable()`. From there, the K2 SmartObject infrastructure takes the `ResultTable`, sends it to the SmartObject, and fills the SmartObject with the data.

```
//This method shows how return a single row of data, this would
//be used for Read and Create methods (when calling Create you will
//want to return primary key of new record)
private void LoadMethod(ServiceObject so, Method method)
{
    //Add in code here to retrieve data from any external data source and
    //load it into the result set for this method.
    so.Properties.InitResultTable();
    so.Properties["MyField1"].Value = 1;
    so.Properties["MyField2"].Value = "Comments";
    so.Properties.BindPropertiesToResultTable();
}
```

The `ListMethod()` is called when a collection of data needs to be returned. In this method the `ResultTable` is accessed directly from the `ServicePackage` and can be filled with data. This could have been done in the previous method.

```
//This method shows how to return a collection of data using a DataTable.
//This would be used for a List method
private void ListMethod(ServiceObject so, Method method)
{
    so.Properties.InitResultTable();
    DataTable resultTable = this.ServicePackage.ResultTable;

    //Write code to fill the ResultTable with data.
}
```

## Extend() Method

This method is not used by most implementations. The purpose of this method is to perform operations that can modify the service instance without requiring the service instance to be stopped and restarted. For example, `Extend()` is used with the SmartBox Service. Designers can modify a SmartObject definition in a design environment, and then when it is deployed to the K2 server, the `Extend()` method is called. The SmartBox implementation of the `Extend` method modifies the SmartObject Service methods and parameters similar to the code written in the `DescribeSchema()` method. The `Extend()` method must also be executed at the appropriate time, which in the case of the SmartBox is during deployment.

```
public override void Extend()
{
    //No implementation required.
}
```

# Summary

K2 SmartObjects provide a flexible architecture in which data can be used inside and outside of K2 processes to make business decisions. The SmartObject Services framework is extensible and can be used to access any LOB data source within an enterprise. K2 blackpearl provides the visual design tools that allow you to quickly model SmartObjects and use them within your workflows and applications. With these tools significant time can be gained back into a project plan allowing designers to focus more on implementing business processes.

The next chapter focuses on how to plan on building process-driven applications using K2 blackpearl processes and SmartObjects. The chapter will concentrate on all the considerations you as a designer need to take before authoring a process. At the end of that chapter and with this information from the SmartObject chapter, you as a designer will have enough information to author your first workflow (which is covered in Chapter 9).

# Effective Process-Driven Application Planning

Codi Kaji

To ensure success, every process-driven application project should be carefully planned to ensure each effort meets its objectives. This chapter will walk you through the steps to ensure that you can build successful processes. The purpose of this chapter is to define the main K2 components and how they fit into effective process design. In previous chapters, you learned about how to gather business requirements, including the data requirements. In this chapter, you'll get back to the business process that you are automating!

This chapter covers the following topics:

❑   Defining your process, including selection criteria for candidate processes and how to effectively diagram your process

❑   Process design principles, including happy and alternate paths

❑   The "Who," including actors and roles

❑   The "What," including activities, events, actions, and outcomes

❑   The "How," including Line and Activity Rules

❑   The "When," including escalations and notifications

❑   Advanced process design, including the Spider Workflow approach

It is important to note that we discussed the data requirements with SmartObjects in Chapter 7. In other words, we talked about the business objects *before* we talked about the process surrounding those entities. A process is meaningless if the right data is not displayed at the right time to the user who needs to make a business decision.

# How to Start

The first step in defining your process is to select one. It is important to narrow down that process to its most simple form. For example, while your end goal may be to automate the entire Employee on-boarding process, start with baby steps. Break down that process into the subprocesses, the ones that can be easily defined. It is important to scope your process just as you would any other development engagement, with clearly defined goals and a small enough scope to be successful. Once you've automated your first process, then you can keep adding processes to your library and will eventually have all your business processes automated.

## *Selecting the Process*

In order to select the appropriate process to start, there are a few criteria that should help you navigate your business processes to find the one to start with. Always remember, any business process automation initiative should have major impact to the end users, to the people who will be using this process. Look for those low hanging fruits first, the applications or processes that people hate to do but must as part of their jobs. By tackling a process that people are unhappy with, you will be able to convert the masses to the business process automation way of life.

Good candidates for process automation involve the following:

❑ **Large number of participants:** Look for a business process that impacts a large number of users, or a process in which a large number of people participate throughout the process lifecycle.

❑ **Large number of instances that must be tracked:** Look for a business process that happens frequently, and where each instance needs to be tracked or reported on. A process that happens once a year probably is not a good candidate to begin with. Instead, look for a process where multiple people start an instance on a daily basis, where they need to know the status of the request or where other people, such as Legal or Audit, need to have visibility into the process.

❑ **Geographically dispersed participants:** Paper-based processes always break down or become more complicated when participants in the process are in different offices, perhaps even different continents. Look for processes that involve faxing documents, or scanning and e-mailing documents for approval.

❑ **Processes that last over long periods of time:** For long-running processes, it is always difficult to remember where the form currently is in the process, who has it, what needs to be done next, and so on. These are prime candidates for automation, as having a reporting mechanism or an escalation process to remind people that a process instance is stalled and waiting for action can really help drive the process to completion.

❑ **Costly mistakes:** Any process that could result in legal ramifications, including fines, or degradation of the business' reputation are also good candidates. Business process automation helps drive consistency and repeatability of a process, thereby ensuring a level of compliance that is not always possible with paper forms or an ad hoc process.

In addition to these criteria, process automation also helps hide the business process from end users. For processes that are particularly complicated, end users do not need to understand the complexities or the various systems that are involved with the business process. Instead, they know how to interact with the process using the forms you build, they know how to get information out of the process using the reports, and that's all they really need to know.

# Drawing It Out

After you've selected the process you are going to automate, find out who the Subject Matter Experts (SMEs) are from the various touch points in the business and schedule a meeting to start down this path. At this point in time, you may want to introduce the K2 technologies, but you may want to just start with a discussion around the current business process, what works and what doesn't work, and then start digging deeper into the mechanics of the process.

Whenever a discussion begins about a business process, someone usually grabs a whiteboard marker and starts drawing boxes and lines on a whiteboard. Or maybe someone cracks open Visio and starts drawing boxes during a meeting. While this is a key step, and usually starts people thinking about how the process works today, and maybe even how it should work in the future, we propose a new way to look at defining your process.

There are really three key considerations when automating a business process:

1. **Data:** Without having the proper data or business entities exposed to the users, they cannot make decisions. Without knowing what information needs to be displayed to the users, you cannot design your forms. Without understanding who needs to see what and when, you cannot define your process. That's why in Chapter 7 you learned about SmartObjects and how to expose your business data into the K2 platform. There are some main concepts to keep in mind, however, as you are drawing out your process. At this point, we really don't care where the data lives. Only that it exists and that people need it to do their jobs. We do care about getting the right data to the right people at the right time. And, we do care if that data should be read-only or if it needs to updated or changed as part of this process.

2. **Forms:** Without really understanding the people, or actors, who will participate in your process, you cannot define how they will need to interact with the data via forms. You will learn about the different forms technologies in Chapter 11, but at this point you will need to define how people will interact with the data, whether in reports, via e-mail, or through an online form. Forms are really just a way to display and capture data. And because we want to get the right data to the right people, we need to understand the security and validation that needs to be present in this form. While reports are not traditionally thought of as forms, a report is just a read-only set of data. Make sure that while you are thinking of how people interact with the data, you do not overlook the reporting requirements as well. Be sure to capture all the data you could possibly need to report on later, or to help you slice and dice the data in the reports.

3. **Process:** The last key to the puzzle is how the data flows between groups of people and/or systems. All the process really does is play traffic cop, routing the appropriate data to the appropriate people in the correct order. Each step in the process should add value to the end user. After a step has been completed, you should never have to return because of missing or invalid data.

This chapter will focus on the details and concepts surrounding the process definition. In order to effectively design an automated process, you will need to have these concepts in your toolbox, to pick and choose from where appropriate.

## Sometimes Paper Is Good

At this point in the process design phase, a good exercise could also be to get all the stakeholders and SMEs in a room and pass around a piece of paper which represents the form. Have them pass it back and forth in the order in which that form needs to travel. Have the business analyst document the order and the interactions, the "who" and the "when." Look for where the process could be improved, where things could be given to more than one person at a time for approvals. Look for redundant steps. Look for where the same person has touched the form multiple times, could these be combined or reordered to reduce redundancy? If data is missing and filled in later, could it be found and incorporated into the process earlier to streamline the process?

During this exercise, the SMEs may realize that they do not know the process as well as they thought. And that no one person knows the process from end to end. That is why these meetings are critical, so that all the information and requirements can be gathered in order to automate the complete, and correct, business process.

Complimentarily to the whiteboard approach, you are in effect designing the activity flow of your process. You start drawing boxes and lines as you start breaking down your business process into logical components. Each block corresponds to an activity in K2. We will define these terms in more detail a little later, but for now, when you are drawing boxes think of them as activities. You can start defining your process at this high of a level, but the more detail that you start capturing in your design, the easier it will be for all your stakeholders to buy into the fact that the process design is correct.

From the whiteboard, it is important to document your process into a diagram. There are several types of diagrams that are used for defining business processes. While your organization may have a template or a preferred method, we will introduce these diagrams to add into your automation toolbox.

## The Block Diagram

The process diagram shown in Figure 8-1 depicts a typical block diagram representing a business process. The type of process represented by the diagram is not important. The manner in which the process is documented makes all the difference in the world to those employees involved.

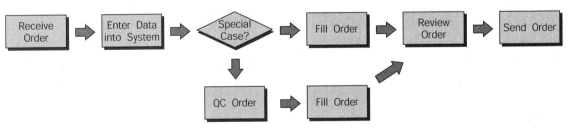

Figure 8-1

Many organizations use the BPMN (Business Process Modeling Notation) standards for creating process flow diagrams. An example of a BPMN diagram is shown in Figure 8-2. While this may have more detail than the block diagram shown in Figure 8-1, it is still just boxes and lines, with some start and endpoints defined. It is still generalized, and still places people a distance from the process, as if they were outsiders looking in.

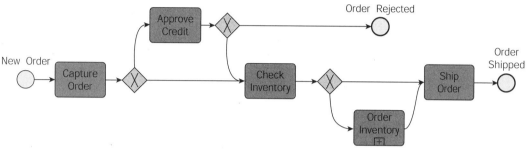

Figure 8-2

## Challenges with the Block Diagram

The people involved in the process can perceive the block diagram as a representation of their value. Any modifications to this diagram, either addition or subtraction, can be received as threatening.

Psychologically, the block diagram is distant and generalized. It invokes a third-person perspective in conversation. Common phrases such as "the process should do this," or "the process should contain that," create a distance between the process and the process participants. This distance makes it difficult to understand the process from the perspective of the people involved.

It is important to use whatever method works best in your organization, whatever people are familiar with for documentation and for understanding the business process. However, because blocks and lines do not translate conceptually into people's minds of tasks and actions, we have found that changing from blocks to people icons is more effective in business process automation efforts.

## *The Pawn Diagram*

By placing more significance on the people who are involved with the process rather than the activities in the process, you can achieve a greater level of buy-in from the stakeholders. By recognizing that processes involve people, and that people are a business's greatest asset, you can place the same level of importance on the actors in the process as on the actual tasks they are performing. These processes now become people-focused, or human-centric, instead of task-based.

The pawn diagram shown in Figure 8-3, places a focus on the process participants and the roles they play within the process. This diagram approach replaces the typical block diagram shapes with a symbol to which all business users can easily relate: a person.

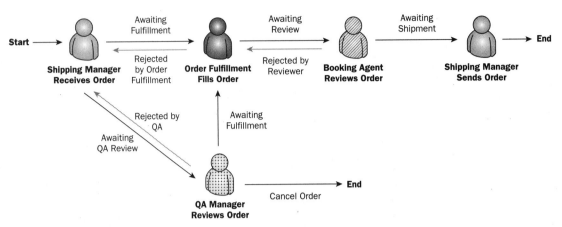

**Figure 8-3**

*Please take note that because the figures in this book are in black and white, we've used different shading and fills to differentiate between and among the pawns in those figures that have them in this chapter. Ordinarily, the different pawns would be represented by using different colors to easily see where each role plays a part in the process.*

## Why a Human-Centric Diagram Works

It is important to understand that process automation isn't simply about implementing the K2 blackpearl technology. It is about managing process participants' securities and insecurities surrounding their role within the process. To the average employee, the word "automation" can conjure up negative thoughts; especially if they value their role within the process and are held accountable and responsible for the output. Most often process participants feel more comfortable discussing a process they understand, rather than a technology that they do not.

Changing blocks to pawns serves as an effective communication pattern among participants because it is a nonintrusive and nonthreatening approach to understanding requirements, and it places the importance on people within the process, rather than the technology being implemented. Only people can optimize and think of new ways of streamlining processes; the technology only enables this. While IT is usually more excited about the technology, the process owners are much more interested in how the process will change and the role they will be playing in its automated state.

By starting with the people who participate in the process and automating the features and functionalities of the system around them, you can create a valuable paradigm shift. Process owners begin to take responsibility of their role within the process. They stop speaking in the third person, (for example, "the process should do this"), and begin to speak in the first person. You'll begin to hear, "In order for me to approve this item, I need the following information," or "After I submit this information, it should be your job to review it and provide feedback." This shift in perspective allows participants to take ownership of the process. They can begin to see how the purpose of automation technology is to help them improve the process.

Furthermore, by switching to first person references, the process designer can start to identify the various roles and workflow participants that will be actors in this process. These actors can be translated into roles or groups based on job function. A pawn should not represent a single person in an organization but rather the role that person plays within the business process. When creating the pawn diagram, you stop thinking about the boxes and start thinking about the actors who perform the tasks, which helps you design the process and implement it that much faster.

These pawn diagrams play a key role for several reasons:

❑ Identifying the touch points for the various actors helps you customize training and communications to those specific audiences.

❑ Testing can use these diagrams to ensure that the process is being routed correctly to the appropriate person or role.

❑ Validating that the process design is fully captured and is accurately represented by the diagram with all stakeholders.

## Basic Process Definitions

While you were defining your process by drawing blocks and lines on the whiteboard, you started to define the process using either a *serial* or *parallel* process without even recognizing it. These types of process definitions just define how the activities are routed, and we will discuss them in depth next.

### Serial Process Definition

A serial process is the simplest form of routing data. Serial routing is defined as a combined set of sequential steps executed in order; one right after the other. Data passes through the process one step at a time and cannot skip steps. Serial processes should be the default approach to process definition. A serial process is shown in Figure 8-4.

Figure 8-4

### Parallel Process Definition

A parallel process differs from a serial process because data can be simultaneously routed to multiple destinations within a single step in the process. A parallel process is often more complex to implement than a serial process because parallel processes require complex data manipulation to split and merge data according to specific business rules. Do not let the complexities of the parallel process definition hinder your intent to implement such a process. K2 blackpearl technology is designed to handle complex data manipulation with ease. An example of a parallel process is shown in Figure 8-5.

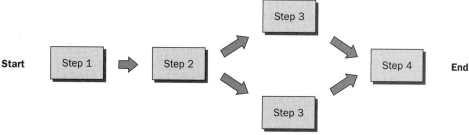

Figure 8-5

199

There are multiple types of parallel processes. Each parallel process is designed to improve the flow of the process in a unique way. Many times, a parallel approval activity can be handled using the built-in capabilities of the Destination Rules, which will be discussed later. For now, as you are drawing your diagram, keep in mind those steps that need to happen in order and which can be split and handed off to multiple people for action at one time.

## Taking the Next Steps

After you have drawn out your diagram, make sure that all the people that were present and involved with the design of the process review it for accuracy. Make sure that all the details were captured appropriately and accurately. Where you uncovered details about data or forms, be sure that those are documented in a requirements document as well. Sometimes, in addition to the pawn diagram, a requirements document that describes the various actors, the actions they will take, and the data or form requirements is possible at this stage in the process definition.

If you have not gotten to this level of detail yet, schedule follow-up meetings. Be sure to get all the stakeholders and SMEs in a room and continue working on the details. By spending the time up front to get to a detailed design of the process, you will save development effort and rework time later. It is worth the extra meetings.

# Process Design Principles

There are several key design principles that will help you document your process. Some of these are K2-specific, and others are principles for business process automation and management. All are important parts of your toolkit in identifying your process and interacting with the stakeholders to accurately design your process, and be able to translate it into the K2 platform after the design is complete.

Remember that in Chapter 2 we defined what Business Process Management meant. In this chapter, we are focusing on a process. A process is defined as a particular course of action intended to achieve a specific result. In the context of workflow, the K2 process is the logical representation of a course of action that must be followed. The process itself is composed of a combination of one or more activities capable of performing the individual logic and routing steps within the process. Each activity may contain one Client Event and multiple Server Events. A Client Event usually enables human to system interaction, while a Server Event usually enables system to system interaction. We will cover events in more detail in a little bit, but for now let's begin with the "flow" in workflow.

## Paths

The next step in the modeling process is to define the relationships between the different actors in the process. Complex processes such as approval processes can have multiple alternatives, depending upon business rules. A process follows one or more paths to completion.

### Happy Path

The happy path is defined as the route the request takes through the process if everything were to run perfectly, and there were no errors or alterations. Essentially, your goal is to identify the most commonly used process path. In Figure 8-6, we've added "start" and "end" identifiers, as well as arrows to describe the happy path.

**Figure 8-6**

Please make note of the following unique aspects. First, not all actors may be required in order to represent the happy path. Some actors may serve supporting roles in alternate flows, and others may simply be discarded when you pose the question, "How would you like the process to flow?" Be careful to understand the value of each actor. Now is the appropriate time to identify a process that is driven by exception, rather than a predictable or optimal flow.

Second, you'll notice that the same actor (Shipping Manager) is shown twice in Figure 8-6. This is by design; in this process the request has to go back to the Shipping Manager for completion at the end of this process. By showing where each actor participates in the process, and by using a different color (or in this black-and-white example a different shade or fill) per actor, you can easily see who plays a role when in the process. In this example, having the Shipping Manager touch this request twice, once at the beginning and once at the end, can facilitate additional discussions. Why is this necessary? Can the tasks be consolidated so that the Shipping Manager only has to touch a request once? This can drive efficiencies by recognizing redundant work by an actor in a process.

## Alternate Paths

Alternate paths are those steps where the workflow branches. For example, the happy path as shown in Figure 8-6 assumes that each actor approves the request. Well what happens if a person declines the request? Or sends it back for rework? Or what if the request is over a certain amount and must go through multiple levels of approval? The alternate paths are designed to capture this information and route the request appropriately.

In order to identify an alternate flow, at each step in the process, ask what other options could occur? For example, if the Order Fulfillment role in the process above cannot fulfill the order, what happens? How do they handle that exception?

Properly defining the alternate paths is critical in fully defining the business process. However, many times these exceptions are handled on a one-off basis. Therefore, until the automated process is actually used, some of these highly unlikely cases may not be discovered. This is why we use an iterative approach when designing process-driven applications. Capturing the happy path and the most common alternate paths will meet the business need 80% of the time and the less likely alternate paths can be added at a later date. K2 handles this flexibility in adding alternate paths through actions and outcomes, which will be discussed in detail later.

One of the first alternate paths that usually comes up in discussion is the scenario where an approver is presented a form with data, and they decide not to approve the content. Usually, the actions available to the approver are Approve and Decline. If an approver declines the data in a specific step within the process, usually the status of the request changes and the request goes back to a previous step, perhaps for rework. Other times, a decline action may end the process. One example of the decline scenario is shown in Figure 8-7.

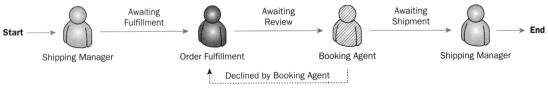

**Figure 8-7**

In this example, the request would go back to the Order Fulfillment actor, perhaps to rework the data or for data to be revalidated before continuing on.

Another common alternate path is if a request needs to be canceled. For example, if the business rules affecting the process or other external factors render the current request no longer applicable, the request should be canceled in its current state. Upon cancellation, data can be restored to a specific state, the status can be changed, or a secondary process can be started. Either way, a cancellation brings the current process to a conclusion. Figure 8-8 displays a cancellation component.

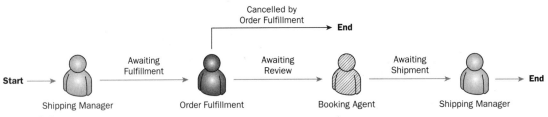

**Figure 8-8**

Notice that the alternate path lines are a different line type (and when viewed in color, a different color). This is to strongly denote the differences between the happy path and an alternate path. Also note that status descriptions have been added to all lines in this process. These statuses can be used as a process field in order for the stakeholders in the process to know exactly where the request is in the process. These statuses should be descriptive, such as "Awaiting Review" or "Declined by Booking Agent" so that, at a glance, the status of the request is known.

## The "Who"

So far in this chapter we've focused on the people-centric workflow concept, and have been using the pawn diagram for examples to show paths and statuses. Let's now look a little deeper at the people part of this process. In any good business process, a pawn should not represent a single person. This represents a single point of failure for your business process. However, in many smaller organizations this is true. A single person may play multiple roles in a process. But, in the pawn diagrams shown earlier, you did not see a person labeled as "Mike" or "Sue," but rather "Shipping Manager." It is important to denote the generic role or job title that person plays in the process rather than the individual's name.

The pawns in the diagrams represent Destinations, which is a rule that K2 blackpearl uses to assign tasks to people or roles. These destinations are created when defining the process, and destination rules will be discussed in more detail later in the chapter. For now, recognize that people play a key role in a business process, and K2 calls these destinations.

## Actors

The first step in the modeling process is to identify the actors that will be participating in the process. You have already done this by abstracting the blocks into people or roles. There may not be a one-to-one correlation between blocks and actors. There can be more or less actors than blocks. There may also be steps in the process that are not done by a person, but rather by a system or an automated task, such as looking up information from the order system.

Figure 8-9 represents a set of actors participating in an example process. Notice that each actor is a different color (or in this black-and-white example, a different shade or fill type) and includes a title. Additionally, you could have an actor that is the server or code, for those activities that do not require a person to intervene, but are a logical component of the process.

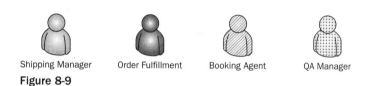

Shipping Manager     Order Fulfillment     Booking Agent     QA Manager

**Figure 8-9**

How do actors in a process translate into users in K2? K2 relies on user providers to bring user information into the context of the K2 platform. K2 configures Active Directory and SQL user providers, but other user providers can be added. The default user provider is Active Directory and uses the "K2" security label. The SQL user provider uses the "K2SQL" security label. Labels are used to identify user providers.

User providers can display users from various systems, such as Active Directory, SQL Server, or any custom user provider that has been developed to work with K2. Once the user provider has been defined, those users are displayed in the Object Browser under the User Browser tab and can be given permissions on processes.

Because we have been careful when defining our actors in the process as generic job titles rather than specific individuals, we have not been defining the individual users who participate in a process, but rather the roles.

## Roles

Users can be added to processes directly as destinations but a more flexible approach is to add users to roles and use the roles as destinations. This way, when responsibilities change, the role membership can be modified without having to redeploy the process definition. Much like groups or roles in other K2 systems, such as Active Directory, roles in K2 blackpearl are groups of users. Unlike other systems, roles in blackpearl can be dynamic if based on SmartObject queries, and they can include users from multiple systems, which is particularly useful if your process involves external participants.

Roles are set up using the Management Console in K2 Workspace, and can be used across business processes. Therefore, it is important when you are designing roles for use in your process that you be specific about the roles. For example, naming a role "HR" is too broad and may confuse other processes designers. A better name would be "HR New Hire Approvers," as this describes both the department and the function being performed, in this case approving new hires.

As mentioned, roles can span user providers, meaning that roles can contain users with different labels. Role membership can also be configured to exclude users. This is useful, for example, when an Active Directory group contains individuals who should not receive notifications or worklist items.

A new role is given a name and one or more role items. These items can be based on the following entities:

❑ Users or Groups from Active Directory or SQL

❑ Other K2 roles

❑ Result from SmartObject methods

As shown in Figure 8-10, all users are included in the Role1 role, except Mike. SmartObject methods can also be included or excluded from the role.

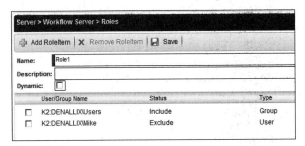

**Figure 8-10**

Users can be added to processes directly as destinations but a more flexible approach is to add users to roles and use the roles as destinations. This way, when responsibilities change, the role can be modified without having to change the process. Chapter 15 will go into more detail on creating and maintaining roles. Destinations will be discussed in more detail later in this chapter.

## Permissions

When role membership changes, users removed from a role will no longer see worklist items associated with the role. Conversely, users added to a role will see worklist items associated with the role after the refresh interval. A refresh interval is the time period associated with a role to query for new role items. The refresh interval is set on a role after it has been used with a process. For example, Figure 8-11 shows Role1 being used in a process with a refresh interval of 10 minutes. This means that every 10 minutes the K2 server will query for changes to the role membership and will adjust the tasks that users see accordingly.

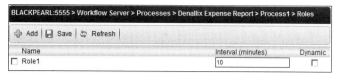

**Figure 8-11**

User and role permissions are resolved using a concept called the *context grid*, which allows for the definition and management of user permissions. For example, a role can be used in the destination rule for an event and all users in that role will see worklist items related to that event. The context grid allows actions to be assigned to users based on their role membership.

Let's discuss the context grid in terms of a scenario. We have an expense report process that allows a form to be submitted for approval by an employee (the originator of the request). The process is configured to route the expense report to the originator's manager. This manager has several actions, such as Approve, Decline, and Rework. The originator may view the form at this stage in the process, as can senior management. Assuming that the manager has not actioned the item in 48 hours, the senior management should now be able to Approve or Decline the request.

Think of the context grid as a way to map the task (in this case, the Manager Approval) and the action (in this case, Approve, Decline, or Rework) as well as who (the user, group, or role) can perform the action (in this case, the manager, or senior management)

## Delegation

A user who has been assigned a task can delegate it to another user, meaning that they can allow their delegate to act on their behalf. This is available from the K2 Worklist, from the worklist item, as shown in Figure 8-12.

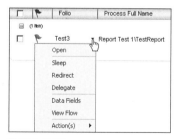

**Figure 8-12**

The delegator can determine which actions a delegate can perform. The work item will appear in both the delegator and delegate's worklist. The first user to select the work item will process the item.

This can be very useful for managers to delegate work to their subordinates, but control which actions they can do. For example, in an expense claim process, a manager can delegate a task to the project manager for review, but since that project manager has no direct approval authority, the manager can restrict the actions to only reject or rework. If the expense claim should be approved, the project manager can notify the manager, at which time the original manager can approve the claim.

## Redirection

Also from the action menu from the worklist item is redirect. This allows a user to send the selected worklist item to someone else to action. The worklist item will be removed from the original user's worklist, and will appear in the redirect's worklist.

This can be very useful for items that should go to another manager for approval. For example, perhaps you have an expense claim process that requires the employee's manager to approve. If the employee has been working on a project run by a project manager and has expenses related to that project, the manager can redirect the expense claim request to the project manager for approval.

# The "What"

After you've defined who is participating in the process, the next step is to identify what they need to do. Remember, as you were drawing boxes and lines on the whiteboard, you were identifying the things that needed to happen. These boxes are what we will define next.

Figure 8-13 shows the structural hierarchy of a K2 solution. A solution is basically a storage container for processes and SmartObjects, and other artifacts (such as forms, Web services, etc.). In a solution, you have a Process. This Process is built up of activities and events, which we will describe in detail soon. When you deploy a K2 solution, you can select which process(es) or artifacts to include in the deployment. However, this goes down to the process level, which is made up in whole by the activities and events within them.

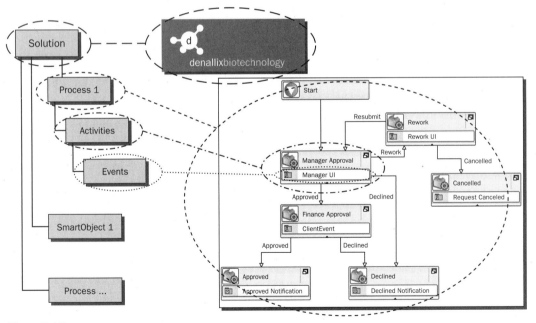

Figure 8-13

## Process

In the context of K2 blackpearl, a process is built using activities and events. A Process Wizard is basically a template for a Process that uses that particular feature. Process Wizards give you a jump start on configuring the workflow.

- ❑ **InfoPath Integration:** The starting place when designing workflows that use InfoPath. This wizard takes you through the steps of adding an InfoPath form to your solution and integrating it as the starting mechanism for the process. If you have an InfoPath form that you want to use within your process, start with the InfoPath Integration Process Wizard to initially associate your workflow with an InfoPath form. Then, you can continue to build your process using any of the Server Events and as many InfoPath Client Events as you need.

- ❑ **SharePoint Events Process:** Allows you to configure a workflow to run in response to certain SharePoint list events, such as a data field added, changed, or deleted, or an item added, changed, or deleted from a particular list or library. This Process Wizard allows the SharePoint list or library to be the starting point for the K2 process and does not require another form to start the process instance.

- ❑ **SharePoint Workflow Integration:** The starting place when designing a workflow that will be a SharePoint workflow and deployed as a feature in SharePoint. The K2 blackpearl workflow can be associated with a library, list, or a content type. The workflow can either begin manually, using the Workflows item within SharePoint or the appropriate Office application, or it can be configured to start automatically when a new item is added or an item is changed.

These wizards set the stage for the process type, and enable K2 blackpearl to integrate tightly with the underlying technology, either InfoPath or SharePoint. You can use one of the above Process Wizards to start off, or you can start with just a blank K2 process and begin designing your process using the building blocks of activities and events.

## Activities

Activities act as the containers for events within a process. An activity within a process can potentially contain Client Events, Server Events, or Interprocess Communication (IPC) events. The business logic includes concepts like: "who must be involved in the activity," and "are there any prerequisites that must be met before workflow participants can start with the activity." Activities are the logical grouping of related events. For example, let's use an example of "Pull from Inventory" as an activity. In the "Pull from Inventory" step in the process, there are actually several tasks that need to take place, such as "Check Inventory Levels at Local Store," "Lookup Inventory in Warehouse," "Decrease Available Inventory by Request Amount," and so forth. The activity groups the related events together.

Activities are also important components in the process because they represent points where decisions are to be made, data is to be delivered, or actions are to be carried out. One of the most important properties of activities is the business rules associated with the activity. These Activity Rules represent the tools used to build business logic into the activity. For an activity to be useful, it must have at least one event associated with it.

Think of activities as the boxes on the whiteboard. They contain the events and all the logic around what needs to happen. The way the activities are connected, or lines, dictates the path of the request through the process.

It is important while designing your process to recognize that activities can group events together, but only events that should be performed by the same entity. For example, in the "Pull from Inventory" activity above, all of the subtasks are performed by the Server, via code. Because they all happen automatically by the K2 server, they can be grouped together. If a task requires a user to intervene, then it should be split into its own activity, so that the Activity Rules can be defined separately. Also, the order in which the events appear within an activity is the order in which they are performed by the K2 server. In Figure 8-14, the "Pull from Inventory" activity is displayed with the appropriate events. The order in which the events will occur is from top to bottom, with the "Check Inventory Levels at Local Store" occurring first, followed by the steps below.

**Figure 8-14**

Now that we know activities are containers for events with business logic surrounding the activities, let's look more in detail at what exactly are events.

## Events

Events are the tasks that can occur within an activity. So while an activity is a box that represents the steps in a process, an event is the item or substep within that activity. In the previous "Pull from Inventory" example, the tasks that take place are actually the events.

Events can be broken down into three key categories:

- ❏  Client Events
- ❏  Server Events
- ❏  IPC Events (Interprocess Communication Events)

---

### Available Events

Available events may differ from those listed here, depending on the product version and designer you are using. The list of events is accurate for the K2 blackpearl 0803 version.

---

### Client Events

The Client Event represents the physical interaction that takes place between a human user and the process instance. Interaction is on an activity-to-activity basis. In combination, these events are used to create collaborative (human-to-human), transactional (human-to-system), and application integration (system-to-system) workflow solutions. Each activity can host only one Client Event, which performs one Client Event action. This approach categorizes tasks into single steps where one user task is handled per activity. Where multiple steps of Client Event interaction are required in a process, the tasks are linked together by successive activities each containing one Client Event.

A Client Event is always tied to a form. There has to be a way for the user to interact with the system. There are several technologies that are available for forms, and in Chapter 11 you will learn more about them. However, out of the box with K2 blackpearl, there are several types of Client Events that are available:

❑   **Default Client Event:** Allows you to select a custom form to be displayed to the user, such as an ASP.NET Web page, a mobile Web page, or an Exchange Form. Using this Client Event allows you to use your custom forms to interact with a K2 process. These forms can be built using the K2 platform API to return information from the K2 platform. Additional information on ASP.NET forms can be found in Chapter 11. Figure 8-15 shows one screen of the Default Client Event Wizard, where you can specify the URL to your Web page.

**Figure 8-15**

❑   **Forms Generation Client Event:** Creates a skeleton ASPX page automatically with the process data fields, including displaying the XML or SmartObject methods. You can modify this page; after the wizard is completed, a folder with all the necessary ASPX and code-behind pages are available on the file system in your solution folder. While the folder is not automatically added to your K2 solution in Visual Studio, you can add it manually and modify the skeleton page. Figure 8-16 shows one screen of the Forms Generation Client Event Wizard, where you can add data fields, XML fields, or SmartObject methods to be displayed in the generated Web page.

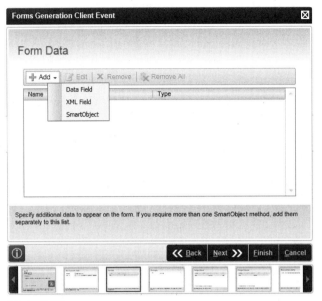

Figure 8-16

❑   **InfoPath Client Event:** Allows you to specify an InfoPath form template and view to complete
a client event. This InfoPath form can be a single form with one or more views shared among
all client events in a particular process, or each client event can use its own form. For more
information about InfoPath forms, please see Chapter 11. Figure 8-17 shows one screen of the
InfoPath Client Event Wizard, where you can specify the Form Template and Client Event View
to display to the end user.

Figure 8-17

❏ **SharePoint Workflow Integration Client Event:** Allows you to use a SharePoint workflow task item as a client event. Mirroring the workflow functionality within SharePoint, end users will not realize they are actioning a K2 process instead of a SharePoint process, but you get the full K2 suite of features, including robust reporting and access to line-of-business (LOB) data, which you do not get with SharePoint workflows. Additional information about the SharePoint integration with K2 can be found in Chapter 12. Figure 8-18 shows one screen of the SharePoint Workflow Integration Client Event Wizard, where you select the Event Name and the Task title that will show up in the SharePoint Tasks list.

**Figure 8-18**

All Client Event wizards have some screens in common. For example, all Client Events have the option of sending an E-Mail Notification to the destination user that a task is waiting their attention. All Client Events also have actions and outcomes that are defined per activity. These will be described in detail a little further in this chapter. And all Client Events also configure the destination user, or the person or people who are responsible for completing this Client Event. Destination Rules will also be covered in a little while. For now, it is important to realize that regardless of the user interface or form that is displayed to the user, notifications, actions, outcomes, and Destination Users are common properties set when configuring all Client Events.

## Server Events

The Server Events execute server-side code. A Server Event has no Client or User interaction. This creates application integration (system-to-system) workflow solutions. Examples of Server Events are the Mail Wizard, and all of the SharePoint wizards (server events for creating a site, list or library, or list item).

Server Events are basically code that executes based on the step in the process, using the data available to the event at that time. There are several Server Events that are available in K2 blackpearl out-of-the-box:

❑ **Default Server Event (Code):** Allows you to write custom C# code to execute on the server. When you use the Default Server Event, an event is added to the process, where you can edit the code. You can use the K2 APIs to access any K2 platform data, or you can access external references, such as Web services. If you can code it, your process can do it. Figure 8-19 shows the Default Server Event on the process design canvas, and how you can edit the C# code behind the event.

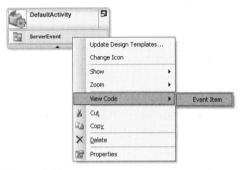

**Figure 8-19**

❑ **Default Server Event (WF):** Allows you to create a Windows Workflow Foundation (WF) sequence activity that will run on the server. Just like the Default Server Event that uses C# code, this event uses a WF schedule for you to customize the event. K2 blackpearl supports the following Windows Workflow Toolbox items:

❑ CallExternalMethod

❑ Code

❑ Compensate

❑ CompensatableSequence

❑ ConditionedActivityGroup

❑ Delay

❑ FaultHandler

❑ IfElse

❑ InvokeWorkflow

❑ Parallel

❑ Policy

❑ Replicator

❑ Sequence

❑ SynchronizationScope

❑ Throw

❑ While

❑ **Mail Event:** Allows you to send an e-mail without waiting for a client response. You can include Process or XML data fields in the e-mail subject or body. This wizard can be used to send notification e-mails of the status of the request to the Originator or other interested parties. For example, if a request has been declined, perhaps that is the end of the process. But, you want to e-mail the Originator of the request the reason the request was declined. Figure 8-20 shows one screen of the Mail Event Wizard.

**Figure 8-20**

❑ **IPC Event:** Allows you to invoke another workflow synchronously or asynchronously. Stands for Interprocess Communication Event. Allows you to call a child process either synchronously, meaning the parent process will wait for the child process to complete, or asynchronously, meaning that the parent process will continue without waiting for the child process. Process data fields can be mapped between the parent and child process. Figure 8-21 shows one screen of the IPC Event Wizard, where you specify the process to call as well as the calling method.

Figure 8-21

❑ **SharePoint Sites and Workspaces Event:** Allows you to create, modify, or delete a SharePoint site. The site template can be one of the built in templates, or you can use your own, custom site definition. This site can be created on any SharePoint Site collection. For example, this wizard could be used to create an automated site provisioning workflow, where after approval, the site is automatically created. Figure 8-22 shows one screen of the Sites and Workspaces Event wizard, where you can specify the Title, Description, URL Name, and Template for a site to be created.

Figure 8-22

❑ **SharePoint Lists and Libraries Event:** Allows you to create, modify, or delete a SharePoint list or library. The list template can be one of the built-in templates, or you can use your own, custom list template. This list can be created on any site. In the automated site provisioning workflow example that was previously covered, you could also use the Lists and Libraries Event to create a set of document libraries, project calendars and tasks lists, and so on in the newly provisioned site. Figure 8-23 shows one screen of the Lists and Libraries Event Wizard, where you can enter the Name, Description, and Template Type for the list or library to be created.

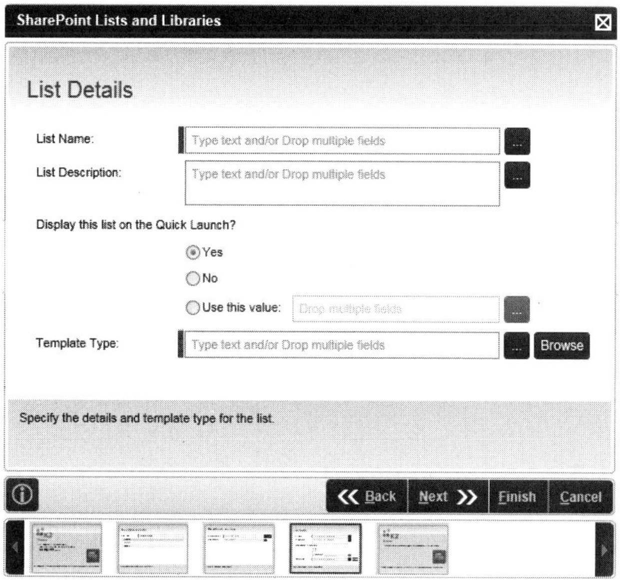

**Figure 8-23**

❑ **SharePoint List Items Event:** Allows you to manipulate a list item within SharePoint, such as creating, copying, or deleting a list item, or retrieving or updated list item metadata. For example, you could use this wizard to change the status of an item stored in a Change Request Register to completed, or delete the list item if the request has been canceled. Figure 8-24 shows the options that you can select from when working with the List Items Event Wizard.

Figure 8-24

❑   **SharePoint Documents Event:** Allows you to manipulate documents within SharePoint, such as uploading, downloading, checking in or out, moving, copying, deleting, or reading, or updating metadata properties. For example, the SharePoint Documents Event Wizard could be used to move a document upon approval, or delete the document if it has been declined. It can also be used to check in a major version of a document upon review and approval. Figure 8-25 shows one screen of the SharePoint Documents Event Wizard, with some of the options that can be performed on a document.

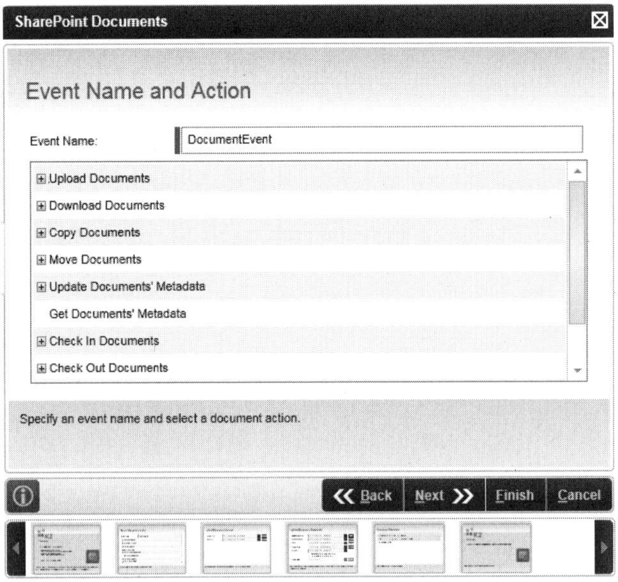

Figure 8-25

❑ **SharePoint Records Management Event:** Send a document to the Record Center or place or release a hold using this wizard. This wizard can be used to send documents to the Record Center, or create a hold. For example, you could create a hold based on a Legal Action workflow, and then create records in the Record Center and place them under that hold. This wizard will only work with Microsoft Office SharePoint Server 2007, as it relies on the records management features of SharePoint. Figure 8-26 shows one screen of the SharePoint Records Management Event Wizard with all the options you could choose from this Event.

**Figure 8-26**

❑ **SharePoint Search Event:** Allows you to search in SharePoint List or Library or across a List or Library Type, and then use the results in the process. You can build elaborate search queries involving multiple fields and Boolean logic. Following the Legal Action workflow example that was previously covered, you could search across the site for all documents with a certain metadata field (for example, where the client matches, or the status is approved), and then store those search results in a content field. Together with the Records Management Event, you could place those documents that met the search criteria on a hold in the records center. The Search Event Wizard will work with both Microsoft Office SharePoint Server 2007 and Windows SharePoint Services 3.0. Figure 8-27 shows one screen of the Search Results Event Wizard, where you enter the Search Filters using fields and Boolean operators to build your search criteria.

Figure 8-27

❑ **SharePoint Publishing Event:** Allows you to create, copy, move, delete, and check in
publishing pages; update and copy page content; and create, update, or delete reusable content.
This wizard will only work with Microsoft Office SharePoint Server 2007, as it relies on the
publishing features of SharePoint. Figure 8-28 shows the various options you can select when
using the SharePoint Publishing Event Wizard.

Figure 8-28

❑ **SharePoint User Management Event:** Allows you to add, change, or delete users, groups, or permissions and change site, list, or library permission inheritance. This Event Wizard can get complicated, as it follows the security mechanisms and the granularity of security properties from SharePoint. In the automated site provisioning workflow example that was previously covered, you could include the User Management Event Wizard to give the Originator of the request access to the newly created site. Figure 8-29 shows one screen of the User Management Event Wizard, where you can select the specific site permissions to grant for a user or group on a SharePoint site.

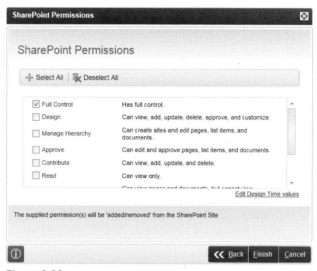

**Figure 8-29**

❑ **SmartObject Event:** Allows you to call a SmartObject method and bind to input or output fields. This event can be used to bind process data to a SmartObject method input to create new records, or to a SmartObject method output for use later in the process. For example, based on a Company Name selected on a form, you may need to pull additional information out of your Customer SmartObject to use in a Mail Event. Figure 8-30 shows one screen in the SmartObject Event Wizard where values from the SmartObject properties are mapped to process data fields.

Figure 8-30

These are the Server Events that are out-of-the-box with K2 blackpearl. Additional wizards can be created using the K2 API and the K2 Wizard framework. For additional information, refer to the K2 Developer Reference.

## IPC Events

IPC Events are a special category of Server Events that allow processes to be called by other processes. This allows for the modular design of processes and allows reuse of common process steps. For example, a parent process will call a child process. There are two types of IPC Events: synchronous and asynchronous.

❏ **Synchronous:** Means that the process will execute in series, meaning that the calling or parent process will wait at this event for the IPC or child process to complete, before it can continue. For example, you are applying for a line of credit on a car. The sales process requires some personal information, this process then performs a synchronous IPC to the credit check process. You now have to wait for the credit check to complete before the sales process is allowed to complete, just in case the client doesn't pass the credit check, in which case they will be unable to purchase the car. A synchronous IPC example is shown in Figure 8-31.

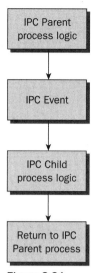

**Figure 8-31**

❑   **Asynchronous:** Means that the two processes can execute in parallel, so the calling or parent process will start the IPC or child process and immediately continue with the next step in the parent process without waiting for a return signal from the child process. For example, think of a purchase order process. Once the request has been approved, the process can hand off the request to a fulfillment process, which in turn checks inventory and fulfills the order, using its own business process and rules. The original purchase order is not concerned with the fulfillment process; therefore it continues on with the invoicing process. This is shown in Figure 8-32.

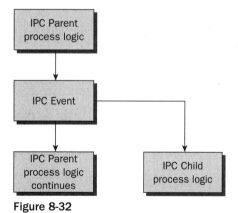

**Figure 8-32**

---

### Important Note about IPCs

The child process is a complete autonomous K2 process, which is defined just like any other K2 process with its own activities, events, lines, and process data fields. The child process definition must already exist before the IPC Server Event can be used. At the time of writing, the child process must also be present in the same Visual Studio solution in order to be called.

---

Due to the fact that the child process is a completely autonomous process, the IPC Event should not be used for creating reusable process modules. The child process must represent a business process within the organization that operates almost independently from the parent business process. You can, however, pass in data fields to the child, as well as pass back return data fields from the child to the parent.

There are several considerations when using IPC Events:

❑ **Incorrect credentials will cause the IPC to fail:** The K2 Server Service Account must have start rights on the child process in order for it to kick-off the process instance. If an IPC fails to start, verify that the permissions are set properly.

❑ **Reporting with IPC Events can be complicated:** With the out-of-the-box K2 reports, you will be able to see that the IPC Event was called, but the data surrounding the activities and events within that IPC process will be stored with the child reporting data, not the parent. Therefore, you will need to create some custom reports in order to show the data from both the parent and child process in a single report.

❑ **Child Processes should be fully operational processes:** IPCs should not be used for parts of processes, but for standalone processes that can be started as steps in other processes. For example, in a car purchasing process, a credit check could be a child process. However, the credit check process could be a standalone process and be started on its own, without having to be called from the parent process.

At the time of writing, there is a limitation within K2 blackpearl that requires the processes to be part of the same K2 project. Therefore, the IPC Event can only call a process on the same physical K2 server where the project has been deployed. Additional information about IPC Events can be found in the K2 blackpearl product documentation.

## Process Execution

When you move from the design environment to the execution environment, you encounter a few new concepts that you need to understand. An understanding of these run-time concepts will also help you in the process design stage.

A workflow process is usually "kicked-off" by a user that completes some kind of form and then submits the form by clicking a Submit button. As soon as the user has submitted the form, the K2 server receives a message that tells the server to Plan or Start a new process. The K2 server will then do this by creating a new Process Instance. From now, the K2 server will push the Process Instance to the various activities by evaluating certain conditions like Line Rules.

As soon as the Process Instance arrives at an activity, the K2 server will create a new Activity Instance. If the activity has any events associated with it, the Server will also create an Event Instance for each event.

During the execution of a process, the K2 server maintains certain properties for each of the Instances that are created. The properties for a Process, Activity, and Event Instance will be discussed next. These properties are surfaced in the K2 Reports and also in the worklist.

## Process Instance

For each Process, the following properties are available per instance during run time:

- ❑ **Process Folio:** A user-friendly name for the Process Instance. It is strongly recommended that the developer assigns a meaningful value to this property. If a value is not assigned to this property by the developer, it will be blank, resulting in all Process Instances having the same Process Folio and making it very difficult to distinguish between the various Process Instances. The Folio also helps users manage their worklists. Think of it as a folder or binder.

- ❑ **Start Date:** The Date and Time when the Process Instance was created, in other words when the user submitted the initial form, for example.

- ❑ **Finish Date:** The Date and Time when the Process reached the last activity in the Process, and K2 flagged the instance as Completed.

- ❑ **Originator:** The name of the user that started this Process Instance, in other words the user that submitted the initial form.

- ❑ **Status:** The current Status of the Process Instance. Possible values include Active, Completed, and Error.

- ❑ **Duration**: How long the process ran or has been running in terms of days, hours, minutes and seconds.

## Activity Instance

For each activity in the process, the following properties are available during run time:

- ❑ **Activity Name:** The name of the activity as defined during design time.

- ❑ **Start Date:** The date and time when the Activity Instance was created.

- ❑ **Finish Date:** The date and time when the activity was flagged as Completed.

- ❑ **Priority:** The priority of this activity as defined during design time. Possible values are High, Medium, and Low.

- ❑ **Status:** The current Status of the Activity Instance. Possible values include Active, Completed, and Error. When an Activity Instance is Active, it is displayed on the worklists of the appropriate users. Note that the Activity Status is different from the status seen in the worklist, which could be Available, Open, or Allocated.

- ❑ **Duration:** How long the activity was or has been active in terms of days, hours, minutes, and seconds.

### Event Instance

For each Event Instance in an activity, the following properties are available during run time:

- ❑ **Event Name:** The name of the event as defined during design time.

- ❑ **Start Date:** The date and time when the Event Instance was created.

- ❑ **Finish Date:** The date and time when the event was completed.

- ❑ **Destination:** Indicates who is responsible for performing this action as defined by the activity's Destination Rule.

- ❑ **Priority:** The Priority of this event as defined during design time. Possible values are High, Medium, and Low.

- ❑ **Status:** The current Status of the Event Instance. Possible values include Active, Completed, and Error.

- ❑ **Duration:** How long the event was or has been active in terms of days, hours, minutes, and seconds.

These properties are surfaced in the K2 Reports and will help communicate the details of what path the process instance followed and each activity and event that the process instance encountered. Therefore, it is critical that you name each activity and event with a descriptive name and give a meaningful Folio for the process instance. Take the time during the designing of your process to identify these titles, keeping in mind that the reports will be the most visible use of these titles and Folios.

## Actions and Outcomes

One of the things you will notice as you build out your K2 blackpearl processes is where you actually set the actions that the User performs and how that action affects the outcome of your activity. So what exactly are actions and outcomes?

Actions and outcomes allow processes to separate what decisions, or actions, users are able to make from the implications, or outcomes, of those actions. Because actions and outcomes are defined outside of the form, maintenance of those decisions and routing logic is simple in K2 blackpearl. In short, *actions* are the decisions that the user can make about the process step. *Outcomes* are K2's way of taking the business decision and deciding where the process moves to next.

Let's discuss a simple example. You have a standard expense claim in your organization that goes through the Finance department. Ask yourself two questions:

1. *What* can Finance do with the Expense Claim?

    - ❑ Approve Request

    - ❑ Decline Request

    - ❑ Query Request

2. What is the possible *outcome(s)* based on Finance's action?

    - ❑ Expense Approved when the business rule is true

❏  Expense Approved but needs further approval (for example, if the first approver's limit is less than the request)

❏  Expense Declined when the business rule is true

❏  Query Expense when the business rule is true

K2 blackpearl allows you to decouple the user interface from the process design. The K2 server will tell the form which actions are available based on the process, and will also tell the form which actions are available to the user. Remember, this concept is called the *context grid*, where only items that the user has permission to see are displayed.

---

### Developer Tip

The form does not store any version information. Using the Workflow.Client API, the worklist object has a collection of actions. You can open the worklist item, pass in the SerialNumber (SN), and retrieve the collection of available actions. Please refer to the K2 Developer Reference or Chapter 11 for code samples on retrieving actions for a worklist item.

---

Based on the action chosen by the user, the outcome of the activity is decided by the K2 server. Regardless of who did what on the form, the process only cares that this outcome evaluates to True, therefore, this is the path to follow. We will talk about configuring lines and rules in a little bit, but the concept that is important here is that you can add new actions without reconfiguring the user interface or the Line Rules, greatly reducing the development time and maintenance of your process.

There are some key points to remember regarding actions and outcomes:

❏  **Action and outcomes are defined in the process, not in the form:**

  ❏  Therefore, if you are adding an action to the process, you do not have to go and change the form; just update the process and the form will pick up the new action.

  ❏  Actions do not care what the user interface is, merely that it exists.

  ❏  Actions and outcomes do not have to be a one-to-one mapping, meaning that one action can trigger multiple outcomes.

❏  **The user interface is rendered automatically with only actions that are available to the user:**

  ❏  The K2 server manages which options are available, based on the process and the user's permissions.

  ❏  Because only the actions that the user can perform are displayed, there is no risk of the user performing an action for which they do not have permission.

  ❏  Because there is no change to the form, there is no risk of a user filling out an "old" version of the form; therefore, no additional training is required.

  ❏  This results in faster development and richer user interfaces.

❏ **Same form can go against multiple versions of the process:**

    ❏ Because the logic is no longer stored in the form, changes to the process logic do not require the User Interface Designer to get involved.

    ❏ Because the form does not change, you do not have to train the users on new forms; no new communications are needed about replacing the form; just update your actions and go!

    ❏ Therefore, the cost to implement and maintain user action logic is dramatically reduced.

Actions and outcomes are defined within the properties of a Client Event. While actions remain part of the event, the outcomes are actually defined within the scope of the activity. So, when a user selects the action in the form, K2 evaluates that action against all of the outcome rules. And, based on the outcome of the activity, the lines are evaluated, and those Line Rules that are True are followed.

We have not discussed lines in detail yet, so let's talk about the various types of lines and rules available in K2 blackpearl.

## The "How"

Lines provide the ability to connect the outcome of one activity in a process to another activity. While a line is a visual representation on the design surface, it also has properties called Line Rules. In fact, many properties of an activity are rules of some kind or another. These Activity Rules represent the tools used to build business logic into the activity, and are the most important properties of an activity.

The set of rules is determined per activity, as shown in Figure 8-33.

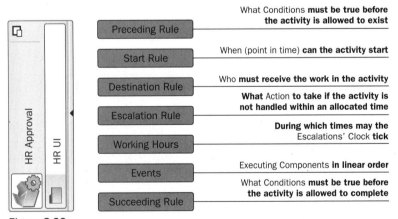

Figure 8-33

The rules follow the order shown in Figure 8-33, and will be described in detail next. As the Activity Rules are defined on the activity, regardless of the events stored within, you can add an empty activity to your design canvas. You can open the Activity Strip by clicking on the down arrow next to the name of the activity or by running the Activity Wizard to see all of the properties of the activity. The Activity Strip, as well as the Activity Wizard icon, is shown in Figure 8-34.

 — Activity Wizard icon

**Figure 8-34**

## *Preceding Rule*

If you want to delay the start of an activity until certain conditions are met, you will define a Preceding Rule. The Preceding Rule is a logical expression that must evaluate to true before an activity can be created. Stated in another way: What conditions must be true before the activity is created for the instance? If the Preceding Rule evaluates to False, none of the other Activity Rules will be evaluated and an instance of the activity will not be created.

A Preceding Rule is not a "wait until this is true" type of rule. Every time a specific line is followed, the Preceding Rule is evaluated once, and if it returns true, then that activity will start (the only remaining question then is when it will start, and that then gets determined by the start rule).

For example, say your process splits into two parallel Activities A and B and then combines them at Activity C. You want both Activity A and B to complete before Activity C is started. You would create a Preceding Rule for Activity C. If Activity A completes, the Line Rule from A to C would evaluate to True, but the Preceding Rule for C would not be true; therefore, Activity C would not begin. Once Activity B completes, the Line Rule from B to C would evaluate to True, and then your Preceding Rule for C would also evaluate to True, and Activity C would begin. Figure 8-35 shows an example of a Preceding Rule based on the previous example.

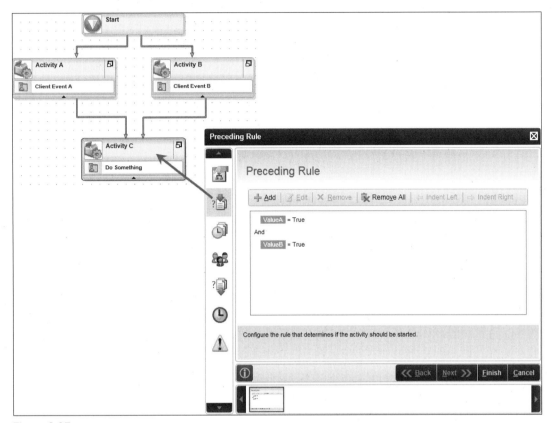

Figure 8-35

Remember, a Preceding Rule is a property of the activity. To set, open the Activity Strip and click on the second icon, or open the activity properties and select the Preceding Rule tab. You can then add your rules based on variables from your process data Fields or SmartObjects, using Boolean logic (And, Or, XOr), and indenting rules to build extensive logic into your Preceding Rule, as shown in Figure 8-36.

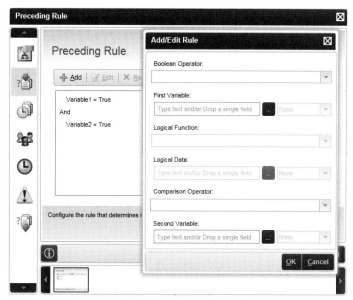

Figure 8-36

## Start Rule

The Start Rule is time-related and dictates when an activity can start. When you think about the Start Rule, think of time. The start of an activity can be delayed by a specified amount of Days, Hours, or Minutes after a base date. The base date can either be the Activity Start Date, or a date value that is kept in a process data or XML field. The Start Rule can only be evaluated if the Preceding Rule evaluated to True.

For example, if you have a business process that should start on the first of every month, use a Start Rule to dictate when the activity should begin. Figure 8-37 shows the Start Rule properties screen. Note that the K2 Object Browser has been expanded by clicking on the arrow on the right-hand side of the wizard. This can be done on any of the K2 wizards to make it easy to drag-and-drop fields onto the wizard screen.

Figure 8-37

## Destination Rule

If the activity involves a Client Event, which in turn has some kind of human interaction, the person or people who are responsible for that event must be specified. By stating who can action the activity, the workflow participants are stored in a Destination Rule. The Destination Rule determines who will receive the events defined in the activity.

We discussed destination users in an earlier section. However, when you set a destination for a Client Event, you are actually modifying the Destination Rule of an activity.

The Destination Rule generally uses the User Browser tab within the K2 Object Browser. This allows you to use users, groups, and roles that have been defined. By default, the User Browser integrates with the configured Security Providers, which out-of-the-box, are Microsoft Active Directory or SQL. Destination Rules can also be one of two types: static or dynamic.

### Static

Static Destination Rules are explicitly defined by dragging a user or group to the destination, as shown in Figure 8-38. You can also mix users, roles and groups into the Destination Users for an activity. However, if you drag a single user into the Destination Rule, if you wish to update the Destination Rule you will need to modify the process definition, make the change, and deploy your process again. This is not a very flexible method, but is very easy when prototyping your process or testing the business logic and routing in your process. You can always go back into the Destination Rule and change to use a dynamic method later.

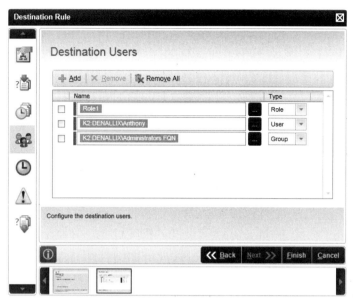

Figure 8-38

## Dynamic

A Dynamic Destination Rule allows the "who will receive the task" to be defined outside of the activity. For example, you can use a process data or XML field as a Destination User. At run time, the value of this data field will be evaluated and the activity will be assigned to the appropriate person or people. This is shown in Figure 8-39.

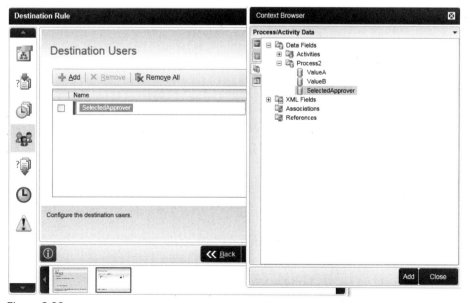

Figure 8-39

Another way of handling Dynamic destinations is by using roles. Although in the Destination Rule, the role will be explicitly defined, because the items that make up that role are defined outside of the process definition, changes can be made without having to export the process again. Roles are defined in the K2 Workspace, as shown in Figure 8-40.

*For more information on how to create roles, please see Chapter 15.*

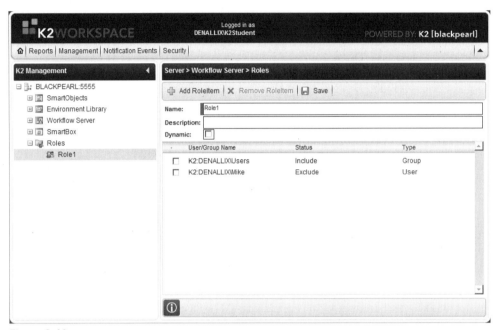

Figure 8-40

## Advanced Destinations

Once the destinations have been defined for the activity, there are some advanced options that can be set. If you go into the Destination Rule page on the Activity Properties, you will see that the Back button is enabled. By clicking Back, you can select to run the Destination Rule wizard in Advanced Mode, which opens up many more options for Destinations.

## Activity Slots

Slots determine how many worklist items can be simultaneously open for the activity. As soon as a user clicks on a worklist item, the status immediately changes from Available to Open and one activity slot is occupied. The number of slots can be limited to a specified number, or a slot can be created for each destination.

For example, creating a slot for each destination can be useful for a voting or collaborative work scenario, which requires all recipients to work on the item. On the Destination Rule Options page, select the "Create a slot for each destination" option, as shown in Figure 8-41. Then, the worklist item will appear on each recipient's worklist, regardless if others have opened it already.

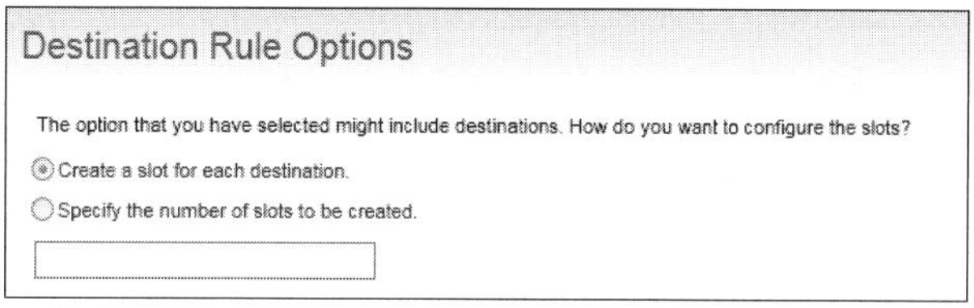

**Figure 8-41**

If no special Succeeding or Line Rules are specified, however, the activity will complete as soon as all of the listed destinations has completed the client event, causing the work item to disappear from all destination users' worklists.

*For more information on some of the advanced destination scenarios, please refer to Chapter 22.*

The other option is to specify the number of slots to be created, as shown in Figure 8-42. For example, if you want to send an item to a group of five people, but only the first two that open the item may work on it, set the number of slots to be created to two.

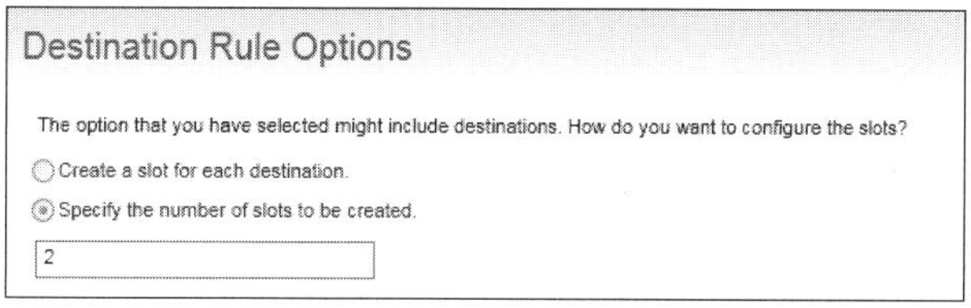

**Figure 8-42**

As soon as the first two users open the work item on their worklists, it is allocated to those users and disappears from the worklist of the other three users.

There are some general guidelines to keep in mind when using multiple slots:

❑ **Succeeding Rule:** If the number of Slots = 1, then no Succeeding Rule is required. However, if the number of Slots > 1, then a Succeeding Rule is required in order to keep the activity from completing before all slots have responded. We will discuss Succeeding Rules in just a bit.

❑ **Data Fields:** Multiple slots will cause the value of a process data field to be overwritten each time a user completes a work item. Use activity data fields to store responses from each user.

❑ **Line Rules:** The Line Rules determine the required direction to follow in the workflow. The direction needs to be modeled around the activity data fields and slots for multiple responses. Line Rules will be discussed in more detail later, but you will need to modify the default Line Rules if you have multiple slots and want the behavior of the process to behave differently based on the activity data fields.

❑ **Actions and Outcomes:** Succeeding Rules and Line Rules are automatically generated and configured according to defined actions and outcomes. By default, all slots will need to select the same action in order for the outcome to evaluate to true. However, this can be changed by modifying the Succeeding Rule.

## Common Scenarios

In order to understand the different Destination Rule options, let's look at a few common scenarios. These scenarios will hopefully help you understand how the slots and Destination Rules can affect the process flow.

Chapter 22 will have additional information on the advanced destination rules. However, there are some common destination options that involve setting destination rules with different slots and combinations, which we will discuss next.

### Scenario #1: First Response Does So for the Group

Figure 8-43 shows an example of Scenario #1. In this scenario, an actor submits a request to multiple destinations simultaneously (A). The first actor to respond to the request (C) does so for the remaining actors (B and D). In this situation, the first response returned from the actors is processed, and the remaining work items are no longer applicable.

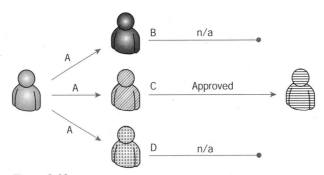

**Figure 8-43**

The First Response approval is beneficial in processes where the request is sent to a destination consisting of a group of people; in our example above, the HR New Hire Role. With a single slot and the default plan (Plan Just Once), as soon as one person opens the worklist item and actions it, the request can continue on in the process without waiting for the others to respond.

### Scenario #2: Process Collectively Unless Declined First

Figure 8-44 shows an example of Scenario #2. In this type of step, an actor submits a request to multiple destinations simultaneously (A). The process requires that each destination in parallel (B, C, and D), review the same items, and provide similar and congruent responses before the request is submitted to the next destination. As responses are received, they are held in a waiting state and verified against the business rule (for example, waiting for the Succeeding Rule to be true). If destination C responds with an action of decline, the entire request is declined and the responses from destinations B and C are nullified.

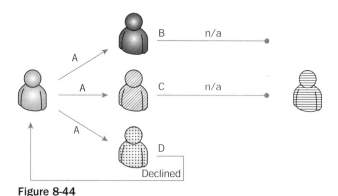

**Figure 8-44**

Scenario #2 is beneficial in situations where a unanimous approval is required. An example might be a purchase agreement that requires engineering, manufacturing, and finance to agree to the terms. Engineering would look at the technical specifications, manufacturing at the service and support terms, and, of course, finance at the financial terms. If any one of these reviews is unsatisfactory then the agreement will need to be renegotiated.

This behavior can be done in K2 blackpearl by adding multiple Destinations to a single activity. The Succeeding Rule would check the actions, and if a "decline" action was performed, the outcome would need to be set appropriately to route the request down the decline path instead of to the next step in the process. Succeeding Rules will be discussed in a little bit.

If, however, you wanted different data to be displayed to each Destination (in this example, engineering, manufacturing and finance), you would need to have three separate activities with three separate Client Events, each mapping to the appropriate user interface.

### Scenario #3: Merge All Responses Before Proceeding

Figure 8-45 shows an example of Scenario #3. In this type of step, an actor submits a request to multiple destinations simultaneously (A). The process requires that each destination in parallel (B, C, and D) reviews the request before the responses are merged together and routed to the next destination.

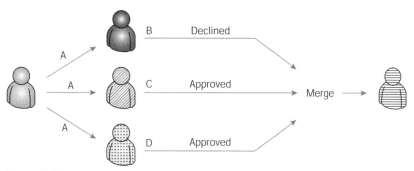

**Figure 8-45**

In this scenario, the process will remain in the step until all destinations have provided input. If one destination is lax in its response, this may delay this specific step and lengthen the overall duration of the process. A classic real-world scenario is an editorial review process where an author submits an article to multiple reviewers, who, in turn, pass along their recommendation to the editor for final review.

In the preceding scenario, you will need to store any data in activity fields rather than process data fields to prevent each destination user from overwriting the others' responses. The Succeeding Rule would wait for all destinations to respond, meaning all slots have responded, but regardless of the actions selected, the process would continue on to the next step.

### Scenario# 4: Merge Similar Responses and Proceed Immediately

Figure 8-46 shows an example of Scenario #4. In this type of step, an actor submits a request to multiple destinations simultaneously (A). The process requires each destination in parallel (B, C, and D) to review specific data within separate sections of the request. Similar responses (for example, approvals) are merged together and routed to the next activity, while other actions (for example, declines) are routed to a different activity.

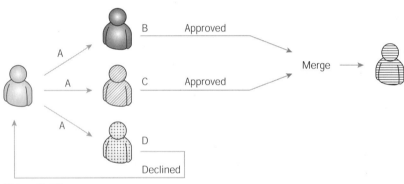

**Figure 8-46**

An example of this type of process is a procurement request. In this example, a hiring manager submits a request for a PC, a phone, and an office chair for a new employee. This request is routed to IT, Communications and Office Supply, where the PC and phone are immediately available and sent on for provisioning. The office chair is unfortunately on back order, and will have to be procured in another way.

While the Succeeding Rule would wait for all slots to respond, the process could go down multiple paths once it has completed this activity. This would be handled with Line Rules, which will be discussed in a later section.

### Additional Information about Destinations

When working with Dynamic destinations such as roles and multiple slots, the behavior of the activity can become very complicated. It helps to write down the desired behavior of the activity when doing your process design. For example, in an HR new hire approval workflow, the activity could go to the entire HR department for processing. However, the first one that opens the worklist item and actions will complete the activity, and the rest of the department should no longer see the worklist item. This would correspond to a Destination Rule where the HR New Hire Role is used for the destination, and the default behavior of a single slot is desired. If however, you required two HR approvals before the activity could complete, you would need to change the number of slots created. The Succeeding Rule should then wait for the two slots to be completed before firing.

## Escalation Rule

Your organization might have a business rule that states a specific activity must be completed within eight (8) hours; if not, some special action must be taken. The Escalation Rule is used to specify when and how this special action takes place.

We will discuss escalations in a later section. However, when you set an escalation you are actually modifying the Escalation Rule of an activity.

## Succeeding Rule

A Succeeding Rule is a logical expression that must evaluate to true before an activity can be completed. Stated in another way: What conditions must be true before the activity is allowed to end?

The logic for when the activity is complete is stored in this rule. This idea ties to the outcomes that were discussed previously. The Succeeding Rule cares about what the outcome of the activity was, but not who actioned it or selected which option in a form. The Succeeding Rule defines the outcome of the activity, which is what the Line Rules that were automatically generated by K2 blackpearl use to evaluate which Line Rules should be followed.

Succeeding Rules are extremely important if you have multiple Activity Slots. A Succeeding Rule can be thought of as the following equation:

```
Succeed (Complete Activity) =
    (Conditions you define) OR (All Worklist Items = Complete)
```

For one slot the Succeeding Rule will evaluate to True as soon as the user completes his work item, regardless of the Condition you defined.

A Succeeding Rule can be used for multiple approvals. For example, a form is sent to three managers for approval. It is required that at least two managers approve, and none reject the form. If the first manager rejects it, the Succeeding Rule can immediately complete the activity, without waiting for the other managers to respond. If the first manager approves the form, the Succeeding Rule will wait for a second approval before completing the activity, leaving the worklist item available for the other managers.

## Line Rules

In addition to the above rules, which are, in effect, properties on the activity, you can also create Line Rules. These are rules that are properties of the Line on the design canvas and can be used to route the business logic for the process. These Line Rules generally occur in a workflow process in a junction point, where the process can flow into one or more directions depending on certain conditions. These are indicated with lines, and conditions are constructed using Line Rules.

When we discussed actions and outcomes in an earlier section, we assumed that if an outcome resolved to True, then that path was followed in the process map. The way that K2 blackpearl handles this is by defining a Line Rule that basically says "If this outcome is true, then this line is also true." By default, K2 blackpearl will create Line Rules that map to each outcome in order to help you quickly design your process. This can be seen in Figure 8-47.

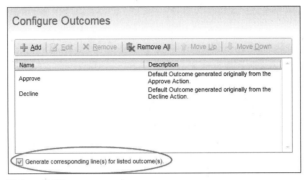

**Figure 8-47**

These default lines will help you easily map your process, and if new actions and outcomes are added to a particular activity, you can generate lines for the newly added option. You can also add new lines, or edit these default lines, to add additional business logic. Basically, if we want the process to follow a specific route we would write a conditional statement that would evaluate to True. On the other hand, the same conditional statement must evaluate to False, if that route must not be followed.

Line Rules are configured by right-clicking on the line and clicking Properties. On the Line Rule Property page of the wizard, you will see the Line Rule that was automatically generated based on the outcome. You can edit or add new conditions to this Line Rule, as shown in Figure 8-48.

**Figure 8-48**

A Line Rule can consist of multiple statements connected with Boolean AND, OR, and XOR operators. Because of operator precedence you will, under certain conditions, want to group statements together with brackets. Consider the following Binary Operations table, and notice the difference in the results columns.

| f1 | f2 | f3 | f1 OR f2 AND f3 | (f1 OR f2) AND f2 |
|----|----|----|-----------------|-------------------|
| 0  | 0  | 0  | 0               | 0                 |
| 0  | 0  | 1  | 0               | 0                 |
| 0  | 1  | 0  | 0               | 0                 |
| 0  | 1  | 1  | 1               | 1                 |
| 1  | 0  | 0  | 1               | 0                 |
| 1  | 0  | 1  | 1               | 1                 |
| 1  | 1  | 0  | 1               | 0                 |
| 1  | 1  | 1  | 1               | 1                 |

You can also indent the operators to create complicated logic statements. Be sure to test each branch in your process definition during the testing phase of your project, to ensure that the process follows the correct path based on the Line Rule logic. It is very easy to make a simple mistake in your Boolean logic that will cause certain branches in your process to never fire.

## The "When"

Once a Process Instance has started, it will basically flow through the defined process using the activities, events, and lines as the map. There are a few K2 features though, that you can use to help the request move smoothly through the process, in particular, escalations and notifications.

### Escalations

One great advantage of automating a business process is the fact that we can, with absolute precision, tell when a specific activity was started. This enables us to enforce a business rule that states how long the activity should take to complete. If the activity takes longer to complete than the expected time, we can use escalations to raise an alert of some kind. The Escalation Rule for an activity determines what must happen if an activity is not completed within a specified time.

The escalation principle applies to both a process and an activity, since an activity that is not completed will prevent an entire process from not completing. Therefore, escalations can be configured at process and activity level.

There are two types of Escalation Rules:

❑ **Escalate On:** Enables the process designer to select either a specific date or a dynamic date. The escalation can be extended further by enabling the option to be repeated.

    ❑ Specifying an escalation date hardcodes a date and/or time by which the escalation will occur. The disadvantage with this option is that once the date is reached, the process will need to be redeployed to the server for new instances of the process to be created. The Specific date functions the same as a hardcoded value. Unless it is changed, the escalation will take place if the date specified has expired.

    ❑ The Dynamic Date option allows dates to come from SmartObjects or process or XML data fields where a date field is provided and the escalation is dependent on the value contained therein.

❑ **Escalate After:** This option is best suited for reusable, short duration escalations, for example, submitting a support request or leave request, where a response is expected within a short time and the lack of action requires a short-term escalation.

    ❑ The Escalate After rule template configures escalations in days, hours, minutes, and seconds. The escalation can be repeated. For example, escalate after eight hours, three times.

    ❑ All fields can be configured using dynamic fields, including SmartObjects or process data or XML fields.

An Escalation Rule determines what to do if the process or activity is not completed within the allocated time. Multiple Escalation Rules can be configured for a single process or activity. An escalation is linked to time elapsed from the start of the process or activity. And, if working hours have been defined, escalations are linked to working hours as well.

## Escalation Types

There are several types of escalations. For processes, activities, and events, the following escalation types are available:

❑ **Default Escalation:** Configures the default escalation.

❑ **E-mail:** Configures an e-mail sent to a recipient for the purpose of managing the process escalation. This can be used as a reminder e-mail that the worklist item is still waiting for action.

At a process level, you can also use an escalation to change the flow of the process:

❑ **Goto Activity:** Configures the process to expire the current activity and move onto the specified activity. For example, you can move the process instance from the Frontline Manager Approval Activity to the Department Manager Approval Activity.

At an activity level, two additional templates are available:

❑ **Expire Activity:** Configures the process to expire the current activity.

❑ **Redirect Activity:** Configures the process to redirect the activity to a different destination user.

You can also use .NET code to manipulate the rule or the escalation action. After you've defined the escalation, you can view the code, as shown in Figure 8-49. The action code can be manipulated using a Windows Workflow Foundation (WF) schedule. The Default Escalation will stub out an empty WF schedule for you to drop the activities you wish to customize the escalation. The rule code also will create a WF schedule, with the rule code embedded as C# code.

Figure 8-49

## When to Use Escalations

Escalations can be effective tools to ensure that your process continues to move forward. For example, escalations can be used to send a reminder e-mail eight (8) working hours after the task has been assigned to a destination user. This reminder e-mail can be sent to the originator as well, to let them know that their request has not been acted upon. Perhaps this reminder happens for three days, after which the task is redirected to an additional user, perhaps to the destination user's manager.

Escalations also can be done on a process level, to perhaps e-mail the K2 administrator or process owner that the request has not completed in a timely manner. In this way, the K2 process can be proactive in letting the administrator or process owner know that there may be an issue, rather than having to watch each process instance closely for bottlenecks.

## *Notifications*

On each Client Event, there is an option to send a notification of the event to the destination user. By default, this notification is an e-mail message, but this can be configured to use other notification engines. This notification is important to factor in to your process design. If you choose not to send a notification to the destination user, how will they know they have a task item? Only if the user accesses their worklist, either through the K2 Workspace or the Worklist Web part, will they see the new worklist item.

Beyond notifying a destination user they have a worklist item, notifications can be important in two other aspects:

❑ **E-mail Events:** Use the Mail Event to send an e-mail. It can be used in any activity and can use any process data or XML fields. This type is used within the process design.

❑ **Notification Designer:** The Notification Designer in the K2 Workspace allows anyone with Process Rights to create additional notifications outside of the process design. Additional information about the Notification Designer can be found in Chapter 20.

It is important to factor in notifications in the process design for several reasons:

❑ To notify the destination user of a worklist task needing action

❑ To remind the destination user that they have not actioned the item in a certain period of time

❑ To keep key stakeholders in the business process informed at each step in the process

❑ To keep the originator informed of their request as it moves through the process

## Working Hours

Working hours can be defined at the K2 server level. This allows the K2 administrator to set up the hours in which to count for escalations and start rules. Remember that you can set escalations on a time basis, meaning that if a user has not actioned the item in a certain time period, an escalation can be performed. Working hours allow you to set up zones to determine when an escalation should be active. The zone also takes into consideration in which time zone the destination user resides.

For example, if your standard business hours are 8 A.M. to 5 P.M., if a request is submitted at 6 P.M. with a 2-hour escalation, the escalation clock does not start until 8 a.m. the following morning. This is important for businesses with set office working hours; for 24x7 Help Desks, this may not be as important.

When setting an escalation, you can choose which zone to use. It is important to remember what the destination of the activity is and select the appropriate zone accordingly.

Working Hours determine during which hours and on which days the "escalation clock" is ticking. Working Hours are configured through the Management Console using Zones.

### Zones

Zones are configured to a Greenwich Mean Time (GMT) zone and have standard working hours for a seven-day week. You can configure the working hours, special dates, and exception dates per zone. More information on configuring zones can be found in Chapter 15.

### Special and Exception Dates

Exception dates can be created for public holidays or all-hands meetings. Special dates can also be configured to set hours where the group is not working, for example at town hall meetings or department-wide meetings. Chapter 15 will also describe special dates in more detail.

# Advanced Process Design

There is another type of workflow design that is common when working with workflow solutions but does not fit the "normal" view of workflow steps.

There are a number of design cases in workflow solutions where the "order of steps" is not known or cannot be determined at design time. An example of this is where certain steps might occur more than once (for example, a specific manager needs to keep reviewing a document until conditions have been met), or where the user is involved in determining the next step of flow of events (for example, a user might wish to route a document directly to the regional manager instead of the departmental manager).

Frequently, during these types of solutions, the workflow designer attempts to solve this by linking each workflow step to each of the possible next steps in the process. However, this can result in a very complex spaghetti workflow process with lines linking everywhere. There, in order to clean up this "ad hoc" style workflow, one of the possible solutions is the Spider Workflow approach.

## Using the Spider Workflow Approach

To some degree, the Spider Workflow approach has been overhyped as the silver bullet for ad hoc workflow. However, this is a logical approach for flexible workflow design, which is why it is discussed here. This solution is very difficult to report on, because of the vast number of Routing Step instances, which makes it difficult to accurately measure the the process. However, with its flexible design, it is a viable solution for ad hoc workflow.

Spider Workflow is a workflow design approach in which the workflow gets handled by a central "router" hub step, and a number of single "spoke" steps. Using this approach, the workflow design is centered on an intelligent central hub step that determines which step (or steps) the workflow should route to next.

The Spider Workflow design could also be described as a hub-and-spoke design.

During the workflow run time, the request will be routed from one spoke to another, until a specific condition is met such that the workflow is complete. In this manner, any spoke can follow a previous one (or even the same spoke more than once if required).

## Building a Spider Workflow

Referring to the diagram shown in Figure 8-50, the Spider Workflow is implemented using the Routing Step as the central activity of the process. This is an activity that contains a single Server Event that evaluates data in order to set an Outcome data field. Each line that emerges from the Routing Step contains a simple Line Rule that checks the value of Outcome to establish whether it needs to be followed or not.

For example, the line that runs from the Routing Step Activity to the Manager Approval Activity could have a Line Rule that checks whether Outcome = Manager Approval, and if true, the Manager Approval Activity would be the next step.

This can continue indefinitely until an exit condition is met. For example, again referring to Figure 8-50, the process might need to continue until all four parties (Manager, Finance, Regional Manager, and CEO) have approved a specific document. In this case, the Routing Step would evaluate the Approval data fields, and if all four of them are set to Approved. then it would set the Outcome data field to Continue, potentially exiting the spider portion and continuing on in the process.

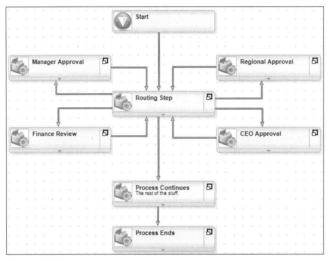

Figure 8-50

## Watching the Spider in Action (an Example)

Because this can be a difficult process definition to understand, let's take a look at an example. This example uses a Corporate Policy Approval process. The originator submits a new policy document to start the process. By default, if the originator does not specify the first approver, the process follows a default order (Manager > Regional > Finance > CEO). So this request is routed to the Manager Approval activity.

The Manager takes a look at the document but feels that the policy is too expensive, so they specify on the form presented that the task must be routed to Finance next. After submitting the form, the Routing Step evaluates the data fields set by the Manager, and routes the task to the Finance Review step.

The Finance team reviews the document and approves the request, but they do not specify the next approver. The Routing Step checks the default order, notices that the Manager has already approved and the next default person is the Regional Manager, so then the request is routed to the Regional Manager.

The Regional Manager is happy with the request, but they see from the process history that the Manager routed it directly to Finance with some concerns. Therefore, the Regional Manager adds some additional comments, and routes it back to the Manager to review the document again.

The Manager gets the document (for the second time), reviews the approval history and comments, and is now satisfied with the document and therefore approves it again. The Routing Step now determines that the only person that has not seen the document is the CEO, so the request is routed to CEO Approval.

The CEO has a look at the request, sees everyone else has approved the document, and approves it.

At this point, the process reaches a specific condition where the Routing Step evaluates all the requirements and establishes that everyone who needs to approve the request has already done so. Therefore, the request is now routed to the Process Continues Activity (where the document might be uploaded to SharePoint, and the originator notified).

This is just a simple run-through of a single process; however, it should be apparent that this process can be approved in any order, any number of times, all driven by the conditions coded into the Routing Step server event.

## *Extending the Design*

This design can be taken further than the simple scenario painted in the previous section. It is relatively easy to extend this solution to allow parallel approvals in the workflow. There is no reason why this document cannot be reviewed by the Regional Manager and by Finance at the same time. The logic in the Routing Step needs to be modified to handle the parallel processing. The process can get as complex as required, and the exit condition will always be "if all conditions have been met, the process can continue."

Extending the design further, the spoke steps could be IPC Events to additional processes. There is a downside to this approach, where the data is passed back to the parent process only after the child process has completed. However, by using SmartObjects to encapsulate the data, this downside is eliminated as SmartObjects can be accessed and updated from anywhere.

# Summary

You have now been introduced to all of the pieces of the K2 process puzzle. You have learned about pawn diagrams, and how translating boxes to people helps with the communication and change management aspects of process automation. You have also learned about the "who," (actors and roles), the "what" (activities, events, actions, and outcomes), the "when" (escalations and notifications), and the "how" (Activity Lines, including Destination Rules and Line Rules) with respect to process design. In the next chapter, you will build your first K2 blackpearl process and put some of these concepts into practice.

# 9

# Creating Your First Workflow

Sergio Del Piccolo

K2 allows for rapid development of process-driven applications using a multitude of tools. Workflows can easily be designed using canvases that allow for graphical development through dragging and dropping of activities. These activities are made up of events and can be joined through connectors known as lines. The graphical output is an illustrated process that is easy to understand, hiding any code that may be required.

Because the solution development lifecycle requires a team comprised of different skills, K2 has developed workflow designers that are aimed at different roles within the team. The K2 Designer for Visio is aimed at the business analyst using a tool that they are familiar with, Microsoft Office Visio 2007. The K2 Designer for Visual Studio is aimed at developers who are not intimidated by Microsoft Visual Studio, and similarly the K2 Designer for SharePoint is aimed at SharePoint business users developing in SharePoint. The folks at K2 have also created a fourth designer, the K2 Studio for developers who do not have Microsoft Visual Studio.

This chapter focuses on creating a workflow using the K2 Designer for Visual Studio. The K2 Designer for Visual Studio is the most sophisticated of the workflow designers, providing an extensive feature set. It allows for the creation of simple workflows, SmartObjects, and complex process-driven applications. Understanding how to use the K2 Designer for Visual Studio creates the necessary foundation required for the development of your applications, regardless of the Designer used.

> *For more information on using alternative design tools like SharePoint and Visio see Chapters 13 and 14.*

This chapter covers workflow implementation using the K2 Designer for Visual Studio. Specifically it:

❑ Introduces the K2 Designer for Visual Studio IDE.

❑ Covers the fundamentals required to construct the workflow: activities, events and lines.

❑ Examines the wizards included for integration into back-end systems.

*At the time of writing the K2 Designer for Visual Studio supports Microsoft Visual Studio 2005. The folks at K2 have informed me that a release for Visual Studio 2008 is planned and should be available by the time this book is published.*

# Getting Started with the K2 Designer for Visual Studio

Open the K2 Designer for Visual Studio by choosing Start ⇨ All Programs ⇨ K2 blackpearl ⇨ K2 Designer for Visual Studio. This launches Microsoft Visual Studio. Next, create a new project by choosing File ⇨ New ⇨ Project. A dialog box appears (as shown in Figure 9-1) with a list of project types to select from. Select K2.

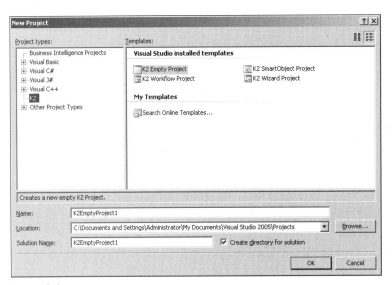

Figure 9-1

There are four K2 templates available when creating a new project, each described in more detail in the following table:

| Template Name | Template Function |
|---|---|
| K2 Empty Project | Creates a new empty K2 Project. |
| K2 SmartObject Project | Creates a new K2 SmartObject Project with a K2 SmartObject (see Chapter 7 for more information on SmartObjects). |
| K2 Workflow Project | Creates a new K2 Workflow Project with a new process. |
| K2 Wizard Project | Creates a new K2 Wizard Integration Project. |

Select the K2 Workflow Project and give the project the following name: **InformationRequest**. Click OK.

A new solution file (InformationRequest.sln) will be created. A subfolder will be created containing the K2 project file (InformationRequest.k2proj) and process file (Process1.kprx).

In the Solution Explorer, right-click the process file (Process1.kprx), and rename it **InformationRequest**.

# Introducing the Visual Studio IDE

The K2 solution and workflow project are created and a new process file is created. Figure 9-2 shows what the Visual Studio IDE will look like.

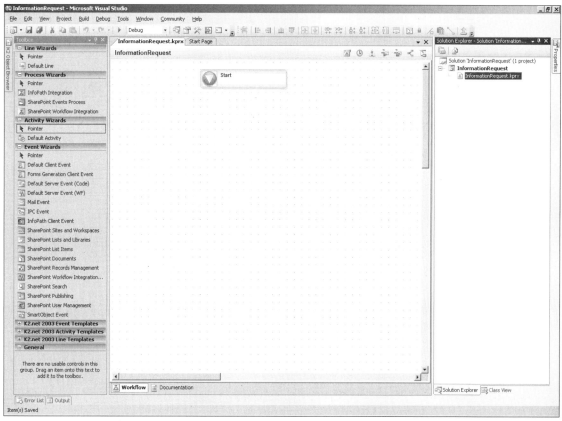

Figure 9-2

Visual Studio contains the following K2 artifacts.

## K2 Studio Designer Toolbar

If the K2 Studio Designer toolbar is not shown by default, using the Visual Studio menu, navigate to View ⇨ Toolbars and select K2 Studio Designer. The toolbar is shown in Figure 9-3.

Figure 9-3

The following table describes the buttons that make up the K2 Studio Designer toolbar.

| Button | Name | Description |
|---|---|---|
| | Align to Grid | Aligns the selected items to the grid. |
| | Align Lefts | Aligns the selected items to the left. |
| | Align Rights | Aligns the selected items to the right. |
| | Align Bottoms | Aligns the selected items to the bottom of the grid. |
| | Align Tops | Aligns the selected items to the top of the grid. |
| | Center Horizontally | Centers the selected items horizontally. |
| | Center Vertically | Centers the selected items vertically. |
| | Decrease Horizontal Spacing | Decreases the horizontal spacing between the selected items. |
| | Increase Horizontal Spacing | Increases the horizontal spacing between the selected items. |
| | Decrease Vertical Spacing | Decreases the vertical spacing between the selected items. |
| | Increase Vertical Spacing | Increases the vertical spacing between the selected items. |
| | Make Same Size | Alters the size of the selected items so that they are all the same size. |

| Button | Name | Description |
|---|---|---|
| | Make Same Height | Alters the height of the selected items so that they are all the same height. |
| | Make Same Width | Alters the width of the selected items so that they are all the same width. |
| | View Code | Shows the XML version of the process .kprx file. |
| | Lock Controls | Locks the selected objects on the design canvas. |
| | Toggle Line Mode | Switches drawing mode from selection to line drawing. Line drawing can also be accomplished by alternate-click drawing. |
| | Collect Copy | Copies an image to the clipboard of items that are selected using a selection box. |
| | Connect Activities | Connects the selected activities with Line Rules. |
| | Deploy | Builds the process and starts the Deploy Project Wizard. |

## K2 Object Browser

The K2 Object Browser displays K2 objects and user-defined objects available to the developer during the development process. These objects include third-party line-of-business (LOB) systems or K2 Objects created by the developers. The K2 Object Browser is shown in Figure 9-4.

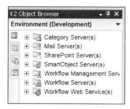

Figure 9-4

The following table describes the tabs contained by the K2 Object Browser:

| Browser | Description |
| --- | --- |
| Environment | Allows for the configuration and maintenance of the working environments of K2 blackpearl. It lists the various servers and services available for configuration and use by the workflow. It also allows the developer to toggle between the various environments, for example, Development, Staging, and Production. |
| User | Lists all of the Users, Groups, and Roles available for use by the workflow. The Users and Groups information is hosted in Active Directory, while roles can be created using the Management Console in the K2 Workspace. |
| Process/Activity Data | Allows for the management of all Process and Activity Data within the workflow. Simply put, Process Data contains data that is available to the workflow for the entire duration of the process instance. Activity Data contains data that is only available during the course of the activity being completed. |
| Workflow Context | Manages the process instances, activities, activity destinations, events, and lines. |

## The Environment Browser

The Environment Browser is used to manage the servers and services that host the K2 Platform resources. A default development environment is used to populate with the desired servers and services used during the development phase. Additional environments can be created that represent the other physical environments, for example, staging and production. This makes it simple to switch between the different environments. Figure 9-5 shows the Environment Browser.

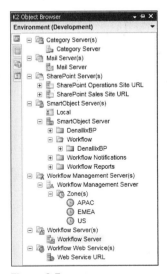

Figure 9-5

The following table describes the servers and services contained in the Environment Browser:

| Server/Services | Description |
| --- | --- |
| Category Server | Provides the hierarchical system for deploying processes and SmartObjects as well as for categorizing reports and notifications. |
| Mail Server | The mail server(s) used by the environment to send e-mail notifications. |
| SharePoint Server | The SharePoint(s) server used by the environment. The SharePoint server node can be expanded to display the lists, document libraries, and so on as subnodes. |
| SmartObject Server | Displays the SmartObjects from the SmartObject server and the local environment. The SmartObject nodes can be expanded to display their methods as subnodes. |
| Workflow Web Service | Displays the Workflow Web Service(s) connection details. |
| Workflow Management Server | Displays the Workflow Management Server(s) connection details. |
| Workflow Server | Displays the Workflow Server(s) connection details. |

To toggle between the environments click on the downward arrow next to the tab name, in this case Environment (Development). Select Environments, which expands to a submenu that lists all of the available environments. Select the desired environment.

## The User Browser

The User Browser exposes all of the Active Directory Users and Groups. While the default provider is Active Directory, other options exist. One that is simple to use is the SQL User Manager. It is installed when K2 blackpearl is configured in the form of a database called K2SQLUM. It is permissible to edit the data within this database to set up your users and groups. The provider used to connect to the User Browser is also extendable allowing developers to create a custom user provider. This is useful should you want to connect to a LOB system that manages your users. The User Browser is shown in Figure 9-6.

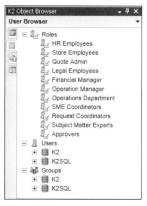

Figure 9-6

The following table describes the contents of the User Browser:

| User | Description |
|------|-------------|
| Roles | K2 Roles (defined in the K2 Management Console) |
| Users | Active Directory Users |
| Groups | Active Directory Groups |

## The Process/Activity Data Browser

The Process/Activity Browser exposes all of the data fields and XML Fields that have been defined for the processes and activities. It also exposes the SmartObject Associations and References. Figure 9-7 shows the Process/Activity Data Browser.

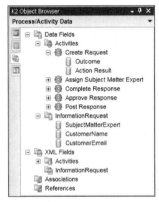

Figure 9-7

The following table describes the contents of the Process/Activity Data Browser in more detail:

| Data | Description |
|------|-------------|
| Data Fields | Data Fields contain custom information related to an activity or process. The activities and processes are displayed as nodes, which in turn can be expanded to display the data fields as subnodes. |
| XML Fields | XML Fields contain custom XML nodes related to an activity or process. The activities and processes are displayed as nodes, which can be expanded to display the XML fields as subnodes. |
| Associations | Associations provide the mapping between SmartObject properties and process data fields. |
| References | Provides a way to add references to SmartObject methods to more easily use SmartObject properties throughout the design of the process. |

To add new data fields, right-click the desired Activity, Process, Associations, or References node, and select Add.

## The Workflow Context Browser

The Workflow Context Browser exposes the workflow instance related fields, as shown in Figure 9-8.

Figure 9-8

The following table describes the contents of the Workflow Context Browser in more detail:

| Instance | Description |
| --- | --- |
| Process | Displays the process instance properties as subnodes. |
| Activity | Displays the activity instance properties as subnodes. |
| Activity Destination | Displays the activity destination properties as subnodes. |
| Event | Displays the event instance properties as subnodes. |
| Line | Displays the line instance properties as subnodes. |

# K2 Toolbox Items

The K2 Toolbox contains K2 blackpearl wizard and components. The following table describes the Toolbox contents in more detail:

| Items | Description |
| --- | --- |
| **Line Wizards** | |
| Default Line | Used in connecting activities to each other. Contains business logic used to control the process flow between activities. |
| **Process Wizards** | |
| InfoPath Integration | Provides the ability to incorporate one or more InfoPath form templates into the workflow to be used as a user interface for workflow actors. |
| SharePoint Events Process | Provides the ability to associate a workflow process with SharePoint list and library events. |
| SharePoint Workflow Integration | Provides the ability to integrate a K2 workflow with SharePoint workflows. K2 blackpearl workflows can be started using the SharePoint browser and Office applications in addition to the K2 Workspace. |
| **Activity Wizards** | |
| Default Activity | Provides a container for workflow events. Events within the activity are processed in the order that they have been added. Events can be moved up or down within an activity. |
| **Event Wizards** | |
| Default Client Event | Defines the user interface for actors to participate in the workflow, for example, a pointer to a Web page. |
| Forms Generation Client Event | Creates a client event and a Web form for user interaction. |
| Default Server Event (Code) | Provides the ability to have a code module that runs on the K2 server. |
| Default Server Event (WF) | Provides the ability to have a Windows Workflow Foundation (WF) module that runs on the K2 server. |
| Mail Event | Creates an e-mail that will be sent by the K2 Server to the relevant parties. |
| IPC Event | Creates an Interprocess Communication (IPC) connection between multiple workflow processes. |
| InfoPath Client Event | Creates an interaction between the process activities and InfoPath forms used as the user interface for workflow actors. |

| Items | Description |
|---|---|
| **Event Wizards** | |
| SharePoint Sites and Workspace | Configures SharePoint sites and workspaces, allowing the workflow to manipulate the sites and workspaces. This includes creating and deleting sites and workspaces. |
| SharePoint Lists and Libraries | Configures SharePoint lists and libraries, allowing the workflow to manipulate the lists and libraries. This includes creating and deleting lists and libraries. |
| SharePoint List Item | Used to create, update, delete, and load metadata from SharePoint lists. |
| SharePoint Document | Configures SharePoint Document Library items, allowing the workflow to upload, delete, move, copy, and load documents from the library. |
| SharePoint Records Management | Configures SharePoint Records Center items, allowing the workflow to send a document to the center, place, and release holds on documents, and delete records. |
| SharePoint Workflow Integration Client | Creates an interaction between the process activities and K2 SharePoint forms used as the user interface for workflow actors. |
| SharePoint Search | Creates a result set of SharePoint documents and/or list items based on search criteria to be used in a workflow process. |
| SharePoint Publishing | Used to create, move, copy, and remove a published page within SharePoint. |
| SharePoint User Manager Server | Used to add and remove SharePoint users and groups. It also manages permissions and resets inheritance. |
| SmartObject Event | Used to execute any SmartObject method, read or write. |

## *K2 Design Canvas*

The K2 Design Canvas provides a drag-and-drop environment to facilitate workflow design. Activities, events, and Line Rules can be dragged from the K2 Toolbox onto the canvas.

# Implementing the Workflow

The workflow that we are going to use for the duration of this chapter is an automated way of dealing with information requests received by a firm and how they deal with responding to the requests. This is a common practice at many large enterprises that need to conform to legislative requirements or stringent corporate governance policies.

## *Workflow Overview*

In most cases when a developer has to start developing a process-driven application such as this, they work from a workflow diagram of the process. Figure 9-9 shows the workflow design that we're going to use to create our first process-driven application using K2 blackpearl.

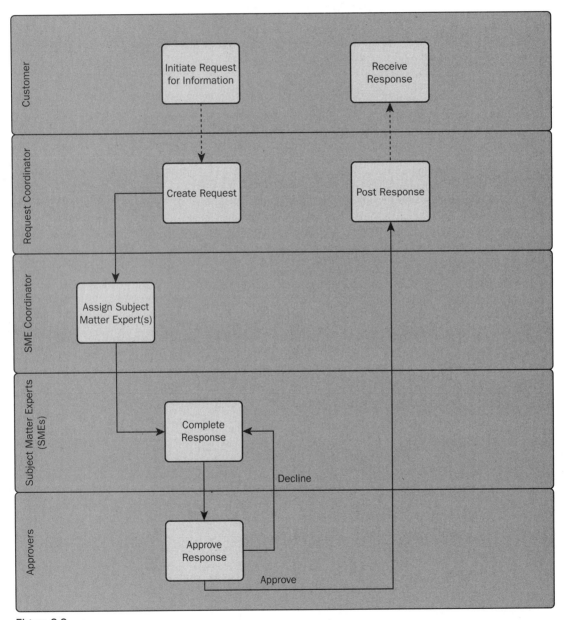

Figure 9-9

The following table explains the workflow and its activities in more detail:

| Activity | Actor | Description |
| --- | --- | --- |
| Initiate Request for Information | Customer | The Customer will initiate a request for information from the enterprise. This can be done manually through an e-mail, a telephone call, or a Web site. We can even have the Web site kick-off the workflow, but for now we'll keep it simple and assume that the Customer will contact the Request Coordinator through e-mail. |
| Create Request | Request Coordinator | Once the Request Coordinator receives the request, they enter the customer's information and start a new instance of the workflow. |
| Assign Subject Matter Expert | Subject Matter Expert (SME) Coordinator | The workflow will create a new task for the SME Coordinator to assign a Subject Matter Expert who will respond to the Information request. |
| Complete Response | Subject Matter Expert | Once the SME Coordinator has assigned the Subject Matter Expert, a new task will be generated for the Subject Matter Expert to complete a response. Once the SME has completed the response, they mark the task as completed and submit it. |
| Approve Response | Approver | A new task is generated for the Approver to approve the Subject Matter Expert's completed response. The Approver has the option to approve or decline the task. If they approve, then a new task is generated for the Request Coordinator to post the response. If they decline, a new task is generated for the Subject Matter Expert to complete their response. |
| Post Response | Request Coordinator | Once the Approver has approved the Subject Matter Expert's completed response, a new task is generated for the Request Coordinator to post the completed response to the customer. Once this has been completed the process ends. |
| Receive Response | Customer | The Customer receives the response from the enterprise regarding their request for information. |

## Adding Roles

The process has a number of roles that each actor falls into as they complete their task. K2 blackpearl provides a way of creating roles and adding users or groups to each role. These roles can be managed from the Management Console and negate the need for Active Directory Groups to be created. Roles contain RoleItems, which are made up of Active Directory Users or Groups, SmartObject queries, or users and groups from a custom user provider. The SQL user provider is supported out of the box, and roles can include or exclude users from multiple user providers.

We're going to add Active Directory Users to our roles. To add the role, navigate to the K2 Workspace (Start ⇨ All Programs ⇨ K2 blackpearl ⇨ K2 Workspace) and navigate to the Management Console (shown in Figure 9-10). On the Management Console, expand the Server and right-click on the Roles. Click Add New Role, enter the role name and description, and add the RoleItems.

Add the following four roles with RoleItems:

| Role Name | Description | RoleItems to Add |
|---|---|---|
| Request Coordinators | Coordinates the Requests for Information received from customers. | Mike (Active Directory User) |
| SME Coordinators | Assigns the Subject Matter Experts to Requests for Information. | Anthony (Active Directory User) |
| Subject Matter Experts | Subject Matter Experts responsible for completion of Information Request responses. | Codi (Active Directory User) |
| Approvers | Approves responses to Information Requests prepared by Subject Matter Experts. | Mike (Active Directory User) |

The end result should look like Figure 9-10.

Figure 9-10

## Testing with Roles

One approach that can be taken to initially test the workflow in a development environment is to add your Active Directory User account as the only RoleItem on each Role. This means that you are the only actor on all of the process activities, and as you step through the activities, the next task generated will be assigned to you. This provides a great way to test the logic of your application. However, when setting up the quality assurance (QA), staging, and production environments, make sure to add different users to Roles.

Another approach is to add the different users to the Roles as outlined previously in the chapter. When you need to test the workflow, either log in as different users (which can be time-consuming) or right-click on Internet Explorer and select Run as the option. Type in the user credentials you're impersonating, and click OK. This launches the browser in the context of that user.

## Adding Data Fields

Data fields are variables within the running workflow. There are two levels of data fields: Process and activity data Fields.

❑   **Process data fields**: Contain information that is available for the entire time that an instance of a process is running.

❑   **Activity data fields:** Are available for the duration that the activity is available. As soon as an activity has been completed, the activity data fields are no longer available.

Data fields are added from the K2 Object Browser. To create data fields:

1.   On the K2 Object Browser, click on the Process/Activity Data tab.

2.   Expand Data Fields, and right-click the Information Request process. Select Add.

3.   A new Add Data Field dialog is displayed. In the Name textbox enter **SubjectMatterExpert**, select String in the Data Type drop-down list, and click OK.

The Add Data Field dialog is shown in Figure 9-11.

**Figure 9-11**

We are going to use this data field to dynamically route a process activity later in the chapter.

## Adding Activities

Now that Roles have been defined, it's time to add the process activities to the K2 Design Canvas. Activities act as containers for one or more events. Where there are multiple events, the events are processed in the order that they have been added to the activity, and all need to be completed prior to the activity being completed.

There are a few ways of adding activities to the canvas.

❑   First, you can drag an event onto the canvas from the K2 Toolbox and a Default Activity is automatically added for you. The wizard for your event is launched as well.

❑   Second, you can drag a Default Activity onto the design canvas from the K2 Toolbox Activity Wizards section. You need to manually launch the Default Activity Wizard.

❑   Third, using your mouse, right-click and hold, then draw an upside-down V (see Figure 9-12). This adds a Default Activity to the design canvas for you. This approach of adding activities or events (M for a Mail Event, S for a Default Server Event) is called *mouse gesturing*. It provides a fun and novel approach to modeling.

**Figure 9-12**

When building out the workflow, you can take a couple of approaches:

❑   One is to build each activity individually, adding all of the required events to it and linking activities to each other with Line Rules as you go (more about Line Rules later in the chapter).

❑   A second is to build all of the activities first, add events to them, and then link all of them at the end.

How you develop your process-driven application will depend on your preference. In order to explain the concepts behind each object (activities, events, Line Rules, and so on) we'll adopt the second approach. Let's get started.

**1.**   Drag a Default Activity from the Activity Wizards section of the K2 Toolbar onto the design canvas.

**2.**   Hovering over the activity with your mouse, click the bolt icon (shown in Figure 9-13) in the lower-right side of the activity to run the default wizard.

**Figure 9-13**

This launches the Activity Wizard, which allows for setting the activity-related properties. We're going to set a couple of the general activity properties and the Destination Rule. General Properties are shown by default (Figure 9-14 shows the Activity General Properties tab of the wizard).

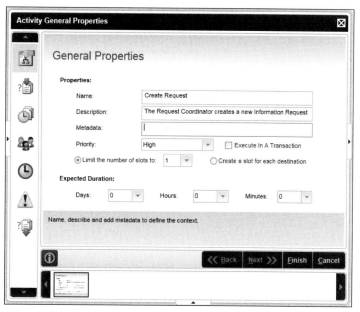

**Figure 9-14**

**3.** On the General Properties tab, set the Name to **Create Request** and the Description to **The Request Coordinator creates a new Information Request**.

**4.** Next, we're going to add a Destination User. The Destination User is the user, group, or role that will be assigned the task at run time. Navigate to the Destination Rule tab by clicking on the Destination User icon (shown in Figure 9-15) in the icon bar on the left-hand side of the wizard.

**Figure 9-15**

**5.** Click the Add button to add a new Destination User. Click the ellipses (. . .) button to bring up the Context Browser, as shown in Figure 9-16.

**Figure 9-16**

6.  Navigate to the User Browser (the second tab on the left, shown as selected in Figure 9-16), expand the Roles, and select Request Coordinators. Click the Add button in the bottom right of the Context Browser. You should end up with what's shown in Figure 9-17.

**Figure 9-17**

**7.** Click the Finish button on the wizard. This closes the wizard.

*You will have noticed that we have set only a couple of the properties on the activity. For more information about all available properties consult the K2 blackpearl documentation or click the blue i (help) button.*

Now that we have added our first activity, we are going to add the rest of the activities as outlined in the following table:

| Tab | Value |
|---|---|
| **Activity #2** | |
| General | 1. Type **Assign Subject Matter Expert** in the Name textbox. |
| | 2. Type **Assign the Information Request response to a Subject Matter Expert** in the Description textbox. |
| Destination Rule | 1. Add the **SME Coordinators** Role. |
| **Activity #3** | |
| General | 1. Type **Complete Response** in the Name textbox. |
| | 2. Type **The SME responds to the Information Request** in the Description textbox. |
| Destination Rule | 1. Add the **Subject Matter Expert** process data field. |
| **Activity #4** | |
| General | 1. Type **Approve Response** in the Name textbox. |
| | 2. Type **The Approvers can approve the response prepared by the SME** in the Description textbox. |
| Destination Rule | 1. Add the **Approvers** Role. |
| **Activity #5** | |
| General | 1. Type **Post Response** in the Name textbox. |
| | 2. Type **The Request Coordinator sends the approved response to the customer** in the Description textbox. |
| Destination Rule | 1. Add the **Request Coordinators** Role. |

To recap, so far we've added the activities required for the workflow, given each a name and description, and set their Destination Rule. The next step is to add events to each activity.

## Adding Events

We're going to start off simple by adding a Forms Generation Client Event to each activity. This event allows us to incorporate client forms for use with each activity. The form is generated as part of the wizard execution process, producing a template or form as a type of framework that can be altered to suit the user requirements.

Customized, audience-specific form templates can also be produced, and these are consumed at design time by the Forms Generation Client Event as part of the design-time process.

*For more information on customizing the client forms see Chapter 11.*

It's time to get started.

**1.** Drag a Forms Generation Client Event to the Create Response activity. This starts the Forms Generation Default Client Event Wizard (shown in Figure 9-18).

**Figure 9-18**

**2.** Ensure that the Run this wizard in Advanced Mode checkbox is not checked. Advanced Mode provides another step to configure in the wizard. In this case, it gives you the ability to alter the default Workflow Server and Workflow Web Services URL configured in your Environment Library. For more information about all available properties consult the K2 blackpearl documentation or click the blue i button. We're good with the default values, so click the Next button.

On the Form Name and Location page, the page name is auto-generated by the wizard and can be renamed for improved usability. Enter **Create_Request** as shown in Figure 9-19. The Internet URL textbox contains the Web Service URL configured in your Environment Library by default.

**Figure 9-19**

3.   Click the Next button, and on the Form Data step add in two data fields. To add the data fields, click the Add button. A new Add Data Source dialog is displayed; click on the ellipses (...) button. This will display the Context Browser. Click on the Process/Activity Data tab and expand the data fields node. Right-click on InformationRequest process and select Add. A new Add Data Field dialog is displayed. It's the same dialog you saw in Figure 9-11 earlier in the chapter.

Enter two new data fields with the following properties as set out in the following table:

| Data Field Name | Data Type | Initial Value |
| --- | --- | --- |
| CustomerName | String | n/a |
| CustomerEmail | String | n/a |

You will notice that these are the same steps used earlier in the chapter when the SubjectMatterExpert data field was added from the K2 Object Browser in Visual Studio. The same functionality is available to you from the wizard.

Once both data fields have been added and selected, the wizard should look like Figure 9-20.

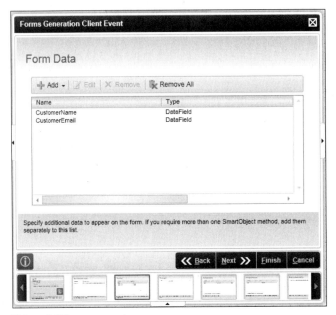

**Figure 9-20**

**4.** Click the Next button to display the Form Layout step. Use the default value of Blank Page. The wizard will list any custom user pages that have been added to the generated forms parent directory.

*For more information regarding custom user pages and the generated forms parent directory, see Chapter 11.*

**5.** Click the Next button to configure the Actions. Actions determine the response that can be given at run time by the actor. Two types of actions exist, Finish and Update. An action of type Finish results in the activity being processed and completed, while an action of type Update merely saves the activity.

Click the Add button. This displays a new dialog prompting you to configure the Action. In the Name textbox, type **Create Request**. In the Description textbox, type in **Create the Request for Information**.

Ensure that the Make the action available without opening the work item checkbox is checked. Also, select the This action will complete the work item radio button. (For more information about all available properties consult the K2 blackpearl documentation or click the blue i button.)

The completed form should look like Figure 9-21.

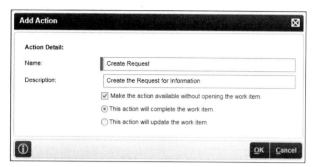

**Figure 9-21**

Click the OK button. The completed step should look like Figure 9-22.

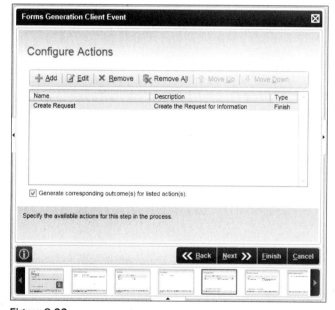

**Figure 9-22**

Ensure that the Generate corresponding outcome(s) for listed action(s) checkbox is checked. This automatically creates the outcome corresponding to your action.

6. Click the Next button to display the Configure Outcomes step. An outcome has been automatically generated for you. Outcomes determine the flow of the process. The completed step should look like Figure 9-23.

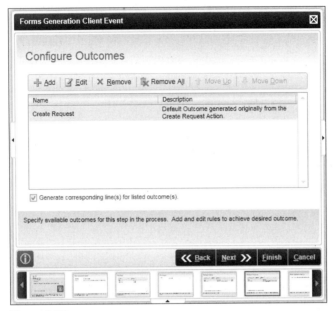

**Figure 9-23**

You will notice that the name of the outcome corresponds with the name of the action. This can be verified by looking at the Description field, which states that the default outcome has been generated from the action with the corresponding name.

Ensure that the Generate corresponding line(s) for listed outcome(s) checkbox is checked. This will automatically create the Line Rules corresponding to our action.

7. Click the Next button to display the Events Notifications Settings step; click Next without checking the Event Notification Settings checkbox.

8. Click the Next button to display the Finished step. Click the Finish button to end the wizard.

Now that we have added our first event, we can go ahead and add a Forms Generation Client Event to the rest of the activities as outlined in the following table:

| Step | Instructions |
|---|---|
| **Assign Subject Matter Expert Activity** | |
| Form Name and Location | 1. Type **Assign_Subject_Matter_Expert** in the Page Name textbox. |
| Form Data | 1. Do not add any data to the form. |
| Form Layout | 1. Use the default Blank Page setting. |
| Configure Actions | Add a new action: |
| | 1. Type **Assign SME** in the Name textbox and **Assign a Subject Matter Expert** into the Description textbox. |
| | 2. Ensure that the Make the action available without opening the work item checkbox is not checked. |
| | 3. Ensure that the This action will complete the work item radio button is selected. |
| | 4. Ensure that the Generate corresponding outcome(s) for listed action(s) checkbox is checked. |
| Configure Outcomes | 1. Ensure the automatically generated Assign SME outcome exists. |
| | 2. Ensure that the Generate corresponding line(s) for listed outcome(s) checkbox is checked. |
| Event Notification Settings | 1. Ensure that the Would you like to send a Notification of the Event to the Destination User(s) checkbox is not checked. |
| **Complete Response Activity** | |
| Form Name and Location | 1. Type **Complete_Response** in the Page Name textbox. |
| Form Data | 1. Do not add any data to the form. |
| Form Layout | 1. Use the default Blank Page setting. |
| Configure Actions | Add a new action: |
| | 1. Type **Complete Response** in the Name textbox and **The information request response is complete** into the Description textbox. |
| | 2. Ensure that the Make the action available without opening the work item checkbox is checked. |
| | 3. Ensure that the This action will complete the work item radio button is selected. |
| | 4. Ensure that the Generate corresponding outcome(s) for listed action(s) checkbox is checked. |
| Configure Outcomes | 1. Ensure the automatically generated Complete Response outcome exists. |
| | 2. Ensure that the Generate corresponding line(s) for listed outcome(s) checkbox is checked. |

*(continued)*

*(continued)*

| Step | Instructions |
|---|---|
| **Complete Response Activity** | |
| Event Notification Settings | 1. Ensure that the Would you like to send a Notification of the Event to the Destination User(s) checkbox is not checked. |
| **Approve Response Activity** | |
| Form Name and Location | 1. Type in **Approve_Response** in the Event Name textbox. |
| Form Data | 1. Do not add any data to the form. |
| Form Layout | 1. Use the default Blank Page setting. |
| Configure Actions | Add the following two new actions: |
| | 1. Type **Approve** in the Name textbox and **The Approver approves the Response for the Information Request** into the Description textbox. |
| | 2. Ensure that the Make the action available without opening the work item checkbox is checked. |
| | 3. Ensure that the This action will complete the work item radio button is selected. |
| | 4. Type **Decline** in the Name textbox and **The Approver declines the Response for the Information Request** into the Description textbox. |
| | 5. Ensure that the Make the action available without opening the work item checkbox is checked. |
| | 6. Ensure that the This action will complete the work item radio button is selected. |
| Configure Outcomes | 1. Ensure that the automatically generated Approve and Decline outcomes exist. |
| | 2. Ensure that the Generate corresponding line(s) for listed outcome(s) checkbox is checked. |
| Event Notification Settings | 1. Ensure that the Would you like to send a Notification of the Event to the Destination User(s) checkbox is not checked. |
| **Post Response Activity** | |
| Form Name and Location | 1. Type in **Post_Response** in the Page Name textbox. |
| Form Data | 1. Do not add any data to the form. |
| Form Layout | 1. Use the default Blank Page setting. |

| Step | Instructions |
|------|--------------|
| **Post Response Activity** | |
| Configure Actions | Add a new action: |
| | 1. Type **Post Response** in the Name textbox and **The response has been returned to the customer** into the Description textbox. |
| | 2. Ensure that the Make the action available without opening the work item checkbox is checked. |
| | 3. Ensure that the This action will complete the work item radio button is selected. |
| | 4. Ensure that the Generate corresponding outcome(s) for listed action(s) checkbox is checked. |
| Configure Outcomes | 1. Ensure the automatically generated Post Response outcome exists. |
| | 2. Ensure that the Generate corresponding line(s) for listed outcome(s) checkbox is not checked. This is the final activity in our process so there is no need for a Line Rule. |
| Event Notification Settings | 1. Ensure that the Would you like to send a Notification of the Event to the Destination User(s) checkbox is not checked. |

# Connecting Activities Using Line Rules

Line Rules are used to connect one activity to another and dictate the flow of the process. Line Rules have the ability to store rule logic. The logic is simply a condition or set of conditions under which the Line Rule evaluates to true. By default, Line Rules return true. These sets of conditions translate into business logic, directing the workflow process to the appropriate destination users.

You need a Line Rule to connect the Start Activity to the first activity in the example process, Create Request. There are a couple of ways you can add this Line Rule.

❑   First, you can click on the Default Line in the K2 Toolbox under the Line Wizards section. Once selected, while holding down the right mouse button, draw a line from the Start activity to the Create Request activity.

❑   The second way of connecting these activities is to hold down the alternate (typically right) mouse button and draw a line from the Start activity to the Create Request activity. This negates the need to use the Default Line in the toolbox.

You might notice that the Create Request activity has a Line Rule attached to the bottom of it. This was created by the Forms Generation Client Event Wizard. You need to connect these Line Rules to their respective activities. Hover the mouse over the Line Rule where the arrow is and click and drag it to the Assign Subject Matter Expert activity. This ensures that the Create Request activity will flow to the Assign Subject Matter Expert activity once it has been completed.

It's time to take a quick look at the logic behind this Line Rule. You can view the logic by right-clicking on the Line Rule on the canvas and selecting Properties. The first tab shows the Line General Properties. Click on the second icon in the icon menu on the left (as shown in Figure 9-24).

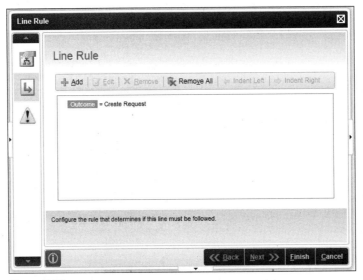

**Figure 9-24**

You will notice that a Line Rule has been added for us. This was done using the Forms Generation Client Event Wizard. You have the ability to add more rules to the line from here if needed.

However, it's time to get on with connecting the activities. Connect the activities to each other using the lines as follows:

| Initial Activity | Line | Subsequent Activity |
|---|---|---|
| Assign Subject Matter Expert | Assign SME | Complete Response |
| Complete Response | Complete Response | Approve Response |
| Approve Response | Approve | Post Response |
| Approve Response | Decline | Complete Response |

Now that the activities are connected, the design canvas should look like Figure 9-25.

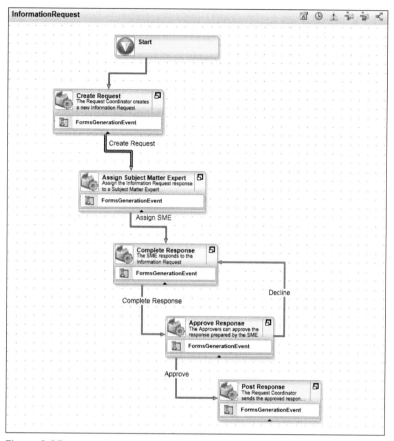

Figure 9-25

## Building and Deploying

You are now ready to build and deploy your K2 Workflow project. You should note, however, that while our goal in this chapter is to create our first workflow, the deployment steps outlined in this section deal specifically with the default deployment on your development environment. Chapters 5, 6, and 10 go into further detail regarding deployment strategies and deploying to multiple environments.

Let's get deployed:

1. Right-click on the InformationRequest solution in the Solution Explorer and select Build. The Build status will be updated in the bottom left of the Visual Studio Status Bar. Once the build is successfully completed, the status will say Build succeeded.

2. Right-click on the InformationRequest project in the Solution Explorer and select Deploy. This will build the project again and initiate the Deploy Project Wizard.

3. Click the Next button to display the Server and Project Settings step as shown in Figure 9-26:

**Figure 9-26**

The Environment drop-down list includes the environments that you are able to deploy to. This may include Development, QA, Staging, and Production depending on your setup. For this example, select the default value: Development.

4. Click the Next button and click the Finish button to commence deployment. The deployment status will be updated in the bottom left of the Visual Studio Status Bar. Once deployment is successfully completed, the status will say Deploy succeeded.

The workflow has now been successfully deployed to the Workflow server. Next you need to set the Process Rights.

## Setting Process Rights

Setting the Process Rights ensures that the process can be accessed by the workflow actors. The following table explains the permissions available:

| Permissions | Description |
|---|---|
| Admin | Allows the user to start and view a process in the Workspace. It also allows the actor to manage the process from the Management Console. |
| Start | Allows the user to start a process. |
| View | Allows the user to view all instances of a process without being an actor in the workflow. This is handy for seeing process reports. |
| View Participate | Allows the user who has been designated as a Destination User to view and participate in the process. They will only be able to view the process and activity data once the activity that they are assigned to has reached them. |
| Server Event | Asynchronous server events wait for a callback from the external system to finish the server event. The user account used by the external system must be granted Server Event permissions for it to be allowed to finish the server event. |

To set the Process Rights you either add the user's Active Directory User account or an Active Directory Group that the user may belong to. The following steps set the Process Rights for users in the example:

1. Navigate to the Management Console in the K2 Workspace.

2. Click on the Workflow Server.

3. Click on Processes.

4. Click on InformationRequest process.

5. Click on InformationRequest below the process.

6. Click on the Process Rights tab.

7. Click the Add button, which opens the Select Users/Groups to assign rights to dialog displayed in Figure 9-27.

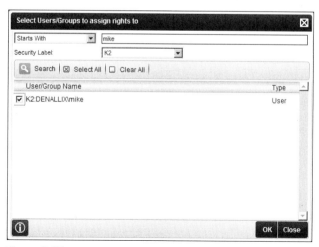

**Figure 9-27**

**8.** Search for your user, check the checkbox next to their name, and click the OK button. Add their Process Rights accordingly. For the example, add the following users and set their permissions accordingly:

| Username | Permissions |
|----------|-------------|
| Codi | Admin |
| Mike | Start, View |
| Anthony | Start, View |

**9.** Click the Save button to persist the permission settings.

Your Management Console should look like Figure 9-28.

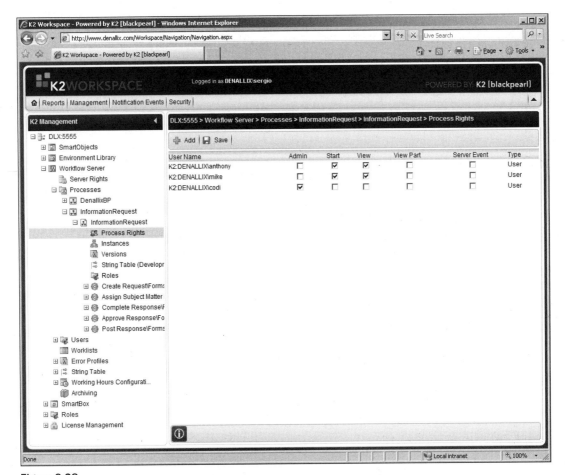

Figure 9-28

# Stepping through the Process

Now that the workflow has been implemented you are ready to step through your process-driven application. This allows you to test for logical errors in the workflow and gives you an opportunity to see what the workflow participants will experience as they complete their tasks.

## Initiating the Workflow

To initiate the workflow, you're going to log on as Request Coordinator, Codi. Alternatively, you can right-click on Internet Explorer and run as Codi.

1. Navigate to the Management Console in the K2 Workspace ⇨ Workflow Server ⇨ Processes ⇨ InformationRequest ⇨ InformationRequest.

2. Click on the Instances tab, and click the Start New button in the pane on the right-hand side of the screen.

   A Create New Process Instance dialog is displayed. Uncheck the Use Date checkbox and enter **IR 1** as the description for the process instance in the Folio textbox. Say that you want to enter some values regarding the customer who made the Request for Information. Click the Load Data Fields button. It loads the process data fields and gives you the opportunity to set their values. Check the two data fields called CustomerName and CustomerEmail. Enter in **Joe Customer** and **joe@customer.com**, respectively. The dialog should look like Figure 9-29.

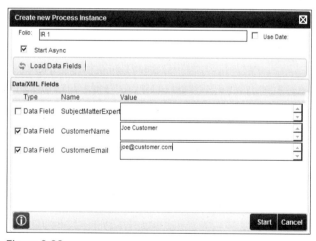

Figure 9-29

3. Click the Start button to create the new process instance. The process instance has created a new activity for Mike to create the request.

## Completing a Workflow Task

When Mike navigates to his K2 Workspace, he will see that he has a new Create Request task. Mike's K2 Workspace should look like Figure 9-30.

Figure 9-30

There are two ways for Mike to complete his task.

❑ Hover over the Folio of the task, IR 1. A small black arrow appears (see Figure 9-31). Click the arrow, and a context menu appears. Click on the Action(s) menu item, and all possible actions are displayed. In this case there is only one, Create Request. To complete the task, click on the action.

Figure 9-31

❑ Click on the Event Name for the task, in this case Create Request. This will open a new instance of your browser with the Web page displayed (the page generated by the Forms Generation Client Event Wizard).

*The Create Request action appears in the context menu on the Worklist because we checked the Make the action available without opening the work item checkbox when configuring the actions of the Forms Generation Client Event. In a case where you did not do so, you would need to click on the Event Name in the Worklist to open the Web form.*

To complete this task, you can use the page generated by the Forms Generation Client Event. Click on the Event Name, and the client-generated page opens in a new browser window. There are a couple of important things to note here:

❑   First, the two process data fields that were populated when creating the instance of this process are displayed. As Mike looks over the form he realizes that the e-mail address was entered incorrectly. Go ahead and change it to be `joe@customer.biz`. When the form is submitted, the data field will be updated with the new value.

❑   The second thing to note is that the form has an Actions drop-down list containing all available actions. In this case there is only one, Create Request.

Mike's form should look like Figure 9-32.

Figure 9-32

Select the Create Request action, and click the Submit button. As soon as the task has been completed, the client page displays a message confirming that the Worklist item action has been completed.

The workflow creates a new Assign Subject Matter Expert task for Anthony. You can complete the task as Anthony by opening a browser under his credentials. Navigate to his task on the K2 Worklist, and click on the Event Name to launch the client form. The form associated with this task has a textbox where you can assign a Subject Matter Expert to complete the response. Anthony enters **DOMAIN\Codi** (enter your domain before the user's name) and selects the Assign SME action from the Actions drop-down list. His form should look like Figure 9-33.

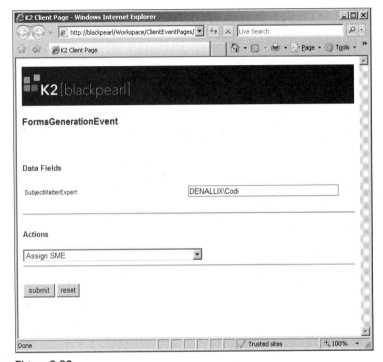

Figure 9-33

The process now creates a new task, Complete Response, for Codi. Remember, the reason this task is going to Codi is because you set the Destination User for this activity to be the value from the SubjectMatterExpert data field. This is an important concept, as you can imagine how powerful this can be. You can have a drop-down list containing several users who are part of a group, and the actor completing this task can select a person at run time.

Log in as Codi and complete her task. Once this task has been submitted, a new Approve Response task is created and assigned to Mike. Take a look as the action available to Mike from his K2 Workspace. Notice now there are two actions available, Approve and Decline, as displayed in Figure 9-34.

Figure 9-34

Depending on Mike's actions one of two outcomes can occur. If he Declines the response, then the workflow is routed back to Codi so that she can have another attempt at completing the response. On the other hand, if Mike approves the response, the workflow is routed to the next activity, Post Response.

Approve the response. A new Post Response task is created for Mike. As soon as Mike has completed the task, the workflow instance has been completed. There you go, one process-driven application later, and you've hardly broken into a sweat.

# Documenting the Process

One useful feature of the K2 Designer for Visual Studio is the Documentation Designer. Look on the bottom left of the design canvas, and you can see a couple of buttons. The first is the Workflow button that displays the K2 Design Canvas. The second, the Documentation button, displays the Documentation Designer. Click on the Documentation button. Figure 9-35 shows the Documentation Designer.

Ensure that the designer is enabled by checking the Designer Enabled checkbox on the top of the Documentation Designer.

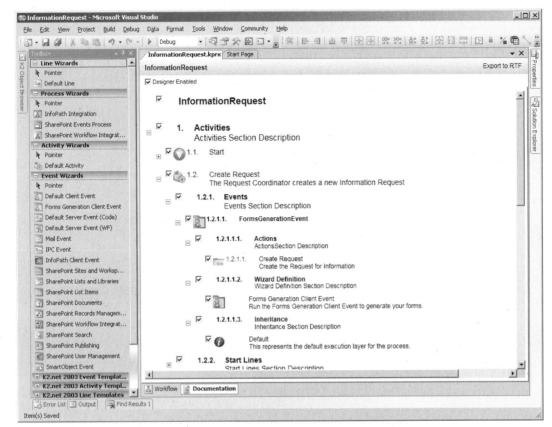

Figure 9-35

The designer lists the workflow Activities, Events, and Line Rules. Each section can be expanded and collapsed. There is a checkbox next to each section that indicates whether to include the section in the documentation or not. To generate the documentation, click the Export to RTF button in the top-right corner of the designer. It opens a Save As dialog allowing you to select a location to save the file to. Figure 9-36 shows the generated RTF file.

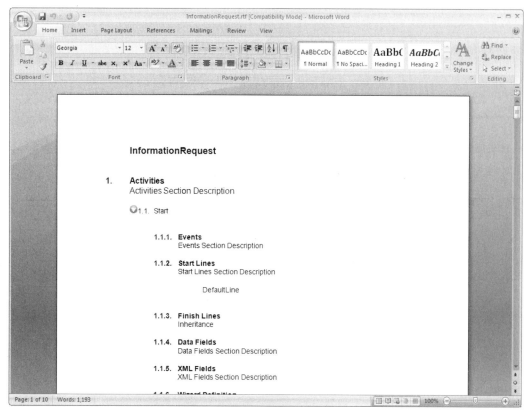

**Figure 9-36**

While you still need to go and complete the documentation for it to make sense, this provides you with a good starting point, ensuring that you don't leave out any of the important details.

# Summary

In this chapter, you've had a chance to become familiar with the K2 Designer for Visual Studio. We introduced you to the K2 wizards and used them to create a new automated workflow using their step-by-step approach. You have seen how to create activities and add events to them, as well as how to join the activities through Line Rules. We walked you through adding roles, setting user permissions, and adding destination users to your activities.

You have now seen how easy it is to create simple client forms for workflow interaction without even writing any code. You initiated a new instance of the workflow, and accessed and altered process data. You used the Document Designer to easily create the documentation related to our process.

Most importantly, you can do all of this without having scratched the surface of K2 blackpearl. As you read through the rest of the chapters, you can think back to this chapter and how you can extend the power of K2 blackpearl even further.

The next chapter now turns to a discussion of deploying your processes and SmartObjects.

# 10

# Deploying Your Processes and SmartObjects

Jason Apergis

K2 blackpearl provides tools that allow designers the ability to quickly and easily deploy processes into development, staging, and production environments. These tools to deploy K2 solutions between environments have immensely simplified the deployment process; however, there are many considerations that must be accounted for. There are multiple ways K2 processes and SmartObjects can be deployed. It's as easy as clicking through a wizard or as advanced as using the K2 API to fully automate the deployment. The K2 deployment platform is built using Microsoft's MSBuild framework providing flexibility that allows development teams to customize, extend, and automate the deployment of K2.

K2 blackpearl has streamlined tasks for deploying processes and SmartObjects into environments. For example, the K2 platform provides the Environment Library server, which contains environment contextual configurations (such as server connection strings) that can be used for a process definition. When deploying processes, the designer has to choose which environment that will be deployed to, and all of the configuration data associated with the selected environment will be deployed with the process. Using the Environment Library server allows designers to easily move processes between development, staging, and production environments because they no longer have to manually go through process and change hardcoded configurations. Think of the K2 Environment Server as a `.config` file management server; however, there are no configuration files as all the data is stored in a database.

Additionally, K2 blackpearl provides features that will package processes and SmartObjects for deployment without requiring designers to create custom deployment projects. These deployment packages can be created and deployed using a wizard, the command line, or K2 blackpearl's API. Plus; once the deployment package is created, it can be used to deploy to any environment without having to rebuild it. Allowing this level of deployment granularity enables development teams to remain agile in the delivery of solutions. This chapter will discuss the mechanics of how to deploy a K2 process and SmartObjects, using the deployment wizard, command line, and the API.

The Environment Library server will be discussed in detail covering how environment variables are defined, how they are used within a K2 process, and how these values are deployed to the K2 blackpearl Workflow server.

This chapter covers the following topics:

❑   Standard deployment of a K2 blackpearl process and SmartObject

❑   Deployment considerations for K2 blackpearl solutions

❑   Environment Libraries, String Tables, and how they should be used in a process

❑   Deploying K2 blackpearl processes and SmartObjects using a MS Build package

❑   Deploying SmartObject Services

❑   Deploying K2 blackpearl processes and SmartObjects using code

# Simple Process Deployment

The K2 platform provides the ability to create deployment packages, which are used to deploy solutions to the server. When using a tool like Visual Studio, a deployment package is created automatically after a successful build. Developers in Visual Studio have become accustomed to creating .NET deployment projects to deploy their solutions; however, this is done for free with K2. The generated deployment packages are built using the MSBuild assemblies from Microsoft and are deployed using the MSBuild infrastructure. This is the only way to deploy a K2 process or SmartObject. They are not deployed like a Web page or a SharePoint Feature, where the files are moved onto a server. All of the K2 project files are deployed directly into the K2 blackpearl server.

It is very important to note that K2 deployment packages are scoped to only deploy the K2 processes and SmartObjects, and will not deploy all things used by the K2 process or SmartObjects. For example, a custom database, a SharePoint site, a Web service, or an ASP.NET Web application will not be deployed as part of a K2 deployment package. However, an InfoPath form or custom DLL library referenced by the Visual Studio project will be deployed.

## Quick Deployment

The simplest way to deploy a K2 project within Visual Studio is to right-click the project name in the solution explorer and then click the Deploy menu item. This will build all of the dependant projects, the K2 project, and, if there are no errors, the Deployment Wizard will begin. Errors will appear in the Error List window. The same Deployment Wizard is used in all K2 blackpearl designer environments (Visual Studio, K2 Studio and Visio). Figure 10-1 shows the first screen of the deployment wizard.

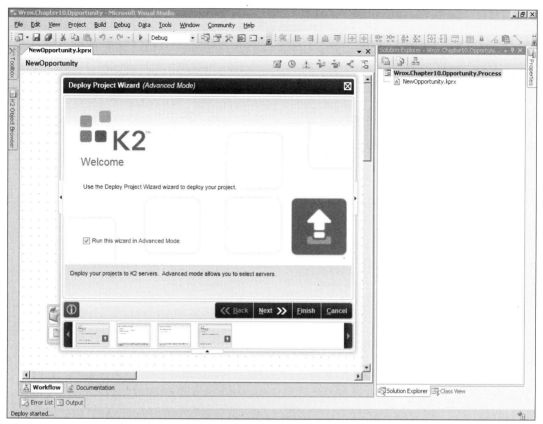

**Figure 10-1**

The next step in the wizard is the Server and Project Settings step. In this step there is an Environment drop-down, which is used to select the environment the project will be deployed to. The Workflow Management Server and SmartObject Server drop-downs are next, and they are used specify the destination of the deployment. These will be configuration values that are stored in the Environment Library and, in most scenarios, there will only be one value in the drop-down (unless there are multiple K2 blackpearl servers in an environment). Finally, there are fields that allow the person performing the deployment to enter in a custom Version Name and Description for the deployment. This information is displayed in the K2 Workspace for later reference about the deployment. Figure 10-2 shows the screen for this step in the wizard.

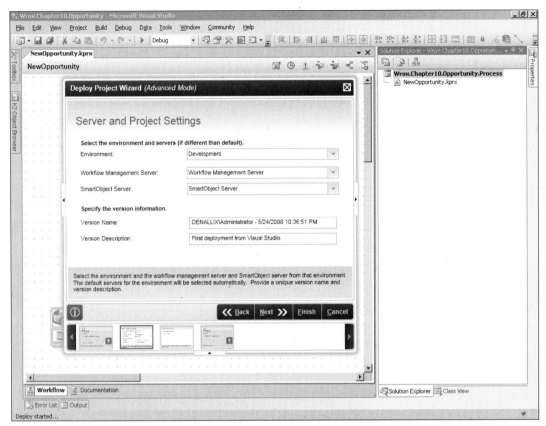

Figure 10-2

The next step in the process will display a listing of all of the processes and SmartObjects that will be deployed. No action can be taken at this point to add or remove processes and SmartObjects as they had to be removed before doing the deployment. Figure 10-3 shows this step in the deployment wizard.

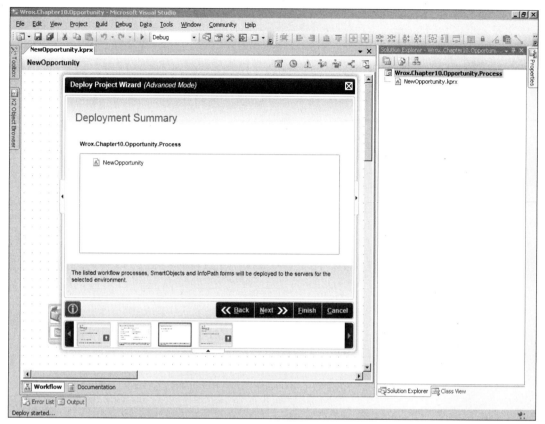

**Figure 10-3**

Once the environment has been selected, the process can be deployed by clicking the Finish button (see Figure 10-4). If this is the first time the process has been deployed, the only thing left to do is go to the K2 Workspace and assign permissions to the process so that users can start initiating process instances. The steps to deploy a K2 solution are relatively simple and both developers and nontechnical designers can execute them.

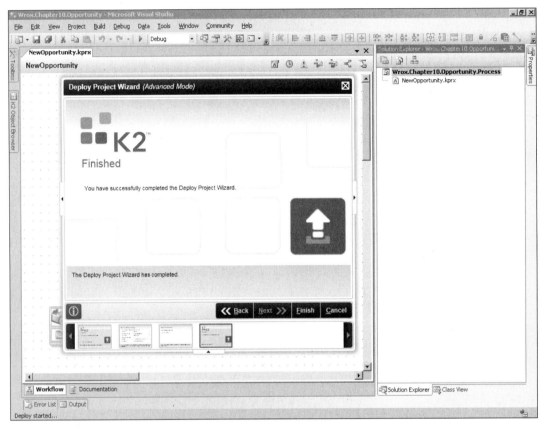

Figure 10-4

This Deployment Wizard that was run in Visual Studio will be the same wizard that is run in other K2 blackpearl design environments such as K2 Studio and Microsoft Visio. In essence, what the Deployment Wizard is doing is running the MSBuild file so that the designer does not have to do a deployment using the command line. The MSBuild file is created whenever a project has been successfully built. This chapter will primarily focus on building and deployment using Visual Studio; however, much of the steps used are very similar within other designer environments.

## Declarative, Not Compiled

It is very important to understand that K2 blackpearl processes and SmartObjects use a declarative model and are not compiled. Declarative programming means that the code describes "what something is like" instead of "how to create it." A well-known example of declarative programming is HTML, where it is used to describe what a Web page should contain, but it does not describe how HTML will be displayed on a screen. An application like a Web browser is responsible for displaying the HTML. The same analogy can be made for K2 processes and SmartObjects. Both of their definitions are basically an XML document that is deployed to the K2 blackpearl server, which is responsible for running a process based on logic described in the process definition (the .kprx file). When a solution is built, the process and SmartObject definitions will be verified to ensure that they are well formed and that code used or referenced can be compiled (like a server-side code event). The .NET code user in the process will be compiled at run time.

Since K2 blackpearl is declarative, process definitions that have been deployed have the ability to be modified on the K2 blackpearl server after deployment. More importantly, a process definition can be modified for a running process instance. For example, there could be a scenario in which data needs to be saved to a database and there are hundreds of process instances currently running on the server. Because the process definition is declarative, a developer can modify the definition of running process instances and then allow them to finish using the modified definition that will save data to a database. Developer and administrative tools to support this capability are planned for a future release of K2 blackpearl.

## Deployment Dependencies

Before a process can be deployed to the server, the K2 blackpearl platform will perform verifications to ensure that process dependencies are in place that cannot be discovered during a build. For example, when building a process, checks will be made to ensure that there are no model declaration errors. However the build cannot check to see if referenced SmartObjects have been deployed to the environment in which the process will eventually be deployed.

Knowing this, there are two steps involved with the deployment of a K2 process. First, the design environment will build the project that creates the MSBuild instructions used by the Deployment Wizard. Second, based on the selected environment, the design environment will check to make sure that all of the necessary server components can be connected, all SmartObjects are generated and deployed, roles that are used have been created, and referenced SharePoint sites and libraries exist. Although this validation in the second step will not check for items such as Web services, ASP.NET sites, dynamically created SharePoint sites, or library locations, and databases. Therefore, a deployment plan should be devised to ensure all components and dependencies are in place before making a process available to business users.

The Environment Library solves the challenge of managing configurations; however it will not validate their presence. It is good practice to ensure that all of dependencies are deployed prior to deploying the K2 process. If the deployment process is complex, due to the number of components that are used by the process, a fully automated build can be created to ensure that all dependencies are verified.

## Verifying Deployment

Once the deployment to K2 blackpearl is complete, there are several ways to verify its success. A simple way to verify that a deployment was successful would be to look at the bottom-left corner in Visual Studio to check if "Deploy succeeded" is displayed on the status bar. Another method is to go the K2 Workspace. Within the K2 Workspace, there is a Management Console page, which can be navigated to from the main menu bar. In the Management Console, the K2 server tree should be opened; it contains a node called Workflow Server. In the Workflow Server node, a subsequent node called Processes exists (see Figure 10-5). This is where all processes that have been deployed to the server are listed. Processes are grouped by K2 Process Project because a single project can have more than one process. For first-time processes, a new tree node for the project is available, which can be expanded to view the processes for the project.

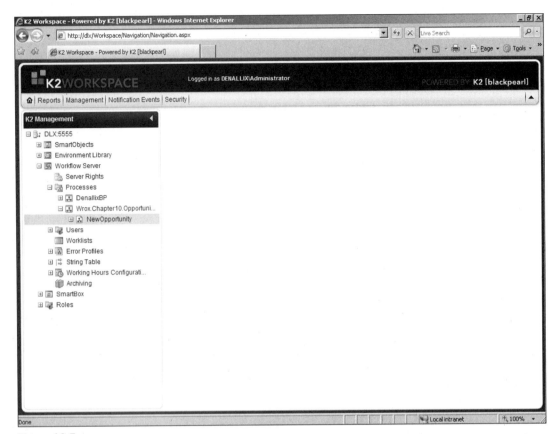

**Figure 10-5**

The Process tree node can be further expanded to view a Versions node. Upon selecting the Versions node, the Versions screen will be displayed, listing all the versions of the process that have been deployed to the server (see Figure 10-6). For each process that has been deployed, a label and description are visible, both of which can have custom text entered at the time of deployment. Additionally, there is a Source column with a Download link that allows for the download of the source code of that particular version. Note that for many reasons this does not replace the need for using source code control tools. This only provides a simple way to access code that has been deployed to the server.

Finally, there is a column named Default, which controls which process version will be used when new processes are instantiated. When a new process is deployed, that version will be set as the default process that all new instances will use. It is possible to change which process is set as the default, for example, if an issue occurred with the newer process version and a prior version needed to be used until a resolution was discovered. Only one process version can be designated as the Default process at any given time; however, the K2 blackpearl server supports the execution of process instances on many versions all at once. It is currently not possible to take a running instance and change which version it runs under. So running process instances will not use the new process definition that was deployed; they will continue to run and must complete the version of the process they were started on. Figure 10-6 shows process versions.

Figure 10-6

## Changing the Process Definition on the Server

It will be possible in the future to modify the process definition of a deployed process directly on the server without having to redeploy the entire process. This will support the ability to add new activities and events to a running process instance if a change must be implemented before the process instance is completed. This is typically referred to as "in flight" changes. For example, this option can be leveraged if an issue is discovered with the process, and the change must be made for all running instances. Typically, it is not possible to stop running instances and create new process instances using a new process version. When this feature becomes available for K2 processes, the changes should be kept to a minimum because it could lead to version control challenges if the changes are not kept in sync with process versions that are in source control. If there is a tactical reason why this should be done, a best practice is to modify the existing process version directly on the server, return to development, add the same change, test it, then redeploy everywhere as a new version of the process. These sorts of changes are to be treated as tactical and thought of as a new version of the process. With this functionality, the K2 platform will provide a powerful capability to fix issues in an ad hoc fashion.

When executing these types of changes, extra care needs to be taken into planning before changes are made. Understanding how these changes could affect external actors to a process, such as a database or SharePoint site, can introduce unanticipated challenges. For example, a new required database field is added. If there are five versions of a process that have been deployed, where each version has several running instances, adding a new required field in the database field will generate errors on insert because those process do not have data for the new required field. In this case, all versions of the process will need to be independently updated with the same exact change to support the insertion or updating of the new value. There are many ways that this could be resolved, but users should recognize that making these sorts of changes in an ad hoc fashion can and will be complicated. It is important to plan changes to the process and address the ways that they affect external dependencies.

## SmartObject and Process Projects

Before deploying a process it is good to plan out the organization of the processes and SmartObjects that will be deployed. It is considered good practice to separate processes and SmartObjects into different projects. This is so because SmartObjects are considered to be reusable data entities that span processes or even extend outside the scope of K2. Knowing that dependencies should be minimized between processes and SmartObjects, it would be a good approach to separate them into their own projects.

## Changing the Name of a Process or SmartObject

Changing the name of a process or SmartObject in Visual Studio will not change the name of the ones that have already been deployed. If the name were changed, the process will be deployed with the new name, but the old one will still remain. This is to support process instances that are running on older versions. If that process refers to a SmartObject using the old name, a run-time exception will occur if the name cannot be found. Knowing this, it is extremely important to devise a naming schema for the processes and SmartObjects before they are deployed. Careful analysis should be made to understand and project future needs as creation of poorly named processes or SmartObjects may lead to confusion later on. A good practice is to use a namespace in the name of the K2 project, just as many people do with their .NET code library Visual Studio projects. A good example would be `Company.Department .K2ProjectType.ProjectName` (`ACME.HR.Process.EmployeeOnboarding` and `ACME.HR.SO .EmployeeOnboarding`). Then, assign good names to the processes and SmartObjects that reside within the project. Regardless of what naming standard is used, make sure that a good, consistent one is adopted.

> Note that K2 project/process names and SmartObject names must be unique. This is again why it is important to implement a strong naming convention.

## Deployment Errors

Errors can occur upon deployment, and it can be challenging to understand the details of the error even though the design environments will give you an error message. One simple way of doing this is to run the MSBuild package that is created as part of the process or SmartObject build in a command window where all of the logs for the deployment will be visible.

If Visual Studio is being used to deploy the K2 process or SmartObject go to Tools, Options from the main menu. Then, in the Options window select, Projects and Solutions, then General in the tree, and check "Show Output window when build starts." Then select the Build and Run node, and select

Diagnostic from the MSBuild project build output verbosity drop-down. This will show all of the same logs that would be seen if the MSBuild package is being executed via the command line.

Finally, another way to investigate issues is to run the K2 blackpearl server in command-line and watching log statements. To do this, first stop the K2 Service using the Service Console. Then from the Start Menu go to All Programs, K2 blackpearl, K2 blackpearl server, right-click the menu item and then click Run As. In the Run As window, enter the username and password of the service account that the blackpearl server runs under. The K2 server will subsequently start up using the service account. Redeploy the process and watch the logs in the command-line window to determine where the error may be occurring. Closing this window will stop the K2 server and it must be restarted again in the Service Console.

*Do not use this operation on a production K2 blackpearl server during peak times of usage.*

# The Environment Library

The Environment Library is an integral component of the K2 platform. Introduced to assist designers in designing processes and managing deployments across development, staging, and production environments, the Environment Library is another server component within the K2 platform. The purpose of this server is to store configuration values that are unique to each server environment. K2 provides several tools that allow both administrators and designers to manage these configuration values. These configurations, referred to as environment variables, can represent items like a K2 server connection string, a database server connection string, a Web service URL, a SharePoint site name, a document library name, or an escalation period of time. By using these environment variables, designers can drag-and-drop configuration values into event wizards to eliminate hardcoded values in the processes.

Environment variables are not mapped to the business process that references them. The concept behind environment variables is that they are a reusable library of configurations that are available to all processes. Because they are reusable, administration of environment variables is easier. A common scenario is that there may be several processes that would reference the same database, for example, a Custom Relationship Management (CRM) database. And in each environment (development, staging, production) the CRM database will be located on a different server. When using the Environment Library, only one connection string variable needs to be created, and then any process can use that variable. If the connection string for the CRM database were to change, all of the processes using the variable would be updated at once.

It is good practice to use as many environment variables as possible in a process definition because K2 provides a myriad of wizards and each and every field in these wizards is configurable. An ellipse button is located next to almost every field in a wizard, and when clicked, it will display the Context Browser. In the Context Browser, the designer simply selects an environment variable, and then it will be referenced by the process. Many of the wizards have fields for the name of a document library, name of a SharePoint site, URL address, document names, destination users, e-mail body configurations, InfoPath form library, and the list goes on.

It would not be correct to assume that every field in the wizard should use the environment variable either. At times, it is more appropriate to use SmartObjects or roles, which are dynamic and can read from external data sources. Environment variables cannot read from any other location other than the

Environment Library. Environment variables can be used for more than just database connection strings and URLs. There may be a dollar threshold on a Line Rule of $500,000 dollars, and this value may change on a regular basis. Instead of hardcoding this, an environment variable may be a good alternative, which can simply be changed without having to redeploy the entire process if the threshold changes (to $750,000, for example). Later on, it would even be better to store such a value in a rules engine and not in the Environment Library. It is important to reinforce that making a process as configurable as possible will help enable the deployment of the K2 process to different environments and its ability to adapt to business changes.

## Architecture of the Environment Library

As previously mentioned, the Environment Library is a server component with several different tools that are available to manage it. All of the environment variables are stored in a SQL Server database and designers have the ability to manage the values within the Environment Library server using K2 Studio, Visual Studio, and K2 Workspace. Figure 10-7 shows an architectural diagram of the Environment Library Server.

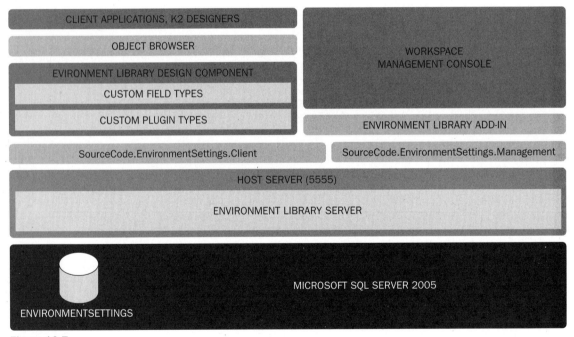

Figure 10-7

Within the K2 Environment Library, there are templates, fields, and environments. Before diving into how these are created and used within a K2 process, it is prudent to define what they are. A template is a logical grouping of fields. A field is a property that can be added to a template which will have a value assigned to it. A template and its fields are analogous to a .NET configuration XML file. Environments are instances of the template and distinct values are assigned to the fields within each environment. For example, development and production URLs to a SharePoint site will be different; however, there is logically only one SharePoint site that the process needs to use. The process will reference the template's field and depending on which environment the process is deployed to, it will use the corresponding value to connect to the SharePoint site.

There are several reasons why the Environment Library has been set up in this fashion. First, since the Environment Library is a server component of the K2 platform, the environment fields are reusable across business processes. To reiterate, there is a high likelihood that a root SharePoint site address will be the same across many K2 processes. This configuration can be reused and defined once, instead of being defined for each and every process. Second, using environments allow process designers to set up all of their fields in a single place and do not have to manage different configuration files in multiple physical locations. Third, since the Environment Library is centrally defined, administrators can create controlled configurations that allow less technical designers to use configurations without requiring them to know how to correctly enter a connection string.

## Creating Templates, Fields, and Environments

To create a new template, the designer must go to the K2 Workspace and open the Management Console. Within the K2 server node, there is a node called Environment Library where the designer can create a new template. By default a template called Default Template will be created (see Figure 10-8).

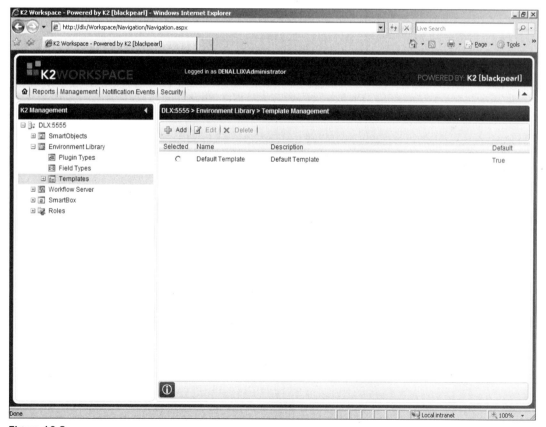

Figure 10-8

Expanding the Environment Library node will show a node called Templates, which when clicked, will open the Template Management page. A designer can add a template by clicking the Add button and providing a distinct name and description. The designer will need to indicate if the template is the default one. Only one template can be designated as the default template, and the default template will be the template selected when a new process is being created. In this case, a new template will be created for the Opportunity process (see Figure 10-9).

**Figure 10-9**

*It is good practice to give the template a strong name. Especially if the template is being created to support a specific process(es). Following the example that was introduced earlier* ACME.HR .Environment.EmployeeOnboarding *would be a proper name. Special characters like a dot are not allowed in a template name.*

After a new template has been created, template fields must be added. This is done by expanding the WroxChapter10OpportunityEnvironment node and selecting the Template Fields node, which will open the Field Management screen (see Figure 10-10). Notice that there are several fields that have been created by default. They are called Field Types, and it is possible to create more of them by going to the Field Types node. Many Field Types are required by K2 blackpearl and must have values because they will be used by the event wizards. For example, the Mail Server field will be used in E-Mail Events, the Web service URL is used in all InfoPath Client Events, and SmartObject Service is used in SmartObject Events. Adding new fields on this screen is again a simple process; the following fields have been added: Opportunity Site, Opportunity Library, and Opportunity File Name. These fields will now be added to every environment that is created from this template and will be set with the default values assigned here.

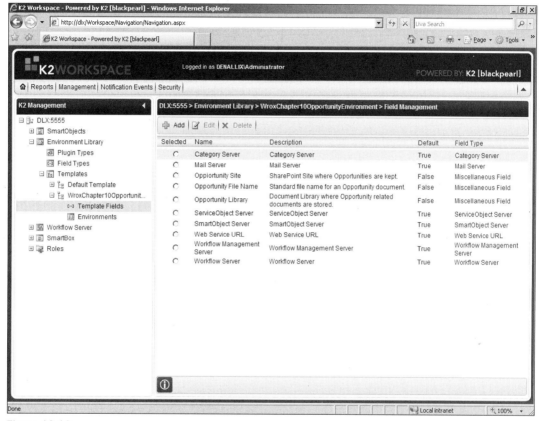

Figure 10-10

In this example, the type for the new fields has been set to Miscellaneous Field and none of them have default values marked as true. Marking one as true would mean that if there are multiple fields of Miscellaneous Type, the one marked true will be the default one used. This does not make sense for the Miscellaneous Type but would be applicable to the Web Service URL field type. This field type is used by the InfoPath Client Event, and whenever the InfoPath Client Event is added to a process it will use the Web Service URL field that is marked as default. If there was a second field of Web Service URL type, it would not be used by the InfoPath Client Event unless the designer was to manually change the event.

Once both templates and fields have completed, new environments can be created for the Opportunity template by selecting the Environments node, which will open the Environment Management screen.

New environments can be added on this screen, and one environment can be designated as the default environment for the template. In Figure 10-11, two environments were created, one for development and one for production.

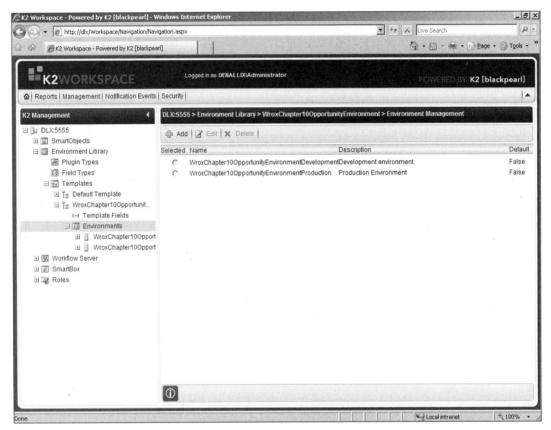

**Figure 10-11**

*It is good practice to give the environment a strong name. Following the example that was introduced earlier,* ACME.HR.Environment.EmployeeOnboarding.Development *would be a proper name. Special characters like a dot are not allowed in a template name.*

After the environments have been created, all of the fields for each environment need to be filled in with data. Figure 10-12 shows the screen where environment field values are managed. It is important to fill in the fields with data before using them inside any of the K2 design environments, as these values will be used and referred to during design. New fields can be added directly to an environment, which will result in a new field being created for the template; subsequently, the new field will appear on every environment for the template. However, changing the value of a field in an environment will only set that value for that environment. The following is a view of the Field Management screen for the development environment. Once this is complete, the Environment Library can be used to compose processes.

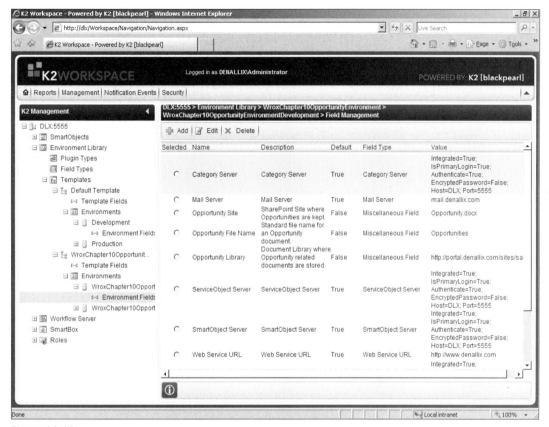

Figure 10-12

## Using Environments

The Environment Library can be used in all K2 design environments, and it is extremely easy to use them. Another great thing about the Environment Library is that a technical developer or administrator can set up templates in an Environment library. Then a designer, who may not be technical, can reference environment fields for their workflows and not be concerned with the details of how to create something like a connection string.

Before working with an Environment Library, a designer must select which environment they want to use. When a new project is created, the default Environment Library will be selected. The Environment Library can be changed using the K2 Object Browser, which shows the current environment displayed at the top. In Figure 10-13 in the K2 Object Browser all of the Field Types from the Environment Library Server are listed as a node in the tree. Within each node will be all of the environment fields of that type.

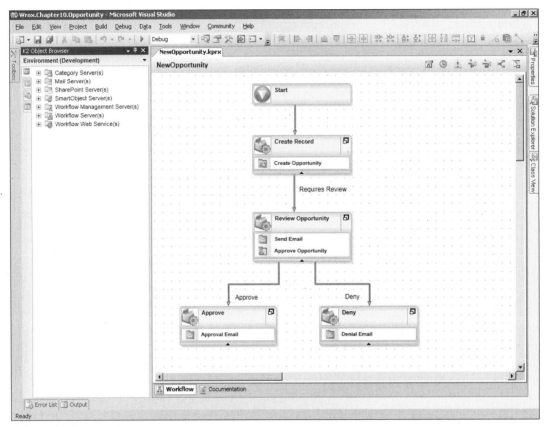

Figure 10-13

If a new sales related process needs to be created, one of the new environments should be selected. To select the new development environment, the new Opportunity template must first be selected. Select the drop-down next to the current environment name and an option will appear to select the template (see Figure 10-14).

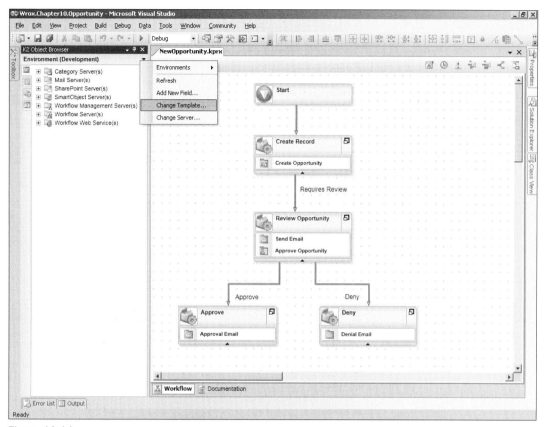

**Figure 10-14**

*If Visual Studio was open while a new template or an environment was created, that template or environment will not be visible until the Object Browser is refreshed. There is a refresh option shown in Figure 10-14. The environments will be refreshed every time the K2 design environment is opened.*

Upon completion, the Change Current Template dialog will appear where the designer can select a template and the environment they want to work with (see Figure 10-15). In this case, the opportunity template and development environment are selected.

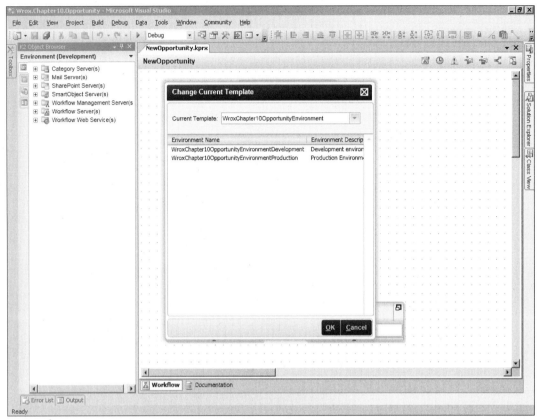

Figure 10-15

It is possible to create environment fields using the K2 Object Browser in Visual Studio, but it is not possible to create new templates and environments, which can only be done inside the K2 Workspace. To add a new field, right-click any of the nodes and then click the add field option. This will open the Add New Field dialog (as shown in Figure 10-16). Fill in the Name, Description, Field Type, default, and Field Value as appropriate. When this is done, the new field will be added to the template so that all environments will have the new field. However, the value that was entered will only apply to the environment in which Visual Studio is running. If a new field was added while using the development environment, the value would be set for the development environment only. The production environment would have the new field, but its value would be blank and needs to be set.

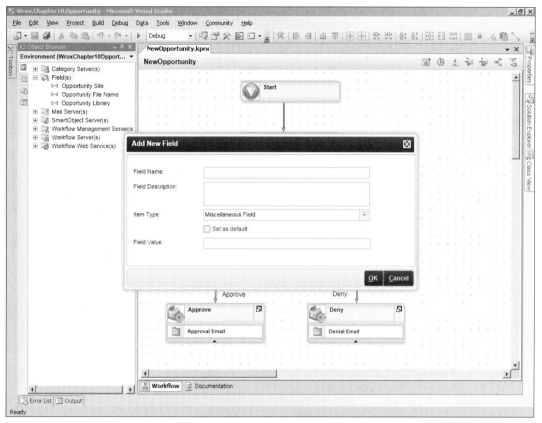

Figure 10-16

Using environment fields in an event wizard is just as simple as selecting which environment to use. Figure 10-17 shows the Upload Document Destination step of the SharePoint Documents event wizard. To select an environment field, click an ellipse next to any field and the Context Browser will open. The designer will simply select a field and then drag-and-drop, it into a field of the wizard. Environment fields are visually identified by a K2 Field Part, which is the green highlight of the environment field name in the wizard. Holding the mouse over the green highlighted area will show the value that is stored in the Environment Library.

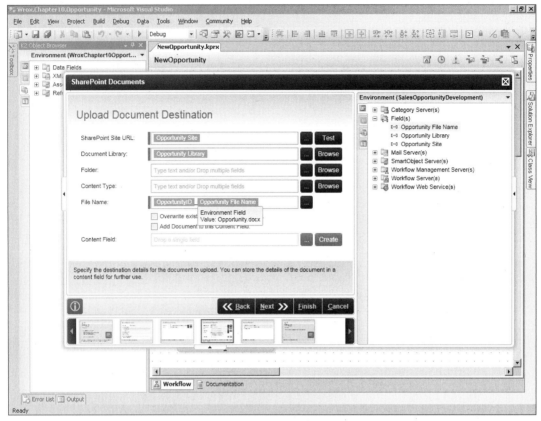

Figure 10-17

In some wizards, the designer will be required to enter design-time values if the values from the environment fields cannot be resolved. For example, this could happen on a SharePoint site URL that does not yet exist because it is generated by the process. If something similar were to occur, the following window will be prompted for the designer to enter a design-time value for the event for design time only. Figure 10-18 shows the window the designer will have to use to enter a value for design-time purposes only.

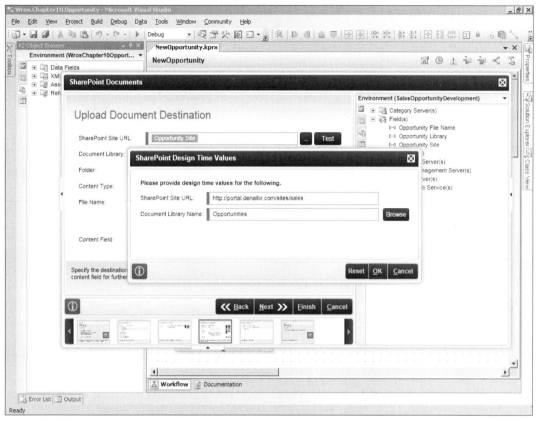

Figure 10-18

## String Tables

After a process has been deployed, the values in the Environment Library are no longer used and values in the String Tables are used by running process instances. During the deployment of the process, the values for the environment are copied into a String Table, and by default, the String Table will be given the same name as the environment. To view the String Table, go to the K2 Workspace by drilling-down to the process and then selecting the String Table node under the process name (see Figure 10-19). All of the values for the String Table are visible and can be edited by selecting the field and then pressing the Edit button.

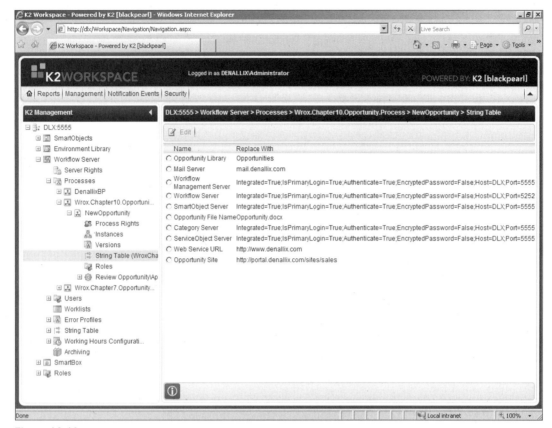

Figure 10-19

Figure 10-19 also shows a node called String Table that is located under the Workflow Server node. This is provided because String Table values can be reused between many processes. Instead of going to the process node to modify a String Table value, an administrator can go to this node and modify the String Table values. Wherever the String Table values are modified the modified, value will be applied to all processes that use the String Table.

## Using the String Table

There are several things that must be understood when managing String Table data. First, String Tables are not used during the design of the process; instead, the Environment Library is used. For example, Visual Studio will connect to the SmartObject Server to get a list of SmartObjects. This connection will be based on the template and environment that Visual Studio is currently running under, not the value in a String Table.

Second, values changed in the String Table will not be reflected in the Environment Library. If values are changed in the String Table, when a process is redeployed the values from the Environment Library will overwrite the values in the String Table. It is highly recommended that if changes are made to a production process's String Table, those identical changes be made immediately in the respective production environment's Environment Library. Remember, all changes to the String Table will affect all processes that use the same String Table name. Be sure that changes to the String Table will not inadvertently cause a run-time error. This will not be an issue if it is planned for ahead of time.

Third, String Table fields can only be edited, they cannot be deleted, nor can new ones be added. As well, String Table values cannot be removed once they have been deployed because all deployed process versions use the same String Table. If a String Table value could be removed, this could cause run-time errors for process instances that are running under a different version.

Fourth, to access values stored in a string through a K2 server-side code, the following can be done. Note that the name of the String Table does not matter because there can only be one String Table that can be used by the process.

```
K2.StringTable["ENVIRONMENT FIELD "]
```

To access the String Table from an external application such as an ASP.NET Web page, the following code can be used. The application will require a reference to the `SourceCode.Workflow.Management` namespace. In this case, the name of the String Table needs to be referenced.

```
WorkflowManagementServer server = new WorkflowManagementServer("blackpearl", 5555);
server.Open();

StringTable stringTable = server.GetStringTable("Production");
```

Fifth, knowing how String Tables work is very important, especially when managing processes that are running in a production environment. String Table values can be shared across processes based on the name of the String Table. The name of the String Table originates from the name of the Environment Library environment. For example, the Default template had an environment named Production. All processes deployed with the Production environment will use the same String Table. This makes management of configuration values extremely easy. For example, if a SharePoint URL needs to be changed an administrator does not need to go to every deployed process and make the change. The administrator only has to do it once and all of the processes using the String Table will be affected.

## Planning Environments and String Tables

The concept of the String Table was first introduced with K2.net 2003 and was carried over to the K2 blackpearl platform. In K2.net 2003, String Tables were a key/value pair; data was defined on the K2 process definition only and were not reusable across processes. This is not the case anymore. At times, it was very helpful to have process-specific configurations that are not shared between processes. For example, there may be a configuration field called Archive Folder, and in different processes the name of that folder may be diverse.

Supporting the ability to have process-specific values is not possible for an Environment Library unless a process-specific Environment Library is created. A process-specific Environment Library is just a standard Environment Library that will only be used by one process. One way to get around creating multiple Environment Libraries would be to give environment variables more qualified names like Finance Archive Folder and Human Resources Archive Folder; however, these fields will now be visible in both processes' String Tables. This can become confusing because administrators will not expect to see Finance configurations in a Human Resources process and vice versa. Another issue that could arise is, down the road, a SharePoint site may need to be partitioned such that Finance and Human Resources are on different site collections using different URLs. If both processes are using the same String Table value for the SharePoint site, the URL data will be stored in the wrong location. Coming full circle, it is important to understand the long-term plan for a process to ensure that it is sustainable, and sometimes the best way to do that is not to use shared Environment Libraries across processes.

> *It is not possible to use multiple environments or String Tables for a process; there can only be one environment used during deployment. It would not be possible to create a global Environment Library and then a process-specific Environment Library, and have the process use both.*

After gaining an understanding of the Environment Library and String Table, a couple of best practices can be determined. It is very important to plan what type of process is being created. First, if the process needs to use configurations and it is acceptable for it to share many of the configurations of other processes, use a single shared template and environment. When K2 is first installed, a template called Default is created with two environments, called Development and Production. More fields and environments can be added with the understanding that all processes using these will share the same values. Second, if there is a need for process-specific configurations, it is recommended that a separate Environment Library template be created, and within the new template, that new environments be created with a strong name as demonstrated earlier.

# MSBuild Package

Environment Library and String Tables are provided by the K2 blackpearl framework to facilitate deploying solutions from environment to environment. Now it is time to take a deeper look into the MSBuild package that is used to deploy processes and SmartObjects. Deploying process and SmartObjects using K2 design tools like the K2 Designer for Visual Studio, the K2 Designer for Visio, or K2 Studio may not always be possible. It is very common that development and production environments may reside on completely different segregated networks where developers and designers are not given permission to use those networks. Even if permission rights are granted, designer tools will not be installed on the machines to deploy processes or SmartObjects. As well, a K2 process may only be a small piece of a larger solution, and custom deployment solutions may need to be created using .NET build projects or installation tools such as InstallShield or Wise. To address the need to deploy a solution outside a K2 Designer, the K2 blackpearl platform supports deployment using the MSBuild utility, which can be executed through a command line.

## Generating a Deployment Package

Creating a deployment package for a K2 project in Visual Studio is simple. Navigate to the solution explorer in Visual Studio, right-click the project, and then click Create Deployment Package. This will generate just the files necessary for a deployment. The files are:

❑ **[K2 project name].exe:** This file contains all of the source code for a K2 Process project, and this file is what will be ultimately deployed to the K2 blackpearl Workflow server. The files can be extracted from the .exe by double-clicking it. This file can later be downloaded from the K2 workspace once it has been deployed. A K2 SmartObject project will not have this file created because .sodx files will be deployed to the K2 SmartObject server.

❑ **[K2 project name].dll:** As mentioned earlier, there is no compiled code for a process however a .dll file is created because it is required by the build operation. This file will be used in the future to contain localized resources for a project, such as names for an activity or SmartObject.

❑ **Deployment folder:** Contains all other files needed for the deployment.

Within the Deployment folder there are the following files:

- ❑ **ProjectDeployments.targets:** Contains steps for deploying a K2 project.

- ❑ **[K2 project name].msbuild:** Provides the MSBuild build engine instructions on what to build and how to build it. This file will be generated by the K2 design tool.

- ❑ **[K2 project name].resources:** .NET resources file.

- ❑ **Bin:** Contains any DLLs that are referenced by the K2 project.

- ❑ **Resources:** Contains resource files that are used by the K2 project.

After creating a deployment package these files can be used to deploy a package to an environment using the MSBuild.exe tool, which is part of the Microsoft .NET Framework 2.0 installation.

## *Deploying a Package*

After generating the MSBuild deployment package using any of the K2 design environments, to deploy the package using the MSBuild utility, do the following. First, go to the \\[Project Folder]\obj\ [Build Type]\ folder and get [K2 project name].exe, [K2 project name].dll and the Deployment folder. These files need to be copied to the destination environment. It is not required that these be actually deployed on the K2 blackpearl server; they just need to be deployed from a computer that has the .NET 2.0 Framework in the same environment where the K2 blackpearl server is running. Second, once these files have been copied to the destination location, the MSBuild utility can now be used to deploy the K2 blackpearl project. The user doing this must have permissions to deploy a solution to the K2 blackpearl server.

There are several properties that can be used with the MSBuild command-line tool to control how the K2 blackpearl project is deployed.

- ❑ **Deploy_Processes:** Deploys the process to the server and by default it is true. If this is set to True, TestOnly must be set to False.

- ❑ **Create_Notifications:** Deploys the notifications that are part of a process.

- ❑ **Create_Workflow_Smart_Objects:** Deploys Workflow SmartObjects for all client-side events and a SmartObject for the process(es) in the project.

- ❑ **Create_Workflow_Reporting_SmartObjects:** Deploys Reporting SmartObjects for every process, activity, and event in the project.

- ❑ **TestOnly:** Used to conduct a test deployment but will stop short of deploying the process and SmartObjects to the server. If this is set to True, the Deploy_Processes property must be set to False.

- ❑ **Deploy_SmartObjects_And_Associations:** Deploys SmartObjects and Associations that have been created between them.

- ❑ **Environment:** Name of the environment that will be used.

To run the build, go to \Microsoft.NET\Framework\v2.0.50727 in a command window and run the MSBUILD command. It is recommended that the command be run in test mode first to see if there are any issues. Upon successful completion, run the command to do the actual deployment.

To run the deployment in test mode run the following command:

```
MSBUILD "[FileName]" /p:TestOnly=True;Environment=[Environment]
MSBUILD "C:\Chapter 10\Deployment\Wrox.Chapter10.Opportunity.Process.msbuild"
/p:TestOnly=True;Environment=SalesOpportunityDevelopment
```

Once the test command succeeds, run the next command to actually deploy the solution.

```
MSBUILD "[FileName]" /p:Environment=[Environment]
MSBUILD "C:\\Chapter 10\Deployment\Wrox.Chapter10.Opportunity.Process.msbuild"
/p:Environment=SalesOpportunityDevelopment
```

The [FileName] property for the MSBuild command is the path for the .msbuild file, which will be located within the \\[Project Folder]\obj\[Build Type]\Deployment folder. The [Environment] property is the name of the environment from the Environment Library that will be used for the deployment of the solution. The name of the environment and its value must be in the .msbuild file, which is generated from the current template and environment that cached in Visual Studio at the time the Create Deployment Package option was selected.

## MSBuild File

There are some other interesting files and information that designers should know about that are created under the \\[Project Folder]\obj\[Build Type]\Deployment folder. Probably the most important file is the .msbuild file. This file contains the instructions for the deployment of the process and when changed, can affect the deployment of the solution. First there are XML nodes for the properties that are used for the MSBuild command line. If no value is specified in the command line, the values specified in the .msbuild file will be used.

```
<PropertyGroup>
    <Deploy_Processes></Deploy_Processes>
    <Create_Notifications></Create_Notifications>
    <Deploy_SmartObjects_And_Associations></Deploy_SmartObjects_And_Associations>
    <Create_Workflow_Smart_Objects></Create_Workflow_Smart_Objects>
    <Create_Workflow_Reporting_Smart_Objects>
    </Create_Workflow_Reporting_Smart_Objects>
</PropertyGroup>
<PropertyGroup>
    <TestOnly></TestOnly>
    <Environment></Environment>
</PropertyGroup>
```

Going down a bit further into the .msbuild file, there will be XML for each environment for the template that is being used with the K2 project. Notice that all of the values were copied out of the Environment Library and placed in this file. If necessary, these values can be changed directly in this file before deployment.

```
<PropertyGroup Condition="$(Environment) == 'Production'">
    <EnvironmentFields>
        <Root Name="Production" xmlns="">
            <Field Name="Mail Server" Value="mail.denallix.com" />
            <Field Name="Web Service URL" Value="https://DLX:443" />
```

```
            <Field Name="Workflow Management Server"
                    Value="Integrated=True;IsPrimaryLogin=True;
                    Authenticate=True;EncryptedPassword=False;Host=DLX;Port=5555" />
            <Field Name="Workflow Server"
                    Value="Integrated=True;IsPrimaryLogin=True;
                    Authenticate=True;EncryptedPassword=False;Host=DLX;Port=5252" />
            <Field Name="SmartObject Server"
                    Value="Integrated=True;IsPrimaryLogin=True;
                    Authenticate=True;EncryptedPassword=False;Host=DLX;Port=5555" />
            <Field Name="ServiceObject Server"
                    Value="Integrated=True;IsPrimaryLogin=True;
                    Authenticate=True;EncryptedPassword=False;Host=DLX;Port=5555" />
            <Field Name="Category Server"
                    Value="Integrated=True;IsPrimaryLogin=True;
                    Authenticate=True;EncryptedPassword=False;Host=DLX;Port=5555" />
            <Field Name="SharePoint Sales Site URL" Value="" />
        </Root>
    </EnvironmentFields>
</PropertyGroup>
```

After `<PropertyGroup>`, there will be nodes for `<DeploymentLabelName>` and `<DeploymentLabelDescription>`. Both of these nodes can be filled in with custom information about the deployment. The rest of the `.msbuild` file contains information about all of the files that are part of the deployment, which should not be modified. Regenerating the `.msbuild` file from Visual Studio is the safest thing to do if major modifications need to be made. There are various other resource files that are located under `\\[Project Folder]\obj\[Build Type]\Deployment`, which are XML definitions of the processes or SmartObjects themselves. It is again recommended not to modify the file and to rerun the Create Deployment Package option in the Visual Studio Solution Explorer.

## Adding Pre- and Postdeployment Tasks

It is possible to create pre- and postdeployment tasks using the MSBuild framework. For example, a K2 process may use a SharePoint document library, and if that document library is not created at run time an error can occur if it is not there. To avoid having to manually create the document library in SharePoint before the process is deployed, predeployment tasks can be added to the MSBuild to create the document library. This could be done simply by creating an MSBuild task that will call the `stsadm` tool, which would use a SharePoint Feature to create a document library on a designated SharePoint Web site. Creating this task is outside of this book, but it is possible.

A very common postdeployment task would be to assign permissions to a process so that it can be used immediately, for example, the `SourceCode.Workflow.Management.WorkflowManagementServer` object, which can retrieve a list of all the processes that have been deployed to a server. Then, once a deployed process has been located, a `ProcSetPermissions` object can be created. This is where users can be given permission to a process and then updated back into the process object on the K2 server. The K2 blackpearl SDK has more specific instructions on how to do these operations and how to incorporate them in the K2 blackpearl MSBuild.

To add pre- and post-MSBuild tasks, the .target files used by K2 need to be modified. When the K2 blackpearl design environment is installed onto a development computer, the following MSBuild target files will be created under \\Program Files\MSBuild\SourceCode\v1.0. These target files contain instructions that are used by the MSBuild framework to deploy a solution:

❑ **ProjectDeployment.targets:** Used to deploy a K2 process or SmartObject project template

❑ **ProjectSystem.targets:** Used to do the core deployment of a K2 project

❑ **Workflow.WizardSDK.targets:** Used to deploy a K2 blackpearl Wizard

When a deployment package is created in a K2 design environment the `ProjectDeployment.targets` file will be copied to the `\\[Project Location]\obj\[Build Type]` folder. This MSBuild instruction file can be modified to include pre- and postdeployment instructions to add new targets to both `<PreDeployDependsOn>` and `<PostDeployDependsOn>`, but never modify the `<CoreDeployDependsOn>`, which is owned by the K2 blackpearl platform.

```xml
<Project xmlns="http://schemas.microsoft.com/developer/msbuild/2003">
  <PropertyGroup>
    <PreDeployDependsOn></PreDeployDependsOn>
    <PostDeployDependsOn></PostDeployDependsOn>
    <CoreDeployDependsOn>PreDeploy;Deploy;PostDeploy</CoreDeployDependsOn>
  </PropertyGroup>

  <Target Name="InitDeploy" Outputs="$(TestOnly);$(Environment)" >
    <CreateProperty Value="$(TestOnly)">
      <Output TaskParameter="Value" PropertyName="TestOnly" />
    </CreateProperty>
    <CreateProperty Value="$(Environment)">
      <Output TaskParameter="Value" PropertyName="Environment" />
    </CreateProperty>
  </Target>
  <Target Name="PreDeploy" DependsOnTargets="$(PreDeployDependsOn)"/>
  <Target Name="PostDeploy" DependsOnTargets="$(PostDeployDependsOn)"/>
  <Target Name="CoreDeploy" DependsOnTargets="$(CoreDeployDependsOn)"/>

  <!-- Custom targets -->

</Project>
```

Changing the `<PreDeployDependsOn>` and `<PostDeployDependsOn>` in the `ProjectDeployment.targets` file in the `\\Program Files\MSBuild\SourceCode\v1.0` folder will affect every deployment package that is created on that development machine. However modifying the `ProjectDeployment.targets` file in the K2 project folder will only affect the single project. Most commonly the `ProjectDeployment.targets` file would be updated in the K2 project folder because pre- and postdeployment instructions will be project specific. Creating MSBuild instructions is outside of the scope of this book, but this shows where custom ones would be added.

*Never modify any of the instructions that are in the* `ProjectSystem.targets` *and* `Workflow.WizardSDK.targets` *files because they are owned by the K2 blackpearl platform and can be updated by future releases.*

### *Environments and String Table Dependencies*

It is important to note that environments and String Tables are not dependent on each other. Templates and environments need to be created only on a development server and do not have to be created on staging or production K2 blackpearl servers. This is because environment fields are only used in the K2 Designers. When the process is successfully built, the environment fields from the current template are pushed into the MSBuild package that is created by the K2 Designer. This MSBuild package will contain all of the environment field values for the template. Then when it is deployed, the values from the MSBuild package are stored in the String Table.

Commonly on a development server there will be an Environment Template with all of the environments such as development, staging, and production with all of the correct values stored. When the MSBuild package is created, all of the files in the Deployment folder need to be simply copied to the correct server, and then the MSBuild package will be deployed via the command line.

The environment field values can be changed directly in the MSBuild package, but it is recommended that if that is done, go back to the K2 Workspace and make the associated change there too, so subsequent builds of the MSBuild package will have the correct environments in place. However, never change the name of an environment field in the MSBuild package because the process definition will have a reference to the name. If the name were to change and the process definition were not updated an exception would occur during deployment. If the name of an environment field must change, go to the K2 Workspace, modify the name of the environment field, and then open the K2 process and rebuild it. This will find all of the places where the old environment field name is used. Change the process to use the renamed environment field, then rebuild and deploy the process.

### *Excluding Items*

It is possible to exclude items from a deployment. This can be done by right-clicking the item in the Visual Studio Solution Explorer and selecting the Exclude from Build menu item. This will put a red X mark next to the item, indicating that it will not be part of a deployment. This must be done before the project is built and the subsequent deployment package is created. This is important because the item will not be built as part of the project and will not be included in the MSBuild deployment instructions. This is why it is not possible to exclude items from the deployment wizard. The deployment wizard is just a nice front user interface for running the `.msbuild` file for users who are not going to deploy using the command line. It is not a recommended solution to exclude items by modifying the `.msbuild` file directly as there can be dependencies that are required at run time. If something needs to be excluded, the item should be excluded by using Visual Studio, rebuilt, and then deployed.

# Deploying SmartObject Services

Using the K2 blackpearl API, developers can author custom SmartObject Services that can be used for SmartObject methods. Once the service has been written, they need to be deployed and registered with the K2 blackpearl server. There are three basic steps to initially deploy a SmartObject service:

1. Build the SmartObject Service DLL.
2. Register the SmartObject Service with the K2 server.
3. Create an instance of the SmartObject Service.

The SmartObject Service is nothing more than an assembly (.dll file) that is compiled and placed in the \\Program Files\K2 blackpearl\ServiceBroker directory. All SmartObject Services will execute from this directory. First, obtain the .dll file for the service and add it to this location. Second, once the .dll has been added to this location, use the BrokerManagement.exe to register the K2 SmartObject Service with the K2 server. The BrokerManagement.exe application is also located within the ServiceBroker folder. Figure 10-20 shows the Service Broker Management tool.

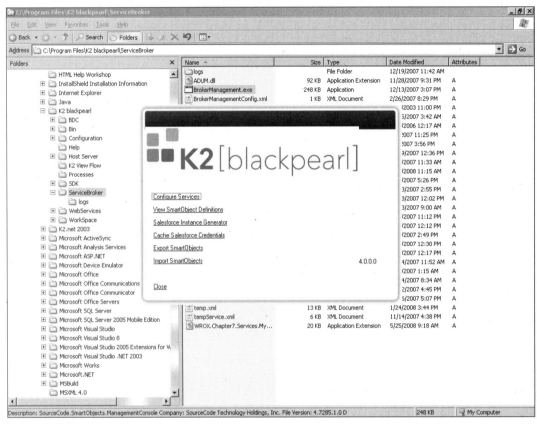

Figure 10-20

When the BrokerManagement.exe application has been started, press the Configure Services link, which will open the Manage Services window. There is a tree of all services that have been registered with the K2 server. To add a new one, right-click the Services node, and select the Register New Service menu item (as shown in Figure 10-21).

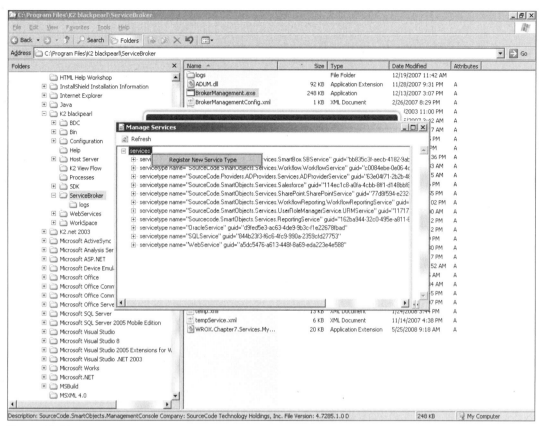

**Figure 10-21**

This will open the Service Type window (shown in Figure 10-22), where metadata associated with the service must be entered. The Type GUID is generated and does not need to be changed. The System Name must be a unique value across all of the services and a Display Name and Description should be provided. Finally, press the ellipse next to the Assembly Path field, which will open a file window to the ServiceBroker directory and the directory's `.dll`. Once this is done, the SmartObject Service will be registered.

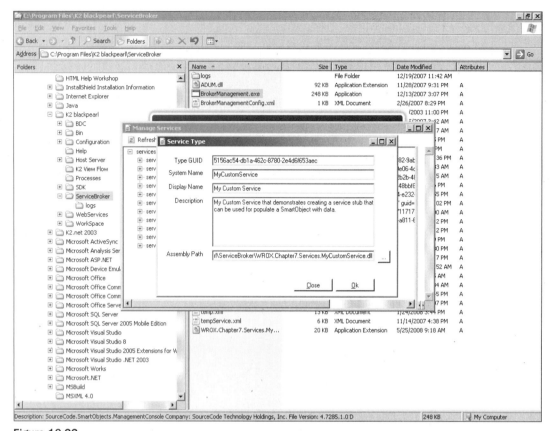

Figure 10-22

A service instance will need to be created for a new service that has been deployed. The service instance is used by the SmartObject method to populate its properties with data. To add a service instance, an administrator will need to go the K2 Workspace, and in the Management Console, open the SmartObjects node. Figure 10-23 shows the SmartObject service types that have been registered with the SmartObject server.

Figure 10-23

To create a new service instance, select the SmartObject Service node, which will then open a window listing all of the service instances that have been created (as shown in Figure 10-24). Clicking the Add button will open the Service Instance Configuration screen, where all of the configuration values for the service can be entered. Custom configurations that were created in the service will be displayed and must be filled-in if they are required. As well, a unique system name and display name must be entered for the service. Once this is completed, the SmartObject service can be used with SmartObjects.

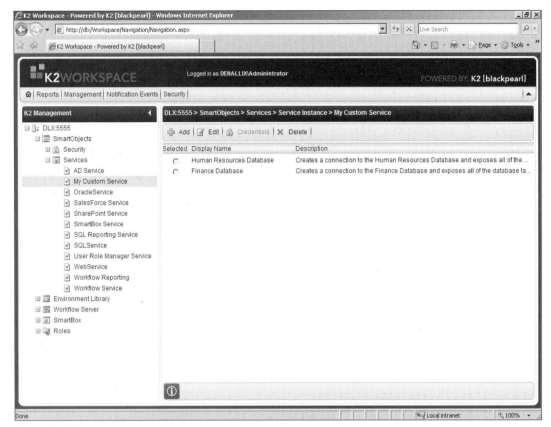

Figure 10-24

If a SmartObject uses a service method that has not been deployed, the SmartObject cannot be deployed. The SmartObject service must be deployed first, and then an instance of the SmartObject service must be created using the same name as the instance for where the SmartObject was created. So if the K2 development server has a SmartObject instance called CRMService, then the production server will need a similar service instance name of CRMService.

Updating a SmartObject Service is not too different from the steps to deploy the SmartObject Service; however, the K2 Service must be stopped so that the updated .dll can be reregistered with the server. To update the SmartObject Service, stop the K2 Service using the Service Console, then move the new .dll into the ServiceBroker directory and then restart the K2 Service in the Service Console. Finally, the BrokerManagement.exe application must be used again to update all of the running instances in order to use the updated .dll. As Figure 10-25 shows, click on the Configure Services link in the BrokerManagement.exe, find the SmartObject service, right-click it, and then select the Refresh All Service Instances menu item.

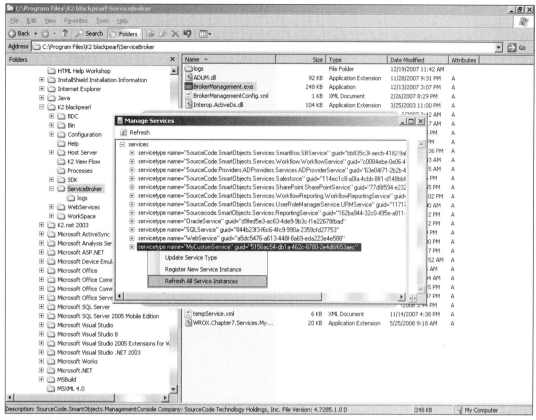

**Figure 10-25**

*If there is a farm of K2 blackpearl servers, this process will have to be done manually on each server in the farm, even if they are load balanced. There is currently no utility that will push this out to every server on the farm. However the service instances that are created in the K2 Workspace will be load balanced.*

## Deploying SmartObjects

SmartObject definitions are deployed to the SmartObject Server in a similar fashion as processes are deployed to the Workflow server. The designer can use the deployment wizard or use the same MSBuild commands to deploy SmartObjects as they would for processes. The `.sodx` file is an XML file that contains the definition of the SmartObject such as all of the fields, methods, and SmartObject Service instances that it will use. This XML file is managed and version controll by the SmartObject server.

When deploying SmartObjects from one server to another, some extra steps may be required. SmartObject Services are deployed to a SmartObject Server and then instances of those SmartObject Services can be created using the K2 Workspace Management Console. The SmartObject Service instances have methods, which are referenced by the SmartObject definition created in a K2 design environment. The SmartObject Service instance is referenced by a GUID, which is contained in the `.sodx` file. This GUID was generated by the SmartObject server when the service instance was created. When a SmartObject is redeployed, for example, from a development to a staging environment, the GUID of the SmartObject Service instance will need to change. This is because even though the SmartObject Service instance has been created in both environments, even with the same name, the GUID will be different. This is required by the K2 SmartObject framework to ensure that there are no conflicts between SmartObject Service instances that reside on different SmartObject servers.

If a `.sodx` file is moved from one environment to another, and this GUID is not changed, an error will occur during deployment similar to the following:

```
"Deploy smartobjects: Task error: SmartObjectServer Exception:
Dependency could not be created. Parent does not exist in this
environment. Check Data property of exception."
```

To resolve the issue, the `.sodx` file must be modified. This error will not occur for all SmartObjects that are moved from one server to another. When K2 blackpearl is initially installed, some SmartObject Service instances will be created by default like the SmartBox and Active Directory. These Service instances have a controlled GUID, which will be the same across all servers. SmartObjects that use these Services will not encounter this error. However, Service instances that are dynamic — like many of the ones on the K2 black market — will counter this issue when it is moved from one server to another.

*If the default Service instances were to ever be removed and then added back again, this error could occur.*

Open the `.sodx` file in a tool like Notepad. There will be section of XML similar to the following (all of the GUID values will be different):

```
<ServiceElementDefinition>
    <Guid>4af9d395-06ad-4eae-a5ea-47bc51eac146</Guid>
    <Name>serviceinstance</Name>
    <Value>e5609413-d844-4325-98c3-db3cacbd406d</Value>
</ServiceElementDefinition>
```

The `Value` node must be updated to the SmartObject Service instance on the environment that this SmartObject is being deployed to. To find the correct GUID value go to the `BrokertManagement.exe` application that is located in `\\Program Files\K2 blackpearl\ServiceBroker`. Run this application and select Configure Services. When the Manage Services window opens, drill-down in the services instances node and select the correct one to which the SmartObject should be mapped. For example, there will be a `serviceinstance` node similar to the following:

```
<serviceinstance name="SmartBoxService"
type="SourceCode.SmartObjects.Services.SmartBox.SBService"
GUID="d9fed5tf-ac63-4de0-9b3c-f1e22678ferr">
```

The GUID from the `serviceinstance` node needs to be updated to the Value node of the `.sodx` file for the SmartObject:

```
<ServiceElementDefinition>
    <Guid>4af9d395-06ad-4eae-a5ea-47bc51eac146</Guid>
    <Name>serviceinstance</Name>
    <Value>d9fed5tf-ac63-4de0-9b3c-f1e22678ferr</Value>
</ServiceElementDefinition>
```

Once this is done, the SmartObject can then be successfully deployed to the new environment. Remember that if this is a composite SmartObject, meaning that more than one SmartObject Service is used by the SmartObject, then all `serviceinstance` GUIDs will need to be updated.

There is a tool on the K2 blackmarket called the ServiceObject GUID Updater. This utility application, supported by the community, will complete all of these steps. It also has a batch feature that is helpful when there are a large number of SmartObjects that need to be updated. As well, K2 plans on releasing some more tools to support this as part of their design environments.

## Deployment through Code

It is possible to create deployment packages and deploy K2 Processes and SmartObjects through code using the K2 blackpearl Deployment framework, which utilizes MSBuild assemblies. This is the same API that is used to provide build functionality within the various designer environments. Using it allows for development teams to create fully automated build scripts or even go as far as creating a continuous integration environment. There are two major steps that must be done to completely deploy a K2 project through code:

1.  Create an MSBuild file that contains all of the instructions necessary to deploy a K2 project. This would entail retrieving all the environment variable values from the Environment server and setting switch statements that would have been done in the command line as previously shown.

2.  Deploy the K2 project to the K2 blackpearl server.

The following code will demonstrate how K2 blackpearl projects can be deployed using code. In this example, a simple Visual Studio Console project will be created and the following libraries must be referenced:

❑   Microsoft.Build.Engine

❑   Microsoft.Build.Framework

❑   SourceCode.EnvironmentSettings.Client

❑   SourceCode.Framework

❑   SourceCode.Workflow.Design

❑   SourceCode.HostClientAPI

Create a class named K2BuildUtility and add the following using statements:

```
using SourceCode.EnvironmentSettings.Client;
using SourceCode.Framework.Deployment;
using SourceCode.ProjectSystem;
using SourceCode.Workflow.Design.EnvironmentSettings;
using SourceCode.Hosting.Client.BaseAPI;
```

To accomplish the task of deploying a K2 project through code, the K2Build class will have two methods called DeployK2() and CreateDeploymentPackage(). Starting with the DeployK2() method, the first thing is to create an object of Project type. This class requires the path to the *.k2proj project file, where a process and/or SmartObjects will reside. Once the project has been loaded, the Project must be built to ensure there are no errors in the process or SmartObject definitions. After building, a DeploymentPackage object must be created and saved, which will create the actual MSBuild file that was discussed previously. The final step is to call Execute() on the package, which will deploy the K2 project to the K2 blackpearl server.

```
public static bool DeployK2(string EnvironmentServer, string DestinationTemplate,
                string DestinationEnvironment, string ProjectPath, string
                OutputPath) {

    bool success = false;

    try
    {
        Project project = new Project();
        project.Load(ProjectPath);

        DeploymentResults results = project.Compile();

        DeploymentPackage package = CreateDeploymentPackage(EnvironmentServer,
            DestinationTemplate, DestinationEnvironment, project, false);
        package.Save(OutputPath, "K2 Deployment Package");

        results = package.Execute();
        success = results.Successful;
    } catch (Exception ex) {
        throw ex;
    }

    return success;
}
```

The CreateDeploymentPackage method was separated from the DeployK2 method because a deployment package may sometimes be the only item that needs to be created. After you make a connection string using the SCConnectionStringBuilder, the Environment Library server is loaded using an EnvironmentSettingsManager object. The EnvironmentSettingsManager object can be used to do anything needed to the Environment Library server, such as creating new templates or environments. However, all that is needed here is to load the `EnvironmentSettingsManager`, using the both the `ConnectToServer` and `InitializeSettingsManager` methods, which will establish a connection to the Environment Library server. Calling the `Refresh` method will actually load the values from the Environment Library server into the object.

```
public static DeploymentPackage CreateDeploymentPackage(string EnvironmentServer,
        string DestinationTemplate, string DestinationEnvironment,
        Project Project, bool TestOnly) {

    //Create connection string to environment server
    SCConnectionStringBuilder cb = new SCConnectionStringBuilder();
    cb.Host = EnvironmentServer;
    cb.Port = 5555;
    cb.Integrated = true;
    cb.IsPrimaryLogin = true;
    cb.Authenticate = true;
    cb.EncryptedPassword = false;
    string envionmentServerConnection = cb.ToString();

    //Retrieve the environments from the server
    EnvironmentSettingsManager environmentManager = new
        EnvironmentSettingsManager(true);
    environmentManager.ConnectToServer(envionmentServerConnection);
    environmentManager.InitializeSettingsManager(true);
    environmentManager.Refresh();
```

Once `EnvironmentSettingsManager` has been loaded, both `EnvironmentTemplate` and `EnvironmentInstance` instances can be referenced. All the field values will need to be extracted and added to the deployment package. After referencing each, the `EnvironmentInstance` object contains all of the field values that will be used to populate the String Table. To get these values from the Environment Library server to the String Table, a `DeploymentPackage` object needs to be created using the `Project.CreateDeploymentPackage()` method.

```
    //Get the template and environment objects.
    EnvironmentTemplate template =
            environmentManager.EnvironmentTemplates[DestinationTemplate];
    EnvironmentInstance environment =
            template.Environments[DestinationEnvironment];

    //Create the package
    DeploymentPackage package = Project.CreateDeploymentPackage();
```

When the `DeploymentPackage` object has been created, a `DeploymentEnvironment` object will need to be created, using the `AddEnvironment()` method on the `DeploymentPackage` object. The `DeploymentEnvironment` will need to take all of the values from the `EnvironmentInstance` `.EnvironmentFields` collection and set it into `DeploymentEnvironment.Properties` collection.

This will ultimately put all of the values into the MSBuild file, which will later be copied to the String Table accessible through the K2 Workspace.

```
//Set all of the environment fields to the package
DeploymentEnvironment deploymentEnv =
        package.AddEnvironment(environment.EnvironmentName);

foreach (EnvironmentField field in environment.EnvironmentFields) {
    deploymentEnv.Properties[field.FieldName] = field.Value;
}
```

Finally, some of the miscellaneous properties of the DeploymentPackage object must be set prior to deployment. The name of the environment being used must be set using the SelectedEnvironment field. This can be any string value and does not have to be the same name as the environment. This value will be used as the title for the String Table; recall that all String Tables that share the same name will share the same values. Both DeploymentLabelName and DeploymentLabelDescription are not actually required; however, it is recommended that they be used to add some description indicating which process or SmartObjects are being deployed. The TestOnly property will control whether the process definition will actually be deployed to the server. Last, both the SmartObjectField and WorkflowManagementServerField connection strings need to be added to the DeploymentPackage, which are retrieved from the EnvironmentInstance. Setting both of these values is extremely important because these values are used to tell the MSBUILD where to deploy the process and SmartObjects.

```
//Set fields on the package
package.SelectedEnvironment = DestinationEnvironment;
package.DeploymentLabelName = DateTime.Now.ToString();
package.DeploymentLabelDescription = "Template: " + DestinationTemplate + ",
        Environment: " + DestinationEnvironment;
package.TestOnly = TestOnly;

//Get the Default SmartObject Server in the Environment
EnvironmentField smartObjectServerField =
        environment.GetDefaultField(typeof(SmartObjectField));
package.SmartObjectConnectionString = "$Field=" +
        smartObjectServerField.DisplayName;

//Get the Default Workflow Management Server in the Environment
EnvironmentField workflowServerField =
        environment.GetDefaultField(typeof(WorkflowManagementServerField));
package.WorkflowManagementConnectionString = "$Field=" +
        workflowServerField.DisplayName;

return package;
}
```

Once both `DeployK2()` and `CreateDeploymentPackage()` have been completed, the following code can be used to deploy a process or SmartObjects project to the K2 server. In this case, the name of where the Environment server is located is called `DLX`. The configuration data in the production environment of the Default Template is being used. The location of the K2 project is specified and the output of the MSBuild files is also specified.

```
K2BuildUtility.DeployK2("DLX", "Default Template", "Production",
    @"C:\Projects\Process.k2proj", @"C:\Projects\Build");
```

*This example showed only how to deploy a K2 process and SmartObject. The same API can be used to deploy SmartObject Services.*

# Summary

You have learned about all of the aspects associated to deploying a K2 process. Even though deploying a K2 process can be a very easy task, forethought needs to be made to ensure that maintainability and sustainability are ensured. Using the Environment Library as shown can streamline deployments. Planning must be incorporated into the way that the Environment Library is used; otherwise, it can become a dumping ground for configurations that are not relevant from one process to another. The architecture of process and SmartObject deployment and how K2 blackpearl utilizes the MSBuild framework to deploy process-driven applications to the server illustrates the extensibility and power of the K2 platform.

The next chapter now turns to working with InfoPath and ASP.NET forms.

# 11

# Working with InfoPath and ASP.NET Forms

Chris O'Connor
Jason Apergis

When you approach a K2 solution, it's important to consider the visual aspects to the process and the end-user experience. ASP.NET and InfoPath are the most common user interfaces for K2 processes.

This chapter covers the following topics:

- ❏ Client event forms within K2
- ❏ InfoPath, ASP.NET, and other forms technologies
- ❏ Pros and cons of InfoPath
- ❏ Pros and cons of ASP.NET
- ❏ Using InfoPath forms
    - ❏ Working with InfoPath data
    - ❏ Advanced InfoPath XML considerations
    - ❏ Modifying the process
    - ❏ Archiving an InfoPath form
    - ❏ InfoPath and SmartObject integration
    - ❏ Good design considerations
    - ❏ InfoPath process deployment

❑ Using ASP.NET forms

  ❑ Initiating a workflow from code

  ❑ Customizing a Web page created via the Forms Generation Client Event

  ❑ Displaying a custom Web page for a workflow task form

  ❑ Completing an activity from code

  ❑ K2 server management from code — process definitions, versions, and activities

  ❑ Viewing processes currently running

  ❑ Viewing a worklist for the current user

# Client Event Forms within K2

Within a traditional ASP.NET Web application, information is displayed to the user who then enters or updates information, and clicks a button to submit. A business layer and subsequent data layer then updates the database and the user continues.

With regard to K2, a workflow process is the business layer, with SmartObjects as the data layer, and forms are used as the presentation layer.

The wording of *forms* gives a perception of a piece of paper, which is often a good way to consider it. A paper-based leave request is an example of a document that would easily translate from a single sheet of paper to a digital-based form.

To include a form within the K2 workflow, a Client Event is added to the process. The "Default" Client Event wizard is shown in Figure 11-1. This allows the designer to enter the form location or choose which form to show.

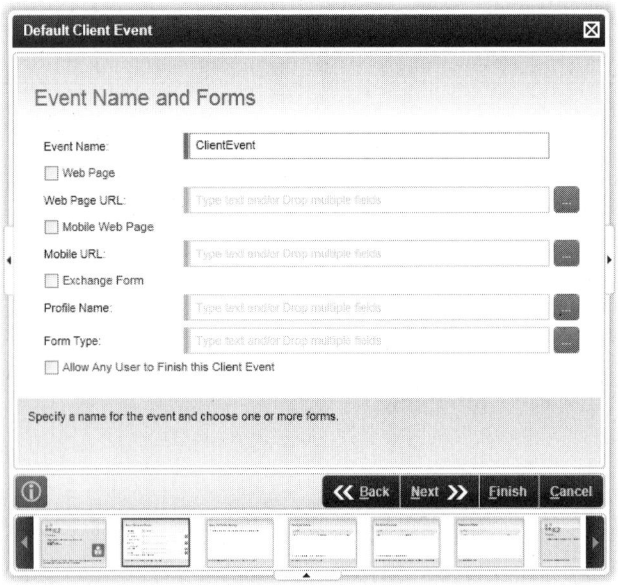

Figure 11-1

As the K2 process is executed, a user task (worklist item) is created for the Client Event. The name and location of the form is included as worklist item *data*, thereby allowing the form to be displayed when a user actions the task.

The user may then enter additional data, provide feedback, and contribute to the information already captured, with any decision made being returned to the K2 workflow. This will then pass the form on to the next person in the workflow or execute the specific workflow logic.

Much as with a paper-based form, there will most likely be sections to be completed by different staff or roles (such as a manager or superior) to enter comments and sign the form.

A form can be designed to have different *views*, with certain fields shown or limited actions available, with the data from the previous step already filled in. This allows the user to focus on nothing more than the specific information required to make a decision.

There are a number of forms technologies that can be used as the presentation layer for the K2 process. The developer or the business user can utilize familiar tools and skill sets to create the user interface for K2 processes in a number of different ways, each with advantages and disadvantages.

> *K2 has no preference for, or dependency on, any of the options that follow. In fact, some processes may not actually need human interaction, such as with system workflow for integration of disparate systems and data sources. Fully functional processes that do not even use forms can be created with K2.*

## InfoPath

An extended member of the Microsoft Office Suite, InfoPath, as is a rich forms designer tool, designed to provide quick and easy creation of essentially paper-based forms for easy data capture and form filling.

Underneath the InfoPath designer (user interface) is an extensive XML schema and data model, into which K2 injects XML nodes and values for interacting with the workflow logic within the process.

Additionally, there is the ability to specify different *views* of the form, to show at certain logic points within the process, or for different security levels.

The workflow decision points known as actions are added to the InfoPath form by the K2 integration, with a combo box added to allow a user to select the relevant outcome when submitting the form.

Within the InfoPath world, there is the option to create *rich-client* forms, which requires users to have the InfoPath product installed on their local PCs or to display the form within a Web browser, using Office Forms Server (often referred to *as InfoPath Forms Services*) and SharePoint to allow for *browser-based* forms.

> *With regard to SharePoint product placement, and licensing, Office Forms Server is available as a separate SKU, although with fairly limited functionality when compared to Microsoft Office SharePoint Server (MOSS), standard or enterprise.*

> *Most implementations of SharePoint and Forms Server will occur via the Enterprise CAL version of SharePoint. This is the assumed environment for the remainder of the chapter — any mention of "Forms Server" is related to the functionality within SharePoint Enterprise, rather than the installation of Office Forms Server (SKU).*

# ASP.NET

If the project or organization has a requirement to provide forms with rich user interfaces, or there is a need to integrate with additional back-end systems, then the choice of Web forms, Web pages, Web services and Web parts developed using ASP.NET is another option.

*Note that the skill set of the organization or project team must be capable of custom code development in order to successfully create, deploy, and maintain forms using ASP.NET.*

Using Visual Studio, you can create custom designed layouts and rich user interfaces including Silverlight, AJAX, and numerous custom controls, as well as create code that can reference namespaces and class libraries as part of the .NET framework and object model.

Using standard .NET languages such as C# and VB.NET, and the rich K2 API and object model, you can create Web pages that programmatically read values within the workflow process to display on screen in whichever text formatting, layout, or graphical design as required.

The Web pages are hosted within IIS, with the corresponding Web page address used within the workflow designer. The K2 process is configured to use the particular Web page URL, and the necessary input parameters (querystring) are provided automatically by the K2 integration. The Web page will then use the values to determine the user task, and the process associated with it.

The actions defined within the process can be shown to users, and then the relevant outcome determined, along with the saving of any workflow data variables users may have entered or updated.

# Other Forms Technologies

There are a number of other forms technologies that can be included in the K2 process designer as Client Event forms. This chapter centers on the main choices of InfoPath and ASP.NET, and so only a high-level overview is provided.

## Exchange Forms

For an organization that uses the Microsoft Outlook Organizational Forms Library within Microsoft Exchange, there can be standard Outlook forms used to deliver the work items to workflow participants.

The K2 process designer will specify the Profile Name used to access the Exchange Server. The Form Type is then specified to link the K2 Processes with the relevant Outlook form (template) within Microsoft Exchange.

*This technology is primarily to retain backward compatibility with K2.net 2003 Exchange Forms.*

## K2 Forms Generation Client

Within the K2 Designer, there is also the Forms Generation Client Event, which allows for some quick browser-based forms to be created automatically, without the need for InfoPath, or custom development of ASP.NET Web pages.

The forms generator is actually a *code* generator, with the result being an ASP.NET page located within the following directory :

```
C:\Program Files\K2 blackpearl\Workspace\ClientEventPages
```

This is underneath the folder for K2 Workspace Web pages, meaning that the forms also reside within the K2 Workspace *Web site* in IIS.

The default user interface created by the generator is rather basic and needs a little polish for layout and graphics. But, the forms are fully functional and can be great to quickly create a simple proof-of-concept (PoC) process. The good news is that the template used can be customized, and additional Form Layouts can be created, as will be shown in the following section.

## Mobile Forms

With an ever-increasing mobile workforce, there may be a requirement to interact with a process remotely using a PDA, SmartPhone, or other such mobile device. InfoPath allows mobile forms to be created automatically, although the form should be designed with fewer fields than a browser-based or InfoPath rich-client design.

Like with ASP.NET Web pages, mobile forms can also be created simply using ASP.NET. They are essentially just Web forms that are sized to a smaller interface and/or use page controls that have reduced functionality and layout. It follows that the techniques detailed in the following sections regarding ASP.NET code and the K2 API will also apply, and they can be used from within Visual Studio as with a "normal" Web application.

When the user views the form, the program code and/or screen controls will determine if it is being shown on a mobile device or Web browser, and display it accordingly.

> When using an InfoPath browser-based form, the rendering of the form is automatically resized for the mobile device. The server will detect the device and adjust the screen resolution and size automatically when browsing to the particular form URL.

The business logic and code behind for the form would contain the same fields being displayed/captured with the larger *normal* ASP.NET form. Of course, the same actions and outcomes would most likely apply, too.

While the same form and code behind may be used, because some ASP.NET controls are able to detect and render content differently, it is generally best to redesign the layout for the smaller form factor.

## WinForms

With the code written for ASP.NET forms, there is no reason this .NET code could not be implemented within a rich-client Windows Form, or even a console application.

The difficulty here is that the integration within the K2 Designer does not exist. Some additional code could be written to interact with the K2 API, and display process data, actions, and outcomes, but this couldn't be directly linked to from within the K2 Process Designer, using the Client Event Wizards.

# Which Should You Choose?

There are many different decisions as to which forms technology to adopt, and there are perfectly valid reasons to use any one of these options, just as there are similar reasons why each should *not* be chosen. The choice will often depend on infrastructure, such as software available, and any budgetary or timing considerations, rather than any specific technical shortfalls of either approach.

The criteria list includes topics such as:

❑   Worker skill set and software tools available (Visual Studio/InfoPath)

❑   System integration

❑   Time to production

❑   User interface requirements

❑   Need/want to integrate with SharePoint

❑   Business logic and code

❑   Deployment

First, let's have a look at some of the pros and cons with regard to the two main contenders — InfoPath and ASP.NET.

## InfoPath Pros

InfoPath is a great Microsoft Office-friendly product, primarily used to design the typical paper-based form. The interface to design forms is simple and intuitive, making it a great choice for business users, and power users alike, without the need to know any code.

The InfoPath designer includes a data source designer with an underlying XML schema file. There are numerous WYSIWYG forms layout tools that allow a user to quickly create professional-looking forms. The completed form contains both the form layout, and data elements and values, in a self-contained XML format.

> *InfoPath has a number of standard template forms allowing the organization to immediately start designing processes such as Expense Claims, Asset Tracking, or Travel Request.*

It's easy to create *views*, which can be targeted using security, such as staff-, manager-, and CEO-level security views, for example. Alternatively, this may be based on logic related to certain business rules — such as "When stock is less than 10,000, display the LowStockDiscount view," with different data fields shown, for example.

Fields within a view can be hidden, read-only, and change colour/font dynamically according to the business rules to be implemented (within the K2 workflow).

Following the design of the various views within InfoPath, the client event inside the K2 Designer is configured with the specific view to show for the particular event. This can be seen in Figure 11-2.

**Figure 11-2**

The data validation capabilities of InfoPath are significant, with rules able to be configured by the user creating the form. Simply using drop-downs, the designer can select that certain field values must be greater than, less than, blank, not blank, match a pattern, and so on, as well as make comparisons between fields, dates, entered values, or using a formula.

These rules can then display a validation message to the user as a screen tip (or, if using rich-client forms, a message box dialog can be used). Users will not be able to submit the form until these validation errors have been corrected, although they can save the form (if the save option for the form has been set) and then update and submit at a later date. The same validation rules will be applied when the user resubmits the form.

The integration with K2 is deep, and provides the ability to modify and design InfoPath forms using the K2 Designer, with tools such as Visual Studio, Visio, or K2 Studio. With the InfoPath form being an XML file underneath, the K2 Designer can easily add nodes, update values, and include details for actions and outcomes.

When the K2 process is executed, the entire XML for the InfoPath form is loaded into a data variable within the process instance, meaning that server code within a K2 Server Event can read, add, and update nodes, and enact changes to the data that is then to be displayed to the user on the form.

A number of Web service data connections are added, to interact with the K2 Web services, upon loading, updating, and submission of the form, depending on the actions and outcomes defined for the process.

A big plus for K2 developers is that the InfoPath files will be included as items within the Visual Studio solution. This keeps all components within the same project, which in turn allows for the use of source control tools such as Team Foundation Server and Visual SourceSafe. InfoPath forms are also relatively easy to deploy, depending on the choice of destination.

InfoPath also allows users to interact with forms using a Web browser. Simply known as browser-based forms, the InfoPath Forms Services (as part of the SharePoint Enterprise installation) allow users to have InfoPath forms shown in a Web browser, rendered using HTML, JavaScript, and CSS. This means that end users (Form Fillers) won't need to have the Microsoft Office InfoPath tool installed.

When using SharePoint and InfoPath, an end user can open an InfoPath form from a document library and have SharePoint events intercepted, which can then initiate a K2 process. This means that the end user simply clicks "New," fills out the form, and once the form is submitted, the K2 workflow commences, using the form data. That seamless integration for initiating workflows is a great feature and one of the reasons that many organizations opt for InfoPath.

Alternatively, using the rich-client InfoPath form allows items saved within a SharePoint document library to be saved locally, meaning there is also an offline capability.

A rich-client InfoPath form can also act purely as an offline file, and has no requirement to coexist with SharePoint at all. These files can be treated as a Microsoft Word or Excel file, allowing a user to e-mail the form within an organization and use the data to interact with a business process on a central K2 server.

Last, the integration with K2 SmartObjects means that the display mechanism for this data can be InfoPath forms. Using a data connection, and mapping fields to the view, the InfoPath form will allow for saving data back to the same SmartObjects upon submission of the form.

## InfoPath Cons

While it would seem that InfoPath is the one to go for, the devil is in the detail. Certainly, there would be many organizations to whom none of the following issues or potential problems apply, and for those organizations, InfoPath is most likely the way to go.

While the InfoPath form layout and data schema designers allow for a great form-style user interface (UI), there can be some pain-points for complex forms related to introducing business logic that requires .NET code, known as the "code behind" within an InfoPath form. There can be deployment difficulties when using .NET managed code, especially for InfoPath rich-client forms.

Bear in mind also, that for browser-based forms, the code choice is limited to .NET languages such as VB.NET, and C#. Scripting languages and code, such as VBScript or JavaScript, cannot be used.

When using InfoPath Forms Services and browser-based forms within SharePoint, the issues with managed code are alleviated somewhat, as the forms become IIS-managed forms and have "full trust" to execute the code behind.

To install such forms, they must first be uploaded within the SharePoint Central Administration site and then activated to a site collection. These are referred to as the Administrator-approved form templates. That may seen as a potential security risk by some; if the security policies of the organizations do not allow for "full trust," then this won't work.

While the InfoPath Forms Services functionality would appear to be a great option, there is a caveat related to licensing and versions of SharePoint. There is a requirement for the *Enterprise* version of SharePoint (Microsoft Office SharePoint Server aka MOSS) — and thus SharePoint Standard Edition can't be used. This is something to consider, especially with regard to the financial aspects of a project, or solution delivery. Alternatively, the Office Forms Server component can be licensed separately, using Windows SharePoint Services (WSS).

Browser-based forms also have a reduced subset of user controls and form design tools. For instance, the Master/Detail control is not supported in browser-based forms. The InfoPath form controls are rendered out as HTML, JavaScript, and CSS when loaded into the browser, and some of the rich-client controls are not able to be formatted as such.

Furthermore, the browser support for InfoPath forms is limited to more recent browsers, from Internet Explorer 6.0 and up, or Firefox 1.5 and above. The functionality may work as expected when using other browsers, but it is not supported.

The authentication model is used to connect to SharePoint, and thus the document library for the InfoPath form will require a security layer. This is limited to using Active Directory (AD) integrated mode security. If forms authentication is required, it cannot be achieved using InfoPath browser-based forms.

Other functions within the rich-client environment are not supported either, including the spell-checker, ink support (for tablet PCs), offline support and custom task panes. To be fair though, none of these would be available within an ASP.NET Web form — this is a difference between rich-client (Windows) and Web applications.

Last, if there is a need to submit forms directly to a database such as Microsoft SQL Server or Microsoft Access, then browser-based forms are not the solution — unless a custom Web service is created to handle submission of data to the database.

However, the good news is that the form can be submitted as an e-mail message, or to a SharePoint library (but not a list), as well as to a Web service.

Lastly, developers wanting to use code within InfoPath need to be aware of the troubleshooting and debugging capabilities being rather specialized, certainly not as simple as clicking "Play" within Visual Studio.

## Browser-Based InfoPath Forms

Some questions to consider:

- ❑ Does the organization have Forms Server or SharePoint Enterprise (licensing)?
- ❑ Does the form operate with managed code? If so, can it then be installed with Full Trust ?
- ❑ Does the form need to submit to a SQL Server database?
- ❑ Do end users need to authenticate using Forms Authentication (not using Active Directory)?

## InfoPath Rich-Client Forms

Some questions to consider:

- ❑ Do all users have InfoPath 2007 installed on their local PC?
- ❑ Do they need to operate without SharePoint?
- ❑ Do end users need or expect a spell-checker or other rich-client functionality?

## ASP.NET Pros

Many organizations implementing a K2 solution would most likely have one or more Web applications already, making use of Internet Information Services (IIS), ASP.NET — and probably SQL Server (required for K2 blackpearl also).

However, not every organization will necessarily have SharePoint (MOSS) and/or InfoPath as part of the infrastructure in place, or standard operating environment (SOE). An alternative may be to create a custom-developed Web site with ASP.NET Web pages and workflow forms, and the K2 API.

The developer or development team will create Web pages within Visual Studio, as with any other Web site, and include class library references for K2 integration. Program code is then included to retrieve, update, and execute an action on the worklist item (user task) within the running workflow instance. In addition to interacting with the K2 server, the custom code approach allows for developers and graphical designers to create the user interface to be shown, and can customize the layout, graphics, fonts, styles, and colors.

Within the K2 Workflow Designer, you specify the page URL to the required Web page, and a querystring with the K2 serial number will be passed to the Web page. This allows the program code to hook into the K2 server, and determine any workflow values and variables, and retrieve the actions and outcomes defined.

Being the ASP.NET program code, there is the full wealth of the Visual Studio toolset, including Server Explorer, debugging, and source control tools, and numerous third-party controls and add-ons. Developers can make use of the full .NET Class Framework, meaning that *any* code can be included from within the most recent versions of the .NET Framework. This allows for the use of WPF, LINQ, AJAX, and so forth, as well as providing the ability to include Web services integration, or connectivity to other servers and systems using the .NET program code.

Any .NET Web control can be used, and there is the ability to include Master Pages and Web parts and have complete HTML and CSS layout options. This allows for visually seamless integration with existing .NET applications. Further possibilities include Silverlight- and AJAX-enabled Web pages.

The project code for the ASP.NET Web site will be included as a separate project to the K2 process and workflow solution, meaning that multiple developers can independently interact with the different pieces of the solution. The integration with source control repositories, such as Visual Source Safe and Team Foundation Server, are the same as for any other Visual Studio project.

Debugging could not be simpler, with the standard F5 key being used to run the Web site with breakpoints easily included, and the ability to view data variables and step through code.

From a project implementation perspective, the only requirement for ASP.NET forms is to have IIS installed and configured, and it is a free add-on as part of the Windows Server environment. This can eliminate costly server licenses for SharePoint, and/or InfoPath, and the K2 Web sites and Web services can happily exist without the need for either SharePoint or InfoPath.

But, the real plus is access to the K2 API. You can code the integration to K2 the same as with System.Data (for ADO.NET), System.Xml, or any other .NET class library.

Here are just a few examples of this:

- ❑ Code can be included within a Web service to initiate a workflow, allowing it to be called from a disparate system such as CRM, or EPM, or another custom back-end application.

- ❑ Existing ASP.NET Web applications can have code added to forms and class libraries to interact with K2, meaning that the investment in legacy applications is not wasted.

- ❑ When the form is being displayed for a task (workitem), the code behind can call to a Web service to retrieve additional information from another system, and display form fields to the end user.

- ❑ Within SharePoint, a custom Web part can be implemented which is a view of the list of tasks from within a process, or a number of processes. For example, the home page for the Marketing department could show a Web part with a list of all current processes underway, and who each task has been assigned to.

- ❑ As seen in Chapter 7 SmartObjects can be used as a source of data for an ADO.NET provider, meaning that a Web page could be coded to have a datagrid that loads data from a SmartObject.

The flexibility of the solution is limited only by the business requirements in place and the skill sets of the development team.

The developer community for K2 is growing rapidly, with a number of open-source projects located in the K2 blackmarket section of `k2underground.com`. Many of these include code samples and snippets that can be integrated into the existing ASP.NET solution.

The ASP.NET form solution provides great power and customization, with almost limitless functionality, user interfaces, and business logic potential, and can be easily integrated into the K2 process and workflow solution.

## ASP.NET Cons

As just described, the major advantage of ASP.NET forms development is the ability to customize and codify anything and everything. Unfortunately, this is also the major disadvantage of this choice. To steal a quote from one of my favorite superhero movies, Spiderman: "With great power, comes great responsibility."

First, there is the need for developers to have the skills and capabilities to program business logic using .NET code, as well as Web pages and screen design using ASP.NET, HTML, CSS, C#, VB.NET, or the like.

Also, there is a greater skill set required to be able to implement and support such a solution. This is beyond the realm of most business users and most likely will require a project team to develop and deploy the solution. There may also be additional staff involved, such as project managers, business analysts, graphic designers, and testers.

The deployment of the K2 process itself will only be part of the entire solution, as the Web site must also be deployed, along with any configuration updates and settings — such as user and security contexts for interacting with K2, and the connection string to connect to the K2 server itself.

With regard to the K2 Process Designer, the Visual Studio projects will be separate, as there is no way to simply add projects to the same solution. This means that there is a segregation of the solution into different constituent parts, requiring some oversight and management to ensure the integrity of the source code.

Custom code will need to be fully defined and documented in a technical specification and be tested and quality checked also, to allow for ease of maintenance for future developers and project teams. This would then necessitate the adoption of and adherence to certain coding standards, and reviews of program code created.

If the solution also interacts with other back-end systems, or databases, then this is further complexity that can have repercussions, depending on the configuration and/or code required.

The deployment of such a solution may not be beyond the skills of a component developer, or a developer capable of creating such a solution, but is certainly more involved than with an InfoPath form deployment.

The deployment phase may have certain risks and issues, such as installation of production servers requiring specialist knowledge and configuration, and may need infrastructure and IT department involvement. Furthermore, moving between environments and servers, for development, test, and production is something else to be considered, as with any implementation.

Simply put, there will be *more* code to be developed and tested, and *more* people involved, or required. This can create potential risks and issues, and have a run-on impact on timeframes, and thus the project delivery cycle is much greater.

And with time = money, and more people, the end result may be an increased cost for the project delivery. (However, there is no requirement for an organization to acquire SharePoint for K2 to operate, meaning potential *reductions* in licensing costs.) This may mean that a greater timeframe is required for the development team to get a solution to production, using ASP.NET.

The simple truth is that there are many traps and pitfalls, with regard to the design and development as well as the project management of such a solution. The timeframe to delivery will be measured in days and weeks, not hours and days, and you should be aware of any deployment and future maintenance considerations before embarking on an ASP.NET forms-based solution. Such problems can be alleviated or lessened with correct planning, design, and forethought.

## Criteria Scorecard

Using the original criteria detailed earlier, and after an overview of the pros and cons of both front-runner forms technologies, there may still be some confusion relating to the best option to choose. The following table examines the capabilities from another perspective.

| Criteria | InfoPath | ASP.NET |
|---|---|---|
| Worker skill set | Relatively easy for business or power users to create forms using InfoPath, without any coding knowledge required | More skills/knowledge required to develop for ASP.NET. <br><br> May require knowledge of C# or VB.NET, HTML, CSS, JavaScript, SQL Server, etc. |

| Criteria | InfoPath | ASP.NET |
|---|---|---|
| System integration | Can submit data and actions directly to K2 workflow via Web services provided.<br><br>Can also submit to SharePoint library or list, or to Microsoft Access, Microsoft SQL Server, and e-mail.<br><br>Can't submit directly to SQL Server when using browser-based forms. | Must include code to create connection, open worklist and submit data and actions to K2 server.<br><br>Other code can be included to integrate to back-end systems, using Web services and/or the .NET and K2 API.<br><br>.NET class libraries allow for the use of Web services, e-mail, active directory, SharePoint, etc. |
| Time to production | Rapid development and deployment<br><br>Can be deployed immediately from within the K2 Designer upon process deployment. | Custom coding, may require longer development and testing time required.<br><br>Potentially requires many developers and team members, resulting in additional costs for the project |
| User interface requirements | Easily configurable validation capabilities and spell-checker, Master/Detail, and other Windows controls.<br><br>InfoPath browser-based forms have fewer controls available, due to requirements for SharePoint Forms Server. | Much greater flexibility and rich UI capabilities, many user controls available, ability to create custom controls.<br><br>Other user interface possibilities such as Silverlight and AJAX. |
| Need/want to integrate with SharePoint | Deep integration with SharePoint, for displaying forms hosted by Forms Server, and for SharePoint event-listening to initiate K2 workflow.<br><br>SharePoint *Enterprise* is required for Office Forms Server. | Doesn't need to integrate or coexist with SharePoint. Only needs IIS and SQL Server (for K2 databases).<br><br>Can mean less licensing costs and infrastructure requirements. |
| Business logic and code | Can become complex with regard to managed code.<br><br>Need "full trust" for code and forms displayed as browser-based.<br><br>Forms can use .NET languages for code. Can't use VBScript or JavaScript for browser-based forms | Custom code can be created for any business logic, or other integration points and data sources.<br><br>K2 API allows for code to redirect, delegate, sleep, and retrieve lists of workflows underway and process definitions. |
| Deployment | When using rich-client forms, InfoPath 2007 must be installed on each user's computer.<br><br>Potential deployment hassles if forms use managed code, for rich-client form.<br><br>For browser-based forms, the InfoPath Forms Services hosting environment requires SharePoint Enterprise licensing. | Deployed as any other Web application.<br><br>Can configure application pools and Web sites within IIS, and include `web.config` settings. |

### Which One to Choose?

There are many reasons that an organization would choose to use InfoPath. If there are certain infrastructure requirements in place, such as SharePoint Enterprise, and users and developers are aware of the differences between the rich-client and browser-based forms approaches, then InfoPath is an ideal choice.

The ability to quickly and easily create what would be typical paper-based forms with no need for code and easy integration with SharePoint is yet another great reason to go with InfoPath.

Of course, it's important to keep things simple with regard to the form design, especially if there may be any need for custom code or for advanced user interface design.

If there is a need for full control over the user interface, both visually, and functionally, including security aspects such as Forms Authentication, and having the full .NET framework available, then the ASP.NET solution may be the better option.

Of course, the development team will have more work on their hands, and they will need certain skills to complete the job — and it may take longer — but there can be some great benefits to be had. Also, there is no specific requirement for SharePoint, which can alleviate some of the infrastructure needs and licensing costs within the organization.

The decision is in your hands; let's go ahead and look at each approach in depth.

# Using InfoPath Forms

Microsoft Office InfoPath is a tool that enables information workers to create forms that can be used to make effective and time-sensitive decisions. InfoPath provides the ability to streamline business processes, capture and validate data-based business rules, to hook into line-of-business (LOB) data, and to work in a flexible environment that accommodates business change. InfoPath is a XML-based Microsoft Office product that allows information workers to author dynamic and interactive forms without requiring the use of development environments like Visual Studio. The power behind InfoPath is an XSD schema, which can either be created by InfoPath or imported into an InfoPath form. Since InfoPath is an XML-based solution, data originating from disparate systems can easily be modified by an information worker.

The value proposition of InfoPath is that information workers can quickly create a form that is used within Office right out-of-the-box. The design experience for InfoPath is "what you see is what you get" (WYSIWYG), empowering information workers to create forms on the fly. InfoPath bridges the traditional gap between software developers and information workers because it does not require a sophisticated development environment or specialized training. InfoPath lends itself well as a tool for capturing data and performing business rules against that data. Some business rules will be enforced for free by the XSD schema, while others are implemented using custom rules, conditional formatting, scripting (JavaScript and VBScript), and .NET code. Once a form has been completed, InfoPath provides several different ways to publish the form template. For instance, an InfoPath form can be sent out via e-mail in Microsoft Outlook, placed on a file share, or published to SharePoint.

InfoPath and SharePoint provides the ability to automate business processes using such elements as e-mails, alerts in a form library, SharePoint Designer, and .NET managed code but more often than not, these tools cannot handle the implementation of enterprise process automation logic. What is commonly needed for building workflow solutions are dynamic user task assignments, task assignment queues, data integration, delegation, escalations, working hours, and process administration, none of which are available when using InfoPath by itself. K2 blackpearl paired with InfoPath provides an extremely exciting solution because InfoPath allows for rapid user interface development using an XML data source, while K2 provides out-of-the-box all of the tools needed to construct a workflow. In essence, the K2 blackpearl platform takes the XML of the InfoPath form and routes it to users and systems based on business rules. Since the XML of the InfoPath form is treated as a generic piece of data, the entire K2 blackpearl platform can be leveraged. K2 provides several wizards and utilities that hook InfoPath forms directly into a K2 process, and the data contained in the form can be modified before and after it's displayed to the user. The integration between InfoPath and a K2 blackpearl process boils down to a series of Web service method calls that are added to the InfoPath form.

## Background

Creating a K2 process that uses an InfoPath form is a relatively simple task using the InfoPath Process Integration and InfoPath Client Event Wizards. Developing InfoPath forms is outside the scope of this book; however, this chapter will cover in detail how an InfoPath form is integrated with K2, design and integration considerations, and how to manage the InfoPath form with K2. This chapter will demonstrate how to create a simple InfoPath approval process. In Figure 11-3, it depicts a process where an InfoPath form is submitted and both a manager and director will need to approve the submission. If either of them were to reject the submission it will go back to the originator for resubmission. Once the process is completed or canceled the InfoPath form will be archived. The process will be built using the Opportunity SmartObjects that were created in Chapter 7.

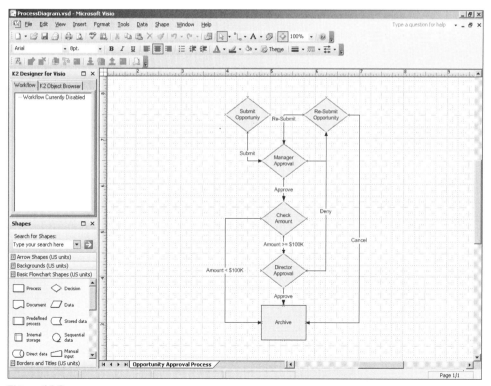

Figure 11-3

## Creating an InfoPath Process

It is good practice to build the InfoPath form first and design the process flow with the business users before construction of the process were to begin. Visio is a great tool for process flow modeling as business users are familiar with its functionality. Forms can be created in InfoPath relatively quickly, and they do not need to be hooked into K2 blackpearl immediately. An analyst can create a form and provide a demonstration to the process owners while walking through the Visio diagrams. Much of the work done in the InfoPath form and Visio diagrams can be reused in the actual construction of the process.

Once the design of the process is completed, the InfoPath form can be integrated with K2; this is commonly referred to as K2-enabling the InfoPath form. When integrated, a copy of the form is added to the solution and used from that point forward. Then the designer can start adding InfoPath Client Events to the K2 process, which will require users to open the InfoPath form and complete actions. Figure 11-4 is a simple form that could be used for a business opportunity approval process. All of the fields are required in the decision-making process and are editable in this view.

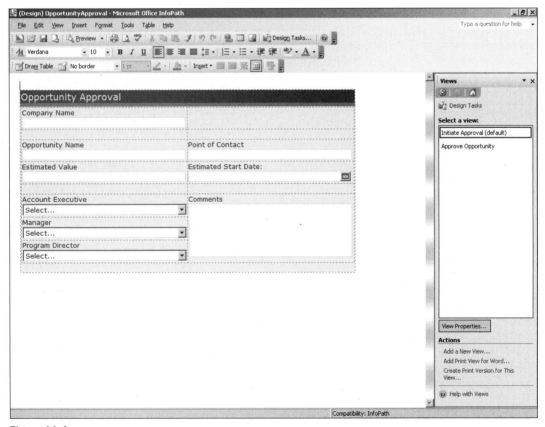

Figure 11-4

In Figure 11-5, a second InfoPath view is created for approvals. InfoPath views provide a way for designers to create multiple views that use the same InfoPath data source. This is valuable because custom views can be created for different users based on the way in which they will work with the data. In the case of the approval view, all of the submission fields are disabled and a new field was added called Action. This field will be used by K2 blackpearl, and it will be dynamically populated with actions that users have permission rights to perform (Approve, Deny, Wait, Cancel, Redirect, etc.). It is important that this field be added to the InfoPath form prior to importing into a K2 blackpearl process because it will be used when configuring the first InfoPath Client Event.

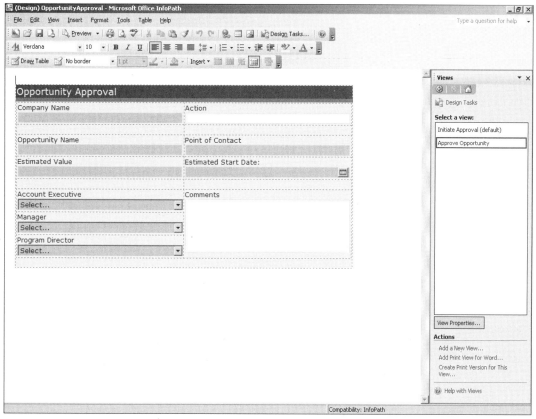

**Figure 11-5**

*Hiding a field in an InfoPath view (for instance, in the approval view) is not a secure way to control data. InfoPath does support using digital signatures; however, there are some limitations with using them with browser-enabled InfoPath forms (for instance they only work with Internet Explorer). Remember, InfoPath is just a user interface on top of an XML document and there is no security on the XML itself. If there are requirements where the data being captured in the form must be secured, a good way of achieving this is to store the data externally in a database and to load the InfoPath form every time it is opened. Another way would be to use multiple InfoPath forms in a single process and place the forms in different form libraries. Then each form library can be given different permissions to ensure that users can only work the data for which they have permission. This second approach will require some more complex code, to split and merge XML in server-side code events.*

Once the form has been created, it can now be integrated with the K2 process. No further actions need to take place with the InfoPath form prior to integrating it with K2. After creating a new K2 Workflow Project, the InfoPath Integration Wizard is used to integrate the InfoPath form with the K2 blackpearl process. To start the InfoPath Integration Wizard, drag-and-drop it from the Process Wizards group in the toolbox onto the design canvas (as shown in Figure 11-6).

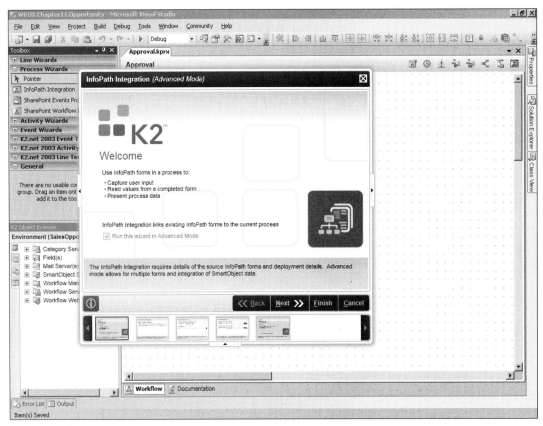

Figure 11-6

The first step is to select an InfoPath form. In Figure 11-7, this is done in the Workflow Form Templates step of the wizard by clicking Add. K2 blackpearl allows for multiple InfoPath forms to be added to the process and additional InfoPath forms can always be added later, but right now, there is only one form to be added.

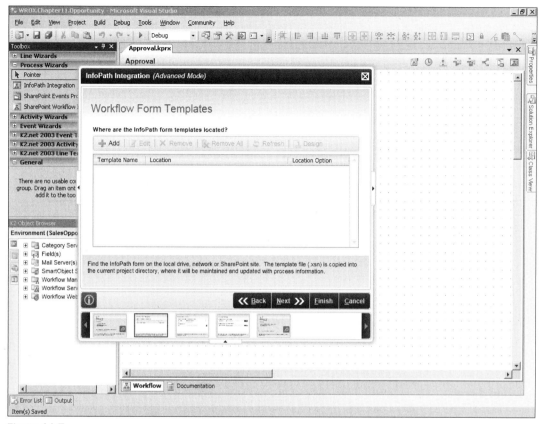

Figure 11-7

In Figure 11-8, clicking Add opens the Add an InfoPath Form Template window. In this window, the InfoPath template file (.xsn extension) must be located. The InfoPath template file can be selected from a local, network drive, already in Visual Studio, or it can be retrieved from the SharePoint site where the InfoPath form may have already been published.

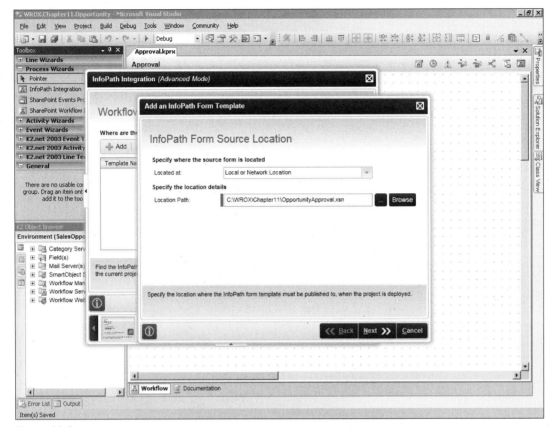

**Figure 11-8**

In Figure 11-9, the next step in the Integration Wizard is to identify where the InfoPath form will be published to when the K2 blackpearl process is deployed. Publishing an InfoPath form basically means deploying the InfoPath template to a common location where it can be opened by a user. Publishing can be done by using the Publishing Wizard that is available inside of InfoPath. In the past with K2.net 2003, publishing the InfoPath form was a separate and manual step. However, with K2 blackpearl, the deployment of the InfoPath form has been automated so the designer does not have to manually go through the InfoPath Deployment Wizard. There are two options available, deploy it to a network share or to a SharePoint form library. Deploying it to a SharePoint form library is the most common scenario. It is highly recommended that environment variables be used and that you avoid hardcoding a URL and form library Name, as the URLs will be different for production and development environments.

*For more information about the Environment Library see Chapter 10.*

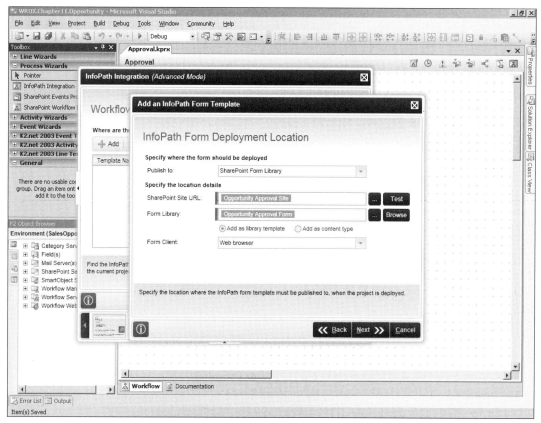

Figure 11-9

Below the Form Library field are two radio buttons that determine if the InfoPath form will be deployed directly to a form library or as a SharePoint content type. A content type is a new feature of SharePoint 2007, used to classify content that is stored inside of SharePoint. For instance, a content type for a purchase request may be created in SharePoint and can then have a template assigned to it. This template can be one of many types of documents such as Word or Excel, but in this case the content type will use an InfoPath form. K2 blackpearl will create the content type and associate the InfoPath form to it whenever the K2 process is deployed. There are a few advantages of using a content type, for instance they can be reused in many form libraries and can be leveraged in MOSS Search.

The remaining fields of this step are the Form Client field, which determines how the InfoPath form will be delivered, either through InfoPath client or through a Web browser. With the release of InfoPath 2007, InfoPath now can be accessed through a browser; however, there are some InfoPath features that are not available and can only be used with the InfoPath client. Using the Design Checker task pane within InfoPath will provide assistance in checking if the form can be deployed to the Web. Browser-enabled InfoPath forms are only available when InfoPath Form Services has been enabled in a SharePoint farm. InfoPath Form Services is packaged as part of MOSS Enterprise but can be deployed separately if MOSS is not needed.

The next step of the wizard is to select SmartObject methods (as shown in Figure 11-10). This step in the wizard allows for any SmartObject method to be executed through InfoPath via a Web service data connection that K2 will add to the InfoPath form. This is commonly used to perform create, read, update, and delete operations on data within an InfoPath form. Right now no SmartObjects will be integrated; however, this is an extremely powerful feature to quickly expose a SmartObject to a business user.

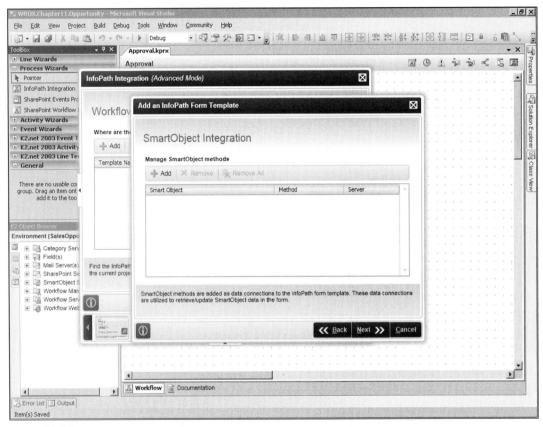

Figure 11-10

Figure 11-11 shows the next step in the wizard, which is to optionally set up the HTML task pane for InfoPath. An InfoPath task pane is nothing more than an HTML file that is made visible on the right-hand side of the screen. A task pane is useful if there is functionality or reference information that should always be displayed to the user regardless of what view they are using. The InfoPath task pane is only available for client-based InfoPath forms. If the task pane is used, a button is placed into the task pane that will allow the user to submit the form to K2. In addition, there will be a link to open the View Process Flow report (note that this link could be added to the InfoPath form itself). For this process, the HTML task pane will not be used. Click Finish to complete the integration of the InfoPath form template.

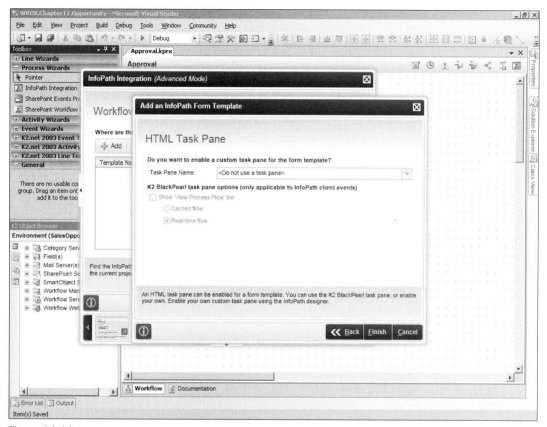

**Figure 11-11**

*The InfoPath task pane and the InfoPath form can be used to provide more complex functionality where controls can be embedded into it and data exchanged between the task pane and the InfoPath data sources. This is done by writing script code; however, this code can become challenging if a lot of functionality is needed in the task pane. If this is the case, something like an ASP.NET form would be a better approach.*

Now that the form has been integrated, the rest of the Process Integration Wizard needs to be completed. When the Add InfoPath Form Template Wizard closes, the InfoPath Integration window is still open and needs to be completed. Clicking Next goes to the Process Start Details step of the wizard (as shown in Figure 11-12). This is the step where the designer must select which InfoPath form view will be used to initiate the InfoPath process. The Form Template field will have all of the InfoPath forms that have been added to the K2 process and the View field will show all of the views for the selected form. Once a form and view have been selected, the Folio field needs be specified.

The Folio field is displayed throughout the K2 Workspace, out-of- the-box reports, administrative screens, and K2 Worklist Web part. The Folio field is used to reference a specific process instance. A default value will always be displayed in the Folio, but it will not have any unique or contextual data associated to the process instance. It is a best practice to put some process-specific data into the Folio field. Commonly, users of K2 blackpearl would like to see a unique identifier number, a start date, or the originator's name, for example, which would help them make a decision as to whether to open the process instance or not. For this process, the company and opportunity names are concatenated together and will be displayed in the Folio name. The values are selected from the XML of the InfoPath form, using the Context browser. Both of these fields are required for initiating the process.

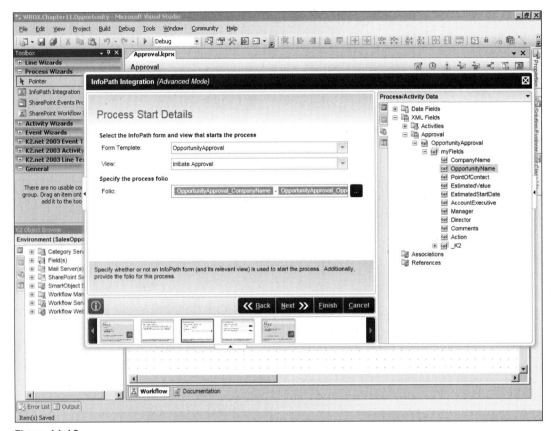

**Figure 11-12**

*It is possible to the set the Folio field after the process has begun in a Code Server Event by using* `K2.ProcessInstance.Folio`. *The Folio field configuration in the wizard will be set prior to the first activity instance being created. Setting the Folio after the process has begun will commonly occur if a unique identifier cannot be generated by InfoPath prior to submission. As well, there may be certain points in the process where the Folio value will need to be changed based on the state of the process instance. It is recommended that the Folio field data being displayed not be highly dynamic.*

The Advanced Settings step of the InfoPath Process Wizard, shown in Figure 11-13, displays both the Workflow server and the Workflow Web services URL prepopulated with environment variables. The Workflow server variable is a connection string to the workflow server, while the Workflow Web services URL is the address where the K2 InfoPath Web service resides. The Web service provides all of the methods that are needed to integrate an InfoPath form with K2. It is not recommended that you hardcode these values. The values of the environment variable set here will be set into the InfoPath form.

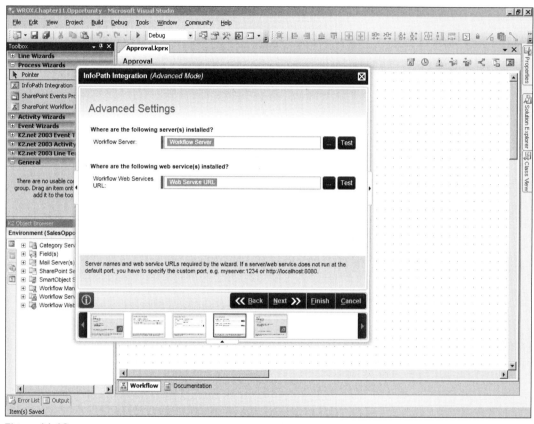

Figure 11-13

On the Finish page of the InfoPath Integration Wizard (as shown in Figure 11-14), the designer is given the choice of starting an InfoPath Client Event by selecting the "Would you like to configure a client event now?" checkbox. This is referred to as wizard chaining where the finishing of one wizard will start another. In this case an InfoPath Client Event wizard will start if this checkbox is checked. This particular business process will require a manager's approval once the InfoPath form has been submitted. Knowing that, checking the checkbox will allow the designer to immediately create the manager approval activity.

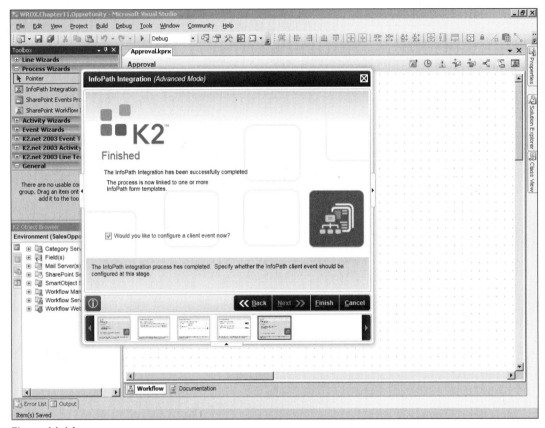

**Figure 11-14**

Click Finish in the InfoPath Integration wizard to start the InfoPath Client Event. The first step of the InfoPath Client Event is shown in Figure 11-15. This is where the manager approval step will be configured.

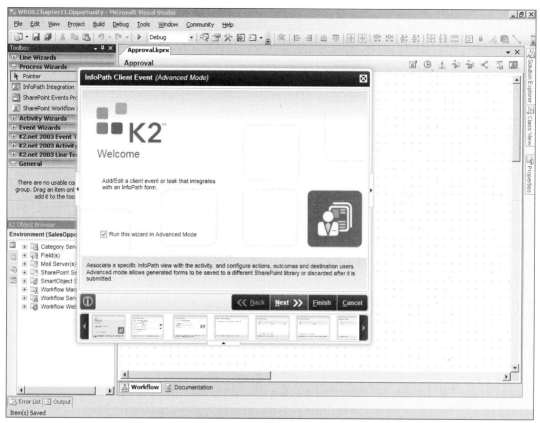

**Figure 11-15**

Clicking Next will move to the General Event Settings step of the InfoPath Client Event Wizard (as shown in Figure 11-16). The Name field will be changed to InfoPath Manager Approval, which is the name displayed on the process view and shown in all of the reports. The Form Template field is used to select which InfoPath form will be displayed to the user. The Client Event View field shows all of the views for the selected form and allows the designer to select which view in the InfoPath form should be displayed. In this case, the Approve Opportunity view will be selected, which is a different view than the one that was used to initiate the process.

The Task Action field allows the designer to select which field in the InfoPath form will be populated with the list of user actions. Some examples of actions are approve, reject, cancel, and so on. To select a field, click the ellipse next to the Action Field. In the Context Browser, go to the Process/Activity Data tab. From there, open the XML Fields node and drill-down into the OpportunityApproval node to select the action field. Remember, the action field was added to the InfoPath form prior to the form's being integrated with K2. It is not possible from this step to add a new field to the InfoPath form. If there is no field, the wizard can be closed and restarted once there is a field.

The action field in the InfoPath form might not be a drop-down before being imported into the K2 process. If the action field is not a drop-down, it will be converted to a drop-down by this wizard. The action drop-down will be populated by Web service, which will retrieve a list of actions from the K2 server. This list of actions will be security trimmed based on the users currently logged in. Only one field per activity can be designated as the action field. Once populated, the user will use this field to make a decision on where the process should go next. In this case, a field called Action was added to the form prior to integration with K2. If the field is not present in the form, cancel this wizard, create the field in the InfoPath form, and start over again. Note, only one field in the InfoPath's form schema can be designated as the action field, regardless of how many views there are.

> *Actions were designed in this fashion so that they are independent of the form user interface whether the form is InfoPath, ASP.NET, or some other platform. This allows designers to add actions to an activity of a process requiring minimal changes to the form. Another advantage is that action security can be easily managed without requiring a single change on the form. For instance, an activity may have approve, deny, and cancel actions. However, the cancel action should only be visible to a specific set up of users. After the K2 process has been deployed, the K2 Workspace can be used to ensure that only a specific subset of users has permission to the cancel action. If the security rules for the action were to ever change, the form would not have to be modified.*

Finally, the "Who is allowed to finish the worklist item?" can be used to determine if all users who have access to the K2 process can complete the event, or if only a designated set of users can complete the event. In this case, "Only the destination user" radio button is selected because only the manager should be allowed to configure this operation.

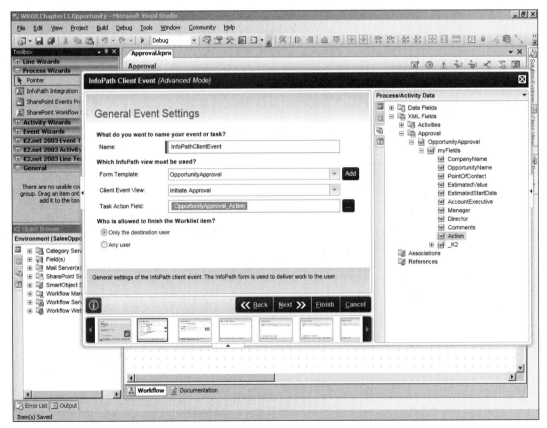

**Figure 11-16**

When you click Next, the prompt shown in Figure 11-17 may appear if the task action field that was selected is not a drop-down. In this case, since the action field is not a drop-down, the wizard will convert the InfoPath field to a drop-down. It is highly recommended that this be done.

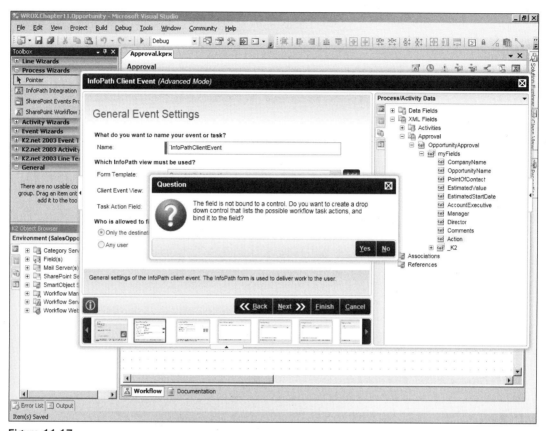

**Figure 11-17**

Figure 11-18 shows the Event Notification Settings step of the wizard, which can be used to send a notification e-mail to all the destination users that a task has been assigned to them for completion. The e-mail message is generic. Using this option does not allow for customization of the message through Visual Studio. The customization of the message can only be done after the process has been deployed in the K2 Workspace and the customizations are specific to the server where the change is made. This is a good, quick way to configure notifications to a process. If more customization is required, a simple Mail Event can be added prior to the InfoPath Client Event.

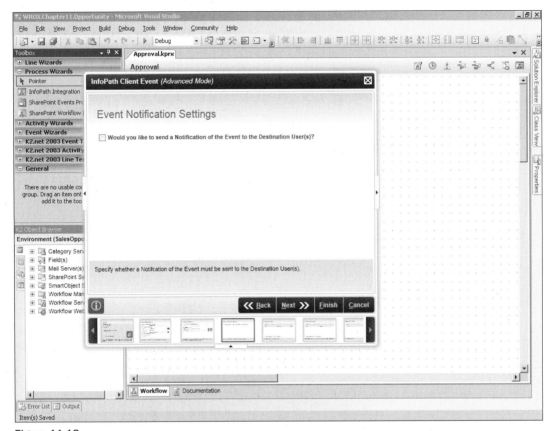

Figure 11-18

The next step of the wizard is the Configure Actions step, where a designer can add actions a user can perform. These actions will be populated into the action field drop-down in the InfoPath form that was created in a previous step. To add an action, click the Add button and the Add Action window will appear. In the Add Action window (as shown in Figure 11-19), there are Name and Description (optional) fields. The Name of the action can be action, deny, delegate, cancel, send to contracts, notify my manager, and the like. It should contain whatever decisions a user may need to make.

There is a checkbox called "Make the action available without opening the work item." Leaving this checkbox checked will ensure that this action is visible in both the SharePoint Worklist Web part and the K2 Workspace Worklist. The user will have the ability to action a worklist item without having to open the InfoPath form. As well, the user will have the ability to do batch actions if there are multiple tasks that have been assigned to them. The Worklist Web part allows users to select multiple items and then complete one-to-many of them without having to click or open each and every task. Unchecking this checkbox will require the user to open the InfoPath form to complete their task, which at times is a good thing. For instance, there may be important legal data in the InfoPath form the decision-maker must read before taking an action.

The last two radio buttons allow the designer to indicate if the action will finish the worklist item or keep it open until the user selects a different action that will complete the InfoPath Client Event. For instance, there may be actions like "approve" and "deny," which should complete the activity. However, an action like "wait" will not make the action complete.

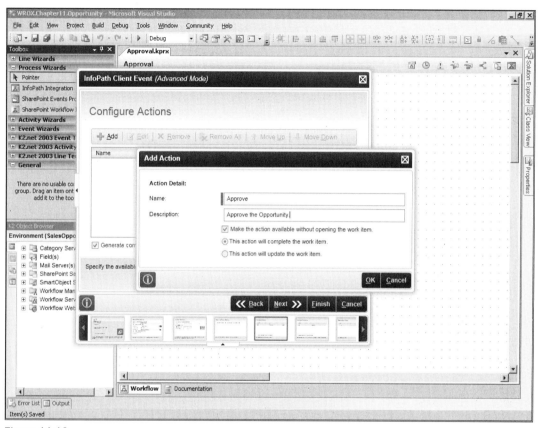

Figure 11-19

For this process, both Approve and Deny actions will be added as shown in Figure 11-20. Once all of the actions have been added, the "Generate corresponding outcome(s) for listed action(s)" checkbox should be checked.

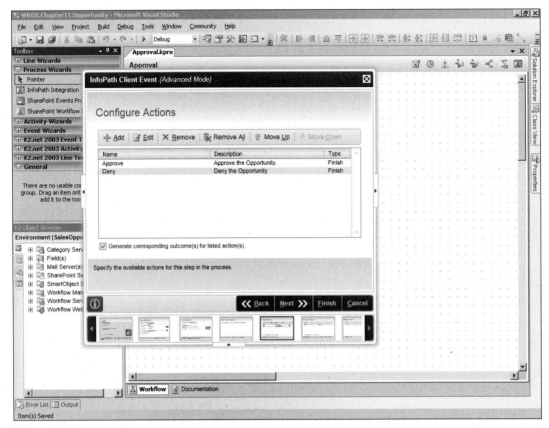

**Figure 11-20**

The next step in the wizard is to Configure Outcomes that are used in the Succeeding Rules for the activity. Succeeding Rules are used by the activity to determine whether the activity is complete or another action needs to be taken. When outcomes are added to an activity, a field called Outcome will be added as an activity-level field. The Outcome field will be populated with the action field value after the user submits the InfoPath form. Checking the "Generate corresponding line(s) for listed outcome(s)" checkbox will generate a line for each outcome. Each line that is generated will have a rule using the Outcome field that will determine which line the process should continue on. Figure 11-21 shows the default outcomes that are generated from the actions.

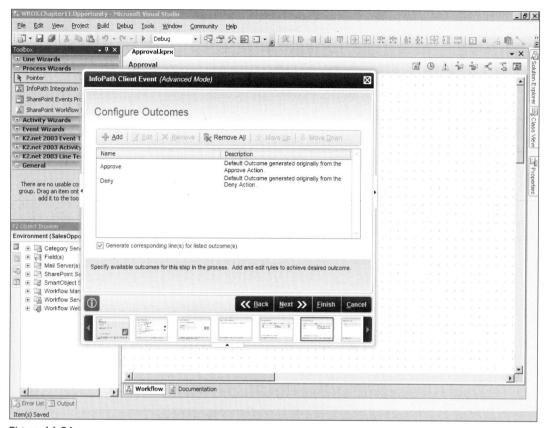

Figure 11-21

*In K2.net 2003 there was no concept of actions. This wizard is setting up all of the Succeeding and Lines Rules that previously had to be manually set up, saving a significant amount of time when creating a process.*

Although it is the default, there is no requirement for a one-to-one mapping between actions and outcomes, which provides a lot of flexibility to support more complex logic. For instance, there may be an Approve or Deny action. However, based on the dollar amount that was approved, the process will need to go down a different path. A simple business rule may be if the dollar amount that was approved is over $100,000, the request form will require a director's approval. Figure 11-22 shows that the new outcome has been added which will check to see if the ActionResult is Approved and if the estimated amount is over $100,000. The dollar amount is located in the XML of the InfoPath form.

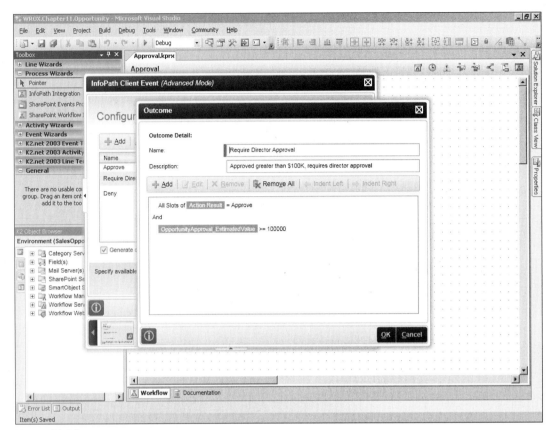

Figure 11-22

Figure 11-23 shows the completed outcome modifications that were made. The original Approved outcome that was generated by the wizard was modified to check if the estimated amount is under $100,000.

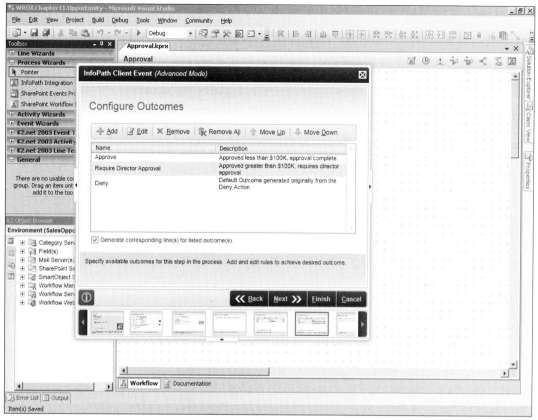

Figure 11-23

Figure 11-24 shows the final step of the wizard is to add Destination Users who are the users assigned worklist items. For this activity, the Destination User will be the manager who was selected in the InfoPath form. To set the Destination Rule with data in the InfoPath from, select the Add button and then click the ellipse to open the context browser. From there, click the Process/Activity Data tab and drill-down into the XML Fields to get the Manager node.

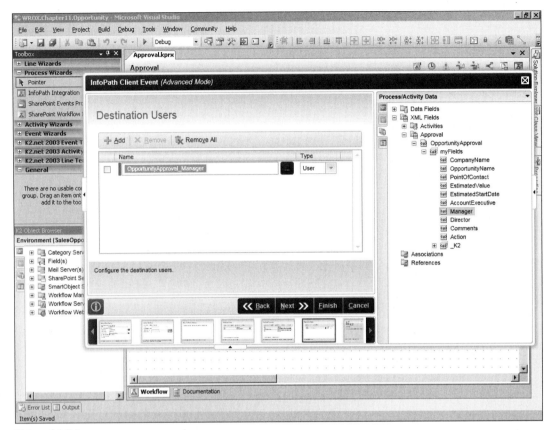

Figure 11-24

Now the wizard is complete, both the InfoPath Integration Wizard and the first InfoPath Client Event will be complete. More InfoPath Client Events can be added to the process by dragging and dropping them on from the toolbox. A new icon will be displayed in the top-right corner of the design canvas. Clicking this will open the InfoPath Integration Wizard and will allow the designer to rerun any of the configurations that were made earlier. Figure 11-25 shows the completed InfoPath process.

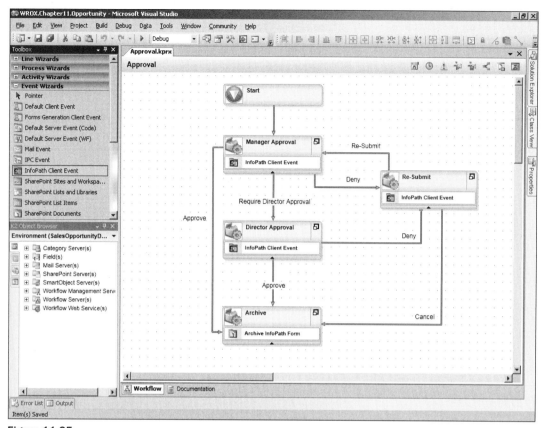

Figure 11-25

## InfoPath Form Integration Details

It is important to understand how the InfoPath form was integrated with the K2 process. First the InfoPath form has now been added to the Visual Studio solution. All changes to the InfoPath form moving forward should be done to the file that is part of the K2 Designer project and not to the file from where the template was originally located. The file in the K2 Designer project is the form that will be synchronized with the K2 process and will be the form that will be published by K2 when the process is deployed. Figure 11-26 shows the updated Solution Explorer in Visual Studio with the InfoPath Form that was integrated into the process.

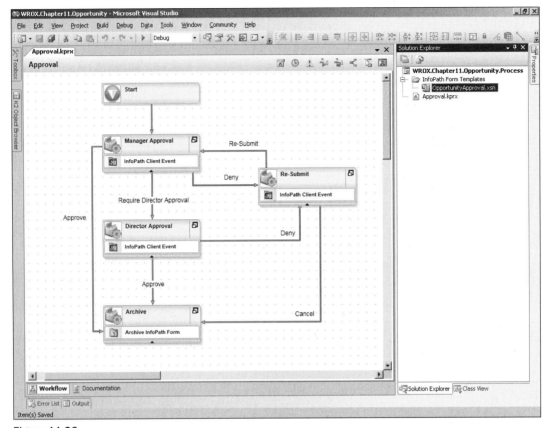

**Figure 11-26**

To make a modification to the InfoPath form, select the InfoPath icon at the top-right corner of the design canvas. The InfoPath Integration menu will appear. Click the Design button to open InfoPath in design mode (as shown in Figure 11-27). The designer can make any needed changes to the InfoPath form. When the InfoPath designer is closed, the form will be resynchronized with the K2 process automatically.

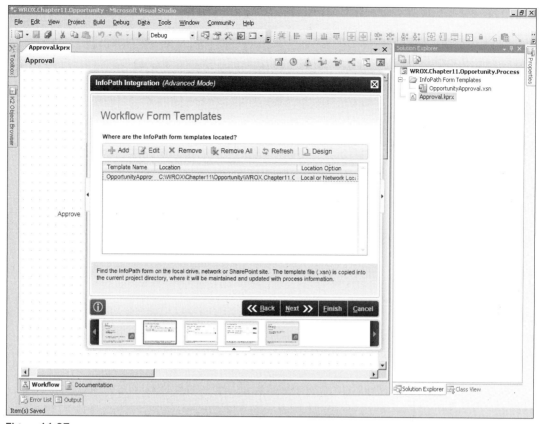

**Figure 11-27**

It is possible to make changes to the InfoPath form outside of Visual Studio. Go directly to the `.xsn` file in the InfoPath Form Templates folder in the Visual Studio project files, open the InfoPath form in design mode, and make the necessary changes. It is extremely important to not go to the original location of where the InfoPath form was selected when it was integrated with the K2 process. Remember when the InfoPath form was integrated with the K2 process, a copy of the `.xsn` file was added to the K2 project itself. Once the changes to the InfoPath form have been completed, the changes to the form must be resynchronized with the K2 process. This is achieved by rerunning the InfoPath Integration Wizard, selecting the form that was modified, and then clicking the Refresh button. It is recommended that this be avoided when possible because the K2 InfoPath Integration Wizard provides the ability to launch the InfoPath form in design mode, and it will ensure that it is always kept in sync with the K2 process. The only time this may be needed is when information workers do not have a Visual Studio, and they require the ability to make changes to the InfoPath form directly.

## InfoPath Form Versioning

InfoPath forms that are integrated with a K2 process are version controlled with that process. Whenever a form is added to a K2 process using the InfoPath Integration Wizard, the name of the InfoPath form template (`.xsn` file) will be made unique. Then that uniquely named file is mapped within the process definition. Within InfoPath, every time the form template is saved, an internal version number within the InfoPath definition is incremented. This version number can be found in the `manifest.xsf` file of the InfoPath form.

*The* manifest.xsf *file is located with the InfoPath form template file. The InfoPath form template file is nothing more than a CAB file with an array of* .xml, .xsd, *and* .xsl *files. The* manifest.xsf *file contains the definition file for the InfoPath form itself. To access this file, open the InfoPath form in design mode and select Save As Source Files under the File menu.*

When updating an InfoPath form through a K2 Designer, the updated form will be resynchronized in several places within the K2 process definition. If the InfoPath form is not resynchronized with the K2 process, definition issues can arise in production because the XML submitted from the InfoPath form will not conform to the XSD definition that is expected by the K2 process. To always avoid this issue, make sure that the InfoPath form is edited from within the K2 project by rerunning the InfoPath Integration Wizard and pressing the Design button.

## Changes to InfoPath

There will also be many changes that are made to the InfoPath form as a result of being added to the K2 process. The first and most notable change to the InfoPath form is that a new group is added to the Main Data Source, called _K2, which has several fields reserved for K2. Figure 11-28 shows the main data source of the OpportunityApproval.xsn form template that was integrated with K2. It is not recommended that any field within this group be manually modified for any reason because these fields and the data within them are owned by K2. If fields are removed or data modified, errors can occur. These fields and the data within them will be managed by K2.

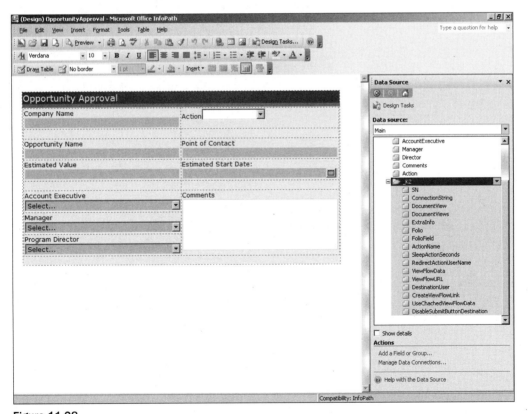

Figure 11-28

A second important change to the InfoPath form is that three new data connections have been added (as shown in Figure 11-29). These data connections are configured to work with K2's InfoPath Web service (located at `<server>/RuntimeServices/InfoPathService.asmx`). The first is called "Can I Submit Workflow Service," which is used to check if the current user has permission to connect to the workflow server. The second is called "Get Workflow Task Actions Service" and will retrieve all of the actions that the current user has permission to. This data connection is used to fill in the action drop-down that was specified in the InfoPath Client Event Wizard. The third is called "Submit Workflow Service" and is used to submit the XML from the InfoPath form to K2 server. The submit Web service method uses the data in the _K2 node to restart the process again with the updated XML in the form.

K2's InfoPath Web service also provides some other helpful methods that can be used in the InfoPath form. There is the "Can I Connect" method that determines if the user has permission to connect to the Web service. There is the Execute SmartObject method, which allows for any method of a SmartObject to be executed in an InfoPath form. Finally there is the Who Am I method, which will return the Active Directory name of the user connecting to the Web service.

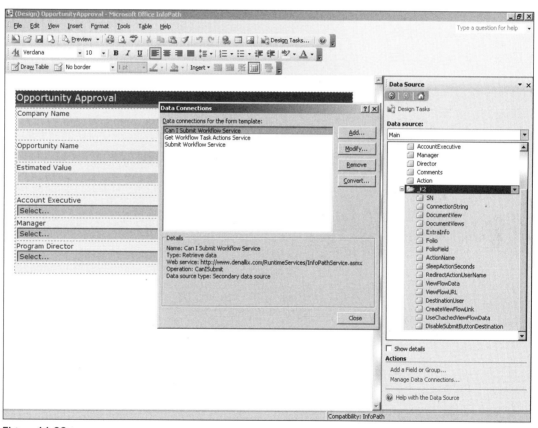

Figure 11-29

Rules were also added to the InfoPath form by K2 that will be executed when the InfoPath form is opened. Figure 11-30 shows the Form Options window selected from the Tools main menu. The Open Behavior of the form can be configured by clicking on the Rules button in the Open and Save section. The InfoPath Integration Wizard will add rules for each view that is in the InfoPath form. These rules are used by the InfoPath Client Event to switch to the correct view the user should see. The InfoPath Client Event will set the DocumentView node (located within the _K2 group) with the view that should be displayed. When the form opens, it will switch the appropriate view. Another rule that will be added is Get Workflow Task Actions, which will call the Web method to get all actions for the current user and populate the Action drop-down with them.

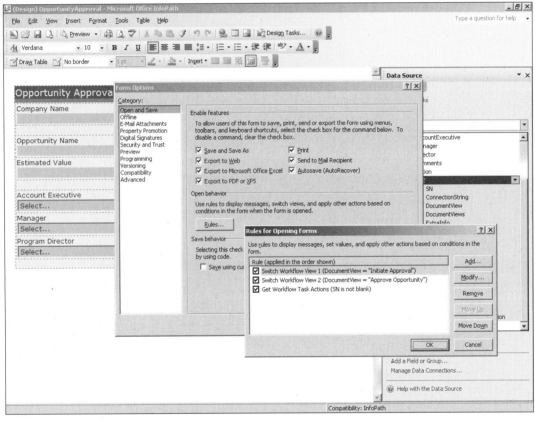

**Figure 11-30**

The last changes made by the InfoPath Integration Wizard can be found under Submit Options. Figure 11-31 shows that the "Perform custom action using Rules" radio button is selected; clicking the "Rules" button will shows the rules that have been configured. The first rule sets the action field value to the _K2 group. The second rule submits the InfoPath form to K2's InfoPath Web service. This is a good place to add other operations that should be completed before the InfoPath form is sent to K2. The last set of changes to the Submit Options is in the advanced section. The "Show success and failure messages" has been selected and the form is configured to close after submission.

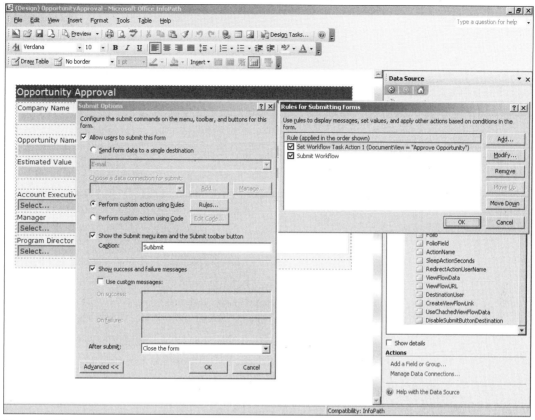

Figure 11-31

*Adding rules after the Submit Workflow rule can lead to undesirable results. For instance if there is data that is saved to a SmartObject using a rule after the Submit Workflow rule, there will be no guarantee that the updated data will be available for Succeeding and Line Rules in the process. It is recommended that you complete all rules before the Submit Rule is executed.*

*Another important thing to know is users will have to be instructed to close their InfoPath form after submission because the K2 process will try to delete the XML file after a user clicks the Submit button. If the InfoPath form remains open, a potential locking error can occur between SharePoint and K2. This is particularly important when using client-based InfoPath forms. This error is not unique to K2, as this is introduced by SharePoint trying to manage two users accessing the same document at the same time. The same error will occur if two users were working with the same document while one has it open and the other tries to delete it.*

Any modifications to changes that K2 made to the InfoPath form can be lost whenever the wizards within K2 are rerun. For instance, if the designer chooses to modify one of the submit or open rules, those changes will be lost when an InfoPath Integration wizard is rerun. However, the designer can add new Submit or Open Rules and those will always remain unaffected.

## Changes to the K2 Process

Changes are not limited to the InfoPath form; there are changes that will be made to the K2 process as a result of running the InfoPath Integration Wizard. The most notable change is that a new process-level XML field has been added to the process. This XML field is created from the XSD schema from the InfoPath form and will contain all of the data from the InfoPath form after each InfoPath Client Event completes. This data can be used anywhere inside of the K2 process, for instance, in places such as Line, Destination, and Succeeding Rules. Figure 11-32 shows all of the XML fields that have been added to the K2 process as a result of the InfoPath form's being integrated.

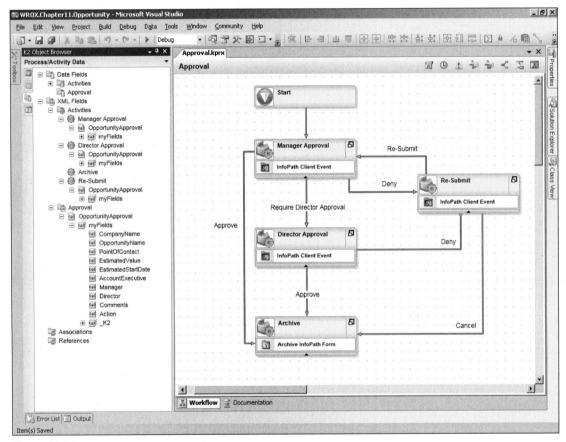

Figure 11-32

It is important to know that the schema of the InfoPath form must be kept in sync with the XSD of the XML fields within K2. Errors could occur at run time if the designer were to add or a remove a field in the InfoPath form outside of Visual Studio and not resynchronize it using the Refresh button in the InfoPath Integration Wizard. A very common error could result from a field's being renamed or possibly removed, which would cause an XPath error. K2 will execute validation measures to ensure that these errors do not occur, but those validations will be based on the XSD schema in the XML field, not the XSD in the InfoPath form. This is why it is very important to keep the InfoPath form and the K2 process in sync with each other.

However, changes associated to the presentation of the form or conditional formatting are safe to make without having to resync it with the K2 process. In these cases, the InfoPath form can be changed and simply republished without having to redeploy the entire K2 process. As a best practice, if there are any changes that need to be made to the InfoPath form other than presentation, the InfoPath form should be resynchronized with the K2 process. Presentation changes do not require a redeployment of the K2 process. However, if the form must be resynchronized because the schema change, the K2 process must be deployed before the InfoPath form can be used.

## Working with InfoPath Data

One thing that may come up when working with an InfoPath process is that the data in the InfoPath form may need to be modified by the K2 process. For instance, in this process, there is one action field on the InfoPath form, and when the manager approves the opportunity, it is then routed to the director for approval. When the director opens the form, the action field will already be marked as approved. It would be better for the action field to be cleared out, forcing the director to make a decision to approve or deny. Clearing out the action XML field can be done by adding a server code event prior to the InfoPath Client Event, as shown in Figure 11-33. To open up the code event-handler, right-click the event, select View Code, and then Event Item. This is where code can be written to access the XML field and modify the XML string.

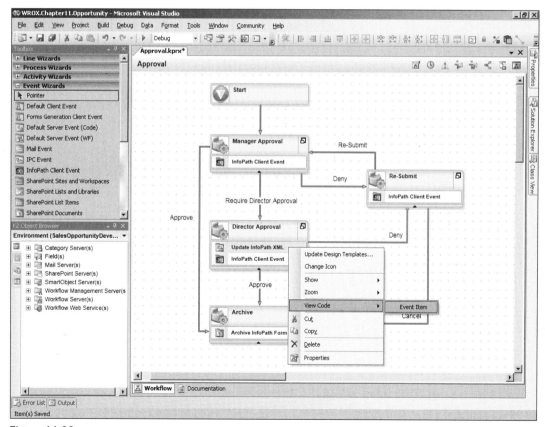

Figure 11-33

The following code shows that the `XmlFields` of the `ProcessInstance` is referenced. The InfoPath XML is subsequently set into a string variable, which is then loaded into an `XmlDocument`. Once the `XmlDocument` has been loaded, an `XmlNamespaceManager` is created, which allows for XPath queries to be executed on the `XmlDocument`. In this case, `//my:Action`, an XPath query, will get the value in the action field and set the action field to empty string. Once the `XmlDocument` has been modified, the XML string needs to be set back into the `ProcessInstance.XmlFields`. If this is not done, the changes that were made will not be committed and shown in the InfoPath form. This is a simple demonstration, but once the developer has access to the XML string, there is a potential to execute more sophisticated operations.

```
//Get the XML Field string
string xml = K2.ProcessInstance.XmlFields["OpportunityApproval"].Value.ToString();

//Load up the XML
XmlDocument doc = new XmlDocument();
doc.LoadXml(xml);

//Create a name space manager for InfoPath
XmlNamespaceManager nsMgr = new XmlNamespaceManager(doc.NameTable);
nsMgr.AddNamespace("my", doc.DocumentElement.GetNamespaceOfPrefix("my"));

//Now set some values
doc.SelectSingleNode("//my:Action ", nsMgr).InnerText = "";

//Now set the value back into the XML Field
K2.ProcessInstance.XmlFields["OpportunityApproval"].Value = doc.OuterXml;
```

Understanding the mechanics of how the XML documents are created and managed by K2 is very important. To view how this is done, right-click any InfoPath Client Event and select view code, and the following Windows Workflow Foundation (WF) process will be displayed (as shown in Figure 11-34). This is the underlying code that is used for the InfoPath process. There are two major steps to the InfoPath client, which are: Create the XML document in SharePoint, and create worklist items for the destination user. To further understand how this works, right-click the WF process and select View Code.

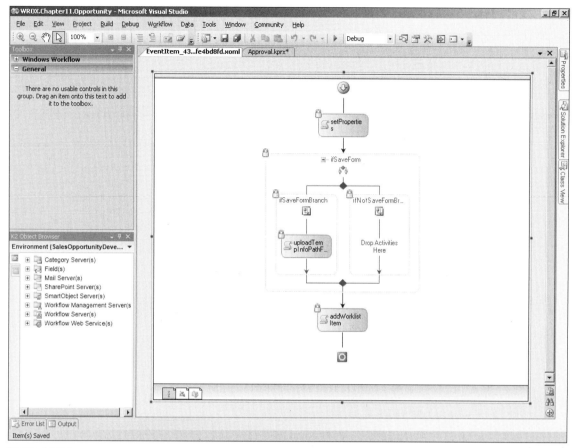

Figure 11-34

## Advanced InfoPath XML Considerations

Before diving deep into how the InfoPath XML is integrated with a K2 process, it is important to understand how the process and activity instances are related. First for every process instance there will be many activity instances. Then for every activity instance, there will be activity instance destinations. The creation of activity instance destinations is driven by the number of slots that will be created, which is based upon the Destination Rules.

What is relevant to this discussion is that for each process instance there is an XML field. As well, each activity with an InfoPath Client Event will also have an XML activity field. The WF process for the InfoPath Client Event, shown earlier, has logic that will take the XML from the process field and copy it in the activity field. Each activity instance destination also has an XML field, which will again be populated from the process XML field. This is done so that each destination user has a copy of the InfoPath document. When the activity completes, the XML from the activity instance destinations will be set back into the process instance XML, and the InfoPath form XML will subsequently be deleted from the form library in SharePoint. The code that deletes the InfoPath form resides in the Succeeding Rule of the activity. This can lead designers into a few traps if the process is not fully understood.

## File Attachments and Database Sizing

The first potential trap is when a code server event is placed after the InfoPath Client Event. If in the server code event the XML needs to be accessed or modified, the XML field from the activity destination must be used and not the process instance XML field. This is because when the XML is submitted from the InfoPath form to K2, the XML is set to the activity destination instance by the K2 InfoPath Web service. When the Succeeding Rule finishes, the XML from the activity destination instance will be set back into the process instance XML. Functions, like Line Rules, which occur after the Succeeding Rule of the InfoPath form, should use the process instance XML field.

Another trap that designers fall into when working with an InfoPath process is database sizing. As mentioned, numerous copies of the XML are created, and if the InfoPath form has a lot of data, this can quickly become an issue. As the number of process and activity instances grows, more and more copies of the XML will be created in the K2 database. A very common issue occurs when file attachments are used in an InfoPath form. A business requirement may be that a document needs to be attached to the InfoPath form so that users can have access to the document when making business decisions.

When files are attached into an InfoPath form, the file is serialized into a Base64 string and stored in the XML of the InfoPath form. This can potentially cause the XML file to be very large. After the XML is submitted to K2, the XML will be copied several times as it goes through the process, along with the serialized file. For example, there may be a process with five activities and on average, three destination users were planned per activity. Potentially 21 copies of the XML will be created: one for the process, five for each activity instance, and fifteen for each activity instance destination. Because there is a 1MB file attachment in the XML of the InfoPath form, this would mean that on average, the K2 database would have provide a minimum of 21MB of storage per process instance. Multiply that for how many process instances there could be, and this could grow tremendously. A good practice is not to store any large amounts of data in the XML of the InfoPath form, especially file attachments. A good workaround is to store the files in SharePoint or an external database, and provide a link back to the document through the InfoPath form.

There are several ways InfoPath forms can save attached files externally. In all cases it boils down to adding a Web service to the InfoPath form. The Web service method will consume the binary representation of the attached file and then store it appropriately. To save an attachment into SharePoint there are several options. For instance a custom Web service could be written that will save the file to SharePoint, the SharePoint Web service could be added to InfoPath, or SharePoint SmartObjects could be added to the form. There is a project supported by the K2 community on the K2 Underground (www .k2underground.com) that will strip file attachments out of an InfoPath form before the XML of the form is submitted to K2. It is important that the attached files be saved externally and then removed from the InfoPath form prior to the submission of the XML to the K2 server.

### Destination Plans

Destination Plans can also lead to some challenges if they are not designed properly. Using the destination plan "Plan Per Destination - All at once" can make things potentially complicated when working the InfoPath XML in code, especially if the Succeeding Rule requires more than one destination user to take an action. Plan "All at once" will create an activity instance destination for every destination user in parallel. If more than one user must take action, and the plan rule is "All at once," there is the potential for data to be lost. For example, if there was an activity that required two managers to approve, and the first manager opened the form and made changes to the XML, they would be making changes to the XML that is assigned to their activity instance destination. When the second manager approved it, they would be making changes to a different copy of the XML, which is for their activity instance destination. When the Succeeding Rule fires, it would take the XML from the last activity instance destination and set it into the process instance XML field. So all data captured by the first manager's XML form would be lost.

The behavior just described was the default behavior of K2.net 2003, but there are several ways this can be avoided with K2 blackpearl. One option is to use the new "Plan just once" Destination Rule, which will only create a single slot that all destination users can use. This is now the default configuration for all Destination Rules in K2 blackpearl. Since there is only one slot, there will only be one copy of the XML, regardless of how many destination users there are. A second option would be to use the plan "One at a time" Destination Rule, which will do serial assignments of the Destination Rules, ensuring only one user at a time accesses the InfoPath XML. This again is new to K2 blackpearl. Third would be to create a purely database-driven InfoPath form using SmartObjects. This issue then becomes irrelevant because users are essentially guaranteed to always be working with the latest data. A final option would be to add some custom code to the Succeeding Rule; however, this could become somewhat complicated because of the need to resolve differences between the new and old XML. The specific situation dictates whether the "Plan just once" or database-driven options will be the best to implement.

## Modifying the Process

Now that the basic process has been built, a requirement can be captured to provide some delegation. This can be done simply by going back to the InfoPath Client Event and rerunning the wizard to add a new action. When the wizard appears, click Next to go to the Configure Actions step in the wizard. Add a new action called Delegate just as before (see Figure 11-35), but this time, the "Generate corresponding outcome(s) for list action (s)" checkbox will not be checked by default. Select it and continue to the Configure Outcomes step of the wizard. A new outcome called Delegate will be created. Select the "Generate corresponding line(s) for listed outcome(s)" checkbox. Finish the InfoPath Client Event Wizard, and the new Delegate line will be generated.

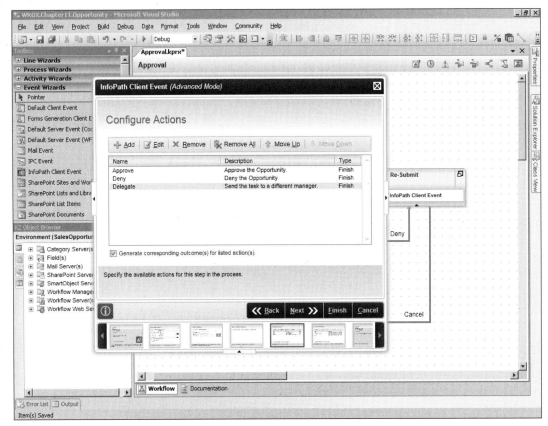

**Figure 11-35**

After adding the new action, take the new generated line and drag it to point back to the activity it started from. Figure 11-36 shows how the process was modified.

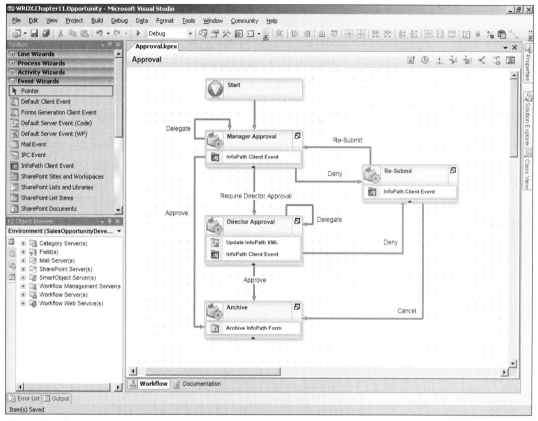

Figure 11-36

Even though delegation functionality is provided in the K2 Workspace, this example shows how flexible and adaptable K2 processes are. Actions and outcomes, new to K2 blackpearl platform, are the power behind this. In K2.net 2003 making this sort of change would have required more work because the line would have had to be manually added, rules would have had to be set, and the InfoPath form would have had to be modified to put the Delegate value into a drop-down.

## Archiving an InfoPath Form

A common requirement for an InfoPath process is that the InfoPath form should be archived when the process is completed. Using SharePoint, the XML can be saved to a form library that is designated as the archive. To save the XML to a form library, the SharePoint Documents Event can be added to the end of the process. Figure 11-37 shows the SharePoint Documents Event being added to the process. The Upload Documents From K2 Field option is selected in the wizard.

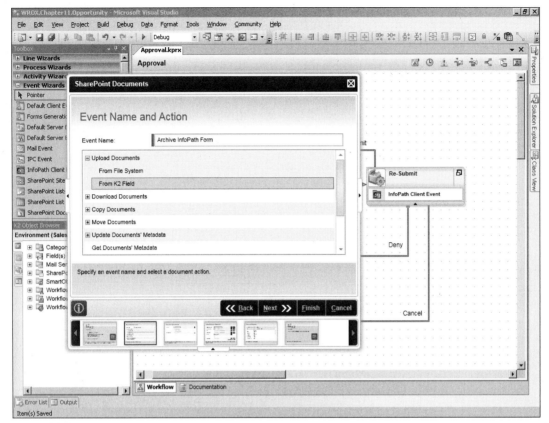

**Figure 11-37**

Figure 11-38 shows the Document Upload Source step of the wizard. This is where the designer selects the InfoPath XML.

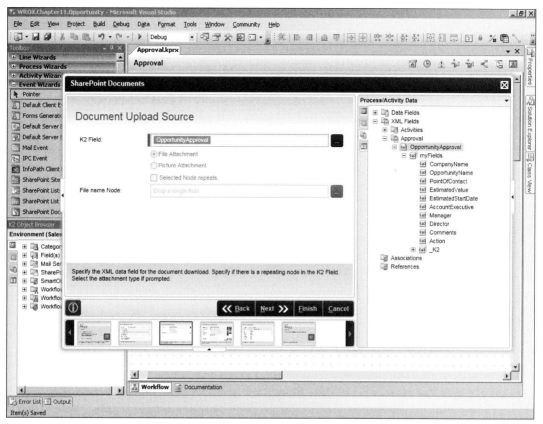

**Figure 11-38**

Figure 11-39 illustrates the final step of the wizard. The Upload Document Destination is where both the SharePoint site and document library are specified. One key thing when configuring this final step is to set the File Name correctly. The file name should contain some sort of unique identifier so when the file is saved to the destination location, it will not overwrite an old one. Finally, add the extension `.xml` to the file name. Once this is done, the InfoPath XML will be saved and be accessible through SharePoint.

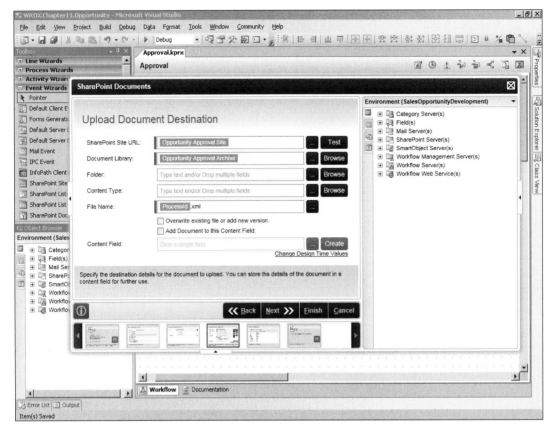

**Figure 11-39**

The archive SharePoint form library must be set up before the process is run. This archive form library will not be created by the K2 deployment package. To set it up, open InfoPath in design mode and publish the InfoPath Form template to the location specified in the wizard. Every time the InfoPath form changes, remember to update the archive form library with the latest version of the InfoPath form template.

If there is a requirement to allow a user to resubmit an archived InfoPath form, this can be achieved by modifying the data in the InfoPath form. To support this requirement, add a server-side code event before the SharePoint Document event that archives the InfoPath XML. In the Code Server Event, add the following code to it. This code will remove the serial number from the _K2 node in the InfoPath form. The serial number is an identifier that K2 generates to uniquely identify process, activity, or event instances. This Serial Number node is set into the form XML in every InfoPath Client Event and is used by the K2 InfoPath Web service. If the serial number is blank, the K2 InfoPath Web service will treat the form as a brand-new InfoPath form submission.

```
//Get the XML Field string
string xml = K2.ProcessInstance.XmlFields["OpportunityApproval"].Value.ToString();

//Load up the XML
XmlDocument doc = new XmlDocument();
doc.LoadXml(xml);

//Create a name space manager for InfoPath
XmlNamespaceManager nsMgr = new XmlNamespaceManager(doc.NameTable);
nsMgr.AddNamespace("my", doc.DocumentElement.GetNamespaceOfPrefix("my"));

//Clear out serial number
doc.SelectSingleNode("//my:SN", nsMgr).InnerText = "";

//Now set the value back into the XML Field
K2.ProcessInstance.XmlFields["OpportunityApproval"].Value = doc.OuterXml;
```

*This is an example of why data within the _K2 node should not be modified unless there is a specific reason to do so. If the serial number value were ever incorrectly removed, a new process instance would be created when, instead, it should have updated the XML and gone to an existing process instance.*

## InfoPath and SmartObject Integration

One of the most exciting things with the introduction of SmartObjects to the K2 blackpearl platform is their integration with InfoPath. In the past, getting data in and out of InfoPath forms required several custom Web services to be written. Now, through SmartObjects, data can be brought in and out of an InfoPath form extremely easily by simply calling any SmartObject method. There two ways SmartObject methods can be added to an InfoPath form. The first is to use the InfoPath Integration Wizard, and the second is to modify the InfoPath form directly using the SmartObject Wizard. Figure 11-40 shows how to add a SmartObject method using the InfoPath Integration Wizard. Once the InfoPath Integration Wizard has been opened go to the Workflow Form Templates window, select the Template Form, and click the Edit button.

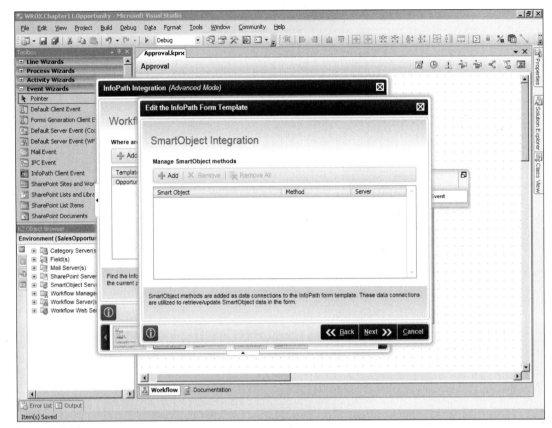

**Figure 11-40**

This will open the Edit the InfoPath Form Template window. The InfoPath Form Deployment Location step will be shown first. Click Next to get to the SmartObject Integration step. This is where SmartObject methods can be added to the InfoPath form. To add a SmartObject method, click the Add button and the Add a SmartObject Method window will appear (as shown in Figure 11-41). Next to the method field, click the ellipse to open the Context Browser. Find the SmartObject method, and click the Add method. In this case, the Opportunity.Create method is added. If the Add to Main DataSource checkbox is checked, the fields from the method will be added to the main data source of the form.

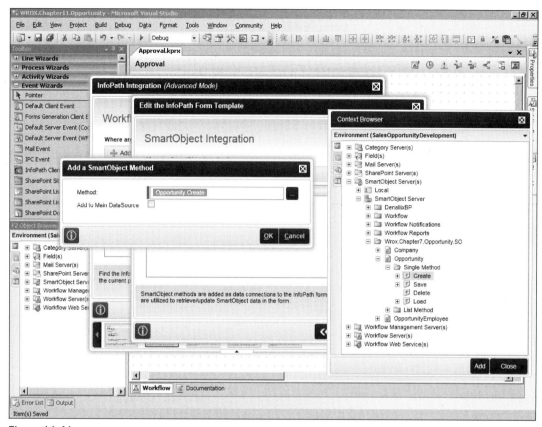

**Figure 11-41**

In Figure 11-42, the `Opportunity.Create`, `Opportunity.GetList`, and `Company.GetList` methods have been added. With these methods, a quick InfoPath form can be constructed that will get all of the opportunities for a company and provide the ability to create a new opportunity for a company.

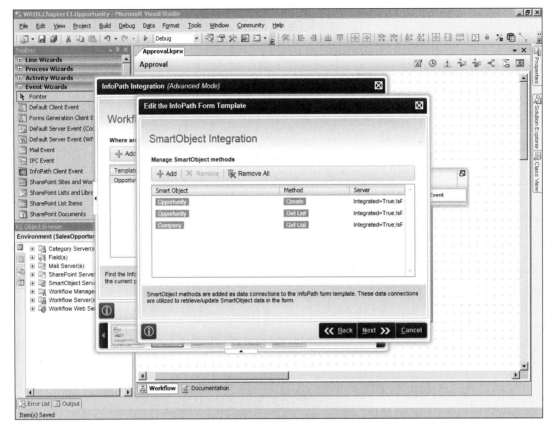

Figure 11-42

The second way SmartObject methods can be added to an InfoPath form is by going to the InfoPath form template (.xsn file), right-clicking it, and selecting the Integrate with SmartObjects option (as shown in Figure 11-43). This will only be available on development machines where the K2 blackpearl design tools have been installed. Selecting this will open the same SmartObject Integration window that was previously shown, but now, SmartObject methods can be added to any InfoPath form regardless of whether or not it is integrated with a K2 process.

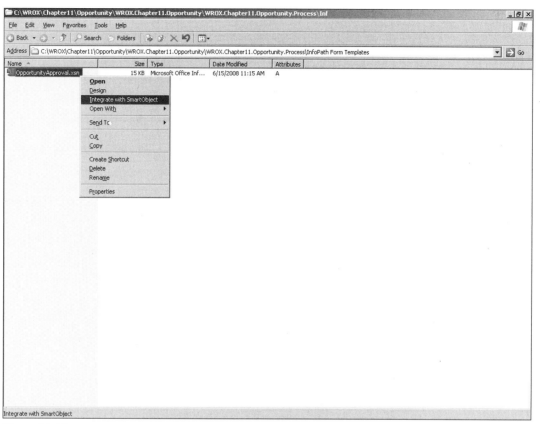

**Figure 11-43**

The SmartObject methods are called by an InfoPath form using a Web service. The following are the data connections that were added to the InfoPath form by K2. Each data connection is named for the SmartObject and method it is associated to, and all of the data connections call the K2 InfoPath Web service ExecuteSmartObjectMethod. Figure 11-44 shows three new data connections that have been added to the InfoPath form.

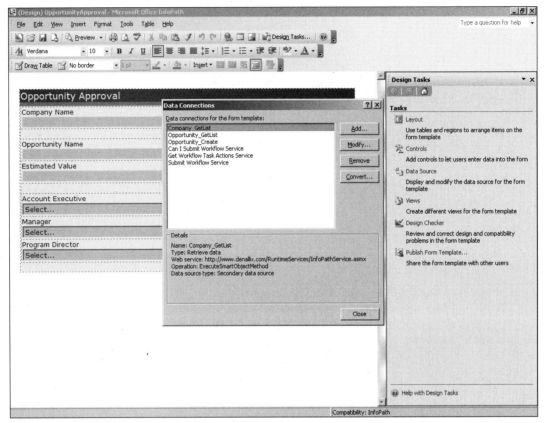

**Figure 11-44**

Since all of the data connections call the same generic Web service, it is good to know how the correct SmartObject method is called. This can be done by looking at the queryFields for the secondary data connection (as shown in Figure 11-45). There is a Locals node with the queryFields. This is where all the connection information to the SmartObject server is located. These values will be set every time the K2 process is deployed with the correct locations in the Environment Library.

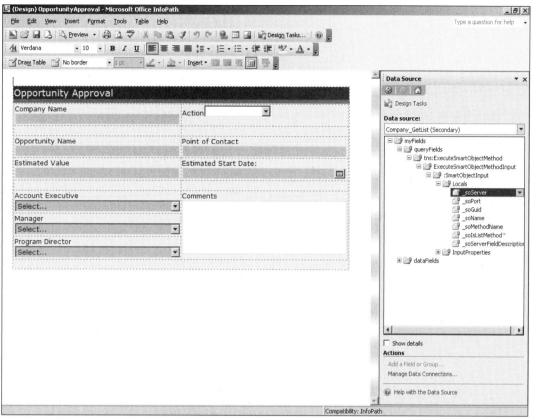

Figure 11-45

Now that the SmartObject methods have been hooked into the InfoPath form using a Web service, the fact that SmartObjects are being used becomes transparent for an InfoPath developer. Figure 11-46 shows a completed InfoPath form that uses the `Company.GetList` method to populate the company drop-down. Once a company is selected, a list of its opportunities is displayed. Finally, there is a section that allows for new opportunities to be added for the selected company. This entire form was constructed in minutes dragging the secondary data source fields on the screen and then adding buttons to call the Web services.

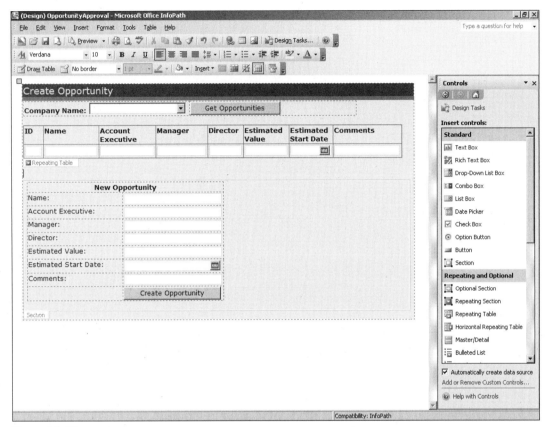

**Figure 11-46**

One important thing to know is that InfoPath forms and SmartObjects should not be used to replace forms that are used to manage large quantities of data. InfoPath forms are great for "form" development, not data management. If there is a business process where data fields will be used to make business decisions, then InfoPath is a fantastic tool to use. However, if the InfoPath form is being used simply as way to access and update data outside of a business process, then it is not the right tool to use. Along that line of thought, there are some limitations when using SmartObjects in InfoPath. For instance, using an InfoPath repeating table to perform batch updates (as in an ASP.NET datagrid) is not supported out-of-the-box and would require some custom code to be added to the InfoPath form. Again, a good general rule is if complex custom code needs to be added to the InfoPath form, it is probably best to transition to ASP.NET.

That aside, the great thing is now InfoPath developers are empowered to integrate with data from multiple locations very rapidly. SmartObjects can be used to bring data from a number of different systems together such as data from SharePoint, ERP systems, mainframes, K2 historical data, and all of the data is shared using an XML document. The InfoPath form does not have to focus on where the data originates from or where it needs to go to. When using SmartObjects, developers no longer have to create custom Web services for a specific InfoPath form. The same SmartObject methods used by the K2 process are now exposed to all applications participating in the workflow, adding continuity to the entire solution.

# Good Design Considerations

There are several design considerations that should be thought about when developing an InfoPath form with K2; for instance, things such as database sizing considerations associated to the data captured in an InfoPath form, managing the data source of the InfoPath form, how to use required fields and InfoPath Views, and whether to use browser-enabled InfoPath forms.

## Storing Data in InfoPath

There are several considerations that must be made when developing an InfoPath form with K2. Probably the first and foremost is where data should be stored, be that in the InfoPath form for the long term or externally in a database. If the business process is simple and there are no strong requirements for historical reporting, it will be sufficient to store the data in the InfoPath form and archive it. If forms are to be stored in a library in SharePoint, a maintenance plan must be created to ensure that the library does not contain more than 2000 items in a single view otherwise performance will degraded. This can be obverted by storing documents in different folders or libraries, for instance, by month completed. If the data in the InfoPath form is considered to be enterprise data and vital to the business, it is highly recommended that the data be stored externally.

If the data is not stored externally in a database, there will be challenges accessing that data. For instance InfoPath forms stored in a SharePoint form library are stored in an XML file. A custom application would have to be written that would parse through all of the XML files in a form library and make it available to an enterprise reporting tool. In the meantime, the K2 database stores the XML data of the InfoPath form, but again, it is stored as XML that must be extracted and queried. Both of these scenarios can become more complicated over the lifetime of the InfoPath form because the XML schema may change. When the schema changes, the parsing of the XML will have to be different for each version. It can also be expected that there will be performance challenges for querying from these data sources in real time.

As mentioned earlier, the introduction of SmartObjects and their integration with InfoPath alleviates this issue. Storing the data externally will allow for much more flexibility when satisfying reporting requirements that will arise over the lifetime of the process. SmartObjects are integrated into InfoPath forms using Web services. It is not good practice to use the secondary data connections of the Web services in the form because there are many limitations within InfoPath. The recommended pattern is to create InfoPath Rules that will load a SmartObject when the form is opened and then move the data from the SmartObject into the main data source. Then before the form is submitted, add more rules that will take the data from the main data source and move it back into the secondary data source. There is even an option, when integrating a SmartObject with InfoPath, to add it to the main data source of the form. What this will do is add the SmartObject method parameters to the main data source of the form. Rules will still need to added to move the data from the main data source to the secondary data source so that data can be sent to the SmartObject Web service.

## Structuring InfoPath Data Source

It is important, regardless of whether or not data is being stored externally, to not pollute the main data source of the form with unnecessary data fields. When working with an InfoPath form, it will become necessary at times to add field or groups to the main data source of the form to support the user interface. A simple example would be a checkbox used to disable or enable some fields on the form. In many cases, the checkbox (and the field it is bound to) has no bearing on the business data captured in the form. It is good practice to keep these sorts of fields separated from the business data that the InfoPath form is capturing. This can be achieved by simply creating a group in the InfoPath main data source called _InfoPath and placing the fields in there.

## Working with Required Fields

One hurdle that developers run into when integrating an InfoPath form with a K2 process is that some fields are required for one activity, but not for another. If a field is marked as required on the main data source, it will be required whenever the form is submitted regardless of what step in the process the InfoPath form is at. A way to get around this is to use the DocumentView field under the _K2 group. This field will always be populated with the name of the view that is being used for the activity. Then the value in the DocumentView field can be used in data validation rules for other fields in the main data source. For instance, a process may have an InfoPath Client Event where a destination user must enter a purchase order number. There could be a requirement that the purchase order number can only be entered by someone in the Purchasing department. If there is a view called "Purchasing Department View," then the purchase order field can have a data validation rule that checks the value for the DocumentView field to see if it is equal to Purchasing Department View and if the purchase order number is blank. Now that this has been done, no other view in the InfoPath form will require the entry of the purchase order number.

## Multiple Forms in a Process

K2 blackpearl now supports the ability to have many forms in a single process, which is a major improvement over K2.net 2003. Having the ability to use multiple InfoPath forms in a process provides process designers with more flexibility. It is common that there will be requirements to support users who have very different InfoPath requirements. For instance there may be complex submission requirements, conditioning formatting, different presentation rules, and security requirements that could lead a designer to want to use multiple InfoPath forms in a process. If this occurs, it is recommended that you use multiple forms in a process.

It does not go without saying that if there are multiple InfoPath forms in a process some extra work will have to be done; if there is common data it must be available in each form. For instance, there may be some header information that must be displayed on every form that is unique to the process instance. Server-side code events could be written to move the data from one place to another, but that will require custom code. A simpler approach would be to use SmartObject to load common data between forms.

## Working with Views

Views in InfoPath allow designers to create a context-specific view of the main data source. An employee's view may be very different than a director's view, but the underlying data is still the same. Views allow the designer to create a user interface geared towards a particular audience. K2 InfoPath Client Events can be configured to select different views based on who the expected destination user will be.

One of the most common concerns with InfoPath is working with views because they can be challenging to manage. Presentation, conditional formatting, and required fields become challenging when the InfoPath form has lots of views, because in many cases they are identical except for a small thing here and there. If that is the case, when modifying the form, you will have to go to each view and make the same changes over and over again. To avoid this, the DocumentView field (discussed earlier) could be used in conditional formatting rules to display a field based on the current activity in the K2 process.

Another challenge when working with InfoPath views is to know when to stop creating views and create a new InfoPath form. For instance completely different data structures or security requirements, or vastly different business rules will drive you to want to create a different form instead of putting everything into a single InfoPath form. If this were to occur, K2 blackpearl does support adding multiple InfoPath forms to a process. If an InfoPath form is split into two different forms and there is shared data, it is possible to add a custom server-side code event that will copy XML data from one InfoPath form to another. If SmartObjects are used in both of the forms, then a server side code event would not be required.

## Using Browser-Enabled or Client-Based InfoPath Forms

With InfoPath 2007 and InfoPath Form Services, it is possible to deliver InfoPath forms over the Web. Users are no longer required to have InfoPath installed on their desktop. While browser-enabled InfoPath forms provide much of the same functionality as the client-based InfoPath forms, there are several considerations that must be made. First, browser-enabled InfoPath forms support several browsers such as Internet Explorer, FireFox, and Mozilla; however, not all versions are currently supported, and the audience who will be using the InfoPath form must be analyzed. Second, there are controls that are not supported with browser-enabled forms, and some controls are limited to specific browsers (please review InfoPath documentation). Other things like spell-checking, add-in menus, and scripting are not supported by browser-enabled forms at all. One feature of client-based InfoPath forms is that they support the ability to allow users to work in a disconnected mode. The InfoPath forms can be saved and filled out locally and then submitted once the user is back online.

Browser-enabled InfoPath forms do not provide as rich a user experience as can be achieved with an ASP.NET form. In today's environment, there is a high expectation placed on Web pages because of the pervasiveness of AJAX, Flash, and Silverlight. InfoPath forms do well at capturing data for basic Web pages, but if there are major presentation requirements or complex user controls that must be implemented, an InfoPath form should not be used.

## Process Mix Mode

K2 processes that use an InfoPath form can utilize other user interfaces in the same process. It is possible to have K2 processes that use InfoPath, ASP.NET, SharePoint, or any other platform to initiate and participate in the same workflow. For instance, there may be an ASP.NET page that users leverage to initialize a submission because the SharePoint site has not been publically exposed. However, there may be several other users who do have access to SharePoint at a certain point in the process, but these users want to use InfoPath. InfoPath Client Events can coincide on the same process where ASP.NET Client Events reside, and if SmartObjects are used, the data captured on both can be accessed easily in both places.

# InfoPath Process Deployment

Chapter 10 discussed all of the details associated with deploying a K2 process and SmartObjects; however, there are several things that must be accounted for when deploying a K2 process that is integrated with InfoPath. Many of the steps are associated to the deployment of the InfoPath form itself.

## Planning Sites and Form Libraries

All SharePoint Site and Form Libraries used by the K2 InfoPath process must be created prior to deployment. In many instances, these locations are not validated as part of the deployment process. A best practice is to have all of the names and the sites they reside in located within the Environment Library. This will ease the redeployment of the K2 blackpearl process between environments.

## Deployment of Data Connections

Deploying a process with an InfoPath form has become much easier with K2 blackpearl. The InfoPath form is now published when the K2 process is deployed. The InfoPath form will be deployed using the same Environment Library variables as the K2 process. All of the data connections in the InfoPath form associated with the K2 InfoPath Web service will be updated during deployment. This is a major improvement from K2.net 2003 because designers are no longer required to make manual changes to the data connections in the InfoPath form when deploying from one environment to another. However, data connections that are not related to K2 will not be updated manually. For example, there could be an InfoPath form that has a direct connection to a SharePoint list. When the form is first developed, it will have a URL pointing to the development SharePoint site. When the form is deployed to production, it will still have the URL for the list that is on the development SharePoint site. The best way to resolve this issue is to publish these data connections to a data connection library on a SharePoint site.

When an InfoPath form is browser-enabled, a data connection library will be created by K2 on the SharePoint site. All of the K2 InfoPath Web service data connections will be stored in the data connection library. Again, this will only be done for data connections that are managed by K2, and all non-K2 ones will have to be manually converted using the process previously described. It is advantageous from deployment perspective to try to convert as many of your data connections to use SmartObjects. Figure 11-47 shows the data connection library created as part of the deployment of the K2 process InfoPath form.

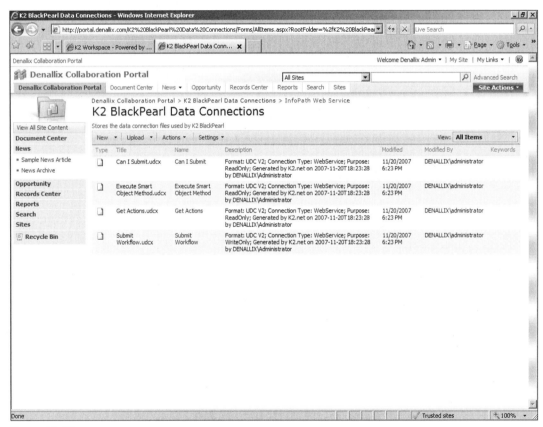

Figure 11-47

## Publishing Promoted Fields

Promoted fields in an InfoPath are fields that will have their values displayed in a column of a form library in SharePoint. The columns will be created when the form is published by InfoPath. When using promoted fields, users will be able to see values that are contained in the InfoPath form without requiring them to open it. This is valuable because, if there are lots of forms in the library, the user can visually scan all of the forms and pick the one to open. When an InfoPath form is deployed by K2, those columns will not appear in the SharePoint form library. One way to make them appear is to manually publish the InfoPath form. This will only have to be done once. If promoted fields need to be updated, the form will have to be republished manually.

When an InfoPath form is modified it will sometimes become necessary to relink the existing InfoPath form instances. It can happen that values in the InfoPath form may not be displayed anymore in the form library; however, new form instances that are added to the form library will have their values shown correctly. To resolve this issue, go to the Form Library Settings and select the "Relink documents to this Library" link, which is located in the Permissions and Management section. Select the entire existing form instance, and relink them. This will then refresh all of the columns in the form library with all of the values in the InfoPath form instances.

## Deploying Browser-Enabled Forms with .NET Managed Code

Deploying InfoPath forms with .NET managed code and K2 can become challenging. InfoPath forms that have .NET managed code must be deployed through MOSS Central Administration. This is a requirement of InfoPath Form Services to prevent malicious code from making its way into the SharePoint environment. InfoPath forms that have .NET managed code are loaded in Central Administration, using the Managed Form Templates link in the Application Management tab. Once the form has been uploaded, Central Administration will push the InfoPath form to site collections as a content type. InfoPath forms that have .NET managed code can be integrated with a K2 process, but a few actions need to be performed prior to deployment.

When integrating the InfoPath form with the K2 process, the form should be hooked to the K2 process by using the InfoPath Integration Wizard before any .NET managed code is added to the form. This avoids any issues that may arise with the location of the .NET managed code project. The .NET managed code project can be added to the K2 solution as another project. Second, when the InfoPath form is integrated using the InfoPath Integration Wizard, make sure that the InfoPath form is deployed as a content type.

When the K2 process is deployed, a few steps need to be taken after process deployment. Even though the deployment of the process will complete successfully and the InfoPath form content type will be created, the InfoPath form will not work. This is because of the fact that the deployed InfoPath form, which had .NET managed code, was not deployed through Central Administration. This is required because MOSS will not allow .NET code to be loaded into the MOSS server unless this is done by a user with administrative rights. The same is true for SharePoint Web parts and Features.

To resolve this, first go to the site collection's Site Content Type Gallery, find the content type that was created by the K2 deployment, and delete it. The name of the content type will be the same name as the form. Next, there will be a library on the same site collection called "K2 blackpearl InfoPath Form Templates." In this library will be all of the InfoPath form templates that were deployed by K2 blackpearl as content types. Download the form template and save it locally. This needs to be done because when the form was deployed, its K2 data connections were converted to use a SharePoint data connection library.

Once the InfoPath form template has been downloaded, open MOSS Central Administration and go to the Application Management tab. In Application Management there is a Manage Form Templates link, and this is where the InfoPath form will be uploaded to SharePoint. Find the InfoPath form that was saved locally, and upload it to the MOSS server. When the status of the form changes to Ready, click the drop-down list arrow on the form's name and select Activate to a Site Collection, which will deploy the InfoPath form as a new content type to a designated site collection. When the form status changes to Deployed, a new content type should be visible in the site collection. This content type can now be used in any form library in the site collection, and the .NET managed code for the InfoPath form will work. The same steps would be followed for any redeployment of the process. K2 will be working with Microsoft to hopefully eliminate the manual steps that are currently required to deploy forms with .NET managed code.

## InfoPath Integration Conclusion

In conclusion, this section demonstrates how easy it is for designers to take an InfoPath form and hook it into a K2 process and automate leveraging the entire K2 blackpearl platform. All the designer needs to do is initially create a form, use InfoPath Integration Wizard to add the form, use the InfoPath Client Event to create steps in the process, and then use actions to define what the destination user can do. K2 provides the ability to create data-driven InfoPath forms using SmartObjects, and K2 has streamlined the deployment of the process along with the InfoPath form. Now processes using K2 blackpearl and InfoPath can be authored and deployed in an extremely rapid fashion.

# Using ASP.NET Forms

Making use of ASP.NET Web Controls, and the familiar C# and VB.NET languages, developers are able to create Web pages that interact with K2 processes as worklist item forms. Additionally, the code can interact with the K2 server to initiate a workflow from a Web service, for example, thereby allowing for integration with external systems.

> *The remainder of this chapter contains some in-depth C# code, which I'm sure that many readers want to see (show me the code!), but bear in mind that K2 blackpearl allows workflows to be created without the need for code. So, for some readers, there may be no real need to delve further. But if it's code you're after, then here it comes.*

The K2 platform has a deep integration with the .NET platform. This includes Windows Presentation Foundation (WPF), Windows Communication Foundation (WCF), and of course, Windows Workflow Foundation (WF), which K2 workflows are built on top of.

In addition, the extensive K2 API allows for developers to treat the K2 infrastructure as a "platform," as well as a "server." For developers who can create a Web page using ASP.NET, it's not much of a leap to add capabilities from the K2 class libraries.

The functionality that will be covered includes a number of specific examples and working prototypes. These will help developers to begin, with the samples available from the Wrox Web site.

The example solutions being covered are:

- ❏ Initiating a workflow from code
- ❏ Customizing a Web page created via Forms Generation Client Event
- ❏ Displaying a custom Web page for a workflow task form
- ❏ Web page to show a list of process definitions and processes underway

*The remaining sections assume that you have sufficient knowledge to code and design the screen elements and program code for an ASP.NET Web page and Web site.*

There are a number of specific namespaces and classes that will be covered. Feel free to have a look at the K2 API and object model from within Visual Studio. There is a very intuitive object hierarchy, with collections of certain classes (such as `Actions` within a `ProcessInstance`).

This chapter covers the following classes; refer to the K2 blackpearl Developer Reference for more details.

- ❏ `SourceCode.Workflow.Client`
  - ❏ `Connection`
  - ❏ `ProcessInstance`
  - ❏ `WorklistItem`
  - ❏ `Action`
- ❏ `SourceCode.Workflow.Management`
  - ❏ `WorkflowManagementServer`
  - ❏ `ProcessSets`
  - ❏ `Processes`
  - ❏ `Activities`

*The following examples make use of C# as the choice of code language for interaction with K2. The same object hierarchy and class libraries can be coded using VB.NET. While the syntax and code statements will differ between C# and VB.NET, the same class libraries are used, and the same functional principles apply.*

## Initiating a Workflow from Code

To initiate the workflow, a Web page will include program code to connect to the K2 server, set the starting parameter values, and initiate the process.

1. Create a standard ASP.NET Web site project, and name it `IRAdmin`.

2. Change the name of the default Web page to `SubmitInfReq.aspx`.

3. Add some ASP.NET controls, including labels, so that the form appears as shown in Figure 11-48. Don't use HTML controls, as the ASP.NET code needs to refer to these controls within event-handlers and properties.

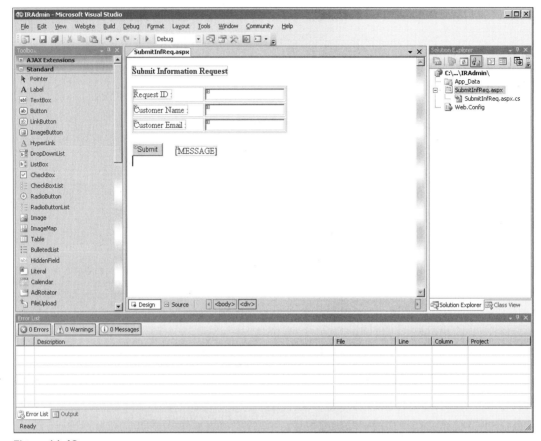

**Figure 11-48**

The next step is to include the code to create a new process instance and submit the workflow. The user will simply enter some values and click Submit.

Double-click the button to create an event-handler code segment:

```
protected void btnSubmit_Click(object sender, EventArgs e)
{

}
```

Add a reference to the K2 assembly, in order to use the namespaces and classes required.

1. Within the solution explorer, click Add Reference and choose the Browse tab.

2. Change folders to `C:\Program Files\K2 blackpearl\bin`.

3. Add a reference to `SourceCode.Workflow.Client.dll`.

4. Within the code-behind view for the page, add the following `using` statement:

```
using SourceCode.Workflow.Client;
```

The code to be added to the `btnSubmit_Click` method will do the following:

- ❑ Create a connection to the K2 server
- ❑ Create a process instance
- ❑ Set the data variables
- ❑ Start the process instance

*The code snippets included here omit any exception handling, such as* `Try...Catch...Finally` *blocks. It would be considered "best practice" to trap any errors found, such as being unable to connect to the K2 server. These code samples are used to describe the code required to interoperate with the K2 API and are not to be viewed as a complete code module.*

The following shows each step:

```
// Declare new K2 Connection & ProcessInstance objects
Connection conn = new Connection();

//Connect to Workflow Server
conn.Open("MyServer");
```

The connection `Open` method allows for a connection using either a server name or a connection string.

If the connection is opened using a server name, the security context used to connect to the K2 server will be the permissions of the *current user*. If this code were to be implemented within a Web service, there would be a user account assigned to the AppPool (IIS configuration). Or, the code could be wrapped within some Windows Impersonate code to change user context and kick-off the workflow.

Alternatively, and arguably easier, the connection parameters for the K2 server (such as server, port number, username, and password) can be specified using a *connection string*. This operates much the same as a SQL Server connection string.

This would usually be stored within a `.config` file but has been hardcoded to illustrate the example.

There are many attributes that can be specified; not all are required:

```
// Declare new K2 Connection & ProcessInstance objects
Connection conn = new Connection();

//create connection string
string connectionString = "Authenticate=true, Host=server,
Integrated=true, IsPrimaryLogin=true, Port=5252, UserID=Administrator,
WindowsDomain=domain, Password=password, SecurityLabelName=K2";

// Connect to Workflow Server
conn.Open(connectionString);
```

The key settings are the `Host`, `UserID`, `Password`, and `WindowsDomain`, as well as `Port`, depending on which K2 server is being connected to.

*The different servers within the K2 environment use a different port, meaning that a* `ConnectionString` *will most likely be required. For instance, the connection to the workflow client server above uses the 5252 port, whereas the* `HostServer` *for the* `WorkflowManagementServer` *operates on port 5555.*

*Additionally, the* `SmartObjectClientServer` *will use the 5555 port. Note that these port numbers can be configured, and thus may have been configured differently within the organization. However, the workflow client server will always use 5252 for backward compatability.*

Now that a connection has been created, the next step is to create a process instance using the connection to the K2 server. This simply requires the name of the process *folio* and name of the process itself:

```
//Create process instance
string name = @"Information Request Workflow\Information Request";
ProcessInstance pi = conn.CreateProcessInstance(name);
```

Again, the process folio and name would most likely be stored within a `web.config` file.

Note there is a further *overload* method for specifying the version of the process, allowing for an integer number corresponding to the version number:

```
string name = @"Information Request Workflow\Information Request";
ProcessInstance pi = conn.CreateProcessInstance(name, [int]);
```

Now that a `ProcessInstance` has been determined, values can be assigned to the process variables using values entered within the fields on the form. This will use the `DataFields` collection within the process instance:

```
// Map the data to the K2 process data fields
pi.DataFields["Request ID"].Value = txtRequestID.Text.Trim();
pi.DataFields["Customer Name"].Value = txtCustomerName.Text.Trim();
pi.DataFields["Customer Email"].Value = txtCustomerEmail.Text.Trim();
```

Last, set the Folio value to something relevant or easily identifiable. This may be an attribute identifying the item in another system or database identity row, for example. Or, simply use the current date and time. In this example, this will be another field from the screen.

Then start the workflow using the `StartProcessInstance` method:

```
// Set the folio
pi.Folio = txtRequestID.Text.Trim();

// Start K2 process instance
conn.StartProcessInstance(pi);
```

There is an overload method for `StartProcessInstance` with an additional parameter to allow for a workflow process to be initiated *asynchronously*. This can be useful for a *system* workflow, and if you do not need to wait for the process to be started:

```
conn.StartProcessInstance(pi, [true|false]);
```

This method actually doesn't return a value, but the ID of the process that was initiated will be updated within the process instance object and can thus be shown in a screen label (as shown in Figure 11-49):

```
// display message to user
lblStatus.Text = "Your new process is number : " + pi.ID;
```

The last thing needed is to close the connection to the K2 server, which will release any resources:

```
// Close Connection
conn.Close();
```

*The program code should* always *close the connection upon completion of the method.*

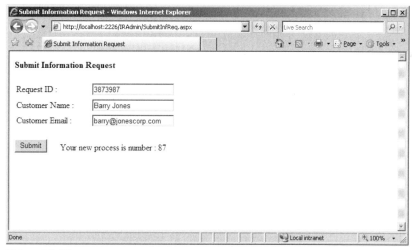

**Figure 11-49**

Here's the same code pieced together:

```
protected void btnSubmit_Click(object sender, EventArgs e)
{
    // Declare new K2 Connection & ProcessInstance objects
    Connection conn = new Connection();

    //Connect to Workflow Server
    conn.Open("MyServer");

    //Create process instance
    string name = @"Information Request Workflow\Information Request";
    ProcessInstance pi = conn.CreateProcessInstance(name);

    // Map the data to the K2 process data fields
    pi.DataFields["Request ID"].Value = txtRequestID.Text.Trim();
    pi.DataFields["Customer Name"].Value = txtCustomerName.Text.Trim();
    pi.DataFields["Customer Email"].Value = txtCustomerEmail.Text.Trim();

    // Set the folio
    pi.Folio = txtRequestID.Text.Trim();

    // Start K2 process instance
    conn.StartProcessInstance(pi);

    // display message to user
    lblStatus.Text = "Your new process is number : " + pi.ID;

    // Close Connection
    conn.Close();

}
```

This is relatively easy to extend and customize, allowing for K2 workflow processes to be initiated using a class or Web service (for example).

Here are some ideas of how to extend the previous concepts:

❑ Create config settings for the K2 server name (or connection string) as well as the process folio and name.

❑ Load additional data fields from an external database, such as SQL Server.

❑ Include the method within a Web service class library, and call it from another system (such as EPM or CRM), passing input parameters for data fields and folio values as required.

❑ After the process is initiated, use the process id value to update some back-end system.

❑ Add the method to a class library (business layer) and call it from a WinForm to initiate the workflow.

## Customizing a Web Page Created via Forms Generation Client Event

As seen in Chapter 9 (refer to Figure 9-18), the forms generation capabilities within K2 allow forms to be created quickly and easily, without the need for any code or InfoPath. An example of this can be seen in Figure 11-50. Admittedly, the forms need a little polish, but they get the job done, and they can be ideal for a quick prototype or testing scenario.

Figure 11-50

There are a few things you can do to customize the form shown:

❑   Update the form look, feel, and code for the Forms Generation page that was created.

❑   Create a new Form Layout template based on the existing Blank Page template.

❑   Create the CSS and HTML layout for the form, affecting new forms.

Within the Workspace Web site created for K2, the Web application contains all the pages and files needed for the K2 Workspace. There is an additional folder added that contains the Forms Generation pages (also known as Client Event Pages). These will have been code generated using the K2 Designer within Visual Studio, and the URL is captured within the K2 workflow.

The IIS Web site is configured to use the following folder for these pages:

```
C:\Program Files\K2 blackpearl\WorkSpace\ClientEventPages
```

The Web site can be opened within Visual Studio, as with any other Web application. When the project is opened, the ASPX page, the class files, and the CSS styles to be applied can be viewed (as shown in Figure 11-51). There can be many customizations, to the layout, and look and feel, and any additional HTML or JavaScript can also be included.

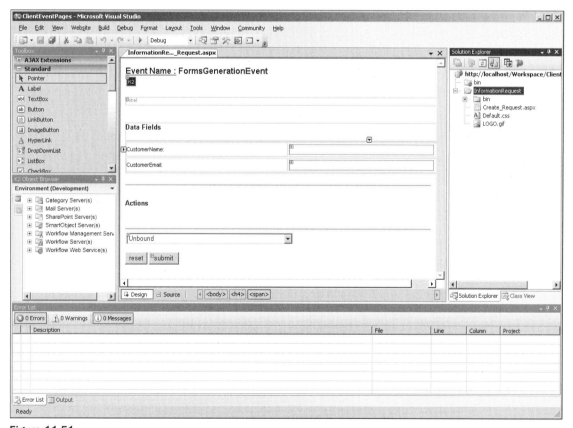

Figure 11-51

Unfortunately, this is actually a *compiled* version of the Web site, so the code can't actually be viewed or edited.

Furthermore, the big downside is that the customizations will be overwritten when the Forms Generation Client Event happens on subsequent deployments. It follows that there must be some way to edit the template or, better yet, to create a new one.

Within the K2 Forms Generation Client Event, the Form Layout initially contains only one item in the combo: Blank Page, as shown in Figure 11-52. New entries can be added to that list of layouts, with different design, formatting and styles, and code behind.

**Figure 11-52**

The template Web page (ASPX) and code used by the Forms Generation Client Wizard can be found in the following folder:

```
C:\Program Files\K2 blackpearl\Bin\Layouts\clientevent\CSharp\1033
```

Within the 1033 folder, there is a folder entitled Blank Page. To create a new template, simply copy the folder, rename it (for example *MyDepartment*), and then update the files within. The name of the *folder* will then appear in the drop-down list of Form Layouts within the K2 Designer.

The styles for the page are contained in the `default.css` file, allowing for customization of fonts, colors, and so on.

The `class.aspx.cs` and `layout.aspx` files contain a number of symbols, which are replaced when the K2 Designer performs the forms generation (see Figure 11-53).

Tags like `$SafeFieldName$`, and `$SafeControlName$` are replaced when the Forms Generation activity processes the Client Event Wizard, and the resulting page is copied to the `ClientEventPages` folder (as shown above).

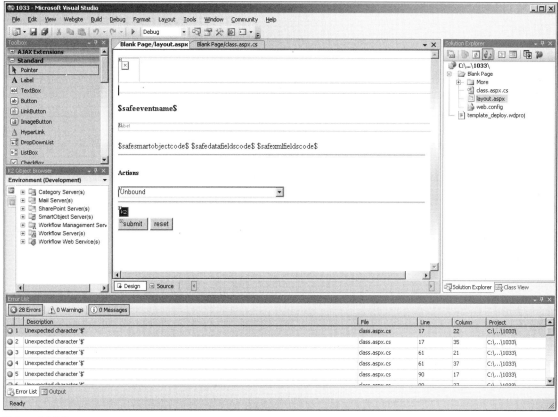

**Figure 11-53**

Feel free to make some changes to the page layout, with your own text, layout, and images, as well as any JavaScript or HTML needed.

> *IMPORTANT! Don't rename the* files; *rename only the* folder. *Also, be aware that Visual Studio will not be able to build or run the project. Visual Studio is just used as an* editor *in this case. Also, take care not to remove the* K2WorklistItemPanel *tag.*

## Displaying a Custom Web Page for a Workflow Task Form

Within the K2 Designer, the Client Event Wizard allows the developer to specify which ASP.NET form to display for the particular user task.

The Workflow Designer will enter the URL of the corresponding Web site/Web page. The Client Event Wizard automatically appends a querystring value, which acts as an input parameter to a page. This value can be seen in the URL of the page (see Figure 11-54).

This identifier is named SN (serial number) and will uniquely identify the worklist item within the K2 server. The K2 API includes automatic security-trimming, meaning that only the allowed user can view the details for the particular task.

The form will be displayed when the user clicks to view the task from within a Workspace or worklist page, or by clicking on a URL provided in an e-mail notification. Program code included within the form will retrieve the worklist item details from the K2 server, using the SN value from the querystring.

Thus, any `DataFields, Actions,` and other process data can be displayed to the user and the action to be applied will be executed on the server.

**Figure 11-54**

As seen in the previous example, there are a few steps required to interact with the workflow:

1.  Create a connection to the K2 server.

2.  Retrieve process data fields to display and update.

3.  Process user action, complete the task, and thus continue the K2 workflow.

    *The example code and functionality will continue the previous example used to initiate the workflow.*

Add another Web page, and rename it `ConfirmReceipt.aspx`.

This Web page will have three labels (not textboxes this time), a drop-down list, and a Submit button. There is also a comments field in which the user can enter any additional information.

Add some ASP.NET controls, including labels, so that the form resembles Figure 11-55.

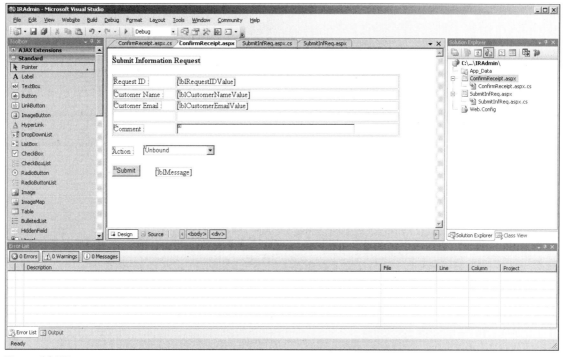

**Figure 11-55**

Add the code to connect to the K2 server and retrieve details for the workflow instance. This will include the data fields and associated actions.

Switch to the code view to add some code to the Page_Load event-handler.

```
protected void Page_Load(object sender, EventArgs e)
{

}
```

First, a reference to the K2 namespace is needed. Scroll to the top of the class library and add the following using statement:

```
using SourceCode.Workflow.Client;
```

Begin the code for the Page_Load event with a connection to the K2 server:

```
// Declare new K2 Connection object
Connection conn = new Connection();

//Connect to Workflow Server
conn.Open("MyServer");
```

Open the specific K2 Worklist item using the SN value from the querystring of the page:

```
//get the serial number
string sn = Request.QueryString["SN"].ToString();

// Get the WorklistItem object
WorklistItem wi = conn.OpenWorklistItem(sn);

// get the process instance object
ProcessInstance pi = wi.ProcessInstance;
```

The WorkListItem object contains a number of properties and collections that allow for the retrieval of data in the process instance, user assignments, and the workflow actions.

The EventInstance and ProcessInstance objects allow you to determine the process folder, name, version, priority, and expected durations, as well as any DataFields, XMLFields, and Actions defined.

For now, some DataField values are retrieved from the ProcessInstance and displayed in the label fields:

```
// Map the data to the K2 process data fields
lblRequestIDValue.Text = pi.DataFields["Request ID"].Value.ToString();
lblCustomerNameValue.Text = pi.DataFields["Customer Name"].Value.ToString();
lblCustomerEmailValue.Text = pi.DataFields["Customer Email"].Value.ToString();
```

Next, the actions are displayed for the workflow step (from the WorkListItem), allowing the user to make a selection. The actions will be loaded into a drop-down list, using simple data binding. The Name field will be displayed, which will also be the key value used when executing the chosen action:

```
// set datasource for drop-down
ddlActions.DataSource = wi.Actions;
ddlActions.DataTextField = "Name";
ddlActions.DataBind();
```

As always, the last step is to close the connection to the K2 server.

```
// Close Connection
conn.Close();
```

Here's the same code pieced together:

```
protected void Page_Load(object sender, EventArgs e)
{

    // Declare new K2 Connection object
    Connection conn = new Connection();

    //Connect to Workflow Server
    conn.Open("MyServer");

    //get the serial number
    string sn = Request.QueryString["SN"].ToString();
```

```
// Get the WorklistItem object
WorklistItem wi = conn.OpenWorklistItem(sn);

// get the process instance object
ProcessInstance pi = wi.ProcessInstance;

// Map the data to the K2 process data fields
lblRequestIDValue.Text = pi.DataFields["Request ID"].Value.ToString();
lblCustomerNameValue.Text = pi.DataFields["Customer Name"].Value.ToString();
lblCustomerEmailValue.Text = pi.DataFields["Customer Email"].Value.ToString();

// set datasource for drop-down
ddlActions.DataSource = wi.Actions;
ddlActions.DataTextField = "Name";
ddlActions.DataBind();

// Close Connection
conn.Close();

}
```

When the user actions the task, the form will appear as follows. Note that the URL has a querystring with the SN value 89_14 (seen in the address bar of the browser in Figure 11-56).

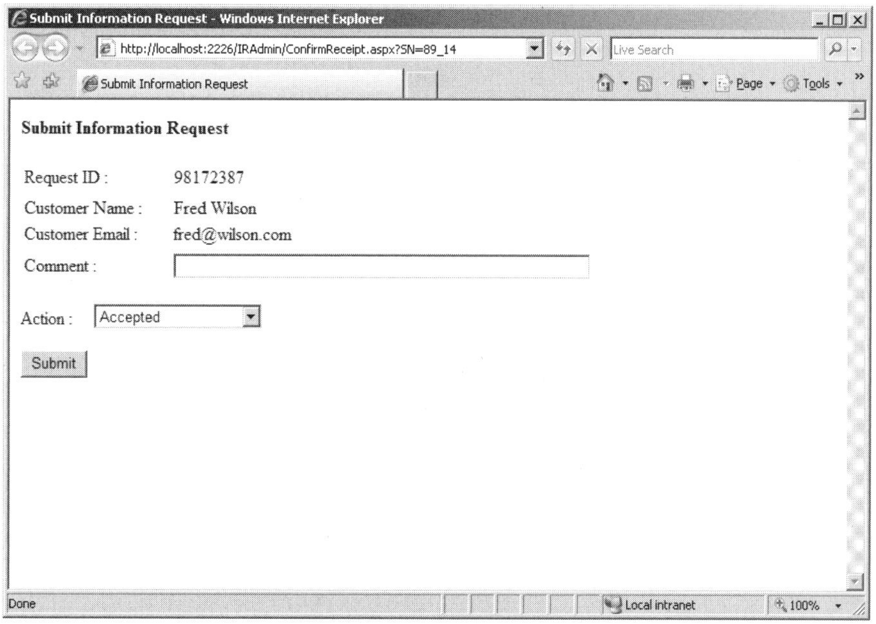

Figure 11-56

## Completing an Activity from Code

To complete the task, the user will enter any necessary details, and choose the action to take, by choosing a value within the drop-down list. The user will then click the Submit button, which runs the code covered next.

The functionality required for this step is:

1.   Create a connection to the K2 server.

2.   Load the `WorklistItem` object for the specific SN (from the querystring).

3.   Execute the action as chosen by the user and thus continue the K2 workflow.

*Much of the code to be included is the same as that used previously — especially with regard to opening a connection to the K2 server and loading the `WorklistItem`. This would most likely be included in a shared class library, or additional class library (DLL).*

The event-handler code for the button is included by double-clicking the Submit button within the Page designer:

```
protected void btnSubmit_Click(object sender, EventArgs e)
{

}
```

The first step is to create a connection to the K2 server:

```
// Declare new K2 Connection object
Connection conn = new Connection();

//Connect to Workflow Server
conn.Open("MyServer");
```

Then open the specific K2 `WorklistItem`, using the SN value as specified within the querystring of the page.

```
// Get the WorklistItem object
string sn = Request.QueryString["SN"].ToString();

// get the worklist item, and process instance (for data fields)
WorklistItem wi = conn.OpenWorklistItem(sn);
ProcessInstance pi = wi.ProcessInstance;
```

The user will have entered some text for the `Comment` field, which needs to be set as the corresponding data variable within the workflow instance. The reference to `ProcessInstance` was created in the previous step, so the `DataField` can be updated using the name of the variable:

```
// Set the Process Data Fields
pi.DataFields["Comment"].Value = txtComment.Text;
```

Of course, the code needs to complete the worklist task and set the `Action` corresponding to the drop-down list value selected. This just uses the name to determine the action and then execute it:

```
// determine the action object for the chosen item
Action action = wi.Actions[ddlActions.Text];

// execute the action
action.Execute();
```

Alternatively, this can be coded as a single statement, without the need to create an `Action` object reference:

```
// execute the action
wi.Actions["Confirm"].Execute();
```

Last, a message is to be displayed to the user and the Submit button on the page is disabled. This prevents the user from resubmitting the form and generating an exception (because the `WorklistItem` will have been closed):

```
// Display message
lblMessage.Text = "The activity has been completed";

// Disable the submit button and close connection
btnSubmit.Enabled = false;
```

The final step, as always, is to close the connection to the K2 server.

```
// Close Connection
conn.Close();
```

Figure 11-57 shows the completed form (after entering a comment and clicking Submit).

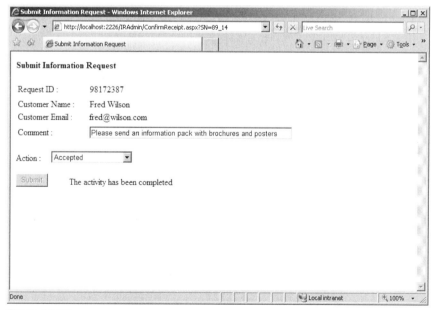

**Figure 11-57**

413

Here's the same code pieced together:

```
protected void btnSubmit_Click(object sender, EventArgs e)
{

    // Declare new K2 Connection object
    Connection conn = new Connection();

    //Connect to Workflow Server
    conn.Open("MyServer");

    // Get the WorklistItem object
    string sn = Request.QueryString["SN"].ToString();

    // get the worklist item, and process instance (for data fields)
    WorklistItem wi = conn.OpenWorklistItem(sn);
    ProcessInstance pi = wi.ProcessInstance;

    // Set the Process Data Fields
    pi.DataFields["Comment"].Value = txtComment.Text;

    // execute the action
    wi.Actions[ddlActions.Text].Execute();

    // Display message
    lblMessage.Text = "The activity has been completed";

    // Disable the submit button and close connection
    btnSubmit.Enabled = false;

    // Close Connection
    conn.Close();

}
```

# K2 Server Management from Code

As shown in the preceding examples, there are numerous namespaces and classes within the K2 API. In addition to the program code to interact with a specific process, such as displaying DataFields and to execute an action, there is also the ability to perform server management tasks.

The following example shows a number of these concepts:

❑   Loading the list of process definitions within the K2 server

❑   Viewing the version of each process and the events and activities for the process definition

❑   Determining a list of all currently running process instances

The first step is to add another Web page to the existing Web site project.

The default Web page can then be renamed K2Manage.aspx.

This Web page has a drop-down list to display a list of processes and a gridview to show details upon selection. It will also include a few buttons to load different details for the process. After adding the necessary ASP.NET controls, the form should look similar to the layout shown in Figure 11-58.

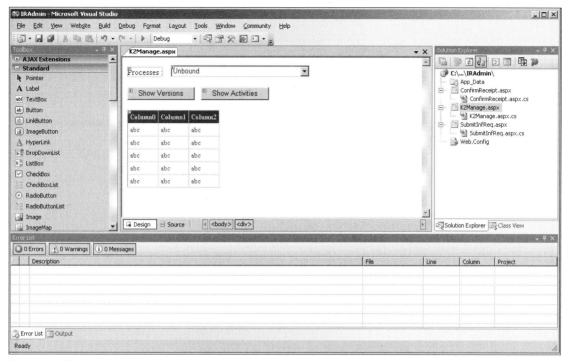

Figure 11-58

## *Loading a Catalog of Process Definitions*

The first step is to add the code to load the details for the page. Switch over to the code view, and add some code to the Page_Load event-handler.

This code is to be run once when the page initially loads, requiring code to check the IsPostBack flag:

```
protected void Page_Load(object sender, EventArgs e)
{
    if (!Page.IsPostBack)
    {


    }
}
```

The code to be included requires the addition of two DLLs:

1. Within the Solution Explorer, click Add Reference and select the Browse tab.

2. Change the folder to C:\Program Files\K2 blackpearl\bin.

3. Add a reference to SourceCode.Workflow.Management.dll.

4. Add a reference to SourceCode.HostClientAPI.dll.

This second DLL contains namespaces and classes required by the `Management` DLL.

Scroll to the top and add the following `using` statements:

```
using SourceCode.Workflow.Management;
using SourceCode.HostClientAPI.BaseAPI;
```

The first step is to create a connection to the K2 server, but with a twist. This time, the connection uses the K2 *Host Server*, which is running on port 5555 (by default).

Instead of creating a `Connection` object, use the `WorkflowManagementServer` class. This requires the server name and the port number as a constructor:

```
//open connection to K2 Host Server
WorkflowManagementServer wms = new WorkflowManagementServer("SERVER", 5555);
wms.Open();
```

The first action is to return a list of all `ProcessSets` within the K2 catalog. This is simply the list of all process definitions that have been deployed to the K2 server:

```
// load list of procsets
ProcessSets ps = wms.GetProcSets();
```

The resulting list of processes will be loaded into the drop-down list using data binding:

```
// assign drop-down to use process sets collection
dropDownListProcSets.DataSource = ps;
dropDownListProcSets.DataTextField = "FullName";
dropDownListProcSets.DataValueField = "ProcSetID";
dropDownListProcSets.DataBind();
```

When the page is loaded, the user will see a list of the processes within the K2 server (as shown in Figure 11-59).

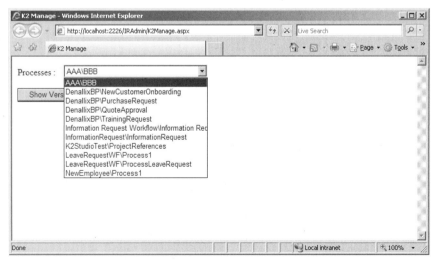

Figure 11-59

Here's the full code snippet:

```
protected void Page_Load(object sender, EventArgs e)
{

    if (!Page.IsPostBack)
    {

        //open connection to K2 Host Server
        WorkflowManagementServer wms = new WorkflowManagementServer
          ("SERVER", 5555);
        wms.Open();

        // load list of procsets
        ProcessSets ps = wms.GetProcSets();

        // assign drop-down to use process sets collection
        dropDownListProcSets.DataSource = ps;
        dropDownListProcSets.DataTextField = "FullName";
        dropDownListProcSets.DataValueField = "ProcSetID";
        dropDownListProcSets.DataBind();


    }
}
```

## Displaying Versions of Process

When the user chooses a particular process definition from the drop-down list, the versions for that process will be loaded into the grid below. All process version information will be displayed, some of which will be used as keys to retrieve other details (as shown in the following example).

The user will click a button to display the details, so the following event-handler is required:

```
protected void btnShowVersions_Click(object sender, EventArgs e)
{

}
```

As previously shown, a connection to the K2 server is included:

```
//open connection to the K2 Host Server
WorkflowManagementServer wms = new WorkflowManagementServer("SERVER", 5555);
wms.Open();
```

The drop-down value determines the specific identifier for the process, as the field procSetID is set as the DataTextValue when the drop-down list is loaded.

```
//determine value selected
int procSetID = Convert.ToInt32(dropDownListProcSets.SelectedValue);
```

Then the collection of Processes is loaded and used to bind to the gridView:

```
//load processes collection
Processes p = wms.GetProcessVersions(procSetID);

//load grid with process versions
gridView.DataSource = p;
gridView.DataBind();
```

Figure 11-60 shows what the output may look like (depending on your processes and server).

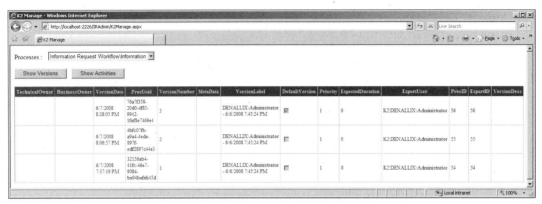

**Figure 11-60**

Here's the same code pieced together:

```
protected void btnShowVersions_Click(object sender, EventArgs e)
{

        //open connection to the K2 Host Server
        WorkflowManagementServer wms = new WorkflowManagementServer
          ("SERVER", 5555);
        wms.Open();

        //determine value selected
        int procSetID = Convert.ToInt32(dropDownListProcSets.SelectedValue);

        //load processes collection
        Processes p = wms.GetProcessVersions(procSetID);

        //load grid with process versions
        gridView.DataSource = p;
        gridView.DataBind();

}
```

## Viewing Activities for a Process Definition

Furthering the previous example, the user can view the list of activities within the process definition for a particular version of the process.

First, create a method for the button event-handler:

```
protected void btnShowActivities_Click(object sender, EventArgs e)
{


}
```

And, of course, open a connection to the workflow server (Host Server):

```
WorkflowManagementServer wms = new WorkflowManagementServer("SERVER", 5555);
wms.Open();
```

Next, the process definition is loaded using the value selected within the drop-down list as the key. The `procSetID` value was set as the `DataValueField` when the drop-down list was loaded:

```
//determine value selected
int procSetID = Convert.ToInt32(dropDownListProcSets.SelectedValue);
```

The `procSetID` value is then used to load a version of the process definition. In this example, the first version of the process is loaded using the collection value of `[0]`. This may or may not be the *default version*, but it will be the *most recent version*.

```
//load the processes for the chosen procset definition
Processes pv = wms.GetProcessVersions(procSetID);

//determine the ID value of the first (most recent) item
int procId = pv[0].ProcID;
```

*The versions are loaded in "reverse date" order, meaning that the first item is the most recently deployed process definition. This is likely to be the* `DefaultVersion`, *although the correct approach would be to check through the versions to see which has the flag for* `DefaultVersion` *set to true (because it may not be simply the most recent).*

Now that the `procId` value has been determined, as opposed to `procSetID`, the list of activities can be loaded into the grid, using data binding:

```
//load activities using procID
Activities activities = wms.GetProcActivities(procId);

//add the results to the grid
gridView.DataSource = activities;
gridView.DataBind();
```

This will display as shown in Figure 11-61.

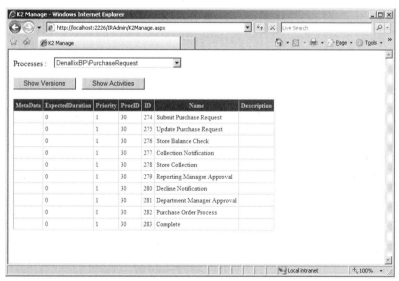

**Figure 11-61**

Here's the code in full:

```
protected void btnShowActivities_Click(object sender, EventArgs e)
{
        WorkflowManagementServer wms = new WorkflowManagementServer("SERVER", 5555);
        wms.Open();

        //determine value selected
        int procSetID = Convert.ToInt32(dropDownListProcSets.SelectedValue);

        //load the processes for the chosen procset definition
        Processes pv = wms.GetProcessVersions(procSetID);

        //determine the ID value of the first (most recent) item
        int procId = pv[0].ProcID;

        //load activities using procID
        Activities activities = wms.GetProcActivities(procId);

        //add the results to the grid
        gridView.DataSource = activities;
        gridView.DataBind();

}
```

Another code example (below) uses the same reference for the `WorkflowManagementServer` to determine the list of `Events` corresponding to an `Activity` (refer to Figure 11-61).

In this instance, the ID column in the grid provides the key for the `ActivityEvents` to be loaded using the `GetActivityEvents` method. To illustrate this, the ID is hardcoded to use the value from the sixth row in the grid — a value of 279 (Reporting Manager Approval).

This could then be loaded to a different gridview, for example:

```
//retrieve events for an activity
int ID = 279;
Events events = wms.GetActivityEvents(ID);

//add the results to the grid
gridView.DataSource = events;
gridView.DataBind();
```

## Viewing Processes Currently Running

The previous code samples show how to use the K2 API to delve into process *definitions*, versions, and their activities and events. The real power of the management namespace and class libraries comes when looking into what's happening on the server at the moment, such as what processes are running and what user tasks are yet to be completed.

Imagine that the marketing department has asked for a Web part to be shown on the home page for its department portal site, with a list of the current processes underway showing the activity name, user assigned, and start date.

*The quickest and easiest way to achieve this is to use a SharePoint Page Viewer Web part with the URL of an ASP.NET Web page containing the code to interact with the K2 server. This also negates the need to install the SharePoint SDK or Visual Studio project templates within the development environment. There are also more hoops to jump through when testing, debugging, and deploying a Web part. An ASP.NET page is a much simpler approach and the results are very similar.*

The steps to achieve this are as follows:

1. Create a connection to the server.

2. Return a list of `WorklistItems` for a particular process `ProcSet`.

3. Show grid columns for the fields: `EventName`, `ActivityName`, `Destination` (User)

The Web page code will make use of a querystring value for `ProcSet` to determine the processes and `WorklistItems` to be displayed. The columns to be displayed in the grid will be specified; this is different from simple data binding, which displays all columns (as in the previous examples).

Within the Visual Studio project, add another Web page and rename it `RunningProcesses.aspx`.

For the page layout, simply add a gridview. Right-click the gridview and choose Auto Layout to change the colors and font sizes.

The form should then look similar to that shown in Figure 11-62.

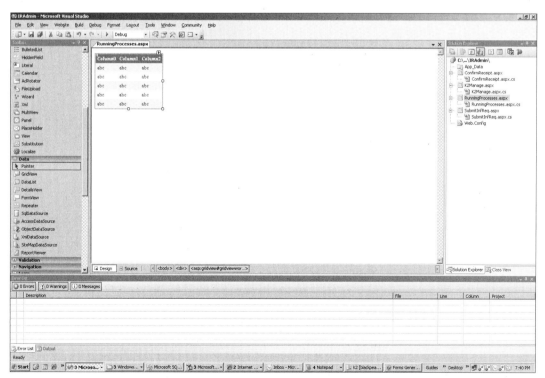

**Figure 11-62**

Switch to the code view for the page. Scroll to the top and add the `using` statement:

```
using SourceCode.Workflow.Management;
```

The `Page_Load` event-handler first needs a check for `IsPostback`:

```
protected void Page_Load(object sender, EventArgs e)
{
    if (!Page.IsPostBack)
    {
        //code goes here


    }
}
```

Once again, a connection to the K2 server is required:

```
// open the connection
WorkflowManagementServer wms = new WorkflowManagementServer("SERVER", 5555);
wms.Open();
```

The querystring value for `ProcSet` is used to retrieve a list of processes. The `GetWorklistItems` method operates as a *search method* with parameters passed as selection criteria (using wildcard values such as %).

The parameters are:

- ❑ From date
- ❑ To date
- ❑ Destination
- ❑ Process name
- ❑ Activity name
- ❑ Event name
- ❑ Folio

> *More information is available from the K2 blackpearl Developer Reference, available at* www.k2underground.com.

For now, some default values for `from` and `to` dates are used, and wildcards will be used for the other parameters that are not required at this stage:

```
// load the querystring value
string procSet = Request.QueryString["ProcSet"].ToString();

// load collection of worklist items underway
WorklistItems wi = wms.GetWorklistItems(DateTime.MinValue,
DateTime.MaxValue, "%", procSet, "%", "%", "%");
```

The following example will use the parameter for `Destination` to retrieve the `WorklistItems` for the current user.

Next, add columns to the gridview and specify the fields to be shown:

```
//ensure columns have been cleared out of the grid
gridviewWorklistItems.Columns.Clear();

//set the data source to the worklist item collection
gridviewWorklistItems.DataSource = wi;

//don't create automatically, will specify
gridviewWorklistItems.AutoGenerateColumns = false;
```

The gridview will have four columns as `BoundFields`, which will be automatically populated when the `DataBind` occurs. The columns to include are `Event Name`, `Activity Name`, the `User`, and `Date Started`:

```
//create a field, and set the data field name, and the column heading
//and add the column
BoundField fldEventName = new BoundField();
fldEventName.DataField = "EventName";
fldEventName.HeaderText = "Event Name";
gridviewWorklistItems.Columns.Add(fldEventName);

BoundField fldActivityName = new BoundField();
fldActivityName.DataField = "ActivityName";
fldActivityName.HeaderText = "Activity Name";
gridviewWorklistItems.Columns.Add(fldActivityName);

BoundField fldDestination = new BoundField();
fldDestination.DataField = "Destination";
fldDestination.HeaderText = "User";
gridviewWorklistItems.Columns.Add(fldDestination);

BoundField fldStartDate = new BoundField();
fldStartDate.DataField = "StartDate";
fldStartDate.HeaderText = "Date Started";
gridviewWorklistItems.Columns.Add(fldStartDate);

//display data on the gridview
gridviewWorklistItems.DataBind();
```

Figure 11-63 shows this page within a Web browser. The address bar shows the querystring value for `ProcSet` is specified as `LeaveRequestWF\ProcessLeaveRequest`, corresponding to the processes to be shown on the Marketing portal site.

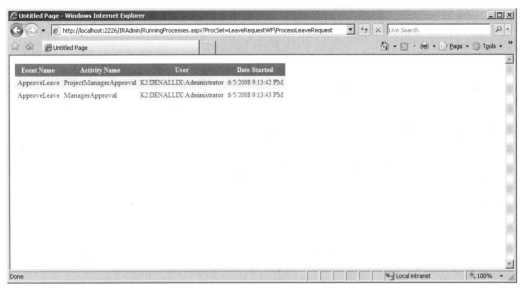

Figure 11-63

The URL shown is then included within the settings for the *Page Viewer Web part* for SharePoint. Figure 11-64 shows the same page within the SharePoint home page.

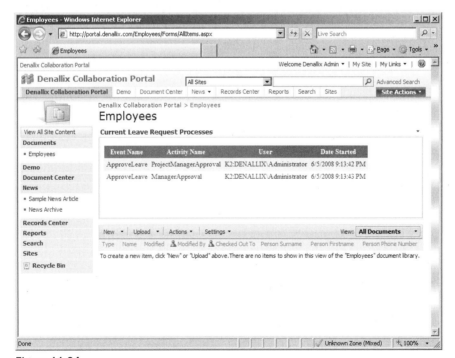

Figure 11-64

Here's the code shown in a single listing:

```
protected void Page_Load(object sender, EventArgs e)
{
    if (!Page.IsPostBack)
    {
        WorkflowManagementServer wms = new WorkflowManagementServer
            ("SERVER", 5555);
        wms.Open();

        // load the querystring value
        string procSet = Request.QueryString["ProcSet"];
        WorklistItems wi = wms.GetWorklistItems
            (DateTime.MinValue, DateTime.MaxValue, "%", procSet, "%", "%", "%");

        gridviewWorklistItems.Columns.Clear();
        gridviewWorklistItems.DataSource = wi;
        gridviewWorklistItems.AutoGenerateColumns = false;

        BoundField fldEventName = new BoundField();
        fldEventName.DataField = "EventName";
        fldEventName.HeaderText = "Event Name";
        gridviewWorklistItems.Columns.Add(fldEventName);

        BoundField fldActivityName = new BoundField();
        fldActivityName.DataField = "ActivityName";
        fldActivityName.HeaderText = "Activity Name";
        gridviewWorklistItems.Columns.Add(fldActivityName);

        BoundField fldDestination = new BoundField();
        fldDestination.DataField = "Destination";
        fldDestination.HeaderText = "User";
        gridviewWorklistItems.Columns.Add(fldDestination);

        BoundField fldStartDate = new BoundField();
        fldStartDate.DataField = "StartDate";
        fldStartDate.HeaderText = "Date Started";
        gridviewWorklistItems.Columns.Add(fldStartDate);

        gridviewWorklistItems.DataBind();

    }
}
```

Of course, the list of processes previously shown can be modified in many ways, including:

❑ Show the `Folio` or `DataFields` for the specific `ProcessInstance`.

❑ Include a link to the `ViewFlow` for the specific process.

❑ Update the layout of the grid, including fonts, colors, column sizing, and so on.

The specific details can be based on business rules or requirements within the organization.

### *Retrieving Processes Currently Running for a Specific User*

In much the same way that the list of `WorkListItems` for a particular *process* was retrieved (in the previous example), the same method can be used to retrieve a list of `WorklistItems` for a particular *user*.

The code example needs one line changed — to include the `Destination` parameter:

```
//set the user name to be used as the Destination
string userName = "DENALLIX\\Administrator";

//load the list of items
WorklistItems wi = wms.GetWorklistItems(DateTime.MinValue, DateTime.MaxValue,
userName, "%", "%", "%", "%");
```

The *current user* could be specified instead of the value selected to load the `WorklistItems` of the logged-on user (`WindowsIdentity`). This requires adding another `using` statement, as in previous examples:

```
using Windows.Security.Principal;
```

The list of `WorklistItems` can then be loaded for the *current* user:

```
//set the user name to be used as the Destination
string userName = Windows.GetIdentity().Name;

//load the list of items
WorklistItems wi = wms.GetWorklistItems(DateTime.MinValue, DateTime.MaxValue,
userName, "%", "%", "%", "%");
```

Either way, the list of `WorklistItems` for the chosen (or current) user will then be loaded into the grid, as with the previous example (running processes).

## *Worklist for Current User*

The previous example is useful for a system administrator or console application — or when a manager needs to view other staff's list of work.

For users viewing their own worklist, there are a number of user interfaces as part of K2 blackpearl. The current tasks can be viewed using the K2 Workspace, SharePoint Web part, and even a Windows Vista sidebar gadget that is available on the K2 black market.

As an alternative, the same details can be retrieved from within custom code and displayed or actioned directly depending on business requirements. Similar code could be used with a Web service or WinForm or perhaps with an application for display on a mobile device.

To retrieve the `WorklistItems` using custom code, we need to jump back to look at the `SourceCode` `.Workflow.Client` namespace (added in previous examples).

This uses the automatic security trimming of the current user who has created the K2 server connection, rather than using program code to specify a username (as seen in the previous example).

Add another Web page to the solution entitled `WorklistForCurrentUser.aspx`.

Within the page designer, add a gridview control. The form should then look similar to that shown in Figure 11-65.

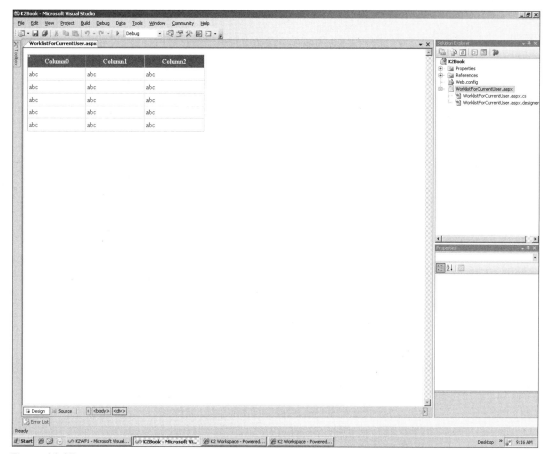

**Figure 11-65**

First, add the namespace to the class by adding the following `using` statement:

```
using SourceCode.Workflow.Client;
```

The first code segment to include is for the `Page_Load` event:

```
protected void Page_Load(object sender, EventArgs e)
{


}
```

Once again, create a connection to the K2 server, as seen in previous examples:

```
//Open Connection
Connection conn = new Connection();
conn.Open("SERVER");
```

The `Worklist` items can then be loaded using a statement that could not be simpler: `OpenWorklist`:

```
//Get Worklist for current Logged on User
Worklist wl = conn.OpenWorklist();
```

The K2 server will automatically determine the *current user* by using Windows Integrated Authentication from the browser or by using the AppPool identity (if it's running within a Web service).

The security trimming related to the particular user context is automatically applied to ensure that only those tasks assigned can be viewed.

The list of `WorklistItems` can then be shown in the grid:

```
gridviewWorklistItems.DataSource = wl;
gridviewWorklistItems.DataBind();
```

The list of columns displayed in the grid will initially be limited to `SerialNumber` and `Data`, which contains the URL of the page to be shown for a client event. Refer to Figure 11-66.

This simply illustrates the `OpenWorklist` method to retrieve the worklist items assigned to a specific user.

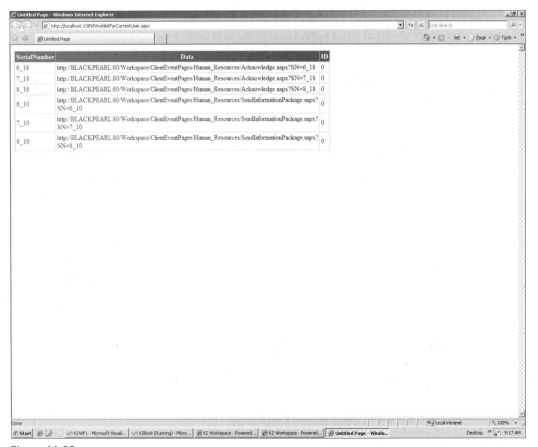

Figure 11-66

To add some detail for the user and show a more *meaningful* list, the code will need to cycle through each `Worklist` item and retrieve the details to display — `ProcessName`, `EventName`, `ActivityName`, `StartDate`, and `Folio`.

The first step is to create a `DataTable` with columns that can then be added to the grid using data binding.

```
//create a data table
DataTable dt = new DataTable();

//add some columns
dt.Columns.Add("SerialNumber");
dt.Columns.Add("ProcessName");
dt.Columns.Add("ActivityName");
dt.Columns.Add("EventName");
dt.Columns.Add("StartDate");
dt.Columns.Add("Folio");
```

The `foreach` statement is used to iterate through all worklist items, with the variable `wli` used for each worklist item in turn:

```
foreach (WorklistItem wli in wl)
{


}
```

Within the `foreach` block, there will be a `DataRow` added to the `DataTable` created previously, with the values from the `WorklistItem` and other values from the sub-objects `ProcessInstance` and `EventInstance`.

```
//create a new row, with columns defined
DataRow dr = dt.NewRow();

//add values from worklist + sub-objects
dr["SerialNumber"] = wli.SerialNumber;
dr["ProcessName"] = wli.ProcessInstance.FullName;
dr["ActivityName"] = wli.ActivityInstanceDestination.Name;
dr["EventName"] = wli.EventInstance.Name;
dr["StartDate"] = wli.EventInstance.StartDate.ToString();
dr["Folio"] = wli.ProcessInstance.Folio;

//add the data row to the data table
dt.Rows.Add(dr);
```

Once the list of `WorklistItems` has been added to the `DataTable`, this can be used as the `DataSource` for the gridview:

```
//bind data table to grid
gridViewWorklistItems.DataSource = dt;
gridViewWorklistItems.DataBind();
```

When the page is shown, the list is loaded, showing only the tasks for the current user. See Figure 11-67.

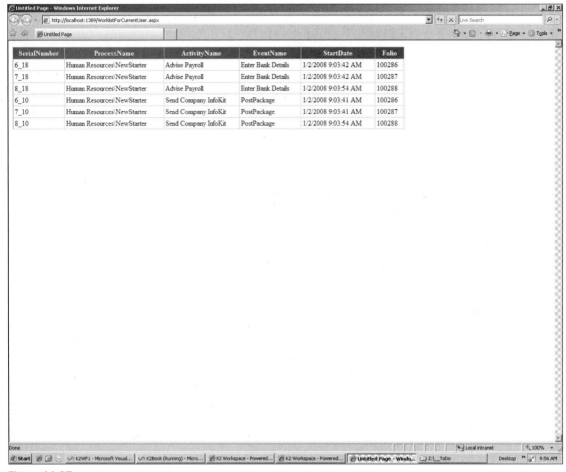

| SerialNumber | ProcessName | ActivityName | EventName | StartDate | Folio |
|---|---|---|---|---|---|
| 6_18 | Human Resources\NewStarter | Advise Payroll | Enter Bank Details | 1/2/2008 9:03:42 AM | 100286 |
| 7_18 | Human Resources\NewStarter | Advise Payroll | Enter Bank Details | 1/2/2008 9:03:42 AM | 100287 |
| 8_18 | Human Resources\NewStarter | Advise Payroll | Enter Bank Details | 1/2/2008 9:03:54 AM | 100288 |
| 6_10 | Human Resources\NewStarter | Send Company InfoKit | PostPackage | 1/2/2008 9:03:41 AM | 100286 |
| 7_10 | Human Resources\NewStarter | Send Company InfoKit | PostPackage | 1/2/2008 9:03:41 AM | 100287 |
| 8_10 | Human Resources\NewStarter | Send Company InfoKit | PostPackage | 1/2/2008 9:03:54 AM | 100288 |

**Figure 11-67**

Here's the full code listing for this example:

```
protected void Page_Load(object sender, EventArgs e)
{
    if (!Page.IsPostBack)
    {
        //Open Connection
        Connection conn = new Connection();
        conn.Open("SERVER");

        //Get Worklist for current Logged on User
        Worklist wl = conn.OpenWorklist();
```

```
//create a data table
DataTable dt = new DataTable();

//add some columns
dt.Columns.Add("SerialNumber");
dt.Columns.Add("ProcessName");
dt.Columns.Add("ActivityName");
dt.Columns.Add("EventName");
dt.Columns.Add("StartDate");
dt.Columns.Add("Folio");

foreach (WorklistItem wli in wl)
{
    //create a new row, with columns defined
    DataRow dr = dt.NewRow();

    //add values from worklist + sub-objects
    dr["SerialNumber"] = wli.SerialNumber;
    dr["ProcessName"] = wli.ProcessInstance.FullName;
    dr["ActivityName"] = wli.ActivityInstanceDestination.Name;
    dr["EventName"] = wli.EventInstance.Name;
    dr["StartDate"] = wli.EventInstance.StartDate.ToString();
    dr["Folio"] = wli.ProcessInstance.Folio;

    //add the data row to the data table
    dt.Rows.Add(dr);
}

//bind data table to grid
gridViewWorklistItems.DataSource = dt;
gridViewWorklistItems.DataBind();

        }
    }
```

Enhancements to this example could involve the following:

❑   Include a hyperlink column with the value loaded from the Data property for the WorklistItem.

❑   Include a column with a drop-down list added to each row, containing the actions available.

❑   Include the code in a Web service, to return a dataset or XML for display in an external system.

❑   Include the code for display within a WinForm or mobile device application.

## Additional Examples

In addition to the samples shown here, the K2 API allows for many more functions related to K2 workflows and the K2 server itself. The specific functionality to be implemented will depend on the requirements for the organization and the design and specifications of the solution at hand.

For example, the API allows for custom code to:

❏     Redirect workflow tasks to a different user

❏     Set processes and tasks to "sleep"

❏     Redirect the current step within the workflow ("Goto Activity")

❏     Configure security, add users, add roles, and so on

❏     Interact with SmartObjects to execute methods or retrieve data for display in a combo or grid

# Summary

When creating the user interface for the K2 process being developed, there are a number of technology choices. Bear in mind that there will be decisions based on the requirements, such as:

❏     Functionality

❏     Maintenance

❏     Skill sets of developers

❏     Time to launch (go live)

❏     Server capabilities and infrastructure

Of course, one of the obvious decision points is related to SharePoint. If the organization doesn't have SharePoint, the only solution is ASP.NET forms and custom code.

> *Using ASP.NET code could mean that forms could also be created using WinForms or even Java Server Pages (JSP) with custom code implemented within Web services to interact with the K2 API (as an example).*

Furthermore, if the organization does not have SharePoint Enterprise, and thus InfoPath Forms Services, browser-based forms will not be an option either. The InfoPath client forms can be used, but that requires installation of InfoPath 2007 on each user's desktop.

Using SharePoint and InfoPath Forms Services allows a process to be initiated from within a document library or some other SharePoint event — and it's a great choice if the infrastructure is available.

ASP.NET provides a wealth of power, allowing developers to use the full .NET Framework and K2 API to interact with processes, manage processes, and use graphical capabilities such as Silverlight, AJAX, and CSS/HTML.

The downside to ASP.NET is that development skills are required, and in most cases, custom code takes longer to develop, test, and implement. That can impact project duration and may require additional resources — including project managers, testers, and database administrators — which may also increase project costs.

This chapter has shown some of the key concepts with regard to forms — using either InfoPath or ASP.NET — with some samples, examples, and information to assist with choosing the correct option.

The next chapter turns to working with SharePoint.

# 12

# Working with SharePoint

Igor Macori

Mike Talley

Microsoft characterizes SharePoint as one of the fastest-selling Microsoft products in the history of the company. Sometimes it's qualified as the fastest-selling server product. In 2008, sales of licenses for SharePoint hit the magical number of $1 billion per year and joined Windows and Office as a heavyweight champion of software sales.[1] Over 100 million SharePoint licenses have been sold. The bottom line is that SharePoint is popular.

It's popular because it allows people to easily collaborate. It's popular because SharePoint, like many Microsoft products, provides the day-to-day functions that many information workers need. It's popular because it's relatively inexpensive, especially if you only need the free Windows SharePoint Services (WSS). It's popular because there's an entire industry that sells templates, solutions, training, and custom development services on top of SharePoint. It's popular because it's powerful.

The K2 blackpearl integration with SharePoint is extensive. If you have only WSS, you get a powerful in-browser interface to build workflows. You also get a mechanism to use data from SharePoint in other applications through SmartObjects. You get list, library, site, and user management. And you get search results that can be used later in the process. K2 blackpoint, which can be thought of as the subset of K2 blackpearl features that integrate with SharePoint, is available if you don't need the other features of the K2 platform. And you can upgrade from K2 blackpoint to K2 blackpearl if that becomes a requirement for your business.

If you have Microsoft Office SharePoint Server (MOSS) 2007, you get more functionality and K2 integration, including publishing, records management, InfoPath browser forms plus all of the standard WSS integration.

While SharePoint includes built-in workflow capabilities based on the Windows Workflow Foundation (WF) and is great for many simple workflows, it does not provide an enterprise-ready platform for automating business processes without a significant amount of development work. Even when adding SharePoint Designer 2007 or Visual Studio into the mix, the workflows that you can create are not readily reusable and cannot provide the extra functionality that an enterprise needs, such as out-of-the-box reporting, dynamic task assignment, and task redirection and delegation. Again, you can accomplish this, but it means more development work. You are also missing security and management building workflows in SharePoint Designer or Visual Studio, but you can accomplish these with more development work. In the end, building with WF requires a significant amount of development work to get to the enterprise-ready state. With K2 blackpearl, the extra, enterprise-class features are already there, and most of your process development is done in a drag-and-drop, visual, and declarative way. If you have to go into code, you will see your WF schedules behind the K2 canvas and can modify, insert, and delete them as you need to.

In this and the next chapter, we will discuss K2 blackpearl features, but as far as the SharePoint integration is concerned, many of the features are also available in K2 blackpoint, which is a less expensive version of the SharePoint-related features of K2 blackpearl. Since it's based on K2 blackpearl, K2 blackpoint processes can be upgraded to K2 blackpearl when the need arises. So keep this in mind as you read this chapter. Anytime we mention K2 blackpearl, the feature is probably in K2 blackpoint as well.

This chapter covers the following topics:

- ❑   Key aspects of SharePoint
- ❑   The differences between WSS and MOSS
- ❑   How K2 integration works
- ❑   K2/SharePoint integration features
- ❑   The K2 Web Designer for SharePoint
- ❑   The K2 Worklist Web part
- ❑   K2 SharePoint/SmartObject integration
- ❑   Creating a workflow in the K2 Web Designer for SharePoint
- ❑   Scenarios enabled by K2 blackpearl

# An Overview of SharePoint

For the purposes of this chapter and the next, we will cover some basic features at a high level. This is not meant to be a complete picture of the features of SharePoint but rather an introduction to some key SharePoint concepts that will help put the K2-integrated features in context.

## Sites and Site Collections

The highest level object in the SharePoint world is the Web application. There is a one-to-one mapping between the Web Application, the Internet Information Services (IIS) Web site, and the SharePoint content database. The next-highest level object is the site collection. It is just what it sounds like — a collection of sites. These can be top-level portals, individual team sites, project workspaces, records centers or publishing sites, just to name a few. Technically speaking, when you create a new site collection you're actually not creating any sites, just the container in which sites can be placed.

A site collection is a useful construct in SharePoint because it allows a group of sites to be treated as a single entity. For example, backing up a site collection makes it simple to backup and restore a set of related sites. Of course you can also back up individual sites if you want.

Sites within a site collection are hierarchically related, meaning that a single top-level portal may have many different child sites, and each of those child sites may have additional child sites of their own, and that list of sites can go on and on. Typically, at the top level you should limit the number of sites to around 125 for SharePoint. For the total number of sites in a site collection, try to limit it to 2000 sites. For whatever reason, 2000 is a magic number in SharePoint because if you start approaching 2000 items in a single SharePoint place — be that sites in a site collection, lists, and libraries in a site, items in a list or library — you risk running into some performance problems. SharePoint scales very well, and many times you will find that you can go beyond these limits quite easily, but keep that number in the back of your head when planning SharePoint site collections. One rule that you can bank on is that if you believe your single Web application database will grow beyond 100GB, try to spin off some of your sites into a new site collection. Break it down by Controlled sites, such as a company's portal structure, and Uncontrolled sites, such as those used for collaboration. Or break it down by regions, or by subsidiaries. Remember, however, that sharing data across site collection boundaries is not easy without a product like K2. For more information about this, see the topic "Plan for software boundaries" on TechNet (http://technet.microsoft.com/en-us/library/cc262787.aspx).

Sites within a site collection can also readily share information, since the content types, permissions, navigation, and security are typically inherited from the parent. You can choose to not inherit the parent's properties when creating new sites. That can be very useful, for example, when building out departmental sites, but the hierarchical relationship will still remain within the site collection. This inheritance of permissions, at least, goes right on down to individual items within a list or library, including folders. Just as when managing permissions on an NTFS file share, you should probably try to manage permissions at the highest level possible (closest to the first folder on the drive, or the first site in the site collection), and use groups and not individual users. But like NTFS, SharePoint allows you to control things on an item-level basis if needed. You can always revert the permissions to inherit from the parent again if you find it getting unmanageable.

## Content Types and Site Columns

Content types are also shared across site collections. They allow you to track metadata and associate workflows and other custom actions with particular pieces of content, as long as you develop those workflows in Visual Studio if you aren't using K2. Everything that you see in SharePoint is associated with a content type, and content types can inherit from each other. If you're familiar with object-oriented programming, content types are very similar in that a content type may inherit a set or properties, or in SharePoint terms "columns," from its parent content type but then extend that content type to include more properties. For example, a Document content type may have a property of Author, while the Chapter content type that is based on the Document content type has Author as well as Title and Page Count.

Content types are used throughout SharePoint to create documents and list items, update properties on content, and to search and locate information based on those properties. The more granular you can make your content types based on your company's core content, the more useful your SharePoint implementation becomes. Keep in mind that content types are shared at the site collection level (but child content types can also be scoped to a lower-level site if required), so if you have multiple site collections you probably don't want to create the same content types multiple times.

A related concept to content type is site column, which can be thought of as the vertical axis to the content type's horizontal axis. It allows you to manage standard data across multiple lists and libraries, on a property-by-property basis. This is useful at times, but plays a secondary role to content types in most implementations. Multiple content types can be associated with a single list or library, meaning that unlike previous versions of SharePoint and the Office Web Server, documents of different types can be stored alongside each other in the same document library but retain their metadata.

## Lists and Libraries

From a SharePoint user perspective, lists, and libraries are the main areas of work in SharePoint. A list tracks information and a library is a place to put documents. Under the covers they are actually the same thing with a slightly different display. Items are added to a list and files are added to a library. Each can have multiple properties based on the type of data being tracked, but basically a document is a type of list item that has a file type associated with it.

In previous versions of SharePoint, before the concept of a content type was introduced, the only way to track data associated with a document or list item was to add them as columns to the library itself. You can still do this with WSS 3.0 and MOSS, but using content types based on your company's information architecture is much more scalable and useful. However, it does take some pre-planning or SharePoint rework if you already have SharePoint running wild in your environment.

## Solutions and Features

WSS 3.0 and MOSS 2007 are built in a modular fashion so that functionality can be added or removed from a particular site or site collection in a very simple and elegant way. This is enabled by two infrastructure features called Solutions and Features. That may sound confusing to call Features a feature of SharePoint, but that's essentially what it is because a SharePoint Feature allows you to package up a set of SharePoint items, such as a library template, a document, a menu item, and a workflow definition, and deploy that as a single package to a SharePoint site. You can also remove that set of items as a group, making the extension of SharePoint much easier to manage.

A SharePoint Solution is a deployable, reusable package that can contain a set of Features, site definitions, and assemblies to apply to sites, and that you can enable or disable individually.

So that is SharePoint at a glance. These are the most important aspects to understand about SharePoint when it comes to deploying and managing it, and for understanding where the K2 integration comes in. Everything else in SharePoint is just a riff on these core concepts.

## What about SharePoint Workflow?

Out-of-the-box, SharePoint offers a handful of workflow templates used to implement simple workflows for lists and document libraries. You can build custom workflows with Microsoft SharePoint Designer 2007 to automate operations in the same SharePoint site.

Microsoft SharePoint does not include a workflow design and creation tool for use in the browser, and it includes only a handful of workflow templates out-of-the-box (one in WSS and five in MOSS, mainly for collecting feedback and gathering signatures and the like). These are useful for a few operations but are not really customizable through Microsoft SharePoint Designer 2007.

When you want to develop customized, complex workflows, reusable in different environments, you must use Microsoft Visual Studio. Developing new custom workflow activities and even workflow templates to use for SharePoint, while possible with Visual Studio, requires technical skills specifically with the Windows Workflow Foundation (WF) that increases the costs and completion time for the project, sometimes by a large factor, depending on your developer skills and resources.

With the additional features offered by K2 blackpearl, process owners are able to realize their advanced, enterprise-class workflow scenarios without asking developers for help. And when they need help, it's easy to share their work. For more information about sharing work, see Chapter 14. For more information about integrating forms with K2 processes, see Chapter 11.

Both SharePoint and K2 blackpearl workflows operate from WF schedules. But WF schedules need a place to run. In other words, an application, whether on a client or server, needs to host the WF framework in order to run WF schedules. For the out-of-the-box SharePoint workflows this is SharePoint. For K2 blackpearl (and K2 blackpoint for that matter), it is the K2 server that hosts the framework and the schedules. This is particularly important from the scalability, maintenance, and isolation perspectives and also from the perspective of accessing SharePoint data across multiple sites and encapsulating workflow activities that might span multiple SharePoint site collections in a single workflow. This, along with all of the other features of the platform, is what raises K2 blackpearl to the level of an enterprise-class workflow platform, and because K2 blackpearl declaratively uses WF schedules as the foundation of its processes, transferring WF development skills to K2 blackpearl is fairly straightforward.

# What Are the Differences between WSS and MOSS?

SharePoint is actually two products, Microsoft Windows SharePoint Services 3.0 (WSS) and Microsoft Office SharePoint Server (MOSS) 2007, whose differences are often unknown, underestimated, and most often misunderstood.

WSS is the free, entry-level Web-based solution that allows information sharing and collaboration services. MOSS extends the features and services offered by WSS, bringing an enterprise-ready feature set to the collaboration foundation provided by WSS.

WSS provides site provisioning and content management, including features for document storage and document management like metadata, versioning, check-in/check-out, mobile device support, and the

Recycle Bin, as well as other collaboration features such as alerts, blogs, and wikis. WSS also includes definitions for a number of different sites, including the Team Site, Document Workspace, Blank Site, Blog, Wiki, and Meeting Workspaces.

MOSS Standard includes the following additional features:

❑ Internet Portals and Web content management. This functionality is partly derived from the retired Microsoft Content Management Server 2002 product and integrated with MOSS.

❑ Enterprise Portal features, with tools for content design and navigation, as Site Directory, Target Audiences, My Sites, and Social Networking.

❑ Enterprise Search tools, through a powerful and fully customizable search engine.

❑ Content lifecycle management, both for Documents and Records.

❑ Other features of MOSS include RSS feeds, a site directory, a site manager, audience targeting, and extra templates and Web parts.

There are a number of features in MOSS, which are known as Enterprise features because they are included in the Enterprise client access license:

❑ **InfoPath Forms Services (IPFS):** Allows users to display Microsoft InfoPath 2007 forms in a Web browser.

❑ **Excel Calculation Services (ECS):** Allows users to publish Excel workbooks to SharePoint sites and perform calculation-intensive operations on a dedicated server. A feature called Excel Web Access displays a spreadsheet in a Web browser.

❑ **Business Data Catalog (BDC):** Allows users to integrate SharePoint with external databases and Web services to add line-of-business (LOB) information. A handful of BDC Web parts are used to browse business data, and MOSS search is able to return this information along with standard SharePoint information.

❑ **Business Intelligence (BI):** Allows users to create digital dashboards and data reporting solutions based on SharePoint and line-of-business information surfaced through the BDC, by employing the BI Web parts, ECS, the Report Center, and Key Performance Indicators (KPIs).

---

### MOSS Standard and MOSS Enterprise

MOSS offers two types of licenses: Standard and Enterprise. For a spreadsheet that lists all SharePoint features by area and the version they are available in, see the Microsoft Office SharePoint Server 2007 products comparison download (http://office.microsoft .com/en-gb/help/HA101978031033.aspx) on Microsoft Office Online. It is extremely important to know which features are included with which license. You can be disappointed if you expect to have browser-based InfoPath forms capabilities, but your company has purchased the Standard SharePoint license. The Microsoft licensing model typically used in business environments[2] requires companies to buy a license for each server in the SharePoint farm and a client access license (CAL) for each connected user or device. This second license, the CAL, can be either the Standard CAL or the Enterprise CAL. Using one or more of the enterprise features requires the full Enterprise CAL. All other MOSS features are included in the Standard CAL, including Search and Web Content Management.

---

Knowing which features are part of WSS and MOSS is necessary for a better understanding of the integration between SharePoint and K2 blackpearl. Many K2 features and wizards work with WSS, but there are a few that work only with MOSS.

The K2 blackpearl installer detects which version of SharePoint you have and installs either the K2 for SharePoint (MOSS) or the K2 for SharePoint (WSS) component. The WSS component includes the following features:

- ❑ K2 Web Designer for SharePoint
- ❑ SmartObject wrappers for SharePoint data
- ❑ SharePoint Workflow integration
- ❑ SharePoint Events integration
- ❑ Sites and Workspaces management
- ❑ User management (permissions)
- ❑ List and Libraries
- ❑ Documents and List Items
- ❑ Process Portals (see the following note)
- ❑ Search Results
- ❑ Administration Components
- ❑ K2 Worklist Web part

*At the time of this writing, Process Portals is a K2 feature that is in beta. They are subsites that include a series of preconfigured Web parts that enable administration and management of K2 processes from within SharePoint. They will not be covered in detail in this chapter or the following chapter.*

The MOSS component includes the following features:

- ❑ SmartObject integration with the Business Data Catalog
- ❑ InfoPath Forms Services
- ❑ Publishing sites and pages
- ❑ Record management

We will not cover every integration point in detail. The SharePoint wizards available in the K2 Designer for Visual Studio and the K2 Designer for Visio will be covered at a high level in Chapter 13. The K2 Help files provide extensive information about the SharePoint integration, including in-depth information about each wizard, what they do, and how to use them, as well as how to configure and manage the K2 SharePoint integration.

## How K2 Integration Works

When the K2 for SharePoint component is installed and configured, a new tab called K2 for SharePoint appears in the SharePoint Central Administration site, as shown in Figure 12-1. This page is deployed as a SharePoint feature, much the same way that most of the K2 integration features for SharePoint are deployed.

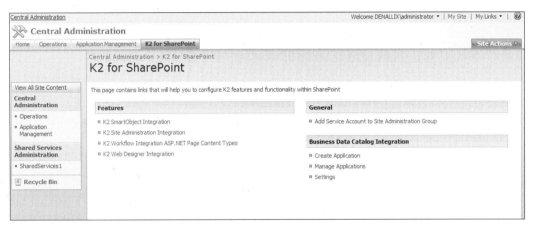

Figure 12-1

From this page you can manage the K2 integration features for content site collections. Content sites are simply site collections that contain SharePoint sites, such as portals, team sites, meeting workspaces and the like, and are unlike sites that are used for Central Administration and the Shared Service Providers. Note that it is not possible to deploy K2 integration features to a particular site in a site collection. You can turn off some of the features individually on the site collection, but that will turn off the features for the entire site collection.

You may be asking "So what do the K2 Integration features provide?" Here is the full list:

❏  **K2 SmartObject Integration:** Allows SharePoint data to be wrapped with a SmartObject, and publishes the Update K2 SmartObject Service definition menu item as pictured in Figure 12-2.

❏  **K2 Site Administration Integration:** Adds the administration links on the Site Settings page.

❏  **K2 Workflow Integration ASP.NET Page Content Types:** Adds the ASP.NET instantiation and task forms to SharePoint for use with SharePoint Workflow Integration processes.

❏  **K2 Web Designer Integration**: Adds the K2 Web Designer link, as shown in Figure 12-3, and the K2 Web Designer for SharePoint design canvas. For more information about working with the K2 Web Designer for SharePoint, see Chapter 14.

Figure 12-2

Figure 12-3

When you deploy a K2 SharePoint Workflow Integration process to a SharePoint site, it will also show up as a feature in the Site collection features page and in the K2 Workflow Integration page, both of which can be found in the Site Collection Administration section of the Site Settings page. There are other K2 features that are displayed in the Site collection features page, but be careful not to deactivate these features here, but rather use the K2 Workflow Integration page for managing workflows. Note that it would be a good practice to name your process in a standard way in order to make managing them easier, especially as the K2 Workflow Integration list grows. In the Site Administration section, you are able to manage K2-integrated SharePoint Events. This integration allows processes to start when an item is added to, updated, or deleted from a SharePoint list or library. The additional links in the Site Settings page allow you to manage workflows and features as needed.

The K2 Worklist Web part is managed as a solution instead of a feature, and is displayed on the Solution Management page of SharePoint Central Administration. Browse to this page by clicking the Operations tab, then the Solution management link in the Global Configuration section of the Operations page. This solution allows you to deploy the K2 Worklist Web part to any SharePoint site collection, even the site collection that hosts My Sites so that users can see their K2 Worklist on their personal My Site.

The K2 features that work with SharePoint communicate with the K2 Server through Web services that are hosted on the same IIS server where the K2 Workspace is installed. Under the RuntimeServices folder, there are two Web services in particular that are used in SharePoint scenarios. The first one, SharePointService, allows the K2 features to pass information between SharePoint and the K2 server. For example, the K2 SharePoint Integrated Workflows maintain tasks in the K2 Worklist as well as in the SharePoint task list. Information about the task is written to SharePoint through the K2 SharePoint Web service. This integration is provided so that SharePoint users do not have to browse to a different location to view their tasks, and it is the same way in which the out-of-the-box SharePoint workflow tasks are maintained. However, users can manage their tasks with either the K2 Worklist in Workspace, the K2 Worklist Web part (in SharePoint), or the SharePoint task list.

Other Web services that come into play when working with SharePoint are InfoPathService and OpenInfoPathTask. The first service allows InfoPath forms, either client-based or browser-based, to communicate with the K2 server to retrieve available actions, SmartObject data, and to submit a task form, among other things. The second one allows an InfoPath task to be opened.

*For more information about working with InfoPath forms, see Chapter 11.*

The remaining section on the K2 for SharePoint page in Central Administration allows you to create a BDC definition for SmartObject data, which is covered in Chapter 13.

# Using the K2 Features for SharePoint

Let's take a closer look at the K2 SharePoint integration features and how they might be used. The administration of these K2 features will not be covered beyond what has been mentioned. The other features, such as the in-browser workflow designer, the worklist Web part, and the SmartObjects integration will be covered in detail here.

The best way to introduce the features of the K2 Web Designer for SharePoint is to step through a simple process. You can try this on a SharePoint site of your own that has the K2 Web Designer available, or just follow along with this section. Either way, you will be able to discover how powerful this tool is by seeing it in action.

## About the Approval Process

The example scenario is a hypothetical approval process for creating a brochure of products and services offered by a fictitious company.

Everything starts from the Work document library, a storage place for all textual and graphical elements that will be part of the brochure. Every element is going to need approval by the Marketing department.

The workflow manages approval of each element. Once approved, these elements are moved into a second document library containing every approved asset. From this point they are sent to artists and art directors who actually create the brochure, and they must be informed when new assets are ready. In the meantime, if the Marketing and Communication department refuses an item, the workflow sends a notification to the author informing him that the item he submitted was not approved. This scenario is shown in Figure 12-4.

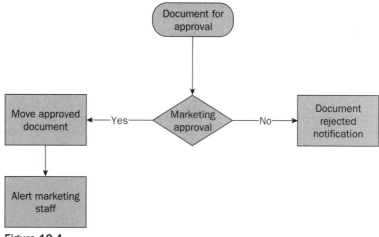

**Figure 12-4**

## *Building the Process*

The first steps set up the environment for the workflow:

**1.** Define a framework for records and data.

**2.** Create the two document libraries (one for work-in-progress assets and the other for approved materials).

**3.** Determine a metadata structure (for example: author, brochure references, status).

These tasks are typically done before you start designing the actual workflow. Now, you can turn to actually designing the workflow:

**1.** When you've created a document library for work-in-progress assets (called Brochure Materials in the example), open the library and start the K2 Web Designer by clicking the menu item on the Settings menu.

**2.** Click the New Process button on the K2 Web Designer page to start the designer. The K2 Web Designer first asks you to specify a Name and an optional Description for the new process in the Process Properties dialog.

This dialog also allows you to define if the process could be manually started by the user. This is a useful option when the library is a working environment where assets will be created, updated, and informally reviewed, and your goal is to let the user start the workflow with a voluntary action when the item is ready for formal approval. You can also choose to automatically start the process when a document is created or modified. In the example scenario, this option is set to its default value, Start Process Manually (see Figure 12-5).

3. Once it is completed, click OK.

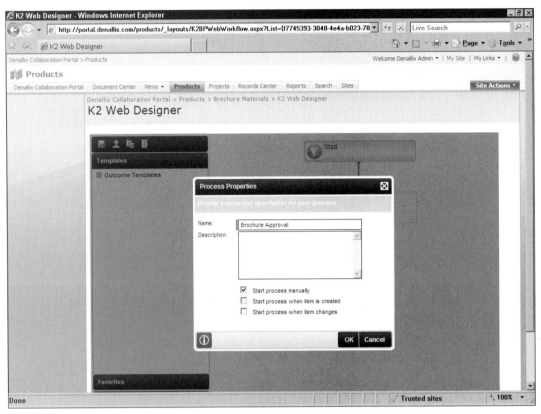

Figure 12-5

4. In the K2 Web Designer, click the Approve — Decline template from the Outcome Templates in the Sidebar and drag the element onto the design canvas.

5. You are asked to specify Activity Properties. Type a Name and an optional Description for the activity (in this case, we named it Marketing Approval), and then click Next.

6. In this step, you will find the predefined actions in the template. You could customize the workflow by adding further actions or by modifying the existing ones. In our scenario, the two available actions, Approved and Declined, are enough to reach the final objective.

7. Nothing else will be modified, so click Next.

8. Every defined action is associated with an Outcome. Click on one of the actions, and then click Edit to customize its behavior (as shown in Figure 12-6).

   An action could be customized depending on the environment, but you can also define specific Outcome Rules. For example, in some scenarios you could define rules allowing the process to move forward only when it is approved by two of the three reviewers. But you're not going to do that now.

9. Click Cancel on this dialog, and then click Finish to confirm your Outcome settings and return to the design canvas.

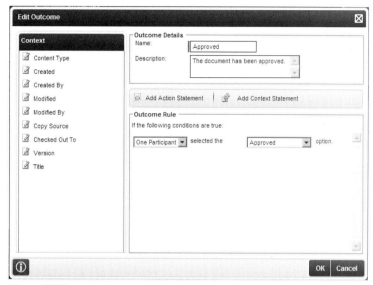

**Figure 12-6**

The design canvas shows the workflow, including the activity you just added and the outcome lines leading from the activity to blank boxes. This allows you to drag two more activities in the two Approved and Declined boxes.

Because of the business logic previously defined, when a document is approved it will be moved into the approved assets library. At the same time, artists and art directors are informed that new assets are available.

1. Open the Wizards section of the Sidebar and select the action Move Document from Document Wizards, then drag the element in the Approved area.

2. When you start a wizard, in the Activity Properties dialog you are asked to specify the activity Name (in our scenario, it's Move Approved Documents). You can also add an optional Description and then click Next.

3. Choose the destination document library (named Brochure Approved in our scenario), as shown in Figure 12-7, and then click Next to define optional Activity Outcomes.

4. In our process, an e-mail notification is subsequently sent to the Marketing department after moving the approved document. So click Add to insert a new Activity Outcome (named Notify), and then click Finish to complete the wizard.

Once again, in the design canvas, you will see a new line and blank box leading from the Approved activity.

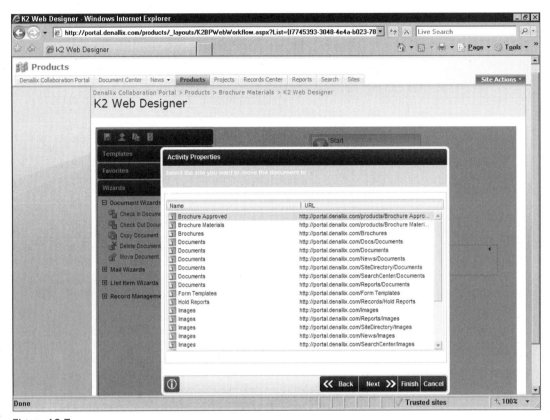

Figure 12-7

To add the e-mail notification feature:

**1.** Drag the Send Mail Wizard from the Sidebar onto the Notify area. The wizard Activity Properties dialog window asks you to specify a Name (Marketing Alerting in our scenario) and an optional Description.

**2.** Click Next to start building a template for the e-mail message.

**3.** Drag the object Process Originator Email from the Object Browser to the From field to define the sender.

**4.** Insert the e-mail address of the receiver in the field To (you can use any e-mail address, even a distribution list such as marketing@denallix.com) and an optional Subject.

**5.** Now you can write the body of the message, alternating fixed text aspects and optional dynamic elements that are dragged into the message body from the Object Browser (as shown in Figure 12-8). When finished writing your e-mail, click Next to define further process options or click Finish to complete the wizard.

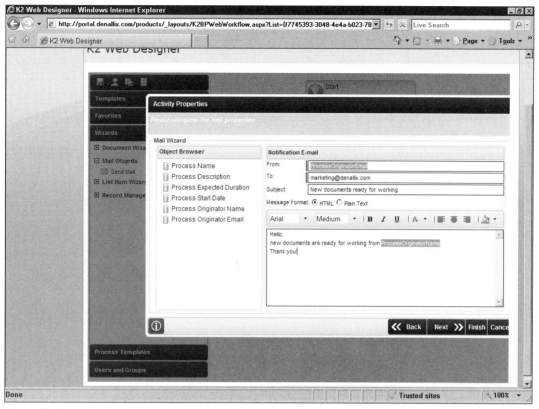

Figure 12-8

To complete the process, you need to define what should happen if the proposed assets are declined. Following the initial analysis, the originator should be notified by e-mail.

1. Drag the wizard Send Mail from the Sidebar into the Declined area and repeat what you did previously to create the message.

2. Use the marketing office e-mail address as the sender and drag the object Process Originator Email in the To field from the Object Browser, then complete the message with a descriptive Subject allowing receivers to easily understand that assets have been declined.

3. You could also add some useful dynamic elements to the message, such as the document Title or its URL, to make identification easier. This is particularly useful if many assets are submitted. Through the Object Browser you could find several elements identifying a document or its author, which is the same metadata in the document library.

4. Click Next to define further options or click Finish to complete the wizard.

The final step of the workflow is defining who will approve the assets:

1. Notice the exclamation mark next to the Marketing Approval block. Click on the icon to access the Destinations window and define the destination users who will approve the assets.

2. Click Add to search for users.

3. Select the option Add users to favorites (as shown in Figure 12-9), if you want to add them in the Favorites list in the Sidebar to make similar actions quicker in the future.

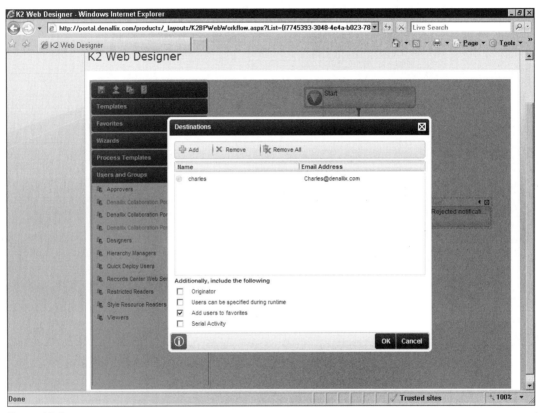

Figure 12-9

4. Click Save at the top of the Sidebar to save the process, as shown in Figure 12-10.

5. Click Deploy at the top of the Sidebar to make the process available and executable in the SharePoint library.

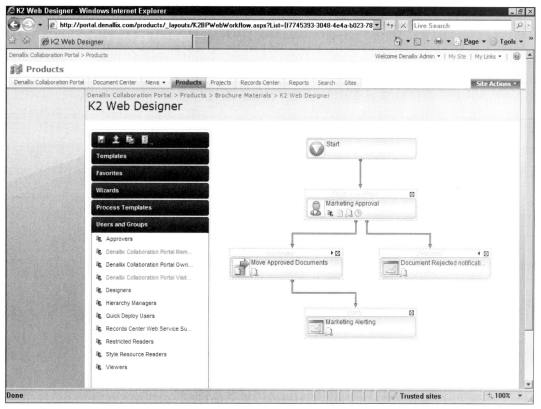

**Figure 12-10**

During the process deployment operation, the K2 Web Designer Build Process Wizard checks if the workflow is complete and warns you about issues or omissions. You should remember that the framework on which SharePoint is based requires at least a Tasks list in the site where the process will be executed as well as a Workflow History list. Both are required by the workflow.

## Starting Workflows Manually

When you design your workflow, you specify how the process will start. While it could be started automatically, we chose to start this particular workflow manually due to the manner in which the assets are created.

To manually execute a workflow associated to a list or a document library, choose Workflows from the item or the document context menu (as shown in Figure 12-11). On the next page you see a list of available workflows; click the workflow you want to start. Note that if every workflow associated with the list or library is an automatically invoked workflow (for example, the manual option is not specified), the Workflows context menu will not appear. However, once the workflow is running, it will be displayed to the right of the item in the main view of the list or library.

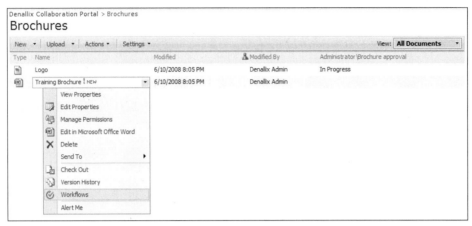

Figure 12-11

# Starting a New Workflow

The Workflows page, which is a standard SharePoint page, allows you to start a new instance of a workflow by choosing among the available ones. You can also check if other workflows are currently running and see further details about the workflow.

The Workflows page, as shown in Figure 12-12, allows you to perform the following actions:

❑    Create new workflows, starting from a workflow template associated to a list or a library.

❑    Access the current status/workflow history.

❑    Check which workflows are currently running.

❑    Check which workflows are complete.

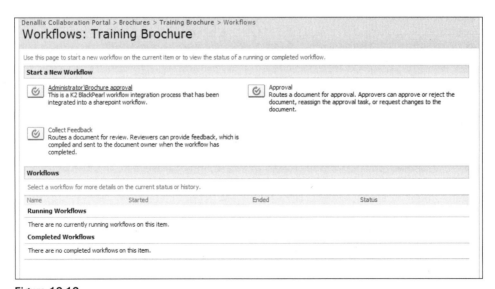

Figure 12-12

After choosing the workflow you want to start, you can set specific workflow template options. For example, you can set the destination users if the option Users Can Be Specified During Runtime was checked during the workflow creation.

After starting the workflow, remember that you can use the status in the document library for the current status of the workflow, the Workflows page in SharePoint, or the View Flow page in K2 Workspace for a more graphical and real-time view of the current process.

## Beyond the K2 Web Designer for SharePoint

Integration between K2 and SharePoint is not limited to the K2 Web Designer for SharePoint. There are several other K2 Designers that allow SharePoint integration, including the K2 Designer for Visual Studio, the K2 Designer for Microsoft Visio 2007, and the soon-to-be-released K2 Studio. These designers share the common wizard interface, which includes many SharePoint-specific wizards. The wizards are divided into four different types for easier understanding.

> Note that you can find the process wizards listed below in the Process Wizards section of the Visual Studio Toolbox, and the rest of the wizards (Client Events, Administration Events, and Content Management Events) are located in the Event Wizards section of the Toolbox.

- ❑ **Process Wizards**

    - ❑ **InfoPath Integration:** Allows one or more InfoPath form templates to be associated and used within the process.

    - ❑ **SharePoint Workflow Integration:** Allows a process to be associated with a list or library.

    - ❑ **SharePoint Events:** Allows a process to be triggered by a list or library event.

- ❑ **Client Events**

    - ❑ **SharePoint Workflow Integration Client Event:** Allows the standard K2 blackpearl task form to be used to action a workflow task.

    - ❑ **InfoPath Client Event:** Allows an InfoPath form associated with a SharePoint library to be used to collect data and action a workflow task. Note that you can also use the InfoPath client event without SharePoint.

- ❑ **Administration Events**

    - ❑ **SharePoint Sites and Workspace:** Allows the creation and deletion of sites and Workspaces.

    - ❑ **SharePoint Lists and Libraries:** Allows the creation and deletion of lists and libraries.

    - ❑ **SharePoint User Management:** Allows the creation, deletion, and updating of user and group rights.

- ❑ **Content Management Events**

    - ❑ **SharePoint List Item:** Allows the creation, deletion, and updating of list items.

    - ❑ **SharePoint Document:** Allows the creation, deletion, copying, moving, and updating of documents in document libraries, even across SharePoint site collections.

❑ **SharePoint Records Management:** Allows documents to be put on hold and moved to a Records Center.

❑ **SharePoint Search:** Allows search criteria to be used to return results that can be used later in the process.

❑ **SharePoint Publishing:** Allows the creation, deletion, and updating of publishing sites and pages.

These wizards and tools are described in Chapter 9, but in the next chapter, Chapter 13, we will describe each wizard in more detail and give you some ideas on how and when you might want to use them.

# Using the K2 Worklist Web Part

One of the most effective solutions to improve usability and integration between K2 and SharePoint is using the K2 Worklist Web part on a SharePoint page. This allows users to access the Tasks list in a more simple and straightforward way than by using the SharePoint task list. See Figure 12-13.

Remember that the K2 Worklist is available within K2 Workspace as well, where you could find some extended features to control the process.

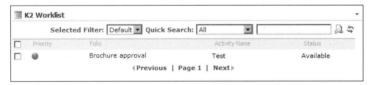

**Figure 12-13**

## Deploying the K2 Worklist Web Part

Installing the K2 Worklist Web part is managed in the same way as installing any SharePoint solution:

1. Browse to the SharePoint Central Administration: Start ➪ All Programs ➪ Microsoft Office Server ➪ SharePoint 3.0 Central Administration.

2. Click the Operations tab.

3. On the Operations page, click the Solution Management link. If the status of k2worklistwebpart solution is already Deployed, you don't have to perform any other actions (skip the step that follows).

4. If that status appears as Not Deployed, click the solution name and then click Deploy Solution. Confirm your action by clicking OK. Note that you must have administrative rights on the SharePoint server to perform this action. If you do not, check the available Web Part list in SharePoint, and if you do not see the K2 Worklist Web part, contact your SharePoint administrator.

## Inserting the K2 Worklist Web Part on a Page

The K2 Worklist Web part is like any other SharePoint Web part. It can be added to any part of a page that supports Web parts, which is just about every page in SharePoint sites. To add the K2 Worklist Web part to a page (if you have the necessary permissions):

1. Click on Site Actions and then select Edit Page to access the page layout.

2. Choose the Web Part Zone available in the page layout where you want to add the K2 Worklist Web part, and then click on the Add a Web Part button to open the Add Web Parts window.

3. Expand the All Web Parts group by clicking on the plus (+) sign.

4. Scroll through the list of the available Web parts to select the K2 Worklist Web part in the group Miscellaneous (Tip: Look for the only Web part with the green icon). Click Add to add the K2 Worklist Web part to the page. See Figure 12-14.

5. Save your modification to the page by clicking Exit Edit Mode under the Site Actions menu (not shown in the figure).

6. Click Publish on the Editing Toolbar near the top of the page if you're using SharePoint Publishing features. Note that this action may be associated with an optional approval process.

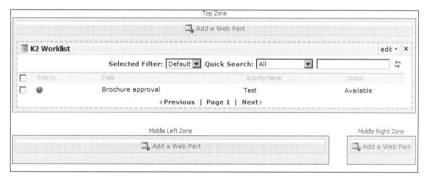

Figure 12-14

Once you have added the K2 Worklist Web part to the page, you must configure its connection to the K2 server.

7. To configure Web part connectivity, click on the down arrow on the top-right corner of the K2 Worklist Web part and then click Modify Shared Web Part.

8. Check your K2 environment connectivity settings from Main Task List Settings in the Web Part task pane as shown in Figure 12-15.

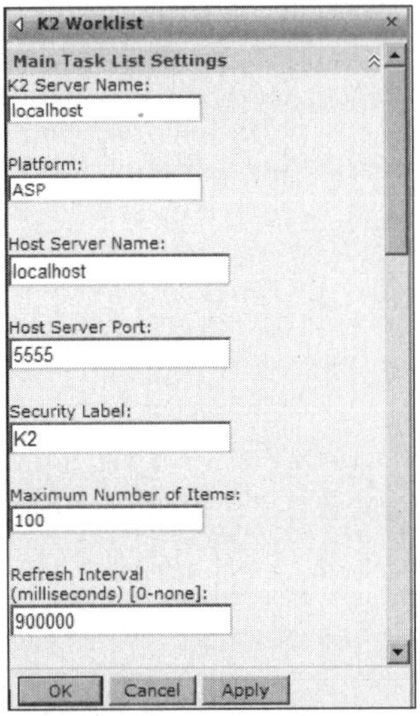

**K2 Worklist**

**Main Task List Settings**

K2 Server Name:
localhost

Platform:
ASP

Host Server Name:
localhost

Host Server Port:
5555

Security Label:
K2

Maximum Number of Items:
100

Refresh Interval
(milliseconds) [0-none]:
900000

OK    Cancel    Apply

**Figure 12-15**

Configuration of the K2 Worklist Web part is handled in a very similar way to configuration of the worklist available in the K2 Workspace. Choose your preferred settings from the Task List Columns section on the Web part task pane. If you select Custom on the Set of Columns drop-down menu, you can choose which columns you want to show and the labels you want to use to display that information on the K2 Worklist Web part, as shown in Figure 12-16.

You can also configure the Group By option, which allows you to manage grouping of tasks — simplifying the user's view of their current tasks. If you think the Web part will show long task lists, enable the Paging option. With Paging enabled, only a few elements will be loaded each time with the Web part, improving performance.

9. When you have finished configuration, click OK to confirm your settings.

10. Publish your page once again (if necessary), using the Publish button on the Editing Toolbar.

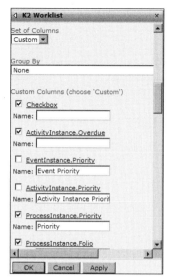

**Figure 12-16**

# Using the K2 SmartObjects Feature

The third and final K2 integration feature that we will discuss here is perhaps the most powerful. Before you explore this feature, make sure that you understand SmartObjects. If necessary, review Chapter 7, which covers what SmartObjects are, how a Service Object relates to a SmartObject, how they can be used, and how the K2 platform can be extended with them.

In the context of SharePoint, just about any piece of user-defined data contained within a site can be wrapped in a SmartObject. If you pause to think about how you can use SmartObjects in processes, even in a process that has no SharePoint integration, you will start to understand the possibilities of using this feature in new scenarios. Beyond processes, you can imagine an application that has no process elements at all, such as a Web site based on SmartObject data, and realize that with this feature — SharePoint data wrapped and exposed through SmartObjects — SharePoint can become a repository for business data that is used elsewhere in your organization. If you don't already use SharePoint in this way, you might consider trying this with a limited scenario. Users find SharePoint so easy to use that they will want to store their data there, but in the past it has been difficult to reuse that data. With the SmartObject integration, that becomes a lot less difficult.

Not only can you retrieve data from SharePoint through a process or through the `SourceCode` `.SmartObjects.Client` API, you can also use the .NET Data Provider for K2 SmartObjects interface. This is a standard ADO.NET component that you can add to any .NET project. The provider allows you to query and update data that is encapsulated by any SmartObject, including those exposed through the SharePoint Service Object.

Installing the SharePoint SmartObject integration feature allows the SharePoint Service Object to create an instance for the SharePoint site where it is deployed. The proper installation of the K2 SmartObjects feature can be verified by:

1. Accessing the SharePoint Central Administration site (Start ⇨ All Programs ⇨ Microsoft Office Server ⇨ SharePoint 3.0 Central Administration).

2. Clicking the K2 for SharePoint tab and then clicking K2 SmartObject Integration.

3. Choosing the Site Collection you want to verify. If you need to activate K2 features, click the Activate button (as shown in Figure 12-17).

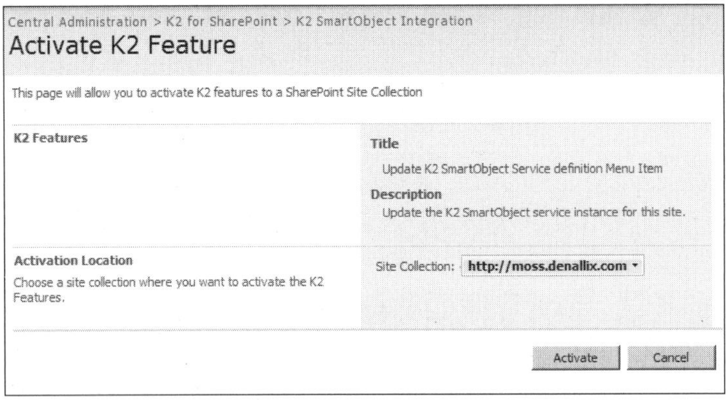

Figure 12-17

Once the feature is deployed to a site, the context menu on the Site Actions drop-down menu will appear, as shown back in Figure 12-2. If you make changes to the SharePoint site from this point forward, such as adding a new list to the site, it may be necessary to update the SmartObject definition to expose that list through the SmartObject Services layer. To do this, click the Update K2 SmartObject Service definition menu item.

# Illustrating Some Example Scenarios

There are many ways you can use the K2 blackpearl integration with SharePoint to enable new scenarios for your company's operations. In the earlier section on SmartObjects, we discussed one important scenario — exposing SharePoint data through ADO.NET and SmartObjects — and now we want to illustrate other ways of using the integration features. Since SharePoint is such a ubiquitous server platform used in many different capacities, it is impossible to list every possible scenario that K2 blackpearl (and K2 blackpoint for that matter) can be employed. But this section provides a small list to get you thinking about some of the possibilities.

The following sections describe some of the scenarios that could be managed through processes. These are just a few examples of what can be accomplished with SharePoint and K2 blackpearl. In Chapter 13, we'll cover more specific information about each wizard and how to use them.

## Site Creation and Maintenance

SharePoint does not really have any native processes that allow users to request a new site. There are some products that allow this very scenario, but with a handful of the administration-focused K2 SharePoint wizards that are available with K2 blackpearl, namely the Sites and Workspaces, User Permissions, and Lists and Libraries, you can create a process to manage and control this common request. You could extend this process further to retire a site via a process once it has lived beyond its intended timeframe.

## Sending Records to the Records Center

Even though SharePoint has a Send To menu option on which you can add the Records Center of a site collection, it requires users to send individual files to the Records Center. Using K2 blackpearl, you could perform a search for files that match a current status, even filtering those records based on the metadata of the content, and send that entire batch of documents to the Records Center in an automated manner. You could also create and delete records Holds in an automated fashion, allowing you to respond to legal or audit requests in a traceable, timely manner.

## Automatic Process-Based Web Publishing

Using the content management features of SharePoint, you could setup a process that aggregates related content from disparate LOB systems, including SharePoint, and publish that information to a SharePoint publishing page. This could be set up to run on a schedule, as part of a process that is initiated by an action that a user must first take, or by the creation of a new item in a SharePoint list or library. You could also use process-based publishing to move pages to different environments, such as from Staging to Production, and update external data connections in the process.

## InfoPath Client or Browser-Based Form to Start and Action Workflows

Having deep integration with InfoPath 2007 and the option to publish forms that will work in the browser means that starting processes and actioning them doesn't require custom forms to be created every time. The flexibility offered with InfoPath forms and InfoPath Forms Services means that business users that are slightly technical can manage their own process forms.

## Business Data Maintenance in SharePoint

One example of using SharePoint to manage business data is using a SharePoint list. The list contains Project Manager contact information for every customer in your organization. Even if your customer data is stored in a separate, line-of-business system (perhaps because project management duties change on a frequent basis), you don't want to update that dedicated field in the LOB system. Keeping it separate and in SharePoint allows the group manager to regularly review and update the information. With the SmartObject feature in SharePoint, you can build a SmartObject containing the customer project manager information and expose that to any .NET application in your organization. This would be a simple implementation, but perhaps you need to incorporate multiple fields from the LOB database into that SmartObject. You would develop a custom service or use one of the out-of-the-box services, depending on the LOB system, for communicating with the LOB system. Adding those SmartObject methods to the SharePoint SmartObject in order to return data from both SharePoint and the LOB system in a single composite SmartObject would allow data from SharePoint and another LOB system to be exposed, managed, and updated through a single interface.

# Operational Benefits of SharePoint Integration

We've covered some of the scenarios enabled by the integration between K2 blackpearl and SharePoint, and the list is by no means exhaustive. There are other operational benefits that come with the integration between K2 blackpearl and SharePoint integration that may not be obvious. The following sections describe the main ones.

## Process Versioning

By default, you don't get much in the way of process versioning when deploying new SharePoint workflows using SharePoint Designer or Visual Studio beyond what you do as a developer to version your assemblies. With K2 blackpearl, each time you deploy a process, the version is updated and every new instance will use the new version. However, already running instances will continue to use the older version of the process until they are completed.

## Process Management

With the upcoming release of Process Portals, you can manage security, see running instances, troubleshoot errors, and even get a graphical representation in real-time of the process in SharePoint. This series of Web parts allows all of the process-based administration that you would normally find in K2 Workspace but through the familiar SharePoint interface.

## Improved Workflow History Reporting

Although SharePoint offers workflow history logs (usually by using the standard Workflow History list), they are not very useful — not even when viewed using Excel pivot tables. K2 adds two key features related to reporting that greatly improve this scenario. First, workflow reporting SmartObjects can be created for every process deployed to a K2 server, including those that integrate with SharePoint. Second, the K2 Report Designer tool in K2 Workspace is a rich environment for creating standard RDL-compliant reports, so the integration between K2, SQL Server Reporting Services, and SharePoint becomes that much easier. And with the option to export these reports to SQL Reporting Services, combined with the SharePoint and SQL Reporting Services integration, enterprise-class reports can be made available within SharePoint for tracking every process in an organization. This is similar to Process Portals but also allows any amount of customization that is required by the business for making better business decisions and optimizing processes based on real-time information.

## Better Usability and Management of Tasks

Using the K2 Worklist Web part, SharePoint can be used as the central place where users can see a list of their tasks. It is a great improvement over the simple task lists that SharePoint typically uses to assign tasks. While these task lists can be spread over main sites in SharePoint farm, the K2 Worklist consolidates all K2 blackpearl tasks in one place, offering much more information and context to the user as well as the ability to batch action related tasks with a few clicks, greatly improving user productivity.

## Integration of LOB Data

Although Microsoft is making improvements to the Business Data Catalog, it is not easy to integrate data in SharePoint from LOB systems. Using K2 SmartObjects, creating the BDC definitions does not require any code or manipulation of long XML files to surface this information in SharePoint.

# Summary

SharePoint is a powerful platform from Microsoft that provides many features necessary for collaboration. When combined with K2 blackpearl, SharePoint becomes a powerful platform for process-driven application development. With K2 blackpearl, SharePoint can become or replace many other enterprise application platforms.

The next chapter will focus on taking advantage of the K2 SharePoint integration features that are available in both WSS and MOSS, including:

❑   An overview of each SharePoint wizard, including what they can be used for and some business scenarios for using them

❑   The Records Center

❑   The Web content management (Publishing) features

❑   The Business Data Catalog

We will also cover some scenarios around using the above features as well as the SharePoint Search Results Wizard. The other SharePoint wizards included with K2 blackpearl and K2 blackpoint are covered extensively in the K2 Help files, so that should be your first point of reference when determining what a particular option on a wizard page can be used for.

# Notes

1.  "SharePoint Joins the Microsoft Pantheon" by Scott Bekker. Redmond Channel Partner, June 1, 2008.

    http://rcpmag.com/columns/article.aspx?editorialsid=2640

2.  For further information about SharePoint licensing, visit these Web sites:

    www.microsoft.com/sharepoint/howtobuy/default.mspx
    https://partner.microsoft.com/US/licensing/licensingchoices/40048861

# 13

# Working with Microsoft Office SharePoint Server

Igor Macori

Mike Talley

In the previous chapter we took a look at the K2 blackpearl features that integrate with SharePoint through the browser, such as the administration pages, the K2 Web Designer for SharePoint, the K2 Worklist Web part, as well as the SmartObject integration. In this chapter we'll turn our attention to the K2 SharePoint integration at design time through the SharePoint wizards available in the other K2 Designers, including what you can do with them and some tips on getting the most out of the K2 SharePoint process and event wizards. We will also take a more careful consideration of the enterprise scenarios enabled by the K2 integration. This chapter covers the K2 blackpearl features you can use to create advanced workflows for SharePoint, including:

❑   Process and SharePoint event integration

❑   Controlling SharePoint content

❑   Administering SharePoint

❑   Enterprise Scenario: Web Content Management

❑   Enterprise Scenario: Using Search Results

❑   Enterprise Scenario: Creating Content Management Rules Using the Records Center

❑   Enterprise Scenario: Interacting with Business Applications and External Databases through the Business Data Catalog (BDC)

# Using the K2 SharePoint Wizards

Let's take a step back and look at all of the SharePoint-related wizards offered with K2 blackpearl. Many of the wizards included in the K2 Designers are there for administrative purposes, such as creating sites, lists, and libraries, and for managing content. In Chapter 9 we introduced all of the wizards available in K2 blackpearl, but here we will look at only the SharePoint-related wizards and give you some ideas on how to use them. There are two wizards, namely SharePoint Records Management and SharePoint Publishing, that rely on MOSS features that may not be enabled due to site configuration or a WSS-only installation. These wizards will still appear in the K2 Designers.

## Process Wizards

We start with the two process wizards:

❑ SharePoint Workflow Integration Process Wizard

❑ SharePoint Events Process Wizard

### The SharePoint Workflow Integration Process Wizard

This wizard allows you to associate a K2 blackpearl workflow with a SharePoint list or library, a publishing library, and a SharePoint content type as shown in Figure 13-1. It uses standard K2 blackpearl SharePoint forms for instantiating and actioning the workflow, so it looks and feels much like an out-of-the-box SharePoint workflow. In combination with this wizard, the SharePoint Workflow Integration Client *Event* Wizard is used to populate the workflow task form with the actions a user can take at a particular point in the process. The available actions are also based on the rights a user has to perform those actions — if users do not have the rights, then that action is not made available by the K2 server.

Figure 13-1

Associating a workflow with a list or library allows you to start the workflow automatically when an item is added to the list or library, and you also have the option of allowing users to start the workflow manually. If you do not specify the manual option, the workflow will not appear in the list of workflows in SharePoint that can be manually started. These options are not mutually exclusive either, so you can have an automatic workflow that can also be manually started.

Associating a workflow with a content type is a particularly powerful mechanism for ensuring that a workflow is automatically started or can be manually instantiated wherever that content type is used in the SharePoint site collection. As your SharePoint implementation grows, having workflows associated with content types allows for the workflow implementation to scale much more easily than if you target specific document libraries. In other words, associating a workflow with a document library is a 1-to-1 relationship, whereas associating a workflow with a content type allows you to have a one-to-many relationship with content wherever it resides on your site collection.

*For more information about SharePoint content types, see "Introduction to Content Types" on MSDN (*`http://msdn.microsoft.com/en-us/library/ms472236.aspx`*).*

## The SharePoint Events Process Wizard

This wizard allows you to instantiate a workflow based on events in lists and libraries, whether that is the structural change to the list or library itself, or an item-level change within the list or library. For example, the first option in this wizard (as shown in Figure 13-2) allows you to instantiate a workflow when a column is added, removed, or updated in a SharePoint list or library. The second option allows you to instantiate a workflow based on a number of different events, for example when an item is added, a document is attached to an item, an item is checked-in, or when a file is converted. For each of these event levels — at the list or library structural level or at the items level — a workflow can be instantiated based on one or more events in the specified list.

**Figure 13-2**

When you choose integration with lists or library events, the available events include:

- ❑ **Field Added:** Occurs when a field is added to the list/library
- ❑ **Field Deleted:** Occurs when a field is deleted from the list/library
- ❑ **Field Updated:** Occurs when a field is updated in the list/library

When you integrate with list or library items, the available events include:

- ❑ **Item Added:** Occurs when items are added to the list/library
- ❑ **Item Attachment Added:** Occurs when attachments are added to a list item in the list/library
- ❑ **Item Attachment Deleted:** Occurs when attachments are deleted from a list item in the list/library
- ❑ **Item Checked-In:** Occurs when items are checked-in to the library
- ❑ **Item Checked-Out:** Occurs when items are checked-out from the library
- ❑ **Item Deleted:** Occurs when items are deleted from the list/library
- ❑ **Item File Converted:** Occurs when files are converted in the list/library
- ❑ **Item File Moved:** Occurs when items are moved from the list/library
- ❑ **Item Unchecked-Out:** Occurs when items are unchecked-out from the library (changes discarded)
- ❑ **Item Updated:** Occurs when items are updated in the list/library

The next step of the wizard is the Metadata Mapping and Folio page, where you can store metadata about the list in a K2 field for later use in the workflow. If you wanted to associate a single workflow with multiple lists and libraries, choose Advanced Mode on the wizard welcome page.

Remember that SharePoint events are mainly suited for automatic workflow processes, not ones that can or should be manually started by users or require some sort of user interaction before the process can begin. If you do require user interaction, use the SharePoint Workflow Integration Process Wizard instead. The SharePoint Events Process Wizard is particularly useful when you always need to start a task when a change is made to the structure of a SharePoint list or library, or an item is added, deleted, or changed. Although the use of SharePoint events' integration is not limited to administrator auditing and alerting, it is particularly useful for these types of scenarios, and they represent workflows that are simple to create. Note that, because of potential negative performance implications, only asynchronous SharePoint events are supported with K2 SharePoint events' integration, which means that certain types of workflows, such as approvals, do not work well with the SharePoint events' integration because the user action has already occurred before an administrator is assigned a workflow task. In other words, there is no mechanism to capture the event and send it for approval. The workflow begins when the event is completed.

Once they are deployed, you can view and manage the K2 SharePoint integrated events by using the K2 Events Integration link in the Site Administration section of the Site Settings page. You can also manage all K2 SharePoint integrated workflows by using the K2 Workflow Integration link in the Site Collection Administration section on the same page. Both of these links are highlighted in Figure 13-3.

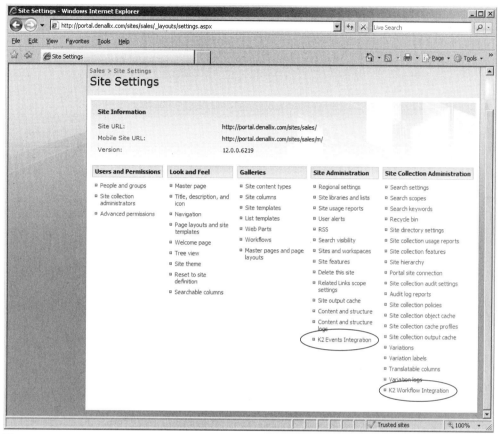

Figure 13-3

## Event Wizards

We now turn our attention to the rest of the SharePoint wizards included with K2 blackpearl. These are the *event* wizards that allow you to perform specific actions with SharePoint entities. One or more events can be added to each K2 activity.

We've already discussed the SharePoint Workflow Integration Client Event Wizard, so we won't be covering that one again. The rest of the wizards do not have a user interface (UI) associated with them; rather they are tools that allow you to do something in SharePoint based on the process you are creating, whether that is moving, copying, or deleting a document; creating a site or a list in a site; or assigning permissions for someone to access a particular SharePoint list. These are just a few examples of what you can automate using K2 blackpearl. Many of these options are also available with K2 blackpoint. We'll break these wizards down into two categories — Administration and Content Management.

## *The Administration Event Wizards*

This class of wizards allows you to automate SharePoint tasks that are typically associated with site designers, site owners, and site and site collection administrators. The power of these three wizards is evident for those readers who already have a SharePoint implementation that has spread like wildfire in their environment and are looking for something to control and manage SharePoint:

❑   SharePoint Sites and Workspaces Event Wizard

❑   SharePoint Lists and Libraries Event Wizard

❑   SharePoint User Management Event Wizard

SharePoint does not have many features in this regard and K2 blackpearl brings the ability to automate site provisioning, list and library creation, and user permissions.

### The SharePoint Sites and Workspaces Event Wizard

This wizard allows you to create and delete SharePoint sites and even update a site's properties, as shown in Figure 13-4. The sites you can create are based on the available site templates in your SharePoint site collection, whether those are out-of-the-box SharePoint templates or custom templates that are installed by an administrator. Note that when updating site properties you are not allowed to change a site's template, only the site properties such as title and description.

Figure 13-4

Using this wizard, you could create a process for site requests, for example, that takes information such as the requested site's title, description and template, and routes that to an appropriate person for approval. Once the request is approved, the site would be automatically provisioned with the template specified in the request form. Combining this with the SharePoint List and Libraries and the SharePoint User Management Wizards, you could also extend this process by creating a company-standard document library and giving all domain users read access to the site.

## The SharePoint Lists and Libraries Event Wizard

This wizard allows you to create, update, and delete lists and libraries, as shown in Figure 13-5. Even though the wizard uses the term "List" in each of the actions, since SharePoint libraries are actually just a special type of list, you can use this wizard to create, update, and delete document libraries as well. Note that updating list properties does not allow you to change an existing list's template.

**Figure 13-5**

As you step through this wizard, you can specify a type of list to create. Again, this is based on the types of lists that are available on the SharePoint site, including custom list types that you have defined. Out-of-the-box SharePoint lists include announcements, calendars, issue tracking, tasks, and links, as well as libraries for documents, forms, wiki pages, and data connections.

Keep in mind that you use this wizard to create both lists and libraries, but to actually create items within a SharePoint list, you use the SharePoint List Items Event Wizard. To create documents within a SharePoint document library, use the SharePoint Documents Event Wizard.

## The SharePoint User Management Event Wizard

This wizard is perhaps the most difficult wizard to understand of all K2 wizards. It is difficult in part because SharePoint security is complex. There are rights, which are the basic things that a user can do. Then there are groups of rights that are referred to as permission levels, and this is what you will see at first glance when managing permissions within the SharePoint UI. These rights can be assigned to individual users or to groups of users, and they can typically be managed at any point within a site collection, from the top all the way down to an individual item in a list or document library. You also have the option, when creating a new SharePoint site, list, or list item, to break the permission inheritance on that SharePoint entity. The SharePoint User Management Event Wizard is just as complex, if not more so.

Figure 13-6 shows the first main page of the SharePoint User Management Event Wizard.

**Figure 13-6**

With this wizard you can perform many SharePoint administrative tasks, such as:

❑ Create or Delete a SharePoint Group.

❑ Give SharePoint Users or Groups access to a site, list, folder, list item, or to another group so that you have nested groups.

❑ Remove SharePoint Users or Groups from a site, list, folder, or item.

❑ Reset the permission inheritance on a site, list, folder, or list item. As you are setting rights, you can also break inheritance at whatever level you are currently configuring.

The SharePoint User Management Event Wizard is one of the only wizards that automatically chains itself, meaning that you can have two user management events that are tied to each other and cannot be individually deleted. This is necessary, for example, when creating a group. Creating it is typically only half of what you need to do with that group. You also must assign some permissions, or rights, to that group. This is where the second instance of the wizard will be used. The wizard is smart in that it will automatically launch itself again when you click Finish the first time through. It will also preselect what action to take because it has some context about what you just did in the previous SharePoint User Management Event Wizard, which makes using the wizard the second time through a bit easier. If you get confused when using this wizard, think about how you would have to manually configure users, groups, and permissions in the SharePoint UI, and then revisit the wizard.

*For more information about SharePoint rights and security, see "Introduction to controlling access to SharePoint sites and site content"* (http://office.microsoft.com/en-us/ sharepointserver/HA102553721033.aspx) *on Microsoft Office Online.*

## The Content Management Event Wizards

The content management event wizards allow you to perform actions on content in SharePoint, whether that is information stored in a list, in a document, in a publishing page, or in the Records Center. We've also included in this section the Search Results Wizard because it is more commonly used when automating content management tasks than SharePoint administration tasks.

- ❑ SharePoint List Items Event Wizard
- ❑ SharePoint Documents Event Wizard
- ❑ SharePoint Records Management Event Wizard
- ❑ SharePoint Search Event Wizard
- ❑ SharePoint Publishing Event Wizard

### The SharePoint List Items Event Wizard

This wizard allows you to create, update, copy, and delete list items in a SharePoint list or library, as shown in Figure 13-7.

Figure 13-7

You'll also notice two options under Update List Items, which also apply to Copy List Items and Delete List Items. These are important options to understand because they can greatly increase the power and dynamic nature of your process design:

❏ **SharePoint List Item:** You will attach the event to a specific item in a SharePoint list or library.

❏ **From Content Field:** This is where the power and flexibility is represented because you can update an item from data stored in the process. This allows you to gather information in a K2 data field or even as the result of a SmartObject query, and then use that data to update, copy, or delete a list item.

---

### Regular versus Advanced Mode

Now is a good time to mention how Regular and Advanced Mode change what you can do in a wizard. It is particularly good to know when it comes to the SharePoint wizards. Every wizard pictured in this chapter is in Regular mode because it's a bit easier to understand some of the options in Regular mode.

The Advanced Mode of a SharePoint wizard generally allows you to perform the action that you are using the wizard for — moving a document or creating an announcement, for example — multiple times. This applies to the wizards where it makes sense. For the Sites and Workspaces Wizard, Advanced Mode doesn't allow you to create multiple sites, but it does allow you to specify if permissions on the new site are inherited or not, and whether the new site shows up in the regular SharePoint navigation.

Handling multiple items may sound like it would be a mess, but it is actually quite powerful and easy to configure. There are many times in SharePoint when you need to work with a series of items, not just a single list entry or a single document. Using the SharePoint wizards in Advanced Mode allows you to work with a set of items in SharePoint and perform the action you specify to each of them individually. For example, with the SharePoint list items, you can specify any number of list items to create. For single operations use Regular mode, but if you need to create multiple list items use Advanced Mode. If you are creating items from a K2 field, use the Add split button in the toolbar to specify the source of the item because, by default, the wizard assumes that you'll want to specify the actual list item details and not base it on a K2 field.

---

### The SharePoint Documents Event Wizard

This wizard, as shown in Figure 13-8, allows you to take many different actions with SharePoint documents, such as:

❏ Copy

❏ Move

❏ Get or Update Metadata

❏ Check In

❏ Check Out

❑   Undo Check Out

❑   Delete

**Figure 13-8**

As with the List Items Wizard, you can perform many of these actions either directly on a document stored in SharePoint, or with a document stored on the file system or in a K2 field. The K2 field option allows for greater power and flexibility because it allows you to specify a document that is stored in a K2 field or in a SmartObject.

The SharePoint Documents Event Wizard allows you to do anything with a SharePoint document that you can do through the UI and more, including checking it in, checking it out, and undoing a document check-out. In addition to that, you can also retrieve the metadata, or properties on a document, which can be stored in a K2 field for later use.

### The SharePoint Records Management Event Wizard

This wizard allows you to create and delete records in a SharePoint Records Center as well as to place a record on hold or remove a hold from a record, as shown in Figure 13-9. It also allows you to create and delete record *holds*. A record hold is a container for SharePoint records that may be subject to litigation, audits, or investigation. A hold overrides a record's information management policy and prevents the record from expiring or being deleted. This ensures that the contents of the record are protected and can be reviewed by legal staff in order to remain in compliance with regulations or ongoing legal matters.

*For more information about records and record holds, see "Introduction to the Records Center site"* (http://office.microsoft.com/en-us/sharepointserver/HA101735961033.aspx) *and "Create a hold to suspend records"* (http://office.microsoft.com/en-us/sharepointserver/HA101735981033.aspx) *on Microsoft Office Online.*

**Figure 13-9**

*Note that this wizard will still be available in designers even when a SharePoint Records Center is not present on the network due to either a licensing restriction of lack of configuration.*

## The SharePoint Search Event Wizard

This wizard allows you to perform a SharePoint search in a specific list or library, and to perform a search across multiple lists and libraries of the same type, as shown in Figure 13-10. When searching across lists or libraries of a specific type, you can also specify the scope of the search. The default scope is the current site as specified in the wizard, but you can expand that scope to include the current site and all subsites, or you can search across the entire site collection.

**Figure 13-10**

Using the SharePoint Search Results, you can specify fairly complex Boolean logic in the Search Filters page. These criteria can be based on dynamic data stored in the process or from the result of a SmartObject query. You can also limit the number of results based on a hardcoded number or data stored in the process. But perhaps the most powerful aspect of this wizard is that it enables you to store the search results in a content field. If you think about it, what good are search results to an automated process if those results can't be used for anything? Storing the results in a content field allows you to use them later for something else, such as copying those documents to a different location, providing a list of search results in an e-mail notification, or putting those list items or documents into the Records Center. Combining the Search Results Event Wizard with other SharePoint event wizards allows you to automate some fairly complex tasks that involve multiple items from a site, a site and its subsites, or the entire site collection.

> *Note that the SharePoint Search Results Event Wizard uses the Collaborative Application Markup Language (CAML) search technology included with all versions of SharePoint, not the standard WSS or MOSS Enterprise Search technology. Using CAML allows K2 to consistently search and do comparisons on SharePoint metadata, which is not something that is easy to accomplish with the other search technologies. However, there may be cases where you want to use the WSS or MOSS search engines. To do this, call the SharePoint Web services using the WSS search (`http://<servername>/_vti_bin/spsearch.asmx`) or MOSS search (`http://<servername>/_vti_bin/search.asmx`) Web services. For more information about these Web services, see "Enterprise Search Query Web Service Overview" (`http://msdn.microsoft.com/en-us/library/ms543175.aspx`) on MSDN.*

### The SharePoint Publishing Event Wizard

This wizard allows you to perform multiple actions with the SharePoint Publishing features, including:

- ❑ Create, copy, move, delete, and check in publishing pages.
- ❑ Get and update publishing page content.
- ❑ Create and update reusable content.

The first page of the wizard, shown in Figure 13-11, allows you to select what you want to do with the SharePoint Publishing features.

**Figure 13-11**

*If you are unfamiliar with what these SharePoint features allow you to do, see "Introduction to Web content management"* (http://office.microsoft.com/en-us/sharepointserver/ HA102406301033.aspx) *on Microsoft Office Online which gives a great overview of how you can use these features.*

With the SharePoint Publishing Event Wizard, you can automate the publishing of Web content, using the power and flexibility of the K2 platform to add more intricate workflows capabilities to the out-of-the-box SharePoint functionality. You can also leverage K2 process data and SmartObject queries to create more dynamic content for those pages.

A scenario-based example of using the SharePoint Publishing Event Wizard is included in the "Using Web Content Management" section later in the chapter, but also keep in mind that when you create a publishing page with this wizard you can also store that content in a K2 content field for later reuse.

# Using K2 SharePoint Integration for Enterprise Scenarios

This section covers the following aspects of the K2 SharePoint integration, including scenarios for illustrating how they might be used in an enterprise:

- ❑ Web Content Management
- ❑ Search Results
- ❑ Records Center
- ❑ The Business Data Catalog (BDC)

BDC does not have a wizard in any K2 designer because it is a SharePoint run-time integration point for K2 blackpearl. It is less about content management than it is about content delivery, because you can deliver information that is stored in SmartObjects directly into SharePoint through the BDC. We'll discuss a scenario in a moment to illustrate the power of this feature.

# Using Web Content Management

SharePoint offers a wide range of features for Web Content Management, allowing users to create intranet and Internet sites that include tools for content publishers and editors. Out-of-the-box, MOSS features a publishing workflow that content editors can use to control and approve content published to a publishing site. K2 blackpearl extends this and the entire publishing feature set by allowing customized publishing workflows for building highly articulated processes that more closely resemble the reviewing and approval needs of enterprises.

## The SharePoint Publishing Features

MOSS includes two different site templates that automatically activate the SharePoint publishing features, but they can be enabled on any SharePoint site, including the team site template, by activating the publishing features. To enable these features, browse to the Site Settings through the Site Actions menu, and then click on Site Features. On this page, enable the Office SharePoint Server Publishing features by clicking on the Activate button as shown in Figure 13-12.

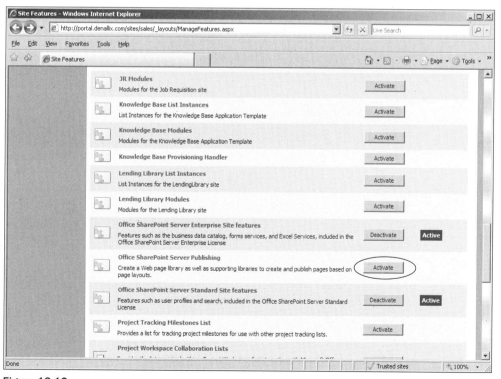

Figure 13-12

After enabling the publishing features, the entire site is automatically updated and the Web Content Management features are available for use. For example, the command Create Page is now available on the Site Actions menu. Use this to create new Web pages linked to specific page Layouts and to manage content with the Web Content Management tools. You will also notice that updating SharePoint pages includes document check-in, an optional approval step, and a publishing step that is different from the standard SharePoint page-editing process.

## An Example Publishing Scenario: Publishing Press Releases

Suppose that you want to create a process for publishing new company press releases. You want to enable an editor to choose a proper page layout and the correct review and approval rules prior to publishing.

1. Start a new K2 Workflow project in the K2 Designer for Visual Studio and drag the SharePoint Publishing Event Wizard from the Visual Studio Toolbox to the K2 design canvas.

2. Check the Run this wizard in Advanced Mode checkbox and then click Next.

3. Type a name for the event in the Event Name field, select the action Create Publishing Page, and then click Next.

4. Type the URL address where the press release will be published and mark the optional Content Field. Alternatively, you could use an Environment Library value or data from the process to dynamically determine the location.

    The Advanced Mode of the wizard also allows you to set a configuration for Page Scheduling, which is useful if you want to automatically publish the content at a particular date and time.

5. After clicking Next, browse the Page Layouts and choose the one you prefer, and then insert a Name and optional Title and Description as shown in Figure 13-13. After you are finished, click Next.

**Figure 13-13**

6. The wizard will then ask you to specify or extend the publishing page metadata.

7. Click Finish to complete the event.

At this point you could add more publishing events to the same activity, such as the Copy Publishing Page or Move Publishing Page actions. This would be useful if you required two different sites for redacting and publishing press releases. The first one would be available on the intranet for editors to preview how multiple pieces of content from different sources looked together on a single page, while the second one would be located on your company's Internet portal, the final destination of every press release.

You could also create an activity to convert press releases. For example, if your editors typically write their press releases using a Microsoft Word template, you could select the Create Page using Converter action to create a new Web page for publishing based on the Word document. In the wizard you would specify the MOSS document conversion service and use the From Word Document to Web Page converter.

Create Reusable Content is a very important action to be aware of as well. Using this action, you could automatically create textual and graphical content that editors could reuse on several different press releases, pages, or on the portal itself, depending on how your intranet, extranet, or Internet sites are configured.

## Using Search Results

SharePoint search comes in a few different flavors and can be the cause of some confusion. SharePoint offers two different search engines in WSS:

❏ CAML search conforms to SharePoint's query schema to search lists for data. CAML search is a declarative search that is similar in concept to a SQL full-text search. CAML queries are also used in rendering list views.

❏ MOSS search is a more powerful search engine that can crawl content, perform indexing, and be scheduled. MOSS extends the SharePoint search service with more options for service configuration, such as incremental crawling, best bets, and the ability to index non-SharePoint content. It is a powerful search engine that can crawl the following sources of content:

   ❏ SharePoint content

   ❏ Web content (intranet and Internet)

   ❏ File shares

   ❏ Exchange Server public folders

   ❏ Any content exposed by the BDC

   ❏ IBM Lotus Notes databases

The search crawler is able to recognize and create indexes for Microsoft Office documents and Web formats, allowing users to execute full-text searches. With the installation of IFilters for specific file types, recognizing these files and indexing their content can be extended, allowing for full-text searches on other formats such as PDF, TIFF, ZIP, and any other file type for which there is an IFilter available.

*Again, as we mentioned in a note earlier in the chapter, remember that the SharePoint Search Results Event Wizard uses the Collaborative Application Markup Language (CAML) search technology included with all versions of SharePoint, not the standard WSS or MOSS Enterprise Search technology.*

## Enterprise Scenario: Accepted Offers Management

Suppose that you would like to manage offer documents prepared by the several Sales offices in the company and store them in a single document library to review offers accepted by customers.

The first solution that comes to mind is the creation of a workflow for each and every Sales Offers document library for every Sales team site around the country. The workflow periodically polls the Offer Status field on the documents, copying documents that have an Offer Status of Accepted to a central document library. A different workflow would consolidate the information and the single consolidated document would be replicated back to each Sales team site.

Alternatively, you could manage offers by using a custom SharePoint content type used within each Sales Offers library on every Sales team site. The workflow could search offer documents across the entire site collection, looking for Accepted offers without needing to take into account how many Sales team sites and Sales Offers libraries there are.

Both solutions would have the same results, but the second option would be more flexible. The first solution is very effective when you can't define a specific content type and in situations where the SharePoint sites are spread across several different site collections or servers.

We can build the first option using the SharePoint Search Event Wizard:

1. Drag the SharePoint Search from the Visual Studio Toolbox onto the K2 design canvas.

2. After the initial welcome step, the wizard will ask you to type an Event Name and choose one of the two available Actions (refer back to Figure 13-10):

   ❑ Search in a SharePoint List or Library.

   ❑ Search across a List or Library Type.

3. Select the action Search in a SharePoint List or Library, and then click Next.

4. Specify the SharePoint Site URL and the Sales Offers library on the Sales team site, and then click Next.

5. Click Add to insert Search Filters — the field or fields to check for a specific value or variable managed through the workflow (see Figure 13-14) as the value *Accepted* in the Offer Status field.

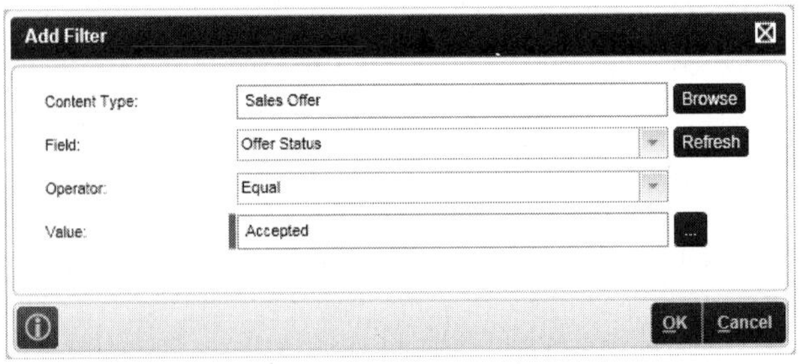

Figure 13-14

At this point in the wizard, you could add other search filters and combine them together to build your query. You have the option to specify Boolean logic and order of operation on your search filter clauses on the same page where you add them.

6. Clicking Next brings you to the final page of the wizard (see Figure 13-15), where you are able to create the content field in which to store the search results. This is the field you will use later in the process to do something interesting with the results of the search.

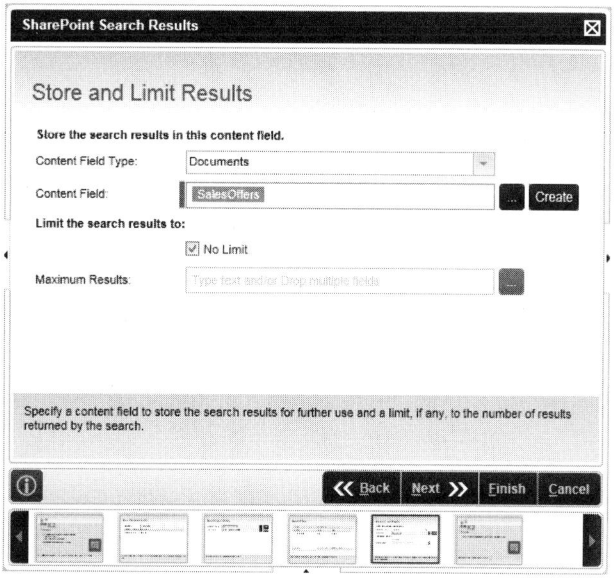

Figure 13-15

On this page you also specify the type of item you are storing, such as documents, list items, records, or publishing pages, and the number of maximum results that you want to keep. Limiting the search results is a good idea if you are searching across the entire site collection. In this scenario, we are creating a workflow for each Sales Offers document library, so limiting the number of results is not an issue. In fact, limiting the results would potentially cause Accepted sales offers to be missed, so you must be aware of how you are using search results and the type of scenario you are using this wizard for in order to achieve the right results.

At this point the search results are stored in the SalesOffers content field. Adding a SharePoint Documents event to the same activity but after the search event would allow you to copy those stored documents to a central location for consolidation. Document consolidation, depending on how your environment is set up, could be a manual process for a sales manager or an automated process if you had the ability to automate this step. SharePoint document conversion may work for this step, converting each Word document into a Web page for later updating. Or you could create reusable content for each document, and then combine those on a single page. Both of these options can be automated with the SharePoint Publishing Wizard.

From there, you would simply create an event to copy the Word or consolidated Web page to each Sales site, using an event per Sales site in order to handle multiple copies of the information.

Other options for using the SharePoint Search Wizard include sending records to the Records Center, which is accomplished in a similar way to the search scenario here, but instead of using the content field of stored documents to copy to a centralized site, you would send the documents to the Records Center, which we will cover next.

# Working with the Records Center

One of the features available in MOSS is the site template called Records Center,[1] a repository for records that you can define rules for document routing, retention and disposal of SharePoint content.

SharePoint allows you to implement more than one Records Center site within your intranet portal, which gives you the flexibility to define a greater number of repositories to use for different archiving and auditing criteria, and answering legal and procedural law requests related to document storage and retention.

> Note that there is a special Records Center URL field that should be configured in the Environment Library, so that it is prepopulated in the wizards and used consistently across processes. For more information about using the Environment Library, see Chapters 10 and 15.

## Using Records and Holds

A record could be represented by any piece of information in SharePoint. Usually files, such as Word documents or Excel spreadsheets, are good candidates for becoming records. But records could also be something such as an e-mail message or an instant messenger chat. Every information element that could support actions and decisions in a business process could be considered a record.

One of the Records Center features is called a hold. Holds are exceptions to normal archiving rules in a Records Center. They are useful tools when it comes to overriding expiration policies, as could be required in compliance audit situations.

The Records Center uses SharePoint content types, one of the most important SharePoint features. Content types allow you not only to define descriptive metadata for specific content in a consistent way but also to create workflows, templates, and policies for information lifecycle management in the organization. You could use content types to specify information types and their proper routing and storing policies in a consistent way.

## Enterprise Scenario: Sales Department Expense Control

Imagine that your corporate office defined new rules for controlling the company's Sales department expenses. Every piece of information related to these costs is now to be archived in anticipation of a possible audit.

An approach might be to have a SharePoint developer create a new feature that could find the documents classified by specific rules and move them into the repository where they are now required to be stored. A similar solution could be developed by people with a deep understanding of the SharePoint API and experience developing SharePoint solutions in Visual Studio.

However, with K2 event wizards you could easily reach these objectives without specific SharePoint development knowledge.

The two actions in the SharePoint Records Management event wizard would be used to define activities for records management:[2]

❑   Sending a document to a Records Center site

❑   Managing holds

To send a document to a Records Center site:

**1.**   Drag the SharePoint Records Management event wizard from the Visual Studio Toolbox to the workflow design canvas.

The first page of the wizard will describe all the possible objectives and offer the Advanced Mode option. The second page allows you to specify a name for the activity and to choose which action to execute.

**2.**   If you want to create records starting from specific SharePoint documents, choose the action Create a Record and then From SharePoint Document, filling in the required fields as shown in Figure 13-16. You must define the SharePoint Site URL, specifying the site where documents are stored, a reference to the Document Library, the optional Folder name, and the document File Name.

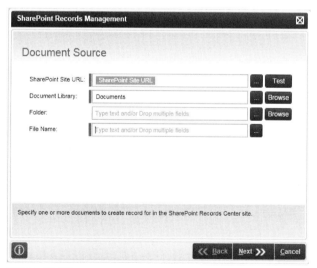

**Figure 13-16**

**3.**   After you have found the elements you want to send to the Records Center, click Next. On the page that appears, you can choose a Records Center other than the default, and if you want to store the resulting records in a Content Field, as shown in Figure 13-17. Do this if you need to use them later in the process.

**4.**   Click Finish to complete the wizard.

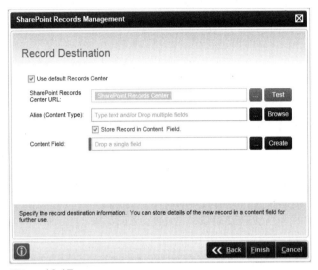

**Figure 13-17**

To create a hold activity:

**1.** Drag another SharePoint Records Management Event Wizard to the workflow design canvas, placing it directly underneath the previous records management event.

**2.** After specifying an Event Name, choose the action Create Hold and then click Next.

**3.** Specify a Record Source, defining the SharePoint Records Center URL. The Hold ID will be used as soon as a hold is released and will include the Title, Description, and Managed By fields (as shown in Figure 13-18).

**Figure 13-18**

You could also combine activities created through the SharePoint Search Event Wizard as previously described. You could build an activity to search for documents with a particular status, such as an expense report that has been approved. Then you could define and execute an action in the workflow to send the approved document to the Records Center.

Like other SharePoint event wizards, running the SharePoint Records Management event wizard in Advanced Mode allows you to specify multiple documents, content fields, or a combination of the two, to create as records, add to a hold, remove from a hold, or delete. The same is true for holds, and by running the wizard in Advanced Mode you can create multiple holds in the same event.

## Using SmartObject Data with the Business Data Catalog (BDC)

One of the most important MOSS Enterprise features is the Business Data Catalog (BDC). It can be used to import external line-of-business (LOB) information into SharePoint from applications such as K2 blackpearl and SAP, and data sources such as SQL and Oracle.

Once you define the BDC application within the SharePoint Shared Services Provider and create the associated XML application definition file, you can import your data source as shown in Figure 13-19.

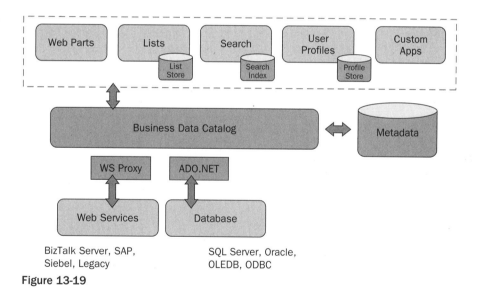

Figure 13-19

BDC applications are generally used in SharePoint for:

❑   Viewing business data through Business Data Web parts

❑   Integrating business data in lists and libraries through business data fields

❑   Searching business data via the MOSS search engine and Business Data Search content sources

Any K2 blackpearl SmartObject could also display data through the BDC. The power in displaying this information through the BDC is twofold: First, it automatically creates the XML application definition for you, which can be a complex process. Second, and perhaps more powerfully, data that is encapsulated in SmartObjects can represent:

❏ Data about a process, such as that used in reporting

❏ Data that is consumed or generated within a process, including LOB data

❏ Data that is surfaced to other nonprocess applications through SmartObjects

When you integrate SmartObject data through the BDC, you create solutions that allow any data contained within a SmartObject to be surfaced in SharePoint without the need for custom development work. For more information about SmartObjects, see Chapter 7.

Out-of-the-box Service objects provided by K2 blackpearl allow you to import data from the following data sources:

❏ Active Directory

❏ SharePoint

❏ Salesforce.com

❏ K2 blackpearl (process reporting)

Refer to Chapter 7 for developing custom SmartObject Services to encapsulate data from other sources through SmartObjects. See Chapter 23 for more information about surfacing data from SAP using K2 connect.

---

### Data and the BDC

It is important to realize that while the BDC can surface business data from many different sources, it is a one-way mechanism. Essentially, the data is read-only. To modify data you must go back to the LOB system to change or update it. While SmartObjects allow data to be queried and updated from LOB systems, when that data is surfaced through the BDC, the data cannot be modified in SharePoint and would have to be modified using the SmartObject directly. This is a limitation of the BDC.

---

## Integrating SmartObjects with BDC

The integration process between SmartObjects and BDC starts with creating one or more SmartObjects with the K2 Designer for Visual Studio. Workflow Reporting SmartObjects can be automatically created for processes. Deploying a SmartObject or Workflow project is the first step, and once it is deployed, creating the BDC application through the K2 for SharePoint tab in the SharePoint Central Administration site is the second step.

Once SmartObject data is integrated with the BDC, the MOSS search engine indexes that data and returns it in the standard search results pages or search Web parts. Keep in mind that SmartObject data that should not be exposed to everyone using MOSS should not be surfaced through the BDC.

Several SmartObjects show data useful for creating reports about process performance, such as number of instances number, average duration, and other information captured by the workflow reporting SmartObjects. This data could be easily used through Business Data Web parts to quickly build process control and monitoring interfaces, which provide information similar to the kind that process portals display.

One of the other advantages offered by Business Data Web parts relates to the execution of data queries through mini-applications. This allows you to link and show data through a Master/Detail view. Rendering these Web parts can also be also customized through XSLT modification and customization, using the tool pane in SharePoint, so a customized view of your process data, or any data encapsulated by SmartObjects, can be highly customized.

## Configuring a K2 BDC Application

To configure a K2 BDC application:

1. Open the SharePoint Central Administration site, and click the K2 for SharePoint tab, as shown in Figure 13-20.

2. Create a new SmartObject BDC application by clicking the Create Application link in the Business Data Catalog Integration section.

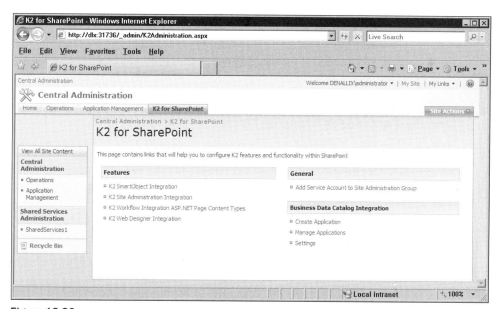

Figure 13-20

3. The Create K2 BDC Application page allows you to choose the SharePoint Shared Service (if there's more than one in your SharePoint Farm) and the SmartObject you wish to use (the list of SmartObjects will help you understand how powerful this integration is).

4. After choosing a SmartObject, the Create K2 BDC application will display the fields to use as Input Parameters elements. You could also define optional Associations with other SmartObjects to include in the same SmartObject BDC application.

5. The last option on the Create K2 BDC Application page enables search crawling (Application Indexing), allowing you to configure settings for the MOSS search engine. Read the warning carefully because you don't want to expose sensitive SmartObject information in search results.

After creating the K2 BDC Application page, you can modify its options through Central Administration K2 for SharePoint by using the Manage Applications link. The K2 Settings link allows you to set K2 Server Settings and retrieve information related to SmartObjects.

BDC Permissions should also be configured. Remember that users accessing SmartObject data through BDC applications need authorization for each application. This setting is found on the BDC management pages in the Shared Services administration site. There are detailed instructions for creating applications and setting this right in the K2 blackpearl Help files.

## Enterprise Scenario: Using Customer Information in SharePoint

There are several practical examples that you can imagine related to business data retrieved through SmartObjects and integrated through use of the BDC. In our scenario we're going to surface customer data in SharePoint that resides within a custom Customer Relationship Management (CRM) system.

Our goal is to have a SmartObject "linked" to business data.[3]

1. The K2 for SharePoint page in the SharePoint Central Administration site allows you to create a K2 BDC Application linked to the *Customers* SmartObject.

2. After creating the SmartObject BDC application and defining user access and authorization, the BDC application can be found in the Business Data Catalogs Applications section located within the Shared Services Administration site, as shown in Figure 13-21. This is where you can explore application settings and available fields.

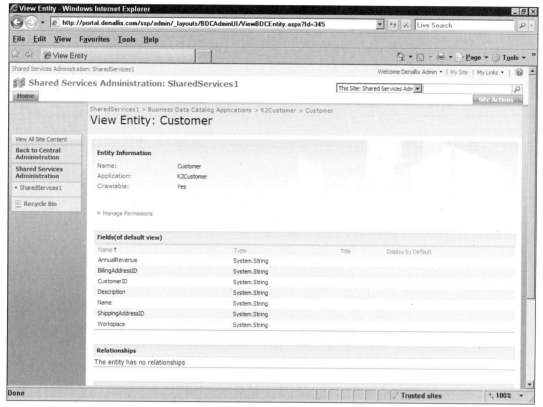

**Figure 13-21**

Once the application is created and authorization is set, users can use the Business Data Web parts and other features described in previous paragraphs to access the SmartObject data.

To test the BDC application:

1. Add a Business Data List Web part to a portal page.

2. Click on the Open the tool pane link to select the Customers SmartObject BDC application.

3. Confirm that data is shown by clicking OK at the bottom of the tool pane.

4. Click Exit Edit Mode to complete the operation.

5. After opening the page, launch a data query using the related toolbar in the Business Data List Web part.

You could also configure a specific Search Content Source to index customer data and make it available through the MOSS search engine.

Metadata based on the customer information could also be added as properties for lists and libraries, which is very similar to adding a custom column to a SharePoint list or library. For instance, you could add data about a customer with an associated offer stored in a document library. To do this:

1. Browse to the library and choose the Create Column command from the Settings menu.

2. Use the page Create Column to choose a Column name, and then select the Business Data option as the column type.

3. Select the BDC application instance in the bottom part of the page through Additional Column Settings, and find the field that you wish to use as library column.

4. After creating the new field, upload a document into the library.

You will notice that the new Customer field (see Figure 13-22) can be queried much like the SharePoint People Picker control; it allows you to browse for and resolve SharePoint users in the same way. Business Data columns allow you to do the same with LOB data (in this case, data that is coming from a CRM system, through a K2 SmartObject and the BDC, and finally into SharePoint).

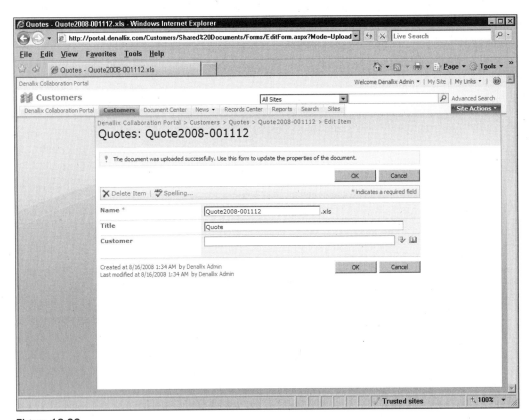

Figure 13-22

The new column also allows you to create different views to sort, filter, or group documents based on the customer name. This provides not only the flexibility to display information but also the consistency with how the customer name appears in SharePoint and your CRM system.

## Integrating Business Information with Microsoft Office Applications

The integration between SharePoint and Microsoft Office System applications allows you to use information retrieved through SmartObject BDC applications in Office documents. To use this feature, access the Document Information Panel or use Quick Parts in applications such as Microsoft Word 2007 (see Figure 13-23). Combining data in this way allows users to see business data and other SharePoint metadata right within the application, which is particularly useful in certain scenarios. You can also customize the Document Information Panels because they are actually InfoPath forms that surface this information. For more information on this, see the Document Information Panel Overview on MSDN (http://msdn.microsoft.com/en-us/library/ms550037.aspx).

You could also use the new field containing business information in any potential workflow, as the customer information is now just another column in your library.

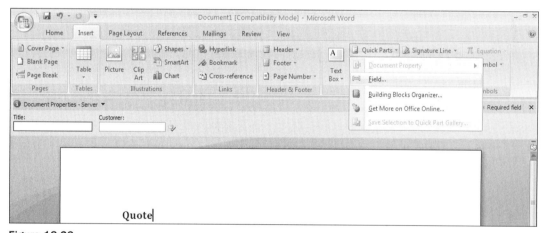

Figure 13-23

There are a limitless number of scenarios for encapsulating LOB information with SmartObjects, surfacing that data in SharePoint through the BDC, and using that integration to display information in ways that, in the past, would have required a significant amount of time and resources. With SmartObjects and the enterprise features of SharePoint, these scenarios become no-code solutions once you have the service layer created from K2 to your back-end server.

*Refer to Chapter 7 and Chapter 23 for more information about SmartObject Services and SAP integration, respectively.*

# Working with InfoPath Forms

One of the last MOSS enterprise features that we'd like to briefly touch on is InfoPath Forms Services (IPFS). IPFS allows InfoPath form templates to be converted and displayed as Web pages within SharePoint. In-depth coverage of InfoPath forms is included in Chapter 11, along with the benefits of using InfoPath compared to ASP.NET forms. If you are using SharePoint, InfoPath forms are the easiest and most convenient way for displaying a custom UI and listing available actions for a process user.

> *Note that even if you don't have the MOSS enterprise features, you can still work with InfoPath forms on SharePoint. You will not, however, be able to render forms as Web pages. K2 blackpearl also integrates with the Microsoft Office Forms Server 2007, a separate SKU that includes only IPFS for InfoPath form rendering in the browser. Since this SKU is separate, it cannot be added on to MOSS like the enterprise features can.*

The biggest benefit that IPFS brings to the table is the ability to fill out InfoPath forms without needing InfoPath 2007 installed on every computer. Though InfoPath 2003 and SharePoint Portal Server had some great integration, the integration between InfoPath 2007 and MOSS is even more powerful with IPFS, allowing you greater number of possibilities to build complex workflows. K2 blackpearl introduces several important features to help you add rich user interfaces via InfoPath forms, whether those are browser-based or client-only forms. These features include:

❑ **Multiple views per form, multiple forms per process:** Allowing you the flexibility to reuse the same form for starting and actioning a workflow, or multiple forms if necessary

❑ **Dynamic action querying for user tasks:** Eliminating the need to update the form when actions change

❑ **SmartObject integration:** Allowing you to add data from SmartObjects to the InfoPath form, which in turn allows for better decision making

❑ **Automatic deployment, versioning and source management:** Enabling you to treat the InfoPath form as part of the process and not worry about how it will be deployed, versioned, and checked in to source control

> *These are the high-level benefits of using InfoPath 2007 forms with your SharePoint workflows. For more information and some caveats about using them, refer to Chapter 11.*

# Summary

As you discover SharePoint's rich and powerful features, you will appreciate the deep integration that K2 blackpearl brings to the table, allowing you to extend and increase your investment in SharePoint.

If you've purchased the Enterprise CAL, you can use every single SharePoint-related event wizard available in the K2 Designer for Visual Studio and the K2 Designer for Visio. These allow you to create no-code solutions to manage SharePoint sites, lists, and libraries, and to control content, all through processes that can provide an immediate and increased return on investment.

If you are just beginning your SharePoint implementation and have never used it before, we hope we've given you some appreciation of the benefits that SharePoint can bring to your organization, and some ideas on how you can use K2 to increase those benefits. If you are a SharePoint expert, we hope that we've given you some new ideas to use when employing SharePoint solutions.

In the next chapter you will take a look at the different K2 Designers available and how they can be used for collaborative process design.

# Notes

1. For further information about Microsoft Office SharePoint Server 2007 Records Center, visit the Web site `http://go.microsoft.com/fwlink/?LinkId=84739`.

2. K2 accesses SharePoint Records Center information through a specific Web service you can reach from the URL `http://yourportal/Records/_vti_bin/officialfile.asmx`. Important: You should check if the K2 blackpearl service account has the proper permissions to access it.

3. Visit the K2 and SAP Web page at `http://www.k2.com/en/displaycontent.aspx?id=107` to find extensions that allow easier integration between K2 and SAP. Also take a look at Chapter 23. If you need guidelines to help you in using Microsoft Dynamics and other platforms, visit the K2 blackmarket at `http://k2underground.com`.

# 14

# The K2 Designers and Collaborative Process Design

Codi Kaji

The K2 blackpearl platform allows for collaborative process modeling by changing the paradigm in which processes are designed. Collaborative modeling allows for a "Big Picture" view of a business's processes, allowing end users, business analysts, and developers to work together to address a broad range of business challenges.

This chapter will discuss the various K2 design surfaces, as well as how the designers work together effectively based on the skill set and role of the project team member. This chapter also covers the following topics:

❑ The roles involved when a K2 process is designed

❑ The designer choices available with K2 blackpearl, including the K2 Designer for Visio, the K2 Web Designer for SharePoint, and the K2 Designer for Visual Studio

❑ Collaborating on a process using the various K2 design tools

## The Right Tool for the Right Person

People are involved in application and process design; that's common sense. What's interesting is the *type* of people that *can* be involved. The K2 platform works process designs declaratively, meaning that the definition of the process is independent of the designer that was used to create it. This allows different design experiences for different types of people with varying technical skills.

Some organizations have fairly rigid standards for building and deploying business solutions. It does not matter whether you mandate that IT must be responsible for all software builds and changes or if you allow other people in the business to actively participate. K2 blackpearl was designed to handle these scenarios and anything in between, as shown in Figure 14-1.

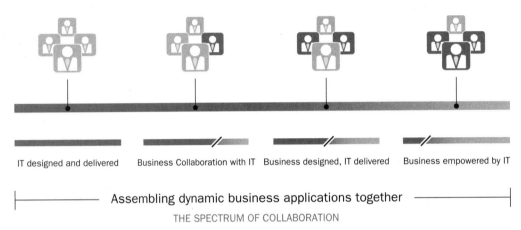

IT designed and delivered  Business Collaboration with IT  Business designed, IT delivered  Business empowered by IT

Assembling dynamic business applications together

THE SPECTRUM OF COLLABORATION

**Figure 14-1**

Because a process designer can have a variety of skillsets, the K2 process designers cater to the various technical and nontechnical user bases. For example, Microsoft Office Visio 2007 can be used to map a process by the business process owner. After the owner has described the process visually, a business analyst can add additional process definition information also using Visio. Once the process has been defined to the limit of their technical capabilities, the process definition can be passed on to a developer to finish the process using Visual Studio.

All K2 design canvases are visual, leveraging drag-and-drop and wizard-driven interfaces to guide designers without requiring significant technical ability. Microsoft .NET Framework 3.0 Windows Workflow Foundation Schedules and associated Microsoft .NET code are automatically created, regardless of designer, for interoperability and extensibility.

K2 provides three types of process designers today, and additional design canvases are planned. Each canvas is targeted at a specific type of person, as shown in Figure 14-2.

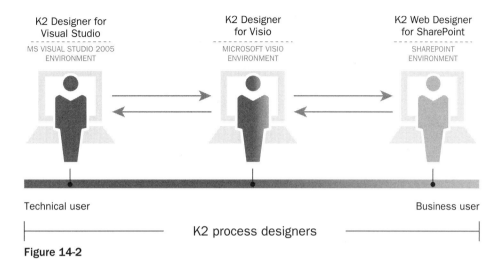

**Figure 14-2**

From left to right, the process designers move from technical complexity to easy use:

❑ The K2 Designer for Visual Studio is for IT professionals comfortable working within the Microsoft Visual Studio 2005 environment.

❑ The K2 Designer for Visio can be used by anyone comfortable with Microsoft Visio, but is generally used by a business analyst.

❑ The K2 Web Designer for SharePoint is for the SharePoint 2007 user or power user who wants to design and run workflows within the SharePoint environment.

Each designer will be discussed in more detail in later sections, as well as the planned designers to be released with later versions of K2 blackpearl. Before we get into detail about the design surfaces, it is important to start with some definitions.

## *Know Your Role*

As defined in Chapter 3, there are several roles that play a part in a K2 automation project. When it comes down to the task of designing the process, there are three key roles or audiences that we will discuss:

❑ Business analyst

❑ Process designer

❑ Developer

While the other roles in a K2 project are important, these three roles are the ones who will actually sit down and design the process using the K2 design tools.

## Business Analyst

While one of the main jobs of the business analyst is documentation of the process, including the business requirements, use cases, form design, and data requirements, K2 allows the business analyst to also play a key role in designing the process. Using tools such as the K2 Designer for Visio, the business analyst can map the process using common business stencils based on the requirements gathered during the design phase of the project.

## Process Designers

The process designer is generally responsible for the design of the application. Many times, a process designer can also be the business analyst and can use tools like the K2 Designer for Visio to develop the business processes. More than just defining the process using shapes, the process designer also connects the shapes with the appropriate K2 wizards to begin to develop the K2 process. For simple processes without requiring custom code, the process designer can completely build the process and deploy. For more complicated processes, the process designer can export the process and send to a developer to enhance.

## Developers

The developer is responsible for developing any custom code that is needed as well as the integration points into line-of-business systems. The developer will use tools such as the K2 Designer for Visual Studio to build on the process designed by the process designer in tools such as the K2 Designer for Visio to incorporate custom code. The developer is also responsible for the creation of SmartObjects, as that functionality is not included within the K2 Designer for Visio.

# Sharing a Process with Other Designers

When working on a business process automation project, many people will be working on the same project. Depending on the scenario, like the example mentioned previously, a business process owner, business analyst, and a developer could all be involved in defining the K2 process. The K2 process definition framework makes sure that the core definition is the same, regardless of the design canvas used to model the process. The framework abstracts the process definition, or the logic and routing information necessary for K2 to run the process, from the view information, or the layout and visual representation of the activities, events, and lines. The process definition framework allows each participant in the process-modeling experience to use the process design tool that best fits their skill sets. At the same time, by having a common definition, participants can collaborate using a variety of tools.

## Why This Works

Every K2 design surface uses the same project file system. All design tools employ the same K2 API to maintain the project (`.kprx`) file and create the supporting build files, whether or not Visual Studio is installed on the machine. The presentation of the workflow integration in each design canvas may be different, but the core pieces that make up the workflow are the same regardless of the design environment. In this way the design of the workflow is completely separated from the visualization of the workflow, which is precisely why collaborative design can occur on the K2 platform.

> ### Create Your Own Design Surface
>
> Though the topic is beyond the scope of this book, you could integrate the same wizard-based visual design canvas in a custom application using the SourceCode .Workflow.Authoring, SourceCode.Workflow.Design, SourceCode.Workflow .VisualDesigners, SourceCode.Workflow.WizardFramework, and SourceCode .Workflow.Wizards assemblies. See the K2 blackpearl Developer Reference for more information about these assemblies, which can be downloaded from the K2 Customer and Partner portal.

The building and deployment of workflows is the same across designers as well. The MSBuild scripts and mechanism by which processes are deployed to a K2 server is exactly the same for every design environment because the same API is used for all designers. Moreover, the K2 Designer for Visual Studio and K2 Designer for Visio (and the K2 Studio designer, not yet released at the time of writing) use the same wizards, so the configuration of processes, activities, and events are the same across designers. This also allows any custom wizards to be used across designers so that business users using K2 Studio or the K2 Designer for Visio can use the same interface as developers using Visual Studio.

Each K2 design surface creates the same project, folder, and file structure. It is the K2 API that defines this structure, which allows the flexibility for multiple designers to work with the same K2 project.

Also, because the visual design of the process and authoring of the process files are separated, there can be a disconnect between the visual model and the process definition. For example, in the K2 Designer for Visio, you may see orphaned activities and events. These orphaned items may have been added in Visual Studio but are not associated to a shape in Visio. Even though they are not visually represented on the canvas, they will be executed as they are represented in the process definition.

Think of this like a blue print to a building. If you were to pull a blue print of your house, you will see the layout of the rooms, entrances, windows, and so on. However, you may not see the details of the electrical or HVAC systems. Even though they are not visually represented in the house blue print, they are defined in another layer and are used within the execution of building the house (and during the day-to-day maintenance of the house, for example when the air conditioning kicks-in).

Using a process designer like the K2 Designer for Visio, you can represent the large activities or human interactions with shapes, much like the rooms in your house. Then, using a designer like the K2 Designer for Visual Studio, you can add in the details for the process, much like the electrical or HVAC systems. When viewing the completely defined process, the technical details may not be represented visually on the Visio page; they are represented within the process definition and will be executed during the run time of the process. Many times the project sponsors or business analysts are not interested in the technical details but only want to see the higher-level overview of the process. Therefore, the visual representation of the process in a Visio diagram is easier for the nontechnical users to understand.

---

**Define a Process Completely via Code**

Because the visual representation and the process definition are independent, you can create a process completely via code without using a visual designer. You can define the `.kprx` using the K2 API, which can then be opened in Visual Studio or imported into Visio. See the K2 blackpearl Developer Reference for more information. Look for the Processes ⇨ Authoring section.

---

## Export and Import Capabilities

As part of the K2 API, process definitions can be exported from the various design surfaces. This creates the necessary project, folder, and file structure so that the process design can be used by the other process designers.

However, there are some limitations on which designers can share processes with other designers. The following list shows the process sharing capabilities of the various K2 blackpearl designers.

- ❑ **Save from the K2 Designer for Visual Studio:**
  - ❑ **K2 Designer for Visio:** Can open and map unbound activities to new shapes.
  - ❑ **K2 Web Designer for SharePoint:** Cannot open.
- ❑ **Save from K2 Designer for Visio:**
  - ❑ **K2 Designer for Visual Studio:** Can open and continue designing with no additional tasks.
  - ❑ **K2 Web Designer for SharePoint:** Cannot open.
- ❑ **Save from K2 Web Designer for SharePoint:**
  - ❑ **K2 Designer for Visual Studio:** Can open and continue designing; process should be deployed as a new process.
  - ❑ **K2 Designer for Visio:** Can open and map unbound activities to new shapes; process should be deployed as a new process.

The reason that the K2 Web Designer cannot open processes designed in the K2 Designer for Visual Studio or the K2 Designer for Visio is based on the limited selection of wizards available within the Web Designer, which will be discussed in detail in a later section. It is strongly recommended that, if a K2 Web Designer process is modified by another design tool, the name be changed before deploying the process again. Because the end user who created the process in the Web Designer can still make changes to the "old" process and deploy it, this can cause issues with the versioning of the process and general headaches. By changing the name of the process before deploying from another designer, you can alleviate this issue and keep the Web Designer process from overwriting the changes.

# Designer Choices

K2 provides a unique process-modeling experience that supports multiple, interchangeable canvases and tools. K2 abstracts the view information from the process definition to ensure that the core process definition is the same, regardless of the canvas or tool. The result is a solution platform that allows each participant in the process modeling experience, regardless of role (for example, business analyst, developer, process owner), to use the modeling environment in which they are most comfortable. We will next talk about the design tools that exist with K2 blackpearl at the time of writing.

## *K2 Designer for Visio*

The K2 Designer for Visio is an add-in for Microsoft Office Visio 2007, bringing the tools available in the K2 Designer for Visual Studio to the Visio environment. By using layers instead of stencils, activities, events, and rules can be associated with any shape on the Visio canvas. This association is not limited to one activity or event per shape. For example, multiple activities can be attached to a single shape if the business requirements and existing drawing require it. This can be useful for drawings that do not model a process but need to be used to build and deploy one, such as a floor plan or an architectural drawing of a network.

Microsoft Visio helps people create professional-looking diagrams of all types. Most software programs of its kind rely on the users' artistic skills to make advanced drawings. But with Microsoft Office Visio 2007, it is as easy as opening a template and dragging the icons and stencils onto the canvas. Many companies already own Visio, and often it is already deployed to the process owners' desktops.

All K2 blackpearl components present in the Visual Studio Toolbox can be inserted on a new or existing Visio drawing. The same wizards available in Visual Studio are used to design specific pieces of a process in Visio, such as adding a SharePoint document event to move or copy a document stored on a SharePoint site.

The K2 Object Browser, which displays the Environment library, process and activity data, and the Workflow Data and User and Roles browsers, is available in Visio as well as Visual Studio. Most processes that can be built in Visual Studio can be built with the K2 Designer for Visio; however, custom code and debugging of processes are not available in Visio.

By using the K2 Designer for Visio, processes can be built and deployed from within the Visio environment. The Visio Designer leverages a familiar tool set and exposes the K2 tools for easy integration of drawings with process modeling. Now the K2 Designer for Visio can take these diagrams and bring them to life. Figure 14-3 below shows an example Visio diagram that has been wired to a K2 workflow.

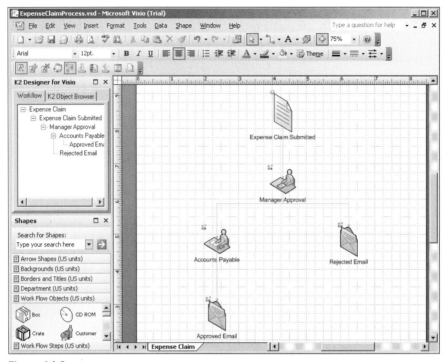

**Figure 14-3**

The K2 information is stored as another layer on top of the Visio diagram. In this way, the original diagram is preserved. You can turn off and on the visibility of the K2 layer so that the additional information (the green lines and K2 icons) does not confuse the viewer with the original K2 layer. For simple diagrams as shown in Figure 14-3, this does not pose an issue. However, with complicated diagrams the additional K2 layer can cause confusion.

The K2 Designer for Visio also takes advantage of easy-to-use wizards. These wizards are the same across many of the design surfaces, including Visio and Visual Studio. By having common wizards, the power of the K2 platform can be leveraged across multiple design surfaces, while allowing the end user to design in a simple Visio-based experience.

The person designing the process can choose between two means of process-enabling Visio diagrams: by activity or by process. A designer can automate processes in an ad hoc fashion, choosing shapes and then binding those shapes to events. For example, a designer might open an existing Visio 2007 diagram and then manually enable activities by selecting the shape, right clicking, and configuring an event (such as sending an e-mail or publishing a document) through a wizard. Alternatively, a designer can create a new process and enable the entire surface, thereby prompting the user to tie the shape to an event or rule when the shape is first dropped onto the design surface.

There are no specific one-shape-to-one-step limitations. This is too restrictive for some advanced processes or those that may follow alternative diagramming methods (for example, a floor plan). Multiple shapes may be used to define various steps, the participants and the decisions to be made. These can be grouped together in Visio and treated as a single K2 activity. Then the process author can begin assigning workflow steps to each stencil item or group of stencil items.

## Audience

The K2 Designer for Visio is intended for a business analyst to use to model processes. However, the design experience is robust enough that developers may choose to model processes using Visio.

In order to be successful with the K2 Designer for Visio, the user should be familiar with Visio concepts, such as using shapes, labels, and lines, as well as K2 concepts such as actions, outcomes, activities, events, and rules.

## Using the K2 Designer for Visio

When the K2 Designer for Visio has been installed on a client machine that has Microsoft Office Visio 2007 already installed, a new K2 toolbar becomes available within Visio. This toolbar is shown in Figure 14-4.

**Figure 14-4**

From left to right, the buttons include:

❑   **Enable/Disable K2 Workflow:** Allow or remove K2 Integration to the Visio drawing.

❑   **Add K2 Workflow Item to Shape:** Bind a K2 workflow item to a shape.

❑   **Remove K2 Workflow Item from Shape:** Remove the binding to a K2 workflow item on a shape.

❑   **Add K2 Workflow Item to Shape on Drop:** Opens the Bind to the Workflow Wizard when dropping a shape on the Visio page.

❑   **Toggle K2 Workflow Layers:** Display or hide the K2 layer on the Visio diagram.

❑   **Toggle Workflow Anchor Window Visibility:** Display or hide the K2 Designer for Visio task pane, including the Workflow and K2 Object Browser.

❑   **Import:** Import an existing K2 workflow to the Visio diagram.

❑   **Export:** Export the Visio designed workflow.

❑   **Deploy:** Deploy the Visio designed workflow to the K2 server.

❑   **Build Manager:** Change the pages and workflow that are used to build and deploy.

❑   **Settings:** Change K2 Designer for Visio settings.

To create a K2 integrated process in Microsoft Office Visio 2007, you must first enable the diagram to support K2 integration. This can be accomplished by clicking on the Enable K2 Workflow button. By enabling K2 integration, any of the shapes in the process can be bound to a K2 blackpearl workflow process. Binding shapes is easy and only requires a few clicks of the mouse.

When you right-click on a shape and select the K2 Integration menu item, the available menu items will be displayed based on the workflow configuration. For example, Figure 14-5 shows a diagram that has been integrated with a K2 workflow. By right-clicking on the start shape, you can change the lines or properties of that shape. The shapes that have been connected to a K2 activity will display a K2 icon next to the shape, as shown below. The icon is displayed on the K2 layer, and if this workflow layer is turned off the icons and lines will be hidden.

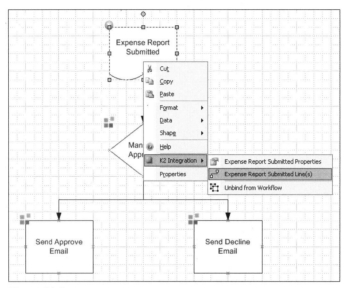

**Figure 14-5**

From a Visio diagram you can build a K2 process from scratch by integrating shapes with new workflow activities. You can bind any shape to any of the available K2 event wizards. The K2 Designer for Visio will walk you through a series of wizards to associate a shape with first the activity, then the Event Wizard. Depending on the event selected, additional sub wizards will be displayed to guide you through the process of configuring the event. These wizards are exactly the same as the wizards that are displayed in Visual Studio.

*For more details on the K2 wizards, please see Chapter 8.*

Once all of the shapes have been associated with workflow events, you need to connect them. Activities are joined by using the K2 Integration menu and configuring the lines. This is different than connecting lines in Visual Studio, as you cannot drag-and-drop the line stubs from actions to connect activities.

## Importing

Rather than building a process from scratch in Visio, a business analyst can also import an existing process that a developer has created in Visual Studio and map the process activities to shapes. Once a process has been imported into Visio, the user can map unbound activities to shapes.

Processes can be imported into Visio by choosing the Import button on the K2 toolbar.

## Exporting

To export a process out of Visio, click on the Export button on the K2 toolbar. Once exported all the files in the specified export location can be handed off to a developer for extending the process. The folder that the process was exported to will contain a complete K2 blackpearl project (`.k2proj` file) and process (`.kprx` file) that can be handed off to a developer for further customization. The project can be opened directly in Visual Studio, modified by the developer, and saved.

Once the developer has finished the modifications, the business analyst will open the Visio diagram and import the new process definition. Any of the already bound activities and lines will display on the K2 layer. Any activities that were added to the process definition in Visual Studio will be displayed as unbound activities. These new activities can be integrated with a shape in Visio for the visual representation. However, the process will still execute correctly even if it is not bound to a Visio shape. Remember, the visual representation layer and the process definition are separate. As long as the process definition is complete, the process will run correctly.

## Collaboration Experience

Processes designed in Visio can be opened within the K2 Designer for Visual Studio, modified, extended, and imported again to Visio for further changes or adjustments. This gives Visio and Visual Studio users the ability to collaborate on process design in comfortable and skill-appropriate environments.

The collaboration experience is bidirectional, meaning the process definition can begin in Visio or in Visual Studio and can be shared back and forth. For example, the business analyst can start from a blank Visio page, design the process using shapes and lines, and then wire up the page to new K2 activities and events. Or, the developer can build a K2 process, which the business analyst can then import into a new or existing Visio diagram and then attach the activities to the appropriate shapes.

For forms development, custom ASP.NET pages cannot be created in Visio. They must be created using a development tool such as Visual Studio. However, the developer can create the necessary pages and give the URL information to the process designer for use within client event wizards in Visio. If an InfoPath form has already been created, the process designer can integrate the Visio diagram with an InfoPath process wizard to fully implement the process using InfoPath forms. Design of the InfoPath form must be done in Microsoft Office InfoPath 2007.

## Extensibility

The K2 Designer for Visio design experience is not limited by what is available out-of-the-box. The platform is intended for collaboration and extension. For example, developers can create custom ASP.NET forms and preconfigured wizards with steps and actions for use by Visio process designers.

Process designers can also work with developers to extend capabilities that can't be solely enabled through available wizards. Processes can be shared by exporting the process from Visio and then opening the process with the K2 Designer for Visual Studio. All of the configured activities, events, and properties from Visio will be accessible from Visual Studio. The developer can use a full set of K2 tools, Visual Studio tools, and custom code to complete the process logic. The developer can check in the file for validation by the process designer. The process designer can reopen the process within Visio. If the developer creates objects that Visio is unable to interpret, the K2 Designer for Visio will allow the user to create associations between a Visio shape and the orphaned object.

## When to Use It

The K2 Designer for Visio is intended for a business analyst to be able to quickly wire up diagrams with key K2 activities and events. The Visio Designer should be used when:

❏ The business analyst needs to take written requirements and turn them into a visual representation of the process flow. By starting with Visio, the visual information about the process can be reused in Visual Studio, making it a jump start for the developer.

❏ The business analyst knows enough about K2 to be able to wire up the diagram with the process definition. You can either start with the diagram or start with a prebuilt process from Visual Studio. At the end, you will have a fully defined K2 process ready to be deployed and tested.

## When Not to Use It

Visio is not the appropriate design surface for all users. The Visio designer should not be used when:

❏ The developer is not familiar or comfortable with Visio. You should use the design surface that you are most comfortable with in order to rapidly develop your K2 processes.

❏ There is custom code that needs to be created behind the wizards. The Visio designer does not expose the code editing capabilities of the K2 platform. The Visual Studio designer is more appropriate when custom code needs to be created. However, if code modules have already been written and exposed as K2 wizards, they can be used within the Visio designer.

❏ SmartObjects need to be created for the first time. The K2 Designer for Visio does not include a design canvas for SmartObjects; these must be created in Visual Studio. However, once a SmartObject has been designed and deployed, it can be used within the Visio Designer from the K2 Object Browser.

# K2 Web Designer for SharePoint

*The information that follows is based on the K2 Web Designer for SharePoint version (1.0) that is currently available with K2 blackpearl 0803 at the time of writing. The Web Designer is undergoing some major changes, which will be discussed in a later section.*

Business users can visually model, build, and deploy processes using the K2 Web Designer for SharePoint, surfaced within SharePoint 2007. The K2 Web Designer for SharePoint is accessible to design workflows for any library or list within a SharePoint site collection. One of the great advantages to using the K2 Web Designer for SharePoint is that the SharePoint context is built in. This means that you can use SharePoint metadata from the list item or document in Line Rules, or use people columns as Destination Rules. Because this context is understood by the K2 Web Designer, as soon as you start designing a K2 process this information is available to you.

In order to accelerate the design process using the K2 Web Designer for SharePoint, Outcome templates are prebuilt to describe the actions that a user can take at a given point in the process. Wizards are also available to define what happens to the SharePoint item (either the document or list item that started the K2 process) as a result of the user's selected action. K2 provides a visual drag-and-drop and wizard-driven interface for building SharePoint-based processes from within the Web browser. SharePoint users can build processes that span documents, sites, libraries, lists, and more, without the need to build forms or understand technical concepts.

The designer is available for Microsoft Office SharePoint Server (MOSS) 2007 and Windows SharePoint Services (WSS) 3.0. Once the feature has been activated on a site collection, the K2 Web Designer for SharePoint is available from any document library or list. The design surface displays within the browser within the same frame as the SharePoint site, as shown in Figure 14-6.

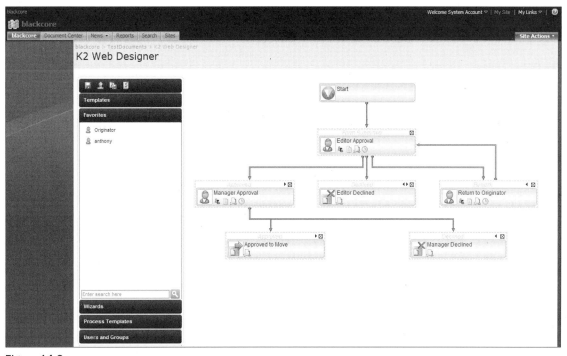

**Figure 14-6**

Because the K2 Web Designer for SharePoint is intended for power users and business analysts, the Sidebar contains a series of Outcome templates and wizards that can be used within the context of the K2 process. This will be described further in a later section.

Because the wizard list is restricted in the K2 Web Designer for SharePoint, this design surface is not as robust as the Visio Designer or the Visual Studio Designer. However, it is easier for an end user to design simple processes that center around a document or list item within SharePoint.

## Audience

The K2 Web Designer for SharePoint is intended for a power user or a business analyst to create simple, SharePoint-based processes. This designer offers a graphical workflow design experience within a Web browser for business users who do not desire or have the skills to write custom code.

The major advantage to hosting the Workflow Designer within the browser is a broad reach to users in an organization. This allows users who do not want or need Visual Studio 2005 or Visio 2007 to participate in K2 workflow design. However, the browser experience is not the same as a traditional Windows-based development environment.

In order to be successful with the K2 Web Designer for SharePoint, the user should be familiar with SharePoint concepts, such as documents, lists, libraries, records management, and permissions, as well as K2 concepts such as actions, outcomes, activities, and events.

Additionally, a SharePoint administrator is required to deploy this service to a SharePoint server farm. While the administrator may not need to know the details around the Web Designer, he or she should be familiar with deploying features within SharePoint. More information about deploying the K2 Web Designer can be found in Chapter 12.

## Using the K2 Web Designer

The K2 Web Designer for SharePoint is available from the Settings menu on any List or Library in a site collection where the feature has been activated. For more information on how to activate the Web Designer feature, see Chapter 12. Figure 14-7 shows the Settings menu with the K2 Web Designer option. This option is only displayed if you have the appropriate permissions.

**Figure 14-7**

After the Web Designer is opened, you will see a list of your personal processes as well as those that have been shared by others. You can select one of the listed processes to Edit, Share, or Export, or you can create a New Process. These options are shown in the toolbar of the K2 Web Designer, as shown in Figure 14-8. If you have opened the K2 Web Designer from a list, only processes that have been designed for lists will be displayed. Similarly, if you are looking at the K2 Web Designer from a document library, the processes that have been designed for document libraries will be listed.

**Figure 14-8**

Sharing a process will allow other users who have permission to use the K2 Web Designer to see the process in the Shared Processes section of the home page. Shared processes can be modified and redeployed by any member of the site with sufficient permissions.

Exporting a process will build the process definition and ensure that only complete processes are exported. Exporting a process creates a self-extracting .zip file (*.exe) that you can save local and then extract. This will create the necessary project and process files that can then be opened directly in Visual Studio, or can be imported into a Visio diagram.

Clicking New Process produces a prompt that asks you for the name of your process and offers different start options, such as start manually, when an item is created or when an item is changed. For a Form Library process, you must have an InfoPath form published to the library before you can create a new process. The start option for an InfoPath process is Start View. After you enter the information, the K2 Web Designer canvas is displayed.

The Sidebar contains all of the features that you can use when designing processes in the K2 Web Designer, as shown in Figure 14-9.

**Figure 14-9**

These Sidebar items will be discussed in detail and include:

- ❏ **Action Menu:** Buttons that allow you to Save, Deploy, Save as a Template, or change the Properties of the process.

- ❏ **Templates:** Outcome templates define the flow of activities for the process.

- ❏ **Favorites:** Ability to store users and groups as favorites gives you a quick reference to frequently used items, to speed up the design experience.

- ❏ **Wizards:** Based on where the process is being designed (a list, document library, or forms library) the list of available wizards will change and be displayed in this menu.

- ❏ **Process Templates:** Ability to use processes that have been saved as templates for quick design reuse.

- ❏ **Users and Groups:** Similar to the User Browser in Visio or Visual Studio, this item will display the SharePoint Users or Groups that can be used within the process.

## Action Menu

Across the top of the Sidebar are the Action Menu buttons. While designing your process, you can save it (strongly recommended to save frequently when designing large processes); deploy it to the K2 server, which allows it to run based on your start options; use the Save as Template option, which allows others to use this process as a starting point when designing new processes; or edit the properties of the process (such as the name, description, and start options).

Deploying the process will launch a wizard to check the process definition for missing information, and upon a successful validation, deploy the process to the K2 server. Any errors found when checking the process will be listed so that you can fix the issue and try the deployment again. The deployment process is similar to deploying projects from other K2 Designers, although it is more automated because the environment context is known. You cannot deploy a K2 Web Designer process to a different SharePoint environment. In other words, you cannot design the process on the test SharePoint URL and deploy it to production. To move between environments, you will have to export the process and deploy it using a different K2 Designer.

## Templates

Outcome templates describe the actions that can be taken by the user and are not able to be modified. The prebuilt templates include the following:

- ❏ Approve-Decline
- ❏ Approve-Decline-More Info
- ❏ Approve-Decline-Review
- ❏ Approve-Decline-Rework
- ❏ Approve-Retry
- ❏ Back
- ❏ Close Outcome
- ❏ No Outcome
- ❏ Retry-Close

By using the Outcome templates, the flow of the K2 process is defined. This basically defines the activities for the K2 process. By dropping a template onto the design canvas, a wizard opens which asks for the activity name and description, as well as the actions and outcomes available as part of this activity. Depending on the template that you used, these are already defined for you. However, you can add, edit, or remove actions and outcomes to customize your process. For more information on actions and outcomes, please see Chapter 8.

## Wizards

Once the activities have been identified, then the events need to be described. Because the K2 Web Designer can only design SharePoint based processes, not all of the K2 Wizards are available within the designer. Based on where the process is being designed (a List, Document Library or Form Library), the available wizards will change. Each wizard uses the context of the item that started the workflow. In other words, if the workflow is set to start when a new item is added, the newly added item becomes the workflow context. The wizards act upon this item.

The wizards are limited according to the following table:

| Document Wizards | Description | Available In |
|---|---|---|
| Check In Document | Checks in the document using the version control feature of SharePoint. | Document Library |
| Check Out Document | Checks out the document using the version control feature of SharePoint. | Document Library |
| Copy Document | Copies the document to the destination document library, but leaves the document in the source document library. | Document Library |
| Delete Document | Deletes the document. | Document Library |
| Move Document | Moves the document from the source document library to the destination document library. | Document Library |
| **Mail Wizards** | **Description** | **Available In** |
| Send Mail | Sends an e-mail notification, and can include metadata from the form, document, or list item. | Document Library List Form Library |
| **List Item Wizards** | **Description** | **Available In** |
| Create List Item | Creates a new list item on a destination list. | Document Library |
| Copy List Item | Copies the list item from the source list to a destination list. | Document Library List |
| Delete List Item | Deletes the list item from the source list. | Document Library List |
| **Record Management Wizards** | **Description** | **Available in** |
| Send Document to Record Center | Copies the document to the Record Center using the Records Management feature of MOSS. | Document Library |
| Place Hold on Record | Places a hold on a document already in the Record Center using the Records Management feature of MOSS. | Document Library |
| Remove Hold from Record | Removes a hold from a document already in the Record Center using the Records Management feature of MOSS. | Document Library |
| Delete Record | Deletes a document from the Record Center using the Records Management feature of MOSS. | Document Library |

Forms libraries must have an InfoPath form published to the library before a workflow can be designed. Only the mail wizard is available when designing a workflow with an InfoPath form. For more complicated processes, do not use the K2 Web Designer.

*For more details on what the SharePoint wizards are used for, please see Chapter 13.*

## Favorites

When you are setting the destinations for the various activities, you have the ability to store the users as favorites, as shown in Figure 14-10. Once a user or a group been added as a favorite, it will display under the Favorites section of the Sidebar. For users or SharePoint groups that you use frequently in processes, it is a good idea to save them as a favorite to quickly drag-and-drop them onto activities to speed up setting the destinations.

**Figure 14-10**

## Process Templates

Once you have designed and configured a process, you can save it as a process template. This allows you to save processes or sections of processes as templates in order to speed up the design process. For example, you can configure a two step approval process where the decline steps send e-mails to the originator and save it as a process template. The next time you are building a process where you have this type of two-step approval process, rather than starting from scratch and configuring the approval steps again, you can drag on the process template and save some time.

A process template creates a copy of the template definition in the process you are designing. It is not a reference back to the original process, so if you change a process it is not reflected in other processes that use it as a template. Process templates cannot be edited, and can only be dropped onto the default "Form Submitted" activity. This means they can be used at the beginning of a process but cannot be stacked as building blocks.

### Users and Groups

The available Users and Groups in the site collection in which you are designing a process will be displayed in the Sidebar. You can drag and drop the SharePoint groups onto an activity to quickly set that group as the destination. Remember that the Sidebar only shows the particular users and groups that have been granted explicit rights to the list or library from which you accessed the K2 Web Designer. If you do not see the group listed that you want to use, try opening the destination properties of the activity. This will let you search for users or groups within the context of your site collection. If you still do not see the group listed, they may not have access to the site collection. Check the SharePoint permissions and try again.

## Collaboration Experience

Processes created in the K2 Web Designer for SharePoint can be exported. This creates the necessary project, folder, and file structure using the K2 API so that the process can be used in the other design surfaces. Once exported, the process can be imported into the K2 Designer for Visio and attached to a diagram. The process can also be opened directly in the K2 Designer for Visual Studio for more sophisticated activities and integration.

Once the process has been modified by Visio or Visual Studio, it can no longer be modified using the K2 Web Designer for SharePoint. This is due to the wizard limitations in the K2 Web Designer. It is also strongly recommended that if a K2 Web Designer process is modified by another design tool that the name is changed before deploying the process again. Because the end user who created the process in the Web Designer can still make changes to the "old" process and deploy, this can cause issues with the versioning of the process and general headaches. By changing the name of the process before deploying from another designer, you can alleviate this issue and keep the Web Designer process from overwriting the changes.

The key to this collaboration experience is communication. Be sure to tell the person who designed the process using the Web Designer that it has been modified and that they should no longer use the Web Designer to make changes, but instead go through the necessary procedures to make changes using the other designers.

## Extensibility

While the same wizards that are used in the other design tools are not used within the K2 Web Designer, there are some extensibility points. However, these are not code-based.

The K2 Web Designer has the concept of templates, whereby a user can save a process as a template. This allows for the process to be designed once and reused. For example, a process is defined and configured to start the same way, perhaps on upload of a document, and based on a form value, a different process can be followed. By saving the starting configuration of a process as a template, the business user can worry about the process after the document has been uploaded rather than the beginning point of the workflow.

The end user can also save items into their Favorites within the K2 Web Designer, making it faster to access commonly used items, such as destinations (users or SharePoint groups). This allows for a customized experience per user.

While the process designed is aware of the SharePoint list or library it has been launched from, a deployed Web Designer process is in actuality a SharePoint feature. Once deployed, the feature is automatically associated with the list or library for which it was designed. However, a deployed workflow is available for use in other lists or libraries throughout the entire SharePoint site collection by associating the feature to the appropriate list. This is another way to design once and reuse the process.

## When to Use It

The K2 Web Designer for SharePoint is a simple design tool that should be used when:

❑ The end user wants to create simple SharePoint-based workflows, where the available wizards are all that are necessary for the process. Remember that the document and list item wizards are reduced in the K2 Web Designer; for use of all the available wizards use a different K2 Designer.

❑ When a process is SharePoint-centric, meaning all items within the process are surrounding a document, list item, or form within SharePoint.

## When Not to Use It

The K2 Web Designer for SharePoint should not be used when:

❑ More complex workflows are required, where the prebuilt Outcome templates are not flexible enough. For example, more complicated workflow design solutions, such as the Spider workflow, cannot be created using the K2 Web Designer. Also, altering the task and workflow history lists for SharePoint workflow integration processes is not possible using the K2 Web Designer.

❑ There is custom code that needs to be created. No custom code or custom wizards can be created for the K2 Web Designer. The Visual Studio designer is more appropriate when custom code needs to be created.

❑ SmartObjects need to be created for the first time. The K2 Web Designer does not include a design canvas for SmartObjects; these must be created in Visual Studio. And, SmartObjects cannot be used within the K2 Web Designer, so any process that will rely on line-of-business data should be designed using another K2 design tool.

❑ Active Directory groups or users who have not been imported into SharePoint groups or users need to be used. Only SharePoint groups and users are available in the User Browser within the K2 Web Designer for SharePoint.

❑ SharePoint administration tasks need to be part of the workflow. The SharePoint Sites and Workspaces and the SharePoint Lists and Libraries wizards are not accessible via the K2 Web Designer. If your process needs to create sites or libraries using these wizards, use another design tool.

# K2 Designer for Visual Studio

The K2 Designer for Visual Studio is a fully integrated extension of Visual Studio 2005 and provides a powerful design experience, allowing access to all of the K2 tooling and the generated Microsoft .NET Framework 3.0 Windows Workflow Foundation Schedules and associated Microsoft .NET code for all appropriate K2 objects.

*At the time of writing, Visual Studio 2008 support is planned and is under development, but only Visual Studio 2005 is supported by K2 blackpearl 0803.*

In the K2 Designer for Visual Studio environment, as shown in Figure 14-11, developers simply drag-and-drop components onto the process-design canvas. Windows Presentation Foundation–based wizards — including wizards for integrating with technologies like SharePoint, sending e-mail and displaying ASP.NET or Microsoft Office InfoPath 2007 forms — guide the developer through configuring the underlying Workflow Foundation schedules, rules, and activities. Developers may use the K2-provided Developer Reference to develop their own custom wizards. Processes built in K2 are extensible. K2 leverages .NET 3.0 — including Workflow Foundation (WF), Windows Communication Foundation (WCF), and Windows Presentation Foundation (WPF) — so developers can open and extend processes within the WF design canvas or directly through custom C# code.

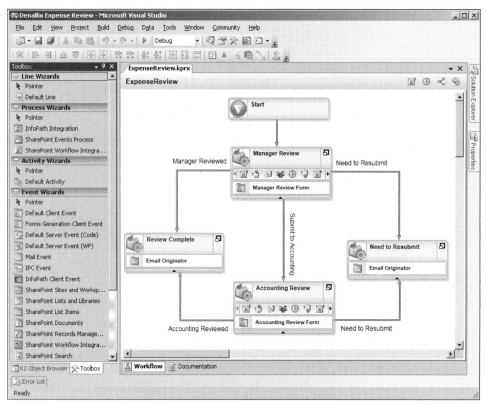

Figure 14-11

As with all of the K2 design tools, wizard-driven templates are made available to the developer, and the developer has the option to access the generated Microsoft .NET components as necessary.

The Solution Explorer exposes the K2 project and associated dependencies. It includes a context menu to build, deploy, and add new items to K2 projects. Behind the scenes, MSBuild is used for building, packaging, and deploying K2 solutions. All project assembly references are automatically added when a new K2 project or process definition is created. K2 projects can also be included in a single solution file with standard .NET artifacts like ASP.NET pages and Windows Forms. InfoPath solutions are integrated into the project system, ensuring the InfoPath form templates files and their associated K2 projects remain in sync for versioning and deployment. Further, developers will have one-click InfoPath design-time access to all InfoPath form templates included within a K2 project.

## Audience

The K2 Designer for Visual Studio is intended for a developer to use to model processes and business entities. In order to be successful with the K2 Designer for Visual Studio, the developer should be familiar with Visual Studio concepts, such as building, setting properties, deploying, and working with error messages, as well as K2 concepts such as actions, outcomes, activities, events, and rules.

## Using the K2 Designer for Visual Studio

Because the K2 Designer for Visual Studio is the preferred K2 Designer for a developer audience, it has been used throughout this book. In Chapter 7 you learned about creating SmartObjects using Visual Studio. In Chapter 9 you were first introduced to using Visual Studio to design K2 processes. Chapter 11 covered creating custom ASP.NET forms for use as client interactions with processes. For more details on how to use the Visual Studio to design processes, SmartObjects, or custom ASP.NET pages, please refer to these chapters.

## Collaboration Experience

Any process designed in the K2 Web Designer for SharePoint or the K2 Designer for Visio may be exported to the K2 Designer for Visual Studio, allowing a developer to enhance those processes. Processes created in the K2 Designer for Visio may also be sent back from Visual Studio, allowing for bidirectional modification of the process by both the business analyst and the developer.

## Extensibility

The K2 design experience is not limited by what is available out-of-the-box. The platform is intended for collaboration and extension. For example, developers can create custom ASP.NET pages and preconfigured wizards with steps and actions for use by other process designers. Using the K2 Developer Reference, custom wizards can be developed and then can be used in the K2 Designer for Visio. For more information on creating custom wizards, see the K2 blackpearl Developer Reference.

Process designers can also work with developers to extend capabilities that can't be solely enabled through available wizards. Processes can be exported from Visio and then opened in Visual Studio. A developer is then able to open the process model and any preconfigured activities directly within K2 Designer for Visual Studio. The developer can use a full set of K2 tools, Visual Studio tools, and custom code to complete the process logic. The developer can check in the file for validation by the process designer. The process designer can reopen the process within Visio. If the developer creates objects that Visio is unable to interpret, the K2 Designer for Visio will allow the user to create associations between a Visio shape and the orphaned object.

## When to Use It

The K2 Designer for Visual Studio is the most robust of the K2 Designers. It should be used when:

❑ The developer is familiar with and comfortable with developing in Visual Studio. Because the K2 Designer for Visual Studio is completely integrated within the Visual Studio IDE, only the new K2 concepts and toolbars need to be understood before developing a K2 process. This provides for a much smaller learning curve for someone who is already familiar with Visual Studio.

❑ SmartObjects need to be created. At the time of writing, the K2 Designer for Visual Studio is the only design tool where SmartObjects can be created, edited, or deployed.

❑ Custom code needs to be integrated with or consumed within a process definition. The K2 Designer for Visual Studio is the only design tool where the WF schedules or underlying C# code are accessible for modification.

❑ Custom ASP.NET pages or Windows applications need to be created for the client events, or user interactions with the process. While these client interactions can be developed in any technology, Visual Studio makes it easy to reference the K2 APIs, and the K2 blackpearl developer reference has sample projects and code examples for use within Visual Studio.

## When Not to Use It

Because the K2 Designer for Visual Studio is designed for a developer, it should not be used when:

❑ A business analyst wants to model a process. Use one of the other design tools rather than spending the time and money to skill up a business analyst on a developer tool.

❑ For simple, SharePoint-driven processes that can be quickly designed using one of the other designer tools. Visual Studio can be overkill and requires a developer interaction. Other K2 Designers, such as Visio or the Web Designer, can be used effectively when the business analyst or power user has the skills and knowledge required to develop the process.

# Future Design Tools

Because the K2 API creates the framework for the project, folder, and file structure for all K2 processes, the design surface possibilities are endless. The K2 Designer for Visio, the K2 Web Designer for SharePoint, and the K2 Designer for Visual Studio are the three canvases that are available with K2 blackpearl 0803. However, additional design surfaces are in the works and will be available with future releases of K2 blackpearl.

*The information provided here on future designers is subject to change, as these design surfaces are still in development. The additional design surfaces will be available in future releases of K2 blackpearl.*

## K2 Studio

With K2 Studio, business users can create process applications within an Office-like application. K2 Studio is a client-side application providing the ability to build a process application using K2's easy-to-use wizards. This benefit allows customers to have a simple design experience, while at the same time leveraging the power the K2 platform has to offer. The K2 Studio designer uses the Microsoft Office look-and-feel, creating a design environment that is familiar and easy to use for business users.

Some of the key features of K2 Studio include:

❑ **K2 Toolbox:** Providing easy access to K2 blackpearl components and wizards, this toolbox displays the K2 Object Browser and Process and Event wizards for easy access to all the K2 values and wizards when designing a process.

❑ **Solution Explorer:** All project assembly references are automatically added for you when you start a new K2 project or process definition. This explorer is similar to the Visual Studio Solution Explorer.

❑ **Process Helper:** To shorten the development cycle, the process helper tool pane shortcuts common wizards into just the minimum requirement information to prototype and build processes faster.

❑ **Visual Process Designer:** An extendable design canvas for visually modeling workflow and business processes. This design canvas is similar to the Visual Studio design canvas.

❑ **SmartObject Designer:** This provides a visual interface that allows developers to build and deploy composite data entities.

❑ **Process Guides:** To assist in the process design, video and step-by-step guides are included to assist first-time process designers in configuring their K2 process.

This standalone application does not require Visual Studio to be installed in order to develop K2 processes and SmartObjects. All the K2 wizards that are available in Visual Studio are also available within K2 Studio. However, you cannot edit code in K2 Studio. You will need Visual Studio in order to modify the WF schedules or code-behind wizards.

Any process designed in K2 Studio may be imported into Visio to wire a Visio diagram, or directly edited in Visual Studio. Because K2 Studio uses the same solution and project file structure as Visual Studio, K2 solutions can be opened in either K2 Studio or Visual Studio for a completely seamless collaboration experience.

K2 Studio is designed for a business analyst to be able to develop K2 processes and SmartObjects easily and effectively. In order to be successful with K2 Studio, the user should be familiar with Office 2007 concepts, such as the ribbon bar and tool panes, as well as K2 concepts such as actions, outcomes, activities, events, and rules.

## *K2 Web Designer 2.0*

The K2 Web Designer will be revamped from its current implementation as the K2 Web Designer for SharePoint. The current version focuses on activities and events as the building blocks for processes. The new version will focus on people rather than activities. For example, in the current version you start building your process by thinking about the outcomes (for example, approve-decline), then you think about what happens to the item (for example, move document, delete item). In the next version, you start building your process by thinking of the people that need to interact with that item (for example, manager approval). As in the pawn diagram discussion in Chapter 8, by moving people to the forefront of the discussion around the business process rather than the blocks and lines that make up the process, it is easier to gain buy-in and approval of the newly automated process.

The next version of the K2 Web Designer will also not be dependent on SharePoint in order to design processes. It will still be SharePoint-aware, allowing processes to be built quickly based on the site collection and list or library from which it is launched. However, the K2 Web Designer will also be a standalone Web site to remove the dependency on SharePoint.

As is the first version, the K2 Web Designer is intended for a business analyst or power user to use to develop process-driven applications. While the design canvas and the paradigm for thinking about the business process may change, the user should still be familiar with SharePoint concepts such as documents, lists, libraries, records management, and permissions, as well as K2 concepts such as actions, outcomes, activities, and events.

# Working Collaboratively

With the various designers available for the project team to use, it is important to understand some guidelines when working on K2 projects collaboratively. As with any technology project, there are challenges that will exist outside of the boundaries of the project. The next sections will discuss the challenges and best practices to successfully work collaboratively with K2.

## Example Scenario

Before we discuss the details, let's walk through an example collaborative development scenario. Let's assume that you've already set up the project team, selected your process to automate (in this example, let's use the HR process for bringing new employees on board), and have held meetings to discuss the business requirements and have documented the use cases.

The business analyst takes the requirements and starts to create the process model using Visio. The diagram has been created using the appropriate shapes to accurately depict the process, beginning with the job posting, the interview process, the offer letter, and so on until the employee has been hired and has started their first day on the job. Once the diagram has been approved by the appropriate stakeholders, the business analyst is ready to start developing the process. They starts wiring up the shapes with the appropriate activities and events, starting with a job posting that has been uploaded to a SharePoint document library on the HR site. Because the business analyst understands the K2 concepts and wizards, they are able to successfully wire up a number of the activities in the process. Once an applicant has applied and interviews have been scheduled (stored on an interview calendar on the HR site), and the decision to extend an offer has been made, the offer is actually created by Payroll using their legacy system for employee payroll, raises, and bonuses.

Because the process has now stepped into the realm of system integration and because the business analyst doesn't know the underlying technology for the payroll system, they needs help from the developer. They can save the Visio diagram, and export the K2 process. When they exports the process, the necessary K2 projects and processes are created automatically. The developer can then open the K2 process in Visual Studio and can develop the necessary code to integrate with the payroll system.

Once the developer has completed the integration tasks, which could use a custom code event for example, or a series of SmartObjects to expose data from and update data to the payroll system, he saves the process and tells the business analyst that their work is complete. They can then import the modified process back into the Visio diagram. All the events that were wired up previously will still be connected. The new events that the developer created (which display as orphaned activities in Visio) can be associated with shapes on the Visio diagram and the business analyst can continue working on the process.

The K2 platform allows for tight collaboration among the members of the team by providing a common framework that defines the K2 solutions, projects, and artifacts. However, the technology can only take you so far in working collaboratively. There are considerations outside of the technology that you should look at.

## Identify Roles and the Plan

A strong part of any successful project is having a clearly defined scope, project plan, and responsibility matrix. By identifying who is responsible for which tasks and when they are due, you can set expectations early on. Additionally, you can use this opportunity to look at the team members and identify their strengths and weaknesses. Use this to help them learn the new tools they will be using, such as the K2 designers or any project-reporting tools you use. If a team member is not going to be a developer, then don't teach them how to use the K2 Designer for Visual Studio. Instead, focus their energies on the K2 Designer for Visio or another design canvas.

By clearly identifying the responsibilities, from our previous example scenario, the business analyst knows that they is responsible for creating as much of the process as they can. Additionally, they knows who the developer is who is responsible for integration with the payroll system. Having this information defined up front, before any work begins on the process automation, will make it easy for team members to work together effectively.

## Manage to the Project Plan

A business process automation project is just like any other project. If you have a large team of people, make sure that boundaries are set early on with responsibilities and deadlines. Hold people accountable for the tasks that are assigned to them, using whatever method works in your environment, perhaps daily status e-mails or weekly status meetings, or perhaps SharePoint or Microsoft Office Project works in your environment to manage projects. Use the tools to help you keep a handle on the project. While it is mainly the project manager's job to make sure that the project is on task, it is the responsibility of every person on the team to know what they should be working on, and when.

Also make sure that you do not create a massive project plan and then never update it. A good project plan is flexible enough to allow for fire drills that come up during a project. It is also updated frequently with status and progress, so that all the stakeholders and team members know at a glance the project status.

## Source Code Control

As with any development project, it is a good idea to check in the code for an application to a source code management tool. This way there is a backup of the working code as well as version control and locking so that changes are not overwritten in a large development team.

With K2 blackpearl 0807, checking in K2 solutions and associated files is integrated and fully working within Visual Studio. Any package (such as Microsoft Visual SourceSafe or Team Foundation Server) that can be integrated into Visual Studio as a source code control provider can be used to check in the K2 projects' code. Be sure to configure Visual Studio to integrate with whichever source control package you use to manage your code.

Throughout this book, we've said that K2 is a declarative model, with no compiled code. But now we're talking about managing source code? When you create a K2 process, you are actually building a .kprx file. This is an XML file which declaratively stores all of the configuration properties and customizations that you make to the process definitions. You need to have only this single .kprx file managed under source code control for your process to be protected. If you have other artifacts, such as SmartObjects, custom ASP.NET pages, or InfoPath forms, these will also be checked in to the source code repository when checking in the K2 project.

When working in a development team, there are a few key points to keep in mind:

❑ Only one person can work on a file at a time. Make sure that you set up your integration with source code control to use exclusive check-out. Because the K2 files are based on XML, only one person should be modifying the file at a time. If you have multiple items within a single solution, one developer can be working on the SmartObjects while another is working on the process definition. However, two developers cannot be working on the same process at the same time.

❑ Merging changes is not supported. Because of the declarative nature of the K2 files, it is very difficult to merge changes based on XML structures. Therefore, make sure that only one person is working on a file at a time.

❑ There is no comparison tool to look at the differences between two versions of a K2 process. You could compare the XML behind the .kprx to look for differences, but this is extremely time-consuming and not intuitive, as there are no visual comparison tools for XML. You could also open the process versions in two different Visual Studio instances and look for changes, but again, this is extremely time-consuming. It is better to enforce exclusive check-outs to ensure that only one person is modifying the process definition at a time.

❑ All of the custom code and modifications made to the process definition are stored within the single .kprx file. When you go and modify the code behind an event or rule, that modification and custom code is actually stored within the .kprx file itself. This is why it is extremely important to back up and enforce proper check-in and check-out of this file to ensure that no changes are overwritten or lost during a collaborative development experience.

❑ Never check in extender projects. All information is stored in the .kprx file, and checking in extender projects just causes issues.

❑ Keep your process definitions in a separate K2 project and solution. This makes it easy for different developers to work on custom ASP.NET pages, SmartObjects, or Service Objects separately from the workflow processes.

If you are working in Visual Studio, the source code management process is fully integrated. However, if you are working on a development team where members are working in other designers (such as the K2 Designer for Visio), you will need to have a developer manually check out the file in order for the team member to be able to modify the process in a designer other than Visual Studio. There is no integration with source code control packages in the other design tools.

---

**Previous Versions of K2 blackpearl**

With K2 blackpearl 0807, this process is seamless and fully integrated. If you are using previous versions of K2 blackpearl, there are issues with checking in the extender projects that are added to the project file structure. Always make sure that you are running the latest released version of K2 blackpearl to ensure that you have the latest fixes and features.

If you are running an older version of K2 blackpearl, you can still check in your K2 projects into source control. Just be sure to only check in the `.kprx` file; do not check in the extender projects that are automatically created by the K2 wizards. These extender projects are recreated as necessary and all customizations and configuration information are stored in the `.kprx` file.

---

## Communicate, Communicate, Communicate

Regardless of the technology you put in place to help manage the source code, if the team does not communicate effectively, you will always run into issues. Set guidelines early on, such as having everyone check in their files at the end of the day, and have everyone get the latest versions as soon as they get in the next day before they start working. Or, set guidelines stating that the project must be built locally before being checked in, thereby helping to make sure that the copy in source code control will always be a working copy.

These guidelines should be set at the beginning of the project, and it's a good idea to remind folks often of the rules. Reminders are a good way to keep these guidelines at the forefront of the project team's mind, to ensure that the team works together effectively.

Also, don't rely on the technology to help drive collaboration. Working closely together (literally, having the project team in close proximity) can help the project team be effective. If the project team is virtual, using tools such as e-mail and instant messaging can help bridge the distance. Having frequent checkpoints such as status meetings or central issues lists are also good ideas to help manage the communication between the project team.

# Summary

The K2 platform's common project framework allows for many design tools and seamless integration between the designers and the project file system. With designers such as the K2 Designer for Visio, the K2 Web Designer for SharePoint, and the K2 Designer for Visual Studio, there is a designer available to match the skill sets on a project team, regardless of the technical abilities. When working collaboratively as a team, it is a good idea to communicate often, manage the project plan, and control the source code and process files using a source code repository. These items will help make the K2 project successful, regardless of the size of the project or team.

In the past several chapters, you have read about how to create processes using the various pieces and components in K2 blackpearl, ending in this chapter with how to collaborate with other process designers. In the next chapter, you will move on to the administration features of K2 blackpearl, including the administration of the K2 server and components.

# Part IV
# Administration of K2 blackpearl

# 15

# Server and Component Administration

Eric Schaffer

This chapter will do two things:

- ❏ Introduce you to the main components that compose a K2 blackpearl environment
- ❏ Guide you in the routine maintenance and administration of these components

Each component serves a specific role and ensuring that these components are operating correctly is an important task for a K2 administrator. This chapter is not an installation guide nor is it a troubleshooting guide. Please refer to the product documentation for installation and troubleshooting information.

## Server Architecture

As a K2 administrator it is important to have a basic understanding of the underlying architecture of the K2 blackpearl server.

At its core the K2 blackpearl server is a service that runs on a Microsoft Windows 2003 server. The service leverages standard Microsoft technology such as the .NET Framework 3.0, Microsoft Message Queuing (MSMQ), Microsoft Distributed Transaction Coordinator (MSDTC), Internet Information Server (IIS), Microsoft SQL Server 2005, and Microsoft SQL Reporting Services.

The K2 blackpearl Service is architected as a pluggable Host Server. This pluggable framework allows the services that support the K2 environment to be developed and managed individually as well as providing a core set of interfaces for the other services to leverage. The framework is also open to developers to build their own services, which provides for a high level of extensibility.

*An example of where this can be useful is with authentication providers. K2 blackpearl ships with two authentication providers (Active Directory and a SQL table–based provider) however an additional provider can be developed and plugged into the Host Server framework.*

Figure 15-1 illustrates the high-level architecture of the Hosted Server framework.

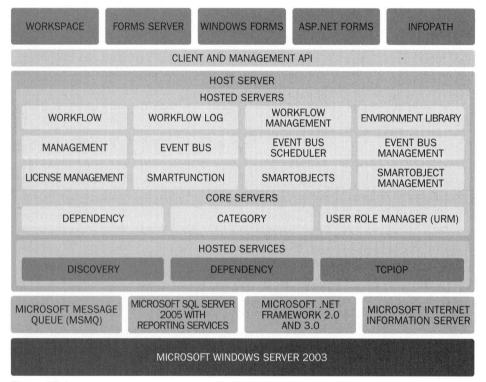

**Figure 15-1**

The following table provides a brief overview of each of the services that run within the Host Server environment:

| Service | Description |
| --- | --- |
| SmartObject Server | Handles the interaction with business entities or SmartObjects in the K2 environment. |
| SmartObject Management | Handles the management of SmartObjects in the K2 environment. |
| Workflow Server | Responsible for the interaction with and execution of the running process instances in the K2 Environment. |
| Workflow Management | Handles the workflow specific management interfaces in the environment. |

| Service | Description |
|---------|-------------|
| Workflow Log Server | Responsible for logging workflow events to the logging database. |
| Management | Handles the general K2 management interfaces in the environment. |
| License Management | Responsible for managing K2 licenses. |
| SmartFunction Server | The rules engine for the K2 environment. It handles the maintenance and execution of business rule entities. |
| Environment Library | Manages the interaction with the environment variables that are used when deploying K2 processes in multiple environments. |
| Event Bus | Responsible for the event system in the K2 environment. This includes server-level events as well as process- and SmartObject-level events. |
| Event Bus Scheduler | Responsible for the scheduling event system in the K2 environment. |
| Event Bus Management | Responsible for the management interfaces surrounding the Event Bus scheduler. |
| Dependency Server | Manages the dependencies between various artifacts (Processes, SmartObjects, SmartFunctions, Environment Variables, and so on) in the K2 environment. |
| Category Server | Manages categorical information for the K2 environment. |
| URM Server | The URM (User Rights Management) server is responsible for authentication and authorization in the K2 environment. |

Communication to and from the Host Server is through a TCP/IP connection on port 5555. The workflow service utilizes a TCP/IP connection on port 5252.

> *It is important to ensure that any firewalls that sit between the K2 blackpearl server and any component or application that needs to connect to the server are configured to allow communication on ports 5555 and 5252.*

The service can be managed through the standard Windows service console. The recommended approach is to run the service as a domain service account rather than as the local service account. The service account needs to have "log on as a service rights" to the server, and it is recommended that this account also be a local administrator on the server. If your security policies do not allow a service account to be a local administrator, please consult the K2 blackpearl *Getting Started Guide* for information on how to configure the specific permissions required.

# Workspace Management Console

The Workspace Management Console is home to the management applications used by system and process administrators to configure everything from the K2 platform to roles per process and user permissions.

When you load the Management tab, the Column Bar contains each management application (see Figure 15-2).

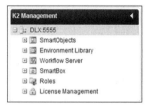

**Figure 15-2**

Most K2 administrative tasks are handled through the Workspace Management Console, and the first part of this chapter covers these administrative functions. However, there are some components in the K2 environment that are administered in different applications, such as the K2 components for SharePoint discussed in the "K2 SharePoint Component Administration" section later in this chapter.

# General Workflow Server Settings

The first job of a K2 administrator is to ensure that the administrative application is properly configured. These general administrative settings can be configured for the workflow server through the Workspace Management Console. To access these settings, right-click the Workflow Server heading and select Edit Settings. The following table explains the settings that can be configured:

| Tab | Description |
|-----|-------------|
| General | Used to configure the general server setting, including the server name and port. |
| Database Settings | Used to configure the database and log database settings, including name and authentication settings. |
| Advanced Settings | Used to set more advanced properties, including thread counts, Microsoft .Net Framework version, Trace settings, and Managed Users settings. |
| User Settings | Used to configure user setting including allowing anonymous users and running dynamic queries. |

The General tab (see Figure 15-3) has settings to point to the appropriate K2 Workflow Server and port. Typical administration will not require changing these settings. There is also a setting for Processors Configuration. This setting applies to processor based licensing models where you would need to specify which processor(s) the K2 workflow server will utilize. For example, if you have a single CPU K2 license on a dual-CPU machine, you need to enter either 1 (to specify that K2 will use processor 1) or 2 (to specify that K2 will use processor 2).

**Figure 15-3**

The Database Settings tab configures the database connections for the workflow server. The K2 blackpearl installation will configure this information for you, but if you migrate your databases or wish to change how the workflow server authenticates connections to the databases, this is the interface where you can make those changes.

The Advanced Settings tab has some additional settings for the workflow server. The following table provides a brief description of each of the settings on this tab:

| Setting | Description |
| --- | --- |
| Thread Count | The number of threads used by the workflow server for process execution. |
| Thread Priority | The priority of threads used by the workflow server for process execution. |
| Framework Version | The .NET Framework version used by the workflow server for process execution. |
| Trace | Legacy setting for configuring server logging. |
| File | Legacy setting for configuring the server logging file name. |
| IPC Retry Count | The number of retry attempts the server will make for failed Interprocess Communication calls. |
| IPC Retry Interval | The interval (in minutes) between retry attempts for failed Interprocess Communication calls. |
| Display Worklist of Managed Users | If this setting is checked users who have direct reports as defined within Active Directory will be able to see and manage the worklists for those users. |
| Worklist Remove | Legacy setting not used by K2 blackpearl. |
| Default Platform | The default worklist platform used by the server. |

The User Settings tab defines settings related to authentication such as whether or not to allow anonymous connections or to be able to use dynamic queues. The other settings are specific to the User Management interface to use with the workflow server and should not be modified unless a custom user management interface has been developed to replace the default interface.

# License Management

Each K2 blackpearl server in your environment requires a valid license key to operate. The license keys are based upon a system key which is a unique machine specific key that is generated by an internal K2 algorithm. Most license keys are perpetual and will only need to be set up once during installation. There are, however, some situations where license keys will need to be updated. For example, if your server hardware changes, then the system key could potentially change and invalidate your existing license key. Another example is if you make changes to your licensing agreement. If you have a 30-day trial key and then purchase licensing you would be able to update your trial key and not have to reinstall the software.

The License Management interface is available in the Management section of the K2 Workspace. The License Management interface (see Figure 15-4) is where you can view and edit your license key.

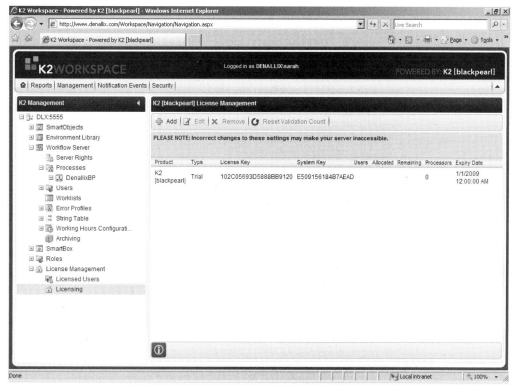

**Figure 15-4**

To edit your license key:

1. Select the key from the list and click Edit.

2. A window pops up where you can enter your new license key.

3. Click OK to apply the changes.

4. The K2 server will need to be restarted for the license key changes to take effect.

There is also a section under License Management called Licensed Users. One of the licensing models available for K2 blackpearl is Named User Model. This interface allows an administrator to see what users are consuming K2 licenses and also remove licenses for users who no longer need access. If you have a Named User license, the number of licenses that have been allocated and the number of licenses that are remaining will be displayed in the licensing interface along with the license key. To remove a license for a user, simply check the box next to the name of the user you wish to remove and click Remove (see Figure 15-5).

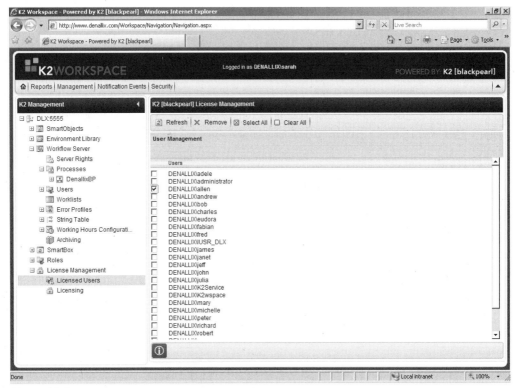

Figure 15-5

You will notice that there is no interface for adding users. Users receive licenses automatically when they log in to the K2 Workspace or into an application that connects to K2.

# Environment Library and String Table Management

The Environment Library at its most basic level is a collection of name-value pairs or fields that process designers can use during the design of processes to simplify deployment to multiple environments. The String Table is the run-time reflection of the Environment Library. For each library template multiple environments can be configured (for example, development, staging, and production). When a process is deployed, the designer selects one of the preconfigured environments, and the values associated with that environment are used to deploy to the selected environment and are also deployed along with the process as String Table values to be used during the execution of the process.

In this section, we will cover the basic administration surrounding the Environment Library. For information about best practices and the usage of the Environment Library when designing a process, please refer to Chapter 10.

In the management section of the Workspace under the Environment Library heading, there are three main management sections:

❑ Plugin Types

❑ Field Types

❑ Templates

Plugin Types allow for additional functionality to be surfaced in the K2 Object Browser (see Figure 15-6). For example, you can dynamically drill through the structure of a SharePoint site in the K2 Object Browser because of the functionality surfaced by the SharePoint Server Plugin. Typical administration will not require the adding, deleting, or editing of these plugin types, but the interface is available for administrators to perform these functions.

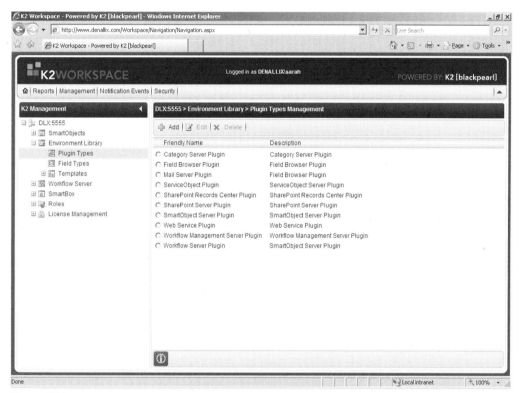

Figure 15-6

The Field Types section is the global list of the types of fields available to be consumed by the Environment Library templates. Each Field Type is associated to a Plugin Type and has a setting to determine if the Field Type should be added to a template by default. Typical administration will not require adding, deleting, or editing field types. If a new plugin type is added, the field types that the add-in exposes will need to be added to the Field Type list.

The Templates section is where administrators and properly privileged developers can define a set of templates and then for each template define the various environments associated with that template. The reason for having multiple templates is that there could be a scenario where there are multiple distinct K2 environments. For example, you might have a development and production environment specifically for the HR department, but the Finance department might have a development, testing, staging, and production environment that is completely separate from the HR department. In this case, a template could be configured for HR and a different template could be configured for Finance. A process designer would then choose the appropriate template in the K2 Object Browser and have the proper environments available.

*For best practices information on configuring your environment templates, please refer to Chapter 10.*

To add a new template:

1. Click Add in the Template Management section.

2. Give the template a Name.

3. Click OK.

Once you have a new template, you can configure which field types are available for this template through the Template Fields management interface (see Figure 15-7).

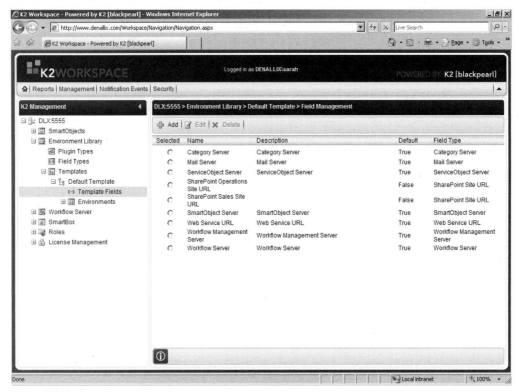

Figure 15-7

For each template, you can define the various environments that are available. To add a new environment:

1. Click the Add button in the Environment management interface for the template (see Figure 15-8).

2. Give the environment a name, and click OK.

Now the new environment will available for configuration.

Figure 15-8

The last step is to assign values to the Environment Fields. This is also where an administrator can modify the values for an environment. For example, if the production SMTP server changes from smtpserver1 to smtpserver2, an administrator would need to change the value for the production Environment Library.

To assign values to the environment fields or change existing values:

1. Select the field in the environment that you would like to modify, and click Edit.

2. Enter the value into the value field, and click OK to save the changes.

It is important to note that the Environment Library is only used during deployment if the values need to be updated during run time; they will need to be edited through the String Table interface that is found under the process management section.

If an environment value changes, it is the administrator's job to update the Environment Library as discussed above to ensure that proper values are used during deployment and also to update the String Table value on the appropriate K2 server so that the proper value is used during run time.

To update the String Table value:

1. Connect to the appropriate K2 server though the management interface. In the case of the SMTP server changing in production, connect to the production K2 server.

2. Under Process Management, click to expand the String Table heading, and select the appropriate String Table. You can edit the fields from this interface.

# Role Management

Roles play an important part of the K2 blackpearl environment because with a role you can manage task participation separately from the process definitions. A role can contain any combination of users and groups that are surfaced through the installed authentication providers. In a standard K2 blackpearl installation the authentication providers include Microsoft Active Directory and a custom SQL table–based authentication provider known as the K2SQLUM. The basic idea behind the K2SQLUM is to allow non–Active Directory users to participate in K2 processes.

In addition to directly specifying users and groups from the authentication providers, you can make use of a SmartObject method that returns a user or users. In this way, you can make the definition of the role dynamic. A common usage of the SmartObject capability is to have a role populated from the contents of a SharePoint list. A SmartObject can be created to return the items of the list, in this case users, and add them to the role.

Role management is surfaced through the Workspace Management Console under the Workflow Server heading. A list of configured roles will be displayed beneath the Roles heading. See Figure 15-9.

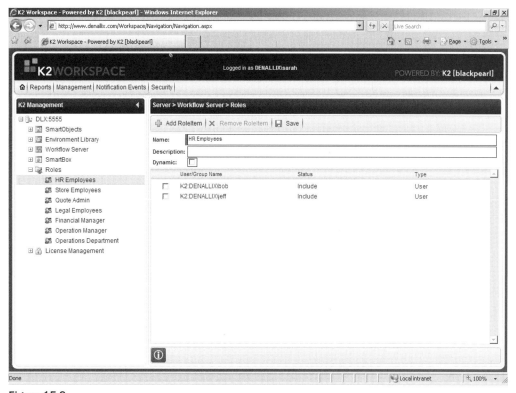

Figure 15-9

You can edit an existing role by selecting it from the list or add a new role by right-clicking the Roles heading and selecting add a new role. The role management interface allows you to specify a name and description for that role. You can also mark whether the role is to be dynamic or not. A dynamic role will reevaluate the role membership whenever users in that role refresh their worklist.

The most common administrative task for a role is to modify the role membership. You can remove role items by checking the boxes next to the items you wish to remove and clicking Remove RoleItem.

To add a role item, click Add RoleItem. This opens an interface with two tabs: Users and SmartObjects. The Users tab allows you to search for any users or groups from any of the installed authentication providers. Once you locate the role items, check the boxes next to the items you wish to add and select whether these role items should be included in or excluded from the role.

*The exclusion capability allows you to define a role, for example, where all users from group A are included as a part of the role except for user B. Without the exclusion capability you would only be able to achieve this same result by specifically adding each user individually from group A except for user B, and then you lose the ability to have the role dynamically add additional users that are added to the group.*

The SmartObjects tab allows you use a return property from a SmartObject call to populate the role. This can be useful if, for example, you want to populate the role with usernames that are stored in a SharePoint list or some other back-end system that you have a SmartObject for. The usernames that are returned will need to validate against the installed authentication providers in order for tasks to be delivered to the users.

Once you are finished making changes to the role, click OK, and then be sure to click Save to save your changes.

When a role is used by a process designer in a process definition, an additional interface for the role is created under the Roles management section for that particular process. The purpose of this interface is to allow you to set the refresh rate of nondynamic roles or manually refresh the role membership. A refresh rate of 0 indicates a dynamic role where the role is refreshed whenever members of the role refresh their worklist.

Refresh rates should be managed carefully as each refresh action for each role will make a connection to the authentication providers and reevaluate the membership. Depending upon the number of roles and the size of the groups this can put a strain on the resources of both the authentication provider and the K2 server. It is typically recommended to have nondynamic roles refresh at most once a day. The administrator always has the capability to manually refresh the role from this interface if necessary.

# Working Hours Management

No, this section will not help you maintain that elusive work-life balance as the title appears to suggest, but it will help manage when escalations and start rules execute for processes that can potentially span the globe. Escalations and start rules in K2 processes can be configured to fire after a period of time has elapsed. These concepts are discussed in more depth in Chapter 8 of this book, but an escalation is essentially a way that a process designer can raise an event when a task or process is taking too long to complete. A start rule is a way for a process designer to delay a step in the workflow for a period of time. Working hours were created to avoid having these types of events fired during non-working hours. The functionality allows an administrator to specify time periods in which the escalation/start rule clock is running. It even allows time zones to be configured so that a process designer can specify which time zone to utilize for a particular escalation or start rule. Administrators and process designers will need to work together to determine that this is all configured properly for the various business scenarios.

As an example, a task that is delivered to a user in Australia should probably not escalate based upon a U.S. time zone because that would likely not correspond to a valid Australian working hour. There may be cases, like a 24x7 support center, where escalations should not be constrained to a specific timeframe and a zone would need to be configured to cater to this scenario.

Working Hours configuration is a relatively straightforward process. In the Workspace Management Console under the Workflow Server heading there is a Working Hours Configuration section. A list of configured Zones will display under the Working Hours section.

To create a new zone, right-click the Working Hours Configuration heading and select Add New Zone. This will open the zone configuration interface (see Figure 15-10).

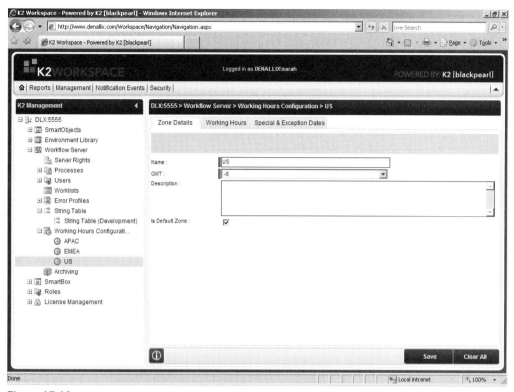

**Figure 15-10**

❏ On the **Zone Details tab**, you can specify the time zone (GMT) and give the zone a Name and Description. Additionally you can mark if the zone is the Default Zone. The Default Zone will be used for escalations and start rules when the process designer does not specifically select another zone.

❏ On the **Working Hours tab**, you are presented with a calendar that is divided into 30-minute blocks. Clicking or clicking and dragging the blocks selects those blocks to be active working hours. Active working hours are denoted by green blocks and non-working hours by black blocks.

❏ On the **Special & Exceptions Dates tab**, you can specify holidays and other date-time ranges to exclude from the working hours zone.

To save your changes to the new zone, click Save at the bottom of the page. The zone will now be available to process designers to use when specifying escalations and start rules. Once you have created the new zone, you can now add users and groups to this zone through the Working Hours Access interface under the Users section of the Workspace Management Console. To add or remove users and groups from a time zone, select the desired time zone from the drop-down list and use the Add and Delete options.

If a user is defined as a part of a particular time zone through the Workspace, then that setting overrides the default time zone for Client Event escalations. For example, if the process designer configures an escalation to use the default time zone on an activity that contains a Client Event, and the user who receives the task at run time is a member of a zone other than the default zone, the escalation will run according to the user's time zone.

# Process Instance Management

As an administrator, it is important that you get a real-time view of the status of process instances that are executing on the server. Through the management interface, there are two ways to get a status view of process instances. You can drill-down to a specific process through the Workspace Management tool and use the instances interface, which will auto-filter for that specific process or you can right-click the Processes heading and select Manage Process Instances. The latter will show all process instances on the server if no filter criterion is specified. Both interfaces will show the same basic information regarding the state of the process instances.

Another way to get status information about process instances is through the reporting interfaces discussed in Chapter 20. Unlike the management interface the reporting interface is a read only view of the process and does not allow for any process instance manipulation.

The status field identifies what state the process instance is in. The following table identifies the various states and what they mean:

| Status | Description |
| --- | --- |
| Active | The process instance is waiting for external input. Typically, this means that a task item has been assigned and the process will continue when the task has been completed. |
| Running | The process instance is actively executing process code. Server events and rule logic fall into this category. A process instance should not typically remain in the running status for very long unless the process contains extensive code-level processing. |
| Stopped | Process instance execution has been paused by an administrator through the management interface. |
| Error | The process instance has entered an error state. |
| Completed | The process instance has completed. (This status is filtered out of the process management interface but will show up in the process reports.) |
| Deleted | The process instance was deleted and the reporting information was maintained. (This status is filtered out of the process management interface but will show up in the process reports.) |

From either interface there are a number of actions that you can take for selected process instances. The following table describes these various actions:

| Action | Description |
|---|---|
| Start | The Start action will resume a stopped instance. The Start action will work only for stopped instances. Along the same lines the Stop action will pause execution of a process instance and will only work for active and running instances. |
| Delete | The Delete action will delete the process instance. When you select to delete a process instance you will be asked whether you want to keep the log entries or not. Deleting the log entries will delete all reporting information about the process instance. Keeping the log entries will keep the reporting information for the instance but show the process in a deleted state. |
| GoTo | The GoTo activity action allows you to move a process instance from its current activity to any other activity in the process definition. This functionality is useful for manually redirecting process flow; however, it does bypass standard process logic and can have unexpected results. For example, if you skip over a step that retrieves values from a back-end system and then the next step uses those values for rule processing, the values could be invalid and cause the process to go to an error state. Much as in programming languages, Goto logic should be used sparingly and with caution. |
| Start New | Start New is available only if you go to the instances section for a specific process. This functionality is provided as a test harness for initiating process instances without having to develop an interface. The test harness even allows you to enter data field values for testing purposes.

To start a new instance of a process, click the Start New button. This will open an interface where you can specify a folio, specify to start synchronously or asynchronously, and provide data field values. Once you have provided the necessary information, click Start to start the new instance. |

# Process Version Management

K2 blackpearl has the ability to run multiple versions of the same process at the same time. This allows process designers to deploy new versions of process without affecting the existing running instances. At a high level, a process instance runs against the version of the process that it was started against until completion, even if a new version of the process is deployed before the existing instance has completed. A complete version history of all deployed processes is maintained by K2 and surfaced to administrators through the management section of the K2 blackpearl Workspace. To view the version history of a specific process through the Workspace, navigate to the process by drilling-down through the Workflow Server and Processes sections to the specific project folder. Once you locate the process expand the process heading and select the Versions section. See Figure 15-11.

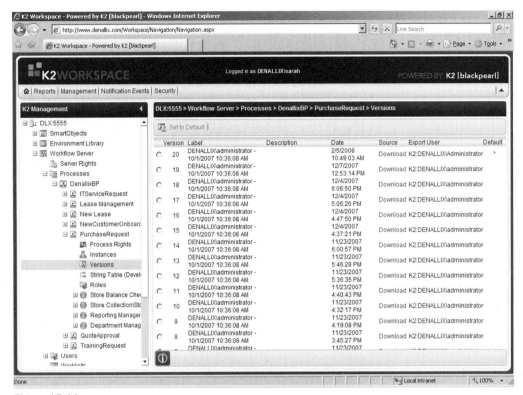

**Figure 15-11**

As shown in Figure 15-11, information is stored about each deployed version of the process. The following table has a description for each of these columns:

| Setting | Description |
| --- | --- |
| Version | The number identifier for the version of the process. |
| Label | The name given to the version of the process by the person who performed the deployment. |
| Description | A description given to the version of the process by the person who performed the deployment. |
| Date | The date and time the process version was deployed. |
| Source | A link that allows the version development files to be downloaded from the server. |
| Export User | The user ID of the user that exported the version of the process. |
| Default | A flag to specify which version of the process will be started by default. |

There is one main administrative task that can be done from this interface and that is to set the default process version flag, which determines which process version will be used for new instances. The K2 `workflow.client` API does support passing a version parameter, which overrides the default flag and allows developers to initiate a specific version of a process.

This interface also allows an administrator to download the source files for any deployed version of the process. This is a handy feature in a disaster situation, where the source files on the process designer's machine are lost. It is not, however, a substitute for source control because it only stores deployed versions of the process, not versions saved through the K2 Designer interfaces.

# Process Error Management

The K2 blackpearl server catches any unhandled exceptions that occur during the execution of process instances. Any process instance that produces an unhandled exception is put into an error state. This halts the execution of that instance and allows the server to continue processing other instances without having to stop everything until the error is resolved. In this section we will briefly discuss the error management capabilities in the Workspace and in Visual Studio. For more information on error logging, please refer to Chapter 19.

A K2 administrator can view a list of all process instances that are in an error state through the Management section of the Workspace. The Error Profiles interface (see Figure 15-12) is located beneath the Workflow Server heading for the desired server.

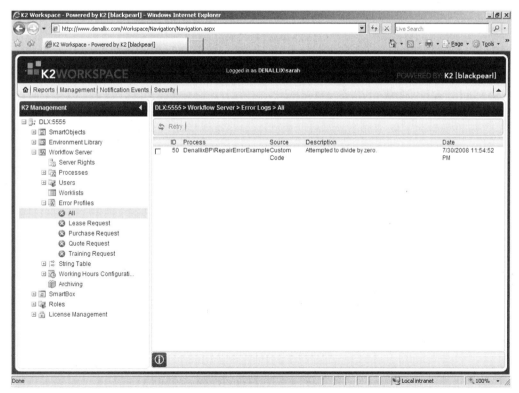

Figure 15-12

Notice that beneath the Error Profiles heading you find a number of error profiles listed. An error profile allows an administrator to configure a filtered view of the errors. The default error profile is the All view, which shows all the errors on the system.

*It can be helpful to create an error profile for each deployed process. This way you can deal with errors on a process-by-process basis.*

To configure a new error profile right-click the Error Profiles heading in the tree view and select Add New Error Profile. A Create New Error Profile page appears.

The Properties tab allows you to give your profile a Name, specify a Processes filter, and select a date range filter.

The Specific tab gives you a list of checkboxes for types of errors. By checking the box for an error type, you are selecting to include that error type in your profile. Deselecting the checkbox for an error type excludes that error type in your profile.

*It is generally not recommended to deselect error types for your profiles unless you are planning to create a filter for each error type. It would be frustrating to know that a process is in an error state but not be able to find the error due to a filter condition.*

Once you have configured your error profile, click Save to save the profile.

To view the new profile (see Figure 15-13), simply click the profile (in our example, RepairErrorExample).

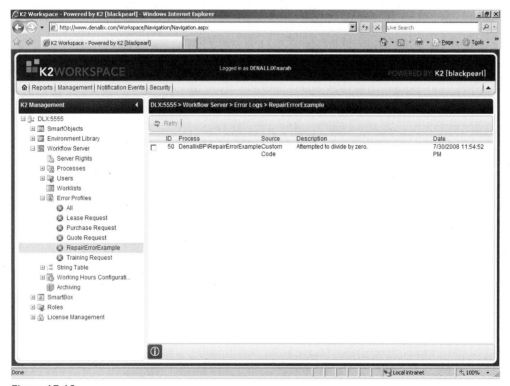

Figure 15-13

As shown in Figure 15-13, the Error Profiles view shows you the process ID, the Process name, the Source event name, and the error Description. Clicking Retry reruns the event that generated the exception for each process instance that is selected in the list. This functionality is helpful for resolving issues like timeouts or file locking.

The Workspace is a great place to ascertain the state that a process instance is in, but it is not a debugging platform. Any issues that require process instance manipulation will need to be dealt with in the K2 Process Management utility within Visual Studio. This tool allows a process instance that is in an error state to be opened, manipulated, and redeployed. Because this capability requires knowledge of the process design and could require code level modifications, a process developer is better suited to perform these repairs than a typical K2 administrator. However, we will briefly cover this capability because it is a powerful tool for resolving run-time errors.

The K2 Process Management utility can be accessed in Visual Studio through the View menu (see Figure 15-14). The utility has three windows:

❑   Environments

❑   Error Profile

❑   View Flow

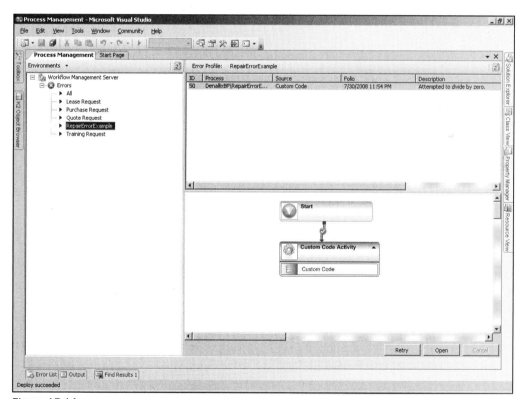

**Figure 15-14**

The Environments window on the left side allows you to select the error profile that you wish to view. The error profiles displayed in this browser are the same profiles that are surfaced through the Workspace Management Console. Selecting a profile in the Environments window populates the Error Profile window on the top right with a list of errors for the selected profile. Selecting a specific error populates the View Flow window on the bottom right to show you a graphical representation of the process instance.

When an error is selected, two options are available.

1.  You can retry the event, which is the same functionality that is surfaced in the Workspace Management Console.

2.  You can open the process instance in the process designer and edit the event item that is causing the problem.

To illustrate the repair error functionality, the process shown in Figure 15-14 is a one-step process with a server event. The code behind the server event attempted to perform a divide-by-zero operation and entered an error state.

We can open the process instance and modify the code.

Once we have completed our corrections, we can redeploy the instance and validate that the instance is no longer in an error state.

Figure 15-15 shows the process now has an additional version associated with it. The changes we made to the process were deployed as a new version, and the instance that was in an error state was reexecuted against the new version of the process.

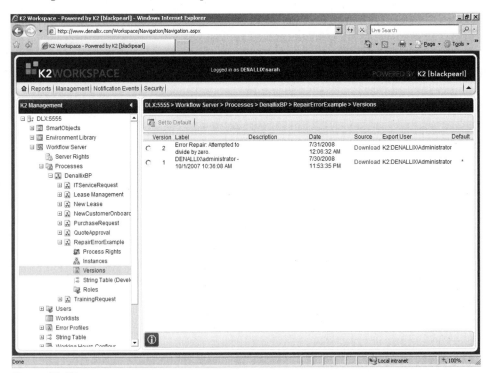

Figure 15-15

*The only process changes that are currently supported through the repair error interface are changes to the event that caused the error. All other process changes will be ignored.*

Repair-error functionality is powerful, but it is important to understand exactly what is happening behind the scenes. When you repair an error, you are directly manipulating the process definition that is stored in the K2 server. These changes do not update the design files that the process designer used to originally deploy the solution, since those files are stored either on the developer's machine or in a source control system. What this means is that if the process designer does not go back and repair the problem in the source files or download the repaired definition from the K2 server, the next version that they deploy will re-introduce the error.

Think of it like a document library. If you take a document that is stored locally on your machine and upload it to a document library and then somebody repairs a spelling mistake in the document stored in the document library, your local copy is out-of-date and uploading the document again will reintroduce the spelling mistake.

# Worklist Administration

K2 users have the ability to manage task items that are assigned specifically to them. K2 administrators on the other hand have the ability manage all task items on the system. This functionality is useful for circumstances where task items are incorrectly assigned to users that are in some way unavailable or unable to redirect the task items. It is also a quick way for an administrator to see how much work is allocated to each user on the system and potentially redirect items to balance the work load.

The Worklists Management interface is located under the Workflow Server heading of the Management Console in the K2 Workspace (see Figure 15-16).

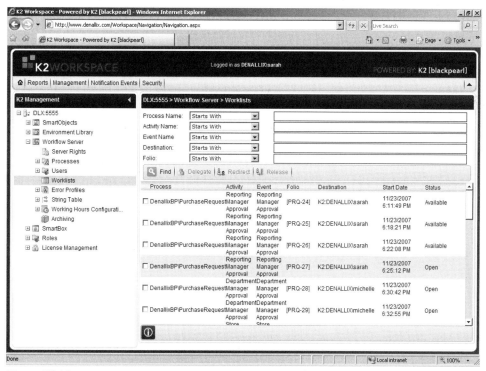

**Figure 15-16**

From this interface a K2 administrator can perform a filtered search of all worklist items that are currently available on the system. You can filter by Process Name, Activity Name, Event Name, Destination, and Folio. For each filter you can specify the type of search comparison from the drop-down list. To see an unfiltered list of task items, leave all the filter criteria blank and click Find.

There are three actions that an administrator can take for selected task items:

❑ Delegate

❑ Redirect

❑ Release

Delegating a task item allows additional defined users to view and perform selected actions on the task item. To perform a delegation:

1. Select the task or tasks you wish to delegate, and click Delegation. This will bring up a search interface where you can search for users to delegate the task to.

2. Once you have searched for and selected the delegated user(s), click Next.

3. On the next screen, select the actions you wish to allow the delegates to perform, and click OK to complete the delegation action.

Redirecting a task item removes the task for the current user and gives the task to the redirect user. To perform a redirect:

1. Select the task or tasks you wish to redirect and click Redirect. This brings up a search interface where you can search for users to redirect the task to.

2. Once you have searched for and selected the redirect users, click OK to complete the redirect action.

Releasing a task item changes the status of the task item from Open/Allocated to Available. This is useful in limited destination slot scenarios where the task does not require that every user in the queue complete the task — for example, when you have a task that is assigned to 10 users but only 1 user out of those 10 needs to complete the item. When the first user opens the task item, the status of the task item for that user is changed from Available to Open. For the other nine users, the task item status is changed to Allocated, which effectively removes the task from their list. Releasing the task item will give the item back to the queue of 10 users and allow another user to open the task item. You can only release tasks that have an Open status. To perform release actions, select the task or tasks that you wish to release and click Release.

# SmartObject Service Management

SmartObject Services are used to create an interface between the K2 platform and business data, whether that be in databases or line-of-business (LOB) systems. As such, SmartObject Services include services that can connect to Microsoft SQL Server, Oracle, SalesForce, Active Directory, and generic Web services among others. These services are application protocols that expose other application properties and methods for use within the K2 platform.

Services are made up of Service Instances and Service Objects. The Service Instances represent the business objects and Service Objects, the properties and methods of the business objects. The services exposed through the K2 platform are the same services that are available in the systems that they originate from and are not recreated.

Some services come standard with the installation of K2 blackpearl. Custom services can be written to interface to other systems and LOB applications. See the K2 Documentation for a detailed list of services that come standard and how to write custom services.

The SmartObjects Services are administered from the Workspace Management Console (see Figure 15-17).

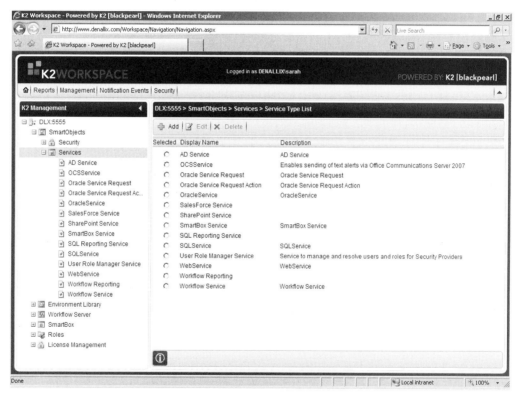

**Figure 15-17**

*Please refer to Chapter 10 for more information on managing SmartObject Services.*

# Archiving

The databases are the most critical components in the K2 blackpearl environment. All state information about completed and running process is stored in the databases. Additionally, all versions of all deployed process definitions and all SmartObject definitions are stored in the databases. The ability to effectively restore a K2 blackpearl environment hinges on being able to restore the databases. Having a good backup strategy for the databases is crucial. In fact it is so crucial that we have dedicated an entire chapter to it. For more information, see Chapter 18.

In this section we will cover archiving, which is the other main database maintenance task. There are two main databases that the workflow engine uses:

❑ K2Server

❑ K2ServerLog

The K2Server database is the transactional database where active and running process instances live. The K2ServerLog database is, as the name suggests, the log database where all the reporting about process instances lives. Archiving focuses on the log database. Unlike the transaction database, the log database will consistently grow over time as more and more process instances are run. At a certain point you will either run out of space for that database or the reporting performance will decrease due to the size of the database. In either of these two cases, the answer is archiving.

The archiving process is fairly straightforward. The first thing you need to do is to create a blank database on the database server where the K2ServerLog database lives. You will be able to move the archive database post-archiving, but the archiving process requires that the databases be on the same server.

*The creation of a new database for archiving purposes will require you to add this database to your disaster recovery plan. For more information on this, please refer to Chapter 18.*

Now that you have your archiving database created, you can navigate to the Archiving application in the Workspace Management console under the Workflow Server heading.

The first thing that the application will ask is how to connect to the database server where the K2ServerLog and Archive database reside. Provide the server name and credentials, and click OK.

To set up the archive, select your K2ServerLog database, provide a date range for instances to be archived, and Select the archive database. The blank archive database will now be updated with the proper tables and structure. After the database is properly formatted, you can click Archive to perform the archive task. Depending upon the amount of data being archived, this process could take some time. It is best to perform this task during off hours because it could degrade reporting performance.

The process of restoring archive data back to the main reporting database is exactly the same as archiving except that you click Restore, which will take the date range reporting information out of the archive database and put it back into the standard reporting database.

# Workspace Web Application Management

The Workspace is the out-of-the-box Web interface for K2 blackpearl. Chapter 20 will introduce you to the various sections of the K2 blackpearl Workspace and show you how to leverage the Workspace functionality. The purpose of this section is to understand the administrative tasks required to keep the Workspace application up and running.

The K2 blackpearl Workspace is a .NET 2.0 Web application that runs on Microsoft Internet Information Server (IIS) and utilizes AJAX programming techniques for a rich user experience.

The Workspace Web application is configured as part of the K2 blackpearl installation. However, it is important as an administrator to understand some of these configuration settings in case they ever need to be manually configured.

All administration of the Workspace application itself is done through IIS. You can access the IIS administration tool by clicking Start and navigating to Administrative Tools. Here, you will find the IIS Manager application.

The location of the Workspace application will depend upon the settings used during installation, but the default location is under the Default Web Site node. To access the Workspace Web application settings, right-click the Workspace node in the tree view and select Properties. This opens the Workspace Properties dialog box.

The Virtual Directory tab shows several settings. These settings are described in the following table.

| Setting | Description |
| --- | --- |
| Local Path | This setting points to the Workspace Site directory under the K2 blackpearl installation path. |
| Application Name | This specifies the name of the application and if changed affects the URL link to the Workspace site. |
| Execute Permissions | This setting specifies the execute permissions and should always be set to Scripts and Executables to ensure proper Workspace functionality. |
| Application Pool | This specifies the application pool that the Workspace application runs under. We will discuss the application pool in more depth later. The default application pool for the Workspace is the K2 blackpearl application pool. |

On the Directory Security tab, make sure that the Authentication and Access Control is properly configured. Click Edit under the Authentication and Access Control section to see the details.

The proper configuration for the Workspace when using Active Directory as the default authentication provider is for only Integrated Windows Authentication to be checked. If Enable Anonymous Access is checked, it will cause authentication problems because the Workspace will not be able to apply any of its security policies.

The ASP.NET tab allows an administrator to change what version of the .NET framework to use for the application. The Workspace is a .NET 2.0 application and should always have that framework selected.

In addition to the settings in IIS, there is a configuration file associated to the Web application (web.config) and it is stored in the installation directory under the Workspace site folder.

Normal administration will not require editing the `web.config` file, but this file does contain a set of environmental keys and connection strings that point to things like the Reporting Server, the K2 server services, the K2 Web services, the K2 SQL databases, and Active Directory. If there are environmental changes that affect the location of these components, then you'll need to manually edit the `web.config` or rerun the K2 blackpearl Configuration Manager.

# Runtime Services Management

A set of Web services is also installed with the K2 blackpearl Workspace and lives under the Runtime Services application in IIS (see Figure 15-18). These services are instrumental in the integration with Microsoft InfoPath and Microsoft Office SharePoint Server and provide other functionality for the Forms Generation Client Event and Out of Office functionality.

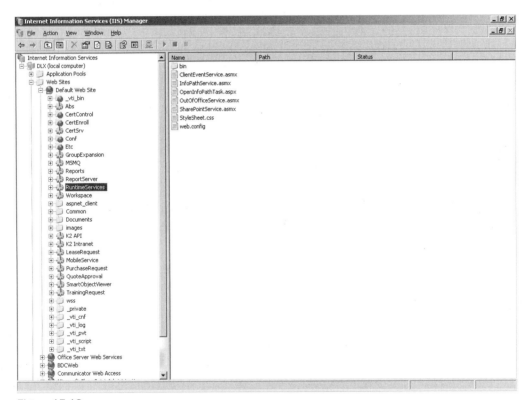

Figure 15-18

The settings for the Web services application should be identical to the settings of the Workspace application except that the Local Path should point to the WebServices/RuntimeServices directory in the K2 blackpearl installation folder.

The Web Services application also has a configuration file (`web.config`) in the Runtime Services directory. Normal administration will not require editing the `web.config`, but there are two settings regarding InfoPath integration that can be set through this configuration file:

❑ **Submit Asynchronously:** This is a flag to set whether an InfoPath submit action should be synchronous or asynchronous.

```
<add key="SubmitAsynchronously" value="false"/>
```

❑ **Start Workflow Asynchronously:** This is a flag to set whether an InfoPath start workflow action should be synchronous or asynchronous.

```
<add key="StartWorkflowAsynchronously" value="true"/>
```

# Workspace Application Pool

The K2 blackpearl installation will create an application pool (named the K2 blackpearl Application Pool) for the Workspace and Runtime Services to run under.

The K2 blackpearl Application Pool can be managed like any other application pool in IIS. The Key setting for the Workspace application pool is the identity that the application pool uses to run the Web sites.

The recommended approach is to us a domain service account to run the K2 blackpearl Application Pool. For correct operation of the K2 Workspace, this account needs to be a member of the IIS_WPG local server group and needs modify rights to the %SYSTEMROOT%\Temp folder. Additionally, the account needs content manager rights in SQL Reporting Services in order to publish any custom Workspace reports to reporting services.

# Workspace Logging

Workspace logging may be required when troubleshooting issues like authentication. The log files that IIS generates are located in the WINDOWS/System32/LogFiles folder. In this folder, you find a folder for each Web site on the server. Folders are identified by `W3SVC<site id>`. For example, the default Web site has a site ID of 1 so the folder is W3SVC1.

# Report Administration

K2 blackpearl reporting is surfaced through the Workspace, but all of the out-of-the-box reporting is Microsoft SQL Reporting Services–based, which means that the reports and the data sources live on the Reporting Services server. This is important to understand as a K2 administrator because there are different interfaces for maintaining the reports than are used for maintaining the Workspace application.

*General usage of the out-of-the-box reports will be discussed in Chapter 20.*

The K2 blackpearl Installation and Configuration Manager installs and configures all of the out-of-the-box reports in SQL Reporting Services. Typical K2 administration will not require making any changes to the reports or their properties, but it is important to understand where the reports reside and what properties are available.

The out-of-the-box K2 blackpearl reports are installed on the Reporting Services server under a Standard Reports folder (see Figure 15-19).

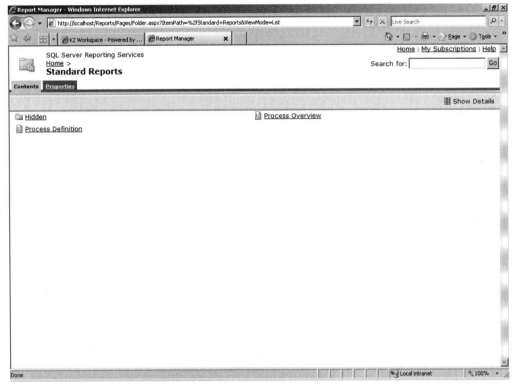

**Figure 15-19**

Two main reports, the Process Overview report and the Process Definition report, are surfaced directly beneath the Standard Reports folder. All other reports live under the Hidden folder. When viewed within Reporting Services by an administrator, each report has four tabs available for managing the report (see Figure 15-20).

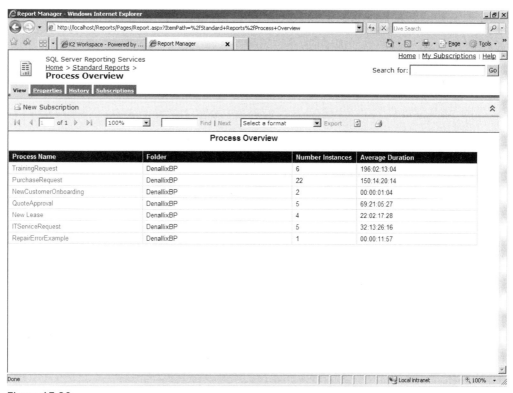

Figure 15-20

❑ **View:** The View tab allows you to view the report as you would through the report view within the K2 Workspace or any other application with a report viewer.

❑ **Properties:** The Properties tab allows you to see and change certain properties about the report. All the functionality surfaced through the Reporting Services interfaces is standard Reporting Services capabilities. We will discuss a couple of the capabilities as they pertain to the proper configuration of the K2 reports, but we will not dive into every aspect of Reporting Services administration.

The Properties tab features several configuration pages. General is the default page. From this page, you can modify the Name and Description of the report. More importantly, you can open the report for editing. Since all of the out-of-the-box K2 reports are simply reporting services reports, administrators can modify the reports to suit their needs whether these needs are aesthetic changes or more complex, query-level changes.

If you need to confirm that a report is using the proper data source, you can do that through the Data Sources page under the Properties tab. For all out-of-the-box K2 reports the data source should point to the `Data Sources/BLACKPEARL` data source.

The K2 blackpearl reports are designed to be real-time reports, but SQL Reporting Services does have the capability to do report caching. Report caching can be configured under the Execution page of the Properties tab. You can configure a caching on a time interval or by a defined schedule.

K2 blackpearl has a security mechanism for determining who has access to see what data through the out-of-the-box K2 reports. If, however, you need to define who can run what reports, you can do that through the Security page. In order for the K2 Workspace to properly leverage the K2 reports, it is important for the account that runs the application pool for the K2 Workspace to have Content Manager access to all the K2 reports.

❑   **History:** The History tab allows you to view any report snapshots that have been generated for the report. The BLACKPEARL data source uses Windows Integrated Security and does not store credentials, so you may find that you are unable to create report snapshots for the out-of-the-box K2 reports.

❑   **Subscriptions:** The Subscriptions tab shows current subscriptions for the logged-in user. As with the history snapshots, you may find that you are unable to create report subscriptions because the BLACKPEARL data source uses Windows Integrated Security rather than storing specific credentials.

# Report Data Source Administration

All of the out-of-the-box K2 reports utilize the BLACKPEARL data source, which is installed under the Data Sources folder (see Figure 15-21).

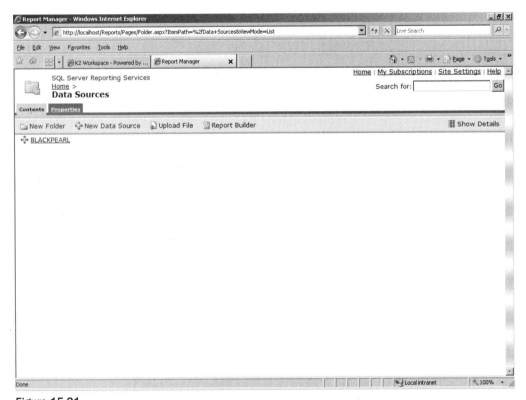

Figure 15-21

Typical K2 administration will not require any modifications to the data source. However, to ensure proper configuration of the data source, we will cover a number of the configuration properties and security settings.

The Properties tab features several important settings (see Figure 15-22). For proper report operation, ensure that the settings are configured as shown in the following table:

| Property | Value |
| --- | --- |
| Name | BLACKPEARL |
| Enable this Data Source | checked |
| Connection Type | SOURCECODE |
| Connection String | Server=[YourK2ServerName];Port=5555;AutoAlias=false |
| Windows Integrated Security | Selected |

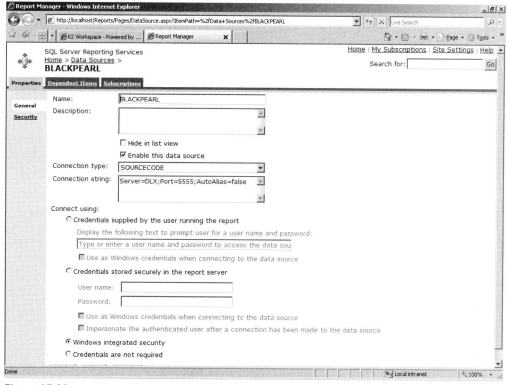

Figure 15-22

Much like the reports themselves, the data source has security to determine what users have access to use the data source. Because we use Windows Integrated Security for the data source, any user that will need to be able to run any of the K2 reports will need browser access to the data source. It is also important to ensure that the account that runs the application pool for the K2 Workspace has Content Manager access to the data source.

# K2 SharePoint Component Administration

K2 blackpearl has extensive out-of-the-box integration with SharePoint Server and Windows SharePoint Services.

All management of K2 blackpearl integration with SharePoint Server and Windows SharePoint Services is done through a K2 for SharePoint administration page (see Figure 15-23) that is added to SharePoint 3.0 Central Administration.

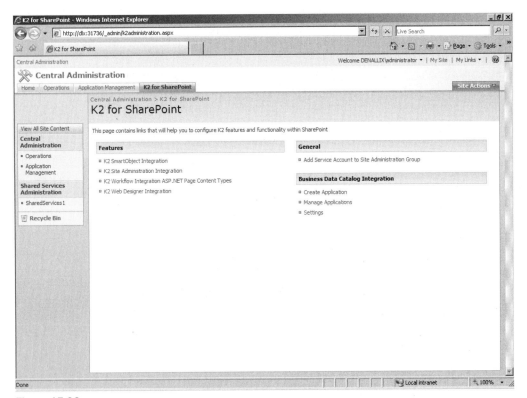

Figure 15-23

## General K2 SharePoint Settings

The General settings section of the K2 SharePoint administration page has one setting that allows you to add the K2 server service account to the site administration group (see Figure 15-24). This setting allows the K2 Server Service account to have the proper permissions to execute actions on the site collection. For example, the K2 process designers allow a user to specify that a SharePoint site be created as a part of a process. During execution of this process the K2 server service account connects to the K2 SharePoint integration Web services that are installed on the SharePoint server and executes the command to create a new site. If the K2 server service account does not have permissions to create sites then this action will fail. It is an important part of K2 SharePoint integration setup to add the K2 server service account to the site administration group.

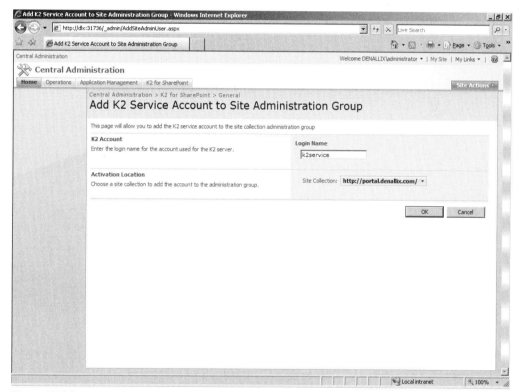

Figure 15-24

## K2 SharePoint Feature Management

Part of the integration of K2 into SharePoint is a number of SharePoint features that can be enabled for your site collections.

## K2 SmartObject Integration

K2 SmartObject integration is a feature that adds a menu item to the Site Actions menu. The menu item, Update K2 SmartObject Service Definition, allows a K2 ServiceObject for the site to be automatically created. This gives a SmartObject designer the capability to leverage SharePoint content on that site through the SmartObject layer.

To enable K2 SmartObject Integration, click the K2 SmartObject Integration link on the K2 for SharePoint administration page, which takes you to a page where you can activate or deactivate the feature for the specified site collection (see Figure 15-25)

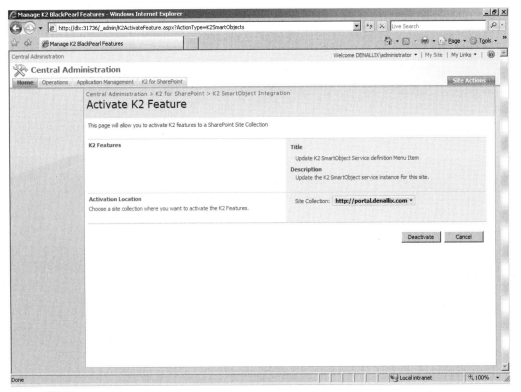

Figure 15-25

## K2 Site Administration Integration

K2 Site Administration Integration is a feature that adds K2 feature administration links to the Site Settings for sites within a site collection. For example, this feature gives you the ability to manage processes that are bound to SharePoint events or manage K2 SharePoint integrated processes.

To enable K2 Site Administration Integration, click the K2 Site Administration Integration link on the K2 for SharePoint administration page, which takes you to a page where you can activate or deactivate the feature for the specified site collection.

## K2 Workflow Integration ASP.NET Page Content Types

K2 Workflow Integration ASP.NET Page Content Types is a feature that allows K2 SharePoint Integrated processes to use the K2 task completion pages that inherit from the out-of-the-box SharePoint task completion pages.

To enable K2 Workflow Integration ASP.NET Page Content Types, click the K2 Workflow Integration ASP.NET Page Content Types link on the K2 for SharePoint administration page, which takes you to a page where you can activate or deactivate the feature for the specified site collection.

## K2 Web Designer Integration

K2 Web Designer Integration is a feature that adds the K2 Web Designer capability to sites within the specified site collection. The K2 Web Designer is accessed by going to a list or library in a site and selecting the K2 Web Designer from the Settings menu (see Figure 15-26).

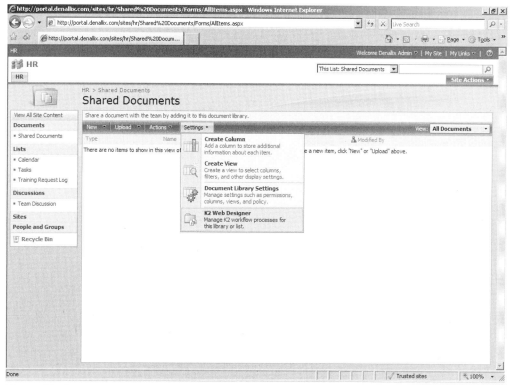

Figure 15-26

To enable K2 Web Designer Integration, click the K2 Web Designer Integration link on the K2 for SharePoint administration page, which takes you to a page where you can activate or deactivate the feature for the specified site collection.

# K2 BDC Application Management

The K2 Business Data Catalog section of the K2 for SharePoint Administration page allows administrators to create and manage K2 BDC applications. BDC applications can be created from any existing K2 SmartObjects. Chapter 13 provides more details on how to create BDC applications.

To manage deployed K2 BDC applications, click the Manage K2 BDC Applications link from the Business Data Catalog section of the K2 for SharePoint Administration page. This takes you to the management page (see Figure 15-27), where you can see a list of K2 BDC applications for the selected site collection. From this interface you can delete any unwanted applications by selecting the application and clicking Delete.

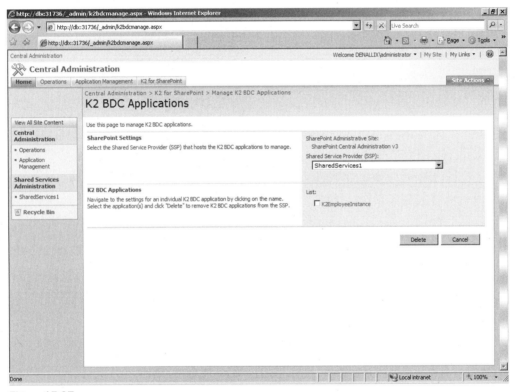

Figure 15-27

There are two configuration settings on the settings page for the Business Data Catalog integration section. The settings, K2 Server Name and K2 Server Port, are set up as a part of the K2 installation and are used by the K2 BDC applications to connect to the appropriate K2 server and execute the BDC SmartObject methods.

# K2 Tasklist Web Part Management

K2 blackpearl provides a Web part for viewing and interacting with task items that are assigned to users by K2 blackpearl processes. To utilize this Web part on SharePoint pages, you will first need to deploy it.

To deploy the K2 Tasklist Web part, navigate to the Operations page in SharePoint 3.0 Central Administration, and click the Solution Management link under the Global Configuration section. Click the K2worklistwebpart in the list of Web parts (see Figure 15-28).

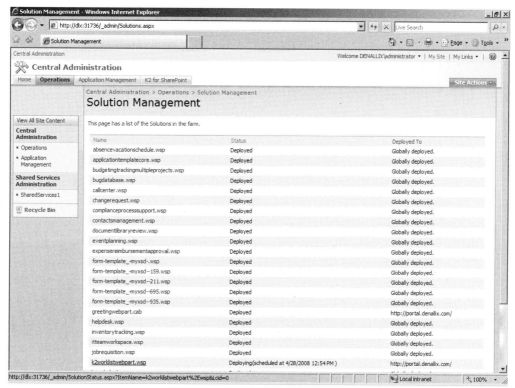

**Figure 15-28**

Then click Deploy Solution (see Figure 15-29).

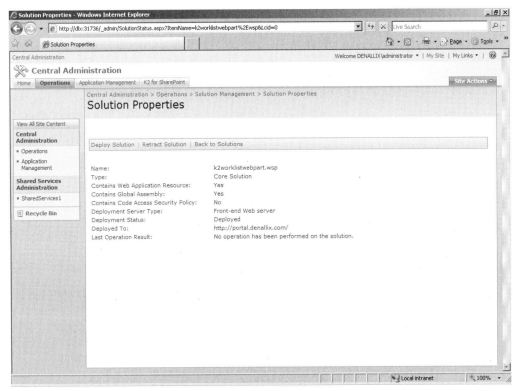

Figure 15-29

The K2 Worklist Web part will now be available for users to add to their SharePoint sites. If for any reason you need to retract the deployment of the K2 Worklist Web part, you can come back into this interface and click Retract Solution.

# The Configuration Manager

The K2 blackpearl Configuration Manager is an environment configuration utility. The Configuration Manager is used during installation to configure the environment for the first time, but it can also be used post-installation to make environment-level configuration changes.

To start the Configuration Manager navigate to the K2 blackpearl folder in the All Programs section of the Windows Start menu and select K2 blackpearl Configuration Manager.

The Configuration Manager uses a wizard interface to guide you through the configuration process. The following table illustrates the changes that can be made through this interface:

| Modification | Description |
|---|---|
| Update License Key | An alternative to the Workspace interface for updating a K2 server license. |
| Workspace Web Site Location | The Web site where the Workspace is or should be installed. |
| Workspace Application Pool Account | The account under which the Workspace application is run. |
| SQL Reporting Services Web Site Name | The Web site where reporting services are installed. |
| SQL Reporting Services Web Site Virtual Directory | The virtual directory on the reporting services Web site where reporting services are installed. |
| Host Service Port | The port which the Host Service uses for communication. The default is 5555. |
| Workflow Service Port | The port which the Workflow Service uses for communication. The default is 5252. |
| E-mail Server Name | The e-mail server that the Workflow Service will deliver task and e-mail notifications through. |
| Database Locations | The locations of the various K2 databases. |
| K2 Administrator Account | The account that should have administrative privileges to the K2 environment. |
| K2 Service Account | The account under which the K2 blackpearl Service should run. |

Configuration Manager changes require a server reboot before taking effect.

# Summary

In this chapter we covered the main components that make up a K2 blackpearl environment and the routine administration associated to these components. We started by looking at the K2 blackpearl Service and how it is a pluggable Host Server that provides flexibility and extensibility. Next, we took a look at the management capabilities surrounding the service, from license management, to error handling, to role management. We also discussed database archiving and the management capabilities for the K2 SharePoint integration components. Finally, we took a look at the Configuration Manager as a way to make high-level configuration changes in the environment.

The next chapter will take a look at security and permission administration in the K2 blackpearl environment.

# 16

# Administering Permissions and Security

**Jason Montgomery**

Security is an important element of any system, and K2 blackpearl has a good offering of security features; however, software security features do equate to a secure system. Like all software, the security of K2 blackpearl goes well beyond the administration and management of authentication (who can login) and authorization (what they can access) or the APIs that provide the use and extensibility of security features, which are all certainly important critical core security features. Instead, the security of any individual system requires a holistic, enterprise-wide approach starting with buy-in from the highest levels of management, mandated to all employees through the policies, including the ability to execute and enforce these policies in an effective manner, while balancing the business needs with the security controls so that information security doesn't present unnecessary barriers to actually getting the work done. What a daunting task! This is because information security is not simply an IT function; it is also a business function.

With that said, there are many facets of information security to cover. When you survey K2 blackpearl, including all the interdependent systems, a picture emerges of an overwhelming task of securing it all — a task that's often ignored due to a lack of knowledge or put off due to time constraints. Since this book is not strictly for developers, this chapter will provide security administration from a business perspective as well as the technical aspects of K2 blackpearl's security administration for K2 administrators and programmers. The first half of this chapter briefly covers a broad spectrum of security principals by providing security awareness. The second half of this chapter delves into the specifics of K2 blackpearl's security offerings and how to best apply those security principals.

This chapter covers the following topics:

- ❏ Defining security
- ❏ Planning a secure K2 blackpearl deployment
- ❏ Deploying a secure K2 blackpearl installation

❑   The K2 blackpearl security landscape

❑   Secure development practices

❑   Troubleshooting security issues

# What Is Security?

According to Breach Security's "Web Hacking Incident Database 2007 Annual Report,"[1] 67% of the incidents in 2007 were for-profit motivated, and in 44% of the incidents, sensitive information was stolen. The trend of security incidents and issues year after year is on a consistent upward trajectory and the increasingly common goal of computer hackers is profit, meaning that the systems and information compromised are likely to be used to cause harm to customers, shareholders, employees, and so on. The report also makes clear that the numbers are only the tip of the iceberg because many incidents aren't publically reported or the organizations are not aware that any security breach or security incident has even taken place. As network and operating systems' overall security improves, attackers are targeting Web applications more and more. Information Security must be taken seriously by all organizations. Organizations must be vigilant to protect employee information, customer information, and internal private or proprietary information.

According to FISMA (Federal Information Security Management Act of 2002, U.S. Code, Title 44, Chapter 35, Subchapter III, § 3542) "information security" is defined as:

> . . . protecting information and information systems from unauthorized access, use, disclosure, disruption, modification, or destruction in order to provide —
>
> (A)   integrity, which means guarding against improper information modification or destruction, and includes ensuring information nonrepudiation and authenticity;
>
> (B)   confidentiality, which means preserving authorized restrictions on access and disclosure, including means for protecting personal privacy and proprietary information; and
>
> (C)   availability, which means ensuring timely and reliable access to and use of information.

These concepts, *integrity, confidentiality,* and *availability,* are commonly referred to as the CIA Triad. When thinking and planning the overall security of any computer system or systems, it helps to view securing them in this light.

## *Integrity*

There are two types of integrity to consider:

❑   **Data integrity:** Which is concerned with data modifications being accomplished properly.

❑   **Source integrity:** Which is concerned with confirming information actually originated from the source that it claims to come from. This also provides nonrepudiation (for example, the sender can't deny that they actually sent a message or performed an action).

## Data Integrity

An example of data integrity would be if a user or system is able to make an unauthorized modification to data as it moves from System A to System B; this would violate integrity; banks, as well as their customers, are especially concerned with data integrity when it comes to fund transfers.

## Source Integrity

With source integrity, in certain situations being able to verify that a piece of information originated from a particular person or system can prevent types of fraud. If messages are forged, much like the problems that plague the Internet e-mail system today, users can easily be tricked into giving up sensitive information (known as phishing). Some ways to help protect against data integrity violations are good data design, the the use of transactional operations, input validation, RAID parity, and mirroring technology, and encryption hash algorithms that can detect the modification of data while in transit or at rest. To provide source security, digital signatures can be used to validate the sender and additionally verify that the message was received unmodified.

# Confidentiality

Confidentiality is all about keeping secrets. Some common methods to help ensure confidentiality are:

- ❑ Authentication
- ❑ Authorization
- ❑ Encryption

For example, if a Human Resources system requires storing Social Security numbers in a database, the application accessing the database and database itself must enforce authentication (users) and authorization (roles) to prevent unauthorized users from accessing that data. However, where most organizations get into trouble is by shrugging off the fact that the database administrator (DBA) as well as the local Administrators group have access (by default the Local Administrators group is added to the sysadmin role in SQL Server). This means that not only can the DBA access the Social Security numbers, but additionally every domain administrator can as well (if the local Administrators' group hasn't been removed from the dbo role in SQL Server and the SQL Server is a domain member). This is when encryption at the data column level must be deployed to prevent those who have access but are not authorized to see the information from doing so. Additionally the Local Administrators' group should be removed from the sysadmin role within SQL Server and replaced with a domain group that represents the SQL DBAs.

In order for an organization to know what data is confidential, it's important to go through a data classification process where all the information within a company is given a classification label (for example, Business Sensitive, Business Confidential, and so on.). Government agencies often already have these classifications defined. Once the information is classified, appropriate controls can be applied to protect data based on policy.

## *Availability*

This concept is straightforward: If the data is not available for some reason, this tenant has been violated. Some examples of availability problems:

❑ The database server is down.

❑ A network switch/router/firewall/cable is malfunctioning or incorrectly configured.

❑ Newly deployed code has bugs and is causing the system or parts of the system to fail or perform poorly or hang.

❑ The server and network are unavailable because a hacker has performed a denial of service (DoS) attack.

Initially, it may not be obvious what availability has to do with information security but when you consider different scenarios, it becomes apparent why availability is in the definition of information security. Consider a business that strictly relies on the Internet, such as an e-commerce company. Every minute the Web site is down, that company is losing potential customers, sometimes permanently as consumers may switch to another, more reliable e-commerce Web site, causing major financial losses. Also consider the military — if a network or system that directly supports soldiers in the field goes down, it could limit their effectiveness or even cost lives. Some ways to protect systems against availability issues:

❑ Making sure to plan for the proper load when building the systems and network

❑ Using network and system redundancy with a backup UPS or power generator

❑ Preventing unauthorized users from accessing critical systems

❑ Preventing developers from deploying code to production systems before software has been adequately tested

❑ Having solid testing processes and procedures before deploying new code

❑ Having a back-out plan if deployed code happens to fail even after testing

❑ Having data stored redundantly (RAID)

❑ Having replacement hardware on hand in the case of a hardware failure

❑ Designing an IT infrastructure that helps mitigate DoS attacks

Also, more extreme scenarios need to be considered. Does the organization have a Business Continuity Plan/disaster recovery plan? How long would an organization survive if the primary networking facility became unavailable for an extended period of time or permanently (for example, fire, hurricane, and so on)? Would the business recover? Chapter 18 will delve more into disaster recovery with K2 blackpearl.

One potential way of mitigating a long term availability failure with K2 blackpearl is by having a backup manual process that doesn't rely on any IT systems. This, of course, would require up-to-date available physical paper copies of any forms needed for a given process. This could allow an organization to function, at least partially, without the system or network for perhaps a few days if needed. It's also critical that employees are familiar with the alternate manual process as well as the automated one. Finally, a method for importing the outcomes of the manual process into the system after it's been restored would be necessary. Certain core features may be missing while it's offline, such as calculations or inventory lookups, so it might not be possible to have a full manual functioning process. This requires careful thought and planning.

## Which Tenet of Security Is Most Important?

It's worth noting that certain types of organizations may focus on one tenant more than the others. For example, the military would be most concerned with confidentiality of information and a financial institution may be more interested in protecting data integrity. This isn't to say that the other tenants of security aren't important or are ignored, it's just that one may stand out as clearly more critical to protect to the organization.

## The Three "A"s

There is also another common security triad used in information security that doesn't completely fall under the CIA Triad that is important for organizations to understand as well. These are *authentication*, *authorization*, and *accounting* (auditing), often called AAA or Triple A.

❑ **Authentication:** Is responsible with identifying the user or system as they access a system. Actual identity can be a challenge to validate; just because a username and password have been presented doesn't necessarily prove the identity of that human or system. It just proves whoever is gaining access to the system knows the credentials needed to log in. To help resolve this difficult issue, multi-factor authentication methods will increase the ability of a system to validate the identity of the user logging in. In certain cases a username and password will suffice; in other cases, multi-factor authentication using Smart Cards can be employed to further assist in protecting assets. Additionally, an account shared between multiple people would violate this principal, since there would be no way to identify the actual person logging in (and no way to provide accounting as defined below).

---

### Multi-Factor Authentication

There are three factors defined for authentication. They are known as something you have (for example, a Smart Card or token), something you know (for example, a password or PIN), and something you are (for example, your fingerprint). In order to have true multi-factor authentication, it must use two of the three factors and the two factors cannot be of the same type.

---

❑ **Authorization:** Speaks to what a user has access to do. These are the roles and privileges assigned to users to allow them to do what they can within a system. It's important to note that it is not the responsibility of a system administrator or database administrator to decide who is authorized to access a given system, data store, Web site, and so on. While it is the administrator's responsibility to grant access, it falls on the Data Owner to permit it. The *Data Owner* would be a top-level business manager that is responsible for that line of business. The *Data Custodian* would be the database and/or system administrators who manage the resource on behalf of the Data Owner.

❏ **Accounting:** Tracks users, as authentication tracks what they do, and records successful and unsuccessful attempts to log in or gain access to specific data. This is critical for auditing systems and accountability. It's what gives administrators and auditors visibility into system abuse, attempted abuse, or problems with a system.

Applying AAA throughout the organization helps protect information assets and additionally provides a way to validate (audit) that assets are protected, or if a breach has occurred or has been attempted.

K2 blackpearl has many features to help facilitate AAA and CIA. Additionally, good software development practices and proper architecture planning and configuration can improve the implementations of CIA and AAA.

# A Very Brief Introduction to Risk Analysis

There's no such thing as 100% security.[2] Or to phrase it another way, there's no such thing as zero risk, so this should not be the goal of information security. Every organization has a threshold of what is an acceptable loss if any of the tenants of the CIA Triad described earlier are violated. A better, more realistic goal is to calculate, estimate, or "ballpark" the level of risk to an enterprise's assets and attempt to lower the risk to these to an acceptable level. Before going any further it's important to mention that there are entire books written on the topic of risk analysis and by no means will the couple of paragraphs here attempt to be exhaustive, but instead hope to convey a framework for thinking about the information security of these systems and how much effort should be applied to a system's security.

Risk analysis helps an organization prioritize where to direct their information security programs based on the goals and priorities of the business itself. Without risk analysis, the security functions within an organization will choose priorities and goals whether they align with the priorities of the business or not; this disconnect can often cause conflict and even confusion within the organization as the functional business units clash with the security controls forced onto the organization. This often results in asymmetric and sometimes odd security policies and controls, and the inconsistent enforcement of security rules imposed on an organization. This isn't to say that when the business priorities align with the security functions of an organization that the security policy and controls won't cause friction within the organization. However, a strong case can be made for such policies and security controls, and thus it will be easier to get buy-in from management as well as support from the employees within the organization. It's important to have a basic, employee-targeted security training program because without it users may be lax or resistant to security controls if they don't understand why they have been put in place.

There are two common approaches to risk analysis — *quantitative risk analysis* and *qualitative risk analysis*:

❏ **Quantitative risk analysis:** Focuses on assigning objective numeric values to assets, enumerating the vulnerabilities and threats to these assets and the probability of these threats occurring. Once these risks are assessed, the cost of each countermeasure is weighed against the value of the assets they protect and economically reasonable safeguards are chosen — all based on the numbers. This can be a difficult and time-consuming approach, since it requires intimate knowledge of assets' worth, as well as intimate knowledge of all the risks, including the probability such risks can occur and the visible and hidden costs it would take to mitigate any given vulnerability. For the inexperienced, such a detailed analysis is time-consuming and has the potential to paralyze the risk assessment process. This process can take so long that by the time the organization is ready to roll out the countermeasures, the environment has changed significantly affecting the outcome of the risk analysis since all the information gathered is now out-of-date. Quantitative risk analysis is often done by a third-party consulting firm that specializes in risk analysis, and/or specialized software packages are used so that the analysis can be completed in a timely fashion.

❑ **The more common approach, qualitative risk analysis:** Focuses not on hard concrete numbers but instead on estimations and even informed opinions. The assets and risks to asset values are ranked categorically or numerically and then dealt with in order of highest risk to lowest risk. This can be done fairly quickly; however, since there aren't hard numbers, it may difficult to tell if a chosen countermeasure is cost-effective.[3]

This brief introduction on risk assessment aside, the important thing to understand about risk analysis is this: *One of the main goals is to help direct the focus to the items requiring the most attention* — those items that are most valuable and have the highest risk. Understanding which assets have higher values/higher risks prevents the wasting of time and money on systems with either little value or on items with low risk. Then time and effort can be put towards administrative controls — that is, the policies, procedures, standards, guidelines, logical or technical controls that are software based, and finally physical controls that protect the IT infrastructure from physical threats in the real world.

This brings us back to K2 blackpearl. Depending on the particulars of a K2 blackpearl implementation in a given environment, it stands to reason that the K2 blackpearl system can have data from just about any system in an enterprise pass through it and/or be stored within it. It also could potentially contain the credentials to pull data from back-end systems as well. Since data from many different systems can be accessible to or stored within K2 blackpearl and a large part of the enterprise may rely on it to function, it has the potential to be a highly valued asset with many potential risks.

All this to say: *Because of the type of data potentially moving through K2 blackpearl and the heavy reliance on K2 as a core system within an enterprise, an organization cannot afford to gloss over the security of such an important core piece of technology, K2 blackpearl, including the systems that K2 blackpearl interacts with and are dependent on.*

# The Security Policy and Regulatory and Legal Compliance

While risk assessments can help guide the security posture and the safeguards placed on particular IT systems, there are other factors that will require additional due care to be taken with IT systems — namely the Security Policy as well as laws and/or regulations that apply to a particular industry, public corporation, or government organization.

## The Security Policy

The Security Policy is an organic document that "states in writing how a company plans to protect the company's physical and information technology assets."[4]

Familiarity with the Security Policy is important because it defines at a high level the expectations placed on employees in the organization to maintain the information security for the organization. Whether they are employees, contractors, or consultants, everyone should be aware of the security posture and policies of the organization. The security policy must be mandatory for ALL employees, no exceptions. If an organization does not have a Security Policy, that also may reveal a bit about its security posture. The responsibility lies with the decision makers at the highest level of an organization to set the security expectations through the Security Policy. Even if one does not exist, it is still important that each individual involved practice due diligence in security, looking to industry standards and best practices. Another important feature of the security policy is that it provides a foundation for enforcement. If an organization has a security policy in place without enforcement, then the policy will not work, and the information security of the organization suffers.[5, 6]

There may also be other documents to be aware of when deploying a new K2 blackpearl installation or designing a workflow for an existing K2 installation. The primary stakeholders must be aware of and current on industry and organizational policies, standards, guidelines, and procedures so care is taken to make sure a deployment can have the authority to operate within an organization. It's not unheard of for a system that meets a functional business need to be built, paid for, and deployed and then have its "authority to operate" pulled and be taken off the network because the system contains unprotected sensitive data or suffers from serious security flaws.

For example, the Defense Information System Agency (DISA) of the U.S. Department of Defense (DoD) has Security Technical Implementation Guides (STIGs) — these in combination with the NSA Guides act as the standard for how to configure computer systems that operate on any DoD network. When a new system is added to the network, it is required to be configured in accordance with these standards. Another example is PCI DSS, the Payment Card Industry (PCI), which is made up of the major credit card companies. It released the Data Security Standards (DSS) as a baseline for securing systems and networks that handle payment-processing information.

Aside from the internal documentation created by an organization (the policies, procedures, policies, guidelines, and standards), there may also be regulations and laws placed on organizations that mandate certain expectations and consequences for failing to protect information within an organization.

## Regulatory and Legal Compliance

Legal and regulatory compliance may dictate how an organization can store, protect, and share data, or perhaps how long it should be stored, what should be logged and audited, and so on. It's critical to talk with the Legal department about the implications of laws on a K2 blackpearl process, especially if it contains sensitive or classified data, personally identifiable information (PII), financials, and so on. Some laws will require auditability, others may require the proper handling of sensitive data, and others yet may require public disclosure of any security incident that happens within an organization.

The following table provides some examples of U.S laws, the industry/organizations they affect, and a brief description of what protection they attempt to provide. Make sure to check not only the laws in the country the organization is headquartered in but also the laws of other countries the organization does business in or has a business presence in, as these laws may also apply to the organization.

| Laws | Industry/Organization Affected | Brief Description |
| --- | --- | --- |
| Privacy Act of 1974 | U.S. federal/state/local government | Helps prevent the abuse of privacy information. |
| FISMA – Federal Information Security Act of 2002 | U.S. federal government and affiliated parties (for example, contractors) | Increases IT Security by mandating a common set of processes for managing and configuring IT systems. |
| The E-Government Act of 2002 | U.S. federal government | Helps protect personal privacy and national security information. |
| HIPPA – Health Insurance Portability and Accountability Act | Healthcare/ health insurance industry | Helps prevent fraud and abuse. |
| Gramm-Leach-Bliley Act | Financial firms | Requires a formal security plan as well as protections for customers to help prevent the exposure of sensitive information. |
| Sarbanes-Oxley Act of 2002 (SOX) | U.S. public company boards; accounting firms | Mandates requirements for financial reporting. |

The bottom line is this: Talk with each stakeholder whose data will be accessed via K2 blackpearl or the business owner of the system being developed. They should be aware of laws and regulations that apply to the organization's industry or organization. Also check with the legal department for laws and regulations that must be followed, and finally make sure to follow industry security best practices when setting up each system that will interface with K2 blackpearl. Practicing due care and due diligence by following industry security standards and best practices can provide protection from negligence. Remember, ignorance will not protect an organization from liability. The final ultimate responsibility for information security falls on the highest-level managers, not the technicians.

# Deploying a Secure K2 blackpearl Installation

Deploying K2 blackpearl can be quite the undertaking, since it has the capability to integrate and interoperate with just about any other system in the enterprise. Before delving into the aspects of security that K2 blackpearl provides within the product, it's important to start with securing the environment K2 will run in. This includes the network infrastructure, server operating systems, and perimeter security such as firewalls.

## *Organize, Plan, Test, and Document*

Get organized! Take the time to plan, document, and map out the K2 blackpearl deployment taking care to include all the software that will integrate with K2 blackpearl, be it Windows SharePoint Server 3.0 (WSS/MOSS), SQL Reporting Services 2005, IIS, and so on . Your organization may already have guidelines for systems documentation requirements. If so, start with those. However, they may not be exhaustive, so it will be helpful to add additional information.

The documentation will start with the deployment plan and architectural template discussed in Chapter 5. Additionally, it will be helpful to document all the additional pieces of information needed to set up and configure the entire infrastructure from scratch. This will also be critical for Business Continuity/disaster recovery (see Chapter 18 for more information on disaster recovery). The K2 blackpearl *Installation Guide* in the K2 blackpearl documentation also contains an Excel Workbook to document the installation process.

The following list contains information that will be helpful to document. This list is not exhaustive, but will provide a good starting point:

- ❑ The DNS names and corresponding IP addresses for each Web site, database server, and also server names (as there may be multiple names and or IPs per system).

- ❑ Internet Information Services sites and applications that will access K2 blackpearl and the corresponding IIS configuration settings.

- ❑ SSL certificates required, including the fully qualified domain name (FQDN).

- ❑ The software and subcomponents and the corresponding systems, based on the architectural template used from Chapter 5.

- ❑ Installation folders where the applications will be installed (security best practices recommend software be installed on a separate drive then the OS partition to protect against canonicalization attacks).

- ❑ Planned application log folders for each server. Also document how verbose each log will be set on which servers for each corresponding service.

- ❑ Service accounts that will run the services of the software being installed.

- ❑ A logical network diagram, including firewall locations and the corresponding network ports that must be opened for the systems to function.

If unfamiliar with the K2 blackpearl installation process and configuration, invest in the time to become familiar with it by installing it on a virtual PC first, taking care to test the installation process, permissions required to install, how the product handles security internally, and operating system privileges required for the proper functioning of the system. Virtualization provides rollback abilities so mistakes can be undone, which can save time if problems are encountered while getting familiar with the software. This virtual image will serve as the proof of concept for an actual deployment and a playground for trying new things, patches, configuration settings, and so on. It's critical to have a level of competence and comfort with software before deploying it on any system for consumption, be it a development, staging, or production system. Once the system has been deployed and adopted, it is often difficult or impossible to make major changes to the installation since it may affect the availability of the system, meaning your organization may have to live with any mistakes you make during deployment.

Familiarity with the software, good documentation, and planning reduces the possibility of making mistakes during the final production installations (including test and/or staging environments) and assists with avoiding skipping important steps in the installation and securing process. This process will also serve to create an architecture diagram of the entire installation,, which is often required as part of a project anyway but is often missing. Not only will this documentation assist in troubleshooting, but it will also help other administrators to understand what's been installed, how it's configured, what accounts are used, and what other dependent systems are involved. This will facilitate understanding of the K2 system and all its interdependencies, improving the organization's ability to troubleshoot issues, especially in the situation where the individual who integrated the servers into the environment is unavailable for some reason. Additionally, take extensive notes during the installation, documenting every step. Complete documentation on how to install and configure each software component as well as each server as it has been configured in the environment will aid in disaster recovery/Business Continuity plans.

If the availability of the K2 workflow engine affects an organization's ability to complete one of its core business functions and ends up creating a work stoppage, financial losses may result. Good up-to-date documentation and training *at least* one other administrator on the K2 blackpearl deployments is critical. For example, assume that the K2 server goes down and there are 75 users sitting with nothing to do, that is, orders aren't getting processed or customers aren't receiving the support or attention they need. If administrators are unable to bring the system back online because the one who did the installation and configuration is on vacation or was a consultant, that can potentially lead to real problems. Since availability is one of the core tenants of security, an unavailable system is classified as a security threat and should be taken into account during the risk assessment, and work should be done to mitigate it to reduce downtime. To help mitigate such risks, it's critical that multiple administrators understand how the K2 system has been integrated into their environment, what servers are involved, and what accounts are used to run the services, and how everything is configured. Also, a solid regularly updated and validated disaster recovery plan should be in place that includes all of the documentation created as part of the installation and system hardening process.

Finally, this documentation will serve as a checklist for all the items that need to be configured and the areas to focus on when securing.

## Securing the Environment

After having planned and mapped out the K2 blackpearl installation and installation completes successfully, the final step is to *harden*, or increase the security, of all the servers and services that have been installed. Depending on the architectural template chosen, there may be only one server to harden or several.

There are industry and government standards for hardening operating systems, with varying levels of protections to implement depending on what the system is used for and the types of information available to the system. Initially, this process can be time-consuming and somewhat overwhelming. The goal is to automate this process as much as possible so it's repeatable and can be done quickly. Once the task is completed, schedule to resecure it on an ongoing basis because over time security settings often are removed or changed by administrators or application patches. If a security configuration change should be made permanent, don't forget to go back and update the documentation and automation files.

There are sources available on the Internet that have security checklists based on industry standards for configuring operating systems, networking equipment, application servers, and so on. By building up a library of Active Directory Group Policies, Security Templates, Registry files (.reg) and scripts, a system (for example, Web server, database server, K2 blackpearl server) can be realistically hardened in a reasonably short period of time. There is a learning curve to server hardening, so it's a skill that needs to be developed, but once an administrator has familiarity with the process, it doesn't take as much time.

There are security benchmarks and scoring tools available as well to help automate the scanning, detection, and configuring of systems. One place to download tools and checklists is The Center for Internet Security (www.cisecurity.org). The NSA and Department of Defense also have guides and checklists available online for the Gold and Platinum security standards for operating systems as well as Security Implementation Guides for server products. The Defense Information Systems Agency's guides are located at http://iase.disa.mil/stigs/index.html and the NSA guides are located at www.nsa.gov/snac.

> There is a level of risk involved with securing any system without understanding the relationship between security settings on the system and the affect it has on the software installed on that system, including the system's ability to communicate with another system on the network. Some recommend security settings can and will completely break either the applications or the servers themselves. Some of the Local Security Policy settings may need to be set domain-or forest-wide to maintain system communication. While automating system security is critical, make sure to test settings or groups of related settings incrementally. That way, if a particular setting breaks something on a server, it's easy to roll back the change and document the incompatibility so that it won't be accidently applied later.

## Principal of Least Privilege

The principal of least privilege is a simple but important concept. The principal is this: Grant only the minimum amount of access required for an account to accomplish the tasks required and no more.

This applies to both users and services. If a user needs visibility to a K2 blackpearl process, it would be inappropriate to grant the user the "process admin" permission, although that would certainly work. The problem is that it would give the user the ability to go beyond what's required of them, and they could potentially cause problems. Instead make sure to grant them the View Participate permission (more on K2 blackpearl permissions later in this chapter).

This principal not only applies to users, but it also applies to service accounts. K2 blackpearl's Host Server runs as a Windows Service; during installation, it is configured with an Identity (typically called a service account). In order for K2 blackpearl to function properly, it needs to be granted certain permissions and privileges within the operating system. What's tempting for most administrators is to just add a service account to the Administrators' group on the local machine to try to solve a problem the service may be having. While this may solve the problem, it also may create a more serious problem. If, by chance, the service has a vulnerability and it gets exploited, then because the service is running with administrative rights, it may not only have administrative access to the computer with the vulnerable service but potentially to the entire domain.

A common argument against applying least privilege is that a user wouldn't do the wrong thing, for example, "Bob would never delete those files with critical corporate data," or "Bob wouldn't steal that sensitive data because we trust him, so we don't mind making him an administrator on that server or granting him rights to those files." There are a couple of problems with this argument. Bob may accidently do something he didn't mean to or if Bob's account is compromised, someone will do something with Bob's account that he shouldn't have been able to. Either way, Bob may be held responsible for the actions on that computer when in actuality, the fault is not necessarily Bob's but with the lax security policy or the implementation of the policy.

The principal of Least Privilege can protect employees, systems, and the organization.

### Reducing the Footprint

This step provides several security benefits. If you reduce the software installed, fewer software patches will be required and therefore administrative overhead will be reduced. This also reduces the potential attack vectors available for hackers to exploit by eliminating potential vulnerabilities and therefore decreasing risk. Last, it will free up system resources (memory, disk, CPU), which will also have a positive effect on the availability of a system.

The principal goes something like this:

❑    Install only software that is required for the server to function.

❑    Disable/uninstall everything else.

The more software installed on the system and the more OS features enabled on a server, the greater the potential that the system will contain vulnerable components to exploit. A skilled hacker could use multiple vulnerabilities in multiple services on the same machine in concert to take a seemly limited exploit and escalate it to full--blown access. So not only should administrators not install unneeded software, they also should uninstall and disable operating system features that aren't required to support the application on the server and additionally disable any Windows Services that are not needed. Once the service is marked Disabled, the Discretionary Access Control List (DACL) for that service should then be modified to only allow two accounts have full control and the rest just have read permissions. This prevents a service from being started. The Windows Service security descriptor and startup modes (Automatic, Manual, and Disabled) can be set using the Security Configuration and Analysis Tool or using the `sc.exe` command-line tool. Using these tools, `.inf` files or batch files can be created to automate this process for many different servers, providing that the accounts being configured are the same across those different servers (for example, Administrators, SYSTEM). The following table shows the permissions that should be granted to a disabled service to prevent it from being started by anyone but an administrator. Save a copy of these files for automating system hardening, and documentation. It will come in handy if the server needs to be rebuilt from scratch.

| Account | Discretionary Access Control List (DACL) Assignment |
| --- | --- |
| Local Administrators | Full Control |
| SYSTEM | Full Control |
| Users | Read |

As mentioned previously, this also provides the benefit of freeing up additional memory and system resources for the server to use, so it's really a win-win.

Make sure to test all settings on a test system first before attempting this on a production system as some services are required for the K2 server to function properly. Some services may need to be reenabled during software installation or patching. For example, in some environments there are requirements to disabled the Scheduled Task Service. Normally this isn't a big deal, but if you are using Clustering Services and an attempt is made to install or patch the cluster aware software, the installation cluster node may require the Scheduled Task Service to automatically kick-off the installation on the other cluster node. In some cases it may be necessary to reenable a disabled service while patching.

## Separation of Duties

Separation of duties provides checks and balances among individuals. It can limit the amount of damage any one person can inflict on an organization, either intentionally or unintentionally. This concept is not foreign to banks, retail stores, or military agencies. Areas where there is a conflict of interest often are good candidates to apply separation of duties.

The common cinematic scene in the war movie comes to mind when the military is ready to launch the nukes; the command comes down separate chains-of-command to two soldiers. They are each given codes to get the keys. Both must enter the keys to retrieve the code and insert their keys and turn them at the same time. This prevents one rogue individual from launching the bomb without a conspiracy.

In information security, IT staff may be separate from the IT security staff: one group would be responsible for the management and administration of IT servers, and the security group would be responsible for auditing and monitoring the security of the systems managed by the IT staff to make sure that the policy was followed.

## Logging

The logging configuration is an important, but often overlooked step. Or if logging has been configured, it isn't monitored. Logs not only help you to troubleshoot issues, which is almost the only time they are reviewed, but they also can identify system attacks, potential availability issues, configuration problems, and other similar types of information. Log files should not be written to the application installation folders, as this often means the privileges within those folders need to be elevated. Instead, the log files should be configured to be on their own. Once the logging verbosity and file locations are configured appropriately, these folders also need to be secured. Only the service accounts for each corresponding service will need the ability to write to them. In order to prevent log tampering, no other accounts should be granted access to these folders except for administrators and the auditing group, if such a group exists within the organization. For the strictest environments, only the auditors should be configured to delete any logs. Administrators should only be granted Read permissions. The service account should be granted Modify or Full Control, depending on how the software manages its log files.

Also make sure the Audit Policy has been configured properly so important events are captured in the Application, Security, and System Event logs. Open the Local Security Settings (`secpol.msc`) MMC. Open Local Policies ⇨ Audit Policy. Figure 16-1 shows an example of a fairly strict audit policy.

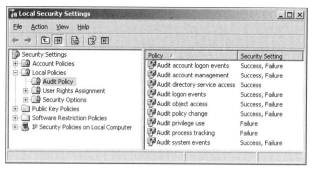

**Figure 16-1**

The log files should be examined on a regular basis, including the Event logs. Anomalies and errors should be investigated and resolved.

*For configuration details on K2 blackpearl logging, see Chapter 19.*

## Permissions and Privileges

To make sure that the principal of least privilege is followed, the goal is to configure the K2 Server Service account and the IIS Worker Group account with the minimum privileges needed on the operating system. Here are the areas to focus on:

❑   Installation privileges

❑   Kerberos configuration (See Chapter 5 on planning an effective deployment.)

❑   Windows operating system privileges

❑   File and folder permissions

❑   Registry permissions

❑   SharePoint permissions

❑   SQL Server permissions

❑   SQL Reporting Services permissions

❑   K2 Workspace permissions

❑   K2 Performance Monitoring permissions

❑   MSMQ permissions

## Installation Privileges

The installation account is the account used to do the K2 blackpearl installation; it should always have administrative privileges on the server where the installation will take place, and with K2 blackpearl it's also helpful to have Domain Administrative permissions so the installer can set up the Service Principal Names in Active Directory to assist with automating the configuration of Kerberos. Additionally, make sure that the account also has sysadmin privileges on the SQL Server so that it can create, configure, and populate the databases. This will allow for a smooth installation. If there is no account that meets these requirements, create one for use during the installation of K2 blackpearl and also use this account for applying product patches and service packs. Leaving this account with such a broad range of permissions in the environment may be risky,, so when it is not in use, disable this account or remove any elevated permissions and reapply them when the account is needed.

## Service Account Privileges

There are several service accounts that will need to be set up and configured for the complete K2 blackpearl installation. The following table lists the server component and the corresponding name that will be used to refer to the service account:

| Component | Service Account Name |
|---|---|
| K2 blackpearl Installer | Installation Account |
| K2 blackpearl server | K2 Service Account |
| K2 blackpearl Workspace | K2 Workspace Service Account |
| Microsoft Office SharePoint Server (MOSS) 2007 | SharePoint Service Account |
| SQL 2005 Reporting Services | Reporting Service Accounts (App Pool Identity and Windows Service Identity) |

For maximum security, each service should be configured to run under a different account. Additionally Authenticated Users or a more limited group will need permissions on different servers as noted in the next section.

### K2 Service Account

The System Account Requirements topic in the K2 blackpearl *Getting Started Guide* recommends that the K2 Service account be granted local administrator rights on the server. From a configuration and management perspective, this makes K2 blackpearl easier to install, configure, and maintain, as just about any request the K2 server makes of the operating system will be granted on the local system because it has a high level of rights and privileges on that system.

From an information security perspective, this may create unnecessary risk and may also be restricted by your organization's security policy. If the K2 Service Account is granted local administrative permissions, any vulnerability in IIS, ASP.NET, or K2 blackpearl could grant a user full administrative access to the system, allowing them to do anything they wished with the server. This does not conform to the principal of least privilege or defense in depth described previously. Instead, remove the K2 Service account from the local Administrators' group. However, understand that additional manual configuration will be required. This section will document the settings needed to grant the least amount of privileges needed to set up.

*To make sure installation completes successfully, make sure that the K2 server has started at least once while the K2 Service account is in the Administrators' group. This will allow K2 to complete some additional setup and configuration tasks that happen the first time the server starts up. If not, you will have to perform these manually. For instance, K2 creates the MSMQ message queues for the Event Bus the first time it starts up.*

> **If for some reason you change the K2 Service account to a different Domain account, K2 blackpearl will no longer have the proper access to the cryptographic keys. It is possible to change the service account to a different user, but be warned that some additional steps will be needed to allow the new service account access to those cryptographic keys. See the section titled "File and Folder Permissions" later in this chapter for more information.**

### K2 Workspace Service Account

When ASP.NET Web sites are hosted in IIS 6.0 and above, they require an identity for the Web application code to execute. All Web applications assigned to that application pool will run as that identity.

### SharePoint Service Account

The SharePoint Service account is the identity the SharePoint Web Site Application Pool runs under. If SharePoint already exists in the environment, this service account will already exist. For K2 blackpearl to integrate properly with SharePoint, additional permissions need to be configured.

### Reporting Service Accounts

There could be potentially two Reporting Service accounts. One is the identity that the Reporting Service Web Site Application Pool runs under. The other is the Account that the SQL Reporting Service runs under. For K2 blackpearl to interface with the Reporting Services, the K2 Service account will need to be granted an appropriate application role within reporting services. SQL Reporting Services accesses a K2 Data Store through a custom provider. By configuring Kerberos and delegation permissions for the Reporting Server, this will allow SQL Reporting Server to impersonate users when they connect to K2, and then K2 permissions will apply when running the reports.

## *Operating System Privileges*

The following table documents the minimum operating system privileges needed to function for K2 blackpearl Service and the IIS Worker Process:

| Account | Privilege |
| --- | --- |
| K2 Service Account | Requires the "Log on as a Service" privilege. |
| K2 Workspace Service Account | Adding this account to the IIS_WPG group will automatically grant it the operating system privileges needed for the K2 Workspace ASP.NET Web site to function. |

To grant the "Log on as a Service" privilege:

**1.** Open the Local Security Settings (`secpol.msc`) MMC.

**2.** Open Local Policies ⇨ User Rights Assignments and double-click Log on as a service.

**3.** Add the K2 Service account to the list.

Figure 16-2 shows an example of the Local Security Policy settings.

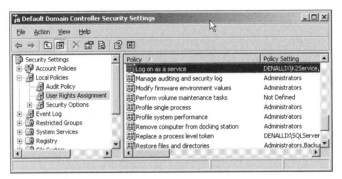

**Figure 16-2**

*The "Log on as a service" right should be granted automatically when setting the Credentials for K2 blackpearl server Service in the Services Console MMC.*

## File and Folder Permissions

The goal in securing the file system is to only allow the service accounts the minimum access to the folders and files required. Before installing any software, including the operating system, all drives should be formatted using the NTFS file systems.

*If installing K2 blackpearl on another drive than %systemroot% (which is typically the C drive), remember that any additional drives created and formatted NTFS are granted excessive permissions. For example, if you are creating a new E drive, make sure to remove all the permissions on the root of that drive except SYSTEM and the local built-in Administrators' group. They should both have Full Control. When installing the software, the installer should set up the proper ACL's for each folder using the accounts specified. Then you manually need to add each service account as well to those drives with Read/Execute permissions.*

The following table documents the file and folder-level permissions required for the K2 Service account on the K2 server:

| Account | Rights | Folder |
|---|---|---|
| K2 Service Account | Full Control | %SYSTEMROOT%\temp |
| K2 Service Account | Full Control | %ALLUSERSPROFILE%\Application Data\Microsoft\Crypto\RSA |
| | | *This setting is NOT typically needed. See the security footnote for a better workaround. |
| K2 Service Account | Read & Execute | %SYSTEMROOT%\Microsoft.NET\Framework\v2.0.50727\CONFIG\ |
| K2 Service Account | Read & Execute | [K2 Install Path]\K2 blackpearl\ |
| | | All subfolders and files, all K2 Logging should be configured to write to a folder outside of this path. |
| K2 Service Account | Modify | [K2 Install Path]\K2 blackpearl\Host Server\Bin\K2HostServer.config |
| | | The service account needs write access to automatically encrypt connection strings in the K2HostServer.config file. |
| K2 Service Account | Create Folders | [K2 Install Path]\K2 blackpearl\Host Server\Bin\ |
| | | Important: Set the Apply onto drop-down to This folder only (Figure 16-3 shows how to configure this setting). |
| CREATOR OWNER | Full Control | [K2 Install Path]\K2 blackpearl\Host Server\bin\ |
| | | Important: Set the Apply Onto to Subfolders only |
| | | When the K2 Service account creates the Work folder, it is the CREATOR OWNER. By granting this permission, it will have full control over the Work subfolder only. |

* WARNING! Granting Full Control to the RSA folder is not recommended, but it will work around a problem created when switching the K2 User Account to run under a different user since the cryptographic key was created while running under the previous account. Instead of changing the ACLs on the RSA folder as the table suggests, fix the problem by reconfiguring the encrypted database connection string section in the K2HostServer.config file by replacing the encrypted section with a new unencrypted section. Then restart the K2 Service, this will trigger the creation of a new RSA cryptographic key with the correct permissions for the new K2 Service accountService account, and then it will rereencrypt the database connection string section.

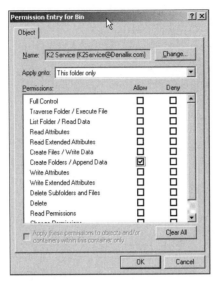

**Figure 16-3**

The following table documents the permissions needed on the K2 Workspace Web server:

| Account | Rights | Folder |
|---|---|---|
| Authenticated Users* | Read and Execute | [K2 Install Path]\K2 blackpearl\Workspace |
| Authenticated Users* | Read and Execute | [K2 Install Path]\K2 blackpearl\WebServices |
| Authenticated Users* | Read and Execute | %SYSTEMROOT%\temp |

* If a subset of Domain Users will be using K2 blackpearl, create a group in Active Directory and assign that instead of Authenticated users. This is especially useful for the development and review environments as only a limited number of users should have access to them.

The following table documents the permissions needed on the SharePoint Web server:

| Account | Rights | Folder |
|---|---|---|
| K2 Service Account | Full Control | %SYSTEMROOT%\temp |
| K2 Service Account | Full Control | %ALLUSERSPROFILE%\Application Data\ Microsoft\Crypto\RSA |
| K2 Service Account | Full Control | %SYSTEMROOT%\Microsoft.NET\Framework\ v2.0.50727\CONFIG |

| Account | Rights | Folder |
|---|---|---|
| K2 Service Account | Write Access | %COMMONPROGRAMFILES%\Microsoft Shared\web server extensions\12 |
| | | Note: If installing SharePoint in a non-standard location, make sure to include that additional path. |
| Authenticated Users* | Modify | %COMMONPROGRAMFILES%\Microsoft Shared\web server extensions\12 |
| | | Note: If installing SharePoint in a non-standard location, make sure to include that additional path. |

* If only a subset of Domain Users will be using K2 blackpearl and the corresponding SQL Reporting Services, create a group in Active Directory and assign that instead of Authenticated users. This is especially useful for the development and review environments as only a limited number of users should have access to them.

The following table documents the permissions needed on the SharePoint Web server:

| Account | Rights | Folder |
|---|---|---|
| SharePoint Service Account | Modify | %SYSTEMROOT%\temp |
| SharePoint Service Account | Write | %COMMONPROGRAMFILES%\Microsoft Shared\web server extensions\12\Layouts\Features |
| SharePoint Service Account | Write | %COMMONPROGRAMFILES%\Microsoft Shared\web server extensions\12\ISAPI |

The following table documents the permissions needed on the SQL Reporting Services Web server:

| Account | Rights | Folder |
|---|---|---|
| Authenticated Users* | Read and Execute | %SYSTEMROOT%\temp |

* If only a subset of Domain Users will be using K2 blackpearl and the corresponding SQL Reporting Services, create a group in Active Directory and assign that instead of Authenticated users. This is especially useful for development and review environments since only a limited number of users should have access.

## Registry Permissions

Grant the listed accounts permissions on the following Registry keys.

For K2 blackpearl server:

| Account | Rights | Registry Key |
|---|---|---|
| K2 Service Account | Full Control | HKEY_LOCAL_MACHINE\SOFTWARE\SourceCode\Logging |

For Microsoft Office SharePoint Server:

| Account | Rights | Registry Key |
|---|---|---|
| K2 Service Account | Full Control | HKLM\SOFTWARE\SourceCode\Logging |

## SharePoint Permissions

In order for the K2 Designer to function within SharePoint, the K2 Service account will need to be granted the Site Collector Administrator role.

| Account | SharePoint Role |
|---|---|
| K2 Service Account | Site Collector Administrator |

## SQL Reporting Services Permissions

Additionally for K2 blackpearl reporting to function, the K2 Workspace Service account will need to be configured as a Content Manager within Reporting Services.

| Account | Role |
|---|---|
| K2 Workspace Service Account | Content Manager |

## SQL Server Permissions

The K2 Web Designer for SharePoint requires specific Database permissions to function. The following table documents the required permissions:

| Permission | Account | Target Object |
|---|---|---|
| db_DataReader | SharePoint Service account | WebWorkflow database |
| db_DataWriter | SharePoint Service account | WebWorkflow database |
| Execute | SharePoint Service account | All Stored Procedures in the WebWorkflow database* |

* Best practice is to create a database role and grant the execute permission for each stored procedure to this role, and add the SharePoint Service account to that role.

## K2 Workspace Permissions

In order for some of the K2 integration with SharePoint to function properly, the SharePoint Service account needs the ability to export Workflows to facilitate the K2 Web Designer for SharePoint. Additionally the SharePoint Service account needs to impersonate users on the K2 blackpearl server so SharePoint can do tasks on behalf of users. The following table lists the Server Rights required for the SharePoint Service account when integrating K2 blackpearl with MOSS or WSS:

| Account | K2 Server Rights |
|---|---|
| SharePoint Service account | Export |
| SharePoint Service account | Impersonate |

## K2 Performance Monitoring Permissions

If K2 Performance Monitoring has been installed, the K2 Service account must be added to the local Administrators' group. Instead, to apply least privilege, there are a group of specific permissions required for the K2 Service account to use the Performance Monitoring and not require being added to the local Administrators' group.

The following table documents the File permissions required to allow the performance monitors to work with K2 blackpearl:

| Account | Rights | Folder |
|---|---|---|
| K2 Service Account | Write Attribute | %systemroot%\system32\lodctr.exe |
| K2 Service Account | Write Attribute | %systemroot%\system32\unlodctr.exe |
| K2 Service Account | Modify | %systemroot%\system32\perfc009.dat |
| K2 Service Account | Modify | %systemroot%\system32\perfh009.dat |

The following table documents the Registry permissions required to allow the performance monitors to work with K2 blackpearl:

| Account | Rights | Registry Key |
|---|---|---|
| K2 Service Account | Read Control<br>Query Value<br>Set Value<br>Create Subkey<br>Enumerate Subkeys<br>Notify | HKLM\SOFTWARE\Microsoft\Windows NT\ CurrentVersion\Perflib |
| K2 Service Account | Read Control<br>Query Value<br>Set Value<br>Create Subkey<br>Enumerate Subkeys<br>Notify | HKLM\SYSTEM\ControlSet001\Services |
| K2 Service Account | Full Control | HKLM\SOFTWARE\Microsoft\Windows NT\ CurrentVersion\Tracing |

## MSMQ Permissions

K2 blackpearl utilizes Microsoft Message Queuing (MSMQ) to support the K2 logging infrastructure as well as the Event Bus. After installation, on the initial run of K2 blackpearl, it creates two message queues for Event Bus called `eventbus` and `eventbus error`. So for the Event Bus to function properly, the K2 Service account requires Create permissions on the MSMQ server (by default the K2 Service account is granted the permissions to create the queues because it's put in the Administrators' group during installation). Once these queues are created, permissions can be relaxed. The following table shows the permissions needed:

| Account | Rights | Queue Name |
|---|---|---|
| K2 Service Account | Receive Message<br>Peek Message<br>Receive Journal Message<br>Get Properties<br>Get Permissions<br>Send Message | `Eventbus` |
| K2 Service Account | Receive Message<br>Peek Message<br>Receive Journal Message<br>Get Properties<br>Get Permissions<br>Send Message | `eventbus error` |

Additionally, if you are using MSMQ Logging, the `HostServerLogging.config` file references a private queue called `private$\SCQueue`. If this queue doesn't exist, the Host Server will attempt to create it, which will require Create permissions to be granted at that time, or an administrator can create the queue manually and then grant the permissions to the K2 Service account directly.

## The Discovery Service

K2 blackpearl comes with a service called the Discovery Service that allows the K2 Workspace or any component that makes an API call to discover the K2 blackpearl servers on the network. The Discovery Service listens on UDP Port 49599 (see `DiscoveryService.config` in the `[K2 Install Path]\k2 blackpearl\Host Server\bin` folder to view or change the default port). When a component wants to discover the K2 servers in the environment, a call to the Discovery API will send out a broadcast datagram to the network. If the broadcast datagram is seen by the Discovery Service running on the K2 blackpearl Service, it will respond back directly to the system that initiated the broadcast and transmit the K2 blackpearl server's hostname, and Host Server port.

In environments with more stringent security requirements, it may be requested that this service be disabled so that it can't be discovered on the network. To disable the Discovery Service, simply remove the `SourceCode.DiscoveryService.dll` from the `HostedServices` in the `[K2 Install Path]\Host Server\bin` folder.

## Securing K2 blackpearl Communications

Security requirements for your specific environment may mandate the confidentiality of data that moves through a K2 blackpearl workflow. If personally identifiable information (PII) — for example, Social Security numbers, birth dates, personal names, and addresses — are fields within the processes or are used by SmartObjects, then communications should be encrypted over-the-wire. Additionally, corporate data or government data that has been assigned a security label — for example, Confidential, For Official Use Only (FOUO), and Sensitive — should also be taken into consideration when making the determination that data should be encrypted over-the-wire.

The architectural template chosen for the K2 blackpearl system architecture will affect the scope of what communication channels need to be encrypted. For example, if you are deploying a single server deployment where everything is installed on one server — K2 blackpearl, SQL Server, SQL Reporting Services, IIS, and WSS or MOSS — the only data that is transmitted over-the-wire will be the Web traffic from Web clients. In this scenario, only the Web traffic will need to be encrypted. However, if you are deploying the medium-scale architecture, there are more points of encryption that will be required.

There are a couple of different approaches that can be used to encrypt data communications for a given K2 topology — TLS/SSL and IPSec. All Web connectivity, including the Web services should use TLS/SSL Certificates, including K2 Workspace, Microsoft Office SharePoint, and SQL 2005 Reporting Services. Additionally all SQL Server connections can also be encrypted using SSL certificates. K2 blackpearl doesn't natively support encrypting its communication channels over-the-wire, so an add-on network encryption technology like IPSec can be used. IPSec is network encryption protocol that is available in Windows Server productions as well as Windows Desktop operating systems and can be used to encrypt data on specific ports and protocols. Additionally, third-party software and hardware can also be used to deploy IPSec communication between servers. Take care to not leave any significant gaps of unencrypted traffic when deploying IPSec with a hardware solution.

An additional layer of protection can be added by requiring Client Certificates on the Web Interfaces for SharePoint, SQL Reporting Services, and the K2 Workspace.

> **Enabling client certificates on the** `http://[k2webserver]/RuntimeServices` **folder in IIS may break certain features of K2 blackpearl or may require an additional level of configuration and/or programming for items that consume these Web services.**

The specifics of how to configure SSL/TLS with IIS, and SQL Server and IPSec with K2 blackpearl are beyond the scope of this book.

See the following links for more information:

❑ **Certificates (IIS 6.0):** `www.microsoft.com/technet/prodtechnol/WindowsServer2003/Library/IIS/f8f81568-31f2-4210-9982-b9391afc30eb.mspx?mfr=true`

❑ **How to Enable SSL Encryption for an Instance of SQL Server by Using Microsoft Management Console:** `support.microsoft.com/kb/316898`

❑ **Configuring a Report Server for Secure Sockets Layer (SSL) Connections:** `technet.microsoft.com/en-us/library/ms345223.aspx`

❑ **IPSec on Microsoft Technet:** `technet.microsoft.com/en-us/network/bb531150.aspx`

Additionally, for WSS 3.0 SSL Configuration, see the WSS 3.0 installation documentation.

# The K2 blackpearl Security Landscape

The second part of this chapter is dedicated to the security features provided with K2 blackpearl:

❑ K2 Security framework

❑ K2 Workspace permissions

❑ K2 Management Console

❑ Environment Library Templates security

❑ SmartObject security

❑ SmartBox security

❑ EventBus security

❑ Programmers and process designers

## K2 Security Framework

K2 blackpearl comes with two authentication providers:

❏ **Active Directory–based authentication:** The Active Directory provider will work with the organization's current Active Directory infrastructure to authenticate users and to provide authorization within K2 using Groups.

❏ **A K2 SQL authentication provider that is in the works (targeted to be released with Service Pack 2):** The K2 SQL provider allows an additional mechanism outside of Active Directory to set up user accounts for users not in Active Directory.

To help identify which authentication provider to use when assigning permissions or logging in, K2 blackpearl attaches a *Security Label* to the identity to associate specific credentials with a specific authentication provider. For example, the K2 SQL Provider uses the label K2SQL; the Active Directory Label uses the K2 prefix as the Security Label.

> *See Chapter 17 for more information on the administration of the security providers included with K2 blackpearl.*

### Security Programming and Extensibility

Additionally, K2 blackpearl is also designed with an extensible pluggable provider model for adding custom user and role providers. This allows flexibility for organizations that need to build or have already built custom authentication or are using an extensible third-party authentication system other than Active Directory. In these situations, a custom provider can be developed and plugged into K2 blackpearl to support other authentication mechanisms. These providers will use a unique security label to identify their use in the environment.

> *See Chapter 17 for information on the building custom security providers for K2 blackpearl.*

## K2 Workspace Permissions

The K2 Workspace is a Web-based interface for K2 server Management. Access to the workspace should be granted based on the principal of least privilege.

By default, all areas of the Workspace are viewable by all users within the domain. To keep the administration overhead for the K2 Workspace permissions low, one approach would be to create a domain group for permissions in the K2 Workspace.

Navigate to the Workspace Permissions by clicking on the Security menu and selecting Workspace Permissions,, as shown in Figure 16-4.

**Figure 16-4**

Figure 16-5 shows the left side menu where there is a list of the Workspace Components for which permissions are granted.

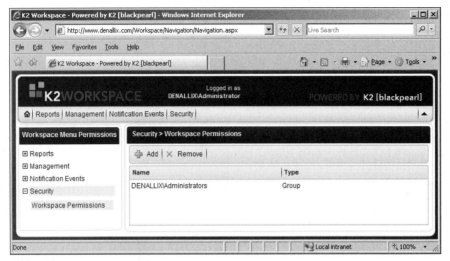

**Figure 16-5**

These items correspond with the top K2 Workspace Navigation Bar (see Figure 16-6).

**Figure 16-6**

The following table shows an example of a quick and easy way to setup the K2 Workspace Permissions:

| K2 Workspace Permission | Domain Group |
|---|---|
| Reports | K2WorkspaceReports |
| Management | K2WorkspaceManagement |
| Notification Events | K2WorkspaceNotification |
| Security | K2WorkspaceSecurity |

Then add the domain groups and/or users using Active Directory Users & Computers that will need access to the required areas of the K2 Workspace.

> By default, the Workspace Security list has no users. When this list is empty, K2 allows full access to the Workspace Security Permission. Once one user has been granted the Workspace Security Permission, all other users are locked out of the Security menu from within the K2 Workspace. Take care to include the K2 administrators first, than additionally add any additional users, if appropriate. The same rule applies to the Reports, Management Console, and Notification Events Security Permissions as well.

# K2 Management Console

The K2 Management Console is the primary interface for managing the K2 blackpearl server. This chapter will only cover the configuration options relating to Rights, Permissions, Users, and Roles. For in-depth coverage of the K2 Management Console, see Chapter 20 on the K2 Workspace and reporting.

## Server Rights

The K2 server Rights (see Figure 16-7) provide an interface to add rights for K2 administrators, grant permissions for process designers, developers, and deployment users to export processes, and grant permission for users to impersonate other users.

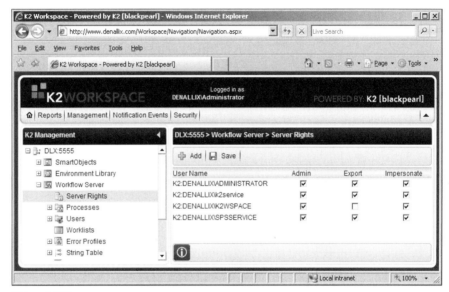

Figure 16-7

| Right | Description |
| --- | --- |
| Admin | This right allows the user to manage all aspects of the K2 Management Console; it also allows the repairing of processes, access to the reports, processes, and process instance data, and more. If it's in the K2 Workspace, the Admin right should grant access to it. |
| Export | Users with this right can deploy processes and SmartObjects to the K2 blackpearl server. |
| Can Impersonate | This right allows users to take actions on events within K2 blackpearl on behalf of another user. |

The ability to impersonate another user is an important privilege within K2 blackpearl. For example, the SharePoint Service account needs to do things on behalf of SharePoint users, so it requires the right to impersonate a user to properly carry out its work on behalf of that user. Additionally, the Impersonate

Right is also often required for server events that need to impersonate users to accomplish some task. Grant this privilege with care, as impersonation has the potential to violate CIA and AAA.

## Process Rights

Process Rights (see Figure 16-8) grant users the ability to participate within a workflow.

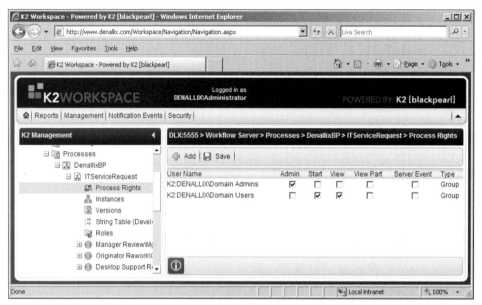

Figure 16-8

The following table shows the five Process Rights. These rights are set on a per-process basis:

| Permission | Description |
| --- | --- |
| Admin | Grants all of the rights below. Additionally is allows the management of the processes in the K2 Management Console. It also grants the ability to repair processes. |
| Start | Start a new instance of the process. |
| View | Allows the user to view any process instance for the process the permission is granted for, enabling reporting on the process in the K2 Workspace. The user is not able to participate in the process itself. |
| View Participate | Allows a participant in the process, for example, the user is defined as the destination user for one of the process activities, to view the details of the process instance. The user will only be able to access process reports and the activity instance once it has reached the activity for which they are a destination user. |
| Server Event | Asynchronous server events wait for a call-back from the external system to finish the server event. The user account used by the external system must be granted Server Event permissions for it to be allowed to finish the server event. |

## Process Action Rights

Each process allows specific rights to be assigned for each action that limit a user's interaction with activities or client events within an activity. These are called Process Action Rights (see Figure 16-9).

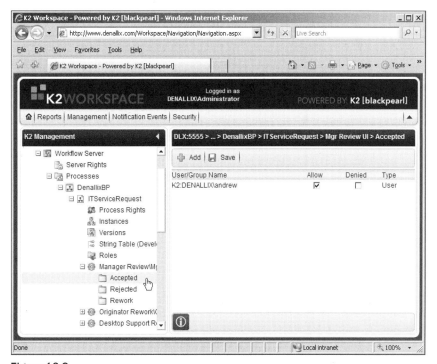

**Figure 16-9**

The following table describes the different Action Rights:

| Action | Name |
| --- | --- |
| Allow | Allows the associated User/Group to view the activity or client event. |
| Denied | Prevents the associated User/Group from accessing the activity or client event. |

## K2 Server Roles

K2 server Roles (see Figure 16-10) allow the ability to create a server-level dynamic container of users that can be resolved at design time or at run time. These roles can then be assigned within a process (see Figure 16-11) to control different actor's roles within the workflow.

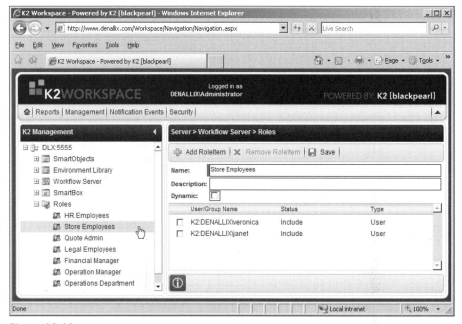

**Figure 16-10**

Take care when setting the role refresh interval. The interval sets the time interval that these roles will be repopulated with current account information from Active Directory. If the time interval is set too long, the accounts could become stale, and users that have been revoked access may still have access causing a breach in confidentiality, or new users that need access to the system won't have access affecting availability.

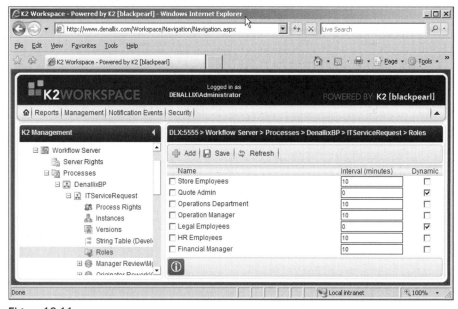

**Figure 16-11**

# Environment Library Templates Security

The Environment Library provides a flexible way to create and store environment specific settings, for example, connection strings, server names, configuration options, for use in multiple environments such as development and production.

*See Chapter 15 for more specific information on the Environment Library.*

The Environment Library templates can potentially contain sensitive information like server names, server usernames and passwords so it's important to apply the principal of least privilege when granted access to these settings. See Figure 16-12 for the Environment Library Template Security settings.

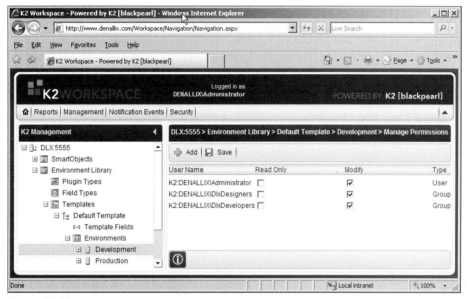

**Figure 16-12**

There are two Template Actions associated with the Environment Library Template Security listed in the following table:

| Template Action | Description |
|---|---|
| Read Only | Allows users to view the environment template settings. |
| Modify | Grants users permission to modify the environment template settings. |

> By default, the Environment Library Template Action List is empty. When the list is empty, K2 will allow full access to all users to the Template Library Templates. Once one Template Action is granted to a user, all other users are locked out of that template from both the K2 Object Browser as well as the K2 Management Console Environment Library Template settings. Take care to include the K2 administrators first, then add the appropriate users. Make sure that at least one user can make changes by granting them the Modify permission.

Grant the developers and workflow designers, at minimum, the Read privilege to any Environment Library Templates that store environment information supporting the development environment they work with. Architects or developers who are in charge of designing and configuring the Environment Library Templates should be granted the Modify right for the development environment templates. If there are multiple environments for different projects under development, it is appropriate to partition those into different Environment Library Templates as well and only grant developers and process designers working on a specific project access to the corresponding Environment Library Templates.

For review/test environments, depending on how the organization is structured, test engineers may be responsible for configuring the review/test environment templates.

Finally, production environments should be set up and configured by the K2 server administrators who are responsible for supporting the production environment. Developers and test engineers should not have access to read or modify the templates on the production server, as an incorrectly configured environment template could potentially cause data integrity issues or availability issues.

## SmartObject Security

SmartObjects have the ability to pull data from disparate systems and make them available through a common interface to K2 blackpearl processes or the .NET Data Provider for K2 SmartObjects. There are two global SmartObject permissions (see Figure 16-13):

❑ Publish SmartObject
❑ Delete SmartObject

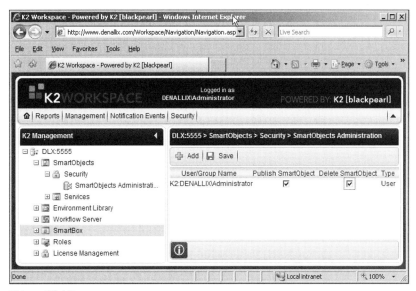

Figure 16-13

The following table defines each one:

| Action | Description |
|---|---|
| Publish SmartObject | Gives the specified user permission to publish a new SmartObject to the server. |
| Delete SmartObject | Gives the specified user permission to delete a SmartObject. |

Apply the principal of least privilege to SmartObjects. On production servers, the ability to publish, and especially, delete SmartObjects should be granted judiciously.

## SmartBox Security

SmartBox is the built-in SmartObject repository for K2 blackpearl that allows rapid development of data storage containers that are made available to processes and programmatic access via ADO.NET. For complete coverage of SmartBox, see Chapter 7. Figure 16-14 shows the security settings for any SmartBox object.

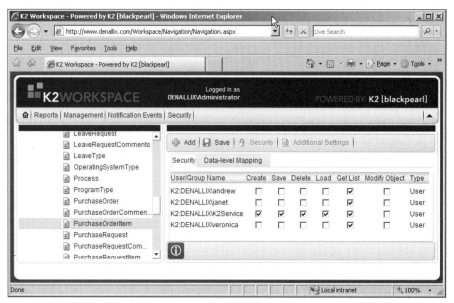

**Figure 16-14**

The following table lists and defines the permissions:

| SmartObject Permission | Description |
| --- | --- |
| Create | Allows users or groups to Create a new record. |
| Save | Allows users or groups to Save changes to a record. |
| Delete | Allows users or groups to Delete a record. |
| Load | Allows users or groups to Select one record. |
| Get List | Allows users or groups to Select a list of records. |
| Modify Object | Users or groups can modify the SmartObject object definition. |

Most of the permissions listed in the table above govern the access control for who can access data in the SmartObject except the Modify Object permission. The Modify Object permissions allow changes to be applied to the SmartObject. Grant Modify Object permission with care on production servers as it can allow for the destruction of data.

## EventBus Security

The EventBus provides K2 blackpearl and API programmers the capability to fire events that are triggered based on various types of schedules (for example, a specific date and time has elapsed) or specific events (for example, a file in a folder being monitored has changed).

In order for new events to be registered within the Event Bus, a valid login is required to the K2 blackpearl server.

## Programmers and Process Designers

There are four interfaces that process designers use to develop new processes for K2 blackpearl:

- ❑ Microsoft Visio 2007
- ❑ Microsoft Office SharePoint 2007 (MOSS)
- ❑ K2 Studio
- ❑ Microsoft Visual Studio

Within these tools are two areas that security settings in K2 blackpearl govern:

- ❑ The K2 Object Browser
- ❑ The ability to export processes and SmartObjects

### The K2 Object Browser

The K2 Object browser allows process designers and programmers to access only the working environments that they have been granted rights to view and/or modify. Additionally, there is the User Browser (which has no restrictions), process/activity data, and the Workflow Context Browser.

Security can and should be maintained on the Environment Library through the K2 Management Console. See the "Environment Library Templates Security" section earlier in the chapter.

### Export Permissions

Only developers and process designers with Export permissions can deploy a K2 process or SmartObjects to the K2 blackpearl server. All programmers and process designers who are responsible for building K2 processes and SmartObjects should have export permissions on the development K2 server. Without Export permissions it's impossible to push processes to the K2 blackpearl server and actually test and debug processes or SmartObjects.

It's important to go through and clean up processes that have been deployed on the development server from time to time, as they tend to become cluttered with unnecessary projects making it difficult to discern the actual projects vs. projects to be deleted. The development team should come up with a naming standard for process, so it can easily tell the difference between "real" projects and abandoned, test, or sample projects.

On the review/test K2 blackpearl server, limit users who can export projects, except a few appropriate users. Since this server is to look more like production, it will be helpful to limit access to make sure it stays organized.

Finally, on the K2 blackpearl production server, the approach taken for assigning permissions will depend on the security posture of the organization. Organizations with less stringent security posture should have only a few individuals with Export permissions on the production server, typically the lead and a couple alternates in the case of their absence. An organization with a stricter security policy will probably not allow the K2 process designers or programmers to have direct access to the production server (separation of duties), so the administrators in charge of the K2 server will need to have the ability to Export and be trained on the process or, instead, the developers will be required to deliver the K2 MSBUILD packages for the processes and SmartObjects. See Chapter 10 for in-depth information on how to create MSBUILD packages for deployment. There should be a test procedure set up in review to test the deployment packages before they are deployed on production.

### Server Debugging

Enabling remote server debugging on a K2 blackpearl server can be an incredibly useful tool; however, on a production server this can open it up to serious security issues. Resist enabling debugging on a production server. If it's deemed necessary, at least be willing to configure it only when it's needed. When debugging is not in use, make sure to disable it.

# Secure Development Practices

Every organization that does software programming needs to subscribe to certain security coding best practices. Here are some areas for further consideration and research:

- ❑ Pay attention to the Open Web Application Security Project (OWASP) Top 10. It documents the most common vulnerabilities, including SQL Injection, Cross Site Scripting (XSS), Cross Site Requires Forgery (XSRF), and more.[7]

- ❑ Use tried and true industry accepted vulnerability mitigation techniques. Don't invent mitigation techniques; it can be challenging to understand every angle of a security vulnerability and protect against them all.

- ❑ Get training on secure programming that targets the programming language used by the organization's development team.

- ❑ Code review; consider both Static Code Analysis products as well as peer review.

- ❑ Follow industry and organizational best practices on handling sensitive data or classified data.

- ❑ Adopt a form of the Security Development Lifecycle developed by Microsoft. (A good resource for looking into this is *The Security Development Lifecycle* by Michael Howard and Steve Lipner [MS Press, 2006]).

This is not a topic to take lightly. Even with the best security policies, system hardening, and security practices, it takes only one security vulnerability in code to put an entire organization's assets at risk.

# Troubleshooting Security Issues

It you decide to take securing the K2 blackpearl server seriously and work to apply the principal of least privilege to the K2 service account, you will most likely run up against some security issues that affect the functionality of the K2 server. For instance, perhaps the Host Service won't start, or perhaps the K2 Service crashes when a certain event happens on the server or certain functionality of the K2 Workspace doesn't function properly. These events may be evidence of a bug or an untrapped error in K2 server, but usually are caused by a failure to grant the K2 Service enough rights or privileges to function properly. Resolving these security issues can sometimes be a challenging task, this section covers concepts that will help with troubleshooting. Some of these are pretty obvious, but they are often overlooked.

## *File and Registry Auditing*

Enable the Audit Policy in the Local Security Policy, and then turn on File auditing as well as Registry auditing in Windows for all failed attempts to access files and Registry data. This is a critical first step in troubleshooting issues related to accessing files/folders and for common Registry keys (`HKLM\Software` and `HKLM\Security`). This will reveal when the K2 Service account or a user can't access something on disk when it needs to. Figure 16-15 shows how to configure auditing of any failure to access a file or folder on the entire C drive for any user. The Failures will show up in the Security Event log.

To enable logging for a drive:

1. Right-click the drive and click Properties.

2. Select the Security Tab.

3. Click Advanced.

4. Select the Auditing tab.

5. In the entry box, type **Everyone** and click OK.

6. In the Auditing Entry for Local Disk (C:) dialog (see Figure 16-15), click the Full Control checkbox in the Failed column, which will automatically check all of the items.

7. Click OK.

Repeat this for all Drives installed in the system. Additionally, follow the same process for auditing all failures for `HKLM\Software` and `HKLM\System` nodes using the Registry Editor (`regedit.exe`).

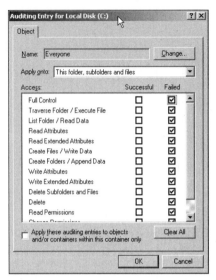

**Figure 16-15**

# Log Files

Review the Windows Application, Security, and System Event logs. Additionally, enable and review specific server log files (for example, K2 blackpearl, Microsoft Office SharePoint, SQL 2005 Reporting Services, and SQL Server 2005 all have different logging mechanisms).

*See Chapter 19 on logging and system reporting for more information on logging options for K2 blackpearl.*

# K2 blackpearl Console Mode

Stop the K2 blackpearl Service, and start up K2 blackpearl in Console mode. Console mode provides real-time logging feedback from the K2 server. The data will be similar to what is output in the K2 Log files, but can be tuned to provide a different level of logging by editing the `HostServerLogging` `.config` file located in the `[K2 Install Path]\K2 blackpearl\Host Server\Bin\` folder.

*See Chapter 19 on logging and system reporting for more information.*

## *Temporarily Add the Service Account to the Administrators Group*

If adding the K2 blackpearl Service account to the Administrators' group and cycling the K2 blackpearl Service seems to fix issues with K2 blackpearl, then chances are there is a right or privilege that has not been granted to the service account. Adding the account to the Administrators' group will prove this theory, but under NO circumstances leave the account in that group. Once you have narrowed it down to a security issue, then that limits the solution to a handful of items that are causing the issue. Review and audit file system and Registry permissions, the Local Security Policy privileges, and the log files to see if it reveals the access that is being denied.

## *Advanced Tools*

If the previous tools aren't providing enough insight, Microsoft provides some more advanced tools like NetMon 3, Process Monitor, and Process Explorer to name a few. These aren't for the inexperienced, as understanding the output and knowing which false positives to ignore takes some experience and expertise. Most often than not, File and Registry auditing and reviewing log files will reveal what the issue is; however, occasionally I've found these tools helpful for getting to the root of an issue.

# Summary

Hopefully, this chapter has expanded some views on information security and challenged others to raise the bar in securing their business and IT infrastructure. It's not an easy task, but it does become easier with practice. System administrators who persevere and work through the task of securing systems will not only learn more K2 blackpearl and Microsoft technologies but will also be better at troubleshooting operating system software configuration and security issues in general. Business owners who persevere by making information security a core tenant of doing business should rest easier knowing they have done more to protect the business, their employees, and customer data from harm.

The next chapter will explore how to administer and configure the default provider that ships with K2 blackpearl, called the Active Directory User Manager provider. Additionally, it will cover how to create, debug, and install custom Security Providers that plug into the Security Framework. Finally, the chapter will cover additional security provider features like Single Sign-On and new providers that will be available from K2 in the future.

# Notes

1. The *Web Hacking Incidents Database Annual Report 2007* from Breach Security. `https://bsn.breach` `.com/downloads/whid/The%20Web%20Hacking%20Incidents%20Database%20Annual%20Report` `%202007.pdf` (You will have to register for free access.)

2. "A Qualitative Risk Analysis and Management Tool — CRAMM" by Zeki Yazar, © 2002, SANS Reading Room. `http://www.sans.org/reading_room/whitepapers/auditing/83.php`

3. "How to Conduct a Risk Analysis" by Shon Harris, © 2006, SearchSecurity.com. `http://` `searchsecurity.techtarget.com/tip/1,289483,sid14_gci1178862,00.html`

4. Definition for *security policy*, © 2003-2008, SearchSecurity.com. `http://searchsecurity` `.techtarget.com/dictionary/definition/what-is-security-policy.html`

5. "A Short Primer for Developing Security Policies" by Michele D. Guel, © 2007, The SANS Institute. `http://www.sans.org/resources/policies/Policy_Primer.pdf`

6. "Information Security Policy — A Development Guide for Large and Small Companies" by Sorcha Canavan, © 2003; 2006, The SANS Reading Room. `http://www.sans.org/reading_room/` `whitepapers/policyissues/1331.php`

7. OWASP Top 10 2007, © 2007 OWASP Foundation. `http://www.owasp.org/index` `.php/Top_10_2007`

# 17

# Administering and Creating Security Providers

Jason Montgomery

No matter how many features a software product has, it always seems to be missing something that would be beneficial or useful in certain situations. K2 blackpearl solves this issue in just about every way by providing a high level of extensibility. K2 blackpearl itself is built on a framework of services that allow for powerful customization, including a Provider model for managing authentication (users who can login) and authorization (roles allowing what users can access). These are called security providers and are also known as User Providers since they expose user information from other systems to the K2 platform. At this time, there is only one functional security provider in K2 blackpearl — the Active Directory User and Role Provider. A SQL Server-based security Provider is currently in the works and should be available around the time this book is published. In most situations, the Active Directory Provider will meet the needs of most organizations. However, situations do arise where having the ability to add a prebuilt custom security provider or even create a custom security provider that ties into third-party systems is desirable. K2 blackpearl utilizes the Provider pattern to allow developers to add their own pluggable custom security providers. Additionally, multiple providers can be used in concert and the K2 system will continue to function as expected allowing for a broad range of interoperability with many different types of systems.

This chapter will explore the administration of the K2 security providers for Active Directory and additionally explore the extensible security provider model for building custom providers to handle custom authentication and authorization within the enterprise. Additionally this chapter will touch on Single Sign-On functionality in K2 and the additional security providers that will be provided by K2 connect.

This chapter covers the following topics:

❏    The Active Directory security provider

❏    The SQL security provider

❏    The security provider API

❏    Single Sign-On (SSO)

❏    Building a custom Security Provider

❏    Installing a custom Security Provider

❏    K2 connect

# The Active Directory Security Provider

The Active Directory security provider allows K2 blackpearl to integrate seamlessly with Microsoft Active Directory to manage users and roles with K2 blackpearl. Active Directory integration is a great feature because most organizations are already heavily vested in Active Directory. By leveraging the existing Microsoft infrastructure that's already handing authentication and authorization for the domain lowers the overall cost of ownership of K2 blackpearl.

By default, the current domain is detected during K2 blackpearl installation and is the only one used to resolve users and groups; other domains within the forest will not be used. However, K2 can be configured to support multiple domains. The Active Directory User Manager, also known as ADUM, has a group of settings that control how it interacts with Active Directory. This section will cover the configuration settings for ADUM in detail.

## ADUM Settings

Most of K2 blackpearl's configuration settings live in the `HostServer` database in SQL Server. There is a table called `SecurityLabels` where the ADUM security provider has settings that control certain aspects of how it interacts with Active Directory. These settings can be enumerated by connecting to the K2 blackpearl SQL Server and running the following query. Make sure that you adjust the database name in the following example to match the name given to the `HostServer` database during K2 blackpearl installation. Take note of the `RoleInit` column; it contains a semicolon delimited list of the ADUM configuration settings.

```
USE [HostServer]

SELECT
  SecurityLabelID,
  SecurityLabelName,
  AuthSecurityProviderID,
  AuthInit,
  RoleSecurityProviderID,
  RoleInit,
  DefaultLabel
FROM
  SecurityLabels
WHERE
  SecurityLabelName = 'K2'
```

An excerpt of the XML data stored in the `RoleInit` column will look something like this:

```
<roleprovider>
<init>ADCache=10;LDAPPath=LDAP://DC=DENALLIX,DC=COM;ResolveNestedGroups
=False;IgnoreForeignPrincipals=False;IgnoreUserGroups=False;MultiDomain
=False;DataSources=&lt;DataSources&gt;&lt;DataSource
Path="LDAP://DC=DENALLIX,DC=COM" NetBiosName="DENALLIX"
/&gt;&lt;/DataSources&gt;;;</init>
<login />
...
</roleprovider>
```

The ADUM initialization settings are listed in the `<init>` node of the XML document. These settings are described in the following table:

| Setting | Definition | Default |
| --- | --- | --- |
| ADCache | ADUM maintains a cache of user and group data retrieved from AD. This value controls the number of minutes a value is cached for. | 10 min |
| LDAPPath | The LDAP Distinguished Name (DN) of the domain, for example, `LDAP://DC=DENALLIX,DC=COM` | The domain DN detected during installation. |
| ResolveNestedGroups | This setting controls the behavior of how groups referenced within another group are resolved. If this value is false, users within a nested group will not be resolved. If it's set to true, K2 will attempt to resolve all users in all nested groups. If this option is enabled, K2 will keep track of circular group references so as to not get stuck in an infinite cycle. | False |
| IgnoreForeignPrincipals | A foreign principal is a reference to a user or group in an external domain outside the forest that has a trust relationship established within the forest. | False |
| IgnoreUserGroups | This setting directs ADUM whether to resolve any groups the user may be a member of. If true, group resolution will not happen for any users. If false, ADUM will resolve the groups the user is a member of. | False |

*(continued)*

**611**

*(continued)*

| Setting | Definition | Default |
|---|---|---|
| MultiDomain | This setting alerts ADUM that it should handle users and groups from multiple domains within the forest. More on this in the next section. | False |
| DataSources | This XML document contains data sources for each domain that ADUM will use to resolve users and groups. For example:<br><br>`<DataSources>`<br>   `<DataSource`<br>`Path="LDAP://DC=DENALLIX,DC=COM"`<br>     `NetBiosName="DENALLIX" />`<br>`</DataSources>` | Both the Path and NetBiosName are set to Domain values detected during the K2 blackpearl install. |

> Serious problems with K2 blackpearl can occur if the `HostServer` database is modified incorrectly. Triple-check configuration changes before applying them and be sure to have a current backup of the database as well as configuration files. Be sure to test the new configuration settings in a development environment before deploying to a production system.

The most common scenario for modifying the configuration settings for ADUM is to add additional support for other domains. The next section will walk you through the process of adding an additional domain that will allow users within that domain to interact and participate in K2 workflows.

## Configuring Support for Multiple Domains

Based on the ADUM configuration settings shown above, it's possible to configure K2 blackpearl to use multiple domains within the forest to resolve users and groups. Additionally ADUM can be configured to resolve users and roles from domains outside of the forest that have one- or two-way trusts established.

Two of the configuration settings in the `<init>` node of the `RoleInit` column will need to be modified in addition to a couple of changes to the K2 Workspace configuration.

The `MultiDomain` property documented previously should be set to True. Additionally, a new `DataSource` node should be added to the `DataSources` XML document that defines the `Path` and `NetBiosName` of the domain being added.

There's another column in the HostServer database that needs to be updated; the AuthInit column contains a list of domains that K2 will authenticate users against.

The following is an example of a SQL Script that will update all the appropriate fields to add multi-domain support for the DENALLIX domain as well as the CENTRAL-DLX domain. Make sure to extract the current settings from your environment, and then merge in the appropriate changes noted in bold/italics in the following example.

```
USE [HostServer]

UPDATE
  [SecurityLabels]
SET
  AuthInit =
'<AuthInit>
  <Domain>DENALLIX</Domain>
  <Domain>CENTRAL-DLX</Domain>
</AuthInit>',
  Roleinit =
'<roleprovider>
<init>ADCache=10;LDAPPath=LDAP://DC=DENALLIX,DC=COM;ResolveNestedGroups
=False;IgnoreForeignPrincipals=False;IgnoreUserGroups=False;MultiDomain
=True;DataSources=&lt;DataSources&gt;&lt;DataSource Path="LDAP://DC=DENALLIX,DC=COM"
NetBiosName="DENALLIX" /&gt;&lt;DataSource Path="LDAP://DC=CENTRAL-DLX,
DC=DENALLIX,DC=COM"
NetBiosName="CENTRAL-DLX" /&gt;&lt;/DataSources&gt;;;</init>
  <login />
  <implementation assembly="ADUM, Version=4.0.0.0, Culture=neutral,
PublicKeyToken=16a2c5aaaa1b130d" type="ADUM.K2UserManager2" />
    <properties>
      <user>
        <property name="Name" type="System.String" />
        <property name="Description" type="System.String" />
        <property name="Email" type="System.String" />
        <property name="Manager" type="System.String" />
        <property name="SipAccount" type="System.String" />
        <property name="ObjectSID" type="System.String" />
      </user>
      <group>
        <property name="Name" type="System.String" />
        <property name="Description" type="System.String" />
      </group>
    </properties>
</roleprovider>'
WHERE
  SecurityLabelName = 'K2'
```

After the `SecurityLabels` table in the `HostServer` database has been updated, there is one final area requiring configuration — the K2 Workspace `web.config` will need updated to take into account the new domain. This file is located in the `[K2 Install Folder]\Workspace\Site` folder.

In the connection string settings of the `web.config` file, add the following to the `connectionString` section, making the appropriate adjustments for your environment:

```
<add name="CNTRLDLX-ADConnString" connectionString="LDAP://CENTRAL-DLX.com" />
```

Finally, in the `membership` section, add a new provider that uses the connection string added in the previous step, as follows — take particular node of the bold/italics text in the example. The `connectionString` name must match the connection string from the previous step,, and the `name` attribute must also be unique.

```
<add connectionStringName="CNTRLDLX-ADConnString"
    connectionProtection="Secure"
    enablePasswordReset="false"
    enableSearchMethods="true"
    requiresQuestionAndAnswer="false"
    applicationName="/"
    description="Central DLX AD connection"
    requiresUniqueEmail="false"
    clientSearchTimeout="30"
    serverSearchTimeout="30"
    attributeMapUsername="sAMAccountName"
    name="AspNetActiveDirectoryMembershipProvider_CentralDlx"
    type="System.Web.Security.ActiveDirectoryMembershipProvider,System.Web,
    Version=2.0.0.0, Culture=neutral, PublicKeyToken=b03f5f7f11d50a3a" />
```

This process can be repeated to add support for as many domains in K2 as is needed.

# The SQL Security Provider

Having Active Directory integration, as discussed in the previous section, is a no-brainer; however, not every user store within the enterprise lives in Active Directory nor can they all be. To help solve this issue, the SQL Role Provider will be a SQL Server-based User and Role Provider, allowing the full administration of the SQL Users and Roles within the K2 Workspace. Users who are outside the scope of the enterprise's Active Directory will be able to have accounts within K2 blackpearl, participate in workflows, and have access to the K2 Workspace using the SQL Role Provider. All the user and role information will be stored in a SQL database. And for those organizations that would rather not have K2 tie into Active Directory at all, the SQL security provider will be the primary security provider, and Active Directory integration will be optional.

As it stands now, the SQL Role Provider is on track to be included with K2 blackpearl SP2, which should be available around the time this book is published.

# The Security Provider API

Not every organization uses Active Directory and not every organization uses SQL Server, so requiring one or the other may be overly restrictive. That leaves a third option — rolling your own security provider to use the existing authentication and authorization mechanisms within your enterprise. K2 blackpearl provides a pluggable architecture that can be added to or replaces the current Authentication and Authorization Providers. Or perhaps your organization uses Active Directory and can rely on ADUM, but there are business requirements that require you to allow business partners to have access to K2 — adding an additional security provider in these situations makes a lot of sense. K2 workflow processes allow the mixing and matching of users from multiple security providers so that you can get the most out of the workflow engine.

This section covers the K2 blackpearl APIs needed for building these pluggable security providers.

# *The Security Provider Object Model*

The K2 blackpearl Host Server, the core server that hosts all of the K2 Services, has an extensible architecture that allows pluggable components. In order for an object to be loaded by the Host Server and also be recognized and used as a security provider, it must implement the IHostableSecurityProvider interface. This interface is built on three other interfaces, the IHostableType interface, the IAuthenticationProvider interface, and the IRoleProvider interface.

All pluggable components that are loaded by the Host Server must implement the IHostableType interface. The Host Server will be able to dynamically load, initialize, and unload objects that implement the IHostableType interface.

Additionally, all K2 security providers require two interfaces to function — one for handling authentication via the IAuthenticationProvider and another for handling User and Role functionality through the IRoleProvider interface. When implementing this interface, additional interfaces need to be implemented that represent the Users and Groups for the custom security provider — more on these later.

These three interfaces, IHostableType, IAuthenticationProvider, and IRoleProvider are all inherited by the IHostableSecurityProvider interface. This main interface, IHostableSecurityProvider, must be implemented in order to create a custom security provider, so it will be important to have an understanding of each interface's function and their relationships. Take a moment to study the following Class Diagram shown in Figure 17-1 to understand these relationships.

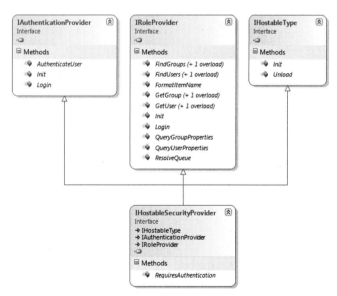

**Figure 17-1**

Notice that there is some overlap in the method interface names, like the Init() and Login() methods. This may cause some initial confusion, but there is good reason for the duplication of functions on these multiple interfaces. For example, three different Init() methods are required — one for each interface. This is because the IAuthenticationProvider and the IRoleProvider are instantiated separately.

*The IAuthenticationProvider and IRoleProvider are instantiated separately by the Host Server, meaning that while they all share the same class definition, they are initialized as separate object instances in memory. That's why each interface has an Init() method defined. If there are similar initialization requirements between the IAuthenticationProvider and IRoleProvider, the code must be repeated in each Init() method. However, any class level objects initialized and assigned in the IHostableType.Init() method are available to the IRoleProvider or IAuthenticationProvider.*

Even though the IAuthenticationProvider and the IRoleProvider are combined into the same final IHostableSecurityProvider interface, ultimately both interfaces do not have to be implemented. Additionally providers can be mixed and matched. Based on the way the security provider configuration is handled and also how each provider is instantiated separately gives them a bit of flexibility allowing them to be completely decoupled. So, for example, if building an IAuthenticationProvider, none of the IRoleProvider interface methods have to be implemented; they could simply throw a NotImplementedException exception. This is also why the Login() method is defined on both the IRoleProvider and the IAuthenticationProvider interfaces. Since each provider can be decoupled, they may use completely different mechanisms to log in to retrieve groups or authenticate users. It's also possible that only one provider may be needed; for example, in certain situations, only the IAuthenticationProvider may be employed without the need for an IRoleProvider.

## A Pluggable Architecture

With the object model defined, the Host Server must have a way to dynamically load and initialize security providers. It employs a plugin architecture based on the Interfaces defined in the object model, combined with the configuration settings in the HostServer database. The actual installation of a security provider is covered in great detail later in this chapter; this section will attempt to map out its architecture.

There is one initial event that triggers a security provider to be loaded by the Host Server. By dropping an assembly containing a specific object type into the securityproviders folder on the K2 server, the next time the K2 Service starts up, it polls this folder for assemblies containing an IHostableSecurityProvider type. Once this file containing this type is loaded by the Host Server, it then records the new security provider by inserting a row into the database. The next and final step is manual — the database needs to be updated to give the security provider a friendly name, called a security label, and to also provide configuration data for the IAuthenticationProvider and the IRoleProvider.

The two tables in the HostServer database that are used to construct a security provider are the SecurityLabels and SecurityProvider tables shown in Figure 17-2. The SecurityLabels table stores a record for each security provider.

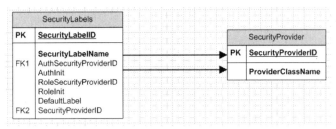

**Figure 17-2**

Based on the table relationships defined in Figure 17-2, a security provider is defined as a unique security label with one Authentication security provider Class and one Role security provider Class, and the corresponding Initialization data for each.

The first field is the `SecurityLabelName`. This field stores the security label, which is the friendly name used by K2 blackpearl to identify a security provider. For instance, `K2` is the security label for the Active Directory provider, and `K2SQL` is used for the K2 SQL Role Manager. So for K2 to identify a user, it will combine the security label with the username, delimited with a colon. For example, for K2 to identify the Administrator account in the Active Directory Domain called DENALLIX using ADUM, the username would be represented as `K2:DENALLIX\Administrator`.

Next is the `AuthSecurityProviderID` column. This is a Foreign Key to the `SecurityProviderID` in the `SecurityProvider` table. This table maps a unique security label to the security provider's Class name. For instance, the security label `K2` in the `SecurityLabels` table relates to a provider class name of `SourceCode.Hosting.SecurityProviders.SSPI` in the `SecurityProvider` table.

The `AuthInit` field coupled with the `AuthSecurityProviderID` field and its relationship to the `SecurityProvider` table provides the Host Server with the information needed to initialize the `IAuthenticationProvider` when the Host Server starts up. The `AuthInit` field contains an XML document containing configuration data used to initialize the `IAuthenticationProvider`. In the case of `SourceCode.Hosting.SecurityProviders.SSPI`, the XML document stored in the `AuthInit` XML column contains the following.

```
<AuthInit>
  <Domain>DENALLIX</Domain>
</AuthInit>
```

Likewise, the `RoleInit` column coupled with the `RoleSecurityProviderID` and the related `SecurityProvider` table provides the Host Server with the configuration information needed to initialize the `IRoleProvider`. An example of the `RoleInit` column data was shown earlier in this chapter when covering how to change the ADUM's Active Directory configuration settings.

With all these pieces put together, when K2 encounters a security label, it looks up the corresponding security provider and passes off control to the security provider based on a coding contract — which is the security provider's Interfaces.

## *IHostableType*

The `IHostableType` interface is used during the startup and shutdown of the Host Server. This interface is straightforward. When the Host Server starts, it calls the `IHostableType.Init()` method on all the installed security providers, and likewise when the Host Server is shutting down, it calls `IHostableType.Unload()` on all installed security providers so they can clean up any resources that need to be freed.

The following table documents the interface members.

| Methods | Description |
| --- | --- |
| Init | Initializes the `IHostableType`. This is called when the Host Server Starts up. |
| Unload | Unloads the Provider. This is called when the Host Server shuts down. |

The `IHostableType.Init()` method is used to pass in context objects from the Host Server , so the `IHostableType` being implemented can access objects like the Configuration Manager or Security Manager or any other server hosted in the Host Server. Additionally, the Host Server context objects `IServiceMarshalling` and `IServerMarshalling` which are passed into the `IHostableType.Init()` method also contain methods for marshalling data between the custom security provider and the Host Server.

The following code snippet shows how to set up a reference to the Configuration Manager, Security Manager, and references to other servers hosted in the Host Server — in this example, the `Logger`. These items are covered in more detail in the next section.

```
using SourceCode.Hosting.Client.BaseAPI;
using SourceCode.Hosting.Server.Interfaces;

public class CustomSecurityProvider : IHostableSecurityProvider
{
 private Logger _logger;
 private IConfigurationManager _configurationManager;
 private ISecurityManager _securityManager;

 #region IHostableType Members

 public void Init(IServiceMarshalling ServiceMarshalling,
                             IServerMarshaling ServerMarshaling)
 {
  // Get a reference to the Configuration Manager Object
  _configurationManager = serviceMarshalling.GetConfigurationManagerContext();

  // Get a reference to the Security Manager Object
  _securityManager = ServerMarshaling.GetSecurityManagerContext();

  // Get a reference to the Logger Object
```

```
   _logger = (Logger)ServiceMarshalling.GetHostedService(typeof(Logger).ToString());
 }

 public void Unload()
 {
  // Perform any clean-up required when the service shuts down
 }
 #endregion
 ...
 }
```

Notice how the `IServiceMarshalling` and `IServerMarshaling` classes provide access to objects in the Host Server in the `Init()` method. In many cases, the `Unload` method may not have any code; it's there to provide the ability to properly handle the freeing or closing of managed and/or unmanaged resources when needed.

# It's All About Context

A security provider doesn't exist in a vacuum; it needs contextual access to functionality provided by objects in the Host Server. The objects of use when developing a custom security provider are the Configuration Manager, the Security Manager, and the Logger.

## The Configuration Manager

The Configuration Manager provides access to server configuration settings such as licensing, current users, the path to the Host Server configuration file to name a few. For most custom security providers, the K2 Configuration Manager won't be of much use. The following code shows how to get a reference to the Configuration Manager through the `serviceMarshalling` argument of the `Init()` method.

```
// Get a reference to the Configuration Manager Object
_configurationManager = serviceMarshalling.GetConfigurationManagerContext();
```

The Host Server's Configuration file, located in `[K2 Install]\Host Server\bin\K2HostServer`
`.config`, can be used to store configuration values using .NET's built-in Configuration framework. For example, to add a connection string that's available to a custom security provider, the following connection string could be added to the `K2HostServer.config` file:

```
<add name="CustomProviderName.Connectionstring" connectionString="Data
Source=DLX;Database=CustomProviderDB; Integrated Security=True" />
```

To retrieve values stored in the Host Server's configuration file, use .NET's Configuration Manger class (`System.Configuration.ConfigurationManager`), like this:

```
string conn =
ConfigurationManager.ConnectionStrings["CustomProviderName.Connectionst
ring"].ConnectionString;
```

What's nice about using the Host Server's configuration file to store connection strings is that K2 will automatically encrypt the `<connectionStrings>` section, protecting any usernames and passwords that exist in that part of the configuration file using the Protected Configuration mechanisms provided in .NET 2.0.

## *The Security Manager*

The Security Manager provides access to different security features of the Host Server, including getting a reference to an authentication provider, access to cryptographic features of the Host Server, and the ability to enumerate the different security and role providers loaded in the Host Server. The following code demonstrates how to get a reference to the Security Manager:

```
// Get a reference to the Security Manager Object
_securityManager = ServerMarshaling.GetSecurityManagerContext();
```

When implementing a custom security provider, the `ISecurityManager.GetSecurityLabelItem()` method can be used to retrieve the initialization data for the custom security provider. This method allows a custom security provider to retrieve the XML-formatted custom configuration settings from the Host Server database.

```
string label = "SECURITY_LABEL";

// Retrieve the Initialization data from the Host Server
// database.
string initData = _securityManager.GetSecurityLabelItem("AuthInit", label) as string;

// Parse the initData to initialize the provider
...
```

The previous example shows how to retrieve the XML initialization data stored in the `AuthInit` column in the `SecurityLabels` table in the `HostServer` database where `SecurityLabelName` is equal to `SECURITY_LABEL`. The security label is the friendly name used to uniquely identify any security provider in K2.

In the introduction to the security provider API earlier in the chapter, it was pointed out that the `IRoleProvider` and the `ISecurityProvider` are separate object instances in memory, which means that fields initialized by one aren't accessible to the other, thus the need for multiple `Init()` methods. However, the Security Manager provides the ability for one provider to access another, and additionally the Security Manager can also provide a reference to any other security provider in the system, given the corresponding security label. The following example shows how to access another security provider running in the Host Server.

```
// Get a reference to the IRoleProvider for the given _securityLabel
IRoleProvider roleProvider =
            _securityManager.GetRoleProviderContext(_securityLabel);

// Get a reference to the IAuthenticationProvider for the given _securityLabel
IAuthenticationProvider authProvider =
            _securityManager.GetAuthenticationProviderContext(_securityLabel);
```

## *The Logger*

Another important item for use when developing a custom security provider is `SourceCode.Logging.Logger`. A reference to the logger allows security providers access to the main Host Server logging mechanism, allowing log messages to be written to the Debug Console, Host Server Log File, System Event log, and so on.

*See Chapter 19 on logging and system reporting for more information on the* `SourceCode.Logging` `.Logger` *namespace.*

The following code shows how to get a reference to the Logger:

```
// Get a reference to the Logger Object
_logger = (Logger) ServiceMarshalling.GetHostedService(typeof(Logger).ToString());
```

The following table lists the logging methods of interest when creating a custom security provider:

| Methods | Description |
| --- | --- |
| LogDebugMessage | Write a message Debug Severity to the Logger. Use this for debugging purposes. |
| LogErrorMessage | Write a message with Error Severity to the Logger. Code that detects errors that are NOT in a `try...catch` block should use this method. |
| LogExceptionMsg | Writes an Exception to the Logger. Use this method to log exceptions in a `try...catch` block. |
| LogInfoMessage | Write an Informational message to the Logger. This is used for writing noteworthy information to the logger. |
| LogWarningMessage | Writes a message with the Warning Severity to the Logger. Used to write warnings to the Logger when encountering certain code conditions that may cause unknown or undesirable behavior. |

The Host Server allows for different levels of logging based on the Logger's Severity configuration set in the `[K2 Install Path]\Host Server\bin\HostServerLogging.config` file. When developing a custom security provider, make sure to enable the Debug Severity to the appropriate logging mechanism. This will allow for any debugging message output from the custom security provider being developed to be logged.

## IHostableSecurityProvider

The `IHostableSecurityProvider` brings an addition of one method called `RequiresAuthentication`. It turns out that the developer need not do much more then always return true.

| Methods | Description |
| --- | --- |
| RequiresAuthentication | This method is a leftover artifact and should always return true. It may eventually be removed from the Interface API. |

## IAuthenticationProvider

The IAuthenticationProvider interface is where the authentication work is done through the AuthenticateUser method. Additionally, the IAuthenticationProvider.Init() method serves an important role as it is how the Authentication provider gets the initialization data from the HostServer database.

The following table documents the IAuthenticationProvider interface:

| Methods | Description |
|---|---|
| AuthenticateUser | Used to authenticate the user. |
| Init | Initializes the IAuthenticationProvider. |
| Login | Used to log in to the underlying security provider store using the provided connection string. Once the Login succeeds, the open connection can be used for authenticating the user if necessary. This method is invoked when the Workflow client opens a connection to the K2 server using this security providers' security label. |

## IAuthenticationProvider Initialization

When K2 instantiates the IAuthenticationProvider, it invokes IAuthenticationProvider .Init(string label, string authInit). The string label contains the security label name and the authInit data, which contains the name of the AuthInit column in the SecurityLabels table. For the following example, assume the AuthInit column in the database contains the XML Document from the DENALLIX domain. The code to initialize a security provider might look something like this:

```
void IAuthenticationProvider.Init(string label, string authInit)
{
  // Retrieve the AuthInit data from the database
  string authInit =
    securityManager.GetSecurityLabelItem("AuthInit", label) as string;

  // Make sure authInit has a value
  if (!string.IsNullOrEmpty(authInit))
  {
    // Retrieve configuration settings from the
    // AuthInit Xml document
    XPathDocument document = new
        XPathDocument(XmlReader.Create(new StringReader(authInit)));

    // Select the Active Directory Domain
    string domain = document.SelectSingleNode("/AuthInit/Domain").InnerText;
    ...
  }
  ...
}
```

Use the `AuthInit` field in the database to store configuration settings or any dynamic settings that should not be hardcoded in the security provider assembly. This will allow configuration changes later without recompiling a new version of the provider.

# Authenticating Users

When the Host Server receives a request for a user to log in/authenticate, the Host Server will call the `IAuthenticationProvider.AuthenticateUser` method on the security provider for the given security label.

The interface defines `IAuthenticationProvider.AuthenticateUser()` as follows:

```
public bool AuthenticateUser(string userName, string password, string extraData);
```

The following table defines each argument:

| Method Argument | Definition |
| --- | --- |
| userName | The name of the user to authenticate. |
| password | The user's password. |
| extraData | This field can contain additional metadata that originates from the client's connection string and is passed through to the security provider on the server. The value of the `AuthData` field in the client's connection string will be assigned to this argument. In many cases it won't be used unless the custom security provider takes the code and explicitly does something with it. |
| Returns | A Boolean value — True if the user is successfully authenticated, false if the user does not succeed. |

The following example creates a connection string and logs in to the K2 server using the Client API:

```
SCConnectionStringBuilder builder = new SCConnectionStringBuilder();
        builder.Host = "DLX";
        builder.Port = 5252;
        builder.SecurityLabelName = "CUSTOM_K2";
        builder.UserID = @"jmontgomery";
        builder.Password = "th1s1smyp4ssw0rdw00t!@";
        builder.Integrated = false;
        builder.IsPrimaryLogin = true;
        builder.AuthData = "extra config metadata";

// Login to the K2 Server
Connection k2Conn = new Connection();
k2Conn.Open("DLX", builder.ToString());
```

The Host Server will receive the request to authenticate the user from the client and will look up the appropriate security provider based on the provided security label name `"CUSTOM_K2"` set in the connection string. The Host Server will then call the `IAuthenticationProvider` `.AuthenticateUser()` method, passing in the following arguments:

```
Username = "jmontgomery"
password = "th1s1smyp4ssw0rdw00t!@"
extraData = "extra config metadata"
```

If the credentials are correct, `AuthenticateUser()` will return true, notifying the Host Server that the user was successfully authenticated. If false is returned, the Host Server will throw an exception back to the client and they will be notified of an unsuccessful login.

## IRoleProvider

The `IRoleProvider` handles all user and role based functions for the security provider. The name `IRoleProvider` may initially cause confusion because of the word "Role" in the name. It not only handles finding roles/groups, it also handles all the user functionality. The following table documents the members on this interface, and each will be explored further as the chapter continues:

| Methods | Description |
|---|---|
| Init | Initializes the provider. |
| Login | This method performs a login to the underlying Role provider data store using the given connection string. Once the login succeeds, the open connection can then be used to retrieve Groups and Users from the underlying Role provider. This method is invoked when opening a connection from a client workflow when using this provider's security label to connect. |
| GetUser | Gets an IUser by username. |
| FindUsers | Searches the underlying security provider data store for users who are members of groupName, or that match the given search criteria in the properties dictionary. Returns an IUserCollection of matches. |
| QueryUserProperties | Returns a dictionary that contains all defined IUser.Properties valid for the security provider's IUser object and the corresponding types. |
| GetGroup | Returns an IGroup object by name. |
| FindGroups | Searches the underlying security provider data store for groups that the userName is a member of, or that match the given criteria specified in the properties dictionary. Returns an IGroupCollection of the matches. |
| QueryGroupProperties | Returns a dictionary containing all defined Properties valid for the security provider's IGroup object and the corresponding types. |

| Methods | Description |
|---------|-------------|
| FormatItemName | Formats usernames in a consistent format. This method is used to normalize all usernames for a provider so that they are consistent. Domain names can be represented user@domain or domain\user. This is a convenience method added for developers to reference within their own classes. The K2 server itself doesn't appear to ever call this method. |
| ResolveQueue | Resolves all users and groups in a destination queue that are listed in the provided XML document. |

## Initializing the Role Provider

The `IRoleProvider`'s initialization works very similarly to the `IAuthenticationProvider` initialization. The difference is that the `IRoleProvider.Init()` method is passed the RoleInit column name instead as the value for the `roleInit` parameter.

The following snippet is an example of an `IRoleProvider.Init()` method:

```
void IRoleProvider.Init(string label, string roleInit)
{
    // Retrieve the RoleInit data from the database
    roleInit =
        this._securityManager.GetSecurityLabelItem("RoleInit", label) as string;

    // Make sure roleInit has a value
    if (!string.IsNullOrEmpty(roleInit))
    {
        // extract Role Providers from Xml document
        ...
    }
    ...
}
```

Once the values are extracted from the RoleInit XML document, they can be extracted and stored in field variables on the `IHostableSecurityProvider` object so that they can be used throughout the class.

Before exploring the specifics of some of the `IRoleProvider` methods, such as `IRoleProvider .FindUsers()` and `IRoleProvider.FindGroups()`, types for Users and Groups must be understood. The `SourceCode.Hosting.Server.Interfaces` namespace has four additional interfaces needed for building custom User and Role objects that work within K2 blackpearl. These interfaces are `IUser`, `IUserCollection`, `IGroup`, and `IGroupCollection`.

## IUser and IUserCollection Interfaces

Figure 17-3 shows the class diagram for the `IUser` and `IUserCollection`. The interface defines the `UserID` and the `UserName` for the user within K2 blackpearl. The `IUser.Properties` dictionary can contain any attributes deemed useful, for example, phone number, address, cell phone, and so on.

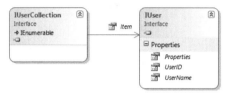

Figure 17-3

The `IRoleProvider.FindUsers()` and `IRoleProvider.GetUser()` methods will return the `IUser` and `IUserCollection` objects. The following table defines the different `IUser` properties:

| Property | Definition |
|---|---|
| UserID | The User ID is used to uniquely identify a user within K2. It combines the security label and the security provider's username separated by a colon ':' — for example, `K2:DENALLIX\Robert`. |
| UserName | The username field contains the security provider's username — for example, `DENALLIX\Robert`. |
| Properties | A dictionary of attributes associated with the user. |

In order for an `IUser` object to function properly in the K2 environment, there are several required properties that MUST be added to the `IUser.Properties` collection. They are listed and defined in the following table:

| Required Properties | Definition |
|---|---|
| Name | The user's name, for example, `Robert Smith`. |
| Description | A description associated with the user. |
| Email | The user's e-mail address for use in notification. |
| Manager | The user's manager — this is used in K2 processes for resolving a user's manager for approval, routing, escalation, and so on. |

Additionally, any number of custom properties can be added to provide additional user data to K2 Processes. For example, K2 allows support for instant messaging and the `IUser.Properties` dictionary contains an attribute called `SipAccount` to facilitate that functionality.

Here is a sample implementation of the `IUser` interface, with only the required properties:

```
class CustomUser : IUser
{
    private IDictionary<String, Object> _properties;
    private string _userID;
    private string _userName;

    #region IUser Members

    public IDictionary<string, object> Properties
    {
        get { return _properties; }
        set { _properties = value; }
    }

    public string UserID
    {
        get { return _userID; }
        set { _userID = value; }
    }

    public string UserName
    {
        get { return _userName; }
        set { _userName = value; }
    }

    #endregion

    public CustomUser(
        string securityLabel,
        string userName,
        string name,
        string description,
        string email,
        string manager)
    {
        _userID = securityLabel + ":" + userName;
        _userName = userName;

        _properties = new Dictionary<string, object>();
        _properties.Add("Name", name);
        _properties.Add("Description", description);
        _properties.Add("Email", email);
        _properties.Add("Manager", manager);
    }
}
```

Notice that the `UserID` is made up of a combination of the security label and the username. This guarantees that the `UserID` for a given provider is unique within the system. Also, the `name`, `description`, `email`, and `manager` properties are the minimum fields required to be added to an `IUser` to properly function within K2. Additional fields can be added to add support for additional functionality in your workflows.

> At the time of writing, the following characters should not be used anywhere in the UserName field due to character filtering in the K2 Workspace. Using any of these characters will cause errors and failures when using a custom user provider within the K2 Workspace.
>
> **Excluded Special Characters:**
>
> ```
> &!@#$%^&*()+=-[]\';,./{}|":<>?_~
> ```
>
> **Always excluded:**
>
> ```
> -:\.&$#@
> ```
>
> This may change in later releases. For current information on filtered characters and for a full list of filtered Chinese characters, please see Knowledge Base Article KB000299 on the K2 Web site.

The other class required is `IUserCollection`.

```
class CustomUserCollection : IUserCollection
{
    private Collection<IUser> _collection;

    public CustomUserCollection()
    {
        _collection = new Collection<IUser>();
    }

    #region IUserCollection Members

    public IUser this[int index]
    {
        get { return _collection[index]; }
    }

    #endregion

    #region IEnumerable Members

    public System.Collections.IEnumerator GetEnumerator()
    {
        return _collection.GetEnumerator();
    }

    #endregion

    public void Add(IUser user)
    {
        _collection.Add(user);
    }
}
```

That's as simple as it needs to be. More functionality can certainly be added, but the two classes stubbed out as shown in the preceding code would be enough to build a complete provider. Next, we explore how to retrieve users and groups.

## IGroup and IGroupCollection Interfaces

Figure 17-4 shows the class diagram for the `IGroup` and `IGroupCollection`. This interface defines the `GroupID` and `GroupName` properties as well as a property collection called `Properties` used for any additional fields that will be made available to the K2 Processes.

**Figure 17-4**

The following table documents the class members of the `IGroup` interface:

| Property | Definition |
|---|---|
| GroupID | The Group ID is used to uniquely identify a group within K2. It combines the security label and the security provider's group name separated by a colon ':' — for example, `K2:DENALLIX\ITUsers`. |
| GroupName | The username field contains the security provider's group name — for example, `DENALLIX\ITUsers`. |
| Properties | A dictionary of attributes associated with the group. |

The `IRoleProvider.FindGroups()` and `IRoleProvider.GetGroup()` methods return `IGroup` and `IGroupCollection` objects.

In order for an `IGroup` object to be compatible with K2, there are two required properties that MUST be added to the `IGroup.Properties` collection. They are listed and defined in the following table:

| Required Properties | Definition |
|---|---|
| Name | The group name |
| Description | A description for the group |

Additional custom fields can be added to the IGroup as well to facilitate additional functionality in K2 processes.

The actual implementation of the IGroup and IGroupCollection is almost identical to the IUser and IUserCollection implementations. The following is an implementation of the IGroup interface:

```
class CustomGroup : SourceCode.Hosting.Server.Interfaces.IGroup
{
    private string _groupID;
    private string _groupName;
    private IDictionary<string, object> _properties;

    #region IGroup Members

    public string GroupID
    {
        get { return _groupID; }
        set { _groupID = value; }
    }

    public string GroupName
    {
        get { return _groupName; }
        set { _groupName = value; }
    }

    public IDictionary<string, object> Properties
    {
        get { return _properties; }
        set { _properties = value; }
    }

    #endregion

    public CustomGroup(string securityLabel, string groupName, string description)
    {
        _groupID = securityLabel + ":" + groupName;
        _groupName = groupName;

        _properties = new Dictionary<string, object>();
        _properties.Add("Name", _groupID);
        _properties.Add("Description", description);
    }
}
```

Notice that the GroupID combines the group's name with the security label. This makes the GroupID unique in K2 for any security provider. Also, remember the Name and Description properties are required for any IGroup implementation. Additional properties can be added to add additional functionality into K2 blackpearl.

The following code is a sample implementation of the `IGroupCollection` interface:

```
class CustomGroupCollection : SourceCode.Hosting.Server.Interfaces.IGroupCollection
{
    Collection<IGroup> _groups;

    #region IGroupCollection Members

    public SourceCode.Hosting.Server.Interfaces.IGroup this[int index]
    {
        get { return _groups[index]; }
    }

    #endregion

    #region IEnumerable Members

    public System.Collections.IEnumerator GetEnumerator()
    {
        return _groups.GetEnumerator();
    }

    #endregion

    public CustomGroupCollection()
    {
        _groups = new Collection<IGroup>();
    }

    public void Add(IGroup group)
    {
        _groups.Add(group);
    }
}
```

These sample implementations of the `IGroup` and `IGroupCollection` interfaces contain all the functionality needed to use them in an actual security provider.

## Retrieving Users and Groups

There are two methods defined on the interface that retrieve one user or one group, each with one overload for extra metadata:

❑   `IRoleProvider.GetUser()`
❑   `IRoleProvider.GetRole()`

Each is defined as follows:

```
// Interface Method Definitions for GetUser
IUser GetUser(string name);
IUser GetUser(string name, string extraData);

// Interface Method Definitions for GetGroup()
IGroup GetGroup(string name);
IGroup GetGroup(string name, string extraData);
```

The following table defines both `FindUser` and `FindGroup`:

| Argument | Definition |
|---|---|
| Name | The exact name of the user or group to retrieve. |
| extraData | Any extra metadata. |
| Returns | Returns one IUser or IGroup that corresponds to the name that was passed in. |

`IRoleProvider.GetUser()` is called, for example, immediately after an `AuthenticateUser()` method is run to retrieve user information.

## Searching for Users and Groups

In order to search the underlying Role provider store for users and groups, a dictionary of properties is provided to the `Find` methods with the corresponding search criteria. In order to be able to implement the search properly, K2 needs to know what `properties` (required and custom) have been defined for the provider.

K2 is able to discover what properties and their corresponding types are defined on the `IUser` and `IGroup` objects of a security provider by calling the `IRoleProvider.QueryUserProperties()` and `IRoleProvider.QueryGroupProperties()` methods. Before every search, K2 queries the properties and then fills in the search criteria to the appropriate ones.

The basic implementation of the `QueryUserProperties()` method, taking into account the required properties, would look like this:

```
public Dictionary<string, string> QueryUserProperties()
{
    Dictionary<string,string> userProperties = new Dictionary<string, string>();
    userProperties.Add("Name", "System.String");
    userProperties.Add("Description", "System.String");
    userProperties.Add("Email", "System.String");
    userProperties.Add("Manager", "System.String");
    return _userProperties;
}
```

A more flexible option, other then hardcoding the list into the Role provider, might be to store a list of the properties in the `RoleInit` XML document so that the list could be changed without recompiling. This is exactly how the `ADUM` security provider is configured.

Similarly, the most basic implementation of the `QueryGroupProperties()` method would look like this:

```
public Dictionary<string, string> QueryGroupProperties()
{
    Dictionary<string,string> groupProperties = new Dictionary<string, string>();
    groupProperties.Add("Name", "System.String");
    groupProperties.Add("Description", "System.String");
    return groupProperties;
}
```

Now that K2 knows what properties the custom `IUser` and `IGroup` objects contain, it can now successfully search for them.

## Searching for Users

The method `IRoleProvider.FindUser()` retrieves a collection of users from the security provider's data store — SQL Server, LDAP, or so forth. There are two interface signatures; one requires two arguments, and the other requires three arguments:

❑   `groupName`

❑   `properties`

❑   `extraData`

```
IUserCollection IRoleProvider.FindUsers(
     string groupName,
     IDictionary<string, object> properties
);

IUserCollection IRoleProvider.FindUsers(
     string groupName,
     IDictionary<string, object> properties,
     string extraData
);
```

The following table defines each argument:

| Argument | Description |
|----------|-------------|
| groupName | When `groupName` is provided, `FindUsers()` will return all users within the provided group. Can be null or empty. When `groupName` isn't provided, the `properties` argument will contain search criteria. |
| properties | Contains a dictionary of search parameters of which `IUsers` to return. Each key in the dictionary corresponds to an item in the `Properties` dictionary of the `IUser`. Each key is always provided, but the value is only provided when a search is to be performed on that property. A wildcard character, the asterisks (*), is provided depending on the type of search to be performed. A search can have multiple wildcards. |
| extraData | While `AuthInit` and `RoleInit` provide static provider configuration, extra data can provide dynamic metadata to modify the behavior of the security provider if needed. This value is typically null. |
| Returns | Returns a collection of `IUser` objects that are a member of the group `groupName` OR a collection of all groups that match the search criteria specified in the `properties` argument. |

When the `groupName` argument is provided, it will contain the exact name of the group to search for. This means that the search criterion is not needed, so the `properties` dictionary can be ignored. Likewise, if the `groupName` argument is null or empty, then a search is being performed, and the exact group name is unknown, so the search criteria will be in the `properties` dictionary. If both the `groupName` and the `properties` dictionary items don't have any values, then a complete wildcard search should be performed of all users in the underlying security provider data store.

## Searching for Groups

The `IRoleProvider.FindGroups()` functions very similar to the `IRoleProvider.FindUsers()` previously described. The following code uses the two interface signatures; one requires two arguments, and the other requires three:

❑   userName

❑   properties

❑   extraData

```
IGroupCollection FindGroups(
    string userName,
    IDictionary<string, object> properties
)
IGroupCollection FindGroups(
    string userName,
    IDictionary<string, object> properties,
    string extraData
);
```

The following table describes each argument:

| Argument | Description |
| --- | --- |
| userName | When userName is provided, FindGroups() will return all the groups the user is a member of. Can be null or empty. When userName isn't provided, the properties argument will contain search criteria. |
| properties | Contains a dictionary of search parameters of which IGroups to return. Each key in the dictionary corresponds to an item in the Properties dictionary of the IGroup. Each key is always provided, but the value is only provided when a search is to be performed on that property. A wildcard character, the asterisks (*), is provided depending on the type of search to be performed. A search can have multiple wildcards. |
| extraData | While AuthInit and RoleInit provide static provider configuration, the extraData can provide dynamic metadata to modify the behavior of the security provider if needed. This value is typically null. |
| Returns | Returns a collection of IGroup objects that the specified user is a member of OR a collection of all groups that match the search criteria specified in the properties argument. |

When the `userName` argument is provided to the `FindGroups()` method, it will contain an exact username that was previously resolved. This allows for a direct retrieval of the user, and the `properties` dictionary of search parameters can be ignored. When the `userName` argument is null or empty, then the search parameters will contain the attributes to search on that match the properties of the `IGroup`.`Properties` dictionary. If the `userName` argument is empty and there are no values for any of the keys in the `properties` dictionary, then `FindGroups` should return all groups from the underlying security provider data store.

## How K2 Workspace Searches a Security Provider

To demonstrate how searching works between K2 and any security provider, we look to the K2 Workspace as it contains Search functionality in many places.

For an example of where `IRoleProvider.FindUsers()` and `IRoleProvider.FindGroups()` are called, see Figure 17-5, which shows the K2 Workspace Search Screen that is used to assign Process Rights to users and groups.

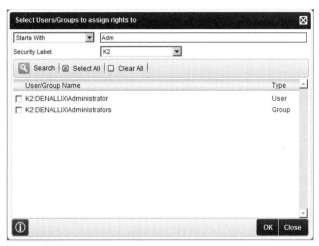

Figure 17-5

When the user fills out the search criteria and clicks the Search button, the K2 Workspace then calls the K2 server and asks the security provider for the registered label, in this case the provider registered with the security label `K2`, to do a partial search for all users and groups whose name starts with "Adm". Both `FindUsers()` and `FindGroups()` are called. The `groupName` and `userName` arguments will both be null; the `properties` dictionary for both will contain all the properties, but only the `Name` property will have a value set; and based on the screen above the value for `Name` will be "Adm*" because the Search Criteria drop-down has the "Starts With" option selected. Notice it found both a user named "Administrator" and a group called "Administrators."

Four possible options control where the wildcard will show up (as shown in Figure 17-6).

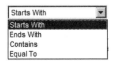

Figure 17-6

The Workspace will add a wildcard in different places, depending on which item is selected in the drop-down shown in Figure 17-6:

❑   **Starts With:** The wildcard will be at the end of the phrase.

❑   **Ends With:** The wildcard will be at the beginning of the phrase.

❑   **Contains:** There will be two wildcards — one at the beginning and one at the end.

❑   **Equal To:** No wildcard will be provided.

Make sure to convert the asterisks' wildcard to the appropriate search symbol used by the underlying security provider data store. For example, if you are passing the phrase with the asterisks' wildcard to an LDAP-based system, the asterisks will work just fine as the wildcard. However, if SQL Server is the underlying data store, the asterisks will need to be converted to percent (%) characters before they can be passed along.

## Resolving Destination Queues

Destination queue functionality is a remnant from K2.net 2003 so the functionality provided in `IRoleProvider.ResolveQueue()` is used to maintain backward compatibility with K2.net 2003. In the case where you have upgraded a K2.net 2003 process or have migrated a K2.net 2003 process to K2 blackpearl, when a process utilizes a destination queue it will call `IRoleProvider.ResolveQueue()`. In most situations for many custom security providers used in K2.net 2003, it's rare that this method will need to be implemented.

Once K2 blackpearl SP2 is released, any custom security provider built for K2.net 2003 should be able to be migrated to K2 blackpearl under its own security label. Some manual steps will need to be performed in K2 blackpearl to register the custom security provider from K2.net 2003 into K2 blackpearl.

The following table briefly describes how `IRoleProvider.ResolveQueue()` should function:

| Argument | Description |
|---|---|
| data | This string contains an XML document that represents the destination queue. |
| Returns | An array of users that are resolved in the queue based on the XML document data. |

The following code shows a sample of the `DestinationQueues` XML document:

```
<DestinationQueues>
  <DestinationQueue>
    <SendToBehaviour Name="Send To" Type="sendto">
      <SendToItem Name="DENALLIX\Sales " Type="group"
              Path="LDAP://CN=Sales,CN=Users,DC=denallix,DC=com" />
      <SendToItem Name="DENALLIX\Operations" Type="organizationalunit"
              Path="LDAP://OU=Operations,OU=Depts,DC=denallix,DC=com" />
```

```
      </SendToBehaviour>
      <SendToBehaviour Name="Send To Manager" Type="sendtomanager">
        <SendToItem Name="DENALLIX\janet" Type="user"
          Path="LDAP://CN=Janet Brown,OU=Operations,OU=Depts,DC=denallix,DC=com"
          />
      </SendToBehaviour>
    </DestinationQueues>
  </DestinationQueue>
```

The `DestinationQueues` XML document contains the following elements:

❑ A Root element called `DestinationQueues` — This contains one or more `DestinationQueue` elements.

❑ The `DestinationQueue` node can contain one or more `SendToBehaviour` elements.

❑ `SendToBehaviour` elements can contain one or more `SendToItem` elements and will have a `Name` attribute and `Type` attribute. The attribute `Type` can be `sendto`, `sendtomanager`, `sendtopeers`, or `exclude`. This behavior element defines rules for how the `SendToItem` elements are to be resolved.

❑ The `SentToItem` element does not contain any child elements or nodes. It has a `Name`, `Type`, and `Path` attribute. The `Name` attribute will contain the name of the user, group, or organizational unit that the `SendToItem` will operate. The `Type` specifies if the `SendToItem` is a `user`, `group`, or `organizationalunit`. The `Path` attribute will contain the path to the `SendToItem`.

An implementation of `IRoleProvider.ResolveQueue()` will need to consume the `DestinationQueues` XML document and resolve all the users based on the behaviors defined in the `SendToBehaviour` elements using the `SendToItems` elements.

## Remotely Invoking the Security Provider

All of the code covered thus far runs server-side within the context of the Host Server. However, sometimes it's necessary to be able to communicate with a security provider from outside of K2 blackpearl. K2 blackpearl provides an API to remotely query to the security providers from any client, locally or remotely over the network.

Adding a reference to `SourceCode.Security.UserRoleManager.Client.dll` assembly will provide access to the `UserRoleManagerServer` object that provides the ability to interface to all security providers on the K2 blackpearl server.

All the methods contained within the `UserRoleManagerServer` object almost exactly mirror the methods on the `IRoleProvider` interface. The difference is that the `UserRoleManagerServer` is agnostic to the security provider being used meaning you can use it to query any of the installed security providers by providing the security label.

The following table documents the methods on the `UserRoleManagerServer`:

| Methods | Description |
| --- | --- |
| FindGroups | Overloaded. Invokes `IRoleProvider.FindGroups()` on the security provider for the specified security label. |
| FindUsers | Overloaded. Invokes `IRoleProvider.FindUsers()` on the security provider for the specified security label. |
| FormatItemName | Invokes `IRoleProvider.FormatItemName()` on the security provider for the specified security label. |
| GetDefaultLabelName | Retrieves the default security label name by querying the `[SecurityLabels]` table in the `[HostServer]` database where `[DefaultLabel]` is set to 1. |
| GetGroup | Overloaded. Invokes `IRoleProvider.GetGroup()` on the security provider for the specified security label. |
| GetLabelProvider | Returns a string that contains the name of the provider. |
| GetLabels | Returns a string array containing all the registered security labels in the Host Server |
| GetUser | Overloaded. Invokes `IRoleProvider.GetUser()` on the security provider for the specified security label. |
| QueryGroupProperties | Invokes `IRoleProvider.QueryGroupProperties()` on the security provider for the specified security label. |
| QueryUserProperties | Invokes `IRoleProvider.QueryUserProperties()` on the security provider for the specified security label. |
| ResolveQueue | Overloaded. These methods are used mainly to support migrated or upgraded K2.net 2003 processes that use destination queues. |

The following is an example of how to use the `UserRoleManagerServer` object to query the default security provider to discover the groups the user "bob" is in:

```
// Create a dictionary of search terms with the criteria for
// searching for a group or groups. This isn't used in this
// scenario, but it is required on the interface.
IDictionary<string,object> groupProps = new IDictionary<string,object>();
groupProps.Add("Name", null); // no search criteria needed
groupProps.Add("Description", null); // no search criteria needed

// Build a connection string to the K2 blackpearl server
SCConnectionStringBuilder connBuilder = new SCConnectionStringBuilder();
connBuilder.Host = "DLX";
connBuilder.Port = 5555;
connBuilder.Integrated = true;
```

```
// Instantiate the UserRoleManagerServer
UserRoleManagerServer roleServer = new UserRoleManagerServer();
roleServer.CreateConnection();

try
{
    roleServer.Connection.Open(connBuilder.ToString());
    // Make sure bob's username is normalized, this will prefix the
    // default domain in front of the username if it's not there already
    // E.g. Denallix\bob
    string userName = roleServer.FormatItemName("bob", "K2");
    // Resolve the Active Directory Groups Bob is in
    IGroupCollection bobsGroups =
                        roleServer.FindGroups(userName, groupProps, "K2");
}
finally
{
    roleServer.Connection.Close();
    roleServer.Connsection.Dispose();
}
```

# Single Sign-On (SSO)

With the basic security provider API covered, an additional important feature of K2 blackpearl's Security Framework worth mentioning is Single Sign-On (SSO). SSO solves an important issue created when accessing many systems that have different authentication mechanisms or even different credential requirements through K2 blackpearl. The role of SSO is to broker all authentication requests to third-party systems on behalf of the logged-in K2 user.

Each user has a SSO Cache that stores their personal set of credentials for access to external systems through K2 blackpearl. The SSO Cache stores the security label of the security provider, as well as user-associated name and passwords used to connect to these other systems. The credentials are encrypted and then persisted permanently. If a user's password changes, K2 will attempt to log in using their old credentials in the SSO Cache. If the login fails, the underlying K2 Security Framework will throw an exception containing the information needed to prompt the user for the new credentials.

For example, while accessing a SmartObject, users may be required to provide credentials for the system from which the SmartObject retrieves data. The first time the user attempts to access that back-end system through the SmartObject, SSO checks to see if the SSO Cache has the required credentials for that user to log in to that specific system. If SSO cannot find the credentials in the SSO Cache, the application using the SmartObject receives a `SourceCode.Hosting.Exceptions.AuthenticationException`. This exception will provide two properties that will supply information needed to ask for the proper credentials. These properties are the `ProviderFriendlyName`, which contains the security label and the `ProviderTypeString`. Based on the friendly name and the provider type, any consumer can prompt the user for credentials and then create a new connection string. When authenticating to a system where the credentials are handled by SSO, the connection string requires the `IsPrimaryLogin` property set to false. Finally a call to `Authenticate(string connectionString)` on the `Connection` object will need to be made on behalf of the user to validate the new credentials. To validate the secondary login properly, the user must already be authenticated using their primary login (with `IsPrimaryLogin` set to true).

Once the user logs in, their credentials are then stored in the SSO Cache, which is a table in one of the K2 blackpearl databases. Once cached, all subsequent authentication requests to that system will be made automatically, on behalf of the user. Credentials cannot be deleted out of the SSO Cache.

Since credentials are the keys to the kingdom, so to speak, it's critical they are secured. K2 blackpearl employs strong cryptography to protect these credentials when they are persisted to the cache. An additional feature planned for future K2 blackpearl release will allow users and/or administrators to choose which credentials to allow to be cached. This will provide flexibility as some policies may prohibit the caching of credentials to particular sensitive systems.

At the time this chapter is being written, the SSO functionality currently only works with SmartObjects. In the future, SSO functionality will work with all K2 blackpearl components.

# Building a Custom Security Provider

A complete custom security provider has been developed as a companion to this chapter and can be downloaded from www.wrox.com. The security provider is built around Active Directory Application Mode (ADAM), which is basically a standalone lightweight but robust LDAP Service based on Active Directory. ADAM is included with Server 2003 R2 and can be downloaded from Microsoft and installed on Windows Server 2003 and Windows XP.

Instead of covering the specifics of the ADAM implementation here, this section will cover the basics and some general approaches that can be used to build a custom security provider.

## Where to Start

To begin developing a custom security provider, Visual Studio 2005 with the K2 Designer for Visual Studio is required. The development environment can be set up either on a standalone Windows XP system targeting a remote K2 blackpearl server, or on a Server 2003 system with K2 server installed locally with all the development tools.

In order to create a custom K2 blackpearl security provider, the following assemblies' references are required: `SourceCode.HostClientAPI.dll`, which can be added via the Visual Studio Add Reference dialog, and `SourceCode.HostServerInterfaces.dll`, which is located in the `[K2 Install Path]\Configuration\Bin` folder on the developer workstation where the K2 Designer for Visual Studio is installed. Additionally, when using the logging functionality in the `SourceCode.Logging.Logger` namespace, add a reference to the `SourceCode.Logging` assembly located in the Add Reference dialog in Visual Studio.

## Code Organization

Since the `IHostableSecurityProvider` is a conglomeration of many different interfaces, I've found it helpful to organize each interface for the core security provider in four different partial classes; this allows clean separation of each of the different logical code sections, making it easily find different segments of code and prevent the class file from growing unwieldy. Remember, partial classes are merged into one class when it's compiled, so don't duplicate any methods or properties. Also, all fields, properties, methods, events, and so on will be visible to all classes that are members of the same partial class.

Add four class files to the newly created custom security provider project. Name them as follows:

❑ `CustomSecurityProvider.IAuthenticationProvider.cs`

❑ `CustomSecurityProvider.IHostableSecurityProvider.cs`

❑ `CustomSecurityProvider.IHostableType.cs`

❑ `CustomSecurityProvider.IRoleProvider.cs`

Then open each file and change the class declaration from:

```
class CustomSecurityProvider
```

To the following:

```
partial class CustomSecurityProvider
```

Then for each file, implement the skeleton interface for the corresponding interface in the file name; for example, to add the `IAuthenticationProvider` interface to the `CustomSecurityProvider`.`IAuthenticationProvider.cs` file, open it in Visual Studio and change it from:

```
partial class CustomSecurityProvider
```

To the following:

```
public partial class CustomSecurityProvider : IAuthenticationProvider
```

Then click the Smart Tag on the `IAuthenticaionProvider` interface, and choose Explicitly implement interface `'IAuthenticationProvider'` (as shown in Figure 17-7).

**Figure 17-7**

This will automatically stub in all of the required `IAuthenticationProvider` interface requirements. Repeat these steps for each interface.

For simplicity, you can choose the "Explicitly implement interface . . . " option for the interfaces that have overlapping identical method signatures. Really, only two specific methods need to be explicitly implemented: `IAuthenticationProvider.Init()` and `IRoleProvider.Init()`.

Finally, once all the partial classes are created and the stub methods are generated, only the `CustomSecurityProvider.IHostableSecurityProvider.cs` class needs the interface `IHostableSecurityProvider` defined, all the other interfaces on the other partial classes can be removed.

# Installing the Custom Security Provider

Once all the stub methods are in place, the custom provider can be installed, and debugging can commence, though without all the methods implemented expect to see errors from the K2 Host Server. Don't install an untested security provider on a production server, as any issues with the provider could affect the availability of the K2 Host Server.

Here is the outline of the process required to install and configure a new security provider:

1.  Stage security provider dependencies.

2.  Stage Host Server configuration settings.

3.  Install the Security Provider library.

4.  Configure the security provider.

5.  Debug the security provider.

6.  Test the security provider. Now let's take a deeper look at each of these six steps.

## Staging Provider Dependencies and Configuration

If the custom security provider has any dependencies, they must be deployed and configured before integrating the security provider library into the Host Server. For example, if the custom security provider requires that a database be created and populated with data, make sure to stage that first.

After all the external dependencies are set up and configured, stop the K2 blackpearl Service.

## Staging Host Server Configuration Settings

After the service is stopped, any K2 blackpearl-specific configuration settings used by the custom security provider need to be installed–for instance, if the security provider depends on Application Configuration settings in the K2HostServer.config, appSettings section or it may have a database connection string stored in the connectionStrings section.

## Installing the Security Provider Library

In the K2 blackpearl Host Server folder, there is a subfolder called securityproviders. This is where the assembly that implements the IHostableSecurityProvider interface goes. After stopping the K2 blackpearl server, copy the new security provider assembly into the [K2 Install Folder]\ K2 blackpearl\Host Server\Bin\securityproviders folder. Make sure to include copying any non-K2 assemblies that aren't installed in the GAC that the custom security provider references.

> As of K2 blackpearl 0807, all custom assemblies must be registered with the Host Server database. See KB000351 titled "K2 blackpearl 0807 Feature and Functionality Changes" for more information.

Here are the steps to register an assembly in the Host Server database for version 0807 and later:

1.  Compile the security provider with a strong name.

2.  Extract the public key token of the security provider using the Strong Name Utility that is bundled with the .NET Framework SDK like so:

```
sn.exe -Tp MySecurityProvider.dll
```

The output will look similar to this:

```
Microsoft (R) .NET Framework Strong Name Utility  Version 3.5.30729.1
Copyright (c) Microsoft Corporation.  All rights reserved.

Public key is
0024000004800000940000000602000000240000525341310004000001000100fb82d933692ba1be803
6122893716e6aaf5b37646111747a2ac2d65956c7b3b93889a715fd3903f680cfd88e244460429caff1
5ae539229b920948d6e1a62103b13c20d8915ec5b014a81de4fc67e9c85c3ac916840382a4dce3a4126
0d828742153b5d967cf9695b11bbc0b16cbdf397bf22302cedb49d3738432f1d8484fca

Public key token is 94606af0c2dd17b7
```

**3.** Add the security provider to the `HostServer` database using the following SQL Command, replacing `MySecurityProvider.dll` and 94606af0c2dd17b7 with the actual assembly name and public key token of your signed security provider dll.

```
INSERT INTO [HostServer].[dbo].[AssemblyRegistration]
(
     [AssemblyID],
     [AssemblyName],
     [PublicKeyToken],
     [Enabled])
VALUES
(
     newid(),
     'MySecurityProvider.dll',
     '94606af0c2dd17b7'
     ,1
)
```

**4.** Make sure to set the `useassemblyregistration appSetting` in the `[K2 Install]\` `Host Server\bin\K2HostServer.config` file as follows:

```
<appSettings>
...
     <add key="useassemblyregistration" value="true" />
...
</appSettings>
```

**5.** Restart the K2 Host Server service.

## Configuring the Security Provider

Once the Security Provider library has been copied and the configuration settings have been set up, start the K2 blackpearl Service. On service startup, the K2 server polls the `securityproviders` folder. If the server finds an assembly that contains an object that implements the `IHostableSecurityProvider` interface, the Host Server will insert a new record in the `SecurityProviders` table in the `HostServer` database for the new provider.

To finish integrating the custom security provider into K2, the `HostServer` database needs to be updated to set the security label name as well as the authentication and roles initialization data (`AuthInit` and `RoleInit` columns). Make sure to give the server a little bit of time to record the new security provider in the database before running the following script; the script will fail if the K2 server either doesn't detect the new security provider for some reason, or if it hasn't had enough time to detect and add the record to the `SecurityProviders` table.

The following sample SQL script can be modified to add a new security label to the `HostServer` database:

```
declare @securityProviderName nvarchar(255)
declare @securityLabel nvarchar(255)
declare @authProviderID uniqueidentifier
declare @securityProviderID uniqueidentifier
declare @securityLabelID uniqueidentifier
declare @authInit xml
declare @roleInit xml
declare @defaultLabel bit

USE [HostServer]

-- This is the security label that will be seen in the K2 Workspace
SET @securityLabel = 'Custom Label Name'

-- This is the Class name of the Provider
SET @securityProviderName = 'Custom.Auth.Provider'

-- Generate a new GUID
SET @securityLabelID = newid()

-- Set up the AuthInit xml document used to initialize the
-- Authentication Provider
SET @authInit = '<authInit />'

-- Set up the RoleInit xml document used to initialize the
-- Roles Provider
SET @roleInit = '<roleProvider><init /></roleProvider>'

-- This is not the system default Label
SET @defaultLabel = 0

-- Extract the Authentication SecurityProviderID for the newly
-- added Provider
SELECT
  @authProviderID = [SecurityProviderID]
FROM
  [SecurityProviders]
WHERE
  [ProviderClassName] = @securityProviderName

-- Extract the Roles SecurityProviderID for the newly
-- added Provider
SELECT
  @securityProviderID = [SecurityProviderID]
FROM
  [SecurityProviders]
WHERE
  [ProviderClassName] = @securityProviderName
```

```
-- Link the SecurityProvider to a new Security Label
INSERT INTO [SecurityLabels]
(
      [SecurityLabelID],
      [SecurityLabelName],
      [AuthSecurityProviderID],
      [AuthInit],
      [RoleSecurityProviderID],
      [RoleInit],
      [DefaultLabel]
)
VALUES
(
      @securityLabelID,
      @securityLabel,
      @authProviderID,
      @authInit,
      @roleProviderID,
      @roleInit,
      @defaultLabel
)
```

At this point, the custom security provider is installed. Check the HostServer log file. There should be an entry making note of the security providers that are loaded. If the K2 blackpearl Service starts and then stops, most likely an exception has occurred in one or multiple `Init()` methods in the provider. These types of issues can be more difficult to troubleshoot because the service isn't up long enough to attach the debugger and the logger may not be up and running to capture messages written to the Logger.

## Debugging the Security Provider

To debug a provider, make sure to copy the `.pdb` file into the `[K2 Install Folder]\Host Server\ bin\securityprovider` folder alongside the security provider assembly.

To debug a custom security provider:

1.  Load the security provider project in Visual Studio.

2.  Click the Debug menu and choose Attach to Process.

3.  Find the K2HostServer.exe in the list, and then click Attach.

*See Chapter 6 for more information on debugging on the K2 blackpearl server.*

If you are developing on a K2 blackpearl server, a decent debugging approach is to configure the Security Provider project in Visual Studio to start the K2 server in Console mode by launching `K2HostServer.exe`. This will require configuring the K2 Service to run successfully under your developer account instead of the normal K2 blackpearl Service Account. Make sure to stop the K2 Service before using this approach.

To configure Visual Studio to directly start and debug `K2HostServer.exe`:

1. Right-click the Custom Security project in the Visual Studio Solution Explorer and choose Properties.

2. Once the Project Properties load, click the Debug tab on the right-hand side.

3. Under Start Action, choose Start External Program, and browse to `[K2 Install Folder]\Host Server\bin\K2HostServer.exe`.

4. Click the Save toolbar button to save the project settings.

Now when you press the Start Debugging toolbar button in Visual Studio, it will start the K2 Host Server with the debugger attached.

Additionally, if you're developing on the K2 server, you can create a post-build event in Visual Studio to copy the latest built version of the custom security provider to the `Host Server\bin\securityproviders` folder in the K2 Installation folder. The security provider has been successfully installed.

To configure Visual Studio to copy the latest version of the security provider assembly and debugging symbols (`..pdb` file) to the `securityproviders` folder after a successful build:

1. Right-click the Custom Security Project in the Visual Studio Solution Explorer, and choose Properties.

2. Once the Project Properties load, click the Build Events tab on the right-hand side.

3. Click the Edit Post-build button.

4. Add the following commands replacing the path that follows with the K2 blackpearl installation path:

```
copy "$(TargetPath)" "c:\program files\k2 blackpearl\Host Server\bin\securityproviders"
copy "$(TargetDir)$(TargetName).pdb" "c:\program files\k2 blackpearl\Host Server\bin\securityproviders"
```

5. Make sure that the Run the post-build event is set to On successful build.

6. Click the Save toolbar button to save the project settings.

7. On the Build menu in Visual Studio, click Build Solution.

If the files are unable to be copied successfully, a build error will be reported. Check the Build Output window to trouble-shoot post-build event Errors. Most likely, any post-build event errors encountered will be because the K2 Host Service is running and has a handle on the custom security provider file, locking it.

There are a couple of other things to avoid when directly debugging on the server. Do not use the K2 Object Browser in the same Visual Studio session you are debugging. It gets deadlocked and the Host Server will have to be killed. Start a second Visual Studio session and use the Object Browser in there.

### *Testing the Security Provider*

To verify that the provider is working:

1. Browse to the K2 Workspace and open the K2 Management Server.

2. Expand the Server node and then the Workflow Server node.

3. Choose Process Rights.

4. Click the Security Label drop-down, and verify the new custom Security Provider label is there.

5. Select the new provider and then click Search. If there are users and/or roles available for the new provider, it will list the users.

6. Verify the new custom security provider's security label shows up in the User Browser in the K2 Object Browser in Visual Studio, Visio, or MOSS/WSS.

7. Once you've verified that the new security label is visible in the K2 Workspace and the K2 Object Browser, test the provider by granting it various permissions to different areas of the K2 Workspace.

8. Finally, create a workflow that uses users and groups from the new security provider. Since there are many different ways to invoke the security providers within K2, make sure to use a broad range of techniques to test a provider. Make sure to include destination queues and dynamic Roles; make sure to also test the resolution of a user's manager.

# K2 connect

K2 connect is an additional layer of functionality that sits on top of K2 blackpearl. Initially Version 1 will provide a security provider that will allow connectivity to SAP. The version after that will add additional connectivity to BizTalk Server and any BizTalk Adapter — which includes Siebel eBusiness Applications, Oracle databases, and any adapter built on the WCF LOB Adapter SDK.

*See Chapter 23 for more information on K2 connect.*

# Summary

This chapter covered the Active Directory User Manager's (ADUM) configurable settings for controlling Active Directory behavior and provided in-depth coverage of how to use the security provider API to build a custom security provider and how to externally invoke the security providers via the Client API. Hopefully, this chapter has illustrated the generous amount of flexibility K2 blackpearl offers for building custom security providers. This extensibility allows K2 blackpearl to integrate into almost any home-grown or third-party systems, leveraging workflow deep within the enterprise.

# 18

# Disaster Recovery Planning

Colin Murphy

Disaster recovery is one of the most important aspects of planning your K2 blackpearl deployment. It is one of those things that you hopefully will never have to actually utilize but that is absolutely critical to any implementation. As you begin planning for disaster recovery and uptime requirements, high-availability planning may also come into consideration as an attempt to minimize the impact of a server failure on your workflows. While this chapter will primarily focus on disaster recovery, an overview of the high-availability options available with K2 blackpearl will also be provided.

Additionally, K2 blackpearl potentially involves many parts, such as:

❑ The process servers

❑ Windows SharePoint Services/Microsoft Office SharePoint Server 2007

❑ IIS (the K2 Workspace)

❑ Line-of-business data (such as that which is accessed by SmartObjects)

❑ Database servers

While this chapter will provide some guidance on these external systems and some considerations that must be taken into account, it will focus only on the K2 specific pieces of the system and the databases which K2 utilizes.

Disaster recovery planning should be a key consideration within every organization, but it can also be an extremely complex process and quite daunting. K2 blackpearl is also a complex product that potentially involves components installed across multiple servers and that likely interacts with other external systems such as SharePoint or other line-of-business (LOB) systems. This chapter attempts to break down the disaster recovery planning process and also provide step-by-step instructions for each K2 component independent of whether it is installed on a standalone server or within a farm.

This chapter covers the following topics:

❑    A general overview of disaster recovery planning

❑    Disaster recovery and K2 blackpearl

❑    Steps to back up and restore K2 blackpearl components

# What Is a Disaster Recovery Plan (DRP)?

A disaster recovery plan (DRP) — also referred to as a Business Continuity Plan (BCP) — is a set of procedures and measures to help ensure that business systems and processes can survive a disaster according to a business's requirements. A DRP typically encompasses three areas of planning:

❑    **Pre-Planning/Mitigation:** Anticipate potential failure points and prepare mitigation strategies where appropriate.

❑    **Continuity:** Develop a plan for how work can continue to be performed while the system is down if necessary.

❑    **Recovery:** Determine the steps required to bring the system back up after a failure and to integrate work performed in the continuity phase back into the system (if necessary).

A disaster recovery plan is also a careful cost-benefits analysis to determine what level of downtime and data loss is acceptable vs. the cost of providing a more robust solution. Your organization may have a Service Level Agreement (SLA) for the application which it might also have to meet. SLAs can be very complex and span a host of service requirements, but a very simple SLA might read:

The system must provide 99.9% uptime within each calendar year.

A 99.9% uptime requirement means that the system can be down a little over eight hours every year, whereas a 99.999% uptime requirement only allows for approximately five minutes of downtime a year! And as you might expect, the difference in cost and resources required to meet the first is far different from the cost and resources required to meet the second.

## Setting the Baseline

You may find it helpful to begin your disaster recovery plan by asking yourself a few simple questions (which may have very complex answers):

❑    What impact would a system failure have on the business?

❑    In the event of a failure, how long can the business reasonably go without the system?

❑    In the event of a failure, what level of data loss is acceptable?

These three questions serve as an excellent starting point for beginning your disaster recovery planning and should also be considered during your initial deployment planning (discussed in Chapter 5).

# Pre-Planning/Mitigation Planning

Mitigation planning primarily revolves around determining potential failure points within your business process and determining what (if any) steps need to be taken to mitigate those potential failures. Within a K2 blackpearl environment, some common failure points to consider might be:

- ❑ **Software Issues:** Server patches, configuration issues

- ❑ **Server Hardware:** Hard drives, power supplies, network cards, RAM, processors, motherboards

- ❑ **Network Infrastructure:** Routers/switches, load balancers, network connection/transmission issues

- ❑ **Local Disasters:** Power failures, fire

- ❑ **Regional Disasters:** Hurricanes, earthquakes, floods

Each issue has a potential mitigation strategy, which may or may not be justified based on your organizations' requirements. Take planning for natural disasters, for example. An example mitigation strategy might be:

Perform tape backups nightly and ship offsite weekly.

Such a mitigation strategy will ensure that, at most, one week of data is lost in the event that the system and all local tapes are destroyed. A mitigation strategy targeted toward no data loss might look something like:

All systems and data will be mirrored in real-time to a duplicate server farm located in a different geography.

This second mitigation strategy will ensure very limited data loss and very good continuity, but the costs associated with such an approach are significant and may not be justified by the processes deployed.

# Continuity Planning

Continuity planning is focused on how the business will continue to operate while the system is down in the event that your mitigation strategies have been ineffective. Common approaches to continuity are:

- ❑ **No Continuity:** No work will be performed until the system comes back up.

- ❑ **Paper/Manual Process:** While the system is down, users will continue to perform their duties through using a manual or paper-based process.

- ❑ **Redundant/Backup System:** While the system is down, users will switch to using a backup system.

There is not necessarily a one-size-fits-all continuity plan, and in many cases, a hybrid approach may also be required. For example, the work involved in bringing a backup system online, switching all users to it, and then migrating the data back into the primary system upon recovery may only be justified for outages lasting long periods of time.

## Recovery Planning

Recovery planning focuses on restoring the system to a working state after a disaster. For simple failures, such as a single drive in a RAID array, this might be as simple as swapping a drive out, while for more severe failures it could involve completely rebuilding a machine or an entire server farm and restoring the data.

It is also important to consider how to merge work that was performed according to your continuity plan back into the system when it is brought back up. This should not be overlooked and can require considerable effort.

## Testing

Once your plan has been established and your disaster recovery procedures are in place, it is extremely important to also test those procedures periodically. No software system is static, and it is very important that the recovery plan be reviewed and tested periodically to ensure that it adequately addresses the needs of the organization.

# Disaster Recovery and K2 blackpearl

K2 blackpearl supports a variety of different configurations, ranging from a single standalone server to large farm configurations consisting of a large number of servers. Additionally, K2 very likely interacts with external systems such a Microsoft Office SharePoint Server (MOSS), LOB, or custom applications. With so many different systems interacting, developing an effective disaster recovery process can prove to be quite challenging.

For that reason, this chapter will discuss the various pieces of K2 that need to be considered, rather than the individual servers on which those components reside. The components which will be discussed are:

- ❑ K2 databases
- ❑ K2 Web Components
- ❑ K2 blackpearl server
- ❑ K2 for Reporting
- ❑ K2 for SharePoint

Additional components that are not K2-specific but that also must be considered in any complete disaster recovery plan are:

- ❑ Forms (ASP.NET/InfoPath)
- ❑ External databases utilized by your K2 processes

## *Backup/Restoration of the Windows Server Machines*

The sections that follow will focus on the individual K2 blackpearl components and provide DR recommendations for each, but it is also critical to have plans in place to be able to restore each server utilized within your install to a clean state (such as restoring the server from a previous backup or a drive image) prior to restoring K2 blackpearl.

*All restoration instructions within this chapter assume that you have a working, baseline Windows 2003 Server.*

## *Database Disaster Recovery Options*

K2's databases are really the heart of your disaster recovery strategy since so much of K2 lives inside of the databases, including workflow instances, process definitions, SmartObject definitions, and environment variables just to name a few. Disaster recovery planning for K2's databases is very similar to the disaster recovery planning one would do for any set of SQL databases.

SQL Server 2005 provides several different disaster recovery options, which can be used for K2 disaster recovery, and those are outlined in the following table:

| Option | Description | Strengths | Weaknesses |
|---|---|---|---|
| Backup and Restore | Creates a backup copy of the database, which can be stored in a safe location. Supports both full and incremental backups. | Backups can be stored to removable storage (such as tape) and do not have to be dependant on network access. | Data added since the last backup will be lost.<br><br>Restoration is not an automatic process<br><br>Database is unavailable while restore is in progress |
| Log Shipping | Similar to replication, data is replicated from one server to another, but the mechanism differs as Log Shipping relies on the transaction log. | Standby server can be brought online more quickly than restoring from backup.<br><br>All schema changes are reflected.<br><br>More efficient than replication.<br><br>Well suited for warm-standby servers or higher latency locations. | Database changes are only shipped after a transaction log backup (some potential data loss).<br><br>Requires additional database server.<br><br>Failover is not automatic. |

*(continued)*

| Option | Description | Strengths | Weaknesses |
|---|---|---|---|
| Database Mirroring | Similar to replication and log shipping, data is replicated from one server to another, but the mechanism differs. | Very low latency. Very quick switchover. | Must be configured per database. Not suited for high-latency connections. Automatic failover possible. Requires additional database server. |
| Database Clustering | Two database servers share the same disk array. | No latency. Automatic failover. | Servers should be in the same geographic location. Requires an additional database server. Increased cost. Share disk array is still a single point of failure. |

*SQL Server 2005 supports one additional option which is sometimes used to replicate data called replication; however, replication is not supported by K2.*

Each solution has strengths and weaknesses, and it will be up to you to determine which option is the best fit for your needs. In almost all scenarios, you will always perform periodic backups and then may additionally utilize one of the other options. For high-availability scenarios, K2 blackpearl supports both clustering and mirroring.

*Because of the complexity involved with configuring these options, this chapter will only focus in detail on the simple backup and restore mechanism for disaster recovery. For more detail on the other disaster recovery options you should consult a book focused on SQL Server 2005 like* SQL Server 2005 Bible *by Paul Nielsen (Wiley, 2006).*

## Backup/Restoration of the K2 blackpearl Databases

The following discussion focuses on the tools that come with SQL Server 2005; however, there are a variety of third-party backup solutions on the market that make database maintenance and backup significantly easier. Though the steps might vary slightly if you are using one of these third-party tools, the information should still be very applicable.

## The K2 blackpearl Databases

K2 blackpearl utilizes 14 distinct databases, which are discussed in greater detail in Chapter 5. Their default names are:

- ❏ Categories
- ❏ Dependencies
- ❏ EnvironmentSettings
- ❏ EventBus
- ❏ EventBusScheduler
- ❏ HostServer
- ❏ K2Server
- ❏ K2ServerLog
- ❏ K2SQLUM
- ❏ SmartBox
- ❏ SmartBroker
- ❏ SmartFunctions
- ❏ WebWorkflow
- ❏ Workspace

*Depending on if your organization utilizes archiving, there may also be archive databases that you must consider as part of your DR strategy (archiving is discussed in Chapter 15).*

Additionally, there are several SQL Server system databases that also should be backed up regularly:

- ❏ Master
- ❏ Model
- ❏ Msdb

## Understanding the SQL Server Backup Model

SQL Server provides three types of backups:

- ❏ Full
- ❏ Differential
- ❏ Transaction Log

The descriptions, strengths, and weaknesses are listed in the following table:

| Option | Description | Strengths | Weaknesses |
|---|---|---|---|
| Full Backup | A complete backup of the entire database. | The quickest and simplest backup to restore. | The slowest backup to perform.<br><br>**Because of K2's architecture, the K2 Service must be stopped in order to perform a full backup.** |
| Differential Backup | A backup of all changes since the last full or differential backup. | Faster to perform than a full backup. | In order to restore a differential backup, you must first restore the last full backup as well as any other differential backups. |
| Transaction Log Backup | A backup of all database changes since the last full/differential backup or transaction log backup. | Generally the fastest backup option.<br><br>Allows for restoring the database to a particular point in time. | Slowest restore.<br><br>In order to restore a transaction log backup, you must first restore the last full backup as well as any differential backups, and any previous transaction log backups. |

An effective DR strategy will usually make use of a combination of all three types to enable the most efficient backup strategy, which allows the minimum amount of acceptable data loss. For example, a typical backup strategy for a system with fairly high transaction volumes might be to perform full backups weekly on Sundays at 3:00 A.M., differential backups daily at 3:00 A.M., and transaction log backups every 10 minutes.

Such a strategy helps ensure that you can restore your database with a minimal amount of effort and will lose at most 10 minutes worth of data.

> *Transaction log backups can be set to a maximum frequency of once every minute. For systems where even that level of data loss in unacceptable, mirroring or clustering should be considered.*

## Performing a Database Backup Manually

SQL Server provides tools that make it quite simple to create backups. These sample steps walk you through performing a simple database backup using one of these tools:

1. Stop the K2 blackpearl service on all application servers.

2. Open up Microsoft SQL Server Management Studio or SQL Server Business Intelligence Studio.

3. Connect to your K2 database server.

4. Find the desired database you wish to back up.

5. Right-click it and select Tasks ⇨ Back Up. See Figure 18-1.

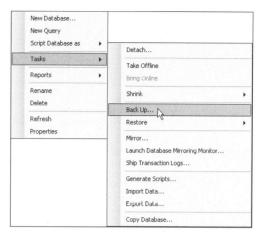

**Figure 18-1**

6.  Ensure that the Backup type is set to Full and name the backup file as desired.

7.  If this is the first time you are configuring your backup, under Destination click the Add button.

8.  Select a desired backup destination location, and click OK.

9.  Click OK.

Repeat for the other 13 K2 databases.

This process can also be scripted so that it can be run from the command line. The following is a sample backup script that will back up all 14 K2 databases to the disk location C:\BACKUP\K2:

```
BACKUP DATABASE [Categories] TO DISK = N'C:\BACKUP\K2\Categories.bak'
WITH NOFORMAT, NOINIT, NAME = N'Categories-Full Database Backup', SKIP,
NOREWIND, NOUNLOAD, STATS = 10
GO
BACKUP DATABASE [Dependencies] TO DISK =
N'C:\BACKUP\K2\Dependencies.bak' WITH NOFORMAT, NOINIT, NAME =
N'Dependencies-Full Database Backup', SKIP, NOREWIND, NOUNLOAD, STATS =
10
GO
BACKUP DATABASE [EnvironmentSettings] TO DISK =
N'C:\BACKUP\K2\EnvironmentSettings.bak' WITH NOFORMAT, NOINIT, NAME =
N'EnvironmentSettings-Full Database Backup', SKIP, NOREWIND, NOUNLOAD,
STATS = 10
GO
BACKUP DATABASE [EventBus] TO DISK = N'C:\BACKUP\K2\EventBus.bak' WITH
NOFORMAT, NOINIT, NAME = N'EventBus-Full Database Backup', SKIP,
NOREWIND, NOUNLOAD, STATS = 10
GO
BACKUP DATABASE [EventBusScheduler] TO DISK =
N'C:\BACKUP\K2\EventBusScheduler.bak' WITH NOFORMAT, NOINIT, NAME =
N'EventBusScheduler-Full Database Backup', SKIP, NOREWIND, NOUNLOAD,
STATS = 10
GO
```

```
BACKUP DATABASE [HostServer] TO DISK = N'C:\BACKUP\K2\HostServer.bak'
WITH NOFORMAT, NOINIT, NAME = N'HostServer-Full Database Backup', SKIP,
NOREWIND, NOUNLOAD, STATS = 10
GO
BACKUP DATABASE [K2Server] TO DISK = N'C:\BACKUP\K2\K2Server.bak' WITH
NOFORMAT, NOINIT, NAME = N'K2Server-Full Database Backup', SKIP,
NOREWIND, NOUNLOAD, STATS = 10
GO
BACKUP DATABASE [K2ServerLog] TO DISK = N'C:\BACKUP\K2\K2ServerLog.bak'
WITH NOFORMAT, NOINIT, NAME = N'K2ServerLog-Full Database Backup',
SKIP, NOREWIND, NOUNLOAD, STATS = 10
GO
BACKUP DATABASE [K2SQLUM] TO DISK = N'C:\BACKUP\K2\K2SQLUM.bak' WITH
NOFORMAT, NOINIT, NAME = N'K2SQLUM-Full Database Backup', SKIP,
NOREWIND, NOUNLOAD, STATS = 10
GO
BACKUP DATABASE [SmartBox] TO DISK = N'C:\BACKUP\K2\SmartBox.bak' WITH
NOFORMAT, NOINIT, NAME = N'SmartBox-Full Database Backup', SKIP,
NOREWIND, NOUNLOAD, STATS = 10
GO
BACKUP DATABASE [SmartBroker] TO DISK = N'C:\BACKUP\K2\SmartBroker.bak' WITH
NOFORMAT, NOINIT, NAME = N'SmartBroker-Full Database Backup', SKIP,
NOREWIND, NOUNLOAD, STATS = 10
GO
BACKUP DATABASE [SmartFunctions] TO DISK =
N'C:\BACKUP\K2\SmartFunctions.bak' WITH NOFORMAT, NOINIT, NAME =
N'SmartFunctions-Full Database Backup', SKIP, NOREWIND, NOUNLOAD, STATS
= 10
GO
BACKUP DATABASE [WebWorkflow] TO DISK =
N'C:\BACKUP\K2\WebWorkflow.bak' WITH NOFORMAT, NOINIT, NAME =
N'WebWorkflow-Full Database Backup',
SKIP, NOREWIND, NOUNLOAD, STATS = 10
GO
BACKUP DATABASE [Workspace] TO DISK = N'C:\BACKUP\K2\Workspace.bak'
WITH NOFORMAT, NOINIT, NAME = N'Workspace-Full Database Backup', SKIP,
NOREWIND, NOUNLOAD, STATS = 10
GO
```

The previous script simply tells SQL Server to perform full backups on all 14 K2 databases. To run the script, utilize the SQLCMD utility from the command prompt:

```
C:\> SQLCMD -s <servername> -i <script file name>
```

*In order to ensure that the backed-up K2 and K2Log databases remain in sync, the K2 service must be stopped prior to performing a full backup.*

## Configuring Automatic Backups

While you may occasionally need to back up databases manually, it is more likely that you will want to configure automatic backups for your K2 databases, which run periodically.

An example schedule might be full backups weekly on Sundays at 3:00 A.M., differential backups daily at 3:00 A.M., and transaction log backups every 10 minutes.

One of the simplest mechanisms for creating backup jobs is to utilize the script generation capabilities of Management Studio.

Follow these steps to create a Full Backup job that runs nightly and an Incremental job that runs periodically during the day:

**1.** Open up Microsoft SQL Server Management Studio or SQL Server Business Intelligence Studio.

**2.** Connect to your K2 database server.

**3.** Expand the SQL Server Agent.

**4.** Right-click Jobs and select New Job. See Figure 18-2.

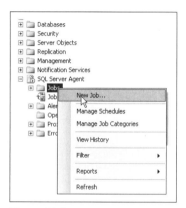

**Figure 18-2**

**5.** Name the Job **K2 Full Backup**.

**6.** Click on the Steps page.

**7.** Click the New button to create a new step.

**8.** Name the step **Stop K2 Service,** and set its type to CmdExec.

**9.** Choose Run As to a proxy which has permissions to start/stop the K2 Service on your K2 server (you may need to first add the proxy and credentials).

**10.** Enter the command sc *<k2ServerName>* stop "K2 [blackpearl] Server" replacing *<k2ServerName>* with your actual server name. If there are multiple K2 servers in your application farm, add an individual line for each server. See Figure 18-3.

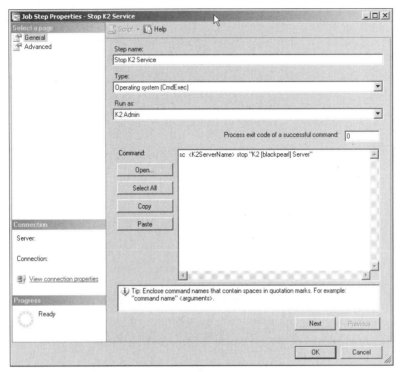

**Figure 18-3**

**11.** Click OK.

**12.** Click the New button to create a new step.

**13.** Name the step **Backup K2 Databases** and set its type to Transact-SQL script (T-SQL).

**14.** Enter the commands to back up each database (an example follows):

```
BACKUP DATABASE [Categories] TO DISK = N'C:\BACKUP\K2\Categories.bak'
WITH NOFORMAT, NOINIT, NAME = N'Categories-Full Database Backup', SKIP,
NOREWIND, NOUNLOAD, STATS = 10
GO
BACKUP DATABASE [Dependencies] TO DISK =
N'C:\BACKUP\K2\Dependencies.bak' WITH NOFORMAT, NOINIT, NAME =
N'Dependencies-Full Database Backup', SKIP, NOREWIND, NOUNLOAD, STATS =
10
GO
BACKUP DATABASE [EnvironmentSettings] TO DISK =
N'C:\BACKUP\K2\EnvironmentSettings.bak' WITH NOFORMAT, NOINIT, NAME =
N'EnvironmentSettings-Full Database Backup', SKIP, NOREWIND, NOUNLOAD, STATS = 10
GO
BACKUP DATABASE [EventBus] TO DISK = N'C:\BACKUP\K2\EventBus.bak' WITH
NOFORMAT, NOINIT, NAME = N'EventBus-Full Database Backup', SKIP,
NOREWIND, NOUNLOAD, STATS = 10
GO
```

```
BACKUP DATABASE [EventBusScheduler] TO DISK =
N'C:\BACKUP\K2\EventBusScheduler.bak' WITH NOFORMAT, NOINIT, NAME =
N'EventBusScheduler-Full Database Backup', SKIP, NOREWIND, NOUNLOAD,
STATS = 10
GO
BACKUP DATABASE [HostServer] TO DISK = N'C:\BACKUP\K2\HostServer.bak'
WITH NOFORMAT, NOINIT, NAME = N'HostServer-Full Database Backup', SKIP,
NOREWIND, NOUNLOAD, STATS = 10
GO
BACKUP DATABASE [K2Server] TO DISK = N'C:\BACKUP\K2\K2Server.bak' WITH
NOFORMAT, NOINIT, NAME = N'K2Server-Full Database Backup', SKIP,
NOREWIND, NOUNLOAD, STATS = 10
GO
BACKUP DATABASE [K2ServerLog] TO DISK = N'C:\BACKUP\K2\K2ServerLog.bak'
WITH NOFORMAT, NOINIT, NAME = N'K2ServerLog-Full Database Backup',
SKIP, NOREWIND, NOUNLOAD, STATS = 10
GO
BACKUP DATABASE [K2SQLUM] TO DISK = N'C:\BACKUP\K2\K2SQLUM.bak' WITH
NOFORMAT, NOINIT, NAME = N'K2SQLUM-Full Database Backup', SKIP,
NOREWIND, NOUNLOAD, STATS = 10
GO
BACKUP DATABASE [SmartBox] TO DISK = N'C:\BACKUP\K2\SmartBox.bak' WITH
NOFORMAT, NOINIT, NAME = N'SmartBox-Full Database Backup', SKIP,
NOREWIND, NOUNLOAD, STATS = 10
GO
BACKUP DATABASE [SmartBroker] TO DISK = N'C:\BACKUP\K2\SmartBroker.bak'
WITH NOFORMAT, NOINIT, NAME = N'SmartBroker-Full Database Backup',
SKIP, NOREWIND, NOUNLOAD, STATS = 10
GO
BACKUP DATABASE [SmartFunctions] TO DISK =
N'C:\BACKUP\K2\SmartFunctions.bak' WITH NOFORMAT, NOINIT, NAME =
N'SmartFunctions-Full Database Backup', SKIP, NOREWIND, NOUNLOAD, STATS =
10
GO
BACKUP DATABASE [WebWorkflow] TO DISK = N'C:\BACKUP\K2\WebWorkflow.bak'
WITH NOFORMAT, NOINIT, NAME = N'WebWorkflow-Full Database Backup',
SKIP, NOREWIND, NOUNLOAD, STATS = 10
GO
BACKUP DATABASE [Workspace] TO DISK = N'C:\BACKUP\K2\Workspace.bak'
WITH NOFORMAT, NOINIT, NAME = N'Workspace-Full Database Backup', SKIP,
NOREWIND, NOUNLOAD, STATS = 10
GO
```

**15.** Click OK.

**16.** Click the New button to create a new step.

**17.** Name the step **Start K2 Service**, and set its type to CmdExec.

**18.** Choose Run As to a proxy that has permissions to start/stop the K2 Service on your K2 server (you may need to first add the proxy and credentials).

**19.** Enter the command sc *<k2ServerName>* start "K2 [blackpearl] Server" replacing *<k2ServerName>* with your actual server name. If there are multiple K2 servers in your application farm, add an individual line for each server.

**20.** Click OK.

**21.** Click on the Schedules page.

**22.** Click the New button.

**23.** Name the schedule entry **Weekly**, and configure its frequency to run Weekly on Sunday at 3:00 A.M. See Figure 18-4.

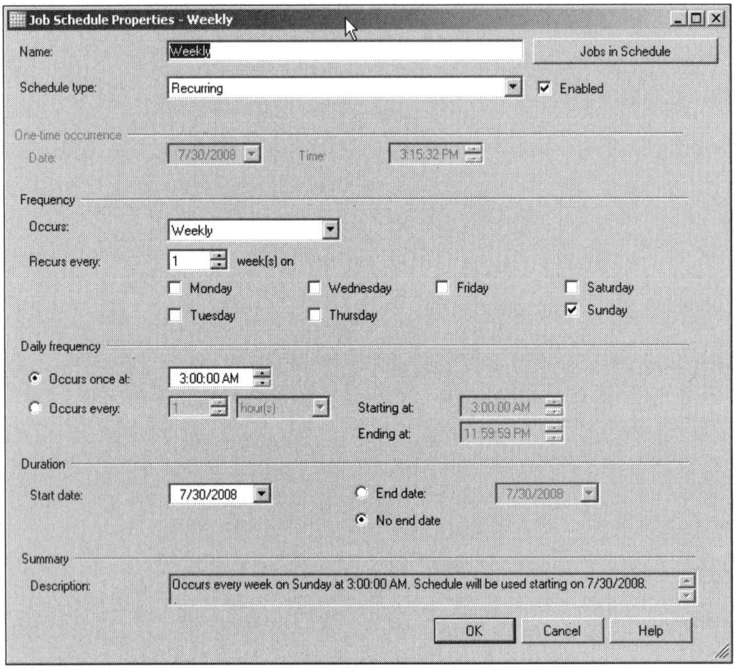

Figure 18-4

**24.** Click OK.

**25.** Click OK.

Now repeat these steps to create a Differential backup job and Transaction Log backup jobs. Differential backups still require the K2 Service to be stopped, but Transaction Log backups do not.

> *I generally recommend a backup schedule that consists of a weekly full backup, a nightly differential backup, and a transaction log backup every 10–15 minutes; however, your organization's needs may vary.*

### Restoring a Database

Restoring a database is also fairly straightforward using the SQL Server 2005 UI.

> **Restoring a database will overwrite all changes since the previous backup!**

1. Stop the K2 Service on all K2 servers.
2. Open up Microsoft SQL Server Management Studio or SQL Server Business Intelligence Studio.
3. Connect to your K2 database server.
4. Find the desired database you wish to restore.
5. Right-click it and select Tasks ⇨ Restore ⇨ Database.
6. Select the point in time to which you wish to restore (the default is the most recent possible).
7. Click OK.

## K2 Web Components

The K2 blackpearl Web Components consist of the Worklist, Management Console, Report Designer, and Notification Event Designer. Generally, these components serve as the "face" of K2 to administrators and users of the system.

There are two primary approaches which can be taken for DRP around the Web Components:

1. Since these components do not contain any kind of unique data or configuration settings (everything is stored in the K2 databases) that will be lost in a disaster, it is fairly simple to reinstall the Web components using the K2 Installation media.
2. Alternately, scheduled backups of the server can occur periodically so that the server can be restored. With this approach, the key areas that must be backed up/restored are the K2 blackpearl installation directory (the default is `"C:\Program Files\K2 blackpearl"`) as well as your IIS Metabase.

### Restoring K2 Web Components

To restore K2 Web Components, follow these steps:

1. Return the Windows machine to a working state.
2. Install the K2 Web Components.
3. (Optional) Restore the K2 blackpearl installation directory from backup.
4. Run the K2 Configuration Wizard.

# K2 blackpearl Server(s)

The K2 blackpearl server(s) handle processing of workflows, SmartObject requests, SmartObject Services, and so on. Unlike the Web Components, there are some customizations of the server that do not live in the server. These customizations are primarily limited to:

❑   Configuration file changes (changes to `.config` or `.setup` files)

❑   Logging files

❑   Custom DLLs such as custom security providers or SmartObject Services

Therefore, it is important to back up the entire K2 blackpearl installation directory (the default is `C:\Program Files\K2 blackpearl`).

> *Reinstalling the K2 Server Components will require obtaining a new license key (even if nothing else on the server has changed). Obtaining a new license key through standard channels can normally take a day; you may find it helpful to request an evaluation key in the meantime. Evaluation keys are valid for 72 hours.*

There are two primary scenarios for restoring a K2 blackpearl environment:

❑   Restoring to a machine with the same machine name (Cold Standby).

❑   Restoring to a new machine (Warm/Hot Standby).

Restoring to a cold standby is fairly straightforward

## Restoring the K2 blackpearl Server Components to a Cold Standby

To restore the server components to a cold standby, follow these steps:

**1.**   Return the Windows machine to a working state.

**2.**   Install the K2 Server Components.

**3.**   Restore the K2 blackpearl installation directory from backup.

**4.**   Run the K2 Configuration Utility and enter an updated license key.

## Setting Up the K2 blackpearl Server Components on a Warm or Hot Standby

Setting up the warm or hot standby environment is a rather involved process. Unlike restoring to a cold standby machine, restoring to a warm or hot standby requires preparation performed on the standby machine prior to the disaster occurring. This preparation is necessary because K2 stores configuration and licensing information within the K2 configuration databases. Since these machines are standby machines and are intended to be running only in the event of a disaster, you need to keep their configuration and licensing details out of the normal, day-to-day database setup. To do this, you first need to back up the production K2 databases, then install standby servers, back up the "standby" version of the relevant K2 databases, and then restore the original production K2 databases.

*A warm standby server is fairly complicated to set up and bring online. A simpler approach is to deploy K2 in a farm configuration and install the K2 blackpearl server Components on two machines in the farm. If you have some need not to run the farm in an active/active cluster, you can simply shut down the second server in the farm. When the first fails, simply bring the other server in the farm online, and the server will begin processing new requests. As a bonus, you shouldn't have to reconfigure external references, since they will have been using the farm name and not the server name.*

*Depending on how you have licensed the K2 software, there may be additional costs associated with configuring a standby server. Contact your K2 representative to determine what license terms are available for this scenario.*

To prepare the server components so that they can be restored in a warm or hot standby scenario, follow these steps:

In your primary environment:

1. Stop the K2 Service on your K2 blackpearl server(s).
2. Perform a full backup of your K2 databases.

In your warm standby environment:

1. Install the K2 Server Components.
2. Run the K2 Configuration Utility.
3. Validate that the environment is working properly.
4. Back up the following two database tables and save this backup to be used in the event of a disaster:
   - ❑ _Server table in K2Server DB
   - ❑ LicenseKeys table in HostServer DB
5. Take the warm standby servers offline.

In your primary environment:

1. Restore the K2 databases from the full backup.
2. Restart the K2 Service on your K2 blackpearl server(s).

## Restoring the K2 blackpearl Server Components to a Warm/Hot Standby

To restore server components in a warm or hot standby, follow these steps:

1. Bring the warm standby environment online.
2. Restore the K2 blackpearl ServiceBroker directory (K2 blackpearl\ServiceBroker) from backup.
3. Restore/deploy any other custom assemblies that your processes may require to the machine.

4. Restore the following two database tables to the database server from the backup taken when setting up the standby environment:

   ❑   _Server table in K2Server DB

   ❑   LicenseKeys table in HostServer DB

5. Update all references to the old machine (external ASPX pages, links to the Workspace, Worklist Web parts in SharePoint, and so on, to point to the new machine name).

6. Start the K2 blackpearl Service.

# K2 for Reporting Services

The K2 for Reporting Services components are installed on your SQL Reporting Services server and are required for the reporting functionality within K2 blackpearl. These components contain no customizations, so can safely be reinstalled after a disaster.

An additional consideration however, is any customized reports which may have been created. These reports are stored within the SQL Reporting Server databases and any backup strategy must also include these databases. The Reporting Service databases are:

❑   `ReportServer`

❑   `ReportServerTempDb`

Similarly to the main K2 databases, you should frequently perform backups of these databases.

### Restoring the K2 for Reporting Services Components

To restore Reporting Services components, follow these steps:

1. Return the Windows machine to a working state.

2. Install the K2 Reporting Components.

3. Restore Reporting Services databases.

# K2 for SharePoint

K2 for SharePoint components are installed on the servers in your SharePoint farm and provide integration between SharePoint and K2 blackpearl. The K2 components do not require any specialized backup considerations outside of your organization's SharePoint disaster recovery procedures. A complete discussion of SharePoint disaster recovery is outside the scope of this book, but SharePoint provides several mechanisms to perform backups and restores including through Central Admin or the command line.

This sample command will perform a farm-level backup of your SharePoint farm:

```
Stsadm.exe -o backup -directory c:\backuplocation -backupmethod full
```

Similarly, this sample command will perform a farm-level restoration:

```
Stsadm.exe -o restore -directory c:\backuplocation -restoremethod overwrite
```

Additionally, you should also perform backups of your SharePoint directory on the file system.

## Additional Components

Many K2 blackpearl workflows are designed to interact with external systems such as Active Directory, SharePoint, LOB databases, or external Web services. These systems are often overlooked as part of the K2 blackpearl disaster recovery plan, since they are likely covered by their own disaster recovery plan/ SLA, but it is very important to also factor these systems in to your continuity planning.

This can be a challenge for administrators, especially since the systems your organization's processes interact with may be extremely fluid. Any new process that is published to the K2 servers might introduce a new external dependency. It is very important, therefore, to have good procedures in place for deployment so that you can understand which external systems could potentially impact your workflows.

For example, imagine that you have a workflow that accesses lookup data from a list in SharePoint in order to determine routing. If SharePoint goes offline, what will happen to workflow process instances that attempt to access this list data? The answer to this question largely depends on the process design, but the likely outcome is that all processes which attempt to access the SharePoint resource will error out and will need to be repaired once SharePoint comes back online. By knowing ahead of time that this workflow has a dependency on SharePoint, you can warn users or take alternative action so that workflows of this type are not started or actioned during the outage.

# High-Availability Planning

During the course of your continuity planning, you might discover that the simple backup/restore paradigm is not sufficient to meet your organization's requirements. K2 blackpearl supports a variety of deployment configurations aimed towards fulfilling high-availability requirements. The following table gives a brief outline of the four basic configurations supported by K2 blackpearl:

| Deployment Type | Description |
| --- | --- |
| Standalone | All K2 components (including database) are installed on a single server. |
| Small Scale | All K2 components except for the database are installed on a single server. The databases are installed on a separate server or a cluster. |
| Medium Scale | All K2 components are installed on multiple servers in a Network Load Balanced environment. The databases are installed on a database cluster. |
| Large Scale | The K2 Workspace is installed on multiple servers that are Network Load Balanced. All other K2 components are installed on multiple servers which are Network Load Balanced. The databases are installed on a database cluster. |

Each configuration provides greater redundancy and performance than the one before it, but also increases in implementation complexity and cost. For more information about these configurations, refer to Chapter 5.

# Summary

Disaster recovery planning is a vital component within all organizations and must be addressed early on in the design process. This chapter has highlighted some of the challenges that arise in disaster recovery planning for a distributed system like K2 blackpearl as well as provided guidance on common disaster recovery steps for the components of K2 blackpearl.

In order to be prepared for a disaster, it is important to begin planning early, to implement disaster recovery procedures, and to validate/test those procedures frequently.

# 19

# Logging and System Reporting

**Shaun Leisegang**

This chapter focuses on logging and system reporting in K2 blackpearl.

❑ **Logging:** Is the process of storing information about events that occurred on the K2 blackpearl server.

❑ **System reporting:** Is the process of collecting and analyzing data to measure the performance of the product, process, or activity against expected results. It is a collection of server, network, and application performance metrics.

Logging allows you to record information about process execution in K2 blackpearl. This information is typically used by workflow developers for debugging purposes, and additionally, depending on the type and detail of information contained in the logging information, by experienced system administrators or technical support personnel to diagnose common problems with K2 blackpearl.

System reporting is done in K2 blackpearl via Windows Performance Monitoring (PerfMon). PerfMon is a tool that goes unused far too often, and when it does get used, it is often misinterpreted. It is a vital and most valuable tool in determining overall system health and activity, and the most common use of PerfMon is to answer the burning question, "Why is my system running slow?" So, in this chapter the various K2 blackpearl counters for PerfMon will be discussed and how these can be used to monitor the overall system health and activity of K2 blackpearl.

# K2 blackpearl Logging

As previously indicated, K2 blackpearl logging is used to store information about various events that have taken place on the K2 blackpearl server.

The base framework for the K2 server components is a hostable runtime environment that provides common infrastructure, such as communication, security, Single Sign-On, session management, logging, high availability, and server component federation.

Several server modules that provide different pieces of functionality are built into the Host Server. Each of these modules can make use of any of the common infrastructure components and are pluggable, allowing for the separation of modules onto different machines to maximize performance. The host environment also allows developers to build their own services that can be hosted within the framework. The server modules included with the platform are as follows:

❑ SmartObject Server

❑ Workflow Server

❑ SmartFunction Server

❑ Category Server

❑ Environment Library

❑ Event Bus

❑ Dependency Server

❑ User Rights Management Server

These server-side components are used for managing the operations of the K2 blackpearl environment. K2 server is one of the principle components responsible for running the processes that are exported to it from the designers. The K2 server requires access to its databases for the successful completion of the process instances and for successful running.

The logging feature is a useful feature common to all Host Servers. By default, messages are logged to a text (*.log) file, but the Host Server is capable of logging to different locations as well, such as the Windows Event log, the console, Microsoft Message Queuing (MSMQ), and SQL. All hosted servers and services use the same Logging Framework.

## Installation Log File

One of the first log files that is created in K2 blackpearl is the installation log file that is created during the installation process.

The K2 blackpearl installation log file allows you to troubleshoot installation issues. Occasionally a problem occurs with the K2 blackpearl setup, and you may have to use the installation log file as one of your tools to determine what the issue is.

During the installation and configuration of K2 blackpearl, a log file is created. Once the Configuration Manager has finished running, a link to the log file detailing the installation is available by clicking on this link surfaced through the Configuration Manager. The content of the installation log file is useful when diagnosing issues with the installation.

The log file is created by the Configuration Manager, and the installation log files can be found in the following location:

```
%PROGRAMFILES%\K2 blackpearl\Configuration\Log
```

The installation log file is called `InstallReport.log`, and an example of an installation log file is shown in Figure 19-1.

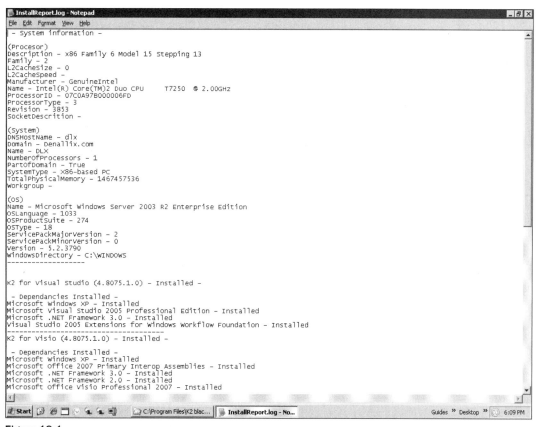

Figure 19-1

The installation log file contains details of the following:

- ❏ System information:
    - ❏ Processer
    - ❏ System
    - ❏ Operating system
- ❏ K2 components and version numbers:
    - ❏ K2 for Visual Studio
    - ❏ K2 for Visio
    - ❏ K2 blackpearl server
    - ❏ K2 Workspace
    - ❏ K2 SharePoint (MOSS) or K2 SharePoint (WSS)
    - ❏ K2 for Reporting Services
    - ❏ K2 Documentation
    - ❏ K2 blackpearl Configuration Manager

In addition to all this information, a detailed list of the relevant dependencies for each component are logged in the Installation log file.

The Installation log file is an excellent resource to debug installation problems with the K2 Support Team and will show details about the original installation, any upgrades to the K2 blackpearl server, and any SharePoint installation.

## Logging Framework

Once your K2 blackpearl installation is up and running, the K2 blackpearl Logging Framework allows you to view details across the several server modules that provide different pieces of functionality in the K2 blackpearl Host Server.

The Logging Framework listens for messages of various severity levels from a range of classes and extensions that interact with it. These messages range from informational messages to error messages to debugging information to warning messages.

The Logging Framework, out-of-the-box, supports recording and displaying these messages in several different locations, including the K2 server console, the K2 server log file, the Event log, an archive extension, and MSMQ.

The Logging Framework is also built with the flexibility to select which loggers are active and the severity levels of each logger. With the flexibility of the Logging Framework, you can turn on or off any standard loggers or custom loggers and set different severity levels to suit the dynamic needs of any business.

K2 blackpearl ships with five different logging extensions. Each extension handles messages differently and should be sufficient for standard business needs. The logging extensions that are shipped with K2 blackpearl are listed in the following table:

| Logging Extension | Description |
| --- | --- |
| ConsoleExtension | When the Console extension is turned on, messages are logged to the K2 server console when the server is running in console mode. |
| FileExtension | When the File extension is turned on, messages are logged to the K2 server log file. |
| EventLogExtension | When the Event log extension is activated, messages are recorded to the machine's Event log. |
| ArchiveExtension | When the Archive extension is activated, messages are logged to SQL Server. This allows queries to be run against logged messages. |
| MSMQExtension | When using the MSMQ extension, messages can be logged to the Microsoft Messaging Queue. A logger can then be set up to monitor the Message Queue for messages and take action when necessary. |

Custom loggers can also be created and plugged into the Logging Framework. These logging extensions are controlled in the HostServerLogging.config file.

## Logging Framework Configuration File

The K2 blackpearl Logging Framework contains its own XML-based configuration file, HostServerLogging .config. This consists of all the Logging Framework configuration settings as well as a list of message categories and specific predefined messages.

The HostServerLogging.config file can be found in the following location:

```
%PROGRAMFILES%\K2 blackpearl\Host Server\Bin
```

The HostServerLogging.config file is a user-friendly and flexible configuration system, one that enables you to easily customize these configuration values postdeployment. Configuration data is stored in plain text files that are both readable and writable. Any standard text editor, XML parser, or scripting language can be used to interpret and update the configuration settings.

At run time, the `HostServerLogging.config` file is used to hierarchically compute a unique collection of configuration settings for each request. These configuration settings are calculated only once and then cached on the server. Any changes to the configuration file are detected and automatically applied to the affected applications. Hierarchical configuration settings are automatically calculated and cached again whenever a configuration file in the hierarchy is changed.

A typical `HostServerLogging.config` file looks as shown in Figure 19-2.

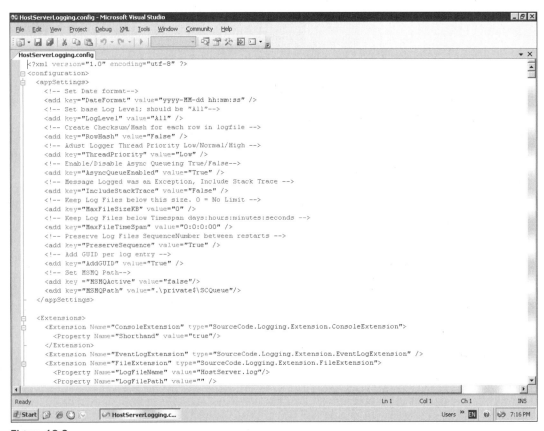

Figure 19-2

The Logging Framework queues the messages in an internal "first in, first out" principle until the logging thread has been scheduled to obtain and process them.

Starting the Logging Framework forces the initialization of internal settings from the `HostServerLogging`
`.config` file. The information in the `HostServerLogging.config` file settings section is stored as key/
value pairs. The K2 blackpearl Logging Framework loads the values from the `HostServerLogging`
`.config` file without the need to change the K2 blackpearl Logging Framework's source code.

The next sections discuss the composition of the `HostServerLogging.config` file.

## The appSettings Section

The `appSettings` section in the `HostServerLogging.config` file contains the general settings for the
Logging Framework, including things such as date formats, log file sizes, and so on.

The `appSettings` section in the `HostServerLogging.config` file looks as follows:

```
<appSettings>
  <!-- Set Date format-->
  <add key="DateFormat" value="yyyy-MM-dd hh:mm:ss" />
  <!-- Set base Log Level; should be "All"-->
  <add key="LogLevel" value="All" />
  <!-- Create Checksum/Hash for each row in logfile -->
  <add key="RowHash" value="False" />
  <!-- Adust Logger Thread Priority Low/Normal/High -->
  <add key="ThreadPriority" value="Low" />
  <!-- Enable/Disable Async Queueing True/False-->
  <add key="AsyncQueueEnabled" value="True" />
  <!-- Message Logged was an Exception, Include Stack Trace -->
  <add key="IncludeStackTrace" value="False" />
  <!-- Keep Log Files below this size. 0 = No Limit -->
  <add key="MaxFileSizeKB" value="0" />
  <!-- Keep Log Files below Timespan days:hours:minutes:seconds -->
  <add key="MaxFileTimeSpan" value="0:0:0:00" />
  <!-- Preserve Log Files SequenceNumber between restarts -->
  <add key="PreserveSequence" value="True" />
  <!-- Add GUID per log entry -->
  <add key="AddGUID" value="True" />
  <!-- Set MSMQ Path-->
  <add key ="MSMQActive" value="false"/>
  <add key="MSMQPath" value=".\private$\SCQueue"/>
</appSettings>
```

The general settings of the `appSettings` section along with a description and their possible values can
be seen in the following table:

| Key | Description | Possible Values |
|---|---|---|
| DateFormat | Use this key to format the Log Entry's date format. All date formats are supported using the standard notation used. | User defined |
| | If this value is left blank, the complete default ISO 8601 format (yyyy-mm-dd hh:mm:ss) will be used. | |
| LogLevel | Each log message has an associated log level. The level gives a rough guide to the importance and urgency of a log message. The log file keeps track of a log level that was specified and discards log requests that are below this level. | All, Debug, Info, Warning, Error |
| RowHash | The RowHash key enables the Row Level Hashing feature. This creates a checksum/hash for each row in the log file, where the information in the row is given a numeric value and calculated to produce a sum. This is then used for security purposes. | True, False |
| ThreadPriority | Every thread has a base priority level. The priority level of all executable threads is used to determine which thread is allocated the next available piece of CPU time. Only when there are no executable threads at a higher level does scheduling of threads at a lower level take place. This key allows one to adjust the Logger Thread Priority to Low, Normal, or High.<br><br>*Note: It is recommended that you set the ThreadPriority to Low as setting the Thread Priority to Normal or High would mean that the thread priority of the K2 blackpearl Logging Framework takes precedence to the K2 blackpearl server activities, making the K2 blackpearl server slower.* | Low, Normal, High |
| AsyncQueueEnabled | Allows you to enable or disable the asynchronous queuing.<br><br>*Note: Set this value to False to ensure that all error messages are logged. This is helpful when a configuration change prevents the Host Server from starting.* | True, False |

| Key | Description | Possible Values |
| --- | --- | --- |
| IncludeStackTrace | Specify whether or not to include a Stack Trace when the message logged was an exception. By default this key will be set to False.<br><br>The IncludeStackTrace key is a useful debugging tool that provides information on the execution history of the current thread, displaying the names of the classes and methods within those classes that had been called at the point when an exception occurred. | True, False |
| MaxFileSizeKB | Specify the maximum size for log files here; a 0 value will specify that there is no limit on the size of the file. When the set maximum size has been reached, a new log file will be created. | User-defined |
| MaxFileTimeSpan | Allows you to keep log files for a specific time span. This is configured in the format days: hours:minutes:seconds. | User-defined |
| PreserveSequence | Allows you to preserve log files sequence numbers between restarts. | True, False |
| AddGUID | Allows you to add a GUID per log entry. | True, False |
| MSMQActive | Allows you to toggle MSMQ between active and inactive. | True, False |
| MSMQPath | Allows you to set the MSMQ path. | User-defined |

## The Extensions Section

The Extensions section in the HostServerLogging.config file contains details around the various logging extensions available for the Logging Framework.

The Extensions section in the HostServerLogging.config file looks as follows:

```
<Extensions>
  <Extension Name="ConsoleExtension"
           type="SourceCode.Logging.Extension.ConsoleExtension">
      <Property Name="Shorthand"
             value="true"/>
  </Extension>
  <Extension Name="EventLogExtension"
           type="SourceCode.Logging.Extension.EventLogExtension" />
  <Extension Name="FileExtension"
           type="SourceCode.Logging.Extension.FileExtension" />
      <Property Name="LogFileName"
             value="HostServer.log"/>
```

```
            <Property Name="LogFilePath"
                    value="" />
            <Property Name="HashAlgorithm"
                    value="CRC32" />
    </Extension>
    <Extension Name="MSMQExtension"
            type="SourceCode.Logging.Extension.MSMQExtension">
            <Property Name="QueuePath"
                    value=".\private$\SCQueue"/>
    </Extension>
    <Extension Name="ArchiveExtension"
            type="SourceCode.Logging.Extension.ArchiveExtension">
            <Property Name="HostServerConfigFileName"
                    value="K2HostServer.config"/>
            <Property Name="ConfigDBConnectionName"
                    value="HostserverDB"/>
    </Extension>
  </Extensions>
```

The Extensions section contains the following extensions and properties; the following table also includes a description and the possible values:

| Extension | Property | Description | Possible Values |
|---|---|---|---|
| ConsoleExtension | Shorthand | With the Shorthand key you can specify that the logged messages that are shown in the console only display a short message of what was logged.<br><br>All the relevant information is still being logged, but it is not being displayed.<br><br>*Note: By default timestamps are added for better debugging purposes. To see the timestamps in the console output, modify the Shorthand value to read False.* | True, False |

| Extension | Property | Description | Possible Values |
|---|---|---|---|
| FileExtension | LogFileName | Allows you to define the file name of the log file created. Define the file name by changing the value to the required file name. | User-defined |
| FileExtension | LogFilePath | Allows you to specify the directory where the log file should be saved. If this value is left blank, the current execution path for the assembly will be used. | User-defined |
| FileExtension | HashAlgorithm | Allows you to specify the Hashing Algorithm. | CRC32, MD5, SHA1 * |
| MSMQExtension | QueuePath | Allows you to set the path to the MSMQ. | User-defined |
| ArchiveExtension | HostServerConfigFileName | Allows you to set the name of the configuration file for the Host Server. | User-defined |
| ArchiveExtension | ConfigDBConnectionName | Allows you to set the database connection name for the specific archive. | User-defined |

* HashAlgorithm values:

**CRC32:** Cyclic Redundancy Code (CRC) is a type of hash function used to produce a checksum that detects errors after transmission or storage. A CRC is computed and appended before transmission or storage and verified afterwards to confirm that no changes occurred. The most commonly used CRC algorithm is CRC-3 used by applications such as Ethernet, PNG, ZIP, and other archive formats. CRC32 produces a checksum with a length of 32 bits.

**MD5:** MD5 is a widely used cryptographic hash function with a 128-bit hash value and is commonly used to validate the integrity of files.

**SHA-1:** The Secure Hash Algorithm (SHA) was developed by the National Institute of Standards and Technology (NIST) with the help of the National Security Agency (NSA). SHA-1 is a cryptographic message digest algorithm similar to MD5. It differs in that it adds an additional expansion operation. The SHA-1 takes a message of less than 264 bits in length and produces a 160-bit message. SHA-1 is used by popular security applications and protocols such as TSL, SSL, PGP, SH, S/MIME, IPSec.

## The ApplicationLevelLogSettings Section

The `ApplicationLevelLogSettings` section in the `HostServerLogging.config` file allows you the flexibility to select which loggers are active and the severity levels of each logger. The Logging Framework gives you the flexibility to turn on or off any standard loggers or custom loggers and set different severity levels to suit the dynamic needs of any business.

The `ApplicationLevelLogSettings` section in the `HostServerLogging.config` file looks as follows:

```
<ApplicationLevelLogSettings>
  <ApplicationLevelLogSetting Scope="Default">
    <LogLocationSettings>
      <LogLocation Name="ConsoleExtension" Active="True" LogLevel="Info" />
      <LogLocation Name="FileExtension" Active="False" LogLevel="All" />
      <LogLocation Name="EventLogExtension" Active="False" LogLevel="Debug" />
      <LogLocation Name="ArchiveExtension" Active="False" LogLevel="Debug" />
      <LogLocation Name="MSMQExtension" Active="False" LogLevel="Debug" />
    </LogLocationSettings>
  </ApplicationLevelLogSetting>
</ApplicationLevelLogSettings>
```

The `ApplicationLevelLogSettings` section contains the log locations, states, and log level details listed in the following table:

| Log Location | Description | Possible Values |
|---|---|---|
| ConsoleExtension | By setting the ConsoleExtension Active flag to True, you enable the relevant log level to the K2 server console. | All, Debug, Info, Warning, Error |
| FileExtension | By setting the FileExtension Active flag to True, you enable the relevant log level for the K2 server log. | All, Debug, Info, Warning, Error |
| EventLogExtension | By setting the EventLogExtension Active flag to True, you enable the relevant log level for the Event log. | All, Debug, Info, Warning, Error |
| ArchiveExtension | By setting the ArchiveExtension Active flag to True, you enable the relevant log level to the specified archive. | All, Debug, Info, Warning, Error |
| MSMQExtension | By setting the MSMQExtension Active flag to True, you enable the relevant log level for the MSMQ. | All, Debug, Info, Warning, Error |

## The Category Section

The Category section in the HostServerLogging.config file allows you to define specific categories of the Logging Framework and allows you to create different categories for different services and events inside K2 blackpearl. This allows you to easily create a relationship between different message entities and categorize them.

The Category section in the HostServerLogging.config file looks as follows:

```
<CategoryList>
   <Category CatID="0" Name="General">
       General Events
   </Category>
   <Category CatID="1" Name="System">
       System Events
   </Category>
   <Category CatID="2" Name="Client">
       Client Events
   </Category>
   <Category CatID="3" Name="Security">
       Security Events
   </Category>
   <Category CatID="3" Name="Communication">
       Communication Events
   </Category>
   <Category CatID="6" Name="SmartFunctions">
       SmartFunctions
   </Category>
   <Category CatID="7" Name="Authorization Provider">
       Authorization Provider
   </Category>
   <Category CatID="8" Name="SmartObjects">
       SmartObjects
   </Category>
   <Category CatID="9" Name="DependencyService">
       Dependency Service
   </Category>
   <Category CatID="10" Name="UserRoleManager">
       UserRoleManager Server
   </Category>
   <Category CatID="11" Name="CategoryServer">
       Category Server
   </Category>
   <Category CatID="12" Name="WorkflowServer">
       Workflow Server
   </Category>
   <Category CatID="13" Name="LiveCommServer">
       Live Communication Server
   </Category>
   <Category CatID="14" Name="EventBus">
       Event Bus
   </Category>
   <Category CatID="15" Name="EnvironmentServer">
```

```
        Environment Server
    </Category>
    <Category  CatID="16" Name="SystemAudit">
        System Audit
    </Category>
    <Category  CatID="17" Name="WorkActivity">
        Work Activity
    </Category>
</CategoryList>
```

The `HostServerLogging.config` file contains a list of possible message categories that can be used when logging messages. These categories are specifically applicable to the K2 blackpearl server and are fully customizable. These categories are especially helpful when saving the log file as a `.csv` file and viewing the logged information in Microsoft Excel.

The individual category entry in this categories' list contains the information in the following table:

| Category ID | Category Name | Category Description |
|:---:|---|---|
| 0 | General | General Events |
| 1 | System | System Events |
| 2 | Client | Client Events |
| 3 | Security | Security Events |
| 3 | Communication | Communication Events |
| 6 | SmartFunctions | SmartFunctions |
| 7 | AuthorizationProvider | Authorization Provider |
| 8 | SmartObjects | SmartObjects |
| 9 | DependencyService | Dependency Service |
| 10 | UserRoleManager | User Role Manager Server |
| 11 | CategoryServer | Category Server |
| 12 | WorkflowServer | Workflow Server |
| 13 | LiveCommServer | Live Communication Server |
| 14 | EventBus | Event Bus |
| 15 | EnvironmentServer | Environment Server |
| 16 | SystemAudit | System Audit |
| 17 | WorkActivity | Work Activity |

## Predefined and Parameterized Messages

The `HostServerLogging.config` file contains a list of predefined and parameterized messages. This includes known Debug, Informational, Warning, or Error messages that can be opened so that they can be used in the planning of firing events or other actions based on known expected messages.

These known messages can be individually configured for severity, category, and forced logging methods. For example a specific known error message can be categorized as "info" and forced to always log to the console and custom logger, regardless of the overall logging level.

A standard message looks as follows:

```
<Message MsgID="27100" Severity="Debug" Category="16" Name="SQLInitSucceed" >
     Sql initialized (Svr:{0}, DB:{1})
</Message>
```

An individual message entry in this predefined and parameterized message list contains the elements in the following table:

| Attribute | Message Sample | Description |
|---|---|---|
| Unique Message ID | `MsgID="27100"` | Used to specify a specific number for the message. |
| Message Severity | `Severity="Debug"` | Used to specify what the specific severity of the message is. |
| Category ID | `Category="16"` | Used to specify what category to assign the message to. |
| Message Name | `Name="SQLInitSucceed"` | Used to specify a specific name for the message. |
| Message Text | `Sql initialized (Svr:{0}, DB:{1})` | Used to specify the message text, including the optional parameters which are also included and can be customized completely for the local requirements. |

## Logging Messages: Custom Run-Time and Static Predefined Messages

The Logging Framework can be used either during run time or to log a predefined message by providing the message ID. Predefined messages can have parameters that must be resolved by the framework.

Logging custom run-time messages is done by the application hosting the Logging Framework, and this calls a logging method, providing the Severity, Name, Source, Text, and Category of a message. The framework then constructs a message object and writes it to the configured logging target(s).

Logging static predefined messages during run time is done by the application hosting the Logging Framework, which calls a logging method, passing only the source and unique attributes of a message. The Logging Framework then retrieves the predefined message for the XML configuration file, based on the unique message ID. The Logging Framework continues to inspect the Severity, Category, and Force Logging directives presented in the attributes of the message.

If the predefined message contains any optional parameters, the Logging Framework resolves these parameters as necessary before writing the message to the forced or configured logging target(s).

## Enabling K2 blackpearl Logging

On the K2 blackpearl server, you can enable detailed logging options to help with troubleshooting and debugging. Changing the logging detail level can be useful when you are attempting to debug problems or if you just want to see what is happening on the K2 blackpearl server.

There are four distinct types of messages that can be surfaced through the Logging Framework. The severity levels of these messages are described in the following table:

| Message Type | Description |
| --- | --- |
| Debug | General debugging information. Useful when trying to trace what is happening on the K2 Host Server. |
| Info | General data about K2 Host Server activity such as sessions starting and users authenticating themselves. |
| Warning | Display warnings from the server. |
| Error | Display data about errors that occur within the server or in components that the server is using. |

To turn on the detailed logging, follow these steps:

1. Open `%PROGRAMFILES%\k2 blackpearl\Host Server\Bin\HostServerLogging.config` with a text editor.

2. In the `appSettings` section, change the values in the following table:

| Default Value | Configured Value |
| --- | --- |
| `<add key="IncludeStackTrace" value="False" />` | `<add key="IncludeStackTrace" value="True" />` |

**3.** In the `ApplicationLevelLogSettings` section, change the values in the following table:

| Default Value | Configured Value |
| --- | --- |
| `<LogLocation`<br>`Name="ConsoleExtension"`<br>`Active="True" LogLevel="Info" />` | `<LogLocation`<br>`Name="ConsoleExtension" Active="True"`<br>`LogLevel="All" />` |
| `<LogLocation`<br>`Name="FileExtension" Active="False"`<br>`LogLevel="All" />` | `<LogLocation`<br>`Name="FileExtension" Active="True"`<br>`LogLevel="All" />` |
| `<LogLocation`<br>`Name="EventLogExtension"`<br>`Active="False" LogLevel="Debug" />` | `<LogLocation`<br>`Name="EventLogExtension" Active="True"`<br>`LogLevel="All" />` |
| `<LogLocation`<br>`Name="ArchiveExtension"`<br>`Active="False" LogLevel="Debug" />` | `<LogLocation`<br>`Name="ArchiveExtension" Active="True"`<br>`LogLevel="All" />` |
| `<LogLocation`<br>`Name="MSMQExtension" Active="False"`<br>`LogLevel="Debug" />` | `<LogLocation`<br>`Name="MSMQExtension" Active="True"`<br>`LogLevel="All" />` |

After you have made your changes to `HostServerLogging.config`, save your changes. The K2 blackpearl Service will need to be restarted in order for this change to take effect and for the K2 blackpearl server to send logging information to the configured locations.

Depending on which logging location you have configured, you can see the detailed logging information by either running the K2 blackpearl server in Console mode, by viewing the K2 blackpearl Server log file, by viewing the Event log, by viewing the Archive, or by viewing the MSMQ.

## Running the K2 blackpearl Server in Console Mode

You can also run the K2 blackpearl server in Console mode by using the K2 blackpearl shortcut (Start ⇨ All Programs ⇨ K2 blackpearl ⇨ K2 blackpearl server). For the K2 server to run in Console mode, the K2 blackpearl Service must be stopped in Services (Start ⇨ All Programs ⇨ Administrative Tools ⇨ Services). When the K2 blackpearl server is run in console mode, it displays information about the Host Server and the components that are currently hosted. The server console is useful when debugging processes and SmartObjects and can display custom debugging messages using a `Console.WriteLine` method in custom code.

To run the K2 server in Console mode follow these steps:

**1.** Open the Services manager (Start ⇨ All Programs ⇨ Administrative Tools ⇨ Services).

**2.** Scroll down to the K2 blackpearl server service, select it, and click the Stop Service button.

3. Once the service shows as stopped, you can close the Services Manager.

4. Right-click on the K2 blackpearl server item in the start menu (Start ⇨ All Programs ⇨ K2 blackpearl), and select Run as (see Figure 19-3).

Figure 19-3

5. Enter the K2 Service account's username and password, and click OK.

This will open the K2 blackpearl server in console mode (see Figure 19-4). Console mode is a useful troubleshooting tool, as all error and informational messages are sent to the console window, so you can watch what is going on. It is important that you run the service as the Service Account in order to accurately troubleshoot permissions and other errors.

Figure 19-4

## Logging to the K2 blackpearl Server Log File

When the File extension is turned on, messages are logged to the K2 blackpearl server log file. This log file is saved to the location specified in the properties of its Logging Framework configuration file.

If no path is specified, the K2 blackpearl server log file can be found in the following location:

```
%PROGRAMFILES%\K2 blackpearl\Host Server\Bin
```

The name of the K2 blackpearl server log file is also taken from the Logging Framework configuration file, and if nothing is specified, the default value for the file is:

```
HostServerYYMMDD_x.log
```

The K2 blackpearl server log file looks like Figure 19-5.

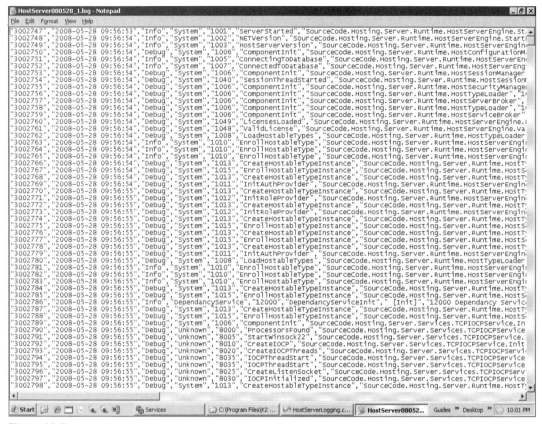

Figure 19-5

## *Viewing the K2 blackpearl Server Log File in Microsoft Excel*

The .csv (comma-separated value) file format is often used to exchange data between different applications. To view the K2 blackpearl server log file in a more usable format, you can save the log file with a .csv file extension, which when opened displays the file in a more accessible format in Excel.

To view the log file in Excel follow the following steps:

**1.** Browse to the log file in the %PROGRAMFILES%\K2 blackpearl\Host Server\Bin directory or in the custom-defined directory stipulated in the Logging Framework configuration file.

**2.** Change the log file's extension from .log to .csv by renaming the file in Windows Explorer.

**3.** Double-click the log file to open the file in Excel.

**4.** The logged information is now displayed in Excel for easy application and reference.

Filters can also be used to organize the information in various ways and to surface and sort the data that is most relevant to you.

## Logging to the Windows Event Log

When the Windows Event log extension is activated, the Logging Framework logs messages to the machine's Event log.

You can access the Event log in one of the following ways:

❑ Start ➪ Administrative Tools ➪ Event Viewer

❑ Start ➪ Run ➪ eventvwr.

Under the Application node in the Event Viewer, you can sort for all messages of source `SourceCode.Logging.Extension.EventLogExtension`. See Figure 19-6.

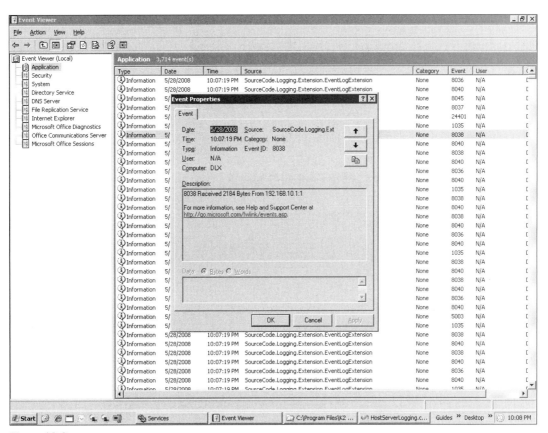

Figure 19-6

## Using the Archive Extension to Log to SQL Server

When the Archive extension is activated, the Logging Framework logs messages to SQL Server. This allows queries to be run against logged messages.

By default, messages are logged to the HostServerDB connection. This can be modified to log messages to another location by changing the properties associated with this extension in the Logging Framework configuration file.

## Using the MSMQ Extension

When you use the MSMQ extension, the Logging Framework logs messages to Microsoft Message Queuing. A logger can then be set up to monitor the Message Queue for messages and take action when necessary. This is useful when you are running multiple K2 blackpearl servers, in a server farm, for example, and one machine is set up to handle all of the logging.

## Extending the Logging Framework

The K2 blackpearl object model is broken down into a few high-level areas:

- ❑ **Assemblies ending with Client:** Are used for working with run-time aspects of K2 entities, such as processes and SmartObjects.

- ❑ **Assemblies ending with Authoring and Design:** Are used during design time for creating entities.

- ❑ **Assemblies ending with VisualDesigners:** Are used for visually representing entities at design time.

- ❑ **And finally, assemblies ending with Management:** Are used for managing servers and services.

Under the **Management** assemblies that the K2 blackpearl platform provides, there are Supporting and Management assemblies. One of these assemblies is SourceCode.Logging.

SourceCode.Logging provides the classes for extending and logging to the K2 blackpearl Host Server log and delivering the output via different mechanisms, such as e-mail, text file, and the console.

The SourceCode.Logging assembly has the following namespaces:

- ❑ SourceCode.Logging
- ❑ SourceCode.Logging.Extension

*For more extensive information on* SourceCode.Logging *see the K2 blackpearl Developer Reference.*

## Custom Logging

If the five out-of-the-box logging extensions that come standard with K2 blackpearl do not meet your business needs, the Logging Framework makes it easy to create a class using the supporting and managing assemblies that plug into the architecture as a custom extension to fit different business needs.

*Creating custom loggers is out of the scope of this chapter, but if you would like to find some examples of custom loggers, please refer to K2 blackmarket. K2 blackmarket was created in order to facilitate project and code sharing in the K2 Underground community. Sharing projects and code with other members of the community can greatly enhance the learning experience as well as reduce the learning curve that is inherently part of getting to know new technologies. You can access the K2 blackmarket through the K2 Underground community Web site located at* www.k2underground.com.

## Kerberos Logging

When you are installing K2 blackpearl in a completely distributed environment where there are separate servers for the database server, K2 blackpearl server, application server, and SharePoint server, the "double-hop" authentication issue often arises.

The double-hop issue has to do with passing of credentials between, for example, a client, the Web server (first hop), and the database server (second hop) for authentication and access.

Often when you encounter the double-hop issue, you may see one of the following errors on the K2 blackpearl server:

```
NT AUTHORITY\ANONYMOUS LOGON
The request failed with HTTP status 401: Unauthorized.
```

When you encounter the double-hop issue, you need to use Kerberos. In a nutshell, Kerberos is a secure ticket-based protocol for authenticating a request. With delegation you simply allow another server/ service to allow a Kerberos ticket to be created for another service on the originating user's behalf. This can be done at the computer level by using full delegation or with constrained delegation. Constrained delegation means that the Kerberos delegation can be executed only against a limited set of services.

*For more information about Kerberos, see Chapter 5.*

The Service Principal Name (SPN) is a name that uniquely identifies an instance of a service to a client within Active Directory. SPNs cannot be duplicated in a given domain and must be specified for each name/alias that can be used to access the host.

Kerberos logging can be very helpful in diagnosing Kerberos authentication issues. Kerberos logging will display errors and notifications in the System Event log. It is a good idea to clear the Events in the System Event log so that new errors and warnings are easier to see.

To enable Kerberos logging on the Web server, perform these steps:

*In these steps, you will edit the Registry settings to enable logging for Kerberos. Modifying the Registry should be done carefully, so please double-check the settings and follow the steps carefully.*

**1.** Open the Registry Editor (Start ⇨ Run ⇨ regedit).

**2.** Navigate to the following node: HKEY_LOCAL_MACHINE ⇨ SYSTEM ⇨ CurrentControlSet ⇨ Control ⇨ Lsa ⇨ Kerberos ⇨ Parameters.

**3.** Right-click on the Parameters item, and create a new DWORD entry with the following property:

> Name: LogLevel
> Value: 1

*If the LogLevel parameter already exists, change the value to 1.*

**4.** Close the Registry Editor.

**5.** Restart the server.

Another useful Kerberos troubleshooting tip is to output a log file for Kerberos. This can be done by adding the following two entries in the Registry:

> *In these steps, you will edit the Registry settings to enable an output log file for Kerberos. Modifying the Registry should be done carefully, so please double-check the settings and follow the steps carefully.*

**1.** Open the Registry Editor (Start ➪ Run ➪ regedit).

**2.** Navigate to the following node: HKEY_LOCAL_MACHINE ➪ SYSTEM ➪ CurrentControlSet ➪ Control ➪ Lsa ➪ Kerberos ➪ Parameters.

**3.** Right-click on the Parameters item, and create a new DWORD entry with the following property:

> Name: KerbDebugLevel
> Value: ff

*If the `LogLevel` parameter already exists, change the value to `ff`.*

**4.** Right-click on the Parameters item and create a new DWORD entry with the following property:

> Name: LogToFile
> Value: 1

*If the `LogLevel` parameter already exists, change the value to `1`.*

**5.** Close the Registry Editor.

**6.** Restart the server.

The Kerberos log file is written to the following location:

```
%WINDOWS%\System32\lsass.log
```

Please be aware that you need to switch off log to file when opening the output file `lsass.log` because of file locking. You can do this by changing `LogToFile` from "1" to "0".From the preceding you can see that K2 blackpearl logging allows you to record information about process execution in K2 blackpearl. This information is typically used by workflow developers for debugging purposes, and additionally, depending on the type and detail of information contained in the logging information, by experienced system administrators or technical support personnel to diagnose common problems with K2 blackpearl.

# K2 blackpearl System Reporting

K2 blackpearl makes use of Windows Performance Monitoring for system reporting, specifically using a tool called System Monitor (`PerfMon.exe`).

PerfMon is a process associated with Windows and is a solution to monitor, manage, and archive thousands of events that are generated by devices across the entire network. This is accomplished by a loadable driver that reprograms devices with performance counters so that user-level code can access these counters, and you can create traces of server activity.

Mastering the System Monitor controls helps you to analyze real-time traces and load and interpret logs. Through System Monitor you can also detect bottlenecks by capturing key performance counters.

The Performance Monitor is an administrative tool used to keep track of a range of processes and provides a real-time graphical display of the results. The Performance Monitor can be used to:

- ❑   Assist with the planning of upgrades.

- ❑   Track processes that need to be optimized.

- ❑   Monitor results from tuning and configuration changes.

- ❑   Analyze a workload and its effect on the resource usage to help identify bottlenecks.

The K2 blackpearl Logging and Performance Monitoring Framework makes use of the Performance Monitor to display specific counters that are relevant to the K2 blackpearl server activities.

## Performance Monitor Interfaces

Microsoft provides two interfaces for System Monitor, PerfMon, and a Microsoft Management Console (MMC) version called Performance Logs and Alerts.

Because of the fact that the MMC version does not allow real-time monitoring, you should only use the MMC Performance Logs and Alerts when you need just logs and alerts. PerfMon should be used when your aim is to collect live data. PerfMon does everything that the MMC version does.

## *Opening the Performance Monitor*

Performance Logs and Alerts (see Figure 19-7) can be opened in the following way:

**1.**  Start ⇨ Run ⇨ mmc.

**2.**  File ⇨ Add/Remove Snap-in ⇨ Add ⇨ Performance Logs and Alerts.

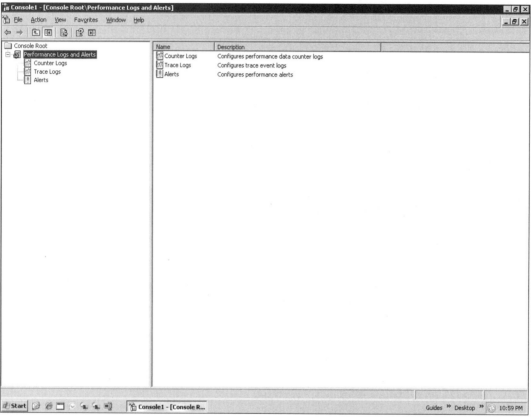

**Figure 19-7**

PerfMon (see Figure 19-8) can be opened in one of the following ways:

❑  Start ⇨ Administrative Tools ⇨ Performance.

❑  Start ⇨ Run ⇨ PerfMon.

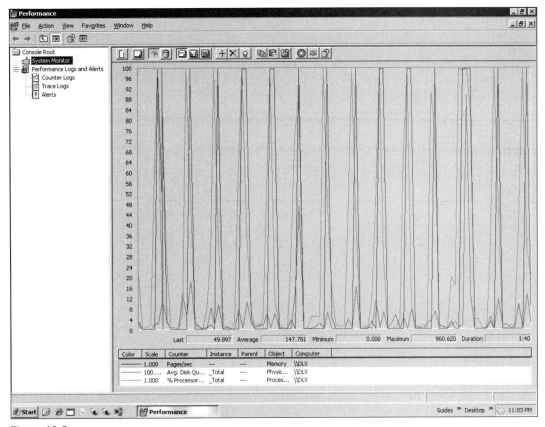

Figure 19-8

Once you launch PerfMon, you will get a graph with a trace that provides you with a graphical display of all system activities. You can use PerfMon to monitor the utilization of system resources and to collect and view real-time performance data in the form of counters for server resources such as processor and memory use.

PerfMon can be used to assist you with the planning of upgrades, the tracking of processes that need to be optimized, the monitoring results of tuning and configuration scenarios, and the understanding of a workload and its effect on resource usage to identify bottlenecks. Bottlenecks can occur on practically any element of the system and may be caused by a malfunctioning resource, the system not having enough resources, or a program that dominates a particular resource.

## Using the Performance Monitor

K2 blackpearl provides K2 blackpearl-specific counters to PerfMon which allow you to monitor the K2 blackpearl server.

In order to activate the newly added K2 blackpearl monitoring functionalities, right-click anywhere on the graph. Select the Add Counters option (shown in Figure 19-9).

Result: The Add Counters dialog box is displayed.

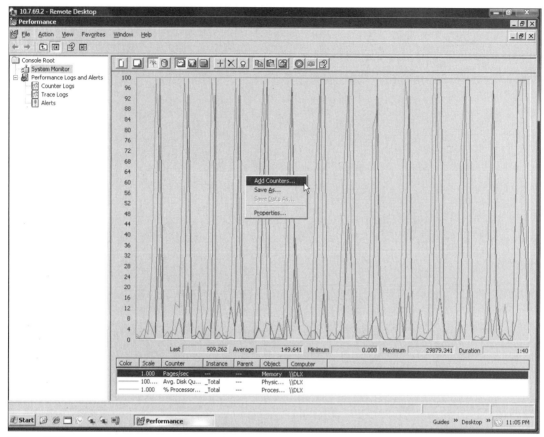

Figure 19-9

You can now add the counters you want to monitor to the Performance Monitor user interface, and K2 blackpearl adds some specific counters that are useful for quickly getting an overall impression of how healthy your system is and where the problems are, if they exist.

The idea here is to see the counters that will be at low or zero values when the K2 blackpearl system is healthy and at high values when something is overloaded. A "perfectly healthy" system would show all counters flat lined at zero. Perfection is however unattainable, so you'll probably never see all of these counters flat-lined at zero in real life.

K2 blackpearl provides you with a number of K2 blackpearl-specific counters to monitor various aspects of the system.

## K2 blackpearl-Specific Counters

The K2 blackpearl Logging and Performance Monitoring Framework has added K2 blackpearl–specific counters to the list generally available in the Performance Monitor. So, generally, the Performance Monitor includes the following K2 blackpearl-specific counters:

- ❏ K2 processes
- ❏ K2 Worklist items
- ❏ K2 Worklists
- ❏ Process memory usage
- ❏ Process modules loaded
- ❏ Process thread counts
- ❏ Transmission Control Protocol (TCP) information

The following table describes the particular K2 blackpearl–specific counters that you have available in the Performance Monitor:

| Counter | Description |
| --- | --- |
| K2 Process Total WaitStart | The total number of K2 processes waiting on a Start Rule (From K2 Transaction DB) |
| K2 Processes Started | The number of K2 processes started by the K2 server |
| K2 Processes Started Per Second | The number of K2 processes started per second by the K2 server |
| K2 Processes Total Active | The number of K2 processes that are currently in an active state |
| K2 Processes Total Completed | The number of K2 processes that are currently in a completed state |
| K2 Processes Total Deleted | The number of K2 processes that are currently in a deleted state |
| K2 Processes Total Error | The number of K2 processes that are currently in an error state |
| K2 Processes Total Escalated | The number of K2 processes that reached an escalation |
| K2 Processes Total Running | The number of K2 processes that are currently in a running state |
| K2 Processes Total Stopped | The number of K2 processes that are currently in a stopped state |
| K2 Worklist Items Finished | The number of K2 Worklist items that were finished by the K2 server |
| K2 Worklist Items Finished Per Second | The number of K2 Worklist items that were finished by the K2 server per second |
| K2 Worklists Opens | The number of K2 Worklists that have been opened by the K2 server |

*(continued)*

*(continued)*

| Counter | Description |
| --- | --- |
| K2 Worklists Opens Per Second | The number of K2 Worklists that have been opened by the K2 server per second |
| Process Memory Usage | The K2 server process memory usage in bytes |
| Process Modules Loaded | The number of modules loaded by the K2 server |
| Process Thread Count | The number of threads running in the K2 server process |
| TCP Bytes Received Per Second | The number of TCP bytes received by the K2 server per second |
| TCP Bytes Received Total | The number of TCP bytes received for the duration of the K2 server running instance |
| TCP Bytes Sent Per Second | The number of TCP bytes sent by the K2 server per second |
| TCP Bytes Sent Total | The number of TCP bytes sent for the duration of the K2 server running instance |
| TCP Concurrent Connections | The number of concurrent client connections for the duration of the K2 server running instance |
| TCP Connections Opened | The number of TCP connections opened for the duration of the K2 server running instance |
| TCP Connections Opened Per Second | The number of TCP connections opened for the duration of the K2 server running instance per second |

So, as you can see, these K2 blackpearl counters give you a great deal of flexibility when it comes to system reporting. You merely need to choose the ones most applicable to your system and add them to the Performance Monitor user interface.

## Adding Counters to the Performance Monitor User Interface

Once you've chosen the counters you want, you can add them to the Performance Monitor user interface as follows:

1. In the Add Counters dialog box, select K2 server from the Performance object drop-down list.
2. Select the relevant counters from the list (see Figure 19-10).
3. Click Add.
4. Click Close.

The performance of the selected counters will now be displayed in the main user interface.

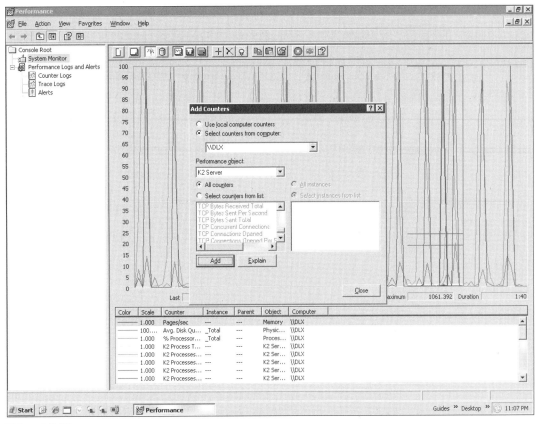

Figure 19-10

## Creating Charts, Alerts, Logs, and Reports

PerfMon lets you create charts, alerts, logs, and reports to monitor an instance of K2 blackpearl.

### Charts

Charts can monitor the current performance of selected objects and counters, for example, the number of K2 Worklists that have been opened by the K2 server per second.

Using a chart can be helpful for the following tasks:

- ❑ Investigating why K2 blackpearl is slow or inefficient
- ❑ Continually monitoring K2 blackpearl to find intermittent performance problems
- ❑ Discovering why you need to increase capacity
- ❑ Displaying a trend as a line chart
- ❑ Displaying a comparison as a histogram chart

Charts are also useful for short-term, real-time monitoring of a local or remote K2 blackpearl server and can be used when you want to monitor an event as it occurs.

## Alerts

You can use PerfMon alerts to monitor the current performance of selected counters. When a counter exceeds a given value, the log records the date and time of the event. An event can also generate a network alert. You can have a specified program run the first time or every time an event occurs. For example, an alert can send a network message to all system administrators that the Process Memory Usage is exceeding the expected limits.

## Logs

Logs allow you to record information on the current activity of selected objects, which allows you to analyze this at a later stage.

Log files provide a wealth of information for troubleshooting or planning. Whereas charts, alerts, and reports on current activity provide instant feedback, log files enable you to track counters over a long period of time. Thus, you can examine information more thoroughly and document K2 blackpearl system performance.

## Reports

Reports allow you to display constantly changing counter and instance values for selected objects. Values appear in columns for each instance. You can adjust report intervals, print snapshots, and export data. Use reports when you need to display the raw numbers.

So, by making use of Windows Performance Monitor and by providing new specific counters, K2 blackpearl allows you to use system monitoring to help you identify where your system problem is coming from. If this tool is used with correct configuration and planning to suit your K2 blackpearl environment, then the system administrator can benefit from being able to tackle problems in less time, thus, making your K2 blackpearl server more efficient.

# Summary

In this chapter we have discussed two key aspects behind the scenes of K2 blackpearl: logging and system reporting.

Logging is the process of storing information about events that occurred on the K2 blackpearl server. It allows you to record information about process execution in K2 blackpearl. This information is typically used by workflow developers for debugging purposes, and additionally, depending on the type and detail of information contained in the logging information, by experienced system administrators or technical support personnel to diagnose common problems with K2 blackpearl.

System reporting is the process of collecting and analyzing data to measure the performance of the product, process, or activity against expected results. Using system reporting you can collect performance data automatically from your K2 blackpearl server. You can view logged counter data or export the data to spreadsheet programs or databases for analysis and report generation, which allows you to query the data and analyze the data as needed for overall performance assessment, trend analysis, and capacity planning.

In the next chapter we look at using the K2 Workspace and the robust reporting capabilities it provides.

# 20

# Using the K2 Workspace and Reporting

Sergio Del Piccolo

The K2 Workspace provides an interface for workflow participants to interact with the process-driven applications developed using K2 blackpearl. Participants are presented with a worklist displaying tasks that have been assigned to them, giving them the ability to manage their worklists and complete their tasks.

The K2 Workspace provides powerful reporting features, allowing for the creation of reports through a simple wizard process. Reports created on the K2 Workspace can be published to Microsoft SQL Server Reporting Services and be edited using any Report Definition Language (RDL)–compliant tools. Reports created by developers using the Reporting Services Report Designer in Microsoft Visual Studio can be imported and shared with the workflow participants.

The K2 Workspace also provides workflow participants, developers, and administrators with the ability to create and manage notification and custom events informing them of important server events that have been executed as the deployed processes run.

Accordingly, this chapter covers the following topics:

❑   Using the K2 Workspace to complete the tasks assigned to you

❑   Viewing and creating reports

❑   Configuring Notification Events

# K2 Workspace Overview

The K2 Workspace is a browser-based interface allowing process participants to manage their worklist and giving them access to view or create workflow related reports. The K2 Workspace contains the K2 Management Console, which can be used by administrators to set security permissions.

Open the K2 Workspace by selecting Start ⇨ All Programs ⇨ K2 blackpearl ⇨ K2 blackpearl Workspace. An instance of your browser will be launched and navigate to the K2 Workspace. Alternatively, in your browser navigate to `http://DomainName.com/workspace/navigation/navigation.aspx` replacing `DomainName.com` with the name of the domain where your workspace is deployed.

As you can see in Figure 20-1, the banner contains the name of current (logged on) participant. This is especially handy when testing and having multiple browser instances where you're signed in as different participants of the process. The Navigation Bar contains the tabs available, each described in more detail in the following table.

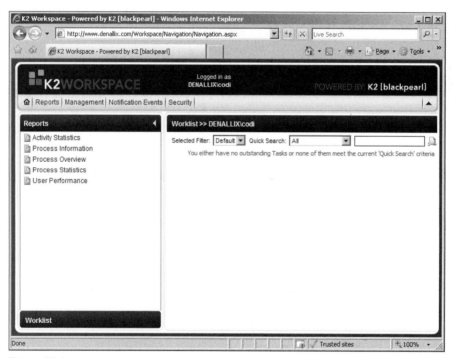

Figure 20-1

| Tab Name | Description |
|---|---|
| Home | The K2 Home Page contains the reports and the participant's worklist with items assigned to the participant. |
| Reports | The K2 for Reporting Services tab contains the Report Designer used to create and save dynamic Web-based reports. Common business objects can be exposed to the K2 platform through SmartObjects. Decision makers and workflow participants can create and save custom reports based on these objects. |
| Management | The K2 Management tab contains the Management Console used for centralized administration of K2 servers, workflow process and instances, security settings, and environment library settings. For more information see Chapter 15. |
| Notification Events | The K2 Notification Events tab contains the Notification Event Designer and Custom Event Designer. The Designers allow the developer to create customizable notifications that are raised when selected events occur. |
| Security | The K2 Security tab contains the Workspace Permissions, which allows for an administrator to configure user access to the tabs contained on the Navigation Bar (excluding the K2 Home Page, which is available to all users). For more information see Chapter 16. |

The Navigation Page contains either menu items or tree views used for navigation depending on the displayed tab. To maximize real estate when working with the K2 Workspace, especially when interacting with the worklist and reports, you can minimize the Navigation Bar and Navigation Page by clicking the arrows on the left-hand side of each control.

The final section is the Workspace, which contains the information that you want to see depending on the displayed tab. In the case of the K2 Home Page, it displays the current participant's worklist and any tasks that have been assigned to them. In Figure 20-1 there are no current worklist items assigned to the user.

During the course of exploring the K2 Workspace, you will find that many of the tabs, wizards and windows contain the button shown in Figure 20-2. Click on the button at any time to get context-sensitive help.

**Figure 20-2**

The K2 Home Page is the default page that will be seen when you open the K2 Workspace
(see Figure 20-3).

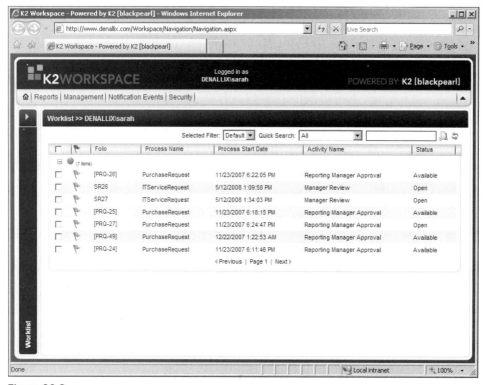

Figure 20-3

# Working with the Worklist

The Workspace by default shows the user's worklist containing items that have been assigned to them, and this space is used to participate in the workflow process.

## Actioning a Worklist Item

There are multiple options open to the workflow participant when they want to complete a task assigned to them. The next sections discuss those options.

### Using Custom Forms

To use custom-developed forms to action the workflow instance, click on the worklist item. If the form associated with this activity is an ASP.NET page or an InfoPath form deployed to SharePoint running Forms Services, a new instance of your browser is launched to display the form.

In the case where the form has been created using InfoPath without Forms Services, the form is displayed in the InfoPath client application. Once the form has been opened, the workflow participant is able to action the activity and move the process instance along.

## Using the Worklist Actions Menu

The worklist item can be opened by hovering over the Folio column and clicking on the drop-down arrow that appears. This displays a context menu. Select Open to open the form associated with the activity, allowing you to act on the task. Alternatively, the workflow can be actioned by selecting from one of the options available through the Action(s) menu item, as shown in Figure 20-4.

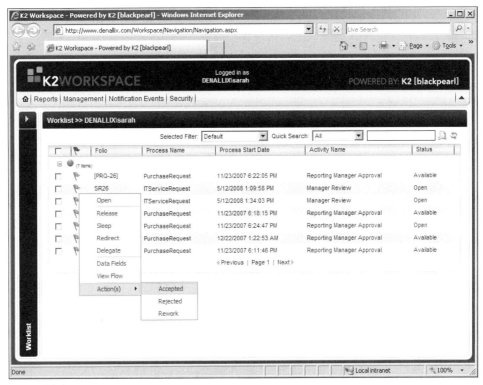

Figure 20-4

*The action items contained in the Action(s) menu need to be made available by the process developer during the development of the process-driven application.*

## Using Batch Actions

You can action multiple process instances at the same time. This is possible by checking the checkboxes of the respective instances (found on the left-hand side of the worklist). Once you select the checkboxes, a Batch Action drop-down list appears above the worklist (on the right-hand side) as shown in Figure 20-5.

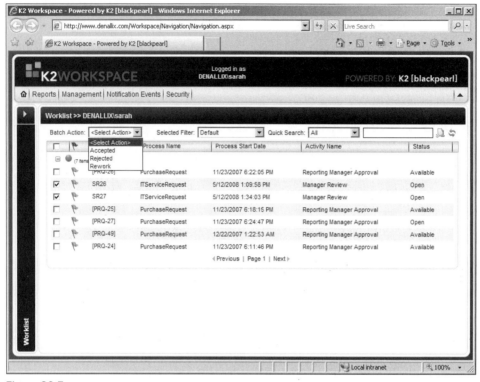

Figure 20-5

The Batch Action drop-down list contains the same options available to the workflow participant as can be found in the Worklist Action Menu.

*If you select process instances from different workflows for batch actioning, the Batch Action drop-down list will not contain any options to select.*

## Suspending a Worklist Item

You can suspend a worklist item for a period of time. To do this, hover over the Folio column and click on the drop-down arrow that appears. This displays a context menu. Select Sleep (shown in Figure 20-4). This opens the Perform Action — Sleep window as shown in Figure 20-6.

Figure 20-6

There are a couple of options available when suspending the activity.

❑ **Relative time:** This allows you to select the duration for which the activity will be suspended. Available options are Days, Hours, Minutes, and Seconds.

❑ **Absolute time:** This allows you to select a date and time until which the activity will be suspended.

Once an activity has been suspended, it disappears from the worklist. After the set duration or selected date has arrived, the item reappears in the worklist, ready for processing.

## Redirecting a Worklist Item

You can also redirect a worklist item. This option is used when a workflow solution allows other participants to assign tasks to a dynamic list of participants. Alternatively, should you be out of the office for a period of time you can clear your current list of assigned tasks prior to leaving the office.

To redirect the activity, hover over the Folio column and click on the drop-down arrow that appears. This displays a context menu. Select Redirect (shown in Figure 20-4). This opens the Perform Action — Redirect window, as shown in Figure 20-7.

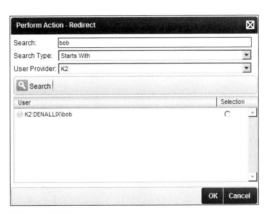

Figure 20-7

The Perform Action — Redirect window allows you to search for and select a user to redirect the worklist item to. Once the item has been redirected, it disappears from your worklist and appears in the new user's worklist.

## Releasing a Worklist Item

In the case where a worklist item has been redirected to a user and that user has not accessed the item, it can be released back to the original user for processing or reassignment. This can be done by hovering over the Folio column and clicking on the drop-down arrow that appears. This displays a context menu. Select Release (shown in Figure 20-4).

## Delegating a Worklist Item

You can delegate tasks to one or more participants. This is quite useful when a batch of tasks has appeared in your worklist, and you need some assistance to complete them, especially if there is a deadline. To do this, hover over the Folio column and click on the drop-down arrow that appears. This displays a context menu. Select Delegate (shown in Figure 20-4). This opens the Perform Action — Delegate window as shown in Figure 20-8.

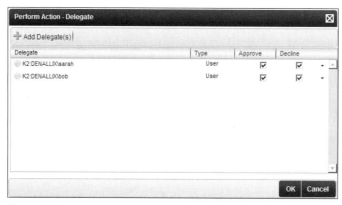

Figure 20-8

To add new participants, click the Add Delegate(s) button. This opens a new window allowing you to search for and select another user to delegate the activity to. Once the delegate(s) has been added, you can assign them permissions with regard to the actions they can perform on the activity. This is useful should you want delegates to be able to only approve tasks leaving the process of declining others to yourself.

To remove delegates, click the downward arrow on the right-hand side of the delegate in the Perform Action — Delegate window and select Delete, as shown in Figure 20-9.

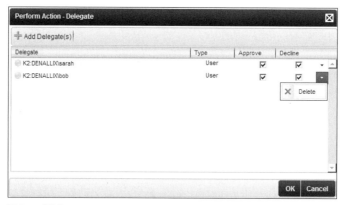

Figure 20-9

## *Viewing Process-Related Data*

During the process instance lifecycle, workflow participants and administrators have the ability to view process-related data. The process-related data is available through the drop-down arrow in the Folio column of the worklist (shown in Figure 20-4).

### Data Fields

Data fields are variables contained within the running workflow. There are two levels of data fields: Process and Activity data fields.

❑   **Process data fields:** Contain information that is available for the entire time that an instance of a process is running.

❑   **Activity data fields:** Available for the duration that the activity is available. As soon as an activity has been completed, the Activity data fields are no longer available.

To view the values of the data fields, hover over the Folio column and click on the drop-down arrow that appears. This displays a context menu. Select Data Fields to open the Data Fields window as shown in Figure 20-10.

*The Click here to view hyperlink shown in Figure 20-10 denotes XML fields. Clicking the hyperlink opens the XML document or the XPATH node.*

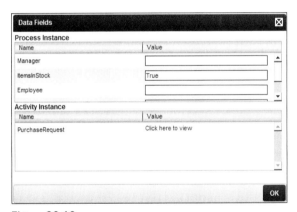

**Figure 20-10**

*The values of the data fields cannot be edited using the Data Fields window.*

### View Flow

The View Flow provides a graphical representation of the flow that the workflow has taken up to the current activity in the process. The View Flow can be seen by hovering over the Folio column and clicking on the drop-down arrow that appears. This displays a context menu. Select View Flow (shown in Figure 20-4). This will open the K2 View Flow window as shown in Figure 20-11.

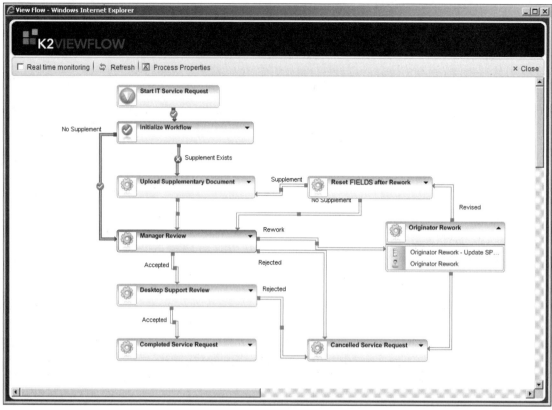

**Figure 20-11**

To understand the flow that the process has taken, the lines are color-coded:

- ❑ **Green:** Lines whose Line Rules evaluated to true.
- ❑ **Red:** Lines whose Line Rules evaluated to false.
- ❑ **No Color:** Bypassed lines or lines that are yet to be evaluated.

Activities are color-coded, too:

- ❑ **Green:** Activities that were successfully completed.
- ❑ **Blue:** The activity that is currently waiting to be completed.
- ❑ **No Color:** Bypassed activities or activities that are yet to be evaluated.

Checking the Real time monitoring checkbox at the top of the K2 View Flow window turns on real-time monitoring of the process. This obviously uses more system resources and should be done only when there is a need for it. Alternatively, select the Refresh button to refresh the View Flow. You also have available reports associated with the process instance. To view the Activity Instances Report (as shown in Figure 20-12), click the Process Properties button at the top of the K2 View Flow window or double-click on the View Flow diagram. Selecting the Activity Name causes the report to drill-down to view more information relating to the activity instance.

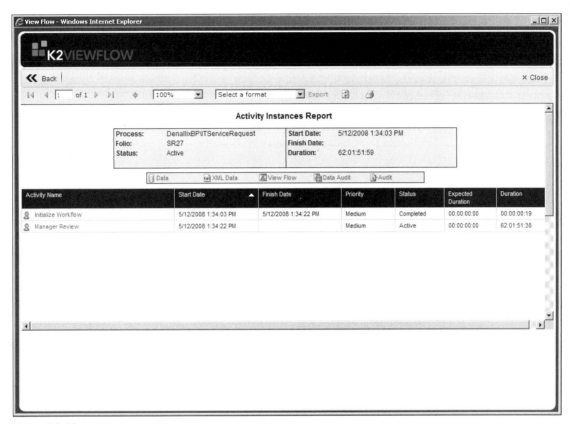

Figure 20-12

# Finding a Worklist Item

In some cases you can have hundreds of tasks to process, and finding a particular instance of the workflow can prove to be a daunting task. There are a few ways to find the elusive task that needs to be completed.

## Sorting the Worklist

The columns in the worklist can be sorted in ascending or descending order by clicking on the worklist headers. Once a column has been sorted, an arrow appears next to the column name indicating whether the column contents are in ascending or descending order, as shown in Figure 20-13 where the worklist items are in ascending order by Folio.

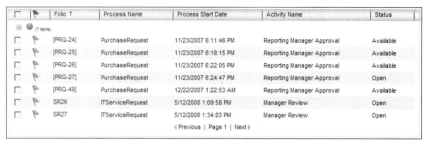

**Figure 20-13**

## Searching the Worklist

Above the worklist items you have several controls available for filtering and searching through the worklist items.

To search through the worklist, select one of the options from the Quick Search drop-down list. It is used to restrict the search criteria against all or one of the columns in the worklist. To the right of the Quick Search drop-down list is a textbox used to enter the search criteria. Figure 20-14 shows the results of searching for "SR" within the Folio column.

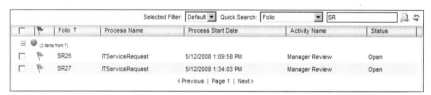

**Figure 20-14**

## Filtering the Worklist

Another control for filtering available to you is the Selected Filter drop-down list. It contains only one value by default — Default. To add new filters, you need to create them. This is done by clicking on the Configuration icon (the second icon from the right on the toolbar above the Worklist icons).

The following are the steps you take to create a new filter, in this case one that returns all active ITServiceRequest process instances.

1. Click the Configuration icon. It opens the Configuration window.

2. Click the Add button to open the Filter Criteria window. Enter a name for the filter in the Filter Name textbox.

3. Click the Add button to open the Filter Criteria Item window shown in Figure 20-15. This allows you to further restrict the data you want to return in the filtered set.

Figure 20-15

Select the field you want to filter against, a compare operator, and enter the filtered value. You can add multiple filter criteria items to narrow down the list as much as needed.

4. Once you are done, the Filter Criteria window should look similar to Figure 20-16. Click the OK button to close the window.

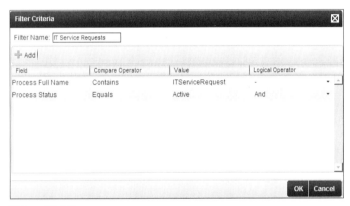

Figure 20-16

5. You are now back at the Configuration window, as shown in Figure 20-17. You have the option to set this new filter as the Default filter shown when we open the K2 Workspace. Click the Next button to go to the next step.

Figure 20-17

**6.** You now have the ability to set the layout of the worklist, as shown in Figure 20-18. The Set of Columns drop-down list allows you to select the columns to be displayed, and the Group By drop-down list allows you to select a property by which to group your worklist items. Selecting the Custom value in the Set of Columns drop-down list enables the list of columns with checkboxes allowing you to select the columns you want returned.

*Changing the layout affects the displayed worklist items regardless of the filter selected.*

To complete the configuration of the newly created filter, click the Finish button.

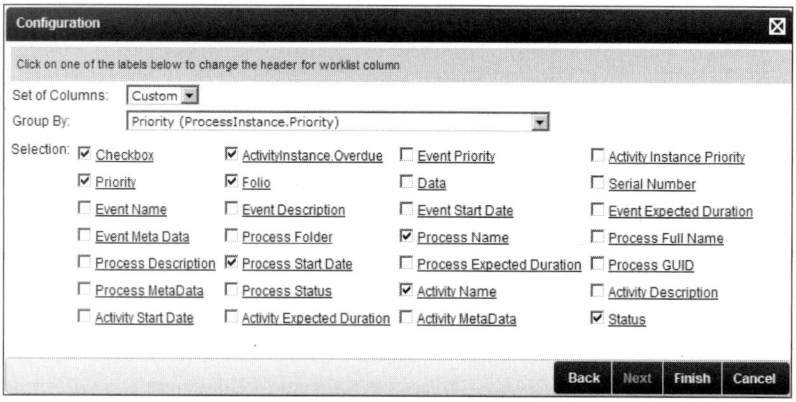

Figure 20-18

You can now select your new filter from the Selected Filter drop-down list, which should return an appropriately filtered worklist.

## Viewing Managed Users' Worklists

Managers have the ability to view the worklists of users who report to them. This is a useful tool in recognizing workers who are overburdened and gives managers the ability to make adjustments so that the process runs as efficiently as possible.

*Viewing managed users' worklists requires users to have their manager configured in Active Directory.*

Here's how you set this up.

**1.** Navigate to the Management Console on the Management tab of the Navigation Bar. Expand the server and right-click on the Workflow server to bring up the context menu. Select Edit Settings. This opens the Configuration Settings for the Workflow server.

**2.** Navigate to the Advanced Settings tab, and ensure that the Display Worklist of Managed Users checkbox is checked as shown in Figure 20-19.

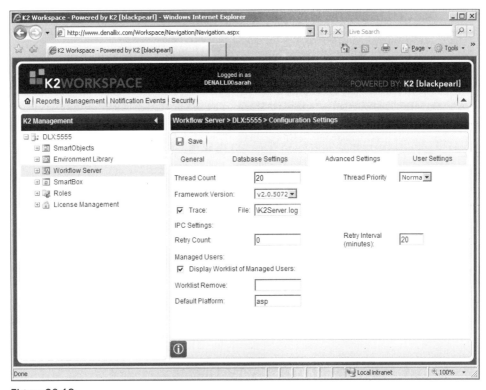

Figure 20-19

# K2 Reporting

The Reports tab allows you to create and run dynamic, Web-based reports using a series of steps to retrieve, filter, and display process data. Reports are created using the Report Designer. SmartObjects are exposed to the reports allowing for real-time data to be viewed.

## Saved and Published Reports

K2 blackpearl makes use of Report Definition Language (RDL) for reports that are created by the Report Designer on the Reports tab. Report Definition Language is an XML schema used to define reports. Reports created by the Report Designer are saved to the Workspace database and do not require Microsoft SQL Server Reporting Services engine to execute. Reports are rendered by the Report Viewer hosted within the K2 Workspace.

Publishing a report requires Microsoft SQL Server 2005 Reporting Services to run the report going forward and allows you to share the report more easily. Furthermore, publishing a report allows you to edit the report in Report Builder or other SQL Server Reporting Services editors.

## Standard Reports

There are some preconfigured reports that have been created for you. These are known as Standard Reports and are visible on the K2 Home Page under the Reports menu in the Navigation Page, as shown in Figure 20-20. The reports have been published to Microsoft SQL Server Reporting Services and can be viewed in the Standard folder and Hidden sub-folder. They use the K2 BLACKPEARL data source, which is created at configuration time of K2 blackpearl. The reports provide statistical data at the process, activity, and workflow participant level.

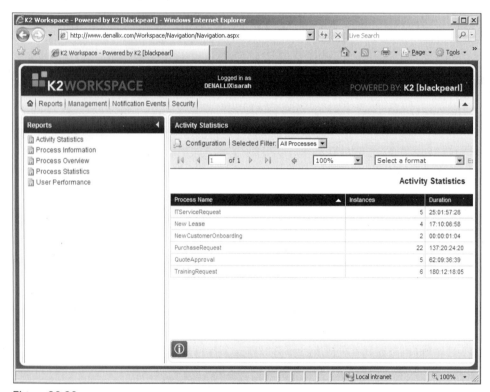

Figure 20-20

The following table explains the five reports that come as Standard Reports in more detail:

| Report Name | Description |
| --- | --- |
| Activity Statistics | A graphical report that provides statistical data about the activities in each workflow process, including the number of activity instances and the average time it has taken to complete an activity. Can be filtered by date range and activity status. |
| Process Information | A graphical report that provides date and process status filters for the selected processes. Can display the average duration of selected processes or the number of instances for each process. |
| Process Overview | Provides the ability to drill-down into processes to see process, activity, and event information, such as slot and audit data. Also provides access to the View Flow report. |
| Process Statistics | A graphical report that provides the ability to drill-down into processes to see statistical data, such as average duration or number of instances. Can be filtered by number of days, weeks, or months, or a particular date range. |
| User Performance | A graphical report that provides the ability to drill-down into processes to display statistical data about process participants, including number of process instances the user actioned and the average time it has taken to complete a task. |

*Because of the fact that some of the data in the reports can be sensitive, there are security permissions that need to be configured for each process to allow workflow participants to view the reports. These permissions are set in the Management Console on the Management tab. See Chapter 15 for more information regarding the Management tab.*

## Using Reports

When you are looking at reports, you have configuration options and drill-down abilities available to you. Above each report there is a Report Viewer Toolbar, as shown in Figure 20-21.

**Figure 20-21**

The toolbar functionality is explained in the following table:

| Button | Name | Function |
|---|---|---|
| | First Page | Navigates to the first page in the report. |
| | Previous Page | Navigates to the previous page in the report. |
| 1 of 1 | Current Page | Displays the current page of the report. |
| | Next Page | Navigates to the next page in the report. |
| | Last Page | Navigates to the last page in the report. |
| | Parent Report | Navigates up the hierarchy to the parent report. This is the case when the user has drilled-down to a sub-report. |
| 100% | Zoom | Sets the size of the report. |
| Select a format Export | Export | Exports the report in the format selected. Format options include XML, CSV, TIFF, PDF, Web, and Microsoft Excel. These options change depending on whether the report has been published or not. If published, then the configured SQL Server Reporting Services options are available. If not published, then the K2 Report Designer contains Microsoft Excel and PDF only. |
| | Refresh | Refreshes the report with the latest data. |
| | Print | Opens a Print Dialog window for report printing. |

A few of the Standard Reports have a Configuration tab, shown in Figure 20-22, allowing for the creation of filters that can be saved for quick access to filtered data. Filters added here are available to all reports that show the Configuration tab.

**Figure 20-22**

You can take the following steps to configure a new filter:

1. Click on the Configure button. This opens the Configuration window, which provides you with the ability to add new filters.

2. Click the Add button to open the Filter Criteria window, as shown in Figure 20-23. Enter the following:

   **Filter Name:** Used to describe your new filter.

   **Process Name:** Used to filter against the processes.

   ": The folder name to filter for.

   ʋutton to continue.

**Figure 20-23**

3. Back at the Configuration window you should see the newly added filter criteria. You have the option to set it as the default filter. Click the OK button to end the configuration. On the Configuration tab, the Selected Filter drop-down list should now contain a new filter to select.

To edit or delete a filter, click the Configuration button on the Configuration tab. In the Configuration window, click the downward-facing arrow in the default column, as shown in Figure 20-24, and select either Edit or Delete.

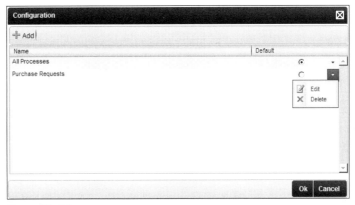

**Figure 20-24**

Now that you've created the report filter, it's time to take a look at the Activity Statistics Report in more detail. Select the Activity Statistics Report from the Navigation Page, as shown in Figure 20-20. From the Selected Filter drop-down list in the Configuration tab (shown in Figure 20-22), select the newly created filter. The report will look similar to Figure 20-25.

Figure 20-25

You can click on the hyperlink in the Process Name column to drill-down further, in this case into Purchase Request. Clicking on the link displays the Report Options page shown in Figure 20-26. The Report Options page enables you to select the data to display and the format in which to do so.

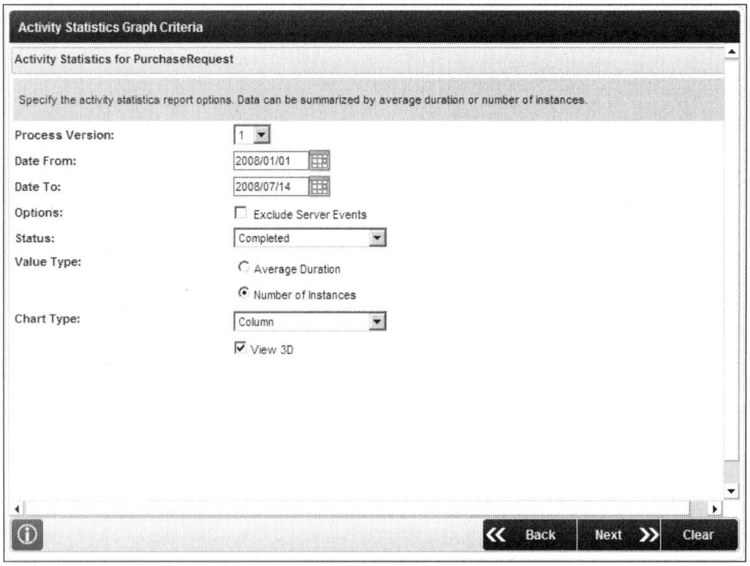

Figure 20-26

The Report Options page for each report in the Standard Reports differs slightly, depending on the report. They all give you the option to select a date range and a chart type. Once the options have been chosen, you click on the Next button to view the report. Figure 20-27 shows an example of the Activity Statistics Report.

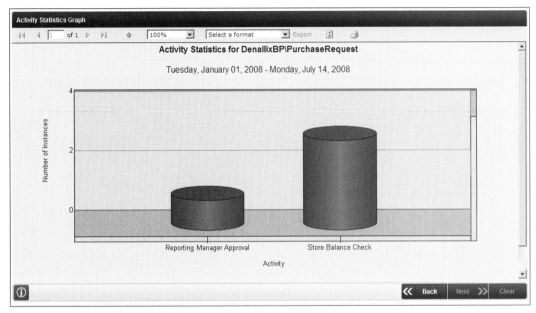

Figure 20-27

## Creating New Reports

Now that you understand how to use the reports, it's time to create a new report and save it for future use. You need to navigate to the Reports ⇨ Report Designer tab on the Navigation bar. Your page should look similar to Figure 20-28.

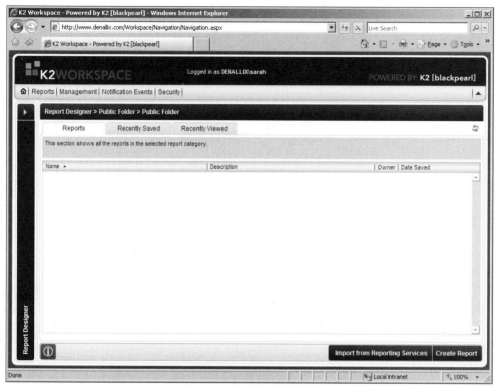

Figure 20-28

The Report Designer lists all saved reports (in this case there aren't any to show yet). Reports can be accessed by all users with access to the Reports tab and with Admin, Start, View, or View Participant Process Rights. The Report Designer contains the report name, a description of the report, the report owner, and the date saved. The columns can be sorted by clicking on the column headers. The Report Designer is made up of the three tabs, described in more detail in the following table.

| Tab Name | Description |
|---|---|
| Reports | Lists all reports with properties. |
| Recently Saved | Lists 20 most recently saved reports. |
| Recently Viewed | Lists 20 most recently viewed reports. |

The Report Designer also allows you to create a new report by clicking the Create Report button, and to import existing reports from Reporting Services by clicking the Import from Reporting Services button.

Use the following steps to create a new report:

1. Click the Create Report button. This launches the Create Report Wizard. The wizard contains a list of the steps it takes to create the report on the left-hand side in the Navigation Page. This changes, depending on the type of report being created. The following table describes the different report types available:

| Report Type | Description |
| --- | --- |
| Tabular | Creates the report in a table structure. |
| Summary | Creates a summary report with totals and subtotals. |
| Matrix | Creates a report with vertical and horizontal axes. |

The first step contains information regarding the report name, description, and report type. Enter a name and description for the report, and select a report type. Click the Next button to continue.

2. The second step allows you to select a SmartObject data source that forms the basis of the report. Expand the folder containing the desired SmartObject, and click on it. The Related Data pane will display the selected SmartObject properties. The properties returned depend on the selected radio button below the pane. There are a couple of choices, described in the following table:

| SmartObject Relation | Description |
| --- | --- |
| Closest Related Data | Displays parent and child SmartObject properties based on the property association between the SmartObjects. For example, if there is a Purchase Order Details SmartObject and a child Purchase Order Items SmartObject, both sets of properties are returned. |
| All Related Data | Displays all SmartObject properties whether directly or indirectly associated to the selected SmartObject. In the Purchase Order example, if the Purchase Order Items SmartObject were selected, the Purchase Order Details SmartObject would be returned as the parent (a direct association) and the Invoice SmartObject would be returned (directly associated with the Purchase Order Details SmartObject, thus indirectly associated with the Purchase Order Items SmartObject). |

On the Related Data pane you check all the checkboxes next to the properties that you want available in the report. This step in the wizard should look similar to Figure 20-29. Click the Next button to continue.

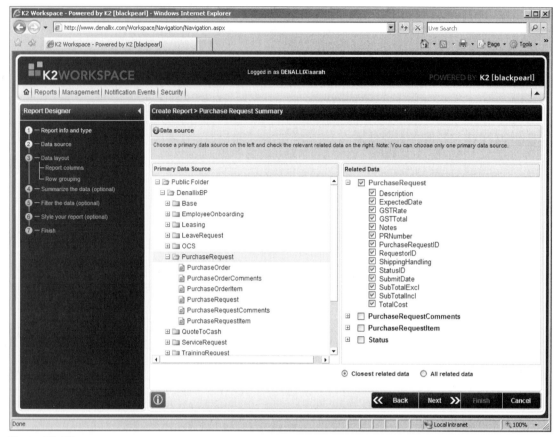

Figure 20-29

3. The third step allows you to design the report layout by dragging-and-dropping the columns onto the report canvas. Drag the desired column to the right-hand side of where it says DROP HERE. Use the Search Report Data textbox to find the SmartObject property. When completed the step should look like Figure 20-30. Click the Next button to continue.

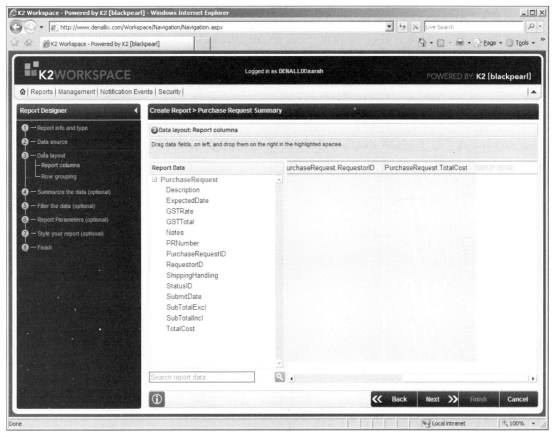

Figure 20-30

4.  The following step allows you to set up the row grouping for the report. This is applicable only to Summary and Matrix reports. Drag the desired property to the report canvas where it says DROP HERE. This groups the report by the chosen property. The completed step should look similar to Figure 20-31.

When you are creating a Matrix report, a column grouping step appears next. It works in the same way as the row grouping step. Since you are creating a Summary report in this example, you won't see the column grouping screen. Click the Next button to continue.

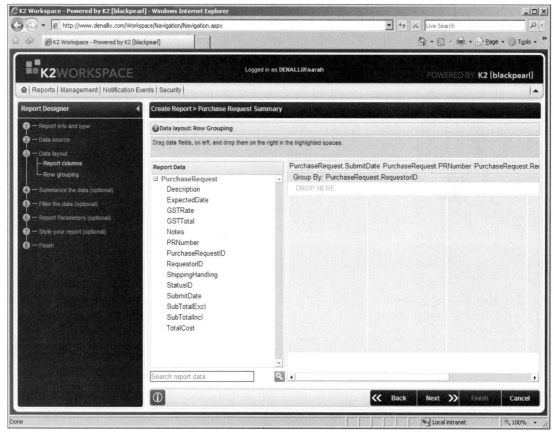

Figure 20-31

5. The steps from here on are all optional and not required to create a report; thus, you can click on the Preview, Save As, and Save buttons at any step. The fourth step allows you to summarize the report data. Drag the desired Summary Filter option to the corresponding report column where it says DROP HERE. Click the Next button to continue.

6. The fifth step allows you to filter the data returned in the report. To create a filter, drag one of the items listed in the Summary Filters list to a Field on the Filter canvas (where it says DROP HERE). Select the appropriate operator value for the Operator drop-down list. The Value options are dependent on the selected property data type. In this example, the value options for a date property allow for the selection of a custom date range. Once all the filters have been added, you can add conditional statements to the filters.

The completed step should look like Figure 20-32. Click the Next button to continue.

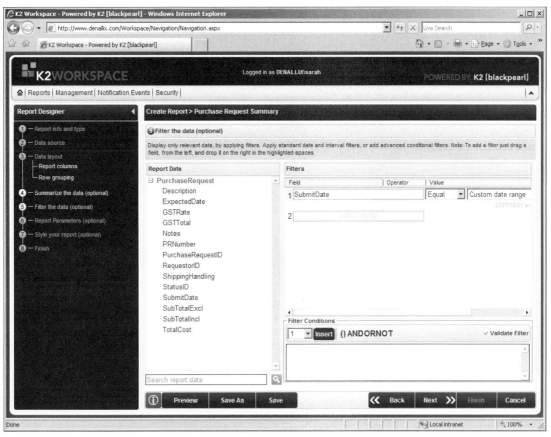

Figure 20-32

7. The sixth step in the wizard allows you to set parameter values for the report. This step appears only if there is at least one SmartObject property that accepts parameters. Enter the parameter value in the Default Value column next to the applicable property. In this example, we are not setting any parameters. Click the Next button to continue.

8. The seventh step allows for setting the formatting style of the report. On the design canvas there is a Formatting Toolbar that allows you to set font, alignment, and color options. Click on a desired column and format the report using the Formatting Toolbar. Click the Next button to continue.

9. The final page of the wizard is a confirmation of the report being created. From here you can choose to view the report, design a new report or publish the report.

   The Save As button is available. This is handy if you have edited an existing report and then want to save it with another name. Click the Finish button to continue.

10. After clicking the Finish button, the report is displayed and looks similar to Figure 20-33.

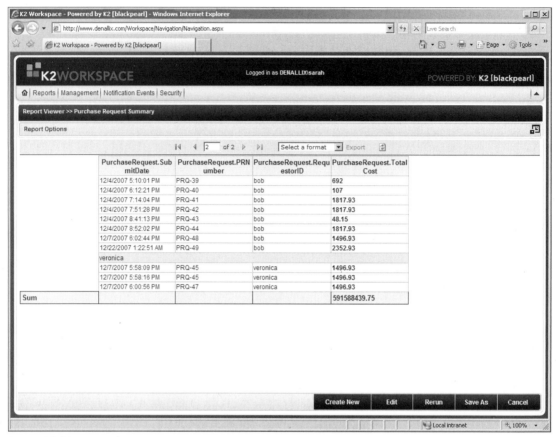

Figure 20-33

**11.** Clicking on the Save As button brings up a Save Report As window. You are prompted to enter the Name of the report and to select a location to save it to. Click the OK button to save the report.

Once the report has been saved, it can be seen on the Reports tab.

You can easily edit, run, or delete existing reports by clicking on the downward arrow that can be found when you hover over the Date Saved column header in the reports list, as shown in Figure 20-34.

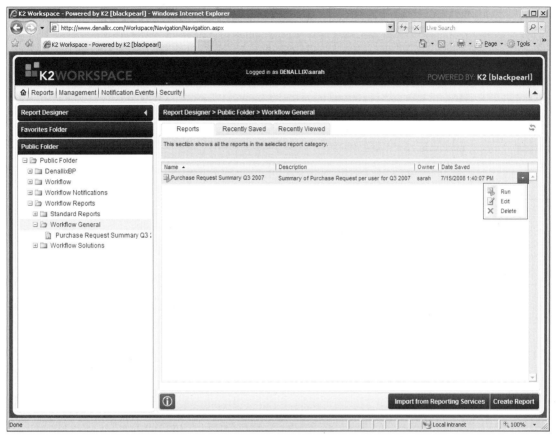

Figure 20-34

When you are viewing a report, you can alter some of the report configuration without editing the report. Click on the icon in the top-right corner of the report (you can see the icon back in Figure 20-33).

This displays the options (Figure 20-35) that can be altered so that you can run the report again using the new configuration settings.

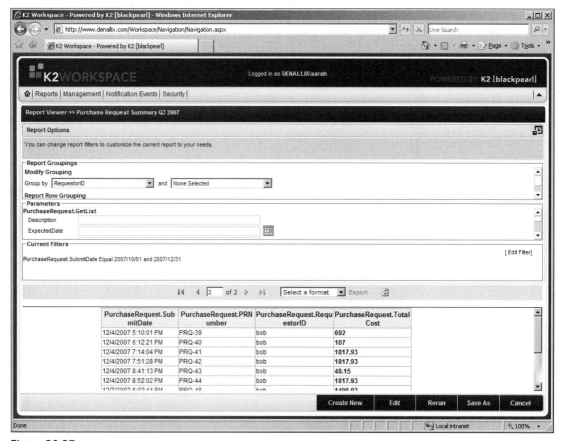

Figure 20-35

You can also add reports to the user's Favorites Folder, allowing for quick access to frequently run reports. This is done by right-clicking on the report in the Public Folder and selecting Add to Favorites, as shown in Figure 20-36.

Figure 20-36

# Working with Reporting Services

K2 blackpearl makes use of Report Definition Language (RDL) for reports that are created by the Report Designer on the Reports tab. It is used by Microsoft SQL Server 2005 Reporting Services and other RDL-compliant authoring tools such as SQL Server Business Intelligence Development Studio and some third-party reporting tools. This means that reports can easily be created in Microsoft Visual Studio 2005, using the Report Designer, and then imported into the K2 Workspace. Similarly, reports created in the K2 Workspace can be exported to Visual Studio 2005.

## Exporting K2 Reports to Reporting Services

Reports that have been published can be exported to Microsoft SQL Server 2005 Reporting Services. Once exported, reports can be edited in Report Builder. This allows for the creation of reports touching multiple data sources, which is useful when the data sources are not exposed to the K2 platform through SmartObjects.

To do this open the Microsoft SQL Server Management Studio by selecting Start ➪ All Programs ➪ Microsoft SQL Server 2005 ➪ SQL Server Management Studio.

When you are prompted to connect to the server, select Reporting Services from the Server type drop-down list and the desired server from the Server name drop-down list.

In the Management Studio expand to the Reporting folder in the Object Explorer, as shown in Figure 20-37. Right-click on the desired report and select Edit Report. This will open a Save Dialog box that can be used to save the report to the desired location. Once saved, the report has been exported and is available to be opened in Microsoft Visual Studio 2005.

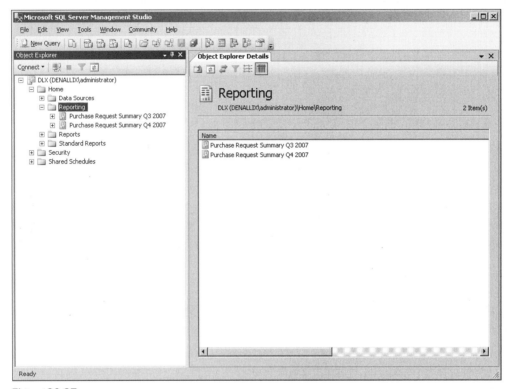

Figure 20-37

## Creating K2 Platform Reports in Visual Studio 2005

You can create Microsoft SQL Server 2005 Reporting Services reports that use SmartObjects as data sources and that can be imported into the Reports tab on the K2 Workspace. Using Microsoft Visual Studio 2005 to create these reports allows you to use all of the features available through the Report Designer. The following section explains how to create such a report.

**1.** Open Microsoft Visual Studio 2005 by clicking Start ⇨ All Programs ⇨ Microsoft Visual Studio 2005 ⇨ Microsoft Visual Studio 2005. Create a new Report Server Project. Right-click on the Reports folder under the project in the Solution Explorer. This opens up the Report Wizard. Click the Next button to continue.

**2.** The next step deals with selecting the data source, as shown in Figure 20-38. Select the New data source radio button and enter **SOURCECODE** in the Name textbox. Ensure that SOURCECODE is selected in the Type drop-down list.

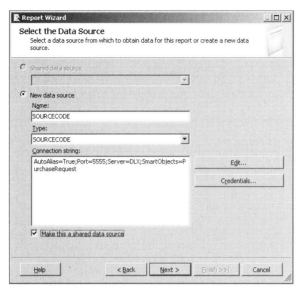

**Figure 20-38**

Click the Edit button to open the Connection Properties window, as shown in Figure 20-39. Set the connection properties to the K2 server, that is, Port Number, Server Name, and required SmartObjects.

**Figure 20-39**

*If the OK button is disabled, click the Change button next to the Data Source textbox. Select the required data source, and click OK.*

To set the SmartObjects, click on the . . . button next to the SmartObject property. This opens the Select SmartObjects window.

Once all of the desired SmartObjects have been selected, click the OK button to return the Report Wizard. Click the Next button to continue.

3. The next step in the wizard allows you to design the query that forms the basis of the dataset used for the report.

Click the Query Builder button to open the Query Builder, as shown in Figure 20-40. Write the query, and click the ! button to see the data returned.

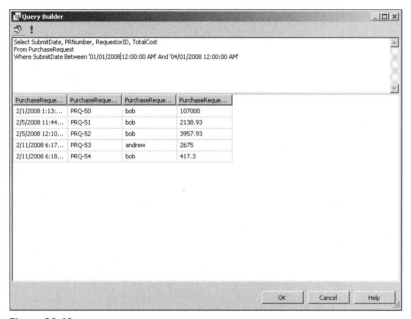

Figure 20-40

Once the process has completed, click the OK button to return to the Report Wizard. Click the Next button to continue.

4. The next step allows you to select the Report Type. Select the report type, and click the Next button to continue.

5. The next step allows you to design the table used to format the report. Select the dataset fields and move them to the desired report field sections, as shown in Figure 20-41. Click the Next button to continue.

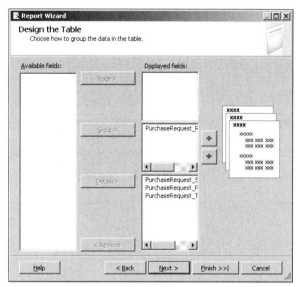

**Figure 20-41**

6. The next step allows you to choose the layout for the table used as the basis of the report. Choose the desired layout. Click the Next button to continue.

7. The next step allows you to choose the style for the table. Select the desired style, and click the Next button to continue.

8. The next step is the final step in the wizard. It allows you to enter a name for the report in the Report name textbox. Check the Preview report checkbox to display the final report and click the Finish button to end the Report Wizard.

9. Microsoft Visual Studio 2005 displays the report, as shown in Figure 20-42. Using the Report Designer the report layout can be altered as desired.

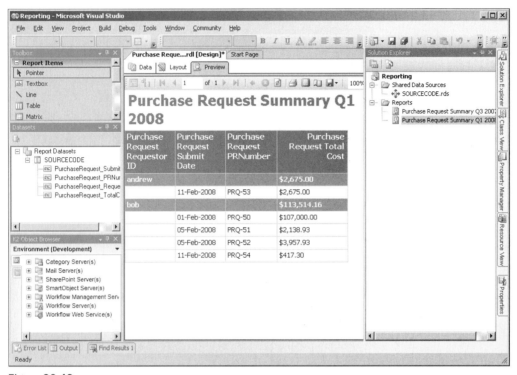

Figure 20-42

**10.** Once you're happy with the report, right-click the project in the Solution Explorer and select Properties. This opens the Property Page dialog, as shown in Figure 20-43. Ensure that the TargetServerURL property is set. Once that is done, right-click on the report in the Solution Explorer and select Deploy. This deploys the report the Reporting Server. It is now ready to be imported into the K2 Workspace.

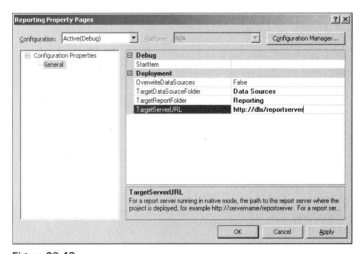

Figure 20-43

## Importing Reporting Services Reports into K2 Reports

To import reports running on Microsoft SQL Server 2005 Reporting Services into the K2 Workspace, click on the Import from Reporting Services button, as shown in Figure 20-44.

Figure 20-44

This opens the Import Reports window, as shown in Figure 20-45. Expand the Reporting Services folders on the left-hand side of the window and navigate to the report that you wish to import. Click on the report, and drag it to the Category in the Category System on the right-hand side of the window. Click OK to continue.

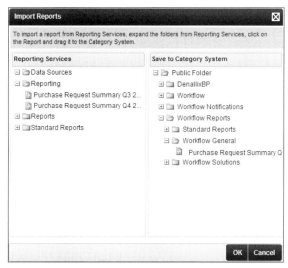

Figure 20-45

Once you've completed these steps, the report will be displayed along with the other reports in the Reports tab of the K2 Workspace.

# K2 Event Notifications

The Notification Events tab of the K2 Workspace allows for the creation of Notification Events that notify users by e-mail of events that occur on the K2 and third-party servers. The events can be raised by third-party servers, from K2 processes, and from single and recurring scheduled tasks. This section gives a brief overview of the notification events and how to create Notification and Custom Events.

There are a number of components that deal with the execution of events and thus Event Notifications. The first is the Custom Event Recorder, which subscribes to the server events, using event handlers. Once an event executes, the event is raised in the Generic Client Recorder.

The Generic Client Recorder retrieves the custom events associated with the event that executed, resolves any actions associated with the custom events, and handles the queuing of the resolved events.

Queuing is processed using transactional queues in Microsoft Message Queuing (MSMQ). From there the events are persisted to the Event database through the Event Bus. Once persisted to the Event database, the resolved events are mapped to action policies. These policies in turn are responsible for sending the notification e-mail and raising any configured custom events.

*For more information on the Event Bus see Chapter 21.*

There are two types of events that the user can create and be notified about upon their execution, Notification Events and Custom Events. Events are created using the Notification Event Designer or Custom Event Designer. These events are simple to create and can be created by workflow participants, developers, or administrators. They can be added to monitor deployed processes without the need for redeploying the workflow solution. It provides a great way to trigger events when you are troubleshooting a deployed process or returning information at peak periods.

*Notification Events can also be created when developing the workflow process. Each activity has a set of Event Notifications Settings that can be configured during the development phase. Setting these sends a notification e-mail to the activity destination users.*

## Notification Events

Notification Events are created using the Notification Event Designer found on the Notification Events tab in the K2 Workspace. Figure 20-46 shows the Notification Event Designer. The Notification Event Designer displays existing events and allows for the creation of new events.

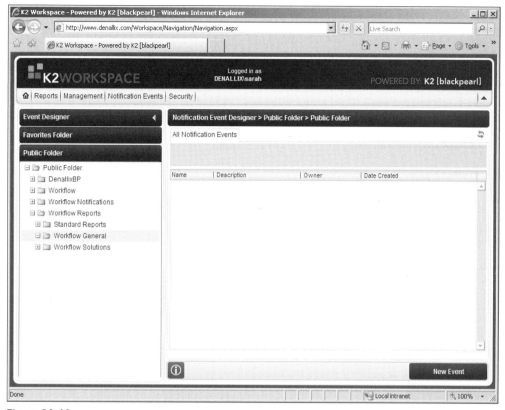

**Figure 20-46**

New events can be created by clicking the New Event button. This is done with the aid of the Add Notification Event Wizard, which walks you through the following steps:

**1.** The first step in the wizard requires the Notification Event name and description. After entering a name and description, select the location for the Notification Event to be displayed. Click the Next button to continue.

**2.** The second step in the wizard deals with selecting the source for the Notification Event, as shown in Figure 20-47. Select the event that you want to subscribe to. It can be from a K2 server or a third-party server. In this example it is from the K2 Workflow server and relates to a deployed process. Click the Next button to continue.

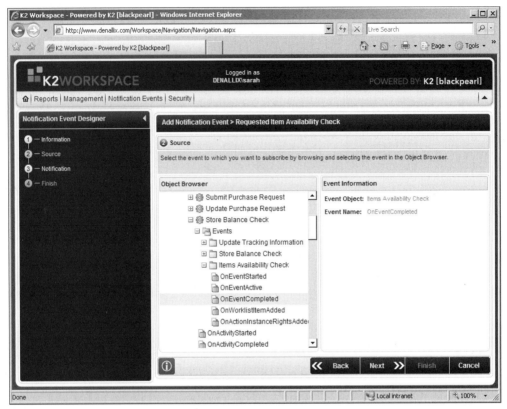

Figure 20-47

3. The third step in the wizard deals with configuring the e-mail notification, as shown in Figure 20-48. You specify the e-mail properties, including the sender, recipient, subject, and body. The body can be formatted in HTML or be plain text. When configuring the e-mail, you can use the Object Browser to drag process fields, data fields, and XML fields to assist in personalizing the e-mail content. Click the Finish button to continue.

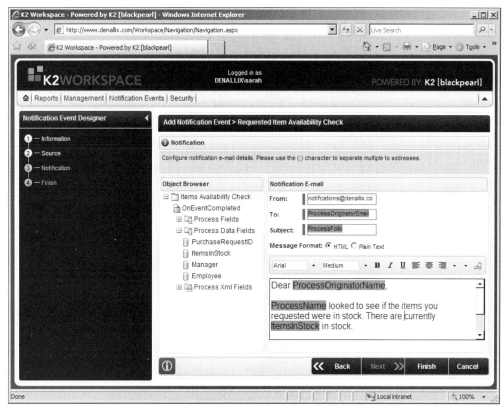

Figure 20-48

4.  The final step in the wizard gives you the option of creating another event or returning to the location that the event has been saved to.

## Custom Events

Creating a Custom Event is done by using the Add Custom Event Wizard. This wizard is similar to the Add Notification Event Wizard, apart from the third step. In the Add Custom Event Wizard the third step is the Custom Event step (as opposed to the Notification step), although it deals with the same functionality, that is, sending a notification e-mail. Figure 20-49 shows the Custom Event step.

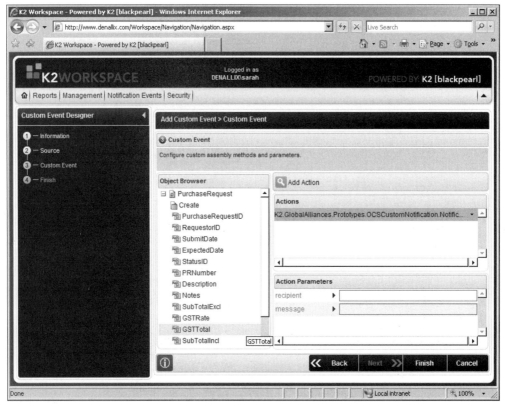

Figure 20-49

To complete this step you click the Add Action button to add an action that will occur when the event subscribed to has executed. The Add Action button opens a dialog that allows you to search for an assembly that you want to reference, the class within the assembly selected, and the method to call. Once you have made a selection, the Action Parameters are populated with the method input parameters. In this case the Send method requires Recipient and Message parameters.

# Summary

In this chapter you've become familiar with the K2 Workspace and all of the functionality it brings with it. First, the chapter covered the K2 Home Page, the page that most visitors to the K2 Workspace see and use. You saw the options available to the workflow participants to manage worklists.

You also were introduced to the reporting capabilities of K2 blackpearl. The K2 Workspace provides simple yet powerful report creating capabilities. The reports are easily imported and exported to Microsoft SQL Server Reporting Services.

You were also introduced to Notification and Custom Events and how to create them. They can provide timely information to participants and administrators alike.

The next chapter introduces the Event Bus. It is a component of the K2 platform that allows notifications and custom assemblies to be called when an event occurs. These events can be raised by third-party servers, from a process, or from a single or recurring schedule.

# Part V

# Advanced K2 blackpearl Concepts and Platform Extensions

# 21

# The K2 Event Bus

### Anthony Petro

The book to this point has shown that K2 blackpearl is an incredible platform for modeling business processes and information. Sometimes factors external to the process can affect its performance or logic and processes should be able to adapt to these events both internal and external to the process. Event monitoring allows users to affect change and address issues that affect the process without having to remodel the process. The K2 Event Bus is the event-modeling platform for K2 blackpearl.

The K2 Event Bus provides the infrastructure and tools to allow business users to model notifications and custom actions based on events in K2 workflow processes, SmartObjects, line-of-business (LOB) systems, and single or recurring schedules. The events are configured to evaluate and execute policies independent of the context of a workflow process or LOB system activity, such as a SmartObject Create method. The policies can range from simple e-mail notifications configured in the K2 Workspace to fully customized .NET code.

This chapter will cover the following topics:

- ❑ Key features of K2 Event Bus
- ❑ K2 Event Bus Architecture
- ❑ Exposing process definitions and data as SmartObjects
- ❑ The K2 Event Bus Scheduler
- ❑ Configuring the Event Bus
- ❑ A walkthrough of using the Event Bus
- ❑ Troubleshooting tips and tricks

# Key Features of the Event Bus

Event-Driven Business Process Management (EDBPM) combines Business Process Management (BPM) with Complex Event Processing (CEP) to bring greater business flexibility, agility, and real-time information to distributed systems.[1] The Event Bus is a key piece of the K2 platform that enables the integration of CEP with BPM. Event-driven scenarios made possible by the Event Bus allow process-driven applications to react to events from line-of-business (LOB) systems and other sources relevant to the business, increasing process flexibility and business agility in response to a changing business environment.

The Event Bus provides rich features for business users and developers alike. The following sections provide a quick overview of the key features of the Event Bus.

## *Open and Extensible Architecture*

The Event Bus provides a set of generic application programming interfaces (APIs) for registering and recording events, mapping and resolving context data, executing policies, and working with message queue systems.

> *Refer to the K2 Developer Reference topics "How to register new events with the Event Bus" for information about scheduling events, and "How to add a 3rd-party Event Recorder to the K2 blackpearl server" for information about raising new events.*

## *Separating Events from Actions*

The Event Bus separates the act of raising an event from the action that must be taken for events that have been raised. This allows more than one event to call the same action.

## *Pluggable Event Systems*

The Event Bus provides a set of programming interfaces that allow any system to be registered as part of the event management toolset. Once a system is registered, users can begin to subscribe to events raised by that LOB system. For example, an organization can configure its proprietary Human Resources applications event for Create New Employee as an event in the Event Bus. Once this HR system is registered, end users can begin to create notifications, or subscriptions, that evaluate when the Create New Employee event is raised from the HR LOB system. The user then has the full power of the Event Bus to determine what conditions of Create New Employee are important to monitor and what actions must be taken when those conditions evaluate to True.

## *Built-In Event Handlers*

The Event Bus is preconfigured with event handlers for K2 Workflow and K2 SmartObjects. The events for the K2 SmartObjects on the K2 server, as well as K2 Workflow events, are made available for users to subscribe to. All the events are available throughout the K2 blackpearl platform, such as reports and forms via the ADO.NET provider and the Notification Events wizards, as shown in Figure 21-1. For more information on how data and events are exposed for K2 Workflow processes, see the "Exposing Process Information through SmartObjects" section in this chapter.

Figure 21-1

# Pluggable Message Queuing

The Event Bus uses message queuing to allow for asynchronous events. All registered events are put on the queue for processing. The events are then pulled from the queue and evaluated to determine if any action needs to be taken. The message queuing infrastructure implements a pluggable architecture that allows any message queuing system to be used by the Event Bus. The Microsoft Message Queuing (MSMQ) interfaces are provided by and used by default by the Event Bus.

# Independent Policy Management

All policies that are evaluated or executed by the Event Bus are created and maintained independently in the policy management system. This allows organizations to manage their business policies independent of the usage of those policies. Users simply consume a policy as part of an event registration process.

*At the time of this writing, the policy management system available is an Event Bus–specific version of the SmartFunction engine. This engine is only available to the K2 Event Bus APIs and UIs and has no additional policy management tooling.*

# Conditional Policies

Although it is possible to register an event and perform an action as a result of that event firing, it is often necessary to apply a policy to the event to determine if an action is necessary given the current condition. The Event Bus allows for the registration of a conditional policy that will be evaluated when the event is fired. Conditional polices are managed independent of the Event Bus, allowing for maximum flexibility within an organization and for modeling events independent of policies and actions.

*Conditional Policies are available only via the API.*

## Action Policies

The action policy allows a business user to configure the action the Event Bus must perform independent of the event system. Typical actions are Send an Email or Start a Workflow Process. The Notification action policy is provided for users with K2 blackpearl.

*See Chapter 20 for an example of how to register for notifications via K2 Workspace.*

## Subscription Model

The subscription model allows users to register for system-level events through wizard-driven tools that abstract the complexity of the underlying data and policies. Typical event management systems require administrator access and intimate knowledge of the underlying system to configure notifications. The subscription model allows business users to take ownership of this configuration.

# Architecture of the K2 Event Bus

The Event Bus component of the K2 platform consists of three hosted servers — the Event Bus Management Server, the Event Bus server, and the Event Bus Scheduler, which are shown in Figure 21-2. The flow of data is shown in the Figure 21-7, but it is important to note here that the Event Bus Scheduler utilizes the `SourceCode.EventBus.ClientRecorder` assembly to schedule events on single or recurring schedules, such as the Last Friday of every Month (see The Event Bus Scheduler section later in this chapter for more details). The scheduler events, along with the recorders for workflow, SmartObjects, and custom events, are processed using Microsoft Messaging Queuing (MSMQ) to either send notifications or call static methods in custom assemblies.

- ❑ **Event Bus Server:** Responsible for the event system in the K2 environment. This includes server level events as well as process- and SmartObject-level events.

- ❑ **Event Bus Management Server:** Responsible for the management interfaces surrounding the Event Bus.

- ❑ **Event Bus Scheduler Server:** Responsible for the management interfaces surrounding the Event Bus scheduling service.

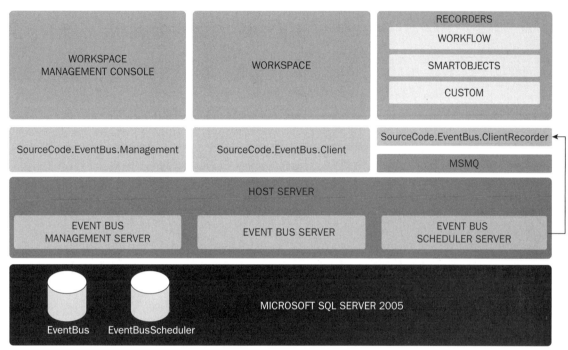

Figure 21-2

## Event Bus Data Flow

The Event Bus has been architected from the ground up with generic components and interfaces throughout the entire platform. All built-in and custom events that are registered with the Event Bus are done so through the Generic Client Event Recorder. This ensures that the tooling provided for managing events and notifications is consistent regardless of the source of the event. To ensure reliable processing of all events without locking or contention issues, the architecture implements the use of a message queue to allow events to be raised independent of their processing. The Generic Client Event Recorder will raise all events that have been registered with the context data that was configured for that event. This happens independent of any processing of the event. The event action and the context data is simply put on the message queue for processing by the Event Bus server.

Figure 21-3 shows how data flows from workflow, SmartObject, and custom Event Recorders through to the message queue (MSMQ) to then be processed by the Event Bus. The processing of events will likely involve a notification or execution of a policy/action or SmartObject method. Typically, these events are configured to send notifications or execute custom code via K2 Workspace, but they can also be programmatically configured.

*Since there is no current tooling in K2 blackpearl, schedules can only be programmatically configured.*

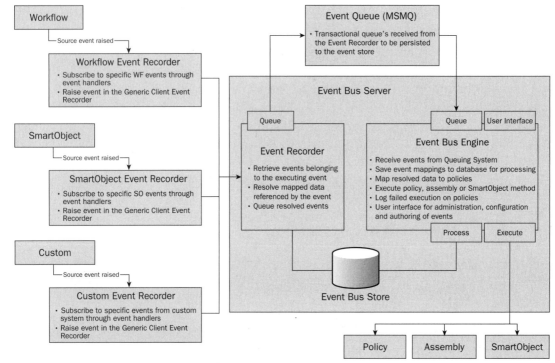

**Figure 21-3**

*The policy aspect of the Event Bus shown in Figure 21-3 is provided by the SmartFunction hosted server. Currently, this server is used only by the Event Bus. It cannot be extended, and it will be superseded by a different policy engine in the future.*

The sample code listed later in this chapter will walk through the various pieces of configuration.

## Event Bus Server

The Event Bus Server (see Figure 21-4) is composed of multiple components and makes up the heart of the event features of the K2 platform. Each component is described in this section.

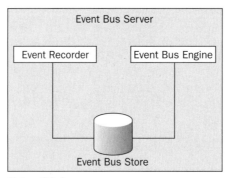

**Figure 21-4**

## *Event Recorder*

The Event Recorder is responsible for actually registering the events that the Event Bus will be listening for. There are several events available through workflow and SmartObject events as well as custom events that implement the Generic Client Recorder interfaces. The registered events will be sent to the configured queue by the Event Recorder.

## *Event Bus Engine*

The Event Bus Engine is the execution engine for the entire event management system. It receives events from the queue, evaluates policies and executes the registered actions. In the case of any exceptions, the Event Bus Engine is also responsible for logging the exceptions.

## *Event Bus Store*

The Event Bus utilizes ADO.NET 2.0 for much of the interaction between the Event Bus server and the Event Bus Store. The Event Bus Store holds the details for all registered events (Workflow, SmartObjects, and Custom) as well as the policies (Conditional and Action). The Event Bus store consists of two main databases: Event Bus and Event Bus Scheduler. Please see the Developer Reference for more information on the databases, tables, and stored procedures that make up the Event Bus Store.

# *Event Recorder*

As Figure 21-5 shows, the Event Recorder serves as the gateway between the Event Bus and source system for the actual events that are being managed. Although the source system is actually where the events happen, it is through the Event Recorder that the events become part of the Event Bus.

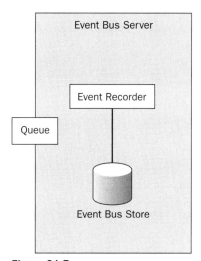

**Figure 21-5**

## System Event Recorder

The events of the source system are exposed to the Event Bus through a custom Event Recorder. All Event Recorders, including the built-in workflow and SmartObject Event Recorders, implement the interfaces of the Generic Client Event Recorder. The system-specific Event Recorders contain the logic for subscribing to events from source system through Event Bus event handlers. These event handlers utilize the Generic Client Event Recorder to raise the events to the Event Bus.

## Generic Client Event Recorder

The Generic Client Event Recorder will retrieve context data belonging to the executing event and provide the ability to store that data. The context data from the events is serialized and deserialized throughout the processing of the event. When the source system raises the event, it will be responsible for storing any context data necessary for processing of the event. This context data is usually configured as part of registering a source system event. To ensure consistent processing of all Event Bus events, the context data is serialized through interfaces in the Generic Client Event Recorder. When the Event Bus processes the source system event, it will utilize these same interfaces to deserialize the context data. The Generic Client Event Recorder is also responsible for the actual queuing of the source system event.

# Event Bus Engine

The Event Bus Engine (see Figure 21-6) provides the gateway between the message queue system, the policy engine, and the user interfaces for configuring the Event Bus.

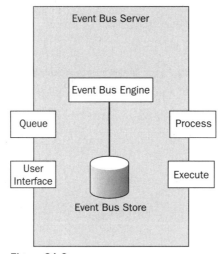

Figure 21-6

## Event Queue

The Event Queue is where all the source system events and their context data are stored. The Event Bus engine utilizes the Event Queue to process events independently of the actual event firing. This allows the source systems to reliably raise all events without waiting for the Event Bus to process those events. The Event Queue will store all the events, and their context data, until it has the cycles to process those events. Ideally, this is within milliseconds of the original event, but under load it may take longer.

The important thing to note is that all events will be processed and the source system will not be affected by this processing.

## Event Store

The Event Store consists of two main databases:

❏ **EventBus:** Stores information about the Event Bus and configured notifications.

❏ **EventBusScheduler:** Stores information about the Event Bus Scheduler, which provides a mechanism to raise events to the Event Bus using single or recurring schedules.

These databases store the list of events that are to be managed by the Event Bus as well as the mappings of their context data. It is important to note that nothing specific to the actual event is stored in the Event Bus store. The specific events and the context data for that event are stored on the Event Queue for processing. Once processed, that event and context data is disposed and no longer accessible.

## Policy Engine

When the Event Bus engine processes events from the queue it will likely execute policies in the form of .NET methods and utilize the context data from the source system. The policies are stored and executed via the SmartFunction hosted server. Failed policy executions are logged and retried. The retry count is configurable and, if exceeded, the Event Bus Engine will log an exception.

*At the time of this writing, the policy engine that currently ships with K2 blackpearl does not support policies other than action policies. Conditional policies are dependent upon future releases.*

Some common failures to watch for include unexpected or missing context data fields and lost connections. Remember that the source system will raise an event and must put the event and the context data on the queue. It is later that the Event Bus engine will process that event with the context data through the execution of policies. Managing for this disconnected processing is key to building custom events.

## Event Administration

The Event Bus engine can be fully managed in code via the APIs. The Event Bus architecture was built from the ground up to ensure flexibility and extensibility. The transparency of the administrative features is a great example of this. The Event Bus currently has business user tooling for creating e-mail notifications for any event managed by the Event Bus. Additionally, there is tooling for executing custom policies in the form of static .NET methods for registered events. This business user tooling is just scratching the surface of the Event Bus administration APIs, and more business user tooling will be available in the future, including registration for schedule-based events.

# Exposing Process Information through SmartObjects

Business processes in organizations typically have two main elements of information that are part of the design-time and run-time process information — the process instance data (what actions were taken for an instance of the process) and the data that is associated with the process instance.

Every business process that is designed in an organization will have certain actions that can be performed on it. These actions are determined when the process is designed. Some of the actions are standard actions, such as Start Process. Others are more specific to the type of process such as Begin Order Approval. A process also generates and contains data during execution. This data is also defined during design time and can be set, but only after an instance of the process is created. So when a user performs an action, such as Start Process for instance, you can first set some data on the instance. This concept of setting data and performing actions is similar to setting properties and executing methods on SmartObjects. This means that exposing processes and data as SmartObjects fits nicely into the SmartObject model. For more information about SmartObjects, see Chapter 7.

Let's walk through the following scenario.

An organization builds an Order Approval process that presents an approver with a form to review the order and determine if it should be Approved or Declined. An e-mail indicating the results is then sent to the Originator of the process.

Most processes consist of a number of activities and events. Some events may require input from a user and are called client events. Other events can be executed without any user interface (UI) and are called server events. The example process has three activities: Order Approval, Order Approved, and Order Declined.

The Order Approval activity has one client event called Approve Order. The Order Approved activity has a server event called Send Approved Email. The Order Declined activity has a server event called Send Declined Email. The full process is shown in Figure 21-7.

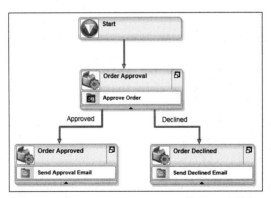

**Figure 21-7**

As with processes, client events can also have actions. In this case the Approve Order client event has actions Approved and Declined. Also like with processes, activities can also have data that are only in the scope for that activity. In the example there is only an Order ID that is defined as data on the process level.

When a process is deployed, SmartObjects are optionally created for the process itself and for each client event in the process. These are the only entities of a process that can have actions performed on them. So in the example there will be a SmartObject created for the Order Approval Process and for the Approve Order client event.

As for the data, because Order ID is defined at the process level, Order ID becomes a property on all entities (process and client events). If Order ID were only defined for the Order Approval activity, it would have been a property of the Approve Order client event SmartObject and not on the Order Approval Process SmartObject (see Figure 21-8).

**Figure 21-8**

Now that you understand where the data for a process sits, let's look at how it flows (see Figure 21-9).

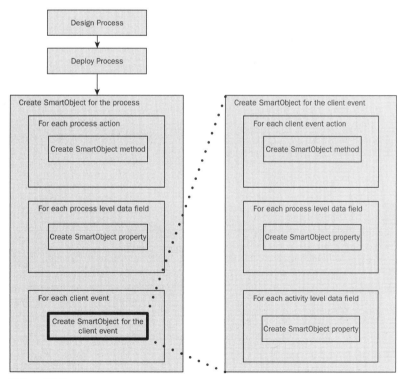

**Figure 21-9**

When the process is deployed, you have a choice to generate the SmartObjects during the deploy task of the process. If you choose not to generate the SmartObjects and later need them, you can always do so manually afterwards. This option is configured on the process properties dialog.

You have the option to choose which objects are created (see Figure 21-10). By default, if you check only Create Workflow SmartObjects and don't specify any other options, this will create only the Process SmartObject and no client SmartObjects. You specifically have to check those you want enabled. Having some of these turned off by default enhances performance and will not put extra load on the server for objects that are never used. Figure 21-10 shows two checkboxes that affect the SmartObjects generated for the process. The same is true concerning the reporting SmartObjects created with Create Workflow Reporting SmartObjects; the only difference is that by default it is checked to be created and you can specify activity objects as well (see the product documentation for more details).

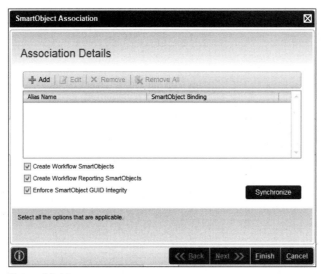

**Figure 21-10**

So how does this apply to the K2 Event Bus?

The ability to represent all business process information — activity instance data, process instance data, data associated with the process that can be both internal and external in a LOB system as business entities — is unique to K2. Once the traditional workflow information is exposed as a SmartObject, all the power of the SmartObject system K2 offers is now available, from dynamic forms and application building to reporting, including intelligent access to all the process information and their related entities without needing to write code or SQL syntax queries to create the relationships, custom applications, other process designs, and the Event Bus to name a few.

# The Event Bus Scheduler

The Event Bus Scheduler is used to schedule time-based events. These could be events that occur on a particular day and time or that recur on a regular basis. Scheduled events are not raised by another system but are created and executed entirely within the Event Bus. LOB systems that raise recurring events can and should probably be used for recurring events that need some interaction with the Event Bus, but if you don't have a system for these events and you would like to give your business users access to a scheduling engine, use the Event Bus Scheduler. Keep in mind that the scheduler will not execute custom code nor will it execute policies for use by the Event Bus.

Events are raised in the same way as in the Event Bus by the use of Event Recorders, and there are two ways of consuming your events as set up by your business users:

1. Schedules can be linked to an Event Bus event in order to execute your policies as the schedules are executed.

2. Custom assemblies can be written to handle your schedules by implementing the appropriate Scheduler interface. These need to be added as Event Recorders in the scheduler configuration file.

The authoring of a schedule uses standard scheduling patterns. The patterns supported by the Event Bus Scheduler are:

❑ Interval

❑ Daily

❑ Weekly

❑ Monthly

❑ Yearly

These occurrence patterns can be used together with an occurrence range to specify the parameters of your schedule. The occurrence range can be specified in one of the following two methods:

❑ Begin and End Dates

❑ Number of Occurrences

By using the predeveloped Event Bus Scheduler Event Recorder, you can create a schedule and link it to an Event Bus policy to be executed. Using the Scheduling API, you can create a schedule with the following code sample:

```
private void SpecificDateSchedule (object sender, EventArgs e)
    {
       SchedClient.ScheduleAuthoring scheduleClient;
       SchedAuth.Schedule schedule;
       int scheduleID = 0;

       try
```

```
      {
        //***** SPECIFIC DATE *****
        schedule = new SchedAuth.Schedule((int)SchedAuth.RecurrenceType.Yearly);
        //Setup Schedule
        schedule.Name = "Specific Date Schedule1";
        schedule.Description = "This schedule executes on 18th of January yearly at
15:39";
        //Setup Range
        schedule.RecurrenceRange.Occurrences = 1; //Could also use the
RecurrenceRange.StartDate and EndDate to specify a range
        //Setup Pattern
        schedule.RecurrencePatternYearly.DayX = 18;
        schedule.RecurrencePatternYearly.EveryXMonth = 01;
        schedule.RecurrencePatternYearly.StartTime = new SchedAuth.Time(15, 39);

        //Open Connection and save schedule
        scheduleClient = new SchedClient.ScheduleAuthoring();
        scheduleClient.CreateConnection();
        scheduleClient.Connection.Open(GetConnectionString());
        scheduleID = scheduleClient.UpdateSchedule(schedule);
        AddSolutionPolicy(scheduleID); //This is where the schedule is linked to the
executing policy
        MessageBox.Show("Done");
      }
      catch (Exception ex)
      {
        MessageBox.Show(ex.ToString());
      }
      finally
      {
        schedule = null;
        scheduleClient = null;
      }
    }
```

To link the schedule created above to an Event Bus policy, the `AddSolutionPolicy` function would be similar to creating Event Bus events, but you would specify a different Event Type, as in the following example:

```
private void AddSolutionPolicy(int scheduleID)
  {
    EBClient.EventAuthoring eventClient;
    EBAuthor.CustomEvent customEvent;
    EBAuthor.PolicyMapping policyMapping;
    EBAuthor.SourceField sourceField;
    try
    {
      //***** Add the Event to Execute for the schedule *****
      //Create Event
      customEvent = new EBAuthor.CustomEvent(
        0,
        "Test Schedule Event",
```

```
            "Description",
            scheduleID.ToString(),
            "OnScheduleExecute",
            (int)SourceCode.EventBus.Common.Enumerators.EventType.Scheduled_Event);
        //Add the action policy
        policyMapping = new EBAuthor.PolicyMapping(0, "C:\\Windows\\SolutionEvent.dll",
"SolutionEvent.Job", "Void TestJob()");

        customEvent.ActionPolicyMappings.Add(policyMapping);
        //Save the custom event
        eventClient = new EBClient.EventAuthoring();
        eventClient.CreateConnection();
        eventClient.Connection.Open(GetConnectionString());
        eventClient.UpdateCustomEvent(customEvent);
    }
    catch (Exception ex)
    {
        MessageBox.Show(ex.ToString());
    }
    finally
    {
        sourceField = null;
        policyMapping = null;
        customEvent = null;
        eventClient = null;
    }
}
```

An example scenario for creating a monthly schedule is to automatically generate a department's sales report and mail the report to all the relevant sales representatives. You could also automatically create a sales discussion meeting if the sales figures are below 10% of the budgeted estimates.

*Note that currently there is no UI to author schedules so everything must be done using the API. Refer to the EventBusScheduler Management Application* http://k2underground.com/k2/ ProjectHome.aspx?ProjectID=90 *on K2 Underground for an example of using the Event Bus Scheduler. It may require a K2 Underground account.*

# Event Bus Configuration Settings

There are several configuration (.config) files that are useful in understanding settings that control how the Event Bus functions:

❑   SourceCode.EventBus.Server.Config

❑   SourceCode.EventBus.Mapping.dll.config

❑   SourceCode.EventBus.ClientRecorder.dll.config

❑   SourceCode.EventBus.EventAdmin.dll.config

This section includes descriptions and important settings for each configuration file.

# SourceCode.EventBus.Server.Config

This configuration file is located at `C:\Program Files\K2 blackpearl\Host Server\Bin` and is used for controlling many aspects of the Event Bus server.

- ❏ `eventbusserverconnection`: Database connection for the Event Bus database.

- ❏ `SmartFunctionconnectionstring`: Host Server connection for the SmartFunction server.

- ❏ `sendmailpolicyname`: Policy name of the SmartFunction to be used to send mail.

- ❏ `sendmailpolicynamespace`: Namespace name of the SmartFunction to be used to send mail.

- ❏ `sendmailpolicymajorversion`: Version number of the SmartFunction to be used to send mail.

- ❏ `sendmailfrom`: The address to be used as the from address for all the worklist item notifications.

- ❏ `notificationtemplatepath`: The path to the notification template to be used for worklist item notifications.

- ❏ `eventbusserverdependencies`: The dependencies needed to be able to successfully handle events for both the workflow and SmartObject events. These class names are used in the Event Bus server to check if these servers are already hosted. If these servers are not successfully hosted, the Event Bus server will idle for a few seconds before trying to determine if the dependencies are hosted, and it will keep on trying to verify these dependencies until they are successfully hosted.

- ❏ `msmqpath`: The queue path to the processing queue.

- ❏ `msmqerrorpath`: The queue path to the error queue.

- ❏ `eventqueuingassembly`: The assembly to be used to retrieve messages from a queue.

- ❏ `eventqueuingtype`: The assembly type to be used to retrieve messages from a queue.

- ❏ `assembliesconfigfilepath`: The path to the configuration file to be used to load the available assemblies that can be used to execute as conditions and actions.

- ❏ `eventbuffersize`: The max item count of the buffer to be used to retrieve items to be processed. This is only used at startup and if there are unprocessed items in the database.

- ❏ `eventpollinginterval`: The interval in milliseconds to be used to release items serviced by multiple servers that might be in an error state. If two servers are used to process items out of the same database, and one server gets an item to process and the server goes down for some reason, then this item will be released after the specified interval, and thus be picked up by the second server for processing.

- ❏ `eventrecorders`: Used to load assemblies to be used for custom recorders. For example, if you want to create a file system watcher to raise events when a file is copied to a specified folder, the Event Bus server can load this file system watcher assembly for you.

- ❏ `mappings`: This section hosts all the data provider and resolver assemblies to be used for creating run-time data and then resolving these values at run time. When adding a third-party system for eventing, this is where you would add the custom data providers. Remember that when adding assembly info in this section, you need to also add the appropriate information to the `SourceCode.EventBus.Mapping.dll.config` file.

# SourceCode.EventBus.Mapping.dll.config

This configuration file is located at `C:\Program Files\K2 blackpearl\Host Server\Bin` and is used for mapping contextual data from the event to the Event Bus.

❑   `resolvers`: This section is where the resolver assemblies need to be added and is also discussed in the mappings description in the SourceCode.EventBus.Server.Config settings section.

❑   `umconnectionstring`: The connection string to connect to the `UserRoleManager` in order to resolve users, roles, and groups.

# SourceCode.EventBus.ClientRecorder.dll.config

This configuration file is located at `C:\Program Files\K2 blackpearl\Host Server\Bin` and is used for managing the generic Event Recorder settings.

❑   `eventqueuing`: If this setting is set to Internal the client recorder will use the default referenced MSMQ message provider. If it is not set to Internal, then the values from the `eventqueuingassembly` and `eventqueuingtype` settings are used to send messages to the messaging queue.

❑   `eventbusclientconnection`: The database connection for the Event Bus database. This is only used to get the policy mappings needed to resolve data for the events to be executed.

❑   `writelog`: If this is set to True then errors will be raised and logged to the Event Bus database.

❑   `logfilepath`: The path to the log file.

❑   `mappingconfigpath`: Path to the mapping assembly configuration file.

# SourceCode.EventBus.EventAdmin.dll.config

This configuration file is located at `C:\Program Files\K2 blackpearl\Host Server\Bin` and is used for controlling some administrative aspects of the Event Bus.

❑   `dependancyconnectionstring`: The connection to the Dependency server. This is used to add dependencies on SmartObjects or SmartFunctions.

❑   `smartobjectdependancyclassid`, `smartfunctiondependancyclassid`, `scheduledependancyclassid`, `eventbusdependancyclassid`, and `dependancyobjectbrowserids`: These will not be discussed here, as these settings should never be changed other than at installation.

❑   `categoryconnectionstring`: The Host Server connection string for categories, which is used to link certain events to a category.

❑   `worklistnotificationcategoryid`, `managementeventcategoryid`, and `runtimeeventcategoryid`: These IDs are used to save worklist item notifications to their respective categories and should not be changed.

# Troubleshooting the Event Bus

The following is a list of things to keep in mind when working with the Event Bus.

❑ Ensure that you can successfully execute the static methods of your Custom Events from a console application before configuring them as Custom Events in K2 Workspace.

❑ Start with simple SmartBox SmartObjects and ensure that all the interfaces are working as expected with Event Bus before configuring the SmartObject to utilize non-SmartBox Service Objects.

❑ Ensure all methods of SmartObjects that utilize non-SmartBox Service Objects work before configuring them for usage in the Event Bus.

❑ Start small with Custom Events. Register a single method with a few simple parameters and output the parameters to the console to get started.

❑ Ensure that your Types can be resolved between the context data represented in the Object Browser and the Action Parameters of the Custom Event or the e-mail fields of a Notification.

❑ Test the code that you expect to raise an event outside of the context of the Event Bus. For example, write a Windows application to make sure that the `FileSystemWatcher` class is raising the Created event for the file filter you've configured.

❑ Test your mapping classes to ensure the Provider and Resolver are processing context data as you expect.

❑ Test your workflow processes by using Management Console in K2 workspace to load process data fields and start a new process — ensure that the process completes without errors.

❑ Enable the Journal option for the "eventbus" and "eventbus error" public queues in MSMQ. Although the data on the queue is not very usable, every event successfully raised via the Generic Client Event Recorder will make an entry in the journal.

❑ Monitor the `ClientEventRecorderError` table in the EventBus database for any errors that may occur with your custom recorders.

❑ Monitor the Event Bus logging information by running K2 blackpearl server in console mode. The Event Bus messages are the ones with Category=14 in the `MessageList` section of the `C:\Program Files\K2 blackpearl\Host Server\bin\HostServerLogging.config` file. See Chapter 19 for more information on configuring K2 blackpearl server for console mode.

❑ Enable your code for debugging in Visual Studio by attaching to the `K2HostServer.exe` process. See the K2 blackpearl Developer Reference for more information on configuring Visual Studio to debug K2 Host Server.

# Walkthrough: Event Bus SMTP Sample

Let's walk through a sample of creating a new custom event based on the arrival of mail in a SMTP folder. The scenario in this example involves a process in which:

❑ A user sends an e-mail to a specific address with a SharePoint search term as the Subject.

❑ The Event Bus Recorder creates an event with context data from the e-mail and adds it to the queue.

❑ The Event Bus creates a new instance of a SharePoint Search process which queries a SharePoint site and sends the user a list of results that match their query.

We must build several components to surface and process the event of receiving an e-mail with the Event Bus. Figure 21-11 shows how these components fit in the overall solution.

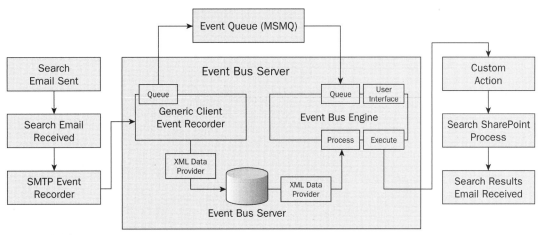

**Figure 21-11**

The provided solution contains three projects related to the registration, configuration, and processing of an e-mail received event and the associated context data from the e-mail. The solution also contains two projects for custom action that will be taken once the e-mail is received, namely the execution of a workflow process.

The five projects are:

❑ `SourceCode.EventBus.Samples.SMTPEventRecorder`: Implements the `IEventRecorder` interface. The `Start` method utilizes the `FileSystemWatcher` .NET Framework classes to monitor the `SearchSharePoint` mailbox and parse the e-mails received for the From address (this will become the search Requestor) and the Subject (this will become the search Keyword).

❑ Once the e-mail is parsed and context data is serialized, Generic Client Event Recorder (`ClientRecorder`) is used to put the event and context data on the queue:

```
RaiseEvent((object)context, "C2815731-5997-4A9F-9837-EBCE48C6FF3F", "SMTP",
"OnMailReceived");
```

❑ `SourceCode.EventBus.Samples.GenericXmlMapping`: Contains the `XmlDataProvider` class to serialize the context data (From and Subject fields) and a `XmlDataResolver` class to deserialize the context data.

❑ `SourceCode.EventBus.Samples.SMTPObjectBrowser`: Implements the `IObjectBrowser` interface. The `ObjectBrowser` class provides the user interface components necessary to allow users to use K2 Workspace to configure Notifications or Custom Events (discussed later in this chapter) for the SMTP Event Recorder.

❏    `SourceCode.EventBus.Samples.SearchSharePointEvent`: Contains the static method `SearchSharePointForDocuments` that is responsible for starting a workflow process and mapping the context data of the event to process data fields.

```
SearchSharePointForDocuments(string keyword, string requestor)
```

❏    `SearchSharePoint`: Contains the SearchResults workflow process that executes a search across document libraries in SharePoint for documents matching the keyword and returns the results in an e-mail to the requestor.

The following steps will help you get the SMTP Event Bus Sample running on your system.

*This example assumes that Visual Studio is installed on the same machine as the K2 server.*

**1.**    Download and open the example solution `SourceCode.EventBus.Samples.SMTP.sln`.

The example assumes that the solution folder has been extracted to the root of the C drive.

All project files and references are configured for K2 blackpearl installed in the default `C:\Program Files\K2 blackpearl` directory. If your directory is different, you will need to change the following:

❏    All project References

❏    All Build Output directories on the projects

❏    All configuration file links in the Solution Items folder

❏    All XML configuration file values listed below

The example assumes that there is an e-mail account `SearchSharePoint` with an SMTP drop at `C:\Inetpub\mailroot\Mailbox\denallix.com\P3_SearchSharePoint.mbx`. Change this value in the `SourceCode.EventBus.Samples.SMTPEventRecorder.dll.config` if necessary.

The sample assumes that the files in the Sample Documents directory are loaded into the Shared Documents library on the `http://portal.denallix.com/sites/sales` site. Reconfigure the SearchSharePoint workflow project to change this location.

*Although the projects are configured to deploy the assemblies to the correct locations automatically, the step to copy the assembly to the appropriate location is listed here for reference.*

**2.**    Deploy the SMTP Event Recorder.

❏    Build the `SourceCode.EventBus.Samples.SMTPEventRecorder` project.

❏    Copy the assembly to `C:\Program Files\K2 blackpearl\Host Server\Bin\ SourceCode.EventBus.Samples.SMTPEventRecorder.dll`.

❏    Add a Recorder to the `<eventrecorders>` section of `C:\Program Files\ K2 blackpearl\Host Server\Bin\SourceCode.EventBus.Server.config` to let the Host Server know about the new recorder. Insert this section above `<mappings>` if it doesn't exist.

```
<eventrecorders>
<recorder name="SMTP Event Recorder"
assembly="SourceCode.EventBus.Samples.SMTPEventRecorder "
type="SourceCode.EventBus.Samples.SMTPEventRecorder.Recorder"></recorder>
</eventrecorders>
```

3.  Deploy the Generic XML Mapper.

    ❏ Build the `SourceCode.EventBus.Samples.GenericXmlMapping` project.

    ❏ Copy the assembly to `C:\Program Files\K2 blackpearl\Bin\ SourceCode .EventBus.Samples.GenericXmlMapping.dll`.

    ❏ Add a Mapping to the `<mappings>` section of `C:\Program Files\K2 blackpearl\ Host Server\Bin\SourceCode.EventBus.Server.config`.

```
<mapping guid="B6477085-403F-4D65-8C58-81A015BE63C0" assemblyfullname="C:\Program
Files\K2 blackpearl\Bin\SourceCode.EventBus.Samples.GenericXmlMapping.dll"
assemblytyperesolver="SourceCode.EventBus.Samples.GenericXmlMapping.XmlDataResolver"
assemblytypeprovider="SourceCode.EventBus.Samples.GenericXmlMapping.XmlDataProvider" />
```

    ❏ Add a Resolver to the `<resolvers>` section of `C:\Program Files\K2 blackpearl\ Host Server\Bin\SourceCode.EventBus.Mapping.dll.config`.

```
<resolver id="B6477085-403F-4D65-8C58-81A015BE63C0" assembly="C:\Program Files\K2
blackpearl\Bin\SourceCode.EventBus.Samples.GenericXmlMapping.dll"
assemblytype="SourceCode.EventBus.Samples.GenericXmlMapping.XmlDataResolver" />
```

4.  Deploy the Object Browser.

    ❏ Build the `SourceCode.EventBus.Samples.SMTPObjectBrowser` project.

    ❏ Copy the assembly to `C:\Program Files\K2 blackpearl\Bin\ SourceCode .EventBus.Samples.SMTPObjectBrowser.dll`.

    ❏ Add an ObjectBrowser to the `<eventbusobjectbrowsers>` section of `C:\Program Files\K2 blackpearl\WorkSpace\Site\web.config`.

```
<objectbrowser id="C2815731-5997-4A9F-9837-EBCE48C6FF3F" displayname="SMTP Object
Browser" assemblyfullname="C:\Program Files\K2
blackpearl\Bin\SourceCode.EventBus.Samples.SMTPObjectBrowser.dll"
assemblytypeprovider="SourceCode.EventBus.Samples.SMTPObjectBrowser.ObjectBrowser"
imageclosed="images/OB/folder_closed.gif" imageopen="images/OB/folder_open.gif"
connectionstring="" />
```

5.  Deploy the Custom Action Event.

    ❏ Build the `SoureCode.EventBus.Samples.SearchSharePointEvent` project.

    ❏ Copy the assembly to `C:\Program Files\K2 blackpearl\Host Server\Bin\ SourceCode.EventBus.Samples.SearchSharePointEvent.dll`.

    ❏ Add an Assembly (for custom notification) to the `<assemblies>` section of `C:\Program Files\K2 blackpearl\Host Server\Bin\SourceCode.EventBus.Assemblies.config`.

```
<assembly displayname="Search SharePoint Process" fullname="C:\Program Files\K2
blackpearl\Host Server\Bin\SourceCode.EventBus.Samples.SearchSharePointEvent.dll" />
```

**6.** Deploy the SearchSharePoint\SearchResults workflow process shown in Figure 21-12.

**Figure 21-12**

Once the previous steps are completed, you should execute an IISRESET and restart the K2 blackpearl server in console mode. You will see the SMTP Event Recorder load (see Figure 21-13).

```
Info    7022 Event Bus Server Loaded Successfully
Debug   7009 Starting Retrieval Thread
Info    7010 MSMQ Thread Listing
Info    7503 Loading SMTP Event Recorder..
Info    7033 SMTP Event Recorder : recorder loaded successfully
Info    7025 All Recorders Loaded
```

**Figure 21-13**

The final steps in this sample involve configuring the new SMTP event to start the workflow process.

**1.** Within K2 Workspace, navigate to Notification Events ⇨ Custom Event Designer and click New Event in the lower-right corner.

**2.** Provide a Name and Description and select a Location (see Figure 21-14), and then click Next.

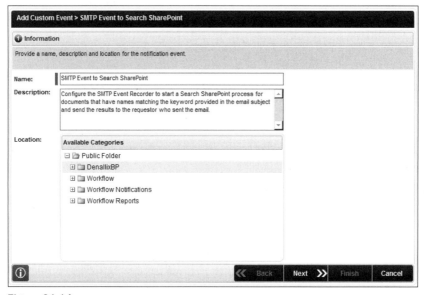

**Figure 21-14**

3. Select the event raised by the SMTP Event Recorder by selecting SMTP Object Browser ⇨ Mail Item ⇨ OnMailReceived (see Figure 21-15), and then click Next.

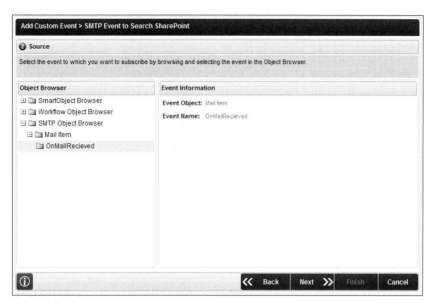

Figure 21-15

4. Configure the Custom Action by clicking Add Action (see Figure 21-16).

Figure 21-16

**5.** Click Search, select Search SharePoint Process from the list of Available Assemblies (see Figure 21-17), and then click Next.

**Figure 21-17**

**6.** Select SourceCode.EventBus.Samples.SearchSharePointEvent.StartProcess (see Figure 21-18), and then click Next.

**Figure 21-18**

**7.** Select SearchSharePointForDocuments (see Figure 21-19), and then click Finish.

**Figure 21-19**

8. Select the From field in the Object Browser on the left, and drag-and-drop it to the requestor field in the Action Parameters section in the lower right (see Figure 21-20). Drag-and-drop the Subject field to the keyword Action Parameter, and then click Finish.

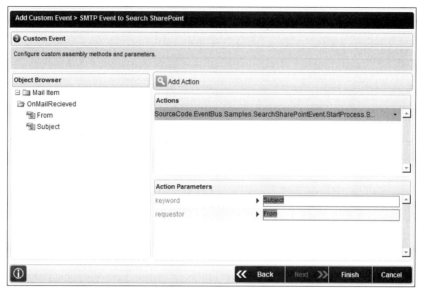

Figure 21-20

9. Click Return to landing.

The configured custom event will now appear in the list (see Figure 21-21).

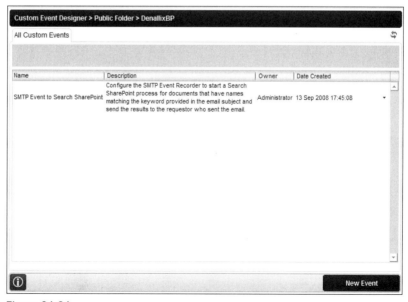

Figure 21-21

The sample is now fully configured. You can verify that everything is working by sending an e-mail with "xbox" in the subject to the SearchSharePoint e-mail address (see Figure 21-22).

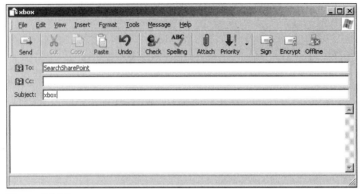

**Figure 21-22**

This will cause an event to be raised to the Event Bus and the SearchResults workflow process to execute sending the e-mail shown in Figure 21-23.

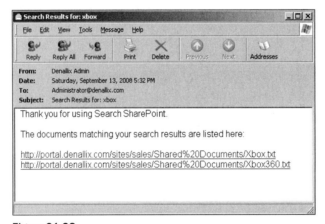

**Figure 21-23**

The SMTP Event Bus Sample is a great example of the extensibility and power of the K2 blackpearl platform. The Event Bus allowed us to easily monitor an external system for events and execute a workflow process, using the contextual data of the event. The application of this concept in the enterprise is very exciting.

# Summary

The Event Bus is a powerful addition to the K2 platform. It serves as a mechanism to allow external LOB system events to affect the K2 platform, to send custom notifications designed in the K2 Workspace, to launch processes based on custom events and data contained within those events, and to schedule recurring events. The Event Bus is a critical component that brings reliable, message-based event processing to the K2 platform. In the next chapter we'll look at how to take advantage of some of the advanced features of K2 blackpearl as well as some advanced process scenarios.

# Notes

1. "Event-Driven Business Process Management" by Rainer von Ammon, et al. `http://debs08.dis.uniroma1.it/pdf/fa-ammon.pdf`

# 22

# Advanced Topics in K2 blackpearl

Holly Anderson

Mike Talley

The K2 blackpearl platform provides tools and wizards that make building process-driven applications very simple. The previous chapters in this book covered the basics that are provided to developers and business analysts for building processes on the K2 blackpearl platform. However, there are additional pieces of functionality in K2 blackpearl that provide an additional level of flexibility in building and maintaining complex applications without having to write an extensive amount of code.

This chapter will cover the following topics:

- ❏ Advanced Destination Rules
- ❏ Advanced actions and outcomes
- ❏ Advanced InfoPath capabilities
- ❏ Troubleshooting

All of the examples in this chapter will be based on an Application Access Request process (see Figure 22-1).

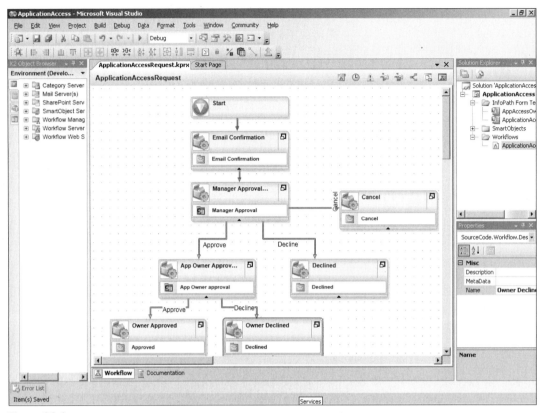

Figure 22-1

The Application Access Request process is an InfoPath-based process that allows a user to request access to one or more applications for another employee. When the request is submitted, an e-mail confirmation is sent to the Requestor and the process is then routed to the employee's manager. After approval from the manager, the request is routed to the appropriate Application Owners, based on the information selected in the InfoPath form. The InfoPath form is deployed to a form library on a SharePoint site. Once approved, an e-mail is sent to the originator letting them know that their request has been approved. During the process, both the Manager and any of the Application Owners have the ability to decline the request, which sends an e-mail to the originator. In addition, a Cancel Request option is available during the Manager Approval step. The process also makes use of several SmartObjects to provide information to the process:

❑ **Employee:** Accesses employee information from Active Directory using the out-of-the-box Active Directory Service Object.

❑ **Applications:** A SmartBox-based SmartObject that holds application information, such as Name and Application Owner.

❑ **ApplicationRequest:** A SmartBox-based SmartObject that holds information about the request instance, including the employee ID and the IDs of the applications that are being requested.

❑ **ApplicationAccess:** A SmartBox-based SmartObject that holds information about the access levels available for a particular application.

# Destination Rules

As described in Chapters 8 and 9, K2 blackpearl provides several options for configuring destinations for human-based tasks. Destinations can be set to individual users, groups, or roles, depending on the needs of the organization. In addition, destinations can be configured to run in parallel or serially and can be configured to accommodate situations where a certain number of members of a group need to respond before moving on to the next task.

All of these options allow for a wide range of scenarios to be solved with the K2 blackpearl platform. However, to provide the most amount of flexibility possible, K2 blackpearl provides several additional options for making destinations dynamic based on information received when the process instance is started. Number of destinations, particular usernames, and so forth, may not all be known at design time but can be planned for using the following options.

## *SmartObjects in Destinations*

K2 blackpearl provides the ability to access information stored in SmartObjects to provide destination user information for process tasks. This information may or may not be filtered based on other information within the process. In the following scenario, an Employee SmartObject is accessed to provide the manager information based on an employee that is selected in the InfoPath form that is used to kick-off the process.

**1.** On the Manager Approval step in the Application Access Request process, click the Destination Users icon in the activity strip (see Figure 22-2).

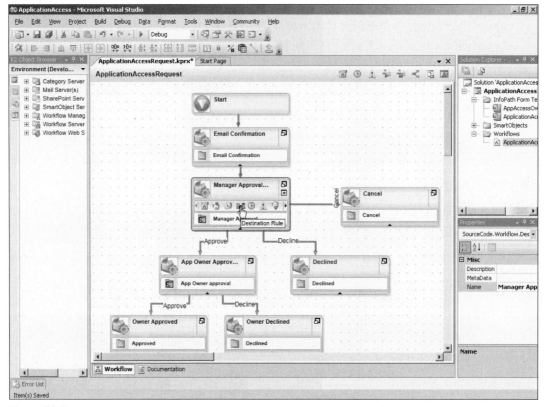

Figure 22-2

2. On the Destination Users screen, click the ellipsis button next to the User field.

3. Expand the SmartObject Server node to access the Employee SmartObject. Select the GetEmployeeDetails list method.

4. This particular SmartObject method required an input parameter to be set for the Employee's information that should be returned. On the window that opens, click the ellipsis button next to the input_username field. Select the Employee Name field (empName) from the Application Request InfoPath form.

5. In the returns section of the screen, select Manager and click OK.

6. Click Finish to complete the wizard.

7. Deploy the process and begin a new instance of the process by accessing the Forms Library on the SharePoint site and filling out the required information.

8. To verify that the correct manager information is retrieved from the SmartObject, open the K2 Workspace and open the Process Overview report. Drill into the appropriate process instance and verify that the destination user for the Manager Approval task is set to the correct manager (see Figure 22-3). In this case, the employee that is requesting access is Codi and her manager is Anthony.

Figure 22-3

## *Using XML Nodes in Destinations*

Another destination configuration option available in K2 blackpearl is the ability to provide destination user information via XML nodes. This allows processes to retrieve destination information from a repeating table within an InfoPath form or other XML-based document. In the following example, the destination users for the Application Owner task are retrieved from a repeating table that has been configured in the InfoPath form.

**1.** On the Application Owner Approval step in the Application Access Request process, click the Destination Users icon in the activity strip.

**2.** On the Destination Users screen, click the ellipsis button next to the User field.

**3.** Drill into the XML field that corresponds to the InfoPath form being used by the process. Select the appOwner field under the Applications node, which is a repeating node.

**4.** Click Finish to complete the wizard.

**5.** Deploy the process and begin a new instance of the process by accessing the Forms Library on the SharePoint site and filling out the required information.

**6.** To verify that the correct application owner information is retrieved from the InfoPath form, open the K2 Workspace and open the Process Overview report. Drill into the appropriate process instance, and verify that the destination users for the Application Owner Approval task are set to the correct owners. In this case, the application owners should be Anthony and Holly. Figures 22-4 and 22-5 show the information as selected in the InfoPath form and the destination users for the Application Owner approval step, respectively.

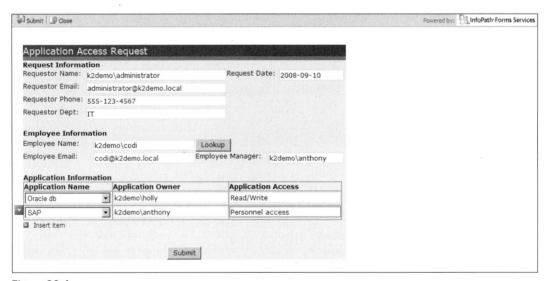

Figure 22-4

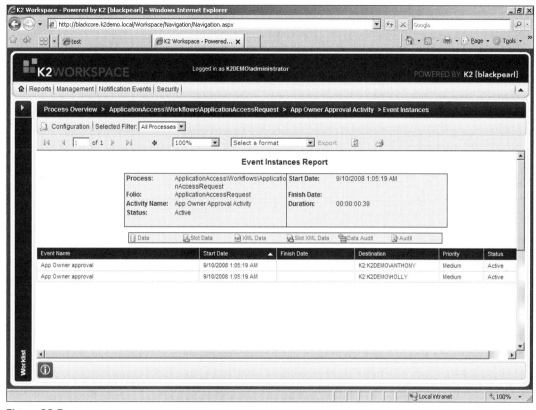

Figure 22-5

# Implications of Activity Plans and Destination Rule Options

You may have some confusion about the options for planning an activity, how to configure Destination Rules, and the effects these different options will have on the events in the activity. K2 blackpearl allows for some extremely powerful ways to plan activities, and the way you set up these rules is determined by your process scenario. For more information about the options, see the whitepaper "K2 blackpearl Roles and Advanced Destination Rules" (www.k2underground.com/files/folders/technical_product_documents/entry20948.aspx) on K2underground.com.

Take the following example of an activity that contains three events:

❑   Mail Event #1

❑   Client Event

❑   Mail Event #2

The default activity plan for all K2 blackpearl activities is Plan Just Once. This type of activity plan allows a single activity instance regardless of the number of users or slots specified. Mail Event #1 and Mail Event #2 will only ever be sent once. The same is true if you do a Plan Per Destination — All at Once, otherwise known as a parallel plan, using the default values, because the worklist item will appear on all user's worklists as soon as the activity is planned.

If you choose the Resolve all roles to users option instead of the Create a slot for each role default option, you will get as many activity instances as you have users in your role. If your role has five users, Mail Event #1 will fire five times. Mail Event #2, however, will fire only the number of times that corresponds to the number of slots you have specified. This is important to understand. The number of slots dictates how many responses are needed during the client event, so if you have five users in your role and only two slots, once two users action their worklist item, the worklist item will disappear from the three other users' worklists, and Mail Event #2 will fire twice because it comes after the client event. If you had something other than a mail event in place of Mail Event #2, such as a SharePoint document copy event, that server event would also fire only twice.

Because of the complexity of options available when configuring advanced Destination Rules, we recommend that you test your process in an environment that closely resembles your business process environment and particularly your users and roles. You can configure the mail events (or server activities) to send mail to a single address so it is easier to test the final outcome of your Destination Rule configuration, but it is important to test what is actually going to happen before deploying a process with advanced activity plans and Destination Rules.

Also keep in mind that the way in which you configure your Destination Rule impacts the way in which data is reported. For example, if you do not specify to resolve roles to users, you will see that your worklist items are assigned to the role instead of individual users, and this may not be desirable. However, resolving roles to users also prevents K2 from dynamically managing the worklists of users in the role. If you create a slot for each role, the report will still list who actually took action on the worklist items, but from an "outstanding task" point of view. You will not see who actually has worklist items assigned to them, and you will either have to know who is a member of the role or look in the Management Console to see the role membership.

# Actions and Outcomes

In previous chapters, actions and outcomes were introduced as the way in which task actions are configured within K2 blackpearl processes. In most cases, the standard action and outcome functionality provided in the K2 blackpearl task wizards provides enough functionality to ensure that a process advances as it should. However, there are some situations that require more advanced functionality regarding how tasks are actioned by the user. The following sections describe a few advanced scenarios that can be handled by the K2 blackpearl platform.

## *More Than Auto-Generated Outcomes*

In most cases, the auto-generated outcomes that are created based on the actions configured will handle all task-actioning needs. However, in some cases, scenarios may come up where actions and outcomes don't match on a one-to-one basis. For example, on an Expense Claim process, perhaps there is a business rule that states that after the manager approval, if the total expenses being claimed are greater than $5000, the process needs to be routed to the VP of finance for an additional approval step. In this case, there are two actions, Approve and Decline, but instead of a one-to-one match for outcomes, there are three possible outcomes, one for Manager Approved — under $5000, one for Manager Approved — above $5000, and one for declined. The K2 blackpearl task wizards make it very easy to configure these types of scenarios without having to resort to writing code. In the scenario below, if the Application Access Request includes a request to access Personnel information within SAP, the request needs to be routed to an HR representative for an additional approval step before moving on to the Application Owner step.

1.    On the Manager Approval step in the Application Access Request process, rerun the task wizard by clicking the Run the default wizard icon on the event (See Figure 22-6).

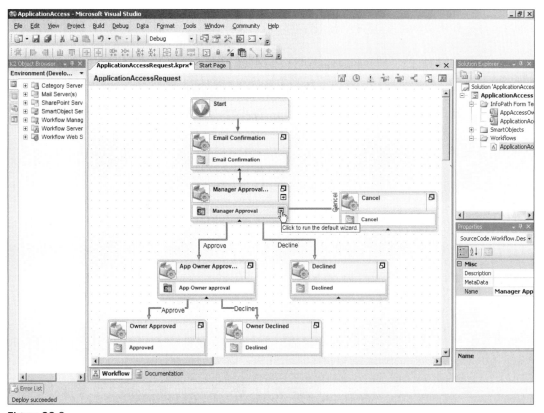

Figure 22-6

**2.** Click through to the Outcomes page. Keep the existing outcomes but add a new one called Approved — Personnel access. Click Add to add a rule to this outcome. In the rule window that opens, set the First Variable field to be the `appAccess` field from the InfoPath form and set that to be equal to Personnel Information. The screen should look like what's shown in Figure 22-7.

Figure 22-7

**3.** Next, modify the existing Approved outcome so that the name is Approved – No personnel access and has a rule that is configured like what's shown in Figure 22-8.

Figure 22-8

**4.** When done configuring the outcomes, click the Generate corresponding line(s) for listed outcome(s) and finish the wizard. You should now have an additional line coming out of the Manager Approval task that can be configured to go to a second level of approval. Your process should look like what's shown in Figure 22-9.

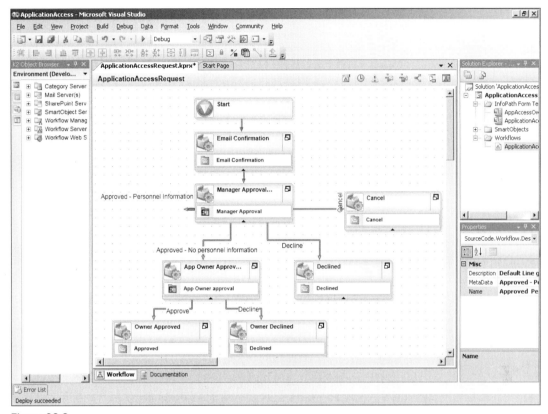

Figure 22-9

**5.** To complete the process, drag an InfoPath client event on to the design canvas and configure the properties so that the event uses the existing InfoPath form and a destination user in the HR group. When complete, the process should look similar to what's shown in Figure 22-10.

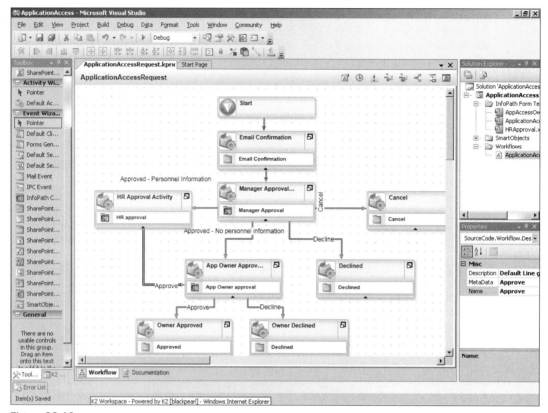

Figure 22-10

# Rights on Actions

Security options have been greatly enhanced in K2 blackpearl, and one of the options now available is to set security on actions for a specific event. This functionality is provided by the K2 Context Grid, which is a matrix of available actions, events, users, and permissions. The management capabilities for the Context Grid are provided in the K2 Management Console and allow an administrator to select specific actions configured on a process to give to users of the process. This functionality allows for administration of users to be added or removed from process tasks without having to modify the process definition if security requirements change in the future.

In the example that follows, the Cancel action on the Manager Approval task will be restricted so that it's only available to the originator of the process.

1. In the K2 Management Console, expand the [ServerName] ➪ Workflow Server ➪ Processes ➪ ApplicationAccess\Processes ➪ ApplicationAccessRequest ➪ Manager Approval Activity and highlight the Cancel action.

2. Click Add to open the Select Users/Groups dialog box.

3. For demonstration purposes, select the user who will originate the process and click OK.

4. Verify that the Allow checkbox is selected, and click Save. The screen should look like that shown in Figure 22-11.

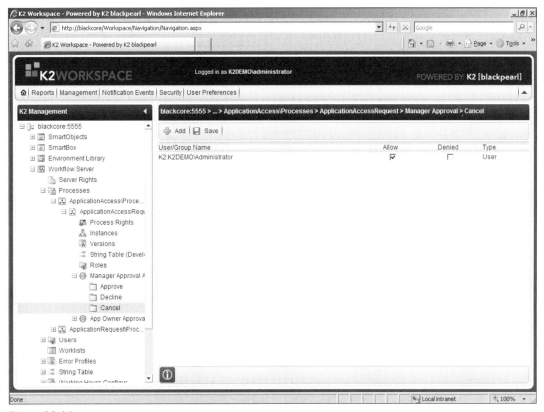

Figure 22-11

5. Kick-off an instance of the project from the SharePoint Forms Library.

6. Log on as the employee's manager to view the available actions for the Manager Approval task. In this example, the employee's manager is Anthony. Notice that in the K2 Tasklist, the only available options for the manager are Approve and Decline (see Figure 22-12).

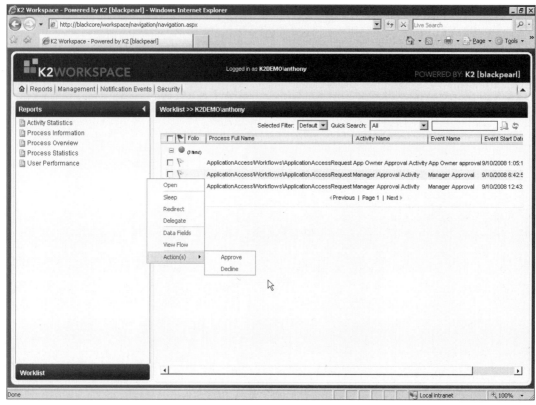

Figure 22-12

7.  Now, open the K2 Tasklist for the originator and view the available actions. Notice that the task shows on the task list with the Cancel action available.

# Advanced InfoPath

K2 blackpearl provides extensive integration with Microsoft InfoPath to provide data capture capabilities for the processes. For more information about the standard InfoPath integration functionality provided with K2 blackpearl, see Chapter 11. Beyond the standard InfoPath functionality, K2 blackpearl can make use of InfoPath forms to provide advanced functionality for complex processes built on the K2 blackpearl platform.

## Multiple InfoPath Forms

In previous versions of the K2 software, processes were restricted to using one InfoPath form for all of the client tasks in the process. Different information could be displayed for different tasks in the process by using the InfoPath View functionality. However, for scenarios that had strict security requirements around data that should be seen by different users of the process, this option was not a viable one. With K2 blackpearl, the InfoPath functionality has been enhanced to allow for multiple forms to be configured on a single process. With this capability, each client task in the process can use a different form if necessary to only show the information appropriate to the user for that task.

In the following example, two InfoPath forms will be configured on the process so that the Manager Approval task uses one form and the Application Owner Approval task uses the second form.

**1.** Rerun the InfoPath Integration Wizard by clicking the InfoPath Integration icon in the upper-right corner of the process designer (see Figure 22-13).

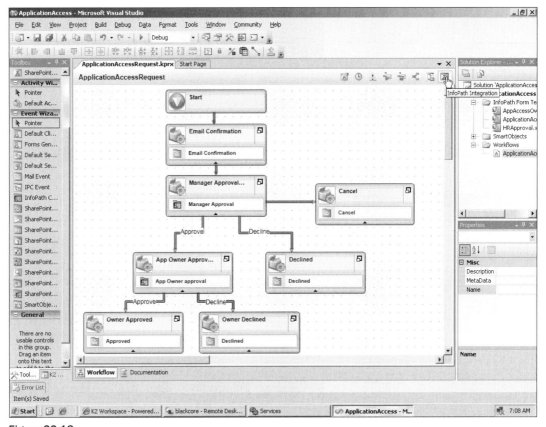

Figure 22-13

**2.** On the Workflow Form Templates screen that appears, configure an additional InfoPath form by clicking Add and following the wizard's steps to add a second form. When complete, the screen should look similar to what's shown in Figure 22-14.

**Figure 22-14**

3.  Rerun the wizard for the Application Owner Approval task. On the General Event Settings screen, select the new InfoPath form template from the drop-down and select the View and Task Action field to use. Once complete, the screen will look similar to what's shown in Figure 22-15.

**Figure 22-15**

**4.** Click Finish to complete the wizard and then deploy the process.

**5.** Start a new instance of the process from the SharePoint Forms Library.

**6.** On the Manager Approval task, verify that the Manager Approval view of the first form is displayed (see Figure 22-16).

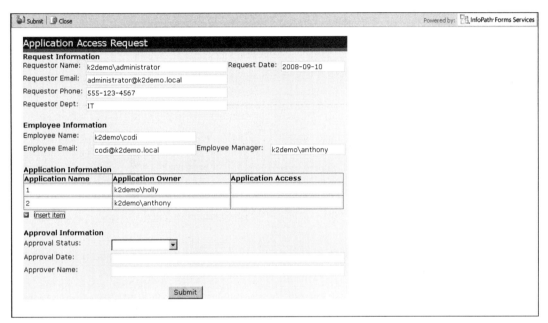

**Figure 22-16**

**7.** Now log in as the Application Owner to verify that the second configured form is displayed (see Figure 22-17).

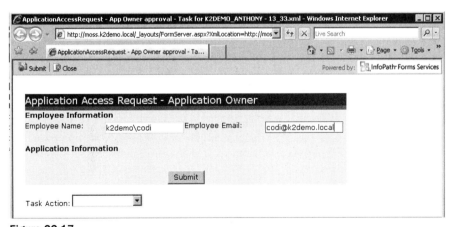

**Figure 22-17**

# Split and Merge

One of the process scenarios that K2 enables is the ability to send client tasks to multiple users for approval, all at the same time. However, the scenario gets complicated if each of those users needs to see slightly different information about the process. For example, in the Application Access Request process, the Application Owner task is routed to each application owner that has been selected in the form. To provide the best possible experience for each of those users, it would be nice to filter the information shown to them so that they only see the application information that they are responsible for. In previous versions of K2, this functionality was possible, but required an extensive amount of coding. The InfoPath form had to be set up with filters to display the information correctly based on the user that was logged in. On top of that, code needed to be written to merge each approver's approval information into the main form so that on the next task, a full picture of the approval process could be seen. This scenario was known as the "split and merge" scenario because the data had to be split across all the users and then merged back into a single view of the form.

With K2 blackpearl, and, in particular, K2 SmartObjects, the "split and merge" scenario has become more simplified. Now, instead of storing all of the relevant process information in the XML document created via the InfoPath form, this information can be stored in a K2 SmartObject. The InfoPath form can then query the K2 SmartObject to retrieve and display the correct information for the user viewing the form. No additional code is required because all relevant information is stored as a SmartObject property and can be displayed in the appropriate way for the task.

In the following example, the Application Access Request process will be modified to use K2 SmartObjects to access the relevant information to display on the InfoPath form for each client task.

1.  On the Submit Request view of the form, modify the InfoPath form so that it includes a connection to the `Create` method on the `ApplicationRequest` SmartObject when the form is submitted. This will add the information about the request as an instance of the `ApplicationRequest` SmartObject. Set the ID of the instance created to the `RequestID` field in the InfoPath form.

2.  On the Manager Approval view of the form, modify the Start Rules so that the `ApplicationRequest` SmartObject is queried to return the information for the appropriate RequestID. Set the return values to display as the appropriate fields on the form. On the Submit button of this view, call the Update method on the `ApplicationRequest` SmartObject to update the `ManagerApproval` field with the value selected in the form.

3.  On the form used for the Application Owner Approval task, modify the form so that on load it queries the `ApplicationRequest` SmartObject to retrieve the information about the request. Include a filter on the SmartObject so that it only returns the application information relevant to the user who is logged in to the InfoPath form, using the InfoPath `UserName` function. On the Submit button, call the `Update` method on the `RequestApplication` SmartObject to update the `ApplicationOwner` field with the value selected on the form.

4.  On the Read Only view of the first form, update the Load Rule for that view to run a query against the `ApplicationRequest` and associated `RequestApplication` SmartObject instances to retrieve all the relevant data for the process. Set the return properties from the SmartObjects to display as fields in the form.

# Troubleshooting

K2 blackpearl provides several different mechanisms for troubleshooting issues with processes and SmartObjects. Troubleshooting tools range from the simple, such as the K2 View Flow or K2 Reporting environment mentioned in earlier chapters, to the more advanced, such as logging and the process management capabilities included in Visual Studio.

More information about the advanced troubleshooting options is available later in the chapter. For information on the K2 View Flow or K2 reporting environments, see Chapter 20.

## Logging

The K2 blackpearl Logging Framework allows K2 server administrators to configure the amount of logging done on each K2 server for K2 processes and K2 SmartObjects and Service Objects. The Logging Framework provides a mechanism for configuring multiple log output locations, and provides support for five output targets by default. The provided extensions are described in the following table:

| Logging Extension | Description |
| --- | --- |
| ConsoleExtension | When enabled, messages will be logged to the K2 blackpearl server console when the server is being run in console mode. |
| FileExtension | When enabled, messages will be logged to a log file. The log file is specified in the properties of the configuration declaration. |
| EventLogExtension | When enabled, messages will be logged to the machine's Event Log. |
| ArchiveExtension | When enabled, messages will be logged to a SQL Server database. By default, messages are logged to the HostServerDB connection, but can be changed in the configuration properties. Logging to a database provides the ability to run queries against logged messages. |
| MSMQExtension | When enabled, messages will be logged to a Microsoft Messaging Queue. This scenario is useful when automatic monitoring tools are used within the environment. |

In addition, custom output locations, such as e-mail, can be added to the system as necessary. For more information about creating a custom logging extension, see the Logging Framework project located on K2 blackmarket: http://k2underground.com/k2/ProjectHome.aspx?ProjectID=2.

Logging settings can be modified to display different levels of log messages. The following table describes the log levels that are available:

| Log Level | Description |
| --- | --- |
| Error | Displays messages about errors occurring within the server or in components that the server is using. Only error messages are displayed at this log level. |
| Warning | Displays general warnings from the server. Both error and warning messages are displayed at this log level. |
| Info | Displays informational messages, such as sessions starting and users being authenticated on the server. Error, warning, and info messages are displayed at this level. |
| Debug | Displays general debugging information and is useful when trying to trace what is happening on the server. Displays error, warning, info, and debug messages at this level. |
| All | Displays all levels of logging information. |

Each level of logging may be useful for different environments in your organization. For example, the development server may be configured to show Debug or All messages to provide developers information about problems that are occurring as they are developing applications. It is important to keep in mind that the level of logging that is selected may affect server performance. The All level of logging is not recommended for a production environment unless it is being used to debug a particular problem during a set period of time.

By default, K2 logging is asynchronous to minimize performance impacts on the server. However, certain scenarios may benefit from synchronous logging, so this setting can be changed as necessary. In addition, all logs can be filtered by namespace to reduce the impact on the server.

## Modifying Logging on a K2 Server

The following example walks through the steps required to modify logging output targets and levels for the K2 server. This scenario will set the logging target to be both console mode and database mode and will set different log levels for each extension.

1. Open C:\Program Files\K2 blackpearl\Host Server\bin, using Windows Explorer.

   *This path may differ in your environment if K2 blackpearl was not installed in the default location.*

2. Open HostServerLogging.config using Notepad or another text editor program.

3. Find the `<ApplicationLevelLogSettings>` section.

4. In the `ConsoleExtension` setting, verify that the Active property is set to `True` and change the LogLevel to `Debug`. The line should look like this:

```
<LogLocation Name="ConsoleExtension" Active="True" LogLevel="Debug" />
```

**5.** In the ArchiveExtension setting, set the Active property to `True` and change the LogLevel to `All`. The line should look like this:

```
<LogLocation Name="ArchiveExtension" Active="True" LogLevel="All" />
```

**6.** Save the changes to the file.

**7.** Restart the K2 server to put the changes into effect.

**8.** Open SQL Server Management Studio.

**9.** Browse to the HostServer database.

**10.** Expand Tables and find the LogArchive database.

**11.** Right-click the database name and select Open Table.

**12.** Verify that the correct log information is being displayed in the database. The database will look similar to what's shown in Figure 22-18.

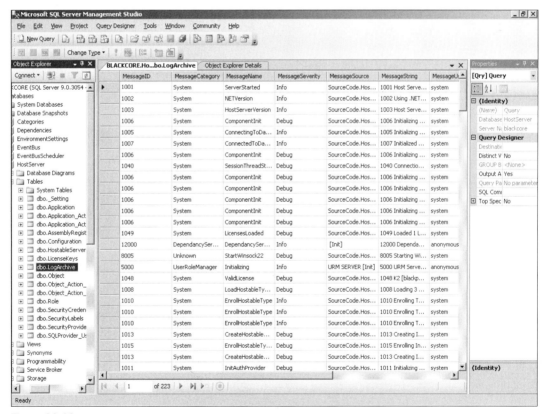

Figure 22-18

## Visual Studio Debugging

Because K2 blackpearl makes use of the Microsoft Visual Studio environment, debugging of K2 processes and K2 SmartObjects or Service Objects is available just as it would be with any other .NET application. The Visual Studio debugger allows a developer to step through the process, SmartObject or Service Object at the code level to troubleshoot errors or to verify that functionality is working properly.

The following scenario will walk through the steps necessary to debug a K2 process. This example will make use of the Application Access Request process previously described.

> *This example assumes that the process source files reside on the K2 server so that debugging can occur on the same environment. If Visual Studio and the source files are running on a separate client machine, it may be necessary to configure the K2 server to allow for Remote Debugging. The following link provides more information:* `http://support.microsoft.com/kb/910448`.

1. Open the Application Access Request project.

2. On the Email Confirmation activity, right-click the Email Confirmation event and select View Code ➪ Event Item.

3. In the XOML designer, right-click the SetProperties activity, and select View Code.

4. Expand the Code Activities section, and add the following code in the `SetProperties_ExecuteCode` method:

```
//adding code for demo
string strFolio = K2.ProcessInstance.Folio;
string requestor = K2.ProcessInstance.Originator.Name;
```

5. Save the changes and deploy the process by right-clicking the project name and selecting Deploy.

6. On the Debug menu in Visual Studio, select Attach to Process.

7. Select the K2HostServer.exe process, and click Attach (see Figure 22-19).

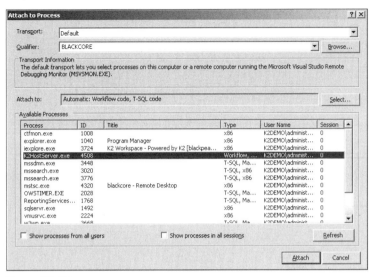

Figure 22-19

**8.** Back in Visual Studio, set a breakpoint on the first line of code that was added in Step 4 (see Figure 22-20).

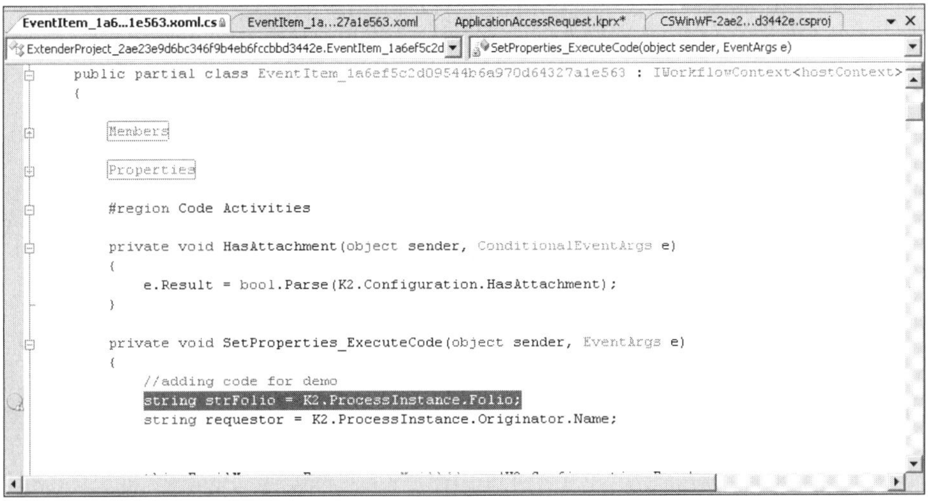

Figure 22-20

**9.** Once the debugger has attached to the K2 process, start a new instance of the process by navigating to the Application Access Request Library on the SharePoint site.

**10.** Step through the code to see the values that are being set and that all functionality is working (see Figure 22-21).

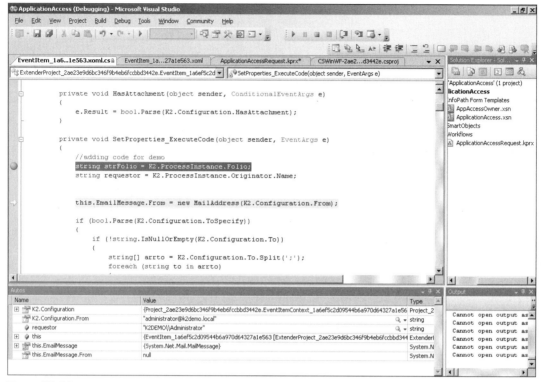

Figure 22-21

# *Error Repair*

K2 blackpearl provides several ways to repair errors that have occurred in a running instance of a process. These tools allow administrators or developers the ability to easily resolve issues that may be caused by environmental issues or process errors that occur because of functionality included in the process.

The first error repair option is the Retry option that is provided in the Error Profile section of the K2 Management Console. The Retry option allows a K2 administrator to retry the part of the process that errored without changing any of the process functionality. This tool should be used on the occasion that the error is not part of process functionality directly but is caused by an external environmental issue. For example, if a process is creating a new item on a SharePoint site but the site is temporarily unavailable, the process may throw an error on that step. Once the SharePoint site is available again, the process can be retried using the K2 Management Console, and the process will continue on to the next step. Figure 22-22 shows the Retry functionality in the K2 Management Console.

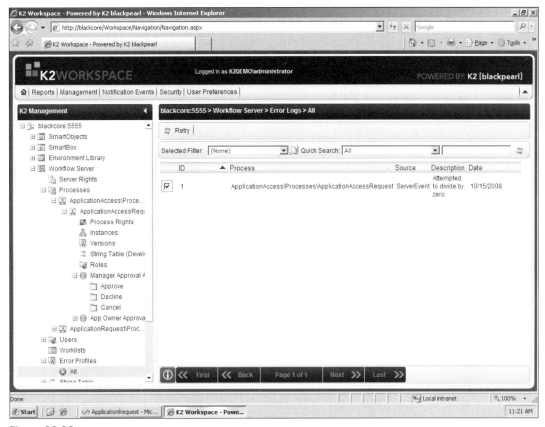

Figure 22-22

The second option is the process management functionality within Visual Studio. This option allows a developer to open the code in the process at the point where the error has occurred. The developer is able to make changes to the functionality and redeploy the process. When the updated process is redeployed, a new version of the process is created on the server and any existing instances that are in error will be retried. In addition, any new instances of the process that are started will use the updated version of the process. Figure 22-23 shows some of the process management functionality.

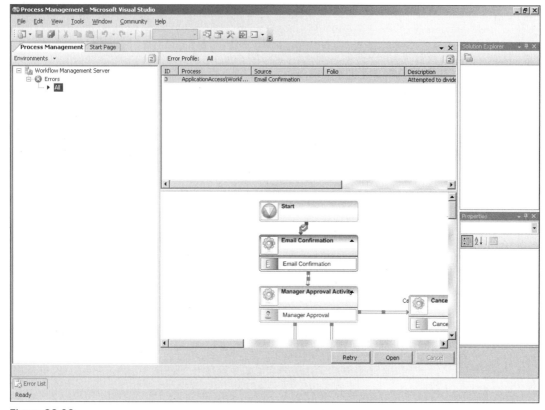

Figure 22-23

In the following example, code is added to the Application Access Request process to force an error when the process is run. Both the retry and process management functionality is used to try to resolve the error.

1. In Visual Studio, right-click the Email Confirmation event and select View Code ⇨ Event Item.

2. In the XOML designer that opens, right-click the Set Properties activity and select View Code.

3. Expand the Code Activities section, and add the following code in the `SetProperties_ExecuteCode` method:

```
//adding code for demo
int a = 100;
int b = 0;
int c = a/b;
```

4. Save the changes and deploy the process by right-clicking the project name and selecting Deploy.

5. Start a new instance of the process by navigating to the Application Access Request Library on the SharePoint site.

6. In the K2 Management Console, expand [SERVERNAME] ⇨ Workflow Server ⇨ Processes ⇨ Application Access ⇨ ApplicationAccessRequest ⇨ Instances. In the right-side window, click Find button to view all the process instances. Note that the most recent instance is in error.

7. Expand the Error Profiles node, and click All to see the current errors.

8. For the most recent instance, note that the error is Attempted to divide by zero. Select the checkbox next to the instance information and then click Retry. The screen will look similar to the one shown in Figure 22-24.

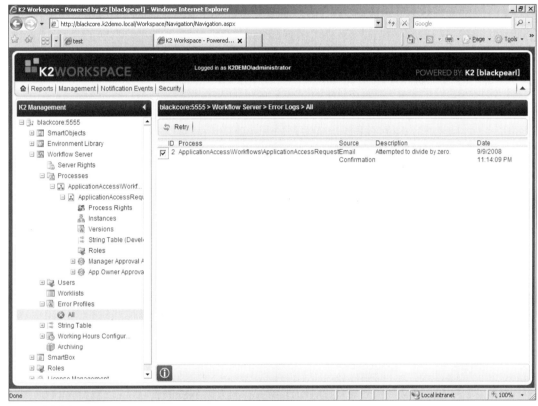

Figure 22-24

9. Note that after the page refreshes, the process instance is still in error.

10. Open Visual Studio and select K2 Process Management in the View menu.

11. Expand Workflow Management Server ⇨ Errors, and select All.

12. Highlight the instance of the process that is in error, and click Open.

13. Once the project has opened to the location where the error occurred, change the code so that the "b" variable does not equal 0 (see Figure 22-25).

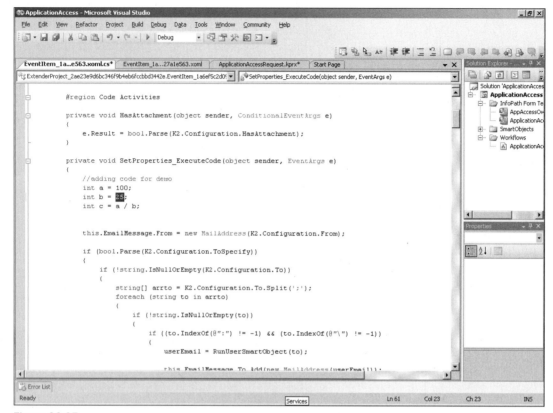

Figure 22-25

**14.** Save the changes, and switch back over to the process management window. Click Redeploy. Give the version a descriptive name, and select Retry all instances.

**15.** Now go back into the K2 Management Console, and verify that there are no errors and that the instance is now active.

# Summary

In this chapter, you have been introduced to several advanced topics on the K2 blackpearl platform. We discussed the advanced options that can be used for configuring destination users, including the use of SmartObject data and data in XML nodes, such as a repeating table node in InfoPath.

In addition, we discussed a few of the advanced options available around the actions and outcomes functionality, including configuring additional outcomes and setting specific security on an action.

InfoPath advanced topics, such as using multiple forms and providing "split and merge" functionality were discussed. And finally, we walked through several troubleshooting options that will help you debug problems that may occur when developing processes on the K2 platform.

These scenarios are certainly not the only advanced functionality that can be provided with K2 blackpearl, but they illustrate some of the most common issues that K2 blackpearl developers face. The K2 blackpearl platform provides numerous tools and functionality that make configuring advanced scenarios very easy, and typically require little to no code be added to the process.

In the next chapter, you'll be introduced to K2 connect for SAP, an add-on for K2 blackpearl. K2 connect for SAP provides a user-friendly interface for developers to model business entities against an SAP environment without having to write code. You will learn about the architecture of K2 connect and will walk through an example of how to build a business entity using the K2 connect for SAP toolset.

# 23

# Introduction to K2 connect

Holly Anderson

K2 blackpearl provides a bridge connecting people and line-of-business (LOB) systems by utilizing SmartObjects. However, even with K2 blackpearl, business users have a difficult time getting to data in complex systems, such as SAP. Users want to read and write SAP data, without involving SAP experts. They want to be able to use SAP data in applications and workflows, view the data in reports, and access it all in a reusable and manageable way. Solutions that provide this type of functionality can be costly and time-consuming. K2 connect for SAP provides the ability to access SAP quickly, giving business users a solution that meets all their needs.

K2 connect for SAP is an add-on component to K2 blackpearl that provides a user-friendly interface for developers to model business entities against an SAP environment without having to write code. The entities can then be surfaced for use within K2 processes, reports, forms, .NET-based applications or Web services, and other applications such as Microsoft Office SharePoint Server. K2 connect decreases development time and improves developer utilization by allowing the SAP experts to work with familiar SAP components such as business application programming interfaces (BAPIs), and provides .NET developers with objects that they can easily access and use within their applications.

The initial release of K2 connect supports accessing SAP R/3 4.6c environments and higher. In subsequent releases, K2 connect will be extended to support any LOB adapter built on Microsoft's WCF framework SDK.

This chapter will focus on K2 connect for SAP, specifically covering the following topics:

❑   The architecture of K2 connect and how it fits in to the K2 blackpearl platform

❑   Creating Service Objects using K2 connect and the K2 Service Object Designer

❑   Creating a K2 SmartObject based on a Service Object created with K2 connect

❑   Advanced topics in K2 connect for SAP

# K2 connect Architecture

K2 connect for SAP is an add-on component to K2 blackpearl that provides additional functionality to the K2 blackpearl platform for integrating with SAP environments. Specific integration points are described in the following sections.

## K2 connect and SAP

SAP provides several interfaces for integrating external applications with an SAP environment. These interfaces include the SAP Remote Function Call (RFC) protocol as well as NetWeaver. The standard adapters that come with K2 connect for SAP support both RFC and NetWeaver. Figure 23-1 shows how K2 connect for SAP interacts with an SAP environment. Notice that just like the SAP GUI, K2 connect sits as a remote application, not installed on the SAP server itself. Using either the RFC adapter or the WSDL adapter, K2 connect interacts with SAP to retrieve information from any BAPIs, such as EmpInfo or CustMaster in this example, that are exposed via RFC or NetWeaver.

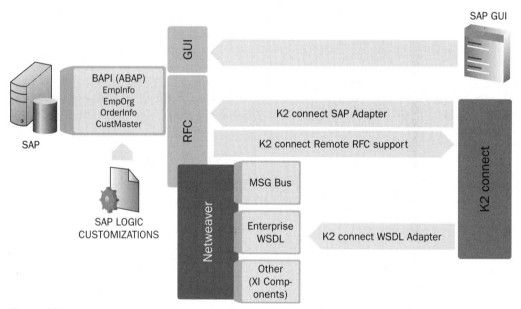

**Figure 23-1**

Any customizations made to the BAPIs in your SAP environment will be available via K2 connect because the K2 connect adapters make use of standard SAP functions to access the data. In addition, because K2 connect is using standard interfaces, you don't have to worry about users accessing SAP data or functions they aren't allowed to see. The K2 SSO framework ensures that each user is authenticated based on his credentials and only exposes information and functionality that is available to the user as determined by SAP.

## K2 connect and K2 blackpearl

K2 connect is an add-on component to K2 blackpearl that extends the Service Object Broker by adding an additional server that can handle the logic of more complex LOB systems, like SAP. Subsequent releases of K2 connect will provide native support for WCF adapters, providing integration with other LOB systems such as Siebel, Customer Relationship Management (CRM), and Oracle databases.

Figure 23-2 shows how the K2 connect server fits into the overall architecture of K2 blackpearl. As depicted in the diagram, K2 connect Server runs as part of the SmartObject Broker inside of the K2 Host Server. Functionality provided by K2 connect allows developers to build Service Objects that can then be used by developers, architects, or business analysts to build SmartObjects that can be used across multiple applications, providing end users with access to the LOB information that is relevant to them. Using either the Runtime API or the Authoring API, K2 surfaces the information retrieved by K2 connect to any K2 user through a variety of mechanisms. K2 Worklist users and K2 Forms users may view the information via the K2 Worklist, K2 reports, or within a form; and K2 developers may use the information to build a process or report using one of the K2 designers.

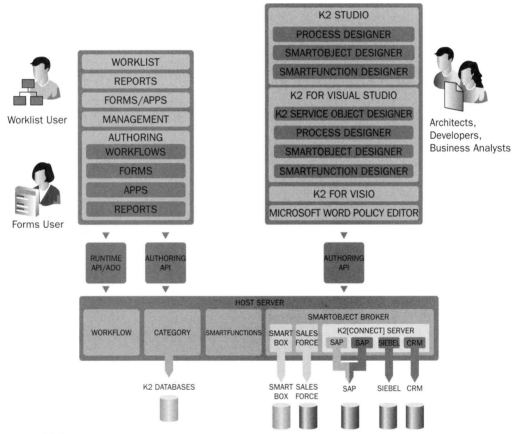

Figure 23-2

## K2 connect and K2 SmartObjects

When K2 connect is used to access an SAP environment, the SAP data and methods are exposed in the K2 SmartObject server as a Service Object. At that point, developers can use the K2 SmartObject Designer to model business entities, using the SAP information. The business entities, or SmartObjects, can comprise data from a single SAP BAPI, multiple SAP BAPIs, or even a combination of data from SAP and another LOB system. Figure 23-3 shows an example of how employee information from multiple back-end sources, including SAP information surfaced through a K2 connect adapter, can be combined using the SmartObject Designer and SmartObject API to create a single employee SmartObject. The SmartObject data is then available for use in applications, forms, and reports.

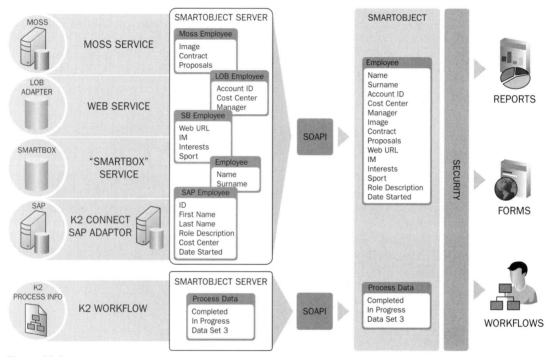

Figure 23-3

*For more information about building SmartObjects and using them in K2 blackpearl applications, see Chapter 7.*

# Using the K2 Service Object Designer

K2 connect for SAP uses the K2 Service Object Designer to provide a developer access to the available BAPIs in SAP. The K2 Service Object Designer is an add-in component to Microsoft Visual Studio, allowing developers to work in a familiar environment. To open the K2 Service Object Designer, open Microsoft Visual Studio from Start ⇨ All Programs ⇨ Microsoft Visual Studio 2005. Create a new project by choosing File ⇨ New ⇨ Project. A dialog box appears with a list of project types to select from. Choose K2 ⇨ K2 Empty Project, and complete the project name information.

A new, empty K2 project is created. To create a new Service Object, right-click the project name in the Solution Explorer. Select Add ⇨ New Item. A dialog box opens with a list of K2 file types to select from. Choose K2 connect Service Object, give the object a name, and select Add.

# K2 Service Object Designer

If the K2 Service Object Designer Explorer does not open, select View ⇨ K2 Service Object Designer. The window that is opened can be docked anywhere within the Visual Studio window. The K2 Service Object Designer provides the interface into all the K2 connect functionality needed to build a Service Object. Figure 23-4 shows the K2 Service Object Designer.

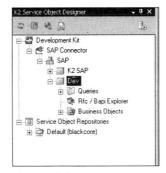

**Figure 23-4**

The K2 Service Object Designer provides three main areas of functionality.

❑   The first is the Development Kit, which provides access to the SAP environments that have been configured in K2 connect. SAP Business Objects are surfaced through this interface in a tree view (see Figure 23-5), and any saved queries that have been built against SAP are available as well.

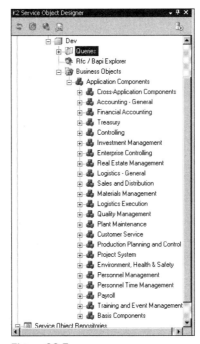

**Figure 23-5**

❑ The second area of functionality is the Service Object Repository (see Figure 23-6), which provides access to all the Service Objects that have been deployed to the K2 connect server.

**Figure 23-6**

❑ Finally, The K2 Service Object Designer provides access to several administrative functions accessible via the icons at the top of the window.

❑ The following table describes the buttons that make up the K2 connect administration functionality available in the K2 Service Object Designer:

| Button | Name | Description |
|---|---|---|
| | Refresh | Refreshes the information displayed in the K2 Service Object Designer. |
| | Configure Destinations | Opens the K2 connect Destination Explorer where new SAP connections can be configured. |
| | Settings | Opens the settings configuration for the K2 Service Object Designer. |
| | K2 blackpearl Settings | Opens the settings for the K2 blackpearl server. |
| | Start/Stop K2 connect Server | Starts or stops the K2 connect Server. |

## K2 Service Object Design Canvas

The K2 Service Object Design Canvas (see Figure 23-7) provides the visual interface for modeling the Service Object against available SAP information. Details about how the design canvas is used will be covered in the next section.

Figure 23-7

# Creating a Service Object with K2 connect for SAP

The following example walks through the basic steps for creating a Service Object with K2 connect. This example will use the Personnel Information Business Object in SAP to create an object that will return Employee information. We will use the `GetList` method of the object to return a list of employees along with specific properties about that employee. The `GetList` method is a read-only method in SAP, but it is important to note that K2 connect can use any BAPI method as long as it has been exposed for use via RFC or NetWeaver. This functionality allows a developer to build applications that not only read information from SAP but are also able to create and update information in SAP.

## *Configuring the Service Object Project*

Create a new empty K2 project by selecting File ⇨ New ⇨ Project in Microsoft Visual Studio 2005. Give the project a name, such as `EmployeeInformationObject`.

Once the project has been created successfully, a Service Object file needs to be added to the project. In the Solution Explorer, right-click the project name and select Add ⇨ New Item and select K2 Service Object. Provide EmployeeServiceObject as the name of the Service Object. The project should now look like the image shown in Figure 23-8.

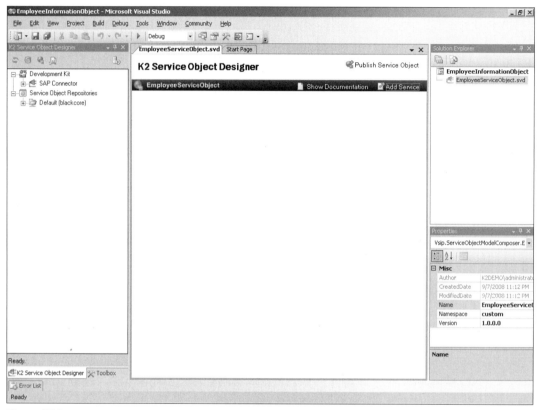

Figure 23-8

## Configuring the GetList Service

The information you need to retrieve about an employee is in the Personnel Information Business Object. This example will use the GetList method of the object to return information about the employee. The following steps will configure the method for retrieving information within the Employee ServiceObject:

1.  In the K2 Service Object Designer, expand the SAP Connector section and select the SAP environment to connect to. A prompt for entering credentials to connect to the SAP server will open.

2.  Enter credentials or select the Predefined User Credentials checkbox (see Figure 23-9) to access SAP.

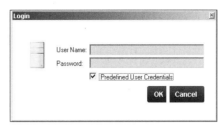

Figure 23-9

**3.** Expand the Business Objects node and navigate down to Application Components ⇨ Personnel Management ⇨ Personnel Administration ⇨ Employee. See Figure 23-10.

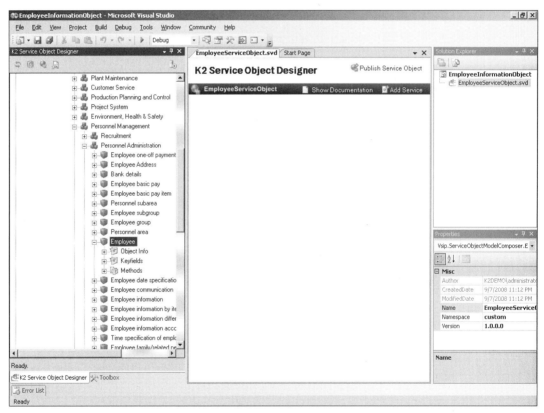

Figure 23-10

**4.** Expand the Methods node. All of the available BAPIs in this Business Object are displayed. This example will use the GetList (BAPI_EMPLOYEE_GETDATA) method. Click the BAPI name and drag it over to the K2 Service Object Designer Canvas to add the method to the Service Object. The project should now look like the image shown in Figure 23-11.

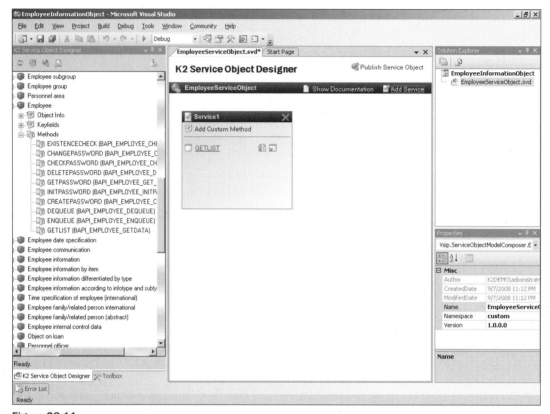

**Figure 23-11**

**5.** Rename the service by double-clicking Service1 and entering EmployeeList.

**6.** Configure the GetList method by clicking the GetList link. Change the Function Name to a friendlier name, such as GetEmpList.

**7.** Configure the input and output parameters for this method. In the Function Interface section, all the parameter fields for this method are listed. The Direction column indicates whether the parameter is an input parameter, is an output parameter, or can be used as both an input and output parameter. Click Clear All to deselect all the parameters and then select the fields that are relevant to this example as indicated in the following table:

| Parameter | Action |
|---|---|
| DATE0 | 1. Check the Date0 field. This field is a required input parameter for the GetList BAPI method. |
| | 2. Click the Friendly Name, and update the name to InputDate. |
| FSTNAME_M | 1. Check the FSTNAME_M field. This field will be used as one of the search parameters to narrow the returned results. |
| | 2. Click the Friendly Name, and update the name to InputFirstName. |
| LASTNAME_M | 1. Check the LASTNAME_M field. This field will be used as one of the search parameters to narrow the returned results. |
| | 2. Click the Friendly Name, and update the name to InputLastName. |
| PERSONAL_DATA | 1. Check the PERSONAL_DATA field. This field is a return parameter that will return the employee information data. |
| | 2. Click the Friendly Name, and update the name to EmployeeInfo. |
| | 3. Notice that the type for this field is not a simple type such as string, but rather a BAPI table ID. This indicates that this field returns a table of data that can be accessed via the Show Structure link. |
| | 4. Click the Show Structure link. Change the Function Name to EmployeeInfo. |
| | 5. Click the Clear All link. Once again, select only the fields relevant to the particular Service Object being worked on. |
| EmployeeInfo BIRTHDATE | 1. Check the BIRTHDATE field. |
| | 2. Click the Friendly Name, and update the name to BirthDate. |
| EmployeeInfo BIRTHPLACE | 1. Check the BIRTHPLACE field. |
| | 2. Click the Friendly Name, and update the name to BirthPlace. |
| EmployeeInfo BIRTHYEAR | 1. Check the BIRTHYEAR field. |
| | 2. Click the Friendly Name, and update the name to BirthYear. |
| EmployeeInfo FIRSTNAME | 1. Check the FIRSTNAME field. |
| | 2. Click the Friendly Name, and update the name to FirstName. |
| EmployeeInfo FROM_DATE | 1. Check the FROM_DATE field. This field represents the employee's employment start date. |
| | 2. Click the Friendly Name, and update the name to EmploymentStartDate. |
| EmployeeInfo LAST_NAME | 1. Check the LAST_NAME field. |
| | 2. Click the Friendly Name, and update the name to LastName. |
| EmployeeInfo PERNO | 1. Check the PERNO field. This field represents the employee's ID in SAP. |
| | 2. Click the Friendly Name, and update the name to EmployeeID. |

After selecting the fields in the `EmployeeInfo` table, the project should look something like Figure 23-12. Notice that BirthPlace, BirthYear, EmployeeID, EmploymentStartDate, and FirstName are all checked.

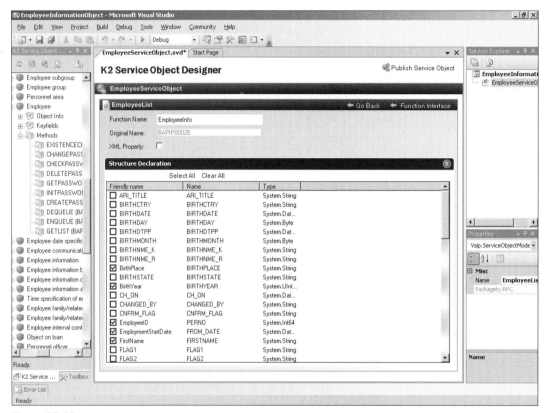

Figure 23-12

8. Click Function Interface to return to the previous screen of parameters. The list of input/output parameters should look something like the one shown in Figure 23-13, with Date0, EmployeeInfo, InputFirstName, and InputLastName all checked.

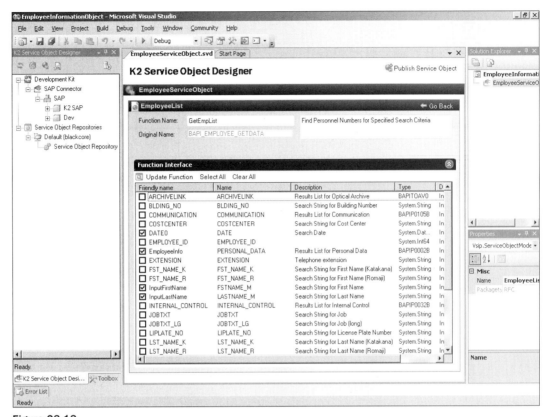

Figure 23-13

# Deploying the Service Object

After selecting the parameters that will be used when calling the GetEmpListmethod, the Service Object is now ready to be deployed. Additional methods or other Business Object information could also be included in the Service Object at this point, but to keep things simple, no additional information will be added.

Click the Publish Service Object link in the upper-right corner of the K2 Service Object Design Canvas. This will publish the Service Object to the K2 server so that it can be consumed by other users. When the Service Object has been published successfully, you'll see the message shown in Figure 23-14.

Figure 23-14

# Creating a K2 SmartObject Based on a K2 connect Service Object

Once a Service Object is created and published to the K2 server via the K2 Service Object Designer, it is now available for use within any K2 SmartObject. In this example, the `EmployeeServiceObject` created in the previous example will be used to create a new Employee SmartObject.

1. Open the EmployeeServiceObject project created in the last example.

2. Add a SmartObject to the project by right-clicking the project name and selecting Add ⇨ New Item.

3. In the dialog box that opens, select K2 SmartObject. Name the new SmartObject Employee. This SmartObject will be based on the SAP information that was added to the EmployeeServiceObject, so the default methods created for this SmartObject need to be removed.

4. Click Advanced Mode in the K2 SmartObject Designer.

5. In the SmartObject Methods section of the designer, click Remove All to remove the default methods.

6. To add a method, click Add in the SmartObject Methods section. The SmartObject Method Wizard opens.

7. In order to set parameters that are passed into the ServiceObject method, the wizard needs to be run in Advanced Mode, so click the checkbox next to Run In Advanced Mode and click Next.

8. On the Method Details screen, give the method a name of Get Employee List, and change the type to List. The properties should look like those shown in Figure 23-15.

Figure 23-15

**9.** On the Method Parameters screen, the parameters that will pass information into the ServiceObject need to be created. Per the previous example, there are three input parameters that need to be configured. Information for each parameter is included in the following table:

| Parameter Name | Parameter Description | Parameter Type |
|---|---|---|
| p_InputDate | Mapped to InputDate field on ServiceObject method. Required by SAP. | Date Time |
| p_InputFirstName | Mapped to InputFirstName field on Service Object method. | Text |
| p_InputLastName | Mapped to InputLastName field on Service Object method. | Text |

After adding the parameters, the Method Parameters screen should look like the one shown in Figure 23-16.

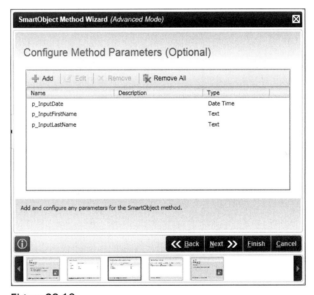

Figure 23-16

**10.** Now the SmartObject method needs to be associated with a corresponding method within a ServiceObject. In this case, the Get Employee List method will use the GetEmpList method from the EmployeeServiceObject. On the Service Object Methods screen, click Add. Click the ellipsis button next to the Service Object Method field.

**11.** In the Context Browser window that opens, drill-down into ServiceObject Server(s) ⇨ ServiceObject Server ⇨ Connect Service for [MachineName] ⇨ EmployeeServiceObject and select the GetEmpList method. See Figure 23-17.

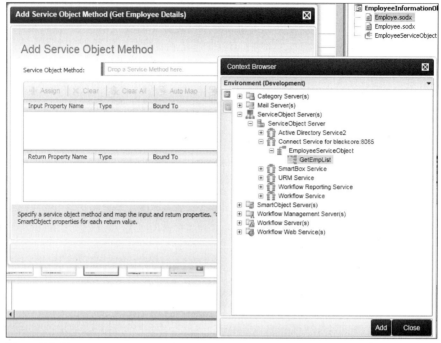

Figure 23-17

All of the input parameters and properties from the ServiceObject method are updated in the interface and can now be associated with parameters on properties on the SmartObject.

12. First, assign the input parameters by clicking the Assign button for each parameter and following the information in the following table:

| Service Method Parameter | Map to Type | SmartObject Property Name |
|---|---|---|
| p_InputDate | SmartObject Method parameter | p_InputDate |
| p_InputFirstName | SmartObject Method parameter | p_InputFirstName |
| p_InputLastName | SmartObject Method parameter | p_InputLastName |

For the remaining properties, corresponding SmartObject properties will be created.

13. Click EmployeeInfo_EmployeeID in the return properties section, and select Assign.

14. Click the Create button. In the SmartObject Property Name field, enter **Employee ID**.

15. Click OK, and then click OK again.

For each additional return property, follow the same steps to configure each SmartObject property, using the information provided in the following table.

| Service Method Property | SmartObject Property Name |
|---|---|
| EmployeeInfo_EmploymentStartDate | Employment Start Date |
| EmployeeInfo_LastName | Last Name |
| EmployeeInfo_FirstName | First Name |
| EmployeeInfo_BirthPlace | Birthplace |
| EmployeeInfo_BirthYear | Birth Year |

**16.** When all properties have been mapped, click OK to close the window. The Service Object Methods screen should resemble the one shown in Figure 23-18.

**Figure 23-18**

**17.** Complete the wizard by clicking Next and then clicking Finish.

At this point, the Employee SmartObject can be saved and deployed to the K2 server. To deploy the SmartObject, right-click the `EmployeeInformationObject` project and select Deploy. The deployment wizard opens allowing the selection of the deployment environment. In this example, deployment will be to the development environment, so click Finish to continue with the deployment process.

Deployment status is displayed in the bottom-left corner of the Visual Studio environment. The deploy is successful when Deploy succeeded is displayed.

The Employee SmartObject can now be used to surface SAP data in any number of applications. The data can be surfaced in an InfoPath or ASP.NET form, a report built with K2 Report Designer, as part of a K2 workflow process, included in another .NET-based application (such as SharePoint Server), or queried directly via the .NET Data Provider for K2 SmartObjects. For more information about using K2 SmartObjects in these different applications, see Chapter 7.

> *In the previous example, K2 connect for SAP was used in a simple scenario to surface employee information from SAP. However, the same basic steps can be followed to provide much more complex functionality based on your organization's needs. Calling multiple BAPI methods from a single Service Object, updating or creating data in the SAP environment, and filtering BAPI results are all possible using the K2 Service Object Designer within K2 connect for SAP. And, all of these tasks can be done without the need to write a single line of code. Specific examples for each of these advanced scenarios can be found in the Developer's Guide that comes as part of the K2 connect for SAP product documentation.*

# Summary

In this chapter, you have been introduced to K2 connect for SAP, an add-on component to K2 blackpearl that provides an interface for modeling business entities against SAP without having to write code. We discussed the architecture of K2 connect and how it fits into the K2 blackpearl platform.

An overview of the K2 Service Object Designer and Design canvas was provided before delving into an example on how to build a simple Service Object using K2 connect for SAP to surface employee information from SAP and how to use that Service Object in a K2 SmartObject to integrate into any application, such as forms, reports, K2 workflow processes, or other .NET-based applications.

Finally, advanced topics in K2 connect were briefly touched upon to provide you with insight into the many possibilities that are opened up with K2 connect for SAP.

By reducing the amount of code necessary to access SAP and by providing easy to use tools, K2 connect for SAP decreases development time and allows business users to access relevant SAP information in a reusable and simple manner.

# K2 blackpearl Tips and Tricks

When we started this book, we wanted to make sure that everyone who read it came away with some good information, not only from the information contained within each chapter but also from the insight each author provides. That in great part explains why the authors were chosen to participate. They come from a variety of fields and have a variety of experiences that should help you take advantage of the K2 platform. To further this idea we have collected various tips, tricks, and "how-to" information from a broader audience, including K2 employees from around the world and community representatives who have discovered some great time-saving techniques. Some of these things you may have seen before on various K2 blogs. Others will be new. We hope you find many of them useful.

## Retrieving the Value from an XML Field Element

By Joseph Dunagan, K2 Consultant

Sometimes you need to get the value from an element within a K2 XML field. This is usually done within a server event. In the following example, I needed to retrieve a URL from a K2-generated XML field. This specific example should work if you do not expect repeating values in the Items node. For scenarios where repeating values are selected, you would need to change the XPath.

```
// get the full XML from the K2 XML field
string strXML = K2.ProcessInstance.XmlFields["SPEventsField"].Value;
// set the XPath to the desired node
string strXPath = "/Items/Item/URL";
// use the helper class to retrieve the value for this element
// (as set in the XPath) for this XML
string strValue = SourceCode.Workflow.Common.XmlHelper.GetXPathValue
(strXML, strXPath);
```

# Super Simple Notes Field with History in InfoPath

**By Joseph Dunagan, K2 Consultant**

It is common for an InfoPath-based process to require the use of a notes field that allows users to add to but not edit the notes history. This is a snap with a couple of rules and one hidden text field.

1.  On the InfoPath form, create three textboxes and one button. All textboxes should be multiline. In my case I named them:

    ❑   NewNote

    ❑   NotesHistory

    ❑   CarriageReturn

    ❑   SaveNewNote (button)

2.  The NotesHistory textbox should be the largest (perhaps 8 or 10 lines; the full width of the form), as it will display all prior notes. This textbox should be set to read-only in its control properties.

3.  I typically make the NewNote textbox large enough for two lines of text (the full width of the form).

4.  The SaveNewNote button should be placed after the NewNote textbox and before the NotesHistory textbox accompanied by a note to the effect of "New notes will only be saved by clicking this button."

5.  The CarriageReturn textbox should be hidden and have its default value set in the function builder to:

    ❑   Type an open quotation mark (").

    ❑   Hold down the Control key and press the Enter key.

    ❑   Type a close quotation mark (").

6.  Finally configure a rule for the SaveNewNote button, including the following Actions:

    ❑   Set a Field's Value ⇨ Field: NotesHistory ⇨ Value (function builder) : concat(today(), ": ", NewNote, CarriageReturn, NotesHistory). Note that NewNote, CarriageReturn, and NotesHistory are inserted using the "Insert Field or Group" button.

    ❑   Set a Field's Value ⇨ Field: NewNote ⇨ Value (leave the value blank).

This button will successfully update the NotesHistory with the new note at the top preceded by the current date.

# Retrieving Process Instance Reporting Data

## By Bob Maggio, K2 Architect

Often you need to access the data that appears within the out-of-the-box K2 Workspace reports from some other custom application. The standard K2 reports are based on a number of SmartObjects that are built into K2, and you can use those same SmartObjects to access the report data.

The first thing is to know what built-in SmartObjects are available and understand the data that you are looking for. You can see the list of SmartObjects in the K2 Object Browser as shown in Figure A-1.

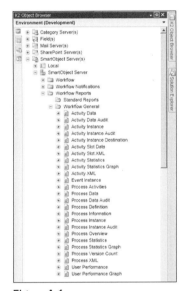

Figure A-1

So if you wanted to get the data from the Activity Instances Report, as shown in Figure A-2, you would find the Activity Instances SmartObject.

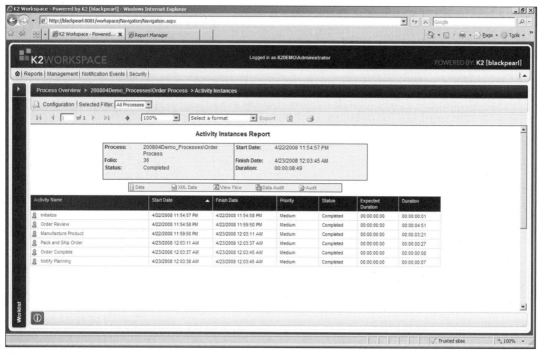

Figure A-2

You can use the `SourceCode.SmartObjects.Client` API to programmatically retrieve information from this SmartObject.

The following is a code sample where I have created a method that accepts a SmartObject name and Process Instance ID and retrieves the data. For the purposes of simplicity of this demo, I am simply doing a `Response.Write` to the ASPX page instead of doing something fancier with the data.

```
private void GetReportData(string strSmartObjectName, int nProcInstID)
{
    SourceCode.SmartObjects.Client.SmartObjectClientServer serverName =
        new SourceCode.SmartObjects.Client.SmartObjectClientServer();
    SourceCode.Hosting.Client.BaseAPI.SCConnectionStringBuilder connectionString =
        new SourceCode.Hosting.Client.BaseAPI.SCConnectionStringBuilder();
    // build a connection string
    connectionString.Authenticate = true;
    connectionString.Host = "localhost";
    connectionString.Integrated = true;
    connectionString.IsPrimaryLogin = true;
    connectionString.Port = 5555;
    // open a K2 Server connection
    serverName.CreateConnection();
    serverName.Connection.Open(connectionString.ToString());
    try
    {
```

```
            // get a handle to the SmartObject
            SourceCode.SmartObjects.Client.SmartObject smartObject =
                serverName.GetSmartObject(strSmartObjectName);
            // specify which method will be called
            smartObject.MethodToExecute = "List";
            // specify input parameters for the method
            smartObject.Properties["ProcessInstanceID"].Value = nProcInstID.ToString();
            // call the method
            SourceCode.SmartObjects.Client.SmartObjectList oSmOList =
                serverName.ExecuteList(smartObject);
            // iterate each smartobject in the collection and do
            // something with the data
            foreach (SourceCode.SmartObjects.Client.SmartObject oSmO in
                oSmOList.SmartObjectsList)
            {
                // for the purposes of this example, I'm
                // just dynamically building out a string
                string strRecord = "";
                foreach(SourceCode.SmartObjects.Client.SmartProperty oProp
                    in oSmO.Properties)
                {
                    strRecord += oProp.Name + ": " + oProp.Value.ToString() + ",   ";
                }
                Response.Write(strRecord + "<br/>");
            }
        }
        catch (Exception ex)
        {
        }
        finally
        {
            // close the connection
            serverName.Connection.Close();
        }
    }
```

When I invoke this method in with the following parameters:

```
GetReportData("Activity_Instance", 4782);
```

I see the following (see Figure A-3), which from a data point of view matches up to the Workspace report.

ProcessInstanceID: 4782, ActivityInstanceID: 8, ActivityName: Initialize, StartDate: 2008-04-22T23:54:57, FinishDate: 2008-04-22T23:54:58, Priority: Medium, Status: Completed ,
ExpectedDuration: 0, Duration: 1,
ProcessInstanceID: 4782, ActivityInstanceID: 15, ActivityName: Order Review, StartDate: 2008-04-22T23:54:58, FinishDate: 2008-04-22T23:59:50, Priority: Medium, Status: Completed ,
ExpectedDuration: 0, Duration: 291,
ProcessInstanceID: 4782, ActivityInstanceID: 26, ActivityName: Manufacture Product, StartDate: 2008-04-22T23:59:50, FinishDate: 2008-04-23T00:03:11, Priority: Medium, Status: Completed ,
ExpectedDuration: 0, Duration: 201,
ProcessInstanceID: 4782, ActivityInstanceID: 37, ActivityName: Pack and Ship Order, StartDate: 2008-04-23T00:03:11, FinishDate: 2008-04-23T00:03:37, Priority: Medium, Status: Completed ,
ExpectedDuration: 0, Duration: 27,
ProcessInstanceID: 4782, ActivityInstanceID: 47, ActivityName: Order Complete, StartDate: 2008-04-23T00:03:37, FinishDate: 2008-04-23T00:03:45, Priority: Medium, Status: Completed ,
ExpectedDuration: 0, Duration: 8,
ProcessInstanceID: 4782, ActivityInstanceID: 53, ActivityName: Notify Planning, StartDate: 2008-04-23T00:03:38, FinishDate: 2008-04-23T00:03:45, Priority: Medium, Status: Completed ,
ExpectedDuration: 0, Duration: 7,

Figure A-3

Obviously this is just a simple example showing how to interact with these SmartObjects. There are other things that you can do with them. For one, if you don't want to write any code, you could use the .NET Data Provider for K2 SmartObjects to bind the results to a control. You can also integrate these objects into InfoPath forms if desired.

Additionally a very useful way to interact with these SmartObjects, and any SmartObjects for that matter, is to use the Amazing SmartObject Tool, which is freely available on the K2 blackmarket (`http://k2underground.com/k2/ProjectHome.aspx?ProjectID=47`) and is included in K2 blackpearl 0807. I highly recommend this tool for anyone developing or working with SmartObjects. (Note: You must create a member account at the site to be able to see the tool.)

# Activity Destination Users Based on a Repeating XML Element

## By Bob Maggio, K2 Architect

One of the lesser known new features of the expanded Destination Rule functionality of K2 blackpearl is the ability to very easily base destination users from a repeating XML node that contains a User ID. In K2 2003 this required a bit of coding in the Destination Rule for each Activity for which you wished to do something like this. With K2 blackpearl this is now a drag-and-drop experience in the process design canvas. This can be a very useful feature in a schema-driven process development effort.

In this example I will show how an InfoPath form can be leveraged to capture a list of users that will then become the basis for the next step's Destination Rule.

1.  Create an InfoPath form and InfoPath-integrated K2 process as normal.

2.  Design the form as per normal.

3.  Add a new repeating Text (string) element to the Main data source, as shown in Figure A-4 (in this example I've named the field "Reviewers").

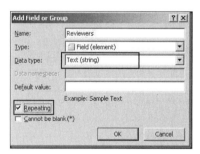

Figure A-4

**4.** I then drag out the repeating text field onto the desired InfoPath view as shown in Figure A-5.

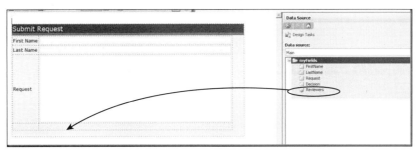

**Figure A-5**

**5.** In this example I then did the following:

❏ Selected Repeating Table when prompted.

❏ Changed the textbox to a drop-down List.

❏ Added content to the drop-down list to allow users to select reviewers from an easily readable drop-down list (with actual Domain\userID as the hidden value), as shown in Figure A-6.

**Figure A-6**

6.  Save and close the InfoPath form.

7.  You should now be back at the Process design canvas and see the message as shown in Figure A-7.

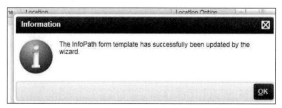

**Figure A-7**

8.  Click OK and then click Finish.

9.  In this example, we then want to change the Destination Rule for the desired activity by clicking on the Destination Rule icon as shown in Figure A-8.

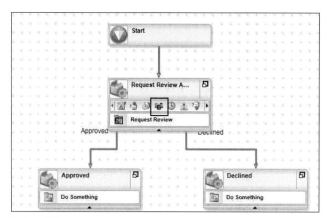

**Figure A-8**

10. With the Destination Rule window open, navigate to the Destination Users window, as shown in Figure A-9.

Figure A-9

11. Click the Add button.

12. Click the ellipse (. . .) button.

13. Navigate to the Process/Activity Data tab within the Context Browser, and then expand the XML Fields node until you find the Reviewers node.

14. Either drag-and-drop the Reviewers node (see Figure A-10) or select the node and click the Add button.

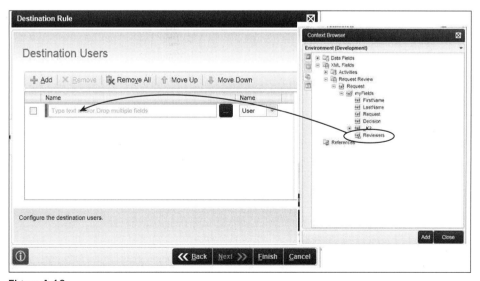

Figure A-10

**15.** Once this has been selected, it should look like Figure A-11.

**Figure A-11**

Now if you deploy the process and then open the form, you can select multiple users (see Figure A-12):

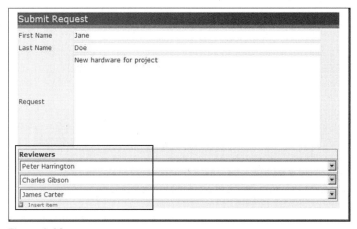

**Figure A-12**

When the process hits the Destination you set up, it will create task rights for each user that appears in that reviewer repeating section. If you review the Activity Instance Destinations Report for this instance, you will see that the three users you selected in the InfoPath form are now destination users for this activity, as shown in Figure A-13.

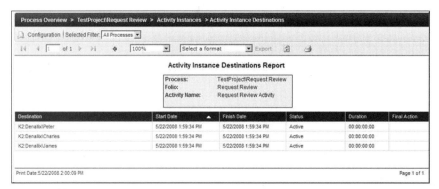

**Figure A-13**

# Differences between Stop and Start, and Sleep

**By Bob Maggio, K2 Architect**

A question that is sometimes asked is "What is the difference between stopping and starting, and sleeping within K2?"

Start and Stop reside at the Process Instance level and are accessible in the K2 Workspace Management tooling or `SourceCode.Workflow.Management` API, both of which require Admin permission. Stop puts an active process instance into a state of `"Stop"`, which prevents it from executing, meaning, for example, that Client Events can't be actioned and escalations won't fire. The process instance is still alive in the sense that it resides in the K2Server transaction database, as opposed to just the K2ServerLog/ reporting database. You can equate this to a pause in the process. Start essentially resumes the process, like pressing play after pausing a movie.

Sleep, on the other hand, is functionality available in the K2 Worklists or through the `SourceCode .Workflow.Client` API, and it operates upon individual worklist items, not at the process instance level. When you sleep a worklist item, it simply changes the status for that specific worklist item to a status of `"Sleep"`. When you sleep a worklist item, you must give K2 a duration or specific date and time to awaken it at, so it doesn't sleep forever.

So what does this mean? By default, the worklists in the K2 Workspace and SharePoint Web part filter out worklist items in a status of Sleep so they won't appear until they are awoken. However, you can change the filter to display these if you'd like. As for escalations, sleep doesn't have any impact on them. In my testing activity, event escalations still fire for a worklist item I have in sleep.

# What Does the Client Event Option "Allow Any User to Finish This Client Event" Mean?

**By Bob Maggio, K2 Architect**

A question was posed recently as to what the "Allow any user to finish this Client Event" checkbox means within a Client Event within K2 Process Designer within Visual Studio (for K2 blackpearl) and K2.net 2003 Studio.

The purpose of "Allow any user to finish this Client Event" goes back to at least K2.net 2003. In my experience this is a rarely used feature, but it can be useful under the correct business requirements.

By default (which means this option is not checked for a Client Event), when a worklist item is attempted to be opened, K2 will validate that the person opening it has the right to do so. If this field is checked, anyone with access to the serial number can potentially open it because K2 will not validate the person opening the task against who it is assigned in the Destination Rule. The thing to keep in mind is that if this option is checked, you still need a destination user because the task will only appear on the Destination User(s) worklist and e-mail notifications will be sent only to the destination users. However, everyone has the physical ability to open and action the task if they know the correct way to access it.

Here is a simplified example. If you have an activity with a Client Event with this "Allow any user to finish this Client Event" option checked that targets John Smith as the destination, and you have e-mail notifications turned on, when the process runs, it creates a worklist item for John Smith (as in it will appear in John's worklist) and sends John an e-mail with the URL to the ASPX page in it. However, John could then forward someone else the e-mail and that other person could click the link and action the item. If this option had not been checked, John could certainly forward the e-mail notification to someone, but when the URL was clicked by that other person, K2 would compare that person's credentials against that of the targeted destinations for this worklist item. Since they would not match, K2 would not permit the task to be opened.

As mentioned, this isn't used too frequently, but I have seen it used in certain situations when someone wanted to assign a task to a primary user, but also wanted to let everyone potentially action the task because those others controlled other aspects of the UI.

# Custom Assembly Versioning within a K2 Process

## By Bob Maggio, K2 Architect

Recently I was asked the following question: "Let's say I have a custom assembly that I include in the workflow project. Later, my requirements change, and I produce a new version of both the workflow and the assembly. Does K2 blackpearl handle the versioning of my custom assembly? In other words, can workflows using the original assembly run side-by-side with the new version?"

The short answer is yes; it behaves exactly as described. The long answer is described in this section to help in better understanding how K2 works.

When you add a reference to a K2 process, the DLL file itself is serialized as binary data to the K2Server database each time you deploy the process. Thus, this DLL is now associated with this specific process definition version. The first time the process is used, K2 server extracts all DLLs (K2-generated and -referenced DLLs) to the K2 work folder. This is typically located at `C:\Program Files\ K2 blackpearl\Host Server\Bin\Work`.

For example, I created a process that referenced a .NET assembly called `MyTestAssembly.dll`. The first time I used this process, it created a folder called `C:\Program Files\K2 blackpearl\Host Server\ Bin\Work\Proc241`. Note the number 241 relates to the ID for the process definition version.

If I look in this folder, I see what's in Figure A-14.

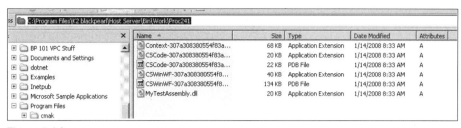

Figure A-14

Here you see all the stuff K2 generates as well as my .NET assembly. Don't be fooled by the date of the .NET assembly. Remember it had been serialized to the database as binary data, so when K2 lays it back down on the disk, it will always have a new date stamp. If I look at the version info on my DLL, I see what's in Figure A-15.

Figure A-15

Now I go and change my DLL and rebuild it. As part of the change, I changed my DLL version to 1.1.1.1. I then reference in my K2 process and then redeploy. Now if I look at my Work folder, I see what's in Figure A-16.

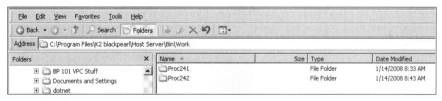

Figure A-16

Notice that we now have two folders side-by-side. Proc241 was my original version, and Proc242 is the new one. If I browse to Proc242, I see what's in Figure A-17.

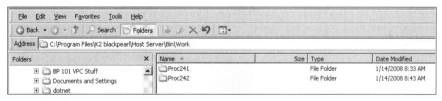

Figure A-17

This looks pretty much the same as what was in Proc241; however, if I look at the version of my DLL, I see the new one (Figure A-18).

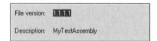

**Figure A-18**

Thus, they should run side by side without issue.

Things were handled very similarly within K2.net 2003, so if you are on a legacy project, the same knowledge can be applied.

# Updating Batch Action/Outcome Results Back into InfoPath Form

### By Johnny Fang, K2 Solutions Manager

This problem came up the other day, and I thought this might be useful to share. The scenario is that when you do a batch selection or quick approval action from the worklist, the outcome is not recorded in the form's audit history. Of course, the process audit history will have it, but in certain cases, the user does not have access to the process history information.

So if you wanted to store the outcome in the InfoPath form data, basically you have to update the value directly within the Succeeding Rules of the client activity.

Here's an example. Edit the code of your succeeding rule. You can get the final outcome by putting this snippet of code inside the Succeeding Rule. Add a `using` statement for `System.Xml` and see the code between the comments. You will have to change the variables to your own form and namespace.

```
      public void
Main(Project_282cb15964ee4ab397715563ff6641a6.SucceedingRuleContext_
369ef228d5e54527b7116b0583eabd22 K2)
        {
        if (SucceedingRuleHelper.AnyOutcomesEvaluatedSuccessfully(K2))
        {
            AllInfoPathTasksFinished(K2);
            K2.SucceedingRule = true;
        // begin custom code
            XmlDocument xmlDoc = new XmlDocument();

            xmlDoc.LoadXml(K2.ProcessInstance.XmlFields["TestForm"].Value);

            XmlNamespaceManager namespaceManager =
                    new XmlNamespaceManager(xmlDoc.NameTable);

            namespaceManager.AddNamespace("my",
```

```
        xmlDoc.DocumentElement.GetNamespaceOfPrefix("my"));

    xmlDoc.SelectSingleNode("my:myFields/my:myDataField",
        namespaceManager).InnerText =
        K2.ActivityInstance.DataFields["Outcome"].Value.ToString();

    K2.ProcessInstance.XmlFields["TestForm"].Value = xmlDoc.OuterXml;
    // end custom code
}
else
{
    InfoPathTaskFinished(K2);
    K2.SucceedingRule = false;
}
}
```

If you are using the Plan Just Once option, you should note that there is only one Activity Instance created with one or more slots tied to it. So if you want to enumerate through the list of actions, here's a code snippet to do this:

```
for (int i = 0; i < K2.ActivityInstanceDestination.ActivityInstance
    .WorklistSlots.Count; i++)
{
    Console.WriteLine("Action Result: " +
        K2.ActivityInstanceDestination.ActivityInstance
        .WorklistSlots[i].DataFields["Action
        Result"].Value.ToString());
    Console.WriteLine("Destination User: " +
        K2.ActivityInstanceDestination.ActivityInstance
        .WorklistSlots[i].User.Name.ToString());
}
```

# Handling Multiple Documents in the K2 blackpearl SharePoint Document Template

**By Johnny Fang, K2 Solutions Manager**

In K2 blackpearl, when you are using the SharePoint Document Template, various functions are supported, such as uploading and downloading documents (multiple documents in Advanced Mode), check-in, check-out, updating of metadata, and so on.

The challenge here is if you need to do this for multiple documents (that is, check-in and check-out), how do you do it? There is no out-of-the-box functionality, but that doesn't mean it cannot be achieved. The following steps show you how, and this technique applies to all functionalities in the Document Template Wizard, including uploading, downloading, and updating of metadata; undo check-out; check-in; and check-out.

**1.** Create the document wizard functionality. In this example, I will be doing recursive check-in of documents based on a Process data field (FileName) passed in. The value stores the documents I want to check in, and the separator ";" is used to distinguishe the various file names, for example: `"doc1.pdf;doc2.pdf"`.

**2.** Go to code view of the event and make the changes to the code as follows.

*Note that only the changes are shown, not the entire code snippet:*

```
foreach (XmlNode checkInItem in checkInItems)
{
    foreach (string docName in
K2.ProcessInstance.DataFields["FileName"].Value.ToString().Split(';'))
    {
    if (bool.Parse(checkInItem.SelectSingleNode("UsePartOfProcessItems").InnerText))
    {
     //....
     checkInSet += "<DocumentName>" + docName + "</DocumentName>";
    //....
     }
     else
     {
    // ....
     checkInSet += "<DocumentName>" + docName + "</DocumentName>";
    // ....
     }
     }
}
```

# Best Practice — Host Server Connections

**By Shaun Leisegang, K2 Presales Manager**

Here are some pointers when you are using the `Connection` object. This object is part of the Base API from which each API inherits (`SmartObjectClientServer`, `SmartObjectManagementServer`, and so on).

The following subsections show some sample code based on three scenarios in which you can connect to the server from the API.

# Scenario 1: Opening and Closing Multiple Connections

This is the most expensive way of using connections and results in the most overhead. After each `Open` method on the `Connection` object, the call is authenticated on the server, and this is what causes the most overhead. This scenario is typically used in a stateless environment where user context does not exist between method calls, for example, Web apps with no sessions.

```
SmartObjectManagementServer _mgmtServer =
    new SmartObjectManagementServer();
SmartObjectClientServer _clientServer = new SmartObjectClientServer();

string _conString =
    "Integrated=True;IsPrimaryLogin=True;Authenticate=True;
    EncryptedPassword=False;Host=blackpearl;Port=5555";

SCConnectionStringBuilder _connBuilder =
    new SCConnectionStringBuilder(_conString);

#region Scenario 1 - Connection for Each operation

//Get SmartObject List...
_mgmtServer.CreateConnection(_connBuilder.ToString());
_mgmtServer.Connection.Open(_connBuilder.ToString());
SmartObjectExplorer smoExplorer =
    _mgmtServer.GetSmartObjects(SmartObjectInfoType.System);
_mgmtServer.Connection.Close();


if (_clientServer.Connection == null)
    _clientServer.CreateConnection();
_clientServer.Connection.Open(_connBuilder.ToString());
SmartObject smo = _clientServer.GetSmartObject
    (smoExplorer.SmartObjects["UMUser"].Guid);
    _clientServer.Connection.Close();

if (_clientServer.Connection == null)
    _clientServer.CreateConnection();

smo.MethodToExecute = "Get_Users";
smo.ListMethods[smo.MethodToExecute].Parameters["Label_Name"].Value =
    "K2";

_clientServer.Connection.Open(_connBuilder.ToString());
SmartObjectList userList = _clientServer.ExecuteList(smo);
_clientServer.Connection.Close();

#endregion
```

## Scenario 2: One Connection Performing Many Operations

This is a much more efficient way of using connections. You can share the `Connection` object between APIs, thereby making it easier to manage the connection.

```
SmartObjectManagementServer _mgmtServer =
    new SmartObjectManagementServer();
SmartObjectClientServer _clientServer = new SmartObjectClientServer();

string _conString =
    "Integrated=True;IsPrimaryLogin=True;Authenticate=True;
    EncryptedPassword=False;Host=blackpearl;Port=5555";

SCConnectionStringBuilder _connBuilder =
    new SCConnectionStringBuilder(_conString);

_mgmtServer.CreateConnection();
_clientServer.Connection = _mgmtServer.Connection;

_mgmtServer.Connection.Open(_connBuilder.ToString());
SmartObjectExplorer smoExplorer =
    _mgmtServer.GetSmartObjects(SmartObjectInfoType.System);
SmartObject smo = _clientServer.GetSmartObject
    (smoExplorer.SmartObjects["UMUser"].Guid);
smo.MethodToExecute = "Get_Users";
smo.ListMethods[smo.MethodToExecute].Parameters["Label_Name"].Value =
    "K2";
SmartObjectList userList = _clientServer.ExecuteList(smo);

_mgmtServer.Connection.Close();
```

## Scenario 3: Using Sessions

If your calling client has state and can manage sessions, this is the way to use it with the `Connection` object. The session connection timeout on the server can be set. However, it does apply to the entire server, which means all servers hosted on that server. The default time is 20 minutes. If a session times out and you make an API call without authenticating (`Authenticate=true`), you will get an exception.

This approach is the most efficient way of handling connections, provided that you have session state.

```
SmartObjectManagementServer _mgmtServer = new SmartObjectManagementServer();
SmartObjectClientServer _clientServer = new SmartObjectClientServer();

string _conString =
    "Integrated=True;IsPrimaryLogin=True;Authenticate=True;
    EncryptedPassword=False;Host=blackpearl;Port=5555";

SCConnectionStringBuilder _connBuilder =
    new SCConnectionStringBuilder(_conString);

_mgmtServer.CreateConnection();
```

```
_clientServer.Connection = _mgmtServer.Connection;

_mgmtServer.Connection.Open(_connBuilder.ToString());
string sessionID = _mgmtServer.Connection.GetResumableSessionCookie();

SmartObjectExplorer smoExplorer =
    _mgmtServer.GetSmartObjects(SmartObjectInfoType.System);
_mgmtServer.Connection.Close();

//Time elapse...

SmartObject smo = null;
try
{
    _connBuilder.Authenticate = false;
    _clientServer.Connection.Open(_connBuilder.ToString());
    _clientServer.Connection.ResumeSession(sessionID);
    smo = _clientServer.GetSmartObject
        (smoExplorer.SmartObjects["UMUser"].Guid);
    _clientServer.Connection.Close();
}
catch (Exception ex)
{
    Console.WriteLine(ex.Message);
}

//Some more time elapse...

if (smo != null)
{
    SmartObjectList userList;
    try
    {
        smo.MethodToExecute = "Get_Users";
        smo.ListMethods[smo.MethodToExecute].
            Parameters["Label_Name"].Value = "k2";
        _clientServer.Connection.Open(_connBuilder.ToString());
        userList = _clientServer.ExecuteList(smo);
        _clientServer.Connection.EndSession(sessionID);
        _clientServer.Connection.Close();
    }
    catch (Exception ex)
    {
        Console.WriteLine(ex.Message);
    }
}
```

# Default Outcomes in Escalations

**By David Loomis, K2 Consultant**

Here's a simple way to set a default outcome for an escalation so the workflow will take to your chosen activity when the escalation fires. I've seen many approaches to accomplish this, but I think this one is the easiest.

Say you have a Client Event (this technique can work with a server or an IPC event with some adjustment) where the user has two choices: Approve or Reject. If the user takes no action after a certain amount of time, you want to automatically take the reject choice.

1. Open the K2 Object Browser and go to the Process/Activity tab.

2. Expand Data Fields ⇨ Activities and then expand the activity that contains your Client Event.

3. Right-click and edit the Outcome field.

4. In the Initial Value field, put the outcome you want to use when the activity expires (Reject in this example, as shown in Figure A-19).

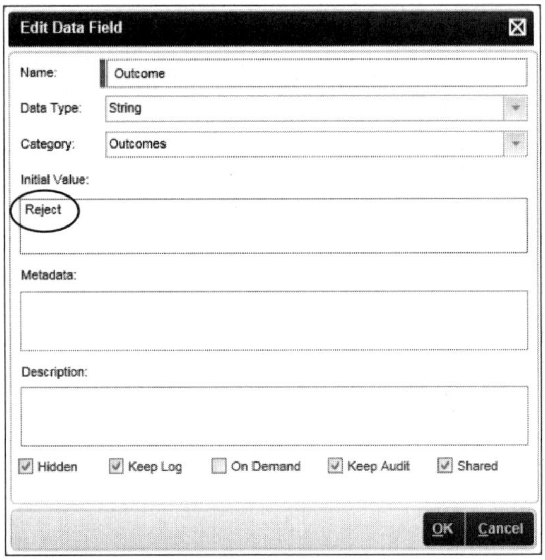

**Figure A-19**

5. Set the activity escalation for the appropriate time and then on the Action Template screen choose Expire Activity, as shown in Figure A-20.

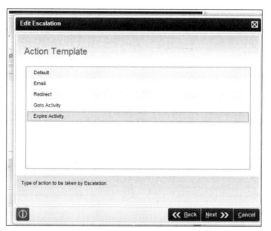

Figure A-20

That's it. When the activity expires, it will take the outcome specified in the initial value. Using this technique, you can also take a path that is not one of the choices given to the user. For example, you can set the initial value of the outcome to Expire and then set up a Line Rule that will branch to activities you want to perform when the user takes no action.

# Adding an IPC Event to a Process from a Different Solution File

### By Harvinder Dhami, K2 User

You create an empty process in your current solution. When you need to IPC to a process that does not exist in the current project, use the data field in the process name in the IPC Wizard. When you click Next, the wizard will ask for a design-time value for IPC. Use the empty process (or any process) here.

When your process runs, populate the data field with the correct process (Project\processname). This way you can use any process as an IPC even if that does not exist in your current solution.

# Asynchronous Server Code Events

### By David Loomis, K2 Consultant

Most K2 developers are familiar with asynchronous IPC events, but fewer are familiar with asynchronous server code events. Although the names sound similar, the two events are quite different. An asynchronous IPC event allows you to start a subprocess and let it continue independently of the main process. An asynchronous server code event is the server-side equivalent of a Client Event. Just like a Client Event, an asynchronous server event allows the process to wait an indefinite amount of time for some action before continuing.

Imagine a workflow where there is a handoff of some task to an external system that takes an unknown amount of time (days or weeks) to complete. Rather than continuously polling the external system for an answer that may take a very long time, the workflow can simply wait until a notification is received. Suppose that a car dealership has developed a K2 process for handling customer orders for custom built-to-order automobiles. The dealership workflow will gather the customer requirements, get appropriate approvals, and then communicate (perhaps using a Web service) with a factory order system that uses BizTalk to process orders. At this point, the factory order system simply acknowledges receipt of the order. The K2 process must wait while the factory order system kicks-off a whole bunch of manual and automated processes in different systems to schedule the car for assembly. The actual completion date for the car depends on such things as factory schedule, the number of other requests pending, and availability of custom parts. When the vehicle has been completed, the factory order system invokes a Web service (or some other mechanism) to tell the dealership's K2 server to continue the process. Once the K2 process continues, an activity can notify the customer that the vehicle is ready for delivery.

## Making an Event Asynchronous

An asynchronous server event is just the tool you need for this situation. How does an asynchronous server event differ from the normal synchronous Code Event? When the workflow engine encounters a *Synchronous* server event it executes the event and then continues the workflow. In an *Asynchronous* event, the workflow engine executes the event and then stops. When you first drag a server code event onto the workflow design canvas, by default it is synchronous. A server code event can be changed from synchronous to asynchronous by adding one line of code to the event as shown in Figure A-21.

```
K2.Synchronous = false;
```

**Figure A-21**

## Completing the Server Event

To notify the workflow the event is complete a key piece of information must be made available to the external system: the serial number of the activity containing the asynchronous server event. Every activity (whether you use it or not) has a serial number that uniquely identifies it. A serial number is similar to the correlation ID used in message queuing. This serial number allows you to use the K2 API to open the correct server item and complete the event using the Finish method of ServerItem.

You can also use the ServerItem class to set process and activity level fields to transfer information back into the workflow. This code could be invoked from a .NET assembly, a Web service, or whatever approach best matches your situation; just add a reference to the SourceCode.Workflow.Client assembly, as shown in Figure A-22.

```
public static void CompleteServerItem(string k2server, string SN)

    {

        if (string.IsNullOrEmpty(SN)) return;


        SourceCode.Workflow.Client.Connection k2conn = null;


        try

        {

            SourceCode.Workflow.Client.ConnectionSetup k2setup = new ConnectionSetup();

            k2setup.ConnectionString = k2server;


            k2conn = new Connection();

            k2conn.Open(k2setup);
```

Figure A-22

The identity used to connect to the K2 server needs to be assigned the right server event for the process in the Management Console (see Figure A-23).

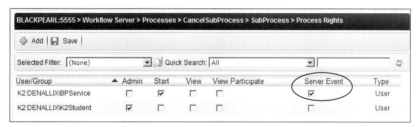

Figure A-23

# Example — Using an Asynchronous Server Event

A common design scenario for workflows is the need to be able to cancel asynchronous IPC processes at any time in response to some action in the main workflow. This scenario typically occurs when the originator decides to cancel a request that has started several independent subprocesses to perform part of the work.

An asynchronous server code event and some other components will be used to implement one possible solution. The basic idea for the solution is that whenever an asynchronous IPC event is started, it will write out information about itself to a SmartObject. When the subprocess ends, it removes the entry. If the main process needs to end, it simply scans the SmartObject for all the currently running subprocesses that belong to it and tells them to finish. The Asynchronous server event will be used in the subprocess to wait for the signal from the main process.

# Example Project

The standalone example that is discussed in this section of the appendix is called "CancelSubTask" and is available in the code download for this book available at www.wrox.com. There are no Web pages for the Client Events; action them using the K2 Worklist. The sample contains two projects: a K2 project and a .NET class library. The K2 project contains two simple workflows (MainProcess and SubProcess) and a SmartObject, ActiveSubProcesses. MainProcess calls SubProcess to do some simulated work using an asynchronous IPC event, passing its process ID. The main process goes on to do some simulated work consisting of a single Client Event. When MainProcess is complete, it signals any subprocesses that are still running to finish.

The class library implements a DLL containing the CompleteServerItem method discussed previously. Complete code is included so you can modify it for your needs. This assembly has been added to the workflow as a project reference, but you could also build a common library of workflow routines like this and deploy them to the Global Assembly Cache. Another option would be to place this code in a Web service.

## SmartObject

ActiveSubProcesses is a very simple SmartBox SmartObject. This SmartObject will contain one row for each currently active subprocess. When the subprocess is entered, it puts a row in this table, and just before it exits it removes the row. The ID field is an autonumber field used as a unique identifier. The ParentID is the process ID of the calling process, while the SubTaskEventSN contains the serial number of an asynchronous Client Event. See Figure A-24.

Figure A-24

At least one value must be passed in from the calling process as a process-level data field: the process ID of the calling workflow. When the main process wants to find any active subprocesses it has started, it can simply request from the SmartObject any rows that match its own process ID.

## The Subprocess

There are two parallel paths from the start of the subprocess; since both Line Rules from Start are true, both paths will be taken. One path (on the left side of Figure A-25) is the normal workflow path that does the actual work of the subprocess. In this example the work is simulated by a single Client Event, but there could be many activities on this path performing the main functionality of the workflow. The other path (on the right side of Figure A-25) contains the logic that waits for the cancel signal from the main workflow. No matter which path completes first, they both go through the Exit activity to remove the entry from the SmartObject.

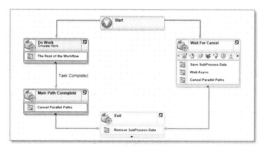

Figure A-25

## Wait for Cancel

This activity waits for a cancellation signal from the parent process. It writes out the serial number of the current activity to the ActiveSubProcesses SmartObject along with the ID of the parent process in the Save SubProcess Data SmartObject event. This path then waits for external action in the Wait Async asynchronous server code event. This path will wait forever until the action is performed or the path is canceled.

## Finishing Subprocesses

When the user completes the Client Event in the main workflow, it moves on to the Cancel Sub Processes activity. This activity invokes the `CompleteServerItem` method described previously for each subprocess in ActiveSubProcesses where the ParentID field matches the MainProcess ProcessID. The advanced Destination Rule for the Cancel Sub Processes activity is set to "Plan Per Slot (no destinations)" and the slots are populated by passing the SubTaskEventSN field from the list method of ActiveSubProcesses.

The Cancel Sub Processes activity contains only one server code event that invokes `CompleteServerItem` method (see Figure A-26). Each slot of the activity receives the SubTaskEventSN in its instance data (see Figure A-27).

```
public void Main(Project_2017b918df674f5eb152cd4f2d86ba03.EventItemContext_792fd70140d24ded96ec5b4c82fbf7e3 K2)
{
    WorkflowHelper.WorkflowUtilities.CompleteServerItem(K2.StringTable['Workflow
```

Figure A-26

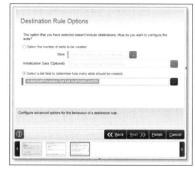

Figure A-27

### Cancel Parallel Paths

When this method is invoked, the asynchronous event Wait Async in the subprocess will complete and the next event, Cancel Parallel Paths, will execute. This event simply invokes the `GotoActivity` method of the process to jump to the Exit activity. Ordinarily, it would be bad practice to use the `GotoActivity` method to control the logic of the workflow, but it does have one useful side effect: It cancels any parallel paths of execution within a process, that is, it causes the normal workflow path to be immediately canceled and the Exit activity begins. The Exit activity has only one SmartObject event that removes the information about this activity from the ActiveSubProcesesses SmartObject.

> *Although the code for the GotoActivity is very simple, you can download the GotoActivity Event Wizard sample from blackmarket to do this without code at* `www.k2underground.com/k2/ProjectHome.aspx?ProjectID=29`. *Again, be sure to create a member account to access the site if you haven't already.*

If the normal path completes before a cancel signal is received from the main workflow, it too invokes the `GotoActivity` method to jump to the Exit activity and cancel the alternate path. If the alternate path is not canceled, it will continue waiting forever, and the subprocess will not finish.

The asynchronous server event can be used to cause a workflow to wait indefinitely until the event is finished via an API call. While waiting, the workflow can be dehydrated so it consumes very little system resources. This behavior can be useful when the workflow must wait for the completion of some long-running external process. This technique can also be used to help coordinate asynchronous subprocesses.

# Dynamic Escalations

I came across a query as to how to make escalation configurations dynamic in K2. The user wanted escalations to be reset when a process data field is changed. He wanted to do this in a Client Event so that the user interface would have update and submit buttons, and as the user made changes to the fields and updates the form, the relevant escalations would be reset accordingly. If the user did not do this within the escalation period, of course, the escalation would fire. If the user makes the update, escalation resets, the next update is expected to happen, and eventually the user submits and completes the event. The process then moves to the next activity.

K2's escalations are bound to an activity at the time of the creation of the activity instance. So the escalation timer value cannot be altered during run time. This means that the way to reset an escalation configuration is to expire the activity and reinstate it.

So how do we achieve what the user wanted?

If you create an activity with a single Client Event and configure the escalation in that activity, then you can create another activity with a server event immediately following the previous escalation activity. You can write code in that server event that can look at what needs to happen based on the updates made in the previous Client Event and set up some data fields with appropriate escalation timer values. Then you can loop back into the escalation activity (when required) and use these data fields to reconfigure the escalation.

The process map will look something like Figure A-28.

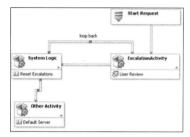

**Figure A-28**

You will also need to create some process data fields; make them hidden and not audited.

In the user interface that corresponds to the Client Event, you can put in some code that will redirect the page to the user's next worklist item from the same process instance, and they will see the same page now with the updated values but belonging to another Client Event.

The code for this redirect will look as follows:

```
con.Open("k2server");
WorklistCriteria crit = new WorklistCriteria();
crit.AddFilterField(WCField.ProcessFolio, WCCompare.Equal,
"folio_of_my_process_instance");
crit.AddFilterField(WCField.ProcessFullName, WCCompare.Equal,
"project\\processname");
crit.AddFilterField(WCField.ActivityName, WCCompare.Equal, "activity_name");
crit.AddFilterField(WCField.EventName, WCCompare.Equal, "event_name");

Worklist wl = con.OpenWorklist(crit);

if (wl.Count > 0)
{
url = wl[0].Data;
}
Con.close();
Page.Redirect(url);
```

Of course, the server event in the activity that follows the escalation activity will have to work out the relevant logic to set the correct escalation timers and Line Rules. Still, you have achieved what you needed to do.

# Looping through an Activity for Each SmartObject List Item

### By Russell Forster, K2 Consultant

Today I discovered a feature within K2 blackpearl, the ability to loop through a list of items and execute a set of events for each item, without having to write a line of code!

A simple Order Processing example can illustrate my business case. For demonstration purposes I assume an Order has multiple Order Items. A K2 Process (Process Order) instance has been started for an individual order. While running this process, we need to spawn a subprocess (Process Order Item) for each Order Item.

I have created a SmartObject (SmartBox) called OrderItems (Figure A-29), which has a List Method returning all Items for a given Order.

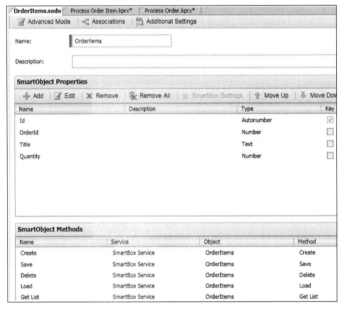

Figure A-29

To see how this looks in K2 see Process Order and Process Order Item processes in Figure A-30.

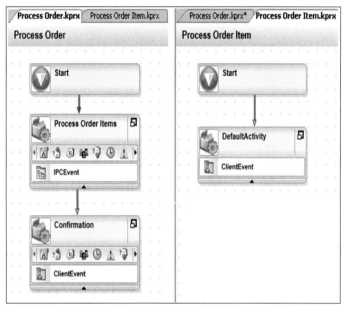

Figure A-30

The Process Order process has one data field:

❑    OrderId (Number)

The Process Order Item process has two Data Fields:

❑    OrderId (Number).

❑    OrderItemId (String) — Note this has to be a string because K2 will pass this value into the process.

You are going to start an instance of Process Order Item for each Item returned by the SmartObject. Within the Process Order Items, set the Destination Rule Option to be Plan per Slot (no destinations).

1.    Select the Id field from the OrderItems SmartObject's List method (see Figure A-31).

Important: The field you select here will be used to identify each loop instance.

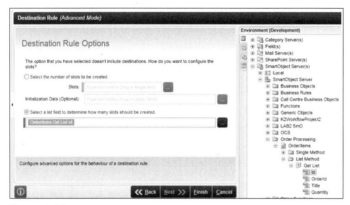

Figure A-31

2. Pass the OrderId (Process Data Field) as an Input for the SmartObject (Figure A-32).

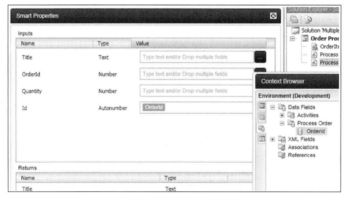

Figure A-32

3. Click Finish.

4. Now when you configure the IPC event, you are able to get the OrderItem's Id Field by accessing the Activity Destination Instance/Instance Data (String). See Figure A-33.

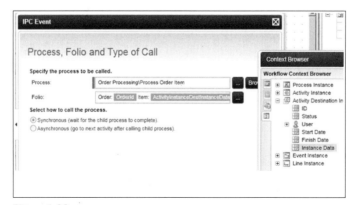

Figure A-33

**5.** You then map the required fields (see Figures A-34 and A-35).

Figure A-34

Figure A-35

**6.** A final step is to configure the Process Order Items Activity Succeeding Rule to ensure all instances have completed by ensuring that All ActivityInstanceDestStatus are now equal to completed as shown in (see Figure A-36).

**Figure A-36**

# Checking If a SharePoint Site or Workspace Exists When Calling CreateWorkspace() Methods

## By Frank Wu, K2 Consultant

The K2 event SharePoint Sites and Workspaces allows the creation of sites under an existing parent site. When the SharePoint site or workspace exists already (they only need to be created once) and when you are calling the CreateWorkspace() method of class K2SPWebs, a typical exception gets thrown as follows:

```
Server was unable to process request. --->
Microsoft.SharePoint.SPException: The Web site address "/MyTestSite" is
already in use. ---> System.Runtime.InteropServices.COMException
(0x800700B7): The Web site address "/MyTestSite" is already in use. at
Microsoft.SharePoint.Library.SPRequestInternalClass.CreateWeb(String
bstrUrl, String bstrTitle, String bstrDescription, UInt32 nLCID, String
bstrWebTemplate, Boolean bCreateUniqueWeb, Boolean bConvertIfThere,
Guid& pgWebId, Guid& pgRootFolderId, Boolean bCreateSystemCatalogs) at
Microsoft.SharePoint.Library.SPRequest.CreateWeb(String bstrUrl, String
bstrTitle, String bstrDescription, UInt32 nLCID, String
bstrWebTemplate, Boolean bCreateUniqueWeb, Boolean bConvertIfThere,
Guid& pgWebId, Guid& pgRootFolderId, Boolean bCreateSystemCatalogs) ---
End of inner exception stack trace --- at
Microsoft.SharePoint.Library.SPRequest.CreateWeb(String
bstrUrl, String bstrTitle, String bstrDescription, UInt32 nLCID, String
bstrWebTemplate, Boolean bCreateUniqueWeb,
```

A resolution for this issue is to apply exception handling and add a `try...catch` block around the `createWorkspace()` method call. To do that, follow these steps:

1. Right-click on SharePoint Sites and Workspaces Event Wizard ⇨ View Code ⇨ Event Item. A Sequential Workflow diagram will be shown, as in Figure A-37.

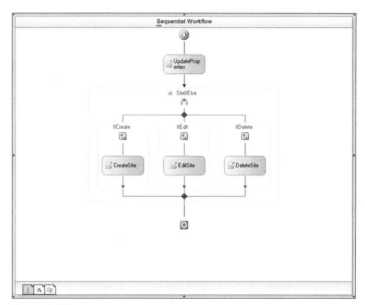

**Figure A-37**

2. Right-click on the box CreateSite ⇨ View Code.

3. Expand the section for `CreateSite_Executecode` and add a `try...catch` block as shown in the following.

```
//This the code to be used to check whether or not an exception is
//thrown by the "CreateSite method in the method itself

private void CreateSite_ExecuteCode(object sender, EventArgs e)
{
    try
    {
        using (K2SPWebs k2SPWebs = new K2SPWebs())
        {
            K2Uri k2Uri = new K2Uri(_siteURL);

            k2SPWebs.Url = k2Uri.FormatURI(true) + "_vti_bin/K2SPWebs.asmx";
```

```
            k2SPWebs.Credentials = _adCredentials.GetCredentials(_siteURL);

            k2SPWebs.CreateWorkSpace(_newServerRelativeURL, _title,
                _description, _webTemplate, _useUniquePermissions, false,
                _useNavigationInheritance);
            AddToProcessField(k2Uri.FormatURI(true), _newServerRelativeURL);
        }
    }
    catch (Exception E)
    {
        Console.WriteLine("<<<<<<<<<<<<<The " + _newServerRelativeURL.ToString()
        + " site already exists>>>>>>>>>>>>>");
    }
}
```

4.  Build and deploy the project.

# Displaying the Name of the Process Instance Originator on Your InfoPath Form

**By Blake Carrigan, K2 Consultant**

When using an InfoPath in a process, you may need to display the name of the process instance originator on certain views of the InfoPath form. However, the process originator is not stored in the _K2 group of fields injected into the form template by K2. This can be accomplished fairly easily using a few lines of code in a default server event as follows:

1.  Add a text field to your InfoPath form that will be used to display the process instance originator name. In this example, the field is called ProcInstOriginator. Make sure to edit the InfoPath form from within the K2 for Visual Studio environment by running the InfoPath Process Integration Wizard and selecting Design.

2.  In the very first activity of your process, add a Default Server Event (Code) as the very first event.

3.  Right-click on the server event and select View Code ⇨ Event Item.

4.  Add the following code to the Main method:

```
//Get the process originator from the K2 context object
string strOriginator = K2.ProcessInstance.Originator.Name.ToString();
//Get the value of the xml field that represents the InfoPath form
string strXmlField = K2.ProcessInstance.XmlFields["InfoPathXMLFieldName"].Value;
//Specify the xpath to the ProcInstOriginator element
string strXmlXPath = "myFields/ProcInstOriginator";
//set the ProcInstOriginator in the xml field based on the xpath.  Returns the
// updated xml field value
string xmlString = SourceCode.Workflow.Common.Utilities.XMLFieldMod.SetXMLValue
    (strXmlField, strXmlXPath, strOriginator);
//Assign the new xml field value back the InfoPath process xml field
K2.ProcessInstance.XmlFields["InfoPathXMLFieldName"].Value = xmlString;
```

Note that, in this example, the process XML field name, `"InfoPathXMLFieldName"`, needs to be replaced with the appropriate value for the XML field name that represents your InfoPath schema. The `strXmlXPath` variable will also need to be set to the appropriate XPath for the element that will be used to display the originator name.

5. Deploy the process.

After you deploy the process and start a new instance, any InfoPath views that contain the `ProcInstOriginator` field will display the process originator name.

# Changing the Default STMP Server Used by K2 blackpearl

**By Blake Carrigan, K2 Consultant**

When K2 blackpearl server is initially installed, the STMP server (e-mail server) is specified in the Configuration Manager Wizard. If the default STMP server needs to be updated post-installation, it is important to understand the difference between the SMTP server configuration information used for a mail event versus the Event Notification mechanism used for a Client Event, in order to update the STMP server in the appropriate place.

E-mail notifications for a Client Event are implemented as notification events that get handled by the K2 blackpearl server Event Bus. The SMTP server used for notification events can be changed by running the Configuration Manager on the K2 blackpearl server. At the E-mail Server Configuration screen, enter the new e-mail server name and complete the Configuration Manager wizard. Alternatively, it is possible to manually update the `smtpServer` setting in the following section of the `Sourcecode .Smartfunctions.Configuration.config` file on the K2 blackpearl server without having to run Configuration Manager.

```
<sourcecode.smartfunctions.configsections.sfconfigsection
connectionstr="SFDBConnection" soServerName="blackpearl"
soServerPort="5555" dependencyServerName="blackpearl"
dependencyServerPort="5555" useDependencyServer="true"
sfDependencyClass="a9345270-a429-4eea-9124-fbe6bc7d2350"
soDependencyClass="9812f4ea-75c9-48c1-83db-578fcce0cbc7"
smtpServer="blackpearl" smtpFrom="system@k2.net" />
```

This file is located in `C:\Program Files\K2 blackpearl\Host Server\Bin\` for a default K2 blackpearl installation. The K2 blackpearl server Service must be restarted for the change to take effect.

A mail event on the other hand is not implemented as a notification event and thus does not get triggered by a specific event that occurs in the K2 system. It simply executes as part of the normal process flow.

The STMP server used by a mail event is configured in the mail event wizard when it is run in Advanced Mode. By default, this is set to the Mail Server environment variable. Unless this has been overridden by hardcoding the server name in the event wizard, to update the STMP server for a mail event simply modify the Mail Server environment setting for the appropriate environment via the of the K2 Object

Browser in Visual Studio. The environment settings can also be modified from the Management Console in Workspace.

*Note that the process will need to be redeployed at which point the Mail Server String Table entry that gets used at run time will be updated accordingly. To avoid redeploying the process, you can update the String Table entry for the Mail Server manually via Workspace.*

# Obtaining the Serial Number for a Worklist Item in a K2 Process

## By Blake Carrigan, K2 Consultant

It may be desirable to include the link for a worklist item in the message body of a mail event rather than using a Client Event notification. By default, a Client Event notification contains a link to the worklist item for each destination user, which includes the serial number on the query string. When configuring a mail event, you must manually build the link to the worklist item in the mail message body. However, the required SN query string parameter (the serial number) is not directly accessible in the Mail Event Wizard.

The serial number is associated with a worklist item and is unique for each destination user of an activity containing a Client Event. It consists of the `ProcessInstanceId` and `ActivityInstanceDestinationId` in the form of `[ProcessInstanceId]_[ActivityInstanceDestinationId]`.

A mail event that precedes the Client Event can be used to send e-mail containing a link to the worklist item by building out the URL for the worklist item in the message body. The URL requires the serial number as a query string parameter and will look something like this:

```
http://[server]:[port]/[path]/[pagename].aspx?SN=[ProcessId]_
[ActivityInstanceDestId]
```

In this example the `[ProcessId]` and `[ActivityInstanceDestId]` for the SN query string parameter can be added to the message body using the Workflow Context Browser tab of the K2 Object Browser. The `[server]`, `[port]`, `[path]`, and `[pagename]` will need to be replaced with appropriate values for your environment.

In addition, the serial number can be obtained in the code behind a server event that precedes the Client Event, using the K2 context object. For example, it could be assigned to an activity level data field as follows:

```
K2.ActivityInstanceDestination.DataFields["SerialNumber"].Value =
    K2.SerialNumber.ToString();
```

When you are using the Plan Just Once Destination Rule option, there will be only one `ActivityInstanceDestination` resulting in a single worklist item that is shared by all the destination users. Thus, the serial number will be the same for all destinations.

When you are using the Plan per Destination option, there will be an `ActivityInstanceDestination` for each destination user, and each user will have a unique serial number. In this case all events that precede the Client Event will be executed once for each user, so data that is unique to the destination user such as the serial number should not be saved to a process level data field.

# Building the URL for a SharePoint Workflow Integration Client Event

### By Blake Carrigan, K2 Consultant

The worklist item for a SharePoint Workflow Integration Client Event points to the Workflow status page in MOSS called `WrkStat.aspx`. This page contains the links for the actual Task List items in SharePoint that allow the user to action the worklist item. All the data needed to build the URL for the `WrkStat.aspx` page is available in the SPIntegrationData process XML field immediately after the process starts.

You may need to include this URL in a mail event rather than use a client notification event. The query string parameters for the `WrkStat.aspx` page can be obtained from the SPIntegrationData field to build out the URL for this page as follows:

```
http://[mossserver]:[port]/[sitepath]/_layouts/WrkStat.aspx?List=[SPInt
egrationData_ListId]&WorkflowInstanceID=[SPIntegrationData_WorkflowId]&
ItemUniqueId=[SPIntegrationData_ItemUniqueId]&taskListId=[SPIntegration
Data_TaskListId]
```

The values between the brackets for the query string parameters correspond to the SPIntegrationData process XML field elements and can be added to the message body using the Process/Activity Data tab of the K2 Object browser. `[mossserver]`, `[port]`, and `[sitepath]` will need to be replaced with appropriate values for your environment.

*Note that the list item ID(s) for the actual task items created on the SharePoint Task List specified in the SharePoint Workflow Integration Process Wizard are not stored in the SPIntegrationData field.*

# Know Your SmartObjects

### By Blake Carrigan, K2 Consultant

Before using SmartObjects in code or in a K2 process, test them using the Amazing K2 SmartObject tool available in the blackmarket section of K2 Underground: `www.k2underground.com/k2/ ProjectLanding.aspx`. Again, be sure to create a member account to access the site if you haven't already.

This tool can be used to execute your SmartObject methods and verify they are functioning as expected before implementing them in an application. It can be extremely useful for isolating and addressing problems specific to your SmartObjects before using them in code, in an InfoPath form, or in a complex K2 process.

Or simply use the tool to explore and understand SmartObjects you may not be familiar with such as the out-of-the-box Workflow Reporting SmartObjects.

It also provides capabilities for creating SmartObjects, deleting SmartObjects, registering Service Types, registering Service Instances, and more. This tool is invaluable for anyone using SmartObjects.

# How to Get a List of the Users and Actions Executed for a Given Process Instance

**By Blake Carrigan, K2 Consultant**

To get a list of every user and action executed against a given process instance or a specific activity use the `Activity_Slot_Data` Workflow Reporting SmartObject that is installed with K2 blackpearl. Often there is a need to display this information on a form at run time for an active process instance, or it may be needed for reporting and auditing of completed and/or active process instances.

The `Activity_Slot_Data` SmartObject has a Destination property that will always get populated with the destination username that actioned the worklistItem. It uses a name-value pair to store the action taken by the user. The `Data_Name` property will be set to the name of the activity data field used for the action result, which by default is Action Result. The `Data_Value` property will be set to the name of the action taken by the destination user. It can be filtered by ProcessInstanceId and/or ActivityInstanceId. Note that this SmartObject does not include a property for the specific activity name, so the `Activity_Instance_Destination` SmartObject should be used to obtain this information.

Take note that the `Activity_Slot_Data` SmartObject does not include a complete list of all destination users for a given activity, just the slot data. For example, assume a situation where an activity has five destinations and two slots. When the activity is complete, the slot data for the activity will consist of two entries, each containing the name of the destination user and the action taken by that user.

The following is a simple code example of how the slot data can be accessed for all activities of a given process instance using the `SourceCode.SmartObjects.Client` namespace. It requires a reference to `SourceCode.SmartObjects.Client.dll` and `SourceCode.HostClientAPI.dll`:

```
// Create a SmartObject ClientServer Object
SmartObjectClientServer soServer = new SmartObjectClientServer();
SCConnectionStringBuilder cb = new SCConnectionStringBuilder();

// Build the connection string
cb.Host = "blackpearl";
cb.UserID = "Administrator";
cb.Password = "password";
cb.Port = 5555;
cb.Integrated = true;
cb.IsPrimaryLogin = true;

// Open the connection to the K2 Server
soServer.CreateConnection();
soServer.Connection.Open(cb.ToString());
```

```
// Get a handle to the 'Activity_Slot_Data' SmartObject
SmartObject soASD = soServer.GetSmartObject("Activity_Slot_Data");
//Specify the method
soASD.MethodToExecute = "List";
// Limit the results to a specific process instance
soASD.Properties["ProcessInstanceID"].Value = "5593";

// Execute the list method and display the Destination user and Action Result for
// each slot
SmartObjectList smoASDList =  soServer.ExecuteList(soASD);
for (int i = 0; i < smoASDList.SmartObjectsList.Count; i++)
{
    if (smoASDList.SmartObjectsList[i].Properties["DataName"].Value ==
       "Action Result")
    {
        Console.WriteLine("----------------------------");
        Console.WriteLine("Destination Name: " +
            smoASDList.SmartObjectsList[i].Properties["Destination"].Value);
        Console.WriteLine("Action Result: " +
            smoASDList.SmartObjectsList[i].Properties["DataValue"].Value);
    }
}
```

# Determining the Destination Users of an Activity in Process Event Code at Run Time

**By Blake Carrigan, K2 Consultant**

It is possible to determine the destination users for an activity at run time if the Destination Rule planning option is set to Plan per destination. This can be done via code behind the Client Event or a server event that precedes the Client Event. The user information is available via the K2.ActivityInstanceDestination.User object, which has properties for the username, FQN, e-mail, and so forth. The following example shows how the destination FQN can be obtained from code in a server event:

```
K2.ProcessInstance.Logger.LogInfoMessage("", "Destination User FQN: " +
    K2.ActivityInstanceDestination.User.FQN.ToString());
```

This example simply illustrates how to access the destination user information by writing it to the K2 logging targets that have been enabled to log messages of type Info. The data could easily be saved to a repeating node of a process XML field for use on a form, and so on.

When you are using Plan per destination, an ActivityInstanceDestination is instantiated for each user, meaning the events that precede the Client Event will execute once for each destination. Thus, saving destination user data to a process-level data field should be avoided as it will be overwritten each time the server event executes. The process data field will ultimately be populated with the data from the last destination user.

*If roles are being used and the Destination Rule is configured to use the Create a slot for each role option, K2.ActivityInstanceDestination.User.FQN will resolve to the role name.*

It is not possible to obtain destination user information when using the default planning option of Plan just once because there is no user context. In this case, there is a single `ActivityInstanceDestination` that belongs to K2Server and no specific destination user. Attempting to execute the preceding code results in an "Object reference not set to an instance of an object" exception, causing the process instance to go into an error state.

However, when you are using Plan just once, it is possible to access the worklist slot data at run time. This can be done via code in a server event following the Client Event to determine the user and action taken by that user:

```
for (int i = 0; i <
K2.ActivityInstanceDestination.ActivityInstance.WorklistSlots.Count; i++)
{
    K2.ProcessInstance.Logger.LogInfoMessage("", "Destination User FQN: " +
        K2.ActivityInstanceDestination.ActivityInstance.WorklistSlots[i]
        .User.FQN.ToString());
    K2.ProcessInstance.Logger.LogInfoMessage("", "Action Result: " +
        K2.ActivityInstanceDestination.ActivityInstance.WorklistSlots[i]
        .DataFields["Action Result"].Value.ToString());
}
```

The Server Event code will run once immediately after the Client Event evaluates to true and will display the user and action taken by that user for each slot configured in the destination rule. The slot data will always contain the name of the destination user, regardless of whether roles are being used.

One side note regarding Plan, because this comes up quite frequently: When you are using a mail event with this option, the Destination User checkbox in the mail event will be disabled, since the single ActivityInstanceDestination belongs to the K2 server and not to a specific destination user.

The preceding `WorklistSlots` example can also be used when you are using Plan per destination, but the server event that follows the Client Event will execute once for each slot, immediately after the worklist item is actioned, rather than executing just once. Again, this is because each user has an `ActivityInstanceDestination`, and when the worklist item associated with it is complete, the Client Event evaluates to true. So, in a multislot situation after the first slot is complete, the preceding code example will display the slot data for that one slot. When the second slot is complete, it will display the slot data for both the first and second slots, and so forth.

# Disabling Deployment of Workflow Reporting SmartObjects

### By Blake Carrigan, K2 Consultant

By default, when a process is deployed from K2 for Visual Studio, process-specific Workflow Reporting SmartObjects, each with a `List` method, will be created for the process, each activity, and each event defined in the process. Every time the process is deployed, a new version of each SmartObject is created.

In an environment such as a development environment where these SmartObjects may never be needed, they can be disabled to reduce the time it takes to deploy the process. When you are deploying processes that contain many activities and events or deploying multiple processes at once, disabling the Workflow Reporting SmartObjects for each process can provide a noticeable improvement in deployment time.

Deployment of the Workflow Reporting SmartObjects is configured for each specific process. With the process open in K2 for Visual Studio, from the process toolbar at the top of the design canvas, click the SmartObject Association icon. In the SmartObject Association dialog uncheck the CreateWorkflow Reporting SmartObjects checkbox and click the Finish button. This will prevent the creation of the Workflow Reporting SmartObjects for future deployments.

When the process is ready for deployment to the production environment, the Workflow Reporting SmartObjects can be enabled again as necessary.

# Using a SmartObject to Populate a Destination Set

## By Blake Carrigan, K2 Consultant

K2 blackpearl provides several advanced techniques for configuring destinations. One such technique involves populating the destination set using a SmartObject. Rather than adding specific individual users to the destination, it is possible to set the destination to the `Get List` method of a SmartObject; specifically to a SmartProperty that returns the destination usernames in a format that is supported by the security provider being used.

The following example does not go into the details of creating and populating a SmartObject but illustrates how a destination can make use of a SmartObject that calls the `Get List` method to return usernames:

1.  Run the Destination Rule Wizard for the desired activity.

2.  At the Destination Users screen click the ellipsis to load the K2 Object Browser. Note that if the Destination Rule Wizard is run in Advanced Mode, at the Destination Sets screen it is necessary to select the appropriate destination (or add a new one), and click Edit to access the dialog where destination users can be added.

3.  From the Environment tab expand the SmartObject server(s) node.

4.  Expand the SmartObject server node.

5.  Drill-down to and expand the SmartObject that stores the destination usernames.

6.  Expand the List Method node.

7.  Expand the node for the Get List method. Note that the list method may have been named something other than Get List when the SmartObject was created.

8.  Select the SmartProperty that stores the usernames that will populate the destination as shown in Figure A-38.

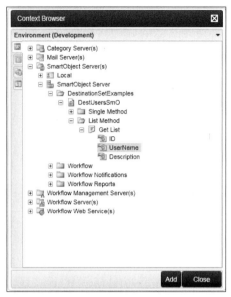

Figure A-38

9. Click the Add button, and the Smart Properties screen will be displayed.

10. If necessary, specify input values to filter the results returned by the Get List method and click OK. The destination Name will be set to the SmartProperty name, and the type will default to User as seen in Figure A-39.

Figure A-39

11. Complete the Destination Rule Wizard.

When you are using the default security provider installed with K2 blackpearl that supports Active Directory, the SmartObject can return usernames in any of the following formats:

```
[Label]:[Domain]\[User]
[Domain]\[User]
[User]
```

When the security label is not specified, the default security label is assumed. For a default installation of K2 blackpearl, the default security label is K2 and is associated with the Active Directory security provider.

When using a SmartObject that returns role names, make sure to set the Type to Role rather than User. As of this writing, using a SmartObject that returns group names is not supported. In addition, the SmartObject should not return a combination of users, groups, and roles.

# Using Mouse Gestures in K2 for Visual Studio to Create Activities and Events

### By Blake Carrigan, K2 Consultant

Mouse gestures can be used to speed up the workflow design process. Rather than dragging an activity or event from the Visual Studio toolbox and dropping it onto the design canvas, the mouse can be used to create the activity or event by holding down the right mouse button and drawing the appropriate letter on the design canvas. For example, drawing an "O" will create a default activity where the "O" was drawn.

It is also possible to use mouse gestures to create events on existing activities by drawing the appropriate letter on the activity.

The following is a list of Mouse Gestures that can be used on the process design canvas:

| Mouse Gesture | Activity/Event Created |
| --- | --- |
| C | Client Event |
| M | Mail Event |
| O | Default Activity |
| P | InfoPath Process Wizard/InfoPath Client Event |
| S | Default Server Event (code) |
| W | Default Server Event (WF) |

# Using K2 Helper Classes to Get and Set Process and Activity XML Fields

### By Blake Carrigan, K2 Consultant

Sometimes it is necessary to get or set the value of a process or activity XML field element in a running process instance. This can be done in code behind a server event using classes in the .NET `System.Xml` namespace, but can be simplified by using the `SourceCode.Workflow.Common` namespace. It includes helper classes with static methods that can be used to get and set K2 XML fields.

The following is an example of how this can be done in code behind a server event:

1. Create a new K2 process in Visual Studio and define a process XML field called SampleXMLField. By default an XmlDocument element will be created.

2. Right-click on the XmlDocument element and select Add.

3. In the Add XML Field or Group dialog, add a new field (element) called SampleXMLElement with a data type of String, and click OK.

4. Right-click on the process XML field node, SampleXMLField, and select Edit.

5. Select the Initial Value tab, click the Generate sample XML file button, and click OK.

6. Add a default server event (Code) to the design canvas and draw a line from the Start activity to the DefaultActivity associated with the server event.

7. Right-click on the serverevent and select View Code ⇨ Event Item.

8. Add the following code to the Main method of the serverevent:

```
// Set the value of a process xml field element using the XMLFieldMod class

// Retrieve the current value of the xml field
string strXml = K2.ProcessInstance.XmlFields["SampleXMLField"].Value;
// Write entire xml string to the console to see the initial value of the
// "SampleXMLElement"
Console.WriteLine("XML Field value: " + strXml);
// Set the xpath for the element to be updated
string strXPath = "XmlDocument/SampleXMLElement";
// Set the new value for element value based on the xpath.  Returns the updated xml
// field value.
strXml =
    SourceCode.Workflow.Common.Utilities.XMLFieldMod.SetXMLValue(strXml,strXPath,
    "TheNewValue");
// Assign the new xml field value back the process level xml field
K2.ProcessInstance.XmlFields["SampleXMLField"].Value = strXml;

// Get the value of a process xml field element using the XmlHelper class

// For illustration purposes, set the strXml variable to null and retrieve it again
strXml = null;
```

```
strXml = K2.ProcessInstance.XmlFields["SampleXMLField"].Value;
// Get the value of the element that was set based on the xpath
string strElemValue = SourceCode.Workflow.Common.XmlHelper.GetXPathValue(strXml,
    strXPath);
//Display the value in the K2 Server console to confirm it displays "TheNewValue"
Console.WriteLine("SimpleXMLElement Value: " + strElemValue.ToString());
```

9.  Save the project and deploy it.

Note that if you start a process instance while the K2 server is running in console mode, you should see output similar to the following when the server event executes:

```
XML Field value: <XmlDocument xmlns:xsi="http://www.w3.org/2001/XMLSchema-instance">
<SampleXMLElement>SampleXMLElement1</SampleXMLElement></XmlDocument>
SimpleXMLElement Value: TheNewValue
```

# I Lost My K2 Workflow Visual Studio Project, Help

**By Blake Carrigan, K2 Consultant**

If you've ever used K2.net 2003, you are probably aware there is no mechanism for retrieving the K2 Studio process file from the K2 database for an exported process. If the process is lost and no backups are available, to export a new version of the process definition would require rebuilding the process from scratch. If you find yourself in a similar situation with K2 blackpearl where the K2 Workflow project source files are no longer available, there is hope.

Each time a K2 blackpearl process is deployed, the project source files are also deployed to a binary field in the _proc table of the K2Server database. The binary file contains the K2 for Visual Studio project file (.k2proj) along with the specific process file (.kprx). For an InfoPath process, the InfoPath form templates are also included. If the project contains SmartObjects, the .sodx files are not included as part of the project source deployed to the database.

Workspace provides an interface for downloading the binary project source file as follows:

1.  From the Management tab select Management Console.

2.  Expand the appropriate K2 blackpearl server node.

3.  Expand the Workflow server node.

4.  Expand the Processes node.

5.  Expand the desired project and process.

6.  Select the Versions node.

7.  In the right-hand pane all versions of the process that have been deployed to the K2 server will be listed. Click the download link for the desired version of the process definition to download the compressed executable file.

Once the project is downloaded and extracted, it can be opened in Visual Studio and redeployed as a new process version.

# Submitting an InfoPath Form Fails with a Generic Error

### By Blake Carrigan, K2 Consultant

When you are using an InfoPath Integration process with Forms Services, form submission failures typically result in the following generic message displayed in a message box: "An error occurred while the form was being submitted."

To effectively isolate and troubleshoot this issue, you need to determine the underlying error. There are a couple of possible ways to obtain the actual exception details.

1.  Review the SharePoint logs on the MOSS front-end server(s).

    By default, the SharePoint logs are located in `C:\Program Files\Common Files\Microsoft Shared\web server extensions\12\LOGS`, but the location can be confirmed via SharePoint Central Administration. In order to capture Forms Services events in the SharePoint logs, you must enable the diagnostic logging for the Forms Services categories in Central Administration.

    Given that large volumes of data can be written to the SharePoint logs in a short period of time, the best way to troubleshoot a form submission problem is:

    ❏ Reproduce the problem.

    ❏ Open the most current SharePoint log.

    ❏ Search from the bottom of the log up for *Forms Server* or *Forms Services* looking for exceptions and warnings.

    The following is an example snippet of a warning logged for a form submission failure. In this case, it's clear that the problem is a result of the user not having Start permissions for the process:

```
Warning  Form submission failed. (User: K2DEMO\administrator, Form
Name: TipsTricks, IP:, Request:
http://moss.k2demo.local/_layouts/Postback.FormServer.aspx, Form ID:
urn:schemas-microsoft-com:office:infopath:TipsTricks:-myXSD-2008-09-
08T20-04-31, Type: DataAdapterException, Exception Message: The remote
server returned an error: (500) Internal Server Error.
System.Web.Services.Protocols.SoapException: Server was unable to
process request. ---> System.Exception: The process cannot be started
due to the following reason: 24408 K2:K2DEMO\Administrator from
192.168.1.103:7 does not have rights to Start Process
TipsTricks\TipsIPProc1Process1
```

2. Often if the error is not specific to Forms Services, if possible, it can be useful to temporarily configure the form library to use the InfoPath client rather than the Web browser, to obtain a more meaningful error message. Rather than the "generic" error you get when using Forms Services, you will get a dialog that contains the underlying exception details, as shown in the Figure A-40.

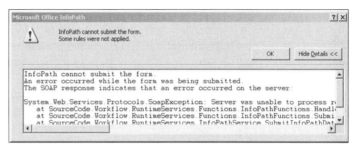

Figure A-40

In this example, if you were to scroll to the right, you would see the same underlying exception message that was logged to the SharePoint logs that you saw previously.

This technique is advantageous in that it is not necessary to dig through the SharePoint logs in an attempt to find the exception.

# Custom Forms and SharePoint Workflow Integrations

### By Chris Geier, K2 Program Manager

I have been asked many questions about our SharePoint integration but none more often that of questions about forms in our SharePoint integrated workflows. During the building of these types of processes you have the option to use a few different types of forms, including automatically generating ASP.NET pages. People often wish to customize the look and feel of these pages beyond what is exposed in the wizards. Fortunately, this is much easier than you think.

When running through the SharePoint Workflow Integration Wizard, make sure that you select ASP.NET as the form technology and generate new ASP.NET pages as the form location. For the rest of the process, run through the wizards as you normally would. After you have your process built, go to where you have saved your project in the file system. You will see a new directory there, which is named CSWebsiteWI by default. Within this directory you will see the pages that K2 blackpearl has generated for you. You can open each one of these files in Visual Studio or even SharePoint Designer. Once it is open in your editor of choice, you can add graphics, change the look and feel, add other fields, use the K2 API, or do virtually anything you need to do. Awesome isn't it?

# Index